Exchange Rates and Global Financial Policies

World Scientific Studies in International Economics

(ISSN: 1793-3641)

Vol. 26 World Trade Organization and International Trade Law: Antidumping, Subsidies and Trade Agreements
by Gary N Horlick (Law Offices of Gary N Horlick, USA & University of Bern, Switzerland)

Vol. 27 European Economic Integration, WTO Membership, Immigration and Offshoring
by Wilhelm Kohler (University of Tübingen, Germany)

Vol. 28 Services Trade Reform: Making Sense of It
by Philippa Dee (Australian National University, Australia)

Vol. 29 The Social Value of the Financial Sector: Too Big to Fail or Just Too Big?
edited by Viral V Acharya (New York University, USA & Centre for Economic Policy (CEPR), UK), Thorsten Beck (Tilburg University, The Netherlands & Centre for Economic Policy (CEPR), UK), Douglas D Evanoff (Federal Reserve Bank of Chicago, USA), George G Kaufman (Loyola University Chicago, USA), & Richard Portes (London Business School, UK & Centre for Economic Policy (CEPR), UK)

Vol. 30 The Role of Central Banks in Financial Stability: How Has It Changed?
edited by Douglas D Evanoff (Federal Reserve Bank of Chicago, USA), Cornelia Holthausen (European Central Bank, Germany), George G Kaufman (Loyola University Chicago, USA) & Manfred Kremer (European Central Bank, Germany)

Vol. 31 Exchange Rates and Global Financial Policies
by Paul De Grauwe (London School of Economics, UK)

Vol. 32 Asian Free Trade Agreements and WTO Compatibility: Goods, Services, Trade Facilitation and Economic Cooperation
by Shintaro Hamanaka (Asian Development Bank, Philippines)

Vol. 33 Economics and Politics of Trade Policy
by Douglas R Nelson (Tulane University, USA)

The complete list of the published volumes in the series can be found at
http://www.worldscientific.com/series/wssie

31 World Scientific Studies in International Economics

Exchange Rates and Global Financial Policies

Paul De Grauwe
London School of Economics, UK

World Scientific
NEW JERSEY • LONDON • SINGAPORE • BEIJING • SHANGHAI • HONG KONG • TAIPEI • CHENNAI

Published by

World Scientific Publishing Co. Pte. Ltd.
5 Toh Tuck Link, Singapore 596224
USA office: 27 Warren Street, Suite 401-402, Hackensack, NJ 07601
UK office: 57 Shelton Street, Covent Garden, London WC2H 9HE

Library of Congress Cataloging-in-Publication Data
Grauwe, Paul de.
Exchange rates and global financial policies / by Paul De Grauwe (London School of Economics, UK).
pages cm. -- (World Scientific studies in international economics, ISSN 1793-3641 ; volume 31)
Includes bibliographical references and index.
ISBN-13: 978-9814513180
ISBN-10: 9814513180
1. Foreign exchange rates. 2. Monetary policy. 3. International finance. I. Title.
HG3851.G6926 2014
332.4'5--dc23
2013038608

British Library Cataloguing-in-Publication Data
A catalogue record for this book is available from the British Library.

In-house Editor: Alisha Nguyen

Typeset by Stallion Press
Email: enquiries@stallionpress.com

Printed in Singapore by World Scientific Printers.

Acknowledgements

The author would like to thank the following publishers, journals and co-authors for granting their permissions to reproduce the chapters in this volume:

Publishers

Cambridge University Press
Routledge

Journals

Australian Economic Review
Banca Nazionale del Lavoro Quarterly Review
Economic Theory
European Economic Review
Financial Times
International Finance
International Journal of Finance and Economics
Journal of Banking and Finance
Journal of Common Market Studies
Journal of Economic Behavior and Organization
Journal of Economic Dynamics and Control
Journal for Institutional Comparisons
Open Economics Review
Public Choice
Scandinavian Journal of Economics
Weltwirtschaftliches Archiv

Co-authors

Yunus Aksoy (Birkbeck College, London)
Michel Beine (University of Luxembourg, Luxembourg)
Hans Dewachter (University of Leuven, Belgium)
Marianna Grimaldi (Sveriges Riksbank, Stockholm)
Magdalena Polan (Goldmann Sachs, London)
Cláudia Costa Storti (European Monitoring Centre on Drugs and Drug Abuse, Lisbon)
J. Spaventa (Deceased in 2012)
Isabel Vansteenkiste (European Central Bank, Frankfurt)
Wim Vanhaverbeke (University of Hasselt, Belgium)

Contents

About the Author

Paul De Grauwe is John Paulson Professor at the London School of Economics. He was a member of the Belgian parliament from 1991 to 2003. He is honorary doctor of the University of Sankt Gallen (Switzerland), the University of Turku (Finland), the University of Genoa and the University of Valencia. He was a visiting professor at various universities: Paris, Amsterdam, Berlin, Kiel, Milan, Pennsylvania and Michigan. He obtained his Ph.D. from the Johns Hopkins University in 1974. He is a research fellow at the Centre for European Policy Studies in Brussels and area director "Macro, Money and Finance" at CESifo in Munich.

Introduction

At the end of the 1960s, and early 1970s it became clear that the Bretton Woods system which was based on fixed exchange rates had become unsustainable. And so in 1973 the major currencies of the world stopped pegging their exchange rates to the dollar. This change in regime led to a search for alternative monetary arrangements. At one extreme, countries let their currencies float freely. In those countries, the foreign exchange markets, instead of politicians, were allowed to determine what the right exchange rate would be. This was the exchange rate regime that major countries adopted *vis-à-vis* each other. At the other extreme, groups of countries started looking for ways to permanently lock their exchange rates among each other. These countries, mainly in Europe, first experimented with a system of regional fixing of their exchange rates. As this only replicated the old Bretton Woods system, it did not last long. The same countries then took the next logical step by entering a monetary union, the Eurozone.

Exchange Rate Economics

The move to flexible exchange rates led to a surge of a whole new branch in economics, i.e., exchange rate economics. This research was very much influenced by the idea that foreign exchange markets were efficient and would lead to better macroeconomic management. This view became embodied in a formidable intellectual construction, the Rational Expectations Efficient Market (REEM) model.

The REEM model provided the dominant mode of thinking about asset markets.This impressive intellectual construction became highly influential and the only model that was taken seriously in academic teaching about the price formation in asset markets (including the exchange market).

In a way this was surprising because the accumulating empirical evidence was not favorable for the REEM model. Many of its predictions were refuted by the data (see Chapter 5). In particular,the prediction that asset prices only change because of news in underlying fundamentals was rejected. Moreover, many empirical phenomena observed in asset markets, e.g., volatility clustering, fat tails in the distribution of the returns, and the profitability of chartist rules, remained unexplained in the REEM model.

This state of affairs inspired me to develop an alternative mode of thinking about the exchange market. My source of inspiration was the behavioral finance literature. The basic philosophy of this modeling approach can be summarized as follows. First, agents experience a cognitive problem when they try to understand the world in which they live. They find it difficult to collect and to process the complex information with which they are confronted. As a result, they use simple rules ("heuristics") to guide their behavior. They do this not because they are irrational, but rather because the complexity of the world is overwhelming. Thus, the agent I assumed was very different from the rational agent assumed to populate our economic models, who is able to comprehend the full complexity of the world, i.e., who has a brain that can contain and process the information embedded in the world in its full complexity.

The second component in my modeling approach was to discipline the behavior of agents, i.e., to impose a criterion that allows some behavioral rules to survive and others to disappear. Thus, in this second stage, I assumed that agents regularly evaluate the behavioral rules they use, and that they do this by comparing the utility of the rule they are using with the utility of other rules. If it turns out that this other rule gives them more satisfaction they are willing to switch to that other rule. In this sense, I introduced rationality in a different way than in the REEM model. It was a selection mechanism based on trial and error in which imperfectly informed agents decide about the best behavior based on their past experiences. This trial and error strategy is probably the best possible strategy in a very uncertain world.

I formalized these ideas in the context of simple models of the foreign exchange market. Chapters 1 to 3 give a flavor of the kind of models that I developed. The main characteristics of these models is that they are non-linear and generate a complex dynamics. One feature that came out of all these models is the sensitivity to initial conditions, i.e., small shocks can generate large and persistent movements in the exchange rate.

These behavioral models also are capable of generating results that closely mimic the main dynamic features observed in the foreign exchange market. First, these models predict that the exchange rate is disconnected most of the time from its underlying fundamentals, and that this disconnect phenomenon is a natural outcome in a world where agents find it difficult to understand the underlying model and use trial and error methods in their forecasting strategies. It is as if the trial and error learning strategies lead to a never ending groping of the market towards the fundamental exchange rate.

Secondly, the behavioral model predicts that frequently (but unpredictably) the exchange rate will be involved in a bubble-and-crash dynamics. These bubbles arise because of the self-fulfilling character of extrapolative forecasting rules:When these rules turn out to be profitable, they attract newcomers who reinforce the upward (or downward) movement, making these even more profitable, attracting newcomers, etc. However, in a stochastic environment the attraction exerted by the fundamental variables overcomes the temporary forces of speculative bubbles, leading to a crash.

Third, the behavioral models of Chapters 1 to 3 mimic the other empirical regularities observed in the foreign exchange markets, i.e., the existence of fat tails in the exchange rate returns, and of volatility clustering. The phenomenon of fat tails implies that very large changes in the exchange rate occur with a frequency that cannot be explained by a normal distribution. The interesting feature of these models is that they generate these fat tails endogenously. They do not assume it to be present in the distribution of the shocks in the fundamentals. The main reason why we obtain these results is that the models produce different equilibria (attractors).

The behavioral models of Chapters 1 to 3 also have important implications for our understanding of how shocks in the fundamentals (the news) affect the exchange rate. My main finding here was that news in fundamentals has an unpredictable effect on the exchange rate. Some times news strongly affects the exchange rate; at other times the same news has no effect whatsoever. In addition, it is essentially unpredictable when news has an effect and when it does not. The fundamental reason for this indeterminacy in the effect of news is that there is no unique equilibrium to which the exchange rate will converge. For example, when the exchange rate is involved in a bubble at the moment the news reaches the market, the news may not affect the exchange rate at all; while at more tranquil times, the same news will strongly affect the exchange rate. Thus, our model predicts that news in the fundamentals has unpredictable effects on the exchange rate. This is also observed in reality. For example, there are many evidences suggesting that news in fundamentals like inflation differentials, the current account, economic growth has unpredictable effects on the euro–dollar exchange rate (see Chapters 4 and 5).

A final implication of the behavioral model concerns the effectiveness of official interventions in the foreign exchange markets. In the traditional REEM model sterilized interventions have no impact on the exchange rates. In the behavioral model this is not so. We find that sterilized interventions can affect the exchange rate, mainly because it can change the behavior of chartists and fundamentalists in the market. In Chapter 6, this effect is empirically verified.

Monetary Integration

The decision of European countries to move towards a full monetary union provided the stimulus for me to engage in the study of the theory of optimal currency areas (Chapter 7) and its empirical evidence (Chapter 8). Most importantly, it led meto study the question of whether the European countries made the right decision to create a monetary union among so many sovereign nations. In my textbook "*The Economics of Monetary Integration*" (Oxford University Press,

1992) I came to the conclusion that the whole project had been too much influenced by political objectives and thus carried a great risk of becoming unsustainable. Unfortunately, this prediction would come out. As it turned out, the absence of a political union in which the monetary union could be embedded was the greatest source of its fragility (Chapter 11).

Later as the Eurozone was put into place, I continued my research on the functioning of monetary unions, in particular the Eurozone. Most of my focus was on identifying the sources of the fragility of the Eurozone (Chapter 11) and how to deal with this fragility (Chapter 12). This led me to formulate a new role for the European Central Bank (ECB). The latter had been created in an intellectual environment provided by the Monetarist Revolution and the Real Business Cycle Theory. In this environment, the central bank was given a minimalist role. All it had to do was to maintain price stability. In doing so, the ECB would make the maximum contribution possible to economic growth and financial stability. There was no need for the central bank to explicitly target growth or financial stability. When markets are kept flexible growth would be maximized provided the central bank kept inflation low. Similarly, a low inflation would allow efficient financial markets to maintain financial stability. My research on exchange markets had warned me that this paradigm was terribly misleading and would blind policymakers from seeing the looming risk of financial instability (Chapter 10).

Instead, I took the view that a central bank has a greater responsibility than keeping the CPI index stable, and that its responsibility includes the need to maintain financial stability, by being a lender of last resort in the government bond markets. Central banks were originally created to deal with the inherent instability of capitalism. They were not primarily set up to maintain price stability. The concern for price stability came only much later. The central bank was given the role of lender of last resort, i.e., a backstop needed to inject liquidity in financial markets when panic after a crash leads everybody to sell assets and to scramble for liquidity.

Right from the start the role of lender of last resort was not restricted to injecting liquidity in the banking sector. It also extended to the government bond markets. The reason is very simple and quite fundamental. It has to do with the existence of a "deadly embrace" between the sovereign and the banks. When the sovereign gets into problems the falling government bond prices threaten the banks, which are the main holders of government debt. When the banks collapse, governments that do not want to let down the banks are threatened with insolvency. If one of the two falls off the cliff, the other one will be pulled down also. As a result, when central banks took on the responsibility of lenders of last resort, it was understood that restricting this responsibility to the banks would be unworkable and would not stabilize the financial system.

Unfortunately, the founders of the Eurozone and of the ECB completely overlooked this essential stabilizing role of the central bank and left the ECB totally unprepared to take on the job of stabilizing the Eurozone. Only in 2012, the ECB, under the leadership of Mario Draghi, took the necessary steps to stabilize the system by promising unlimited support of the government bond markets of the Eurozone.

My research of the Eurozone also included operational matters such as how to set the conversion rates at the start of the union so as to make sure that the right conversion rates are selected (Chapter 9). It also involved an analysis of how the asymmetries in the system should be incorporated in setting optimal monetary policies for the union as a whole (Chapter 13).

Macroeconomics and Monetary Policy

Since its inception, booms and busts have characterized capitalism. The central issue in macroeconomics therefore is why these booms and busts in economic activity and in prices occur. Every macroeconomic theory must be capable of explaining these facts.

The explanation given by mainstream macroeconomics, in particular by New Keynesian macroeconomics, fails to impress. In essence, the story told by the New Keynesian macroeconomics is that these fluctuations arise because of large exogenous shocks. The latter have the effect of forcing rational agents to change their optimal consumption and productions plans, but since they cannot adjust their plans instantaneously, prices and output adjust with lags. It is the combination of external shocks and slow adjustment that produces cyclical movements.

Thus, why did the world get into a recession in 2008–2009? The answer of the New Keynesian model builders is that in 2007 a large external shock arose in the form of a sudden and unexpected increase in risk aversion. This change in risk perception then, like a hurricane, worked its way through the economy and produced a deep recession. In this sense, mainstream macroeconomics has produced a "hurricane theory" of the business cycle.

The failure of mainstream macroeconomics to provide an endogenous explanation of booms and busts, in which a bust is the result of a previous boom, and a boom the result of a previous bust has everything to do with the underlying paradigm of mainstream macroeconomics. This is the paradigm of the fully informed utility maximizing agent who does not make systematic mistakes. Large booms or large busts can only be created by large external shocks to which these rational agents then will react (Chapter 17).

Much of my research in macroeconomics has focused on developing an endogenous explanation of the business cycle. I have tried to do so by developing a behavioral macroeconomic model (Chapters 18 and 19).

The behavioral model in these chapters is based on an enlarged concept of rationality. In mainstream macroeconomics, rationality is narrowly defined as utility maximization of agents who do not exhibit cognitive limitations, and as a result, can solve incredibly complex problems of optimization and information processing. The starting point of the behavioral model is that agents have limited cognitive abilities. These limitations force them to use simple rules (heuristics). Rationality is then introduced as a willingness of agents to learn by switching to alternative rules in order to improve their performance. Thus, moving away from the narrow rationality concept of mainstream macroeconomics does not imply that one is condemned to model irrationality where everything becomes possible.

The behavioral macroeconomic model of Chapters 18 and 19 is capable of generating endogenous business cycle movements.

It generates large movements in output (booms and busts) without having to rely on large exogenous shocks. The underlying mechanism that produces these movements are the waves of optimism and pessimism ("animal spirits") that are generated endogenously and that have a self-fulfilling property. Periods of tranquility during which "animal spirits stay quiet" are followed (unpredictably) by periods when "animal spirits take over," i.e., large movements of optimism or pessimism lead the economy in a period of boom and bust.

These results have implications for the optimal conduct of monetary policies. In general, I find that while inflation targeting remains important, it is not sufficient to stabilize the economy. An explicit objective of stabilizing output is equally necessary to "tame the animal spirits." In fact, I find that in order to be successful in stabilizing inflation, the central bank should also explicitly aim at stabilizing output (Chapter 18). Central banks have a greater responsibility than just stabilizing the CPI.

The behavioral model of Chapters 18 and 19 allows us to better understand the recent macroeconomic developments in the world. The "Great Recession" of 2008–2009 was not the result of an exogenous shock, but resulted from excessive optimism that built up before 2008 and led to unsustainable consumption and investment. When the turnaround occurred, pessimism set in and led to a deep recession. When this interacted with banks taking excessive risks during the boom and becoming excessively risk averse during the downturn one has the recipe for large booms and busts (Chapter 16).

Traditional macroeconomic theory has been built up on a number of cherished theories. One of the most important ones is the quantity theory of money. This says that in the long run there is a proportional relationship between inflation and money growth. I subjected this theory to a number of empirical tests. I found that this theory holds only if one has countries with very high inflation rates in the sample. When restricting the sample to low inflation countries (less than 5 percent inflation per year) there is no trace of a proportional relation between inflation and money growth (Chapter 14).

The corollary of the proportionality between inflation and money growth is that in the long run output growth is not affected by money growth. I subjected this second proposition of the quantity theory and also found it wanting (Chapter 15). Thus, it appears that one of the most cherished pieces of theory in macroeconomics has only poor empirical support.

PART I

EXCHANGE RATE ECONOMICS

Theoretical

Chapter 1

Chaos in the Dornbusch Model of the Exchange Rate

Paul De Grauwe and Hans Dewachter

1. Introduction

Ever since the empirical breakdown of (linear) structural exchange rate models, the predominant view on exchange rate dynamics has been based on the "news" model. In this model the only sources driving the exchange rate are random events.[1]

Recent research has revealed some problems with the "news" model. First, there appears to be more structure in the time series of the exchange rate than the pure stochastic model can account for. This additional structure has been found in most exchange rates. See, for example, Cutler, Poterba and Summers (1990) who report significant autocorrelations in the exchange rates at different lags.

Second it appears that many, if not most, movements in the exchange rates cannot easily be accounted for by observable "news." In an analysis of high-frequency exchange rate data, Goodhart (1990) documents that very often the exchange rate does not respond to observable news, and that many exchange rate movements cannot be associated with news.

Published in *Open Economics Review*, 4, 351–379, 1993.
We are grateful to Caspar De Vries and Daniel Gros for useful suggestions. Financial assistance from the Centre for Economic Policy Research, the Ford Foundation and the Alfred Sloan Foundations is gratefully acknowledged.

[1] Frenkel and Mussa (1985), Levich (1985), Mussa (1984).

This recent empirical research suggests that in addition to random shocks, there are other driving forces in the exchange market that are important to understand its dynamics. In this paper, we will focus on a (non-linear) speculative dynamics, in which the behavior of "chartists" and "fundamentalists" plays a prominent role. The analysis will be performed in the context of a structural model, the Dornbusch model, which has become the most popular textbook model of the exchange rate.[2] It will be shown that this model together with a simple non-linear speculative dynamics is capable of generating a complex behavior of the exchange rate which is unpredictable, even in the absence of random shocks. Such behavior has been called "chaotic."[3] In addition, the model will be used to analyze the behavior of the exchange rate when random events ("news") occur with low frequency.

The remainder of the paper is organized as follows:

In Section 2, we present the model. Section 3 reports the basic properties of the model. It will be shown that the model is able to generate chaotic motion. In Section 4, we report the results of monetary policy shocks. Section 5 points out the importance of low-frequency stochastic shocks for some regions in the parameterspace of the model. Finally, Section 6 briefly discusses the properties of the price level and the interest rate.

2. The Model

2.1. *The Dornbusch Model*

The version of the Dornbusch model that will be used in this paper consists of the following building blocks:

a) *The money market equilibrium condition*

$$Ms_t = Y_t^a \cdot P_t \cdot (1 + r_t)^{-c} \tag{1}$$

[2] Dornbusch (1976).

[3] In a previous paper, one of the authors used a partial equilibrium model of the exchange rate. The chaotic results obtained there also depended on the existence of a J-curve effect, see De Grauwe and Vansanten (1990). Here we discard the assumption of a J-curve. This should make the results stronger.

where P_t is the domestic price level in period t, r_t is the domestic interest rate, Ms_t is the (exogenous) money supply, Y_t is the (exogenous) level of domestic output.

b) *The open interest parity condition*

$$E_t(S_{t+1})/S_t = (1 + r_t)/(1 + r_{ft}) \tag{2}$$

where S_t is the exchange rate in period t (the price of the foreign currency in units of the domestic currency), $E_t(S_{t+1})$ is the forecast made in period t of the exchange rate in period $t+l, r_{ft}$ is the foreign interest rate.

2.1.1. *Goods market equilibrium*

The long run equilibrium condition is defined as a situation in which purchasing power parity (PPP) holds, i.e.:

$$S_t^* = P_t^*/P_{ft}^* \tag{3}$$

where S_t^* is the equilibrium (PPP) exchange rate, P_{ft}^* the foreign and P_t^* the domestic steady state value for the price level in period t.

The short-term price dynamics is assumed to be determined as follows:

$$P_t/P_{t-1} = (S_t/S_t^*)^k \tag{4}$$

$$\text{where } k \geq 0$$

That is, when the exchange rate exceeds its PPP-value, S_t^*, the domestic price level increases. Put differently, when the currency is undervalued this leads to excess demand in the goods market tending to increase the price level. The opposite occurs when the exchange rate is below its PPP-value (an overvalued domestic currency). Note that we assume full employment so that adjustment towards equilibrium is realized through price changes.

2.2. *The Speculative Dynamics*

We assume that there are two classes of speculators. One class is called "chartists," the other "fundamentalists." See Frankel and

Froot (1986) for a first attempt at formalizing this idea. A recent microeconomic foundation of this assumption is provided by Cutler, Poterba, and Summers (1990). Empirical evidence about the importance of these types of speculators is found in Allen and Taylor (1989) and Frankel (1990).

The "chartists" use the past of the exchange rates to detect patterns which they extrapolate into the future. The "fundamentalists" compute the equilibrium value of the exchange rate. In this model, this will be the (steady state) PPP-value of the exchange rate. If the market rate exceeds this equilibrium value they expect it to decline in the future (and *vice versa*). Another way to interpret this dual behavior is as follows. The "chartists" use the past movements of the exchange rates as indicators of market sentiments and extrapolate these into the future. Their behavior adds a "positive feedback" into the model.[4] As will become clear, this is a source of instability. The fundamentalists have regressive expectations, i.e., when the exchange rate deviates from its equilibrium value they expect it to return to the equilibrium. The behavior of the fundamentalists adds a "negative feedback" into the model, and is a source of stability.

A second feature of the speculative dynamics assumed in the model is that the weights given to "chartists" and "fundamentalists" are made endogenous. More specifically, it will be assumed that when the exchange rate is close to the equilibrium (fundamental) rate, the weight given to the fundamentalists is at its lowest, whereas the chartists then have a maximal weight. When the market rate deviates from the equilibrium rate, the weight given to the fundamentalists increases with that deviation. That is, when the exchange rate continues to deviate from its fundamental value, fundamental analysis becomes increasingly important. There comes a point that

[4]Note that chartists themselves may believe that these movements are unrelated to the fundamentals. They consider these market movements to be important pieces of information reflecting other agents believes about market fundamentals.

it will overwhelm technical analysis in forecasting future exchange rates.

This assumption can be rationalized by introducing the idea that expectations made by fundamentalists are heterogenous, i.e., each fundamentalist makes a different calculation of the equilibrium rate (see also Cutler, Poterba and Summers, 1990). If we assume that these calculations are normally distributed around the true equilibrium rate, we can conclude that when the market rate is equal to the true equilibrium rate, the high and low forecasts made by fundamentalists will offset each other (so that also their buy and sell orders will be offsetting). As a result, when the market rate and the fundamental rate coincide, the fundamentalists have a low weight in determining the movements of the exchange rate. These then will be dominated by the chartists. When, however, the market rate starts deviating from the fundamental rate, say it increases, those who have made a low forecast for the equilibrium rate will increasingly dominate the market. If the market rate has increased sufficiently, all fundamentalists will consider that market rate to be too high, and will expect it to go down in the future. Their weight in the formation of market expectations will be high, so that the weight given to the chartists becomes correspondingly small.

We now implement these two assumptions about the speculative dynamics as follows. We write the change in the expected future exchange rate as consisting of two components, a forecast made by the chartists and a forecast made by the fundamentalists:

$$E_t(S_{t+1})/S_t = (E_{ct}(S_{t+1})/S_t)^{m_t}(E_{ft}(S_{t+1})/S_t)^{1-m_t} \tag{5}$$

where $E_t(S_{t+1})$ is the market forecast made in period t of the exchange rate in period $t+1$; $E_{ct}(S_{t+1})$ and $E_{ft}(S_{t+1})$ are the forecasts made by the chartists and the fundamentalists, respectively; m_t is the weight given to the chartists and $1-m_t$ is the weight given to the fundamentalists.

We assume that the chartists extrapolate recent observed exchange rate changes into the future, using a moving average procedure, i.e.:

$$E_{ct}(S_{t+1})/S_t = (S_t/S_{t-1})^d \cdot (S_{t-1}/S_{t-2})^e \cdot (S_{t-2}/S_{t-3})^f \tag{6}$$

where the coefficients d, e, and f are the weights of the moving average.

Admittedly this is a very crude assumption, and chartists typically use more sophisticated rules (in our further research we hope to study the implications of using more sophisticated chartists' forecasts). The use of simple rules, however, is not necessarily a disadvantage if we can show that very complex behavior of the exchange rate is possible even if chartists use these very simple forecasting rules.

The fundamentalists are assumed to calculate the equilibrium exchange rate (i.e., the exchange rate that leads to equilibrium in the model). In our model this is the PPP-rate. They will then expect the market rate to return to that fundamental rate (S_t^*) at the speed h during the next period, if they observe a deviation today, i.e.:

$$E_{ft}(S_{t+1})/S_t = (S_t^*/S_t)^h \tag{7}$$

As indicated earlier, the weights given to chartists and fundamentalists are assumed to be endogenous and to depend on the deviation of the market rate from the fundamental rate.[5]

There are several ways one could implement this assumption. We will make m_t in Eq. (5) a negative function of the deviation of S_t from its equilibrium value S_t^*, using the following specification

$$m_t = n/(1 + b(S_{t-1} - S_{t-1}^*)^2) \tag{8}$$

where $0 < n < 1$ and $b > 0$.

[5] In De Grauwe and Vansanten (1990) these weights were assumed to be fixed.

Graphically, we can represent this specification as follows:

Chaos in the Dornbusch model of the exchange rate

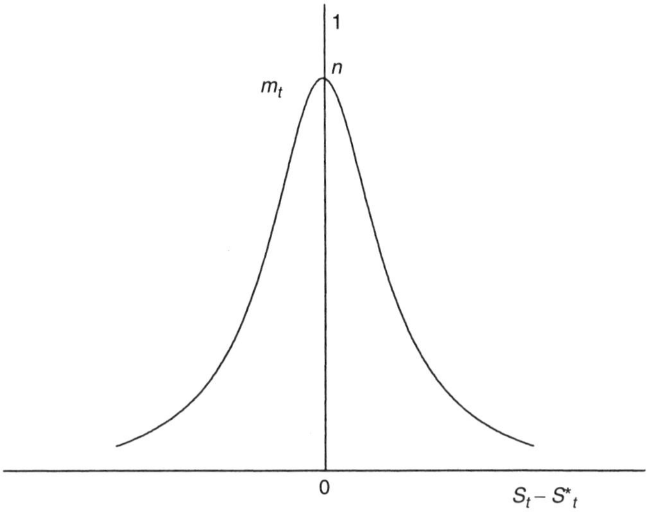

From this figure, it can be seen that when the market exchange rate is close to the fundamental rate the weight given to the chartists attains its maximum. This maximum is set at the value n (which is at most equal to 1). When the market rate deviates from the fundamental rate this weight tends to decline. For very large deviations it tends towards zero. The market expectations will then be dominated by the fundamentalists. Note also that the parameter b determines the speed with which the weight of the chartists declines. This coefficient can also be interpreted as measuring the sensitivity of the fundamentalists' expectations with respect to the deviations between the market and the fundamental exchange rate increases. With a high b the curve in Figure 1 becomes steeper.

From the preceding it may appear that we have introduced a lot of "ad-hoc" assumptions in constructing the model. First, the specification of Eq. (8) determining the changing weights of chartists and fundamentalists may seem rather special. Other functional forms could be used. In appendix we present an alternative functional form, and we show that the main results of the paper remain intact. Second, and more fundamentally, we have not derived the specifications of the behavior of the speculators from an explicit optimizing framework. As a result, expectations cannot be called rational. Our defence here is to plead guilty, and to ask the reader to follow us so as to see how far such a non-linear specification of the speculative dynamics can go in explaining exchange rate movements. We want to show that the speculative dynamics which we assume here (and for which there is an increasing amount of empirical evidence) allows us to construct models that come closer toward understanding reality than the structural models that have been used up to now. In addition, we will show that in our model economic agents have no incentives to invest energy in trying to detect the dynamics of the underlying model. Thus, it becomes reasonable to assume that they use simple rules of thumb (like PPP) in computing the equilibrium rate.

We now proceed toward solving the model.

2.3. *Solution of the Model*

Substituting (6), (7) and (8) into (5), and (5) into (2) and using (3) we obtain an expression for $(1+r)$, which can be substituted in (1). This yields the following equation:

$$P_t \cdot P_t^{*-ch(1-m_t)} \cdot (S_t^{-h(1-m_t)} \cdot E_{ct}(S_{t+1}/S_t)^{m_t})^{-c} = Z_1 \qquad (9)$$

where $Z_1 = MsY^{-a}(1+r_f)^c P_f^{-c(1-m_t)}$ and brings together all the exogenous variables. Equation (9) describes the equilibrium in the money market together with interest parity.

Using (3) we rewrite Eq. (4) as follows:

$$S_t^{-k} \cdot P_t^{(1+k)} \cdot P_{t-1}^{-1} = Z_2 \qquad (10)$$

where $Z_2 = P_f$, which without loss of generality can be set equal to 1.

The system of Eqs. (9) and (10) fully describes the dynamics of the model. We can solve it for the endogenous variables P_t and S_t. This yields:

$$P_t = Z_{1t} \cdot P_t^{*ch(1-m_t)} \cdot (S_t^{-h(1-m_t)} \cdot E_{ct}(S_{t+1}/S_t)^{m_t})^c \qquad (11)$$

and

$$S_t = ((G_2 G_1)^{-1} \cdot S_{t-1}^{-f1} S_{t-2}^{-f2} S_{t-3}^{-f3} S_{t-4}^{-f4})^{(1/f1)} \tag{12}$$

with

$$\begin{aligned}
f_0 &= (cdm_t - ch(1 - m_t))(1 + k) - k \\
f_1 &= (1 + k)cm_t(e - d) - (cdm_{t-1} - ch(1 - m_{t-1})) \\
f_2 &= (1 + k)cm_t(f - e) - c(e - d)m_{t-1} \\
f_3 &= -fcm_t(1 + k) - c(f - e)m_{t-1} \\
f_4 &= cfm_{t-1} \\
G_1 &= (Z1_t^{(1+k)}/Z1_{t-1}) \\
G_2 &= P_t^{*(1-ch(1-m_t))(1+k)}/P_{t-1}^{*(1-ch(1-m_t))} \\
m_i &= n/(1 + b(S_{t-i} - S_{t-i}^*)^2)
\end{aligned}$$

The exchange rate is determined by its own past, the lagged prices, and the exogenous variables Z_1 and Z_2.

As can be seen from (11) and (12) the solution of the model is a complex system of non-linear difference equations. An analytical solution to this system cannot be derived. In the next two sections we will simulate the behaviour of this model. Our interest in the model is first to know whether it is capable of generating an unpredictable dynamics (Section 3). More specifically, we ask the question under what parameter values the system will exhibit "chaotic" behavior. Second, we are interested in the interaction between the deterministic dynamics of the model with the occurence of stochastic shocks (Section 5).

3. Existence of Chaos

In this section, we turn to the question of the type of solutions the model is able to generate under different parameter values. We study under what configuration of parameters the model produces a chaotic movement of the exchange rate.

Let us first define chaotic motion. (We use the definition as provided by *Devaney* (1989)). A function like Eq. (12) is chaotic if:

(a) it has sensitive dependence on initial conditions
(b) it is topologically transitive
(c) periodic points are dense.

The intuition of this definition can be explained as follows. According to (a) a slight change in the initial conditions will (if sufficient time is allowed for) lead to a time path of the exchange rate which bears no resemblance whatsoever with the original time path. As will become clear, this has far-reaching implications for the predictability of the exchange rate. (b) implies that the consecutive exchange rates produced by iteration of Eq. (12) will eventually move from one arbitrarily small neighborhood to any other. Condition (c) introduces an element of regularity. It ensures that the exchange rate will remain within certain bounds around the steady state value (a strange attractor). Conditions b and c together also imply that the exchange rate has infinite periodicity, i.e., no cycles repeat themselves exactly.

Unfortunately there are no known methods to detect chaos, in an analytic way, in a difference equation of higher order like (12). One can use the characteristics (a) and (b), however, to detect chaos in an experimental way, i.e., through iterations of Eq. (12). In particular we will simulate the model and analyze whether the sensitivity to initial conditions holds (condition (a)). We analyze this by generating a minor difference in the initial condition of the system. If the system is not chaotic the solutions should asymptotically be equal. Second, we analyze the periodicity of the solution, by checking whether cycles in the exchange rate repeat themselves.

This simulation approach has an obvious weakness. Since any simulation is finite in length, it is impossible to discriminate between chaos and solutions with a periodicity equal to the length of the simulation plus one.

A pragmatic solution to this problem is to consider simulation runs that are long enough. Here we chose to simulate the model over a period of 7,000 observations. As a result, the difference between chaos and solutions that have a periodicity of 7,000 or more becomes purely academic since agents will not be able to detect a periodicity higher than 7,000. The Dornbusch model we use here typically has as a unit of time, a month (possibly a week).[6] Therefore, it would take at least 140 years (if the unit of time is a week) for a solution with periodicity 7,000 to start a new cycle, and to be detectable. We consider such solutions to be equivalent to chaos.

The number of combinations of parameters is very large. Therefore, we restrict ourselves to an analysis of the parameters underlying the behavior of the speculators (the parameterfield (n, b)). The other parameters, in particular the income elasticity and the interest elasticity are fixed ($a = 0.5$, $c = 0.8$).[7]

By setting $Z_1 = Z_2 = 1$ we have a steady state for the five tupple $(S_t, S_{t-1}, S_{t-2}, S_{t-3}, S_{t-4})$ in the point $(1, 1, 1, 1, 1)$. This steady state solution is independent of specific parameter positions in the parameterfield (n, b). Because of this independence we can evaluate the model characteristics in the neighborhood of $(1, 1, 1, 1, 1)$ for different parameter values.

We disturb the steady state for different values of (n, b) and analyze the behavior of the model from this moment on. The solution is either a stable one (the system returns to the pre shock position) or an unstable one (the system tends to a new position). In both cases, the dynamics can be characterized by periodicity, by a limit cycle or by a chaotic motion.

The simulation results are presented in Table 1. We indicate the kind of solution we obtain for different combinations of the parameters n and b. The interpretation of the table can best be explained by considering an example: Take the second column. For values of $n \leq 0.5$ and $b = 10$, we obtain stable solutions. When n is increased

---

[6]The Dornbusch model has a goods market dynamics in which deviations from PPP are partially corrected during the next period. Therefore it implies a lot of time aggregation. Put differently, the model is not suited to describe, say, hourly or daily exchange rate movements.

[7]The simulation results presented in the paper were generated with the following weights for the chartists' moving average weights: $d = 0.6$, $e = 0.3$ and $f = 0.1$. As is shown in Appendix, the choice of these weights does not alter the main results of the paper. The other parameter values of the model are: $a = 0.5$, $c = 0.8$, $h = k = 0.45$.

to 0.55 the solution of the model exhibits a periodicity of 2 (i.e., each cycle repeats itself after two periods). When n is increased further the periodicity of the solution increases. With $n = 0.7$ we obtain an 4-period solution. Chaos is obtained by increasing n further (for example, $n = 0.74$ leads to chaos). There are values for n that will lead to explosive solutions. These solutions are obtained when $n = 0.8$ or higher. Thus, the model is capable of generating all the types of solutions possible.

Table 1 also illustrates the role of chartists and fundamentalists in the dynamics of the solution. In general, we find that an increase in the weight given to chartists (the parameter n) changes the solution from stable to cyclical and chaotic. Sufficiently high weights given to chartists can even make the system explosive. Consequently, one can also conclude that an increasing weight given to the fundamentalists reduces the likelihood that chaos or instability is obtained.

The role of chartists and fundamentalists is also apparent in another way. As we move to the right in Table 1, the sensitivity

Table 1. Characteristics of the model in the (n, b) space.

n							
1.0	E	E	E	E	E	CH	CH
0.95	E	E	E	E	CH	CH	CH
0.90	E	E	E	E	CH	CH	CH
0.85	E	E	E	E	P16	P8	P8
0.80	E	E	E	E	CH	CH	CH
0.78	E	CH	CH	CH	CH	CH	CH
0.76	E	CH	CH	CH	CH	CH	CH
0.74	E	CH	CH	CH	CH	CH	CH
0.72	E	CH	P2	P2	P2	P2	P2
0.70	E	P4	P2	P2	P2	P2	P2
0.65	E	P2	P2	P2	P2	P2	P2
0.60	E	P2	P2	P2	P2	P2	P2
0.55	E	P2	P2	P2	P2	P2	P2
0.50	S	S	S	S	S	S	S
0.40	S	S	S	S	S	S	S
	0	0.01	0.1	1	100	500	1000
					b		
		(in thousands)					

Where S is the stable solution, Pi displays periodicity i, CH is the chaotic solution, E refers to explosiveness.

of the fundamentalists' expectations with respect to the deviations between the market and the fundamental exchange rate increases. We also observe that this movement leads to a reduction of the unstable region and an increase of the region of chaotic motion.

In Figure 1, we present a few examples of chaotic motions for different configurations of the parameters. Note that the exchange rate fluctuates around a constant steady state value because we assume that the fundamentals are unchanged during the simulation, and the fundamentalists are aware of this. In the later section, we analyze the model when fundamentals are allowed to change.

In order to show the sensitive dependence on initial conditions we simulated the model assuming first an initial shock in the exchange rate of 2.1 percent. We repeated the experiment with the initial shock equal to 2.2 percent. An example of the results of both experiments are shown in Figure 2 (for the parameter configuration $n = 0.79$, $b = 2,000$). We obtain similar results for all the chaotic solutions indicated in Table 1.

Figure 3a shows, as an example, the phase diagram of the chaotic exchange rate series of Figure 2 (assuming an initial disturbance in the exchange rate of 2.1 percent). The horizontal axis shows S_t and the vertical axis S_{t+1}. The diagram presents the 6,000 observations of one simulation experiment. Note that each observation falls in a different point, a characteristic of chaotic motion. No cycle repeats itself. And yet, there is a lot of structure in the phase diagram. This is illustrated further by a blow-up of the same diagram in Figure 3b.

The examples of Figures 1 to 3 illustrate the nature of chaotic motion. We ran simulations of 7,000 periods during which time no cycle repeated itself. More importantly, a small difference in initial condition leads after a few periods to time paths of the exchange rate which are completely different. It is in this sense that exchange rate movements in this model are unpredictable. In order to forecast the exchange rate using this structural model we would need to know the initial condition with a degree of precision that is unattainable in social sciences.

In fact, we need to know not only the initial conditions with extreme precision, but also the parameter values of the structural

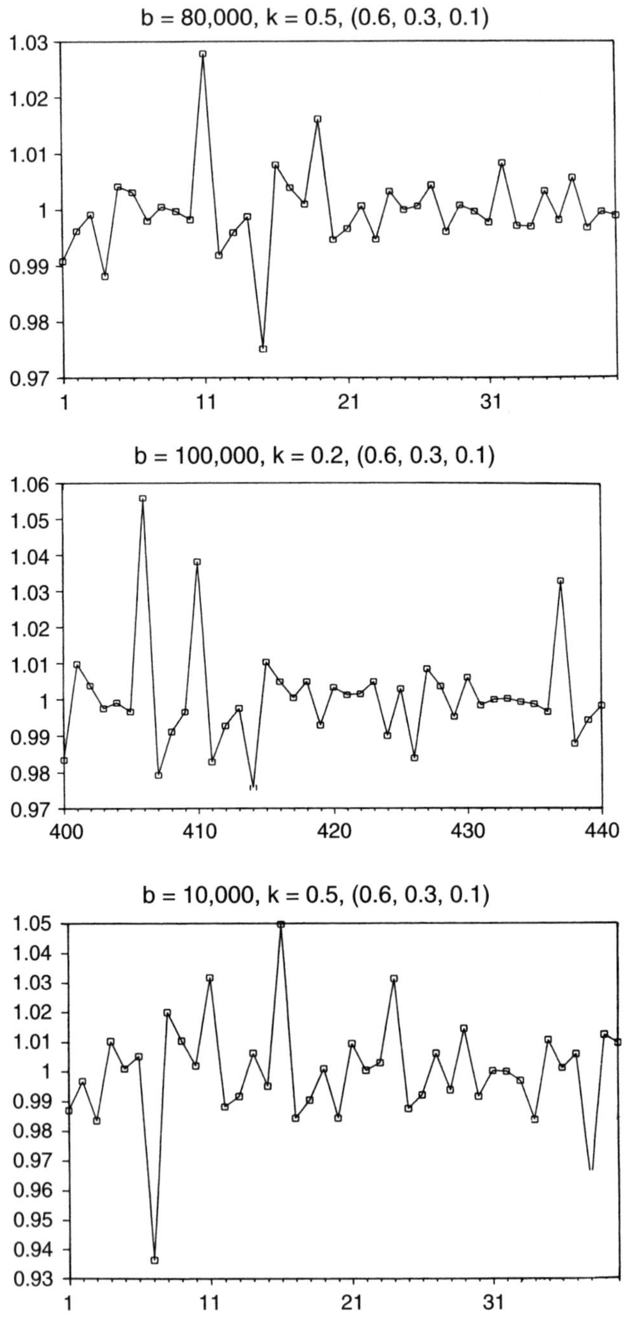

Figure 1. Chaotic motion of the exchange rate.

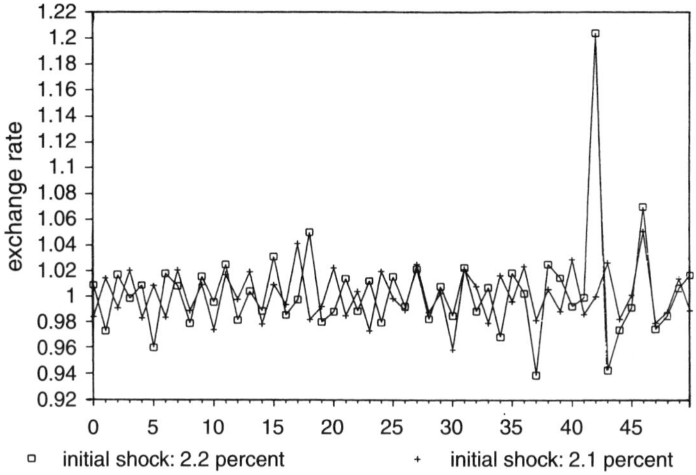

Figure 2. Dependence of initial conditions with chaos.

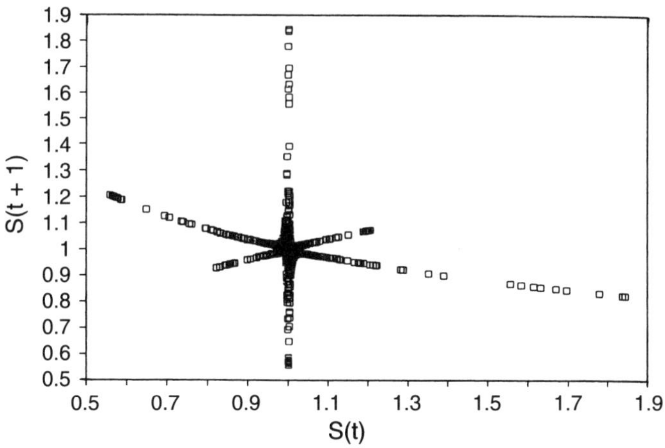

Figure 3a. Phase diagram of chaotic motion.

model with the same kind of precision in order to be able to predict the exchange rate. We illustrate this by presenting two simulations in Figure 4. The first simulation is the same as in Figure 2 (with initial condition: a shock of 2.2 percent in the exchange rate). In the second simulation we have decreased one parameter (n) by 0.5 percent. This second simulation can be interpreted as coming from a model

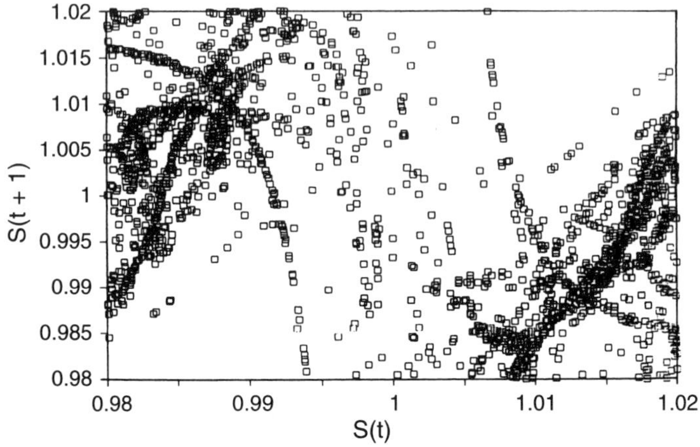

Figure 3b. Phase diagram of chaotic motion (blow-up).

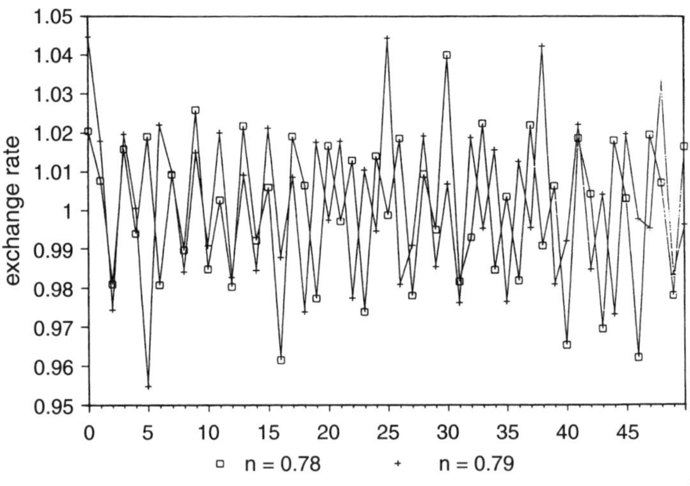

Figure 4. Sensitivity on measurement error simulation 2450 to 2500.

in which a slight measurement error has been made compared to the true model underlying the first simulation. The results of Figure 4 indicate that the slight measurement error produces a completely different time path of the exchange rate. This implies that in order to be able to use the model for predictive purpose we would have to know its underlying structural parameters with an extreme degree of precision. Under those conditions it is also unlikely that economic agents will have incentives to invest time and money in order to obtain information about the underlying structure of the model. The slightest error in the information processing will make it useless.

We will return to the problem of predictability of the exchange rate in a later section where we analyze the behavior of the model in an environment in which stochastic shocks occur "once in a while."

4. Effects of Money Supply Changes

In this section, we analyze how exogenous disturbances affect the solution of the model. We will focus here on permanent changes in the domestic money stock.

An important characteristics of the Dornbusch model is that its steady state solution exhibits typical monetarist results. In particular, an increase of the domestic money stock by x percent leads to an increase of the exchange rate and the domestic price level by the same x percent. Thus, in the steady state PPP and the quantity theory holds, so that money is neutral in the long run.[8]

A second characteristics of the model is that the dynamics of the adjustment after the shock depends on the initial conditions. We illustrate this by applying a permanent increase in the domestic money stock of 5 percent. We do this in two simulations that have different initial conditions. The results are shown in Figure 5. The shock in the money stock of 5 percent, occurs in period 10 in both simulations. The only difference is that the initial conditions for the exchange rate differ (by 0.1 percent). We observe that the time path of the exchange rate looks quite different in both simulations. The steady state value of the exchange rate, however, is the same in the two simulations.

Note also that the exchange rate does exhibit the overshooting phenomenon. Following the news in the money stock, the new

[8]It can be shown that in the steady state ($S^* = S_{t-i} = S_{t-j}$, for all j and i) the monetarist properties are satisfied, since $S^* = Ms^* = P^*$.

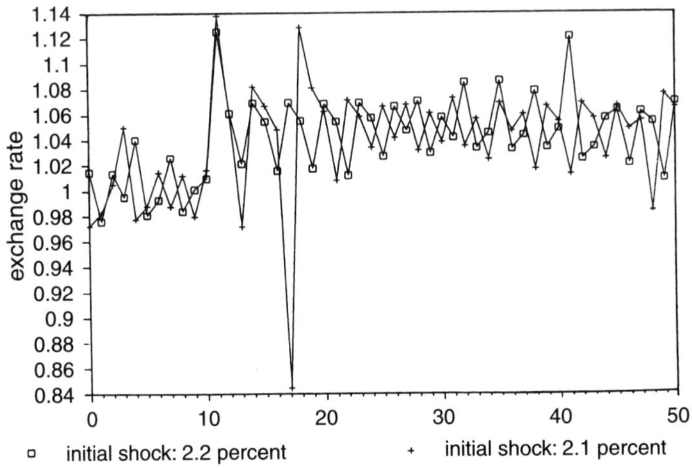

Figure 5. Permanent Shock in the Money Stock (5 percent) Simulation 95 to 130.

exchange rate overshoots its new steady state value. Thereafter the exchange rate moves around the new "strange attractor."

An interesting feature of Figure 5 is the fact that there are several periods during which the exchange rate moves as much or even more than during the period when the "news" in the money stock occurs. As a result, for an outside observer of the time series of Figure 5 it is not immediately obvious that in period 10 (when the shock in the money stock occurs) a change in a fundamental has occurred. It will take some time before this becomes clear. When the size of the disturbance is large relative to the inherent dynamics of the time series the fundamental change that occurs in period 10 can be inferred more quickly. We illustrate this phenomenon in Figure 6 where we assume that the increase in the money stock in period 10 is 10 percent (instead of 5 percent).

5. The Role of News in the Exchange Rate Dynamics

In the model analyzed so far we have established that for certain parameter values chaotic motion can occur. The characteristics of this dynamics is that it is unpredictable. We achieved this result without having recource to stochastic disturbances. In reality of course, "news" occurs and can be an important driving force of the exchange

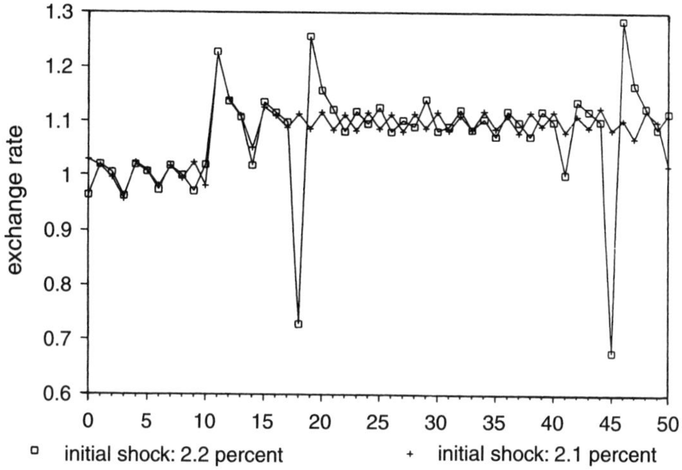

Figure 6. Permanent shock in the money stock (10 percent) simulation 95 to 130.

rate. In this section, we therefore introduce news. We will take the view, however, that "news" does not occur every period. This seems to be more realistic than to assume that news occurs every period.

We will simulate the model assuming that random shocks occur in the money stock. These random shocks occur infrequently, i.e., most of the time there is no disturbance. Once in a while, there is a random shock in the money stock.

The simulations were constructed as follows. First we specify a random walk, i.e.:

$$Ms_t = Ms_{t-1} + u_t \tag{17}$$

with u_t uniformly distributed with mean 0 and variance 0.1.

We perform this experiment using frequency 1/5 and 1/15, i.e., the change in the money stock occurs every 5 and 15 periods respectively. Between these periods no change in the money stock occurs.

We apply these shocks to the model that has as a solution an 8-period cycle. We do this to show that periodic solutions together with infrequent news are sufficient to generate complex dynamics. This then should hold a fortiori when we embed this infrequent news in the chaotic area. To show the latter we have also applied the money stock shocks to the model in the chaotic region. The resulting time series of these simulations are shown in Figures 7 to 9.

The results of Figures 7 and 8 confirm that infrequent occurrence of news (i.e., news every five periods) is sufficient to eliminate most of the systematicity in the movements of the exchange rate. Note,

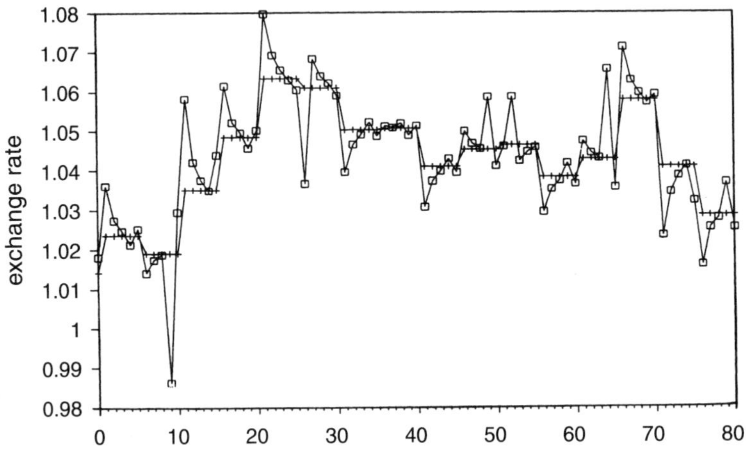

Figure 7. Simulation of the exchange rate with news frequency 1/5 embedded in period 8 solution.

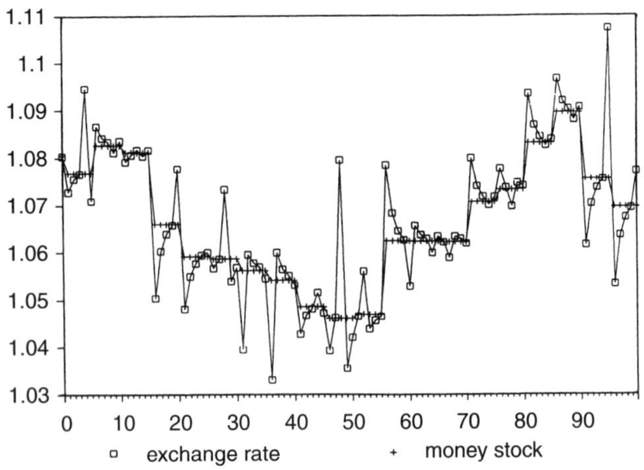

Figure 8. Simulation of the exchange rate with news frequency 1/5 embedded in chaos solution.

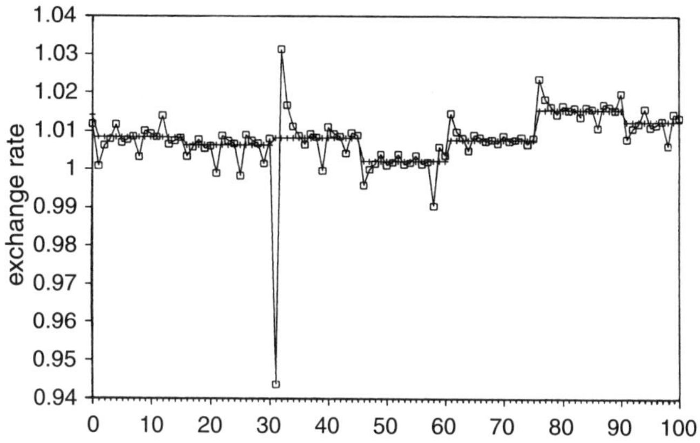

Figure 9. Simulation of the exchange rate with news frequency 1/15 embedded in period 8 solution.

however, that if the frequency with which news occurs is much lower than the periodicity of the cycle, the exchange rate often returns into a preditable periodicity. This is the case with a news-frequency of 1/15 in a model that exhibits a 8-period cycle as is illustrated in Figure 9.

The main reason why we do not need news to occur every time period to generate unpredictable exchange rate movements has to do with the nonlinear nature of the model. The latter is able to generate autonomous dynamics. Even when the latest relevant news brought the model in a low periodic field, the exchange rate will have a non-periodic solution before it displays its asymptotic characteristics and therefore it will be non predictable if the frequency of the news is such that it brings the model into another state before the asymptotic solution is displayed.

There is another noteworthy aspect to the results of Figures 7 and 8. It appears that although the news in the money stock has quite often a substantial impact on the exchange rate, there are also many periods during which shocks in the money stock do not seem to affect the exchange rate very much. In addition, many large changes in the exchange rate occur at times when there is no news in the money stock. (The latter result was also found in the previous section which discussed the effects of permanent changes in the money stock.) These results are consistent with the recent empirical studies Charles Goodhart (see Goodhart, 1989, 1990) who showed that many exchange rate changes of the major currencies could not easily be traced back to observable news. Our model allows us to understand this empirical phenomenon.

6. Some Preliminary Empirical Tests

Out of the large empirical literature concerning the exchange rate one dominant result emerges, i.e., unit root tests applied to exchange rates cannot easily be rejected.

A first test of our model therefore consists in applying unit root tests to the simulated exchange rates. Failure to reject the unit root hypothesis can then be interpreted as evidence (albeit preliminary) that the model's prediction of exchange rate patterns is not in contradiction with observable exchange rate behavior.

In order to test for unit roots we applied the augmented Dickey–Fuller test to the simulations of the model with infrequent news (1/5) using both the model under the 8-period cycle and under chaos.

We first estimated an equation of the form:

$$\Delta S_t = a_1 S_{t-1} + a_2 \Delta S_{t-1} + a_3 \Delta S_{t-2} + a_4 \Delta S_{t-3} \tag{18}$$

We tested the null hypothesis that $a_1 = 0$. The regressions of equation (18) were performed on simulation samples of different sizes. The results are presented in Table 2. In none of the different cases can we reject the null hypothesis of a unit root, i.e., the t-values are well below their critical Dickey–Fuller values.

Despite the fact that we cannot reject the unit root hypothesis, some structure in the time series of the exchange rates exists. This can be seen from the estimated coefficients a_2, a_3 and a_4 (and their standard errors) of Eq. (18) as presented in Table 3. These results suggest that there is autocorrelation in the exchange rate series, and that the random walk may not be the appropriate model to characterize exchange rate movements. A number of

Table 2. Test of $H_0 = 0$ in Equation (18).

sample size	a_1	t-value	$R2$	DW	Q(20)
model with 8-period cycle					
500	−0.000032	−0.07	0.4	2.1	22.7
1,000	−0.000086	−0.32	0.3	2.1	72.2
3,500	−0.000016	−0.11	0.3	2.1	80.3
model with chaos					
500	−0.0004	−0.2	0.5	2.1	35
1,000	−0.0004	−0.3	0.5	2.1	80
3,500	−0.0001	−0.2	0.4	2.1	100

Table 3. Coefficients a_2, a_3 and a_4 in Equation (18).

sample size	a_2	a_3	a_4
model with 8-period cycle			
500	−0.73	−0.48	−0.27
	(0.04)	(0.05)	(0.04)
1,000	−0.69	−0.45	−0.24
	(0.04)	(0.04)	(0.03)
3,500	−0.64	−0.40	−0.22
	(0.02)	(0.02)	(0.02)
model with chaos			
500	−0.86	−0.60	−0.30
	(0.03)	(0.04)	(0.03)
1,000	−0.86	−0.61	−0.29
	(0.04)	(0.04)	(0.03)
3,500	−0.81	−0.56	−0.28
	(0.02)	(0.02)	(0.02)

Note: the numbers in brackets are standard errors

recent empirical studies have also tended to reject the random walk hypothesis to describe the observed exchange rate movements of the major currencies.[9]

[9]See Cutler, Poterba and Summers (1990).

7. Chaos in the Price Level and in the Interest Rate

In this section, we analyze the dynamics of the interest rate and the price level. Our main result is that a chaotic motion of the exchange rate implies that the interest rate and the price level also exhibit chaotic motion. We illustrate this feature for the interest rate in Figure 10. This is the simulated interest rate under the same conditions as those prevailing for the exchange rate in Figure 1. Note that the vertical axis shows the difference between the domestic and the foreign interest rate. Since the latter is assumed to be constant, the numbers can be interpreted as the changes in the domestic interest rate. Figure 11 presents the simulated price level.

Figures 10 and 11 show the movements of the domestic interest rate and the domestic price level assuming the two different initial conditions as in Figure 1. We obtain the same qualitative result, i.e., a small disturbance in the initial conditions leads to a completely different time path of the interest rate and price level, making these variables difficult to predict.

Finally, note that although the qualitative results are the same, both the interest rate and the price level display a smaller volatility than the exchange rate.

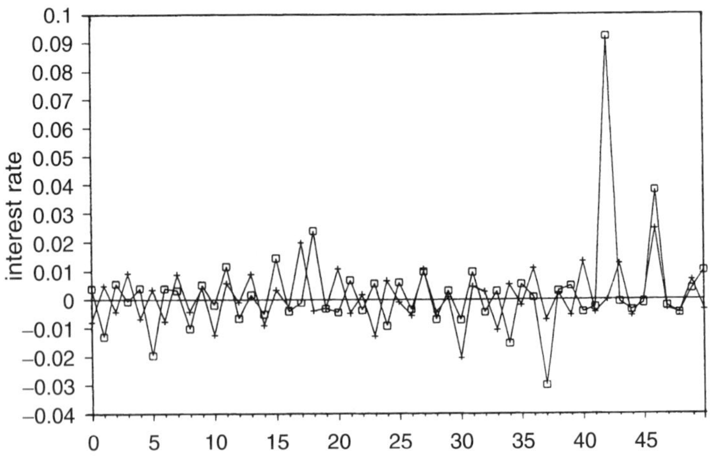

Figure 10. Chaotic motion of the interest rate.

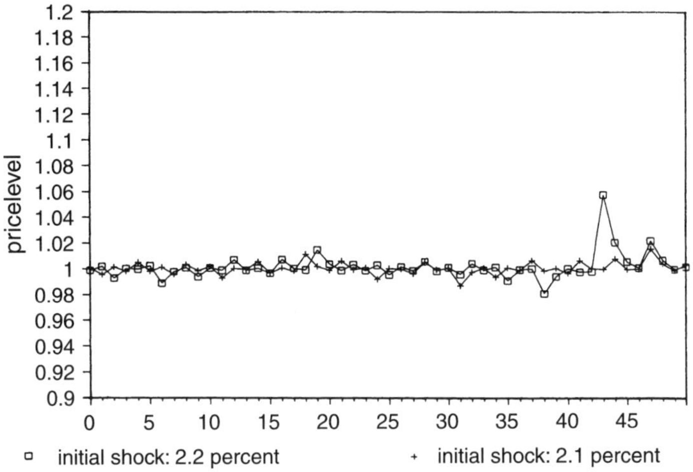

Figure 11. Chaotic motion of the pricelevel.

8. Conclusion

In this paper, we have constructed a monetary model of the exchange rate based on the celebrated *Dornbusch* model. We have added a speculative dynamics in which "chartists" and "fundamentalists" interact and in which the weight given to these two classes of speculators changes depending on the market circumstances. The forecasting rules we have assumed for these two groups of speculators are extremely simple, if not crude. The "chartists" are assumed to extrapolate recent changes in the exchange rate using a simple moving average procedure, whereas the fundamentalists base their expectations on simple PPP calculations. We show that these simple rules implemented in the Dornbusch model are sufficient to produce very complex exchange rate behavior (chaos). These exchange rate changes are essentially unpredictable, despite the fact that the underlying model is deterministic.

The model does not generate chaos for all parameter values. For some plausible parameter values we found a cyclical behavior of the exchange rate, in other words a predictable behavior. We did find, however, that when "news" is infrequent, i.e., its frequency is not much higher than the periodicity of the exchange rate, this is sufficient to make the time series of the exchange rate unpredictable. In this connection, we found that although "news" in the money stock most often has strong effects on the exchange rate, at other times it fails to have much perceptible effect on the exchange rate. In addition, quite often turbulence in the exchange market occurs without any "news."

The results of our model allow to develop a more sophisticated view of the role of news in the foreign exchange market. The "news-paradigm" that has dominated thinking about the foreign exchange market, requires "news" to occur whenever the exchange rate changes. This has led to the situation in which market observers search for news whenever the exchange rate moves. As a rule, these observers will detect some random event which can be made responsible for the "inexplicable" movement in the exchange rate.

The results of our model lead to a different view. The speculative dynamics produced by the interaction of speculators using different pieces of information is capable of generating a complex dynamics which we do not fully understand. Although "news" remains important, we do not need to invoke it to explain *every* observed movement of the exchange rate. Many such movements are unrelated to the occurence of news, but follow an (as yet) not fully understood dynamics. Our model therefore can be considered to provide a synthesis view of the "news" model that up to recently dominated academic thinking, and the more popular view that exchange rate movements are driven by a speculative dynamics. The latter view has acquired some academic respectability recently by the work (among others) Shiller (1984), *Delong et al.* (1990).

Another implication of our model is that initial conditions matter. This is of particular importance to evaluate the effects of monetary disturbances. We found that the same monetary shock has quite different effects on the dynamics of the exchange rate depending on the circumstances (initial conditions) in which it is applied.

A final implication of the results of our model relates to the rational expectations assumption. We have found that very small measurement errors in the estimation of the underlying structural model completely change the exchange rate dynamics predicted by the model. This feature destroys the usefulness of structural models for predictive purposes. It may also explain why the out-of-sample forecasts made by structural models have most often been worse than "random-walk" forecasts (Meese and Rogoff, 1983).

The rational expectations assumption has been based on the idea that economic agents use all relevant information, including the knowledge concerning the underlying structure of the model in which these agents operate. In our model, however, there is no incentive for economic agents to invest time and effort to gain knowledge about the underlying structural model. In order for this knowledge to be useful for predictive purposes, it would need to have a degree of precision which (today) is impossible to attain in the social sciences. It is therefore likely that economic agents use easy "rules of thumb" to compute the fundamental rate, and that they do not bother to use sophisticated structural models for predictive purposes.

Appendix

In this Appendix, we present some results of our model using a different specification of Eq. (8). We maintain the same basic assumption, i.e., that as the exchange rate moves away from its fundamentals, the weight given to the fundamentalists tends to increase, so that the weight of the chartists declines.

Here we selected a log-linear functional form as follows:

$$\begin{aligned} m_t &= n - b(|\log(S_{t-1}) - \log(S^*_{t-1})|) \qquad (8') \\ &\qquad \text{for all } m_t > 0 \\ m_t &= 0 \quad \text{for } m_t < 0 \end{aligned}$$

where n is the maximum value given to the weight of the chartists. This weight tends to decline as the "misalignment" between the market and the fundamental exchange rate increases. For some critical value, it becomes zero.

We simulated this version under the same parameter values as the original model. As in the case of the model discussed in the main text we foud regions of parameters for which a chaotic solution obtains. As an example we produce such a solution (for $n = 0.82$ and $b = 100$).

As can be seen from Figure A1 the qualitative feature of the chaotic results in the paper can be found as well in this version of the model. The sensitivity on initial conditions is maintained in this version of the model.

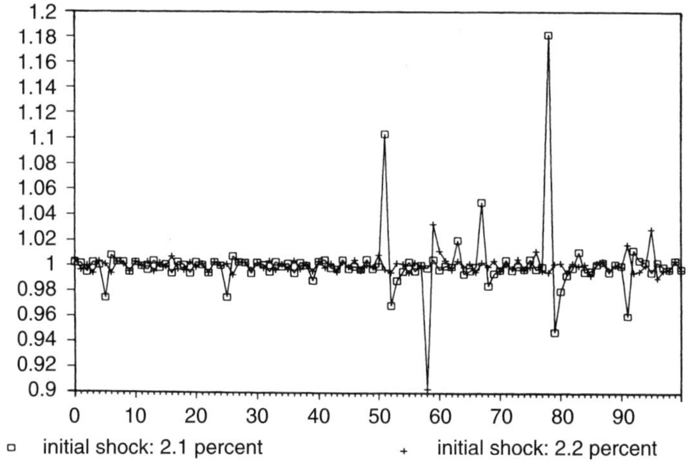

Figure A1. Sensitive dependence on initial conditions simulation 900 to 1000.

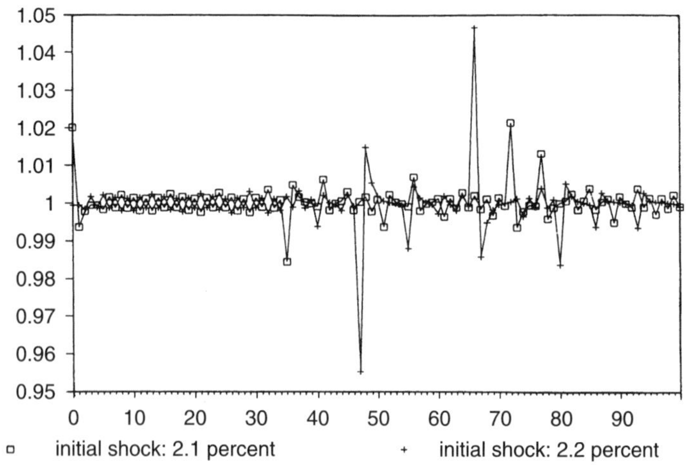

Figure A2. Sensitive dependence on initial conditions simulation 900 to 1000.

We also analyzed the extent to which the results are sensitive to the assumption that "chartists" use a 3-period moving average. Experimentation with different lags leads to the conclusion that our results are not sensitive to the choice of the lag. As an example we show the time series of the exchange rate in a model where chartists use a one period moving average (i.e., $d = 1$, $e = f = 0$). See Figure A2 (we have set $n = 0.85$). The results show the same sensitivity on initial conditions.

References

Allen, H and M Taylor (1989). Charts, noise and fundamentals: A study of the London foreign exchange market. CEPR Discussion Paper No. 341.

Bilson, JFO and RC Marston (1984). *Exchange Rate Theory and Practice.* Chicago, IL: University of Chicago Press.

Cutler, D, J Poterba and L Summers (1990). Speculative dynamics. NBER Working Paper No. 3242.

De Grauwe, P and K Vansanten (1990). Deterministic chaos in the foreign exchange market. CEPR Discussion Paper No. 370.

Delong, B, A Shleifer and L Summers (1990). Waldmann: Noise trader risk in financial markets. *Journal of Finance.*

Devaney, R (1989). *An Introduction to Chaotic Dynamical Systems*, 2nd Edition. Boston, MA: Addison Wesley.

Dornbusch, R (1976). Expectations and exchange rate dynamics. *Journal of Political Economy*, 84, 1161–1176.

Frankel, J and K Froot (1986). The dollar as a speculative bubble: A tale of chartists and fundamentalists. NBER Working Paper No. 1854.

Frankel, J (1989–1990). Chartists, fundamentalists and trading in the foreign exchange market. NBER Reporter, Winter, pp. 9–12.

Frenkel, J and M Mussa (1985). Asset markets, exchange rates and the balance of payments. In *Handbook of International Economics*, Vol. II, RW Jones and PB Kenen (eds.). Amsterdam: North-Holland.

Goodhart, C (1990). News and the foreign exchange market, LSE financial market group. Discussion Paper No. 71.

Levich, R (1985). Empirical studies of exchange rates: Price behaviour, rate determination and market efficiency. In *Handbook of International Economics*, Vol. II, R Jones and P Kenen (eds.). Amsterdam: North-Holland.

Meese, R and K Rogoff (1983). Empirical exchange rate models of the seventies: Do they fit out-of-sample? *Journal of International Economics*, 3–24.

Mussa, M (1984). The theory of exchange rate determination. In *Exchange Rate Theory and Policy*, JFO Bilson and R Marston (eds.). Chicago, IL: University of Chicago Press.

Scheinkman, J and B Lebaron (1989). Nonlinear dynamics and stock returns. *The Journal of Business*, 62(3), 311–337.

Shiller, R (1984). Stock prices and social dynamics. *Brooking Papers on Economic Activity*, (2), 457–498.

Chapter 2

Heterogeneity of Agents, Transactions Costs and the Exchange Rate

Paul De Grauwe and Marianna Grimaldi

1. Introduction

Traditional exchange rate modeling has been based on the efficient market rational expectations paradigm. It is increasingly evident, however, that this model is rejected by the data. There is a whole list of empirical puzzles that the traditional model fails to explain. The first and foremost empirical puzzle has been called the "disconnect" puzzle, i.e., the exchange rate appears to be disconnected from its underlying fundamentals most of the time. Goodhart (1989), Goodhart and Figlioli (1991) and more recently Faust *et al.* (2003) found that most of the changes in the exchange rates occur when there is no observable news in the fundamental economic variables.

Published in *Journal of Economic Dynamics and Control*, 29, 691–719, 2005.
We are grateful to Volker Böhm, Yin-Wong Cheung, Hans Dewachter, Roberto Dieci, Marc Flandreau, Cars Hommes, Philip Lane, Thomas Lux, Richard Lyons, Michael Moore, Ronald McDonald, Assaf Razin, Piet Sercu, Peter Sinclair, Jan Tuinstra and Peter Westaway for comments and suggestions. The comments of two anonymous referees are also gratefully acknowledged.
Keywords: Exchange rate; heterogenous agents; transaction costs; chaos; sensitivity to initial conditions.
JEL classification: F31, F41

This finding contradicts the efficient market rational expectations models, which imply that the exchange rate can only move when there is news in the fundamentals.

The exchange rate disconnect puzzle was also implicit in the celebrated Meese and Rogoff's studies of the early 1980s (Meese and Rogoff, 1983) documenting that there is no stable relationship between exchange rate movements and the *news* in the fundamental variables.

Other empirical anomalies have been uncovered over the years. One anomaly relates to the existence of excess volatility (Baxter and Stockman, 1989; Flood and Rose, 1995). Other puzzles are that the distribution of the exchange rate returns exhibit fat tails and volatility clustering (see de Vries, 2001; Lux, 1998; Lux and Marchesi, 2000). These empirical anomalies have also been observed in other financial markets (see Hommes, 2001). This evidence is difficult to rationalize in existing exchange rate models, since there is little evidence of fat tails and volatility clustering in the fundamental variables that drive the exchange rate in these models.

There is a need for other modelling approaches of the exchange rate. Our modelling approach combines two insights. The first one focuses on the presence of non linearities that arise from the existence of transaction costs in goods markets. Recent research has stressed the importance of transactions costs in the goods market for our understanding of the dynamics of exchange rate adjustments (Obstfeld and Rogoff, 2000; Engel, 2000; O' Connell, 1998; Michael, Nobay and Peel, 1997; Kilian and Taylor, 2001; Sarno and Taylor, 2002).

The second insight highlights the role of the heterogeneity of agents, who use incomplete information and who have different beliefs about the future exchange rate.[1] Recently, heterogeneity of agents was also introduced in rational expectations models (see Bacchetta and van Wincoop, 2003). The implication of rational expectations in models with heterogeneous agents is that it creates

[1]It should be noted that the heterogeneity of agents' expectations has been recognized as being important to explain the dynamics of asset prices, including the exchange rate (see De Long *et al.*, 1990; Frankel and Froot, 1986; Brock and Hommes, 1998; Lux and Marchesi, 2000; Hommes, 2001).

"infinite regress," i.e., the exchange rate depends on the expectations of other agents' expectations, which depends on the expectations of the expectations of other agents' expectations, and so on, *ad infinitum.* This leads to intractable mathematical problems except under very restrictive simplifying assumptions. Although this approach is intellectually satisfying, it is unclear that it is a good representation of what agents do in the exchange market. It requires these agents to solve a mathematical problem to which mathematicians have as yet been unable to give a general solution. This seems to us as imposing too large an informational burden on individual agents.

Our approach contrasts with this rational expectations approach in that agents use simple rules, the "fitness" of which is then controlled *ex post* by checking their profitability,[2] and by switching to the more profitable rules.

The paper is organized as follows. In Sections 2 and 3, we present the theoretical model. In Sections 4, 5, 6 and 7, we analyze its features, while in Section 8 we show the empirical relevance of the model. We conclude with some general implications for the exchange rates of the major currencies.

2. A Simple Non-Linear Exchange Rate Model

In this section, we develop a simple non-linear exchange rate model. We start by defining the fundamental exchange rate. This is the exchange rate that is consistent with equilibrium in the real part of the economy. In a very simple model, this could be the PPP-value of the exchange rate. In more elaborate models (e.g., the monetary model, or the Obstfeld–Rogoff new open economy macro model (Obstfeld and Rogoff, 1996), this fundamental exchange rate could be determined by the interaction of more variables than the price levels. We leave the modelling of the fundamental exchange rate outside the scope of this paper, and we will assume that the fundamental

[2]See Brock and Hommes (1998) for an application to the stock market. By stressing the use of simple rules, this approach comes close to the one of behavioral finance (Shleiffer, 2000).

exchange rate behaves like a random walk without drift.[3] This implies

$$s_t^* = s_{t-1}^* + \varepsilon_t \tag{1}$$

We now introduce the assumption that the agents have heterogeneous beliefs. We assume two types of agents, which we will call *fundamentalists* and *chartists.*[4]

The *fundamentalists* compare the present market exchange rates with the fundamental rate and they forecast the future market rate to move towards the fundamental rate. In this sense, they follow a *negative feedback* rule.[5] We will make the additional assumption that they expect the speed with which the market rate returns to the fundamental rate to be determined by the speed of adjustment in the goods market, θ which we assume to be constant. This leads us to specify the following rule for the fundamentalists:

$$E_{f,t}(\Delta s_{t+1}) = -\theta(s_t - s_t^*) \tag{2}$$

where $E_{f,,t}$ is the forecast made in period t by the fundamentalists using information up to time t, s_t is the exchange rate in period t, and $\theta > 0$.

The *chartists* are assumed to follow a *positive feedback* rule, i.e., they extrapolate past movements of the exchange rate into the future. Their forecast is written as:

$$E_{c,t}(\Delta s_{t+1}) = \beta \sum_{i=0}^{T} \alpha_i \Delta s_{t-i} \tag{3}$$

where $E_{c,,t}$ is the forecast made by the chartists using information up to time t, Δs_t is the change in the exchange rate, $\sum_{i=0}^{T} \alpha_i = 1$, and $0 < \beta < 1$ to ensure dynamic stability.

---

[3]Introducing a drift does not change the nature of the model, nor its results. We also experimented with an AR(1) process for the fundamental rate. This did not affect our results.

[4]This way of modelling the foreign exchange market was first proposed by Frankel and Froot (1986). It was further extended by De Long *et al.* (1990) and De Grauwe *et al.* (1993) and more recently Kilian and Taylor (2001). For evidence about the use of chartism, see Taylor and Allen (1992).

[5]Note that this is also the approach taken in the Dornbusch model.

As can be seen, the chartists compute a moving average of the past exchange rate changes and they extrapolate this into the future exchange rate change. The degree of extrapolation is given by the parameter β. Note that the chartists do not take into account information concerning the fundamental exchange rate. In this sense, they can be considered to be pure *noise traders* (see De Long *et al.*, 1990).

Our choice to introduce chartists' rules of forecasting is based on empirical evidence. The evidence that chartism is used widely to make forecasts is overwhelming (see Cheung *et al.*, 1999; Taylor and Allen, 1992). Therefore, we give a prominent role to chartists in our model. It remains important, however, to check if the model is internally consistent. In particular, the chartists' forecasting rule must be shown to be profitable within the confines of the model. If these rules turn out to be unprofitable, they will not continue to be used.

The next step in our analysis, therefore, is to specify how agents evaluate the usefulness of these two forecasting rules. The general idea that we will follow is that agents use one of the two rules, compare their profitability *ex post* and then decide whether to keep the rule or switch to the other one. Thus, our model is in the logic of evolutionary dynamics, in which simple decision rules are followed. These rules continue to be followed if they pass some "fitness" test (profitability test).

In order to implement this idea, we follow the procedure proposed by Brock and Hommes (1997, 1998) which is based on discrete choice theory. Thus, the fractions of agents using chartist and fundamentalist rules are a function of the relative (risk adjusted) profitability of these rules, i.e.,

$$n_{ct} = \frac{\exp \gamma(\pi_{c,t-1} - \sigma_{c,t-1})}{\exp \gamma(\pi_{c,t-1} - \sigma_{c,t-1}) + \exp \gamma(\pi_{f,t-1} - \sigma_{f,t-1})} \tag{4}$$

$$n_{ft} = \frac{\exp \gamma(\pi_{f,t-1} - \sigma_{f,t-1})}{\exp \gamma(\pi_{c,t-1} - \sigma_{c,t-1}) + \exp \gamma(\pi_{f,t-1} - \sigma_{f,t-1})} \tag{5}$$

where $\pi_{c,t-1}$ and $\pi_{f,t-1}$ are the net profits of the chartists' and fundamentalists' forecasting rule in period $t-1$. Chartists and fundamentalists make a profit (loss) when they correctly (wrongly) forecast the direction of the exchange rate movements. The profit (loss) they make equals the one-period return of the exchange rate. We assume that fundamentalists bear a fixed cost for collecting information on the fundamental variable while chartists' information is costless. Thus

$$\pi_{f,t-1} = \pi'_{f,t-1} - C$$

where $\pi'_{f,t-1}$ *is the* gross profit of fundamentalists and C_i is the fixed cost of collecting information on the fundamental.

The variables $\sigma_{c,t-1}$ and $\sigma_{f,t-1}$ are measures of the risk associated with the forecasting rule of the chartists and fundamentalists, respectively. The most obvious definition of these measures of risk is the weighted average of the squared (one period ahead) forecast errors made by chartists and fundamentalists respectively:

$$\sigma_{i,t} = \sum_{k=1}^{\infty} \lambda_k [E_{i,t-k}(s_{t-k+1}) - s_{t-k+1}]^2 \tag{6}$$

where λ_k are geometrically declining weights.

This definition of the risk leads to a problem for the fundamentalists, however. The latter make a forecast based on the distance between the market exchange rate and the fundamental rate (the misalignment). As a result, when the exchange rate departs from its fundamental, the squared forecast error of using a fundamentalist rule increases. Thus, if we use Eq. (6) as a measure of risk for the fundamentalists, it implies that the stronger the misalignment, the riskier the use of a fundamentalist forecast will be perceived to be. This is quite implausible. One would expect that as the degree of misalignment increases, the confidence in making forecasts based on a fundamentalist rule also increases. In order to take this feature of fundamentalists forecasts into account we amend Eq. (6) for the fundamentalists as follows:

$$\sigma_{f,t} = \frac{\sum_{k=1}^{\infty} \lambda_k [E_{i,t-k}(s_{t-k+1}) - s_{t-k+1}]^2}{1 + (s_{t-1} - s^*_{t-1})^2} \tag{7}$$

where $(s_{t-1} - s^*_{t-1})$ is the misalignment. The logic behind this specification is that with increasing misalignment the fundamentalists attach less importance to the short-term volatility as measured by the one period ahead forecast error, and they become increasingly confident that the exchange rate will revert to its fundamental value.[6] Note that in the neighbourhood of the fundamental exchange rate the risk variable converges to the same value as in Eq. (6).

Equations (4) and (5) can now be interpreted as follows. When the risk adjusted profits[7] of the chartists rule increases relative to the risk adjusted profits of the fundamentalists rule, then the fraction of the fundamentalists in the market increases, and *vice versa*. The sensitivity with which the chartists' and fundamentalists' fractions adjust to the relative profitability of the forecasting rules depends on the parameter γ. With an increasing γ the fraction of chartists (fundamentalists) who switch to the more profitable forecasting rule increases. In the limit when γ goes to infinity agents will select the most profitable rule instantaneously. When γ is equal to zero the fraction of chartists and fundamentalists is constant and equal to 0.5. Thus γ is a measure of inertia in the decision to switch to the more profitable rule.[8]

The market expectation of the exchange rate change can be written as a weighted average of the expectations of chartists and fundamentalists, i.e.:

$$E_t \Delta s_{t+1} = -n_{ft}\theta(s_t - s^*_t) + n_{ct}\beta \sum_{i=0}^{T} a_i \Delta s_{t-i} \tag{8}$$

where n_{ft} and n_{ct} are the weights of fundamentalists and chartists respectively.

The realised change in the market exchange rate in period $t+1$ equals the market forecast made at time t plus some white noise

[6]For a similar approach see Chiarella *et al.* (2002).

[7]Note that the risk adjusted profits can be interpreted as Sharpe ratios.

[8]This specification of the decision rule is often used in discrete choice models. See for example Brock and Hommes (1997) and Lux (1998).

errors (i.e., the *news* that could not be predicted at time t):

$$\Delta s_{t+1} = -n_{ft}\theta(s_t - s_t^*) + n_{ct}\beta \sum_{i=0}^{T} a_i \Delta s_{t-i} + \varepsilon_{t+1} \tag{9}$$

3. The Model with Transactions Costs

There is an increasing body of theoretical literature stressing the importance of transactions costs in the goods market as a source of non-linearity in the determination of the exchange rate (Dumas, 1992; Obstfeld and Rogoff, 2000). The importance of transaction costs in the goods market has also been confirmed empirically (Taylor, Peel, and Sarno, 2001; Kilian and Taylor, 2001). It should be noted that transaction costs in the goods market remain sizeable because a large component of most tradable goods is non-tradable (see Obstfeld and Rogoff, 2000).

We therefore introduce transaction costs into the model and we assume that the fundamentalists take the existence of transaction costs in the goods market into account, i.e., they behave differently depending on whether the exchange rate is within or outside the transaction costs band. When the exchange rate deviations from the fundamental value are smaller than the transaction costs in the goods markets, there is no mechanism that drives the exchange rate towards its equilibrium value. As a result, they expect the changes in the exchange rate to follow a white noise process ε_t. The best they can do is to forecast no change. More formally,

$$\text{when } |s_t - s_t^*| < C, \quad \text{then} \quad E_{f,t}(\Delta s_{t+1}) = 0.$$

In the second case, when the exchange rate deviation from its fundamental value is larger than the transaction costs C (assumed to be of the "iceberg" type), then the fundamentalists follow the same forecasting rule as in Eq. (2). More formally,

$$\text{when } |s_t - s_t^*| > C \text{ holds, then Eq. (2) applies.}$$

This formulation implies that when the exchange rate moves outside the transaction costs band, market inefficiencies other than transaction costs continue to play a role. As a result, these inefficiencies prevent the exchange rate from adjusting instantaneously. In our model, these inefficiencies are captured by the fact that the speed of adjustment in the goods market is not infinite (Eq. 2).

4. Solution of the Model

In this section we investigate the properties of the solution of the model. We first analyze the deterministic part of the model so as to obtain a better insight into the characteristics of the solution that is not clouded by exogenous noise. We use simulation techniques since the non-linearities do not allow for a simple analytical solution. We select "reasonable" values of the parameters, i.e., those that come close to empirically observed values. As we will show later these are also parameter values for which the model replicates the observed statistical properties of exchange rate movements. We will however analyze how sensitive the solution is to different sets of parameter values.

We first concentrate on the fixed point solutions of the model. We find that for a relatively wide range of parameters the solution converges to a fixed point (a *fixed-point attractor*). However, there are many such fixed points (attractors) to which the solution converges depending on the initial conditions.[9] We illustrate this feature in Figure 1, where we show the exchange rate in the time domain for a particular set of parameters and different initial conditions. We find that the exchange rate converges to a different fixed point depending on the initial conditions. (In the next section, we perform a sensitivity analysis to check the general nature of this result). We show this feature in Figure 2 in a different way by plotting the fixed-point solutions (attractors) as a function of the different initial conditions. On the horizontal axis, we set out the different initial conditions. These are initial shocks to the deterministic system. The vertical axis shows the solutions corresponding to

[9]Note that the initial condition that is changed refers to the one period lagged exchange rate.

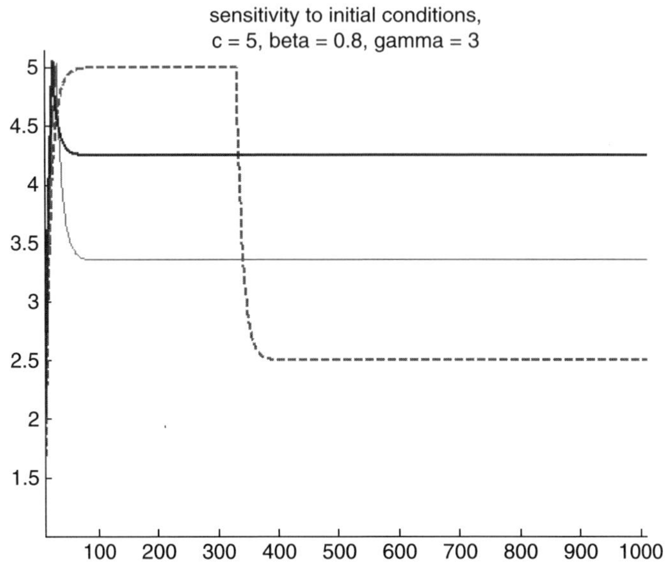

Figure 1.

Note: The parameters α_i and λ_k were defined as geometrically declining weights with $\rho = 0.6$; $C_i = 0.05$. These parameter values were kept unchanged in all the simulations reported here. A sensitivity analysis revealed that the results are not very sensitive to these parameter values.

these different initial conditions. Note that small changes in the initial conditions lead to large and discontinuous displacements of the attractors. This characteristic is a natural result of the non-linear nature of our model. We return to this to give an interpretation to this phenomenon.

5. Sensitivity Analysis

We obtain a multiplicity of fixed-point solutions for a relatively broad range of parameters. We find that the extrapolation parameter of the chartists, β and the intensity of choice parameter γ are of crucial importance. In Figure 3, we show the fixed-point attractors for different combinations of parameter values of β and γ.

It can be seen that we obtain a multiplicity of fixed-point attractors, each one depending on the initial shock. It should also be noted

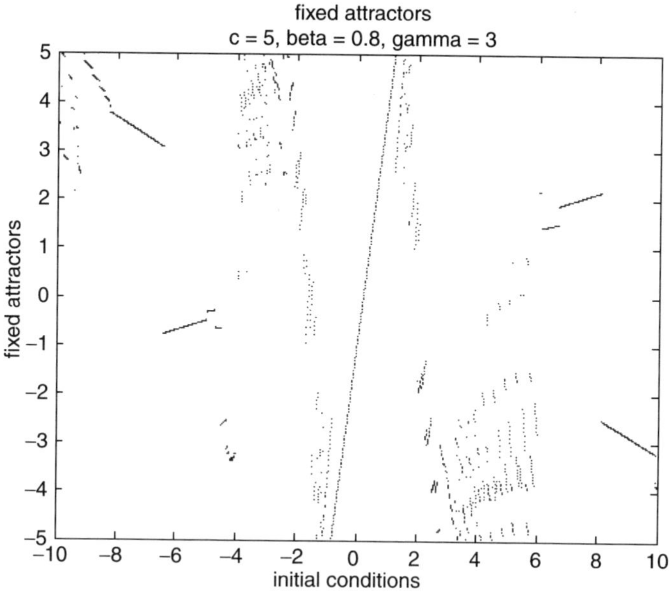

Figure 2.

that the fixed-point attractors lie within the transaction costs band. The intuition is that any fixed-point solution outside the transaction costs band would create an inconsistency, which can be described as follows. Outside the transaction costs band the fundamentalists' behavior leads to a mean reverting process of the exchange rate, moving the latter towards the transaction costs band. Thus, if a fixed point solution were observed outside the transactions cost band, this would mean that the fundamentalists would fail to move the exchange rate toward the band. Once inside the band, the fundamentalists' dynamics disappears. The only dynamics then comes from the chartists who drive the exchange rate to some attractor within the band. The exact position of this attractor depends on the entry point of the exchange rate in the transactions cost band, and this depends on the initial shock.

We next perform a more extensive sensitivity analysis. We analyze how changes in some important parameters of the model affect the nature of the solution. We first do a sensitivity analysis with

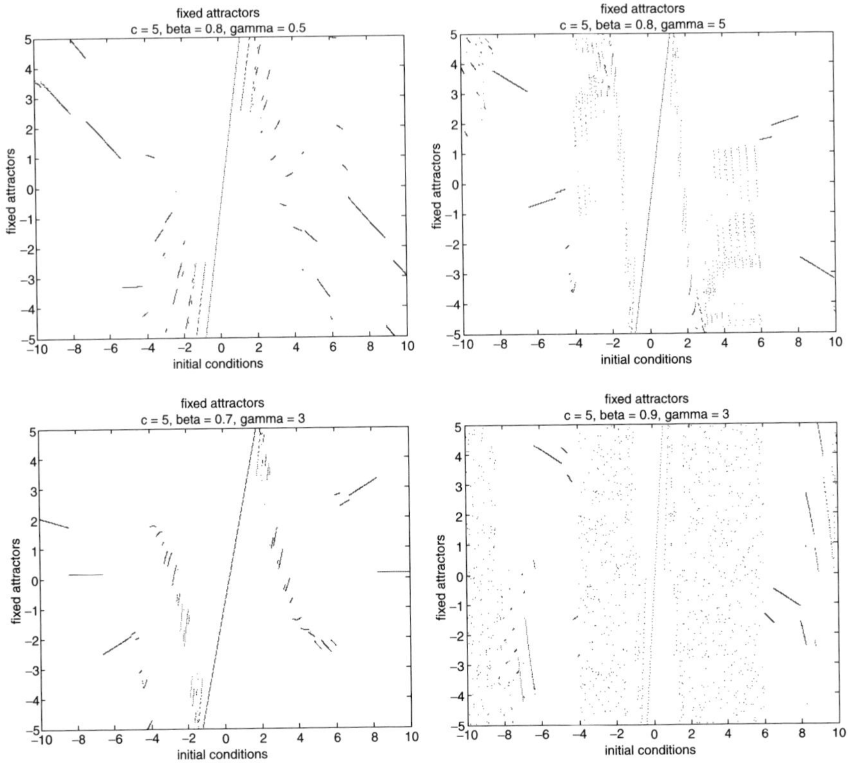

Figure 3.

respect to transaction cost parameter C. In Figure 4, we show the attractors as a function of transaction costs. We observe that as transaction costs increase the band in which the fixed point attractors are located increases correspondingly. The important aspect of Figure 4 is that small changes in the transaction costs lead to a large and discontinuous displacement of the fixed attractor. This feature was also found when we plotted the fixed attractors for different initial conditions (see Figures 2 and 3).

Next we perform a similar sensitivity analysis by allowing changes in γ, the intensity of choice parameter. In Figure 5, we show the equilibrium exchange rate (attractor) as a function of γ. We observe that for relatively low values of γ we obtain fixed-point solutions. For intermediate values of γ we obtain a chaotic region, i.e., the

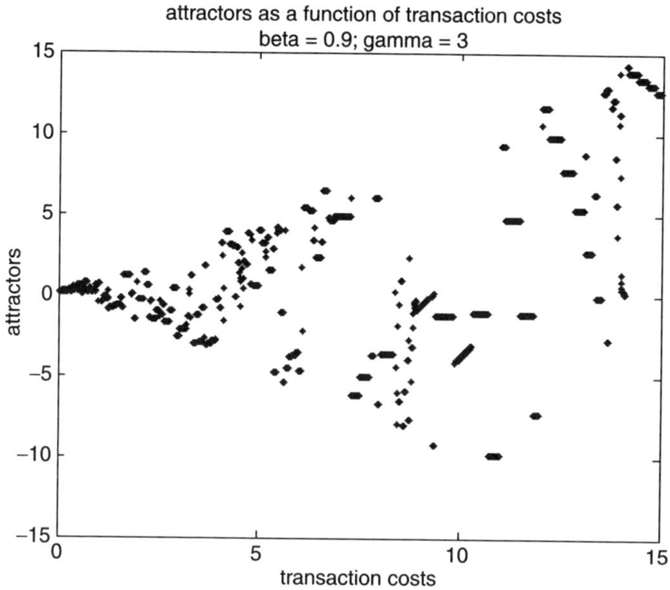

Figure 4.

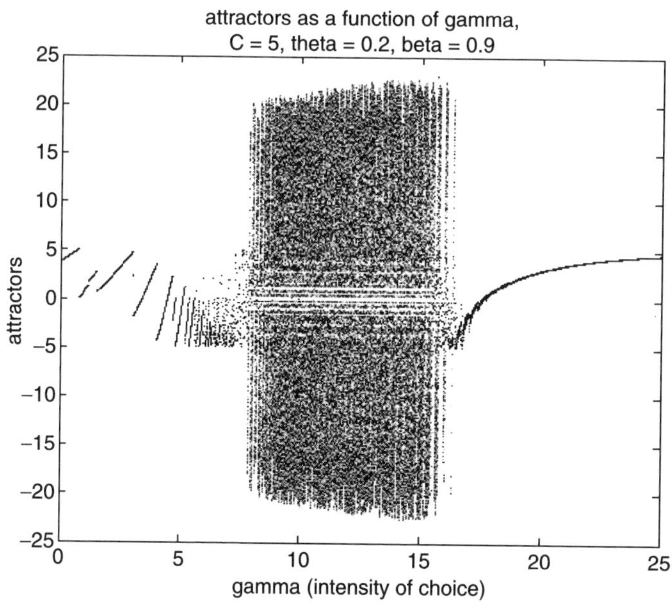

Figure 5.

exchange rate moves within a strange attractor. For high values of γ we return to fixed-point solutions.[10] These, however, are "well-behaved," i.e., they lie on a continuous line. This means that small changes in the parameter γ stop having discontinuous effects on the equilibrium exchange rate. Thus, when agents react forcefully to the relative profitability of the forecasting rules the system converges to a unique fixed-point solution.

Finally in Figure 6, we show the sensitivity of the equilibrium exchange rate with respect to the extrapolation parameter of chartists, β. For values of $\beta < 0.95$ we obtain fixed point attractors. In this region, we obtain the same characteristic that we observed in the sensitivity analysis with respect to the transaction cost, i.e.,

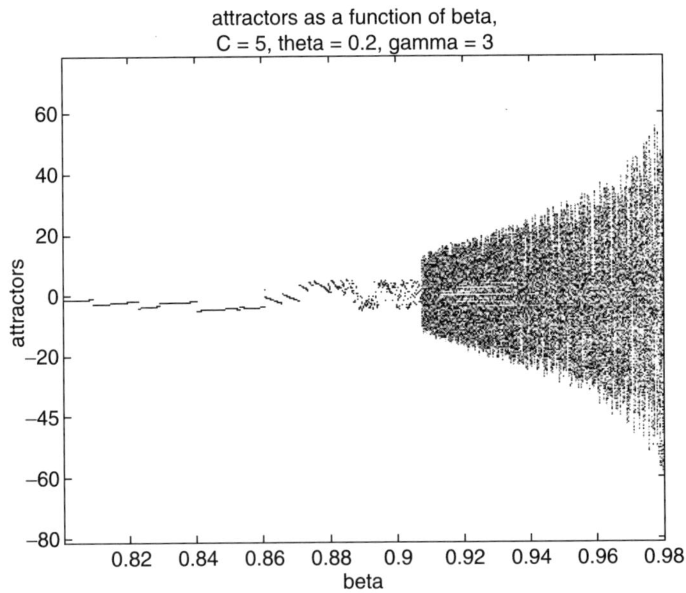

Figure 6.

[10]It should be pointed out that the numerical values of γ that move us in and out of chaos depend on the initial conditions of the simulation runs, and on the other parameters of the model. In all simulations, however, we obtain three regions: a multitude of fixed points for low values of γ, chaotic attractors for intermediate values of γ, a unique fixed point for high values of γ.

a small change in the parameter leads to discrete jumps in the equilibrium exchange rate. When β exceeds 0.91, we enter a chaotic region.

The empirical evidence about the existence of deterministic chaos in the foreign exchange rate market is weak (see Guillaume, 1996; Schittenkopf, Dorffner and Dockner, 2001). Therefore, we will focus the analysis of the model on parameter values that do not lead to deterministic chaos. We will show that in combination with stochastic shocks this model is capable of producing a dynamics that exhibits many of the features of chaotic dynamics despite the fact that the deterministic solutions of the model are fixed points.

6. The Stochastic Version of the Model

We now introduce stochastic disturbances to the model. These disturbances affect the fundamental, which is assumed to be a random walk. In addition, as can be seen from Eq. (9), there is exogenous noise leading to forecast errors of chartists and fundamentalists. We simulate the model with a certain combination of parameter values that we refer to as the "standard case." This includes setting $c=5$, $\beta=0.9$, $\theta=0.2$ and $\gamma=3$. Our results hold for a wide range of parameter values. As mentioned earlier, these are parameter values that do not produce deterministic chaos.

A first feature of the solution of the stochastic version of the model is the sensitivity to initial conditions. In order to show this, we first simulated the model with the "standard" parameter values and then with the same parameters setting but with a slightly different initial condition. In both cases, we used identical stochastic disturbances. We show the time paths of the (market) exchange rate in Figure 7. We observe that after a certain number of periods the two exchange rates start following a different path. This result is related to the presence of many fixed-point attractors in the deterministic part of the model, which are themselves dependent on the initial conditions (see Figure 3, which shows how slight differences in initial conditions can lead to fixed-point attractors that are very far apart). As a result, the two exchange rates can substantially diverge because attracted by fixed-points that are located in different basins

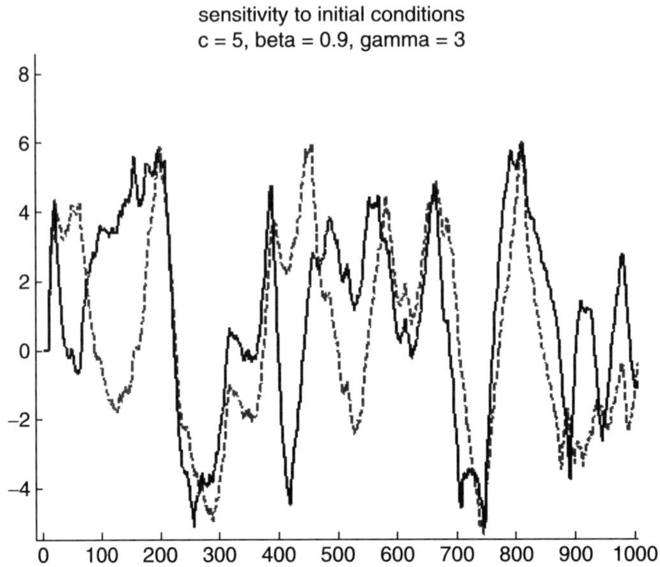

Figure 7.

of attraction. The interesting feature of this result is that the combination of exogenous noise and a multiplicity of fixed-point attractors creates chaos-like dynamics without chaos being present in the deterministic part of the model.

7. The Effect of Permanent Shocks

In this section, we analyze how a permanent shock in the fundamental exchange rate affects the market exchange rate. In linear models, a permanent shock in the fundamental has a predictable effect on the exchange rate, i.e., the coefficient that measures the effect of the shock in the fundamental on the exchange rate converges after some time to a fixed number. Things are very different in our non-linear model. We illustrate this by showing how a permanent increase in the fundamental is transmitted to the exchange rate. We assumed that the fundamental rate increases by 10, and we computed the effect on the exchange rate by taking the difference between the exchange rate with the shock and the exchange rate without

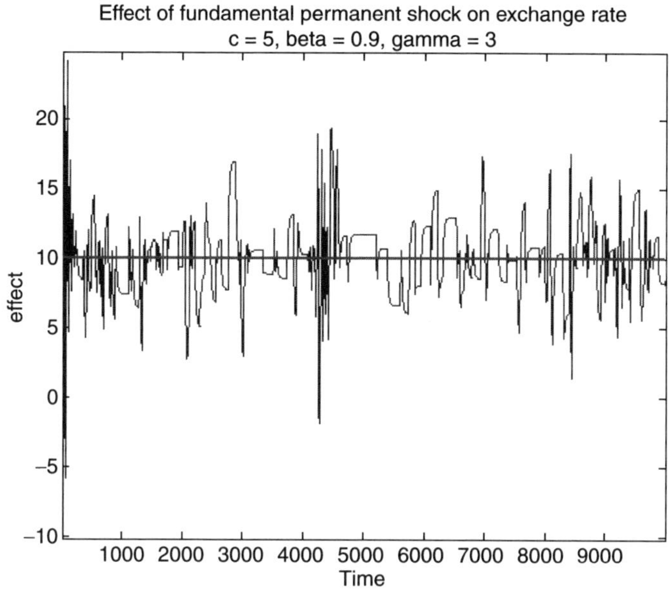

Figure 8.

the shock. The simulations of these two exchange rates are done using the same exogenous noise. In a linear model, we would find that in the long run the exchange rate increases by exactly 10. This is not the case in our model. We present the evidence in Figure 8 where we show the effect of a permanent shock of 10 in the fundamental rate on the exchange rate for our standard set of parameter values.

The most striking feature of these results is that the effect of the permanent shock does not converge to a fixed number. In fact, it follows a complex pattern. Thus, in a non-linear world, it is very difficult to predict what the effect will be of a given shock in the fundamental, even in the long run. Such predictions can only be made in a statistical sense, i.e., our model tells us that *on average* the effect of a shock of 10 in the fundamental will be to increase the exchange rate by 10. In any given period, however, the effect could deviate substantially from this average prediction.

The importance of the initial conditions for the effect of a permanent shock in the fundamental can also be seen by the following

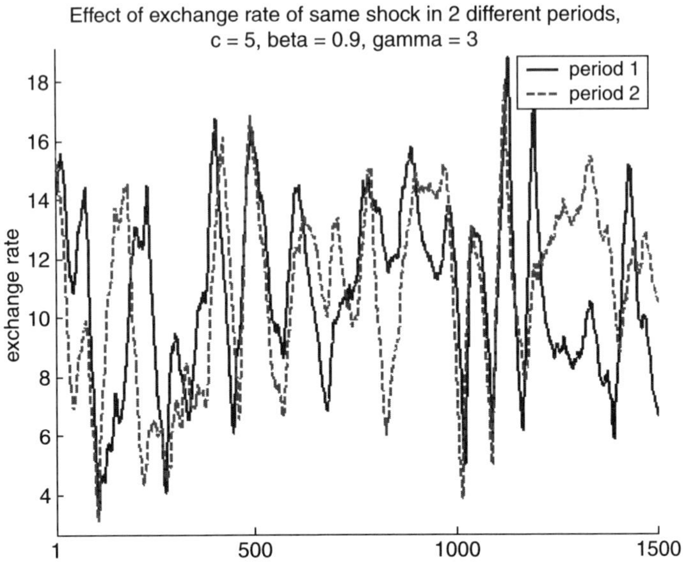

Figure 9.

experiment. We simulated the same permanent shock in the fundamental but applied it in two different time periods. In the first simulation, we applied the shock in the first period; in the second simulation we applied it in the next period. The exogenous noise was identical in both simulations. Thus, the only difference is in the timing of the shock. We show the results in Figure 9.

We observe that the small difference in timing changes the future history of the exchange rate. As a result, the effect of the shock measured at a particular point in time can be very different in both simulations. Thus, history matters. The time at which the permanent shock occurs influences the effects of the shock.

Note however that in a statistical sense, timing does not matter. When we compute the *average* effect of the same shock in the two simulations over a sufficiently long period of time we obtain the same result, i.e., the exchange rate increases by 10 on average. The time period needed to make valid statistical inferences, however, is large. We illustrate this in Figure 10 by the frequency distributions of the effects of the same shock in the two simulations obtained over two

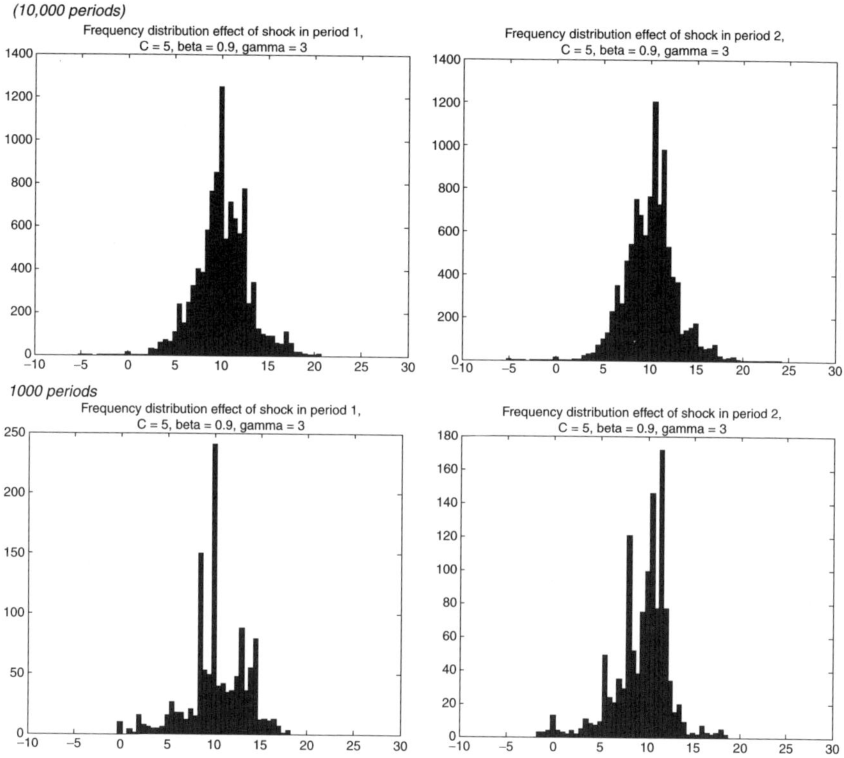

Figure 10.

different simulation runs, the first one containing 10,000 periods, the second one 1,000 periods.

An important aspect of Figure 10 is that when computed over a sample of 1,000 periods, the distribution of the effects is irregular and quite different for the two simulations. Only when the sample becomes very large (10,000) do we obtain "well-behaved" distributions permitting statistical inferences about the effect of the same shock.[11]

Our results help to explain why in the real world it appears difficult to predict the effects of changes in the fundamental exchange

[11]We computed tests of normality of the distribution (Kolmogorov–Smirnov test, and Lillie test). We rejected normality in all cases. Thus, the usual significance tests that assume normality of the distribution (t-test and F-test) are not appropriate here.

rate on the market rate, and why these effects seem to be very different when applied in different periods. In fact, this is probably one of the most intriguing empirical problems. Economists usually explain the difficulty of forecasting the effects of a particular change in one exogenous variable (e.g., an expansion of the money stock) by invoking the *ceteris paribus* hypothesis, i.e., there are usually other exogenous variables changing unexpectedly, preventing us to isolate the effect of the first exogenous variable. In our model, the uncertainty surrounding the effect of a disturbance in an exogenous variable is not due to the failure of the *ceteris paribus* hypothesis. No other exogenous variable is allowed to change. The fact is that the change in the exogenous variable occurs at a particular time, which is different from all other times. Initial conditions (history) matters to forecast the effect of shocks. Since each initial condition is unique, it becomes impossible to forecast the effect of a shock at any given point in time with any precision.

8. Empirical Relevance of the Model

In this section, we analyze how well our model mimics the empirical anomalies and puzzles that have been uncovered by the flourishing empirical literature. We calibrate the model such that it replicates the observed statistical properties of exchange rate movements. The parameters of the model that do this are those that we used in the previous sections. As was noted there, typically these are parameter sets that do not produce deterministic chaos We start with the "disconnect puzzle."

8.1. *The Disconnect Puzzle*

The "disconnect" puzzle (see Obstfeld and Rogoff, 2000) states that the exchange rate is disconnected from its underlying fundamentals most of the time.[12] It was first analyzed by John Williamson

[12] In its original formulation the disconnect puzzle has two dimensions. One says that the exchange rate is disconnected from its fundamental. The second dimension relates to the fact that real variables (for example, the trade account) do not react to the changes in the exchange rate. In this paper, we only analyze the first dimension.

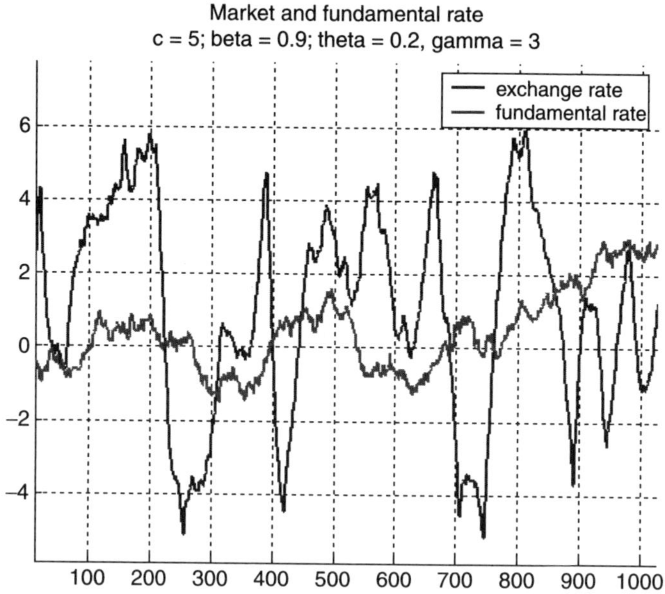

Figure 11.

(1985) who called it the "misalignment problem." This puzzle was also implicit in the celebrated Meese and Rogoff's studies of the early 1980s documenting that there is no stable relationship between exchange rate movements and the *news* in the fundamental variables.

Our model is capable of mimicking this empirical regularity. In Figure 11, we show the market exchange rate and the fundamental rate for a combination of parameters that does not produce deterministic chaos. We observe that the market rate can deviate from the fundamental value substantially and in a persistent way. Moreover, it appears that the exchange rate movements are often disconnected from the movements of the underlying fundamental. In fact, they often move in opposite directions.

We show the nature of the disconnect phenomenon in a more precise way by applying a cointegration analysis to the simulated exchange rate and its fundamental using the same parameter values as in Figure 11 for a sample of 8,000 periods. We found that there is a cointegration relationship between the exchange rate and its fundamental.[13] Note that in our setting there is only one fundamental variable. This implies that no bias from omitted variables can occur.

In the next step, we specify an EC model in the following way:

$$\Delta s_t = \mu(s_{t-1} - \gamma s^*_{t-1}) + \sum_{i=1}^{n} \lambda_i \Delta s_{t-i} + \sum_{i=1}^{n} \varphi_i \Delta s^*_{t-i} \tag{10}$$

The first term on the right hand side is the error correction term. The result of estimating this equation is presented in Table 1 where we have set $n = 4$.[14]

We find that the error correction coefficient (μ) is very low. This suggests that the mean reversion towards the equilibrium exchange rate takes a very long time. In particular, only 0.6% of the adjustment takes place each period. It should be noted that in the simulations we have assumed a speed of adjustment in the goods market equal to 0.2. This implies that each period the adjustment in the goods market is 20%. Thus, the nominal exchange rate is considerably slower to adjust toward its equilibrium than what is implied by the speed of adjustment in the goods market. This slow adjustment of the nominal exchange rate is due the chartist extrapolation behavior.[15] From

Table 1. Parameter estimates of EC model (Equation 10).

Error correction term		Δs_{t-i}				Δs^*_{t-i}			
μ	γ	λ_1	λ_2	λ_3	λ_4	φ_1	φ_2	φ_3	φ_4
−0.006	1.001	0.53	0.19	0.09	0.06	0.06	0.02	−0.01	−0.01
−15.4	*24.8*	*52.7*	*16.6*	*7.80*	*6.1*	*4.9*	*1.3*	*−1.3*	*−0.4*

Note: The sample consists of 8000 periods. The numbers in italics are t-statistics. $R^2 = 0.63$

[13]We first performed a unit root test on the simulated exchange rate. We could not reject the existence of unit root. Next, we tested for cointegration using the Johansen cointegration procedure (see Johansen, 1991). We assumed that there is no deterministic trend in the data. However, we do allow the intercept different from zero.

[14]The number of lags has been chosen according to the information criteria, such that the error term is white noise.

[15]Cheung *et al.* (2001) have provided evidence indicating that the slow speed of adjustment towards to PPP is not so much due to the slow speed of adjustment of prices in the goods market but to the slow speed of adjustment of the nominal exchange rate.

Table 1, we also note that the changes in fundamentals have a small and insignificant impact on the change in exchange rate. In contrast, the past changes in the exchange rate play a significant role in explaining the change in exchange rate.[16] These results are consistent with the empirical findings using VAR approach, which suggests that the exchange rate is driven by its own past (see De Boeck, 2000).

We also performed a cointegration analysis for shorter sample periods (1,000 periods). We find that in some sample periods the exchange rate and its fundamental are cointegrated, in other sample periods we do not find cointegration. This is in line with the empirical evidence indicating that in some periods the exchange rate seems to be disconnected from its fundamental while in other periods it tightly follows the fundamentals.[17]

The results reported in this section use a particular numerical value for the transactions costs, i.e., $C = 5$. An implication of this choice is that the exchange rate remains within the transaction cost band most of the time. In fact, in the simulation reported in Figure 11, the exchange rate remains within the transactions cost band 97% of the time. Thus our explanation of the misalignment puzzle relies very much on the existence of a relatively wide band of transactions costs compared to the variability of the underlying fundamentals. Is this a reasonable explanation for the existence of misalignments? Our claim is that it is the right one for the currencies of the industrial countries like the US, Japan and the European countries. There are two pieces of evidence that substantiate this claim.

First, transactions costs in international trade continue to be substantial, as important empirical evidence shows. In particular, several recent empirical studies report the continued existence of large price differentials for the same traded goods across borders (see Haskel

[16] It should be noted that our results are akin to what was found in stock markets, i.e., that in the short-run the exchange rate under-reacts to news, while it overreacts in the long run. See Schleiffer (2000).

[17] See Obsteld and Rogoff (2000). See also De Grauwe and Grimaldi (2001) for a survey of the empirical evidence. In De Grauwe and Vansteenkiste (2001), we present additional empirical evidence.

Table 2. Inter-country price dispersion for selected products (excluding VAT), 2000.

Supermarket products	
EVIAN MINERAL WATER	43 percent
REXONA DEODORANT	21 percent
SENSODYNE TOOTHPASTE	21 percent
MARS BARS (SINGLE)	21 percent
MARS BARS (MULTIPACK)	22 percent
COCA COLA	21 percent
PEDIGREE PAL DOG FOOD	10 percent
PLENITUDE FACE CARE	21 percent
COLGATE TOOTHPASTE	14 percent
BONNE MAMAN MARMELADE	19 percent
Electronic products	
PHILIPS AUDIO SYSTEM	28 percent
SONY AUDIO SYSTEM	38 percent
CANON CAMCORDER	32 percent
PANASONIC PORTABLE CD	40 percent
PHILIPS PORTABLE CD	56 percent
PIONEER CD PLAYER	34 percent
SONY CD PLAYER	28 percent
PHILLIPS TV (14 inch)	41 percent
SONY TV (14 inch)	33 percent
PANASONIC TV (28 inch)	25 percent
PHILIPS TV (28 inch)	61 percent
JVC VCR	30 percent
PANASONIC VCR	22 percent
SONY VCR	44 percent

Source: European Commission, *Price dispersion in the internal market*, and *Price differentials for supermarket goods in the EU*. Both documents can be downloaded from www.europa.eu.int
Note: Price dispersion is defined as the percentage difference between the most expensive and the cheapest item.

and Wolf, 2001 and Engel and Rogers, 1995). In Table 2, we provide additional evidence. We show the price dispersion of a sample of identical products in the European Union.[18] We observe that price

[18]Similar price differentials exist for other product groups. The large price differentials for cars are notorious. Interestingly, The Economist magazine, which champions the cause of free competition, applies differences in its subscription rates of 20% across the Eurozone (in 2003).

differentials of up to 40% occur both in the category of foodstuff and of electronic products. This indicates that producers apply "pricing to market." Such pricing strategies, however, can only be applied successfully if transaction costs prevent arbitrage. Thus, the large observed price differentials suggest that transactions costs for traded goods are large and of the order of 20% to 40%. In addition, for many services, which are non-traded goods, transactions costs are even higher. See Obstfeld and Rogoff (2000) who argue that transactions costs are key to understanding the major puzzles in international economics.

Second, the size of the shocks in the fundamentals driving the exchange rates of the major currencies is typically small. These fundamentals include inflation differentials, differentials in interest rates, in growth rates of the money stock, and in growth rates of output. These differentials are typically a few percentage points per year. Thus, one can conclude that the exchange rates of the major currencies move in an environment in which the shocks in the fundamentals is relatively small compared to the size of transactions costs. As a result, the exchange rates of these currencies move most of the time within a band within which few opportunities exist for goods market arbitrage. This considerably weakens the mean reversion dynamics on which fundamentalism is based.

It is important to analyze the dynamics of the exchange rate under different combinations of transactions costs and size of shocks in fundamentals. After all, there are many countries in the world where the size of the shocks in fundamentals is very large compared to transactions costs (e.g., Latin American countries that have experienced triple digit inflation rates and growth rates of their money stocks). The way we proceed is to simulate the model under different assumptions about the size of transactions costs, while keeping the size of the shocks unchanged. (Note that we could also vary the size of the fundamental shocks while keeping the transactions cost unchanged. This gives qualitatively the same results[19]). We then

[19]In Section 9, we show such an exercise.

Table 3. Transaction costs and speed of adjustment.

Transaction cost (C)	Error correction coeff (μ)	Percent of time outside transaction cost band
0.5	−0.062	44 percent
1.0	−0.044	25 percent
2.5	−0.016	7 percent
5.0	−0.006	3 percent

apply the same error correction model on the estimated exchange rate as in Eq. (10). We show the coefficients of the error correction term (which is a measure of the speed with which the exchange rate returns to its fundamental value) in Table 3. We observe that there is an inverse relationship between the size of transaction costs and the speed of adjustment. With low transactions costs (relative to the size of fundamental shocks) the speed of adjustment is high; with high transaction costs the speed of adjustment is low. Thus, in a world where the transaction costs are small relative to the size of the fundamental shocks misalignments are quickly corrected. In such a world, the exchange rate is pushed outside the transactions cost band frequently (see last column of Table 3) so that the mean reverting forces originating from goods market arbitrage are forceful.

Thus, our model generates an empirical regularity (the "disconnect" puzzle) that has also been observed in reality. We can summarize the features of this puzzle as follows. First, over the very long run the exchange rate and its fundamentals are cointegrated. However, the speed with which the exchange rate reverts to its equilibrium value is very slow. Second, in the short run the exchange rate and its fundamentals are "disconnected," i.e., they do not appear to be cointegrated. Third, the nature of the disconnect puzzle changes depending on the relative size of transactions costs versus the size in the fundamental shocks. When the size of fundamental shocks is small relative to transactions costs, misalignment is relatively long and protracted. This is the case with the currencies of the major industrial countries. When the size of the fundamental shocks is large relative to transactions costs, misalignments although large are quickly corrected. The empirical evidence substantiates these results (see Sarno and Taylor, 2002) who show that when the size of the shocks to the PPP-relation is large, the speed of adjustment toward PPP is also high).

8.2. *Fat Tails and Excess Kurtosis*

It is well known that the exchange rate changes do not follow a normal distribution. Instead, it has been observed that the distribution of exchange rate changes has more density around the mean than the normal and exhibits fatter tails than the normal (see de Vries, 2000). This phenomenon was first discovered by Mandelbrot (1963) in commodity markets. Since then, fat tails and excess kurtosis have been discovered in many other asset markets including the exchange market. In particular, in the latter the returns have a kurtosis typically exceeding 3 and a measure of fat tails (Hill index) ranging between 2 and 5 (see Koedijk, Stork and de Vries, 1992). However, it has also been detected that the kurtosis is reduced under time aggregation (Lux, 1998). This phenomenon has been observed for most exchange rates. We checked whether this is also the case with the simulated exchange rate changes in our model.[20]

The model was simulated using normally distributed random disturbances (with mean = 0 and standard deviation = 1). We computed the kurtosis and the Hill index of the simulated exchange rate returns. We computed the Hill index for 5 different samples of 2,000 observations. In addition, we considered three different cut-off points of the tails (2.5%, 5%, 10%). We show the results of the kurtosis and of the Hill index in Table 4. We find that for a broad range of parameter values the kurtosis exceeds 3 and the Hill index indicates the presence of fat tails. Finally, we check if the kurtosis of our simulated exchange rate returns declines under time aggregation. In order to do so, we chose different time aggregation periods and we computed

[20]It should be noted that models similar to ours have been applied in the stock markets. These models have been able to replicate fat tails and excess kurtosis observed in these markets. See Hommes (2001).

Table 4. Measure of fat tails: The Hill index.

Parameter values	Kurtosis	Median Hill index (5 samples 2000 observations) 2.5 percent tail	5 percent tail	10 percent tail
$C = 5$, beta = 0.9, gamma = 5	11.21	3.28	3.07	2.56
$C = 5$, beta = 0.9, gamma = 3	10.39	4.30	4.23	3.89
$C = 5$, beta = 0.8, gamma = 3	11.91	4.45	4.71	4.20
$C = 5$, beta = 0.8, gamma = 5	13.92	4.47	4.59	4.15
$C = 1$, beta = 0.9, gamma = 3	8.79	5.37	4.97	4.36
$C = 2.5$, beta = 0.9, gamma = 3	7.07	4.78	4.36	3.57
$C = 2.5$, beta = 0.8, gamma = 3	10.5	6.54	5.35	4.35

Table 5. Kurtosis under time-aggregation.

Parameter values	1 period returns	10 periods returns	25 periods returns	50 periods returns
$C = 5$, beta = 0.9, gamma = 5	11.21	4.75	3.79	4.73
$C = 5$, beta = 0.9, gamma = 3	10.39	9.93	3.19	2.28
$C = 5$, beta = 0.8, gamma = 3	11.91	17.69	3.01	2.97
$C = 5$, beta = 0.8, gamma = 5	13.92	14.65	3.86	2.85
$C = 5$, beta = 1, gamma = 1	9.32	9.01	9.07	2.56
$C = 1$, beta = 0.9, gamma = 3	8.79	8.56	4.01	3.78
$C = 2.5$, beta = 0.9, gamma = 3	7.07	6.43	3.22	2.45
$C = 2.5$, beta = 0.8, gamma = 3	10.5	13.2	2.92	2.67

the kurtosis of the time-aggregated exchange rate returns. We found that the kurtosis declines under time aggregation. In Table 5, we show the results for different parameter values (including low values for the transactions costs C).

These results suggest that the non-linear dynamics of the model transforms normally distributed noise in the exchange rate into exchange rate movements with tails that are significantly fatter than the normal distribution and with more density around the mean. Thus our model mimics an important empirical regularity, i.e., that exchange rate movements are characterised by tranquil periods (occurring most of the time) and turbulent periods (occurring infrequently).

8.3. *Volatility Clustering*

The last empirical regularity we investigate concerns the clustering of volatility. It has been widely observed that the exchange rate returns show a GARCH structure, i.e., there is time dependency in the volatility of the exchange rate returns (see Lux and Marchesi, 2000; Hommes, 2001; Kirman and Teyssière, 2002). In order to check if our model is capable of reproducing this statistical property, we tested for GARCH structures in the simulated exchange rate returns. We first computed the autocorrelation function (ACF) of the absolute returns of the simulated exchange rate returns for a broad range of parameter values. In Figure 12, we show the ACF for a particular set of parameters. At first glance, Figure 12 suggests that the ACF dies out slowly, i.e., that the volatility in the exchange rate returns has a long memory. In order to confirm whether this visual impression is

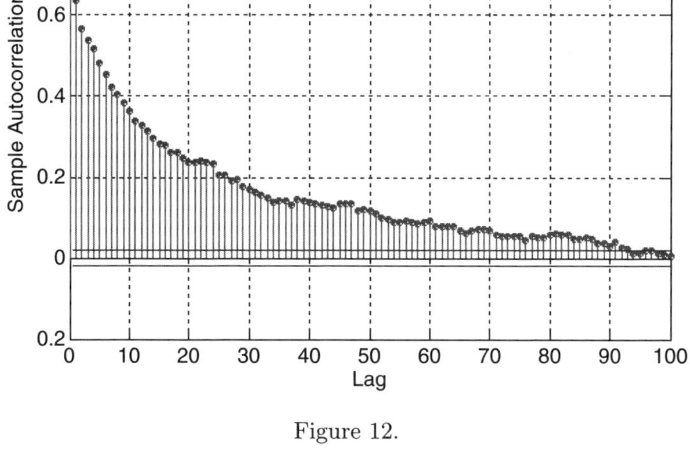

Figure 12.

Table 6. Serial correlation tests residuals ARMA(2,1).

	F-value	p-value	F-value	p-value
	Model I		Model II	
Breusch-Godfrey LM test	14.8	0.000	10.5	0.005
ARCH test	68.03	0.000	71.7	0.000

Model I: $C = 5$, beta = 0.9, gamma = 3
Model II: $C = 2.5$, beta = 0.9, gamma = 3

correct, we proceed as follows.[21] First, we compute the ACF for the raw returns (see Figure 14 in Appendix). The wave-shape suggests an ARMA process for the returns. Thus, we estimate an ARMA model and we find that an ARMA (2,1) performs best. (The results of estimating this model on the returns are also shown in Appendix 1). We then tested for serial correlation in the residuals. These tests are shown in Table 6 for two different sets of parameters. We conclude that we should reject serial correlation in the error term.

The next step consisted in testing for GARCH effects in the exchange rate returns. In order to do so, we chose a GARCH (2,1) specification[22]:

$$\Delta s_t = a + \varepsilon_t$$
$$\sigma_t^2 = b + \alpha\varepsilon_{t-1}^2 + \delta_1\sigma_{t-1}^2 + \delta_2\sigma_{t-2}^2$$

where ε_t is the error term, a is a constant and σ_t^2 is the conditional variance of the returns. We estimated this model using the simulated exchange rate returns. We present the results in Table 7 for different values of the extrapolation parameter β.

We observe that the GARCH coefficients, α, δ_1 and δ_2, are significantly different from zero implying that there is volatility clustering in the exchange rate returns. In addition, we find that for values of

[21] We also computed the rate of decay of the autocorrelation function by estimating an equation $\rho(\mathrm{k}) = \mathrm{k}^{d-1}$ where $\rho(\mathrm{k})$ is the autocorrelation coefficient at lag k. We applied this to the absolute returns. We found that d = 0.48 and significantly different from zero, suggesting a significant departure from exponential decay. (Note that d = 0 for exponential decay, and d = 1 for uniform distribution of the autocorrelations).

[22] We also estimated a GARCH (1,1). The results are very similar.

Table 7. GARCH model.

	I	II	III	IV
a	0.003	−0.003	0.004	0.002
	(2.6)	(−2.5)	(3.5)	(1.2)
b	0.003	0.002	0.003	0.003
	(14.5)	(14.1)	(15.8)	(12.3)
α	0.35	0.33	0.26	0.34
	(19.1)	(31.8)	(22.7)	(15.6)
δ_1	0.44	0.49	0.41	0.37
	(8.5)	(18.5)	(8.2)	(6.3)
δ_2	0.14	0.18	0.18	0.18
	(3.7)	(5.6)	(4.6)	(4.1)

I: $C = 5$, beta = 0.9, gamma = 3; II: $C = 5$, beta = 0.9, gamma = 5; III: $C = 5$, beta = 0.8, gamma = 3; IV: $C = 2.5$, beta = 0.9, gamma = 3.
Numbers in parentheses are t-statistics.

β close to 0.9 the sum of α, δ_1 and δ_2, which is a measure of the degree of inertia of the volatility, is close to one. This implies that the effect of volatility shocks dies out slowly. Thus, our model is capable of reproducing a widely observed phenomenon of clustering and persistence in volatility.

9. Is Chartism Evolutionary Stable?

An important issue is whether chartism survives in our model. Put differently, we ask the question under which conditions chartism is profitable such that it does not disappear. It should be noted that there is a broad literature that shows that technical analysis is used widely, also by large players (see Wei and Kim, 1997).

We investigate this issue by analysing how chartism evolves under different conditions. In Figure 13, we show the average chartists' weight for increasing values of the intensity of choice parameter γ in two different environments concerning the variance of the shocks in fundamentals, a low and a high variance regime.[23] We obtained the

[23]We obtain qualitatively the same results when we keep the variance of the shocks constant while varying the transactions costs C. What matters is the size of the shocks relative to transactions costs.

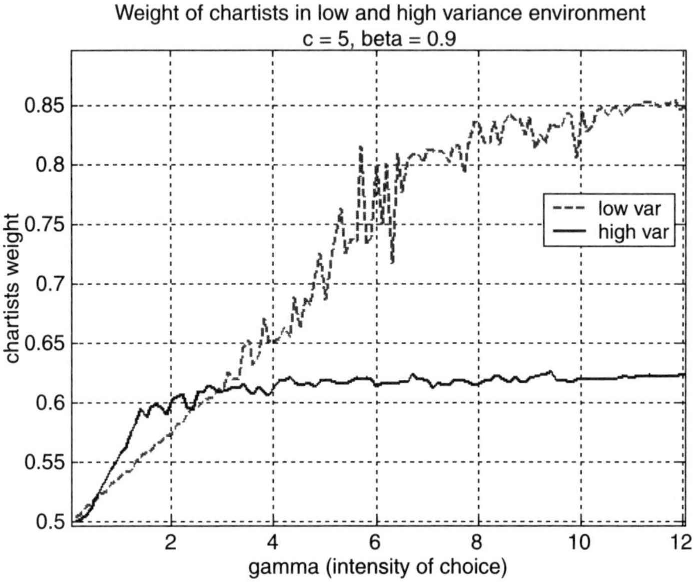

Figure 13.

Note: In high variance regime the variance of the shocks in the fundamentals is 10 times the variance in the fundamentals of the low variance regime.

chartists weights by simulating the model over 10,000 periods and computing the average weight over the last 5,000 periods. Our first finding is that chartism does not disappear, i.e., in all simulations for many different parameters configurations we find that the weight attached to chartists never goes to zero. Second, for a wide range of parameter values we find that the chartists' weight fluctuates around a market share, which exceeds 50%. For high values of γ the chartists' weight approaches 90%. Third, when the shocks are large relative to the transactions cost band, the weight of chartists is considerably lower. This is in line with our previous results. When the fundamental shocks are large relative to transactions costs, the exchange rate is often driven outside the transaction cost band. As a result the goods market dynamics will often be operative, making fundamentalist forecasting relatively profitable. This reduces the scope for chartism.

These results are consistent with the empirical evidence of the importance of chartism in foreign exchange market (Taylor and Allen, 1992). And they also suggest that Chartism is evolutionary stable.

10. Conclusion

In this paper, we developed an exchange rate model, which has the following features. First, it introduces a non-linearity in the dynamics of the foreign exchange market that finds its origin in the existence of transaction costs in the goods markets. Second it allows for heterogeneity of the agents' beliefs. In particular, it assumes that agents use different forecasting rules, and that they switch to the most profitable one after evaluating their relative profitability. The model does not assume rational expectations. The problem of rational expectations models with heterogeneous agents is that it creates an "infinite regress" problem, thereby imposing an unreasonable informational burden on individual agents. Therefore, we find it more useful to assume that in a highly complex world agents use simple forecasting rules and evaluate the 'fitness' of these rules ex post.

The model generates a multitude of fixed-point attractors depending on the initial conditions. By adding exogenous noise the model produces a dynamics that resembles a chaotic one, although the deterministic part of the model is not chaotic. This feature has interesting implications. First, there is sensitivity to initial conditions, which implies that a small disturbance can drive the exchange rate on a different path. Second, the effect of a permanent shock in the fundamental exchange rate is largely unpredictable, i.e., one cannot forecast how the shock will affect the exchange rate in any particular point of time, but one can predict the *average* effect. It also implies that the exact timing of the shock matters. History matters.

The empirical relevance of the model is a measure of its quality. Therefore, we analyzed to what extent our model is capable of reproducing the exchange rate puzzles that we observe in reality. The first puzzle we analyzed is the "disconnect puzzle." This puzzle relates to the fact that the exchange rate movements are disconnected, most of the time, from the movements of the underlying fundamental variables. In our model, "disconnection" is a natural outcome when the variance of the underlying fundamentals is small compared to the size of the transactions costs in the goods market. We argued that this is the regime in which the currencies of the main industrialised countries find themselves in. In contrast, when the size of the fundamental shocks is large relative to the size of the transactions costs, the exchange rate is less disconnected from the underlying fundamentals.

Second, fat tails and excess kurtosis, which have been detected in the exchange rate returns, are generated by our model. In other words, our model generates a dynamics of the exchange rate with *intermittency* of high and low turbulence periods.

A third empirical regularity concerns the volatility clustering and persistence of exchange rate returns. We found GARCH effects in the simulated exchange rate returns that come close to the observed GARCH effects in the real life exchange rate returns.

A fourth empirical regularity is the continuing existence of chartists. This cannot easily be rationalised in the efficient market rational expectations model. In our model where chartists and fundamentalists continuously switch to the most profitable forecasting rule, chartists tend to dominate the market.

Some implications of these findings are the following. The exchange rates of the major currencies are subject to relatively small shocks in the underlying fundamentals (e.g., inflation differentials are almost zero). Compared to these shocks the transactions costs in the goods markets can be said to be relatively large (see Obstfeld and Rogoff, 2000, on this), i.e., a large part of goods and services are non-traded (or difficult to trade) because the cost of shipping them across borders is quite high. Thus, the regime confronted by the exchange rates of the major industrialised countries comes close to the regime we have identified to be the one where exchange rates are disconnected from fundamentals, and where excess volatility and speculative noise is produced by chartists' activity. Put differently, the movements of the exchange rates of the industrialised countries are likely to be clouded by a non-linear speculative dynamics that makes it difficult if not impossible to explain this or that movement of these exchange rates.

Appendix 1: Diagnosis of GARCH Structure in the Simulated Exchange Rate Returns

In this Appendix, we present the autocorrelation function of the simulated exchange rate returns (Figure 14) and the ARMA (2;1) estimation on these returns (Table 8).

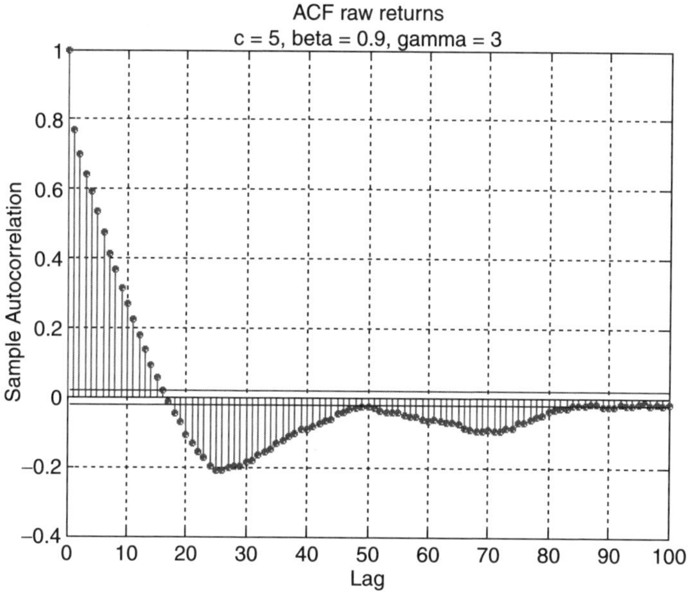

Figure 14. Autocorrelation function of simulated exchange rate returns.

Table 8. Estimation of ARMA(2,1) on simulated returns.

Variables	Coefficient	*t*-statistic
Constant	−0.001	−0.14
AR(1)	0.856	28.74
AR(2)	0.044	1.83
MA(1)	−0.362	−12.71
R-squared	*0.60*	

References

Bacchetta, P and Evan Wincoop (2003). Can information heterogeneity explain the exchange rate determination puzzle? NBER Working Paper No. 9498.

Baxter, M and A Stockman (1989). Business cycles and the exchange rate regime: Some international evidence. *Journal of Monetary Economics*, 23, 377–400.

Brock, W and C Hommes (1997). A rational route to randomness. *Econometrica*, 65, 1059–1095.

Brock, W and C Hommes (1998). Heterogeneous beliefs and routes to chaos in a simple asset pricing model. *Journal of Economic Dynamics and Control*, 22, 1235–1274.

Cheung, Y, M Chinn and I Marsh (1999). Has do UK based foreign exchange dealers think their markets operate? CEPR Discussion Paper No. 2230.

Cheung, Y, K Lai and M Bergman (2001). Dissecting the PPP puzzle: The unconventional roles of nominal exchange rate and price adjustments. Paper presented at CES-Ifo Conference, Munich.

Chiarella, C, R Dieci and L Gardini (2002). Speculative behaviour and complex asset price dynamics. *Journal of Economic Behaviour and Organization*, 49, 173–197.

De Boeck, J (2000). The effect of macroeconomic "news" on exchange rates: A structural VAR approach. Mimeo: University of Leuven.

De Grauwe, P, H Dewachter and M Embrechts (1993). *Exchange Rate Theory: Chaotic Models of the Foreign Exchange Markets*. Oxford, UK: Blackwell.

De Grauwe, P and M Grimaldi (2001). Exchange rates, prices and money: A long-run perspective. *International Journal of Finance and Economics*, 6(4), 289–314.

De Grauwe, P and I Vansteenkiste (2001). Exchange rates and fundamentals. A non-linear relationship? CESifo Working Paper No. 577.

de Vries, C (2000). Fat tails and the history of the guilder. *Tinbergen Magazine*, 4, 3–6.

De Long, JB, A Schleiffer, LH Summers and RJ Waldmann (1990). Noise trader risk in financial markets. *Journal of Political Economy*, 98(4), 703–738.

Dumas, B (1992). Dynamic equilibrium and the real exchange rate in a spatially separated world. *Review of Financial Studies*, 5(2), 153–180.

Engel, C and J Rogers (1995). How wide is the border? International Finance Discussion Paper No. 498.

Engel, C (2000). Long run PPP may not hold after all. *Journal of International Economics*, 57(2), 243–273.

Faust, J, J Rogers and J Wright (2001). Exchange rate forecasting: The errors we've really made. International Finance Discussion Papers No. 741.

Flood, R and A Rose (1995). Fixing the exchange rate regime: A virtual quest for fundamentals. *Journal of Monetary Economics*, 36(1), 3–37.

Frankel, J and K Froot (1986). The dollar as a speculative bubble: A tale of fundamentalists and chartists. NBER Working Paper No. 1963.

Goodhart, C (1989). News and the foreign exchange market. LSE Financial Markets Group Discussion Paper, 71.

Goodhart, C and L Figlioli (1991). Every minute counts in the foreign exchange markets. *Journal of International Money and Finance*, 10, 23–52.

Guillaume D (1996). Chaos, randomness and order in the foreign exchange markets. PhD Thesis K.U. Leuven, Leuven.

Haskel, J and H Wolf (2001). The law of one price. A case study. CESifo Working Paper No. 428.

Hommes, C (2001). Financial markets as complex adaptive evolutionary systems. *Quantitative Finance*, 1, 149–167.

Johansen, S (1991). Estimation and hypothesis testing of cointegration vectors in Gaussian vector autoregressive models. *Econometrica*, 55, 1551–1580.

Kilian, L and M Taylor (2001). Why is it so difficult to beat the random walk forecast of exchange rates? Mimeo: University of Warwick.

Kirman, A and G Theyssière (2002). Microeconomic models for long memory in the volatility of financial time series. *Studies in Nonlinear Dynamics and Econometrics*, 5(4), 281–302.

Koedijk, K, P Stork and C de Vries (1992). Differences between foreign exchange rate regimes: The view from tails. *Journal of International Money and Finance*, 11, 462–473.

Lux, T (1998). The socio-economic dynamics of speculative markets: Interacting agents, chaos, and fat tails of return distributions. *Journal of Economic Behavior and Organization*, 33(2), 143–165.

Lux, T and M Marchesi (2000). Volatility clustering in financial markets: A microsimulation of interacting agents. *International Journal of Theoretical and Applied Finance*, 3(4), 675–702.

Meese, R and KS Rogoff (1983). Empirical exchange rate models of the seventies: Do they fit out of sample? *Journal of International Economics*, 14, 3–24.

Michael, P, R Nobay and A Peel (1997). Transaction costs and non-linear adjustment in real exchange rates: An empirical investigation. *Journal of Political Economy*, 105(4), 862–879.

Obstfeld, M and K Rogoff (1996). *Foundations of International Macroeconomics.* Boston, MA: MIT Press.

Obstfeld, M and K Rogoff (2000). The six major puzzles in international macroeconomics: Is there a common cause? NBER Working Paper No. 7777.

Sarno, L and M Taylor (2002). *The Economics of Exchange Rates.* Cambridge, UK: Cambridge University Press.

Schittenkopf, C, G Dorffner and E Dockner (2001). On nonlinear, stochastic dynamics in economics and financial time series. *Studies in Nonlinear Dynamics and Econometrics*, 4(3), 101–121.

Schleiffer, A (2000). *Introduction to Behavioural Finance.* Gloucestershire: Clarendon Press.

Taylor, M and H Allen (1992). The use of technical analysis in the foreign exchange market. *Journal of International Money and Finance*, 11, 304–314.

Taylor, M, D Peel and L Sarno (2001). Non-linear mean reversion in real exchange rates: Towards a solution to the purchasing power parity puzzles. CEPR Discussion Paper No. 2658.

Wei, S-J and K Jungshik (1997). The big players in the foreign exchange market: Do they trade on information or noise? NBER Working Paper No. 6256.

Williamson, J (1985). The exchange rate system. *Journal of Banking and Finance*, 9(2), 333.

Chapter 3

Exchange Rate Puzzles: A Tale of Switching Attractors

Paul De Grauwe and Marianna Grimaldi

The rational expectations efficient market model of the exchange rate has failed empirically. In this paper, we develop a model of the exchange rate in which agents use simple forecasting rules. Based on an ex post evaluation of the relative profitability of these rules they decide whether to switch or not. In addition, transactions costs in the goods market are introduced. We show that this simple model creates great complexity in the market which is characterised by the fact that the exchange rate is disconnected from its fundamental most of the time. Finally, we show that this model mimicks most of the empirical puzzles uncovered in the literature.

1. Introduction

The rational expectations efficient market model developed during the 1970s has dominated our thinking about exchange rates.

Published in *European Economic Review*, 50, 1–33, 2006.

We very grateful for useful comments to Volker-Bohm, Yin-Wong Cheung, Hans Dewachter, Robert Dieci, Marc Flandreau, Philip Lane, Thomas Lux, Richard Lyons, Ronald McDonald, Michael Moore, Assaf Razin, Piet Sercu, Peter Sinclair and Peter Westaway. We also gratefully acknowledge the comments and suggestions of two anonymous referees.

Keywords: Exchange rate; heterogeneous agents; technical trading; transaction costs.

JEL classification: F31, F41

This model led to the following propositions. First, exchange rate changes can only occur because of unexpected movements (*news*) in the underlying fundamental economic variables (inflation, output growth, interest rates, etc.). Second, the link between exchange rates and fundamentals is a stable one. Well-known examples of the rational expectation efficient market model is the monetary model, the Dornbusch model (Dornbusch, 1976) and the portfolio balance model. Although these models continue to be popular and maintain a prominent place in textbooks, they have failed empirically. The most notorious empirical rejection was made by Meese and Rogoff at the beginning of the 1980s (Meese and Rogoff, 1983). This led to a large empirical literature that uncovered a number of empirical puzzles concerning the behaviour of the exchange rate, which could not be explained by the "news" models.

The first and foremost empirical puzzle has been called the "disconnect" puzzle, i.e., the exchange rate appears to be disconnected from its underlying fundamentals most of the time. Goodhart (1989), Goodhart and Figlioli (1991) and more recently Faust *et al.* (2003) found that most of the changes in the exchange rates occur when there is no observable news in the fundamental economic variables.

Other empirical anomalies have been uncovered over the years. One is the puzzle of "excess volatility" of the exchange rate, i.e., the volatility of the exchange rate by far exceeds the volatility of the underlying economic variables (Baxter and Stockman, 1989; Flood and Rose, 1995).

Another puzzle is that the distribution of the exchange rate returns is not normal, Most of the empirical findings document that the exchange rate returns have fat tails (see de Vries, 2001; Lux, 1997, 1998; Lux and Marchesi, 1999, 2000). This evidence is difficult to rationalise in existing exchange rate models, since there is little evidence of fat tails in the fundamental variables that drive the exchange rate in these models.

The empirical failure of the exchange rate models of the 1970s has led to new attempts to model the exchange rate. These attempts have led to three different modelling approaches. The first one uses the Obstfeld–Rogoff framework of dynamic utility optimisation of a representative agent. This approach although promising is stili waiting for empirical confirmation (Obstfeld and Rogoff, 1996).

A second approach starts from the analysis of the microstructure of the foreign exchange market (Evans and Lyons, 1999; Lyons, 2001). This approach has led to new insights into the way information is aggregated and is important for the understanding of the short-term behaviour of the exchange rate.

Finally, a third approach recognises that heterogeneous agents have different beliefs about the behaviour of the exchange rate. These different beliefs introduce non-linear features in the dynamics of the exchange rate. This approach was initiated by Frankel and Froot (1987) and further developed mainly in the context of stock prices (Kirman, 1993; Brock and Hommes, 1997, 1998; Lux, l998; Le Baron *et al.*, 1999; Gaunersdorfer and Hommes, 2003). Our paper is based on this third approach.

Recently, heterogeneity of agents has also been introduced in rational expectations models (see e.g., Bacchetta and van Wincoop, 2003). The implication of rational expectations in models with heterogeneous agents is that it creates "infinite regress," i.e., the exchange rate depends on the expectations of other agents' expectations, which depends on the expectations of the expectations of other agents' expectations, and so on, ad infinitum. This leads to intractable mathematical problems except under very restrictive simplifying assumptions. Although this approach is intellectually satisfying, it is unclear that it is a good representation of what agents do in the exchange market. It requires these agents to solve a mathematical problem to which mathematicians have as yet been unable to give a general solution. This seems to us as imposing too large an informational burden on individual agents.

Our approach contrasts with this rational expectations approach in that agents use simple rules, the "fitness" of which is then controlled ex post by checking their profitability, and by switching to the more profitable rules. In order to formalize this idea, we will use a switching mechanism which is very close to the mechanism proposed by Brock and Hommes (1997) in their seminal article. In addition, we make use of the recent empirical evidence, which has stressed the importance of transactions costs in the goods market for our understanding of the dynamics of exchange rate adjustments (Michael, Nobay and Peel, 1997; O' Connell, 1998; Obstfeld and Rogoff, 2000; Engel, 2000; Kilian and Taylor, 2003). We show that our model is capable of replicating the empirical puzzles and anomalies uncovered in the last decade by the empirical exchange rate literature.

The paper is organized as follows. In Section 2, we present the theoretical model. In Sections 3, 4 and 5 we analyse its features, while in Sections 6, 7 and 8, we analyze its empirical predictions. We conclude in Section 9.

2. The Model

In this section we develop a simple non-linear model of the exchange rate. The model consists of three building blocks. First, agents decide the optimal portfolio using a mean-variance utility framework. Second, they make forecasts about the future exchange rate based on simple rules. Third, they evaluate these rules ex-post by comparing their risk-adjusted profitability (Brock-Hommes, 1997).

2.1. *The Optimal Portfolio*

We assume agents of different types i depending on their beliefs about the future exchange rate. Each agent can invest in two assets, a domestic and a foreign one. The agents' utility function can be represented by the following equation:

$$U(W_{t+1}^i) = E_t^i(W_{t+1}^i) - \frac{1}{2}\mu V_t^i(W_{t+1}^i) \tag{1}$$

where W_{t+1}^i is the wealth of agent of type i at time $t+1$, E_t^i is the expectation operator of agent of type i, μ is the coefficient of risk aversion and $V_t^i(W_{t+1}^i)$ represents the conditional variance of wealth of agent i. The wealth is specified as follows:

$$W_{t+1}^i = (1+r^*)s_{t+1}d_{i,t} + (1+r)(W_t^i - s_t d_{i,t}) \tag{2}$$

where r and r^* are respectively the domestic and the foreign interest rates, s_{t+1} is the exchange rate at time $t+1$, $d_{i,t}$ represents the holdings of the foreign assets by agent of type i at time t. Thus, the first term on the right-hand side of (2) represents the value of the foreign portfolio in domestic currency at time $t+1$ while the second term represents the value of the domestic portfolio at time $t+1$.

Substituting Eq. 2 in 1 and maximising the utility with respect to $d_{i,t}$ allows us to derive the optimal holding of foreign assets by agents of type i:

$$d_{i,t} = \frac{(1+r^*)E_t^i(s_{t+1}) - (1+r)s_t}{\mu\sigma_{i,t}^2} \tag{3}$$

where $\sigma_{i,t}^2 = (1+r^*)^2 V_t^i(s_{t+1})$. Thus, the optimal holdings of the foreign asset depend on both the heterogenous beliefs about the future level of the exchange rate and its variance. Note that our model is more general than the influential model of Brock and Hommes (1997, 1998) who studied the case of constant and equal variances for all types of agents.[1]

The market demand for foreign assets at time t is the sum of the individual demands, i.e.:

$$\sum_{i=1}^{N} n_{i,t} d_{i,t} = D_t \tag{4}$$

where $n_{i,t}$ is the number of agents of type i.

Market equilibrium implies that the market demand is equal to the market supply X_t which we assume to be exogenous.[2] Thus,

$$X_t = D_t \tag{5}$$

Substituting the optimal holdings into the market demand and then into the market equilibrium equation and solving for the exchange rate s_t yields the market clearing exchange rate:

$$s_t = \left(\frac{1+r^*}{1+r}\right) \frac{1}{\sum_{i=1}^{N} \frac{w_{i,t}}{\sigma_{i,t}^2}} \left[\sum_{i=1}^{N} w_{i,t} \frac{E_t^i(s_{t+1})}{\sigma_{i,t}^2} - \Omega_t X_t\right] \tag{6}$$

[1]Gaunersdorfer (2000) extended the Brock–Hommes model by allowing time varying but homogenous beliefs concerning the variances. Chiarella and He (2002) extended the model to allow for time varying and heterogenous beliefs about varainces.

[2]The market supply is determined by the net current account and by the sales or purchases of foreign exchange of the central bank. We assume both to be exogenous. In an extension of this paper we intend to endogenise the market supply.

where $w_{i,t} = \frac{n_{i,t}}{\sum_{i=1}^{N} n_{i,t}}$ is the weight of agent i, and $w_t = \frac{\mu}{(1+r^*)\sum_{i=1}^{N} n_{i,t}}$. In the following we will set $r = r*$.

2.2. *The Forecasting Rules*

We assume that there are two types of agents: chartists (technical traders) and fundamentalists. Here we specify how fundamentalists and chartists form their expectations of the future exchange rate. Then we will specify how they take into account the risk as measured by the variances.

The fundamentalists base their forecast on a comparison between the market and the fundamental exchange rate, i.e., they forecast the market rate to return to the fundamental rate in the future. In this sense they use a negative feedback rule that introduces a mean reverting dynamics in the exchange rate. The speed with which the market exchange rate returns to the fundamental is assumed to be determined by the speed of adjustment in the goods market. Thus, the forecasting rule for the fundamentalists is:

$$E_t^f(\Delta s_{t+1}) = -\psi(s_{t-1} - s_{t-1}^*) \tag{7}$$

where s_{t-1}^* is the fundamental exchange rate at time $t = 1$, which is assumed to follow a random walk and $0 < \psi < 1$. Note the timing of the information set. In the Walrasian market equilibrium framework used here, the market clearing exchange rate depends on forecasts of s_{t+1}. When forming this forecast agents have not yet observed s_t. As a result, they use the most recent observed exchange rate, s_{t-1}.

In addition, the fundamentalists take the existence of transaction costs in the goods market into account. There is an increasing body of theoretical literature stressing the importance of transactions costs in the goods markets as a source of non-linearity in the determination of the exchange rate (Dumas, 1992; Sercu, Uppal and Van Hulle, 1995; Obstfeld and Rogoff, 2000). The importance of transaction costs in the goods markets has also been confirmed empirically (Taylor, Peel and Sarno, 2001; Kilian and Taylor, 2003). In addition, it should also be remembered that a large component of most tradable goods has a local service component which increases the transaction costs in trading goods internationally (see Obstfeld and Rogoff, 2000).

We therefore introduce these transaction costs into the model and we assume that the fundamentalists behave differently depending on whether the exchange rate is within or outside the transaction costs band. When the exchange rate deviation from its fundamental value is larger than the costs of transacting goods and services, C (assumed to be of the "iceberg" type), the fundamentalists know that goods arbitrage will function, thereby driving the exchange rate towards its fundamental value. As a result, they will expect that the exchange rate will be driven to its fundamental value in the future. Thus, they use the forecasting rule as in Eq. 7. More formally,

$$\text{when } |s_t - s_t^*| > C \quad \text{holds, then Eq. 7 applies.}^3$$

However, when the exchange rate deviations from the fundamental value are smaller than the transaction costs in the goods markets, fundamentalists know that there is no mechanism that drives the exchange rate towards its equilibrium value. As a result, fundamentalists expect the changes in the exchange rate to follow a white noise process and the best they can do is to forecast no change. More formally,

$$\text{when } |s_t - s_t^*| < C, \quad \text{then } E_t^f(\Delta s_{t+1}) = 0.$$

The chartists (technical traders) forecast the future exchange rate by extrapolating past exchange rate movements. Their forecasting rule can be specified as:

$$E_t^f(\Delta s_{t+1}) = \beta \sum_{i=1}^{T} \alpha_i \Delta s_{t-i} \tag{8}$$

Thus, the chartists compute a moving average of the past exchange rate changes and they extrapolate this into the future exchange rate change. The degree of extrapolation is given by the parameter β. Note that in contrast to the fundamentalists they take into account

[3]Note that since $\psi < 1$ market inefficiencies other than transaction costs continue to play a role when the exchange rate moves outside the transaction costs band. As a result, these inefficiencies prevent the exchange rate from adjusting instantaneously.

information concerning the fundamental exchange rate only indirectly, i.e., through the market exchange rate. In this sense, they can be considered to be noise traders. In a way this chartist rule can also be seen as reflecting herding behaviour, i.e., chartists closely watch the movements of the exchange rate as a way to detect "market sentiments." If the latter are positive, they buy; if they are negative, they sell (Brunnermeier, 2001).

Our choice to give a prominent role to chartists' rules of forecasting is based on empirical evidence. The evidence that chartism is used widely to make forecasts is overwhelming (see Cheung and Chinn, 1989; Taylor and Allen, 1992). It remains important, however, to check if the model is internally consistent. In particular, the chartists' forecasting rule must be shown to be profitable within the confines of the model. If these rules turn out to be unprofitable, they will not continue to be used. We return to this issue when we let the number of chartists be determined by the profitability of the chartists' forecasting rule.

We now analyze how fundamentalists and chartists evaluate the risk. The latter is measured by the variance terms in Eq. 6, which we define as the weighted average of the squared (one period ahead) forecasting errors made by chartists and fundamentalists, respectively. Thus,

$$\sigma^2_{i,t+1} = \sum_{k=1}^{\infty} \theta_k [E^i_{t-k}(s_{t-k+1}) - s_{t-k+1}]^2 \tag{9}$$

where $\theta_k = \theta(1-\theta)^k$ are geometrically declining weights ($0 < \theta < 1$), and $i = c, f$

However, fundamentalists and chartists perceive the risk in a different way. In particular the fundamentalists are assumed to take into account the deviation of the exchange rate from the fundamental in addition to the forecasting error. We will call the deviation of the market exchange rate from its fundamental, the misalignment. Thus the fundamentalists' risk term can be written as:

$$\sigma^2_{f,t+1} = \frac{\sum_{k=1}^{\infty} \theta_k [E^f_{t-k}(s_{t-k+1}) - s_{t-k+1}]^2}{1 + (s_t - s^*_t)^2} \tag{10}$$

where $(s_t - s^*_t)$ is the misalignment.

The logic behind this specification is that the fundamentalists consider the fundamental exchange rate as a benchmark for computing their forecasted returns. At the same time, consistently with the way in which they forecast, fundamentalists take into account the fundamentals also when they have to evaluate the risk associated with their forecasted exchange rate. Therefore, the larger is the misalignment the less the fundamentalists will attach importance to the short-term volatility as measured by the one-period ahead forecasting error. Put differently, as the misalignment increases, the fundamentalists become increasingly more confident that the exchange rate will revert to its fundamental value. As a result, their risk perception declines. In contrast, the misalignment does not affect the risk perception of the chartists. The reason is that the latter only take into account the past movements of the exchange rate to forecast the exchange rate. As a result, the fundamental exchange rate plays no (direct) role in this forecasting exercise. The logical implication is that the fundamental exchange rate does not play a (direct) role in determining the risk of the chartists either.

2.3. *Fitness of the Rules*

The next step in our analysis is to specify how agents evaluate the fitness of these two forecasting rules. The general idea that we will follow is that agents use one of the two rules, compare their (risk adjusted) profitability *ex post* and then decide whether to keep the rule or switch to the other one. Thus, our model is in the logic of evolutionary dynamics, in which simple decision rules are selected. These rules will continue to be followed if they pass some "fitness" test (profitability test). Another way to interpret this is as follows. When great uncertainty exists about how the complex world functions, agents use a trial and error strategy. They try a particular forecasting rule until they find out that other rules work better. Such a trial and error strategy can be considered to be a rational strategy when agents cannot understand the full complexity of the underlying model.

In order to implement this idea, we use the concept of a switching mechanism as proposed by Brock and Hommes (1997). Such a mechanism consists in making the weights of the forecasting rules a function of the relative profitability of these rules, i.e.[4]:

$$w_{c,t} = \frac{exp[\gamma\pi'_{c,t-1}]}{exp[\gamma\pi'_{c,t-1}] + exp[\gamma\pi'_{f,t-1}]} \tag{11}$$

$$w_{f,t} = \frac{exp[\gamma\pi'_{f,t-1}]}{exp[\gamma\pi'_{c,t-1}] + exp[\gamma\pi'_{f,t-1}]} \tag{12}$$

where $\pi'_{c,t-1}$ and $\pi'_{f,t-1}$ are the risk adjusted returns made by technical traders' and fundamentalists' forecasting the exchange rate in period $t-1$, i.e., $\pi'_{c,t-1} = \pi_{c,t-1} - \mu\sigma^2_{c,t-1}$ and $\pi'_{f,t-1} = \pi_{f,t-1} - \mu\sigma^2_{f,t-1}$.

Equations 11 and 12 can be interpreted as follows. When the risk adjusted return of the technical traders' rule increases relative to the risk adjusted return of the fundamentalists rule, then the share of agents who use technical trader rules increases in period t, and vice versa. The parameter γ measures the intensity with which the technical traders (chartists) and fundamentalists revise their forecasting rules. With an increasing γ agents react strongly to the relative profitability of the rules. In the limit when γ goes to infinity all agents choose the forecasting rule which proves to be more profitable. When γ is equal to zero agents are insensitive to the relative profitability of the rules. In the latter case, the fraction of technical traders and fundamentalists is constant and equal to 0.5. Thus, γ is a measure of inertia in the decision to switch to the more profitable rule.[5]

We depart from the Brock–Hommes switching mechanism in the way we define profitability. Brock–Hommes define profitability to be the total earnings (profits) on the optimal foreign asset holdings. We define the profitability as the one-period earnings of investing \$1 in the foreign asset. More formally,

$$\pi_{i,t} = [s_t(1+r^*) - s_{t-1}(1+r)]sgn[E^i_{t-1}((1+r^*)s_t - (1+r)s_{t-1})] \tag{13}$$

---

[4]This specification of the decision rule is often used in discrete choice models. For an application in the market for differentiated products see Anderson de Palma and Thisse (1992). The idea has also been applied in financial markets Brock Hommes (1997). A variant of this rules was developed by Lux (1998).

[5]The psychological literature reveals that there is a lot of evidence of a "status quo bias" in decision making (see Kahneman, Knetsch and Thaler, 1991). For this reason we will not set $\gamma = \infty$.

where

$$sgn[x] = \begin{cases} 1 & \text{for } x > 0 \\ 0 & \text{for } x = 0 \\ -1 & \text{for } x < 0 \end{cases} \quad \text{and} \quad i = c, f$$

Thus, when agents forecasted an increase in the exchange rate and this increase is realized, their return is equal to the observed increase in the exchange rate (corrected for the interest differential). If instead the exchange rate declines, they make a negative return which equals this decline (because in this case they have bought foreign assets which have declined in price).

We use a concept of profits per unit invested (return) for two reasons. First, our switching mechanism 11 and 12 selects the fittest rules. It does not select agents. To make this clear, suppose that chartists happen to have more wealth than fundamentalists so that their total profits exceeds the fundamentalists' profits despite the fact that the chartist rule happens to be less profitable (pet unit invested) than the fundamentalist rule. In this case, our switching rule will select the fundamentalists rule although the agents who use this rule make less profits (because their wealth happens to be small) than agents using chartist rules. Second, in our definition of profitability agents only have to use publicly available information, i.e., the forecasting rules and the observed exchange rate changes. They do not have to know their competitor's profits.

3. Solution of the Model

In this section, we investigate the properties of the solution of the model. We first study its deterministic solution. This will allow us to analyze the characteristics of the solution that are not clouded by exogenous noise. The model consists of Eqs. (6) to (13) together with the transaction cost condition. In general, its non-linear structure does not allow for a simple analytical solution.

3.1. *The Steady State*

We analyze the steady state of a simplified version of the model. For the sake of simplicity we assume that chartists only take one lag into account.[6] We also assume that transactions costs in the goods market are zero, i.e., $C = 0$. In addition, we set $X = 0$, and normalize the fundamental rate, $s_t^* = s^* = 0$. We can then write equation 6 as follows:

$$s_t = s_{t-1} - \Theta_{f,t}\psi s_{t-1} + \Theta_{c,t}\beta(s_{t-1} - s_{t-2}) \tag{14}$$

where

$$\Theta_{f,t} = \frac{w_{f,t}/\sigma_{f,t}^2}{w_{f,t}/\sigma_{f,t}^2 + w_{c,t}/\sigma_{c,t}^2} \tag{15}$$

and

$$\Theta_{c,t} = \frac{w_{c,t}/\sigma_{c,t}^2}{w_{f,t}/\sigma_{f,t}^2 + w_{c,t}/\sigma_{c,t}^2} \tag{16}$$

are the risk adjusted weights of fundamentalists and chartists, and

$$w_{f,t} = \frac{exp[\gamma\pi_{f,t-1} - \mu\sigma_{f,t}^2]}{exp[\gamma\pi_{c,t-1} - \mu\sigma_{c,t}^2] + exp[\gamma\pi_{f,t-1} - \mu\sigma_{f,t}^2]} \tag{17}$$

The Eqs. 9 and 10 defining the variance terms can also be rewritten as follows:

$$\sigma_{c,t}^2 = (1-\theta)\sigma_{c,t-1}^2 + \theta[E_{t-2}^c(s_{t-1}) - s_{t-1}]^2 \tag{18}$$

$$\sigma_{f,t}^2 = (1-\theta)\sigma_{f,t-1}^2 + \theta\frac{[E_{t-2}^f(s_{t-1}) - s_{t-1}]^2}{1 + (s_{t-1})^2} \tag{19}$$

Using the definition of the forecasting rules 7 and 8, this yields

$$\sigma_{c,t}^2 = (1-\theta)\sigma_{c,t-1}^2 + \theta[(1+\beta)s_{t-2} - \beta s_{t-3} - s_{t-1}]^2 \tag{20}$$

$$\sigma_{f,t}^2 = (1-\theta)\sigma_{f,t-1}^2 + \theta\frac{[(1-\psi)s_{t-2} - s_{t-1}]^2}{1 + (s_{t-1})^2} \tag{21}$$

[6]One can easily add additional lags without altering the steady state analysis.

With suitable changes of variables it is possible to write the system as a 6-dimensional system. Set

$$u_t = s_{t-1}$$
$$x_t = u_{t-1} (= s_{t-2})$$

The 6 dynamic variables are $(s_t, u_t, x_t, \pi_{c,t}, \sigma^2_{c,t}, \sigma^2_{f,t})$. The state of the system at time $t-1$, i.e., $(s_{t-1}, u_{t-1}, x_{t-1}, z_{t-1}, \pi_{c,t-1}, \sigma^2_{c,t-1}, \sigma^2_{f,t-1})$ determines the state of the system at time t, i.e., $(s_t, u_t, x_t, \pi_{c,t}, \sigma^2_{c,t}, \sigma^2_{f,t})$ through the following 6-D dynamical system:

$$s_t = [1 + -\beta - \Theta_{f,t} + (\psi + \beta)]s_{t-1} - (1 - \Theta_{f,t})\beta u_{t-1} \tag{22}$$
$$u_t = s_{t-1} \tag{23}$$
$$x_t = u_{t-1} \tag{24}$$
$$\pi_{c,t} = (s_t - s_{t-1})\text{sgn}[(u_{t-1} + \beta(u_{t-1} - x_{t-1}) - s_{t-1})(s_t - s_{t-1})] \tag{25}$$
$$\sigma^2_{c,t} = (1 - \theta)\sigma^2_{c,t-1} + \theta[(1 + \beta)u_{t-1} - \beta x_{t-1} - s_{t-1}]^2 \tag{26}$$
$$\sigma^2_{f,t} = (1 - \theta)\sigma^2_{f,t-1} + \theta\frac{[(1-\psi)u_{t-1} - s_{t-1}]^2}{1 + (s_{t-1})^2} \tag{27}$$

where

$$\Theta_{f,t} = \frac{w_{f,t}/\sigma^2_{f,t}}{w_{f,t}/\sigma^2_{f,t} + w_{c,t}/\sigma^2_{c,t}} \tag{28}$$

and

$$w_{f,t} = \frac{exp[\gamma\pi_{f,t-1} - \mu\sigma^2_{f,t}]}{exp[\gamma\pi_{c,t-1} - \mu\sigma^2_{c,t}] + exp[\gamma\pi_{f,t-1} - \mu\sigma^2_{f,t}]} \tag{29}$$
$$\pi_{f,t-1} = (s_{t-1} - u_{t-1})\text{sgn}[((1 - \psi)x_{t-1} - u_{t-1})(s_{t-1} - u_{t-1})] \tag{30}$$

A characteristics of the steady state is that the exchange rate is constant. As a result, the variance terms go to zero. This also implies that in the steady state, the risk adjusted weights of the fundamentalists and chartists are of the form $\Theta_{f,t} = \frac{\infty}{\infty}$ and $\Theta_{c,t} = \frac{\infty}{\infty}$.

Rewriting these weights as follows:

$$\Theta_{f,t} = \frac{w_{f,t}}{w_{f,t} + w_{c,t}(\sigma^2_{f,t}/\sigma^2_{c,t})} \tag{31}$$

and

$$\Theta_{c,t} = \frac{w_{c,t}(\sigma^2_{f,t}/\sigma^2_{c,t})}{w_{f,t} + w_{c,t}(\sigma^2_{f,t}/\sigma^2_{c,t})} \tag{32}$$

One can show by numerical methods that in the steady state the expression $\sigma^2_{f,t}/\sigma^2_{c,t}$ converges to 1.[7] We show this in Appendix 1 where we plot the ratio as a function of time in a typical simulation run. This implies that in the steady state $\Theta_{f,t} = w_{f,t}$ and $\Theta_{c,t} = w_{c,t}$. Note that $w_{f,t} + w_{c,t} = 1$.

The steady states of the system are now obtained by setting

$$\begin{aligned}(s_{t-1}, u_{t-1}, x_{t-1}, \pi_{c,t-1}, \sigma^2_{f,t-1}, \sigma^2_{c,t-1}) &= (s_t, u_t, x_t, \pi_{c,t}, \sigma^2_{f,t}, \sigma^2_{c,t}) \\ &= (\bar{s}, \bar{u}, \bar{x}, \bar{\pi}_c, \bar{\sigma}^2_f, \bar{\sigma}^2_c)\end{aligned}$$

in the dynamical system (22–27).

There is a unique steady state where:

$$\bar{s}, \bar{u}, \bar{x} = 0, \;\; \bar{\pi}_c = 0, \;\; \bar{\sigma}^2_f, \bar{\sigma}^2_c = 0$$

Notice also that at the steady state:

$$\bar{w}_c = \frac{1}{2}, \;\; \bar{w}_f = \frac{1}{2}, \;\; \bar{\pi}_f = 0$$

i.e., the steady state is characterized by the exchange rate being at its fundamental level, by zero profits and zero risk, and by fundamentalist and technical trader fractions equal to $\frac{1}{2}$.

With this dynamical system it is not possible to perform the local stability analysis of the steady state with the usual techniques, based upon the analysis of the eigenvalues of the Jacobian matrix evaluated at the steady state. The reason is that the "map" whose iteration generates the dynamics is not differentiable at the steady state.

[7] It does not appear to be possible to show this by analytical methods.

3.2. *Numerical Analysis*

The strong non-linearities make an analysis of the model's global stability impossible. Therefore, we use simulation techniques which we will present in this and the following sections. We select "reasonable" values of the parameters, i.e., those that come close to empirically observed values. In Appendix 2, we present a table with the numerical values of the parameters of the model and the lags involved. As we will show later, these are also parameter values for which the model replicates the observed statistical properties of exchange rate movements. We will also analyse how sensitive the solution is to different sets of parameter values. The dynamical model used in the numerical analysis is the same one as in the previous section except for the fact that $C > 0$ and except for the number of lags in the chartists' forecasting rule. We now return to the specification of the chartists's rule as given by Eq. (8). As a result, (14) becomes

$$s_t = s_{t-1} - \Theta_{f,t}\psi s_{t-1} + \Theta_{c,t}\beta \sum_{i=1}^{T} \alpha_i \Delta s_{t-i} \tag{33}$$

where $T = 5$. Thus, the full model with all its lags is a 10-dimensional dynamic system.

We first concentrate on the fixed point solutions of the model. We find that for a relatively wide range of parameters the exchange rate converges to a fixed point (a fixed-point attractor). However, there are many such fixed points (attractors) to which the exchange rate converges depending on the initial conditions. We illustrate this feature in Figure 1 where we plot the fixed point solutions (attractors) for the exchange rale as a function of the different initial conditions. These were obtained from simulating the model over 10,000 periods. We found that after such a long period the exchange rate had stabilized to a fixed point (a fixed attractor). On the horizontal axis we set out the different initial conditions. These are initial shocks to the exchange rate in the period before the simulation is started.[8] The vertical axis shows the solutions for the exchange rate

[8]There are longer lags in the model, i.e., five. Thus, we set the exchange rate with a lag of more than one period before the start equal to 0. This means that the initial conditions

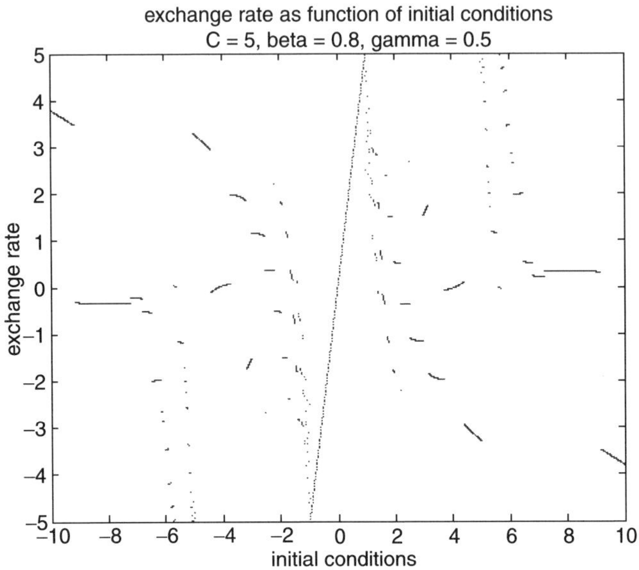

Figure 1.

corresponding to these different initial conditions. Note the complex pattern of these fixed point solutions, with many discontinuities.[9] This has the implication that a small change in the initial condition can have a large effect on the solution. This feature lies at the heart of some of the results that are obtained with this model relating to the unpredictability of the effect of shocks in exogenous variables. We return to this phenomenon in Section 7.[10]

It should also be noted that the fixed-point attractors lie within the transaction costs band. The intuition is that any fixed-point solution outside the transaction costs band would create an inconsistency, which can be described as follows. Outside the transaction costs band the fundamentalists' behavior leads to a mean reverting process of

are one-period shocks in the exchange rate prior to the start of the simulation. All the other lagged dynamic variables are set equal to 0 when the simulation is started.

[9]With a high value of γ results are qualitatively similar.

[10]The numerical values of the simulations are shown in Appendix 2.

the exchange rate, moving the latter towards the transaction costs band. Thus, if a fixed point solution were observed outside the transactions cost band, this would mean that the fundamentalists would fail to move the exchange rate towards the band. Once inside the band, the fundamentalists' dynamics disappears. The only dynamics then comes from the chartists who drive the exchange rate to some attractor within the band. The exact position of this attractor depends on the entry point of the exchange rate in the transactions cost band, and this depends on the initial shock.

4. Sensitivity Analysis

In this section we perform a sensitivity analysis. We do this by showing bifurcation diagrams that relate the solutions to different values of important parameters of the model. We concentrate on the extrapolation parameter used by the chartists, β, on the sensitivity of the switching rule, γ, and on transactions costs C.

4.1. *Sensitivity with Respect to β*

The left panel of Figure 2 shows an example of such a bifurcation diagram. On the horizontal axis we set out different values of the extrapolation parameter β. On the vertical axis we show the solutions for the exchange rate. This is the exchange rate obtained after 10000 periods, given an initial shock to the exchange rate.[11] We observe the following. For low values of β, we obtain unique fixed point solutions. When β reaches a value of approximately 0.9, we enter the chaotic region. This is characterised by infinitely many solutions for each value of β. These points correspond to strange attractors within which the exchange rate then travels.

Figure 2 (upper panel) only provides a visual indication of the existence of a chaotic region. One can detect the existence of chaos more rigourously by calculating the largest Lyapunov exponent. This measures the rate of divergence of nearby trajectories. A positive largest Lyapunov exponent indicates chaos (see Rosenstein *et al.*,

[11]The initial shook in the one period lagged exchange rate was +2. All the other lagged dynamical variables ware set to 0.

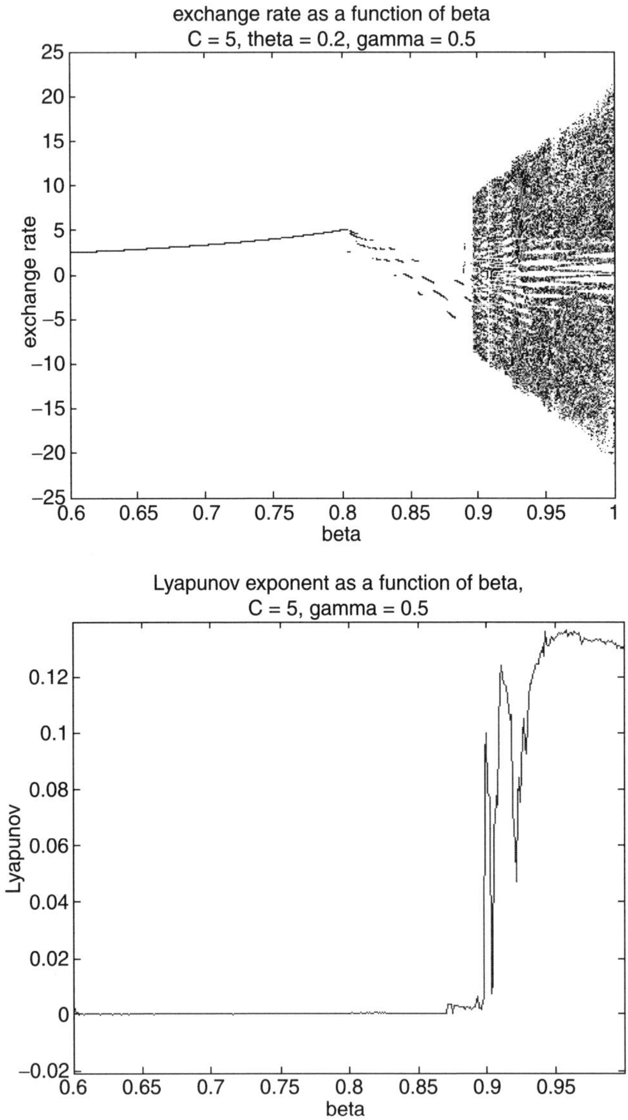

Figure 2.

1992 and De Grauwe *et al.*, 1993 for a discussion of Lyapunov exponents). Since we have access to the equations generating chaos (and thus we know the dimension of the system) it is relatively simple to estimate the largest Lyapunov exponent. It is given by the following expression:

$$\lambda_1(i) = \frac{1}{T-1}\sum_{t=1}^{T-1} \ln \frac{d_t(i)}{d_t(0)} \tag{34}$$

where $d_t(i)$ is the (Euclidian) distance between the tth pair of nearby trajectories after i iterations, and $d_t(0)$ is the reinitialized distance at each point t.[12] We have set $i = 1$ which is a conservative measure, i.e., we compute the distance at each iteration. We show the results of computing the largest Lyapunov exponents in Figure 2 (lower panel). The latter confirms the visual impression of the left panel of Figure 2, i.e. for values of β exceeding 0.9 the largest Lyapunov exponent becomes positive. The exact value of β at which this happens depends on the other parameters of the model and on the initial conditions. Note also that for values of β below 0.9 we obtain a Lyapunov exponent which is zero. This result is due to the coexistence of fixed point attractors. In the absence of chaos (e.g., when $\beta = 0.8$ and $\gamma = 0.5$) we obtain one separate fixed point for each initial condition (see Figure 1). This means that when computing the Lyapunov exponent for two nearby trajectories we will find that these trajectories keep a constant distance in the steady state. As a result, the largest Lyapunov exponent must be zero.

The importance of the initial conditions in determining whether the exchange rate will enter the chaotic domain is illustrated in Figure 3 on the left panel, where we fix $\beta = 0.9$ and vary the initial conditions. The upper panel of Figure 3 is constructed in the same way as Figure 1 and shows the steady state exchange rate (attractor) as a function of the initial value of the exchange rate (initial conditions) while the lower panel exhibits the corresponding Lyapunov exponents. We now observe that the different initial conditions lead to switches in and out of the chaotic region. This feature suggests that there are attractors (some fixed points, others strange attractors) located in different basins of attraction. The border line between these different basins is itself complex. As a result, small differences in

[12]Note that since we have a 10-dimensional system the distance between the two nearby trajectories is computed as the (Euclidian) distance of the 10 variables at each point t.

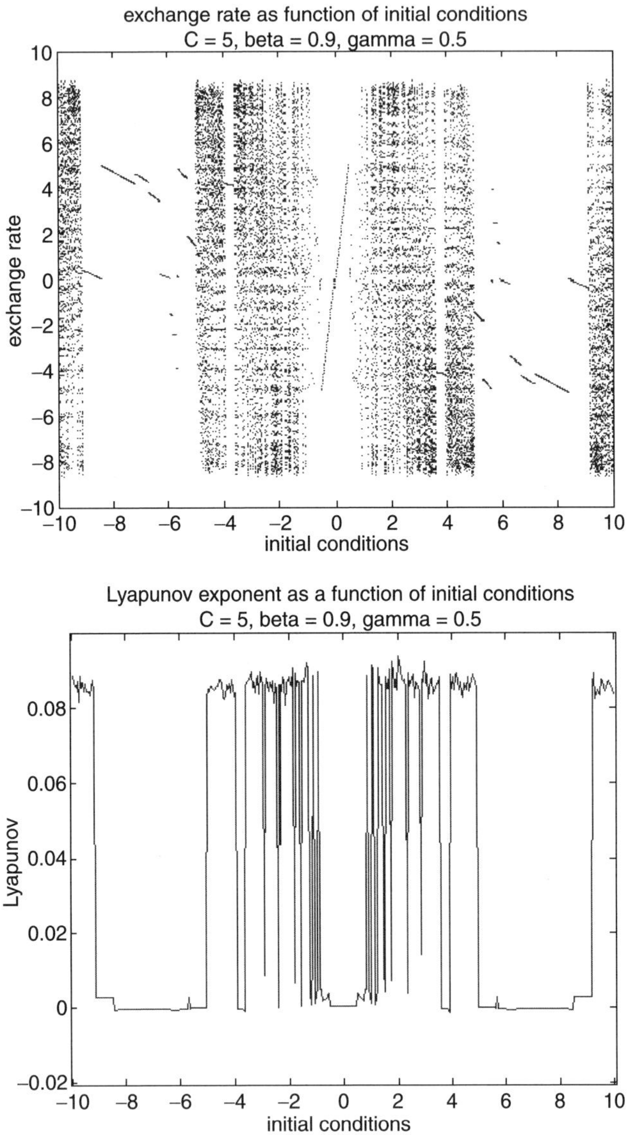

Figure 3.

the initial conditions can lead the system towards different attractors some of which are fixed point attractors, others chaotic attractors.

These features illustrate the great complexity in the exchange rate dynamics. As will be analysed in greater detail later, this complexity has many different implications. It acts as a veil obscuring the transmission of exogenous shocks (e.g., shocks in the fundamental exchange rate) into the market exchange rate. It has the potential of producing regime switches triggered by small disturbances. Finally, this complexity greatly complicates the making of standard statistical inferences from the distribution of the exchange rate changes.

4.2. *Sensitivity with Respect to γ*

In this section, we analyse the sensitivity of the solutions with respect to changes in the parameter γ which measures the sensitivity of the switiching rules with respect to profits ("intensity of choice"). We show the results in Figures 4(a) and (b) for two different values of the extrapolation parameter, β. When β is sufficiently low ($\beta = 0.8$) we obtain fixed point solutions for all values of γ (Figure 4(a)). When $\beta = 0.9$ which as we have seen in the previous section, constitutes the boundary value between fixed point and chaotic solution, variations in γ lead the solutions to switch in and out of chaos (Figure 4(b)). The latter is also confirmed by the Lyapunov exponents shown in Figure 4(c). Thus, changing γ produces similar effects as changing the initial conditions. Note, however, that for small values of γ we obtain fixed point solutions.

4.3. *Sensitivity with Respect to Transactions Costs*

We also investigated the importance of transaction costs. In order to do so, we produced similar bifurcation diagrams as in the previous sections. We now set out the transactions costs on the horizontal axis while we fix β and γ. As in the previous case, we find that when β is sufficiently smaller than 0.9 we obtain fixed point solutions for all values of the transactions costs.[13] In Figure 4(d) we show the case of $\beta = 0.9$. We observe switching in and out of chaos. This is confirmed by Figure 4(e) which shows the largest Lyapunov exponents for the same values of the transaction costs. Note that as transactions costs increase the spread of the possible solutions increases.

[13]We do not show this bifurcation diagram here. It can be obtained from the authors.

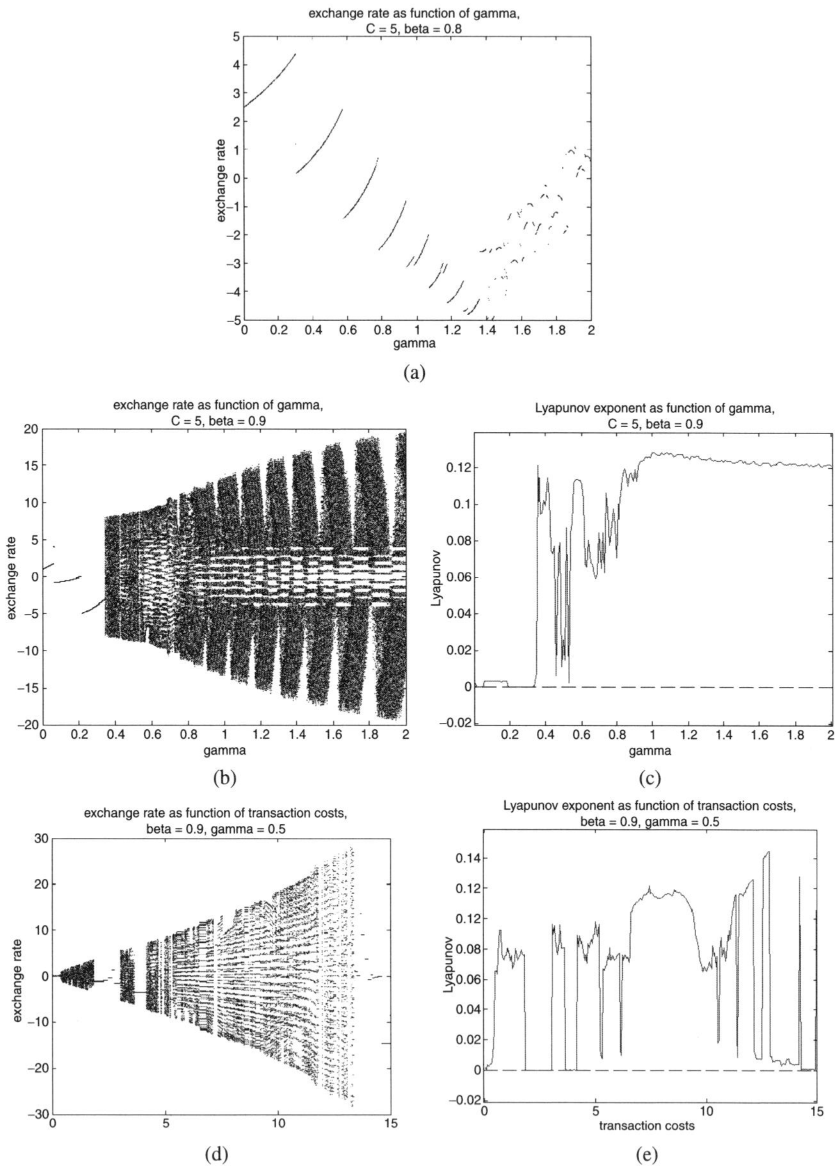
exchange rate as function of gamma,
C = 5, beta = 0.8
exchange rate
gamma
(a)
exchange rate as function of gamma,
C = 5, beta = 0.9
exchange rate
gamma
(b)
Lyapunov exponent as function of gamma,
C = 5, beta = 0.9
Lyapunov
gamma
(c)
exchange rate as function of transaction costs,
beta = 0.9, gamma = 0.5
exchange rate
(d)
Lyapunov exponent as function of transaction costs,
beta = 0.9, gamma = 0.5
Lyapunov
transaction costs
(e)

Figure 4.

The empirical evidence in favour of deterministic chaos is not very strong. Sometimes deterministic chaos has been detected in the data, but most often no such dynamics has been found (Guillaume, 2000; Schittenkopf, Dorffner and Dockner, 2001). Therefore, we will focus the analysis of the model on parameter values that do not lead to deterministic chaos. We will show that in combination with stochastic shocks this model is capable of producing a dynamics that exhibits many of the features of chaotic dynamics despite the fact that the deterministic solutions of the model are fixed points. In addition in Section 6 we will calibrate the model in such a way that it reproduces the main statistical properties of exchange rate movements. It will be shown that the parameters that mimick these statistical properties best do not produce deterministic chaos.

5. The Stochastic Version of the Model

We now introduce stochastic disturbances to the model. In our model, these disturbances appear in that we assume that the fundamental exchange rate behaves as a random walk, i.e., $s_t^* = s_{t-1}^* + \epsilon_t$, where ϵ_t is iid with mean $= 0$ and standard deviation $= 0.1$.

We simulate the model with a combination of parameter values that we refer to as the "standard case." This includes setting $c = 5, \beta = 0.9$ and $\psi = 0.2$. and $\gamma = 0.5$. See also the table in Appendix 2 for the other parameters. (Similar results are obtained for a wide range of parameter values. In addition, it will be shown in Section 6 that these parameter values reproduce the statistical properties observed in exchange rate movements).

A first feature of the solution of the stochastic version of the model is the sensitivity to initial conditions. In order to show this, we first simulated the model with the "standard" parameter values and then we simulated the model with the same parameters setting but with a slightly different initial condition, i.e., $s_0 = +3$, and $s_0 = +3.01$. In both cases we used identical stochastic disturbances driving the fundamental. We show the time paths of the (market) exchange rate in Figure 5(a).

We observe that after a certain number of periods the two exchange rates start following a different path. This result is related

(a)
(b)
(c)

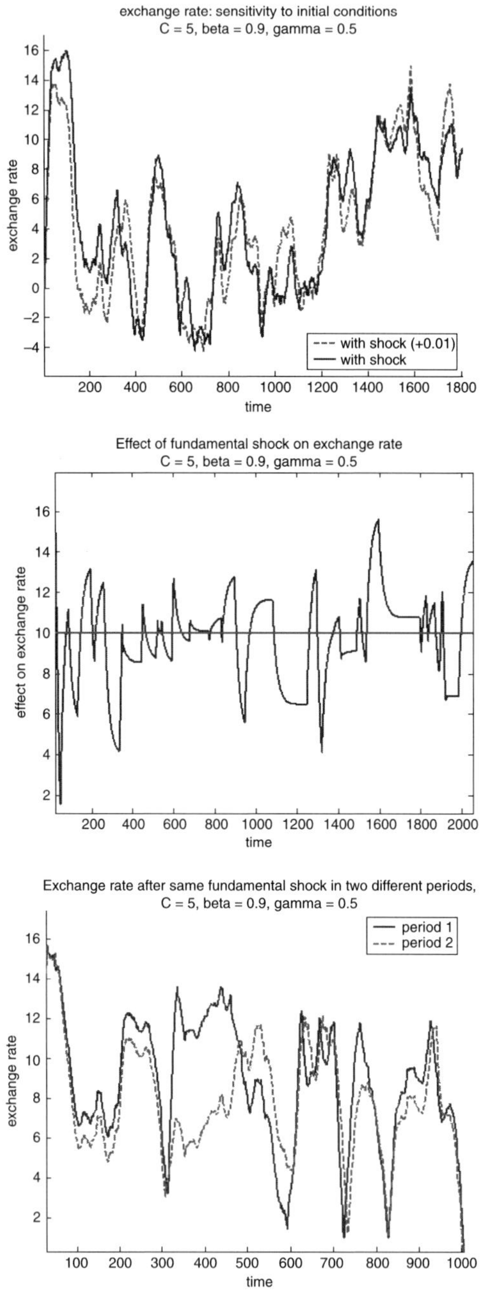
exchange rate: sensitivity to initial conditions
C = 5, beta = 0.9, gamma = 0.5
exchange rate
time
with shock (+0.01)
with shock
Effect of fundamental shock on exchange rate
C = 5, beta = 0.9, gamma = 0.5
effect on exchange rate
time
Exchange rate after same fundamental shock in two different periods,
C = 5, beta = 0.9, gamma = 0.5
period 1
period 2
exchange rate
time

Figure 5.

to the presence of many fixed-point attractors in the deterministic part of the model, which are themselves dependent on the initial conditions (see Figure 1 which shows how slight differences in initial conditions can lead to fixed-point attractors that are very far apart). As a result, the two exchange rates can substantially diverge because they are attracted by fixed-points that are located in different basins of attraction. The nice aspect of this is that we obtain a result that is typical for chaotic systems, however, without chaos being present in the deterministic part of the model. The combination of exogenous noise and a multiplicity of fixed-point attractors located in different basins of attraction creates sensitivity to initial conditions, a feature which is also found in chaotic dynamics.

A second feature of the model relates to the way shocks in the fundamental exchange rate are transmitted into the market exchange rate. In linear models a permanent shock in the fundamental has a predictable effect on the exchange rate, i.e., the coefficient that measures the effect of the shock in the fundamental on the exchange rate converges after some time to a fixed number. Things are very different in our non-linear model. We illustrate this by showing how a permanent increase in the fundamental is transmitted to the exchange rate. We assumed that the fundamental rate increases by 10, and we computed the effect on the exchange rate by taking the difference between the exchange rate with the shock and the exchange rate without the shock. In a linear model we would find that in the long run the exchange rate increases by 10. This is not the case in our model. We present the evidence Figure 5(b) where we show the effect of the same permanent shock of 10 in the fundamental rate on the exchange rate. The simulations are done assuming exactly the same stochastics in the scenario with as without the permanent shock in the fundamental exchange rate. Thus, there is no exogenous noise in the model that could blur the transmission process from the fundamental rate to the exchange rate.

The most striking feature of these results is that the effect of the permanent shock does not converge to a fixed number. In fact, it follows a complex pattern. Thus, in a non-linear world it is very difficult to predict what the effect will be of a given shock in the fundamental, even in the long run. Such predictions can only be made in a statistical sense, i.e., our model tells us that the effect of a shock of 10 in the fundamental will be to increase the exchange rate by 10 on average. In any given period, however, the effect could deviate substantially from this average prediction.

The importance of the initial conditions for the effect of a permanent shock in the fundamental can also be seen by the following experiment. We simulated the same permanent shock in the fundamental but applied it in two different time periods. In the first simulation we applied the shock in the first period; in the second simulation we applied it in the next period. The exogenous noise was identical in both simulations. Thus, the only difference is in the timing of the shock. We show the results in Figure 5(c).

We observe that the small difference in timing changes the future history of the exchange rate. As a result, the effect of the shock measured at a particular point in time can be very different in both simulations. Thus history matters. The time at which the permanent shock occurs influences the effects of the shock.

Our results help to explain why in the real world it appears so difficult to predict the effects of changes in the fundamental exchange rate on the market rate, and why these effects seem to be very different when applied in different periods. In fact, this is probably one of the most intriguing empirical problems. Economists usually explain the difficulty of forecasting the effects of a particular change in one exogenous variable (e.g., an expansion of the money stock) by invoking the *ceteris paribus* hypothesis., i.e., there are usually other exogenous variables changing unexpectedly, preventing us to isolate the effect of the first exogenous variable. In our model, the uncertainty surrounding the effect of a disturbance in an exogenous variable is not due to the failure of the *ceteris paribus* hypothesis. No other exogenous variable is allowed to change. The fact is that the change in the exogenous variable occurs at a particular time, which is different from all other times. This difference is due, among others, to the fact that at each point in time there is a different composition of chartists and fundamentalists in the market, which itself is due to different past performances of chartists and fundamentalists forecasting rules. As a result, the same fundamental shock applied at different time periods is "perceived" differently in the market, e.g. at one moment there are fewer fundamentalists than at another moment so that the same fundamental shock gets less attention. Thus, initial conditions (history) matters to forecast the effect of shocks. Since each initial condition is unique, it becomes impossible to forecast the precise effect of a shock at any given point in time.

Finally, it should be stressed that the uncertainty about the effect of a permanent shock in the fundamental only holds in a particular environment that is related to a low variance of the noise. In a later section, we will analyze how different environments concerning the variance of shocks affect the results.

6. Empirical Relevance of the Model

In this section we analyze how well our model replicates the empirical anomalies and puzzles that have been uncovered by the empirical literature. We calibrate the model such that it replicates the observed statistical properties of exchange rate movements. The parameters of the model that do this are those that we used in the previous sections. As was noted there, typically these are parameter sets that do not produce deterministic chaos. All the simulations reported in this section are stochastic in that the fundamental is driven by a random walk as specified in the previous section. We start with the "disconnect puzzle."

6.1. *The Disconnect Puzzle*

The "disconnect" puzzle was popularized by Obstfeld and Rogoff (2000). It states that the exchange rate is disconnected from its underlying fundamentals most of the time.[14] It was first analyzed by John Williamson (1985) who called it the "misalignment problem."

[14]In its original formulation the disconnect puzzle has two dimensions. One says that the exchange rate is disconnected from its fundamental. The second dimension relates to the fact that real variables (for example, the trade account) do not react to the changes in the exchange rate. In this paper, we only analyze the first dimension.

This puzzle was also implicit in the celebrated Meese and Rogoff studies of the early 1980s documenting that there is no stable relationship between exchange rate movements and the news in the fundamental variables. Goodhart (1989) and Goodhart and Figlioli (1991) found that most of the changes in the exchange rates occur when there is no observable news in the fundamental economic variables. This finding contradicted the theoretical models (based on the efficient market hypothesis), which imply that the exchange rate can only move when there is news in the fundamentals.

We simulated our model to check whether it can replicate this empirical regularity. In Figure 6, we show the market exchange rate and the fundamental rate for a combination of parameters that does not produce deterministic chaos. (Our results hold equally well for a large set of parameter values). As described before, the fundamental rate is driven by a random walk. We observe that the market rate can deviate from the fundamental value substantially and in a persistent way. Moreover, it appears that the exchange rate movements are often disconnected from the movements of the underlying fundamental, and that they often move in opposite directions.

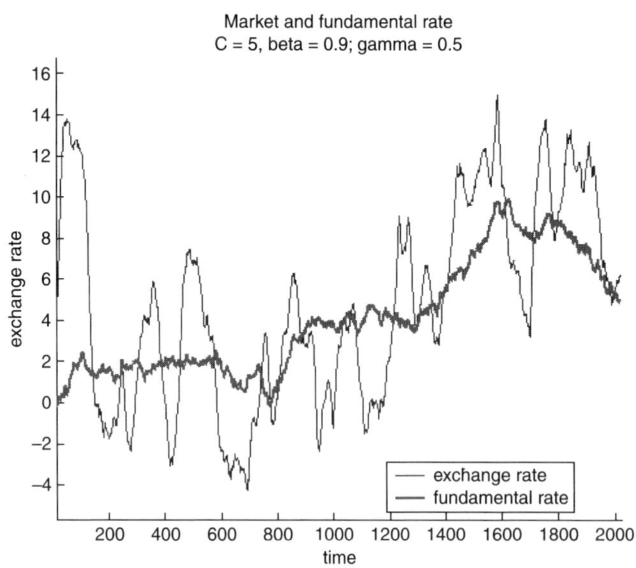

Figure 6.

The previous evidence is impressionistic. In order to show the nature of the disconnect phenomenon in a more precise way we applied a cointegration analysis to the simulated exchange rate and its fundamental using the same parameter values as Figure 6 for a sample of 8,000 periods. We found that there is a cointegration relationship between the exchange rate and its fundamental. Note that in our setting there is only one fundamental variable. This implies that no bias from omitted variables can occur.

In the next step we specify a EC model in the following way:

$$\Delta s_t = \eta(s_{t-1} - \delta s_{t-1}^*) + \sum_{i=1}^{n} \vartheta_i \Delta s_{t-i} + \sum_{i=1}^{n} \phi_i \Delta s_{t-i}^* \qquad (35)$$

The first term on the right hand side is the error correction term. The result of estimating this equation is presented in Table 1 where we have set n = 4. We find that the error correction coefficient (η) is very low. This suggests that the mean reversion towards the equilibrium exchange rate takes a very long time. In particular, only 0.3 percent of the adjustment takes place each period. It should be noted that in the simulations we have assumed that fundamentalists estimate the speed of adjustment in the goods market (ψ) to be 0.2. Thus, based on their belief about the speed of adjustment in the goods market they expect the exchange rate to have a speed of adjustment towards its equilibrium of 20 percent in each period. However, the nominal exchange rate is considerably slower to adjust towards its equilibrium than what is implied by the estimated speed of adjustment in the goods market. This slow adjustment of the nominal exchange rate is due to the chartists' extrapolation behaviour. This phenomenon has been observed in reality. Cheung *et al.* (2002) have recently discovered that most of the slow mean reversion of the real exchange rate is due to slow adjustment of the nominal exchange rate and not of the goods prices.

From Table 1, we also note that the changes in fundamentals have a small and insignificant impact on the change in exchange rate. In contrast, the past changes in the exchange rate play a significant role in explaining the change in exchange rate. These results are consistent with the empirical findings using VAR approach, which

Table 1. Error correction model.

Error correction		Δs_{t-i}				Δs^*_{t-i}			
η	δ	ϑ_1	ϑ_2	ϑ_3	ϑ_4	φ_1	φ_2	φ_3	φ_4
−0.003	0.92	0.32	0.20	0.13	0.08	0.03	0.02	0.01	0.01
−5.9	*4.9*	*22.8*	*13.7*	*8.7*	*5.9*	*1.9*	*1.0*	*0.6*	*0.1*

suggests that the exchange rate is driven by its own past (see De Boeck, 2000).[15]

Thus, our model generates an empirical regularity (the 'disconnect' puzzle) that is widely observed in reality. We can summarise the features of this puzzle as follows. First, over the very long run the exchange rate and its fundamentals are cointegrated. However, the speed with which the exchange rate reverts to its equilibrium value is very slow. Second, in the short run the exchange rate and its fundamentals are "disconnected", i.e. they do not appear to be cointegrated. Our model closely mimics these empirical regularities.

6.2. *The "Excess Volatility" Puzzle*

In this section we discuss another important empirical regularity, which has been called the "excess volatility" puzzle, i.e., the volatility of the exchange rate by far exceeds the volatility of the underlying economic variables. Baxter and Stockman (1989) and Flood and Rose (1995) found that while the movements from fixed to flexible exchange rates led to a dramatic increase in the volatility of the exchange rate no such increase could be detected in the volatility of the underlying economic variables. This contradicted the "news" models that predicted that the volatility of the exchange rate can only increase when the variability of the underlying fundamental

[15] We also performed a cointegration analysis for shorter sample periods (1,000 periods). We find that in some sample periods the exchange rate and its fundamental are cointograted, in other sample periods we do not find cointegration. This is in line with the empirical evidence indicating that in some periods the exchange rate seems to disconnected from its fundamental while in other periods it tightly follows the fundamentals.

variables increases (see Obstfeld and Rogoff, 1996 for a recent formulation of this model).

In order to deal with this puzzle, we compute the noise to signal ratio in the simulated exchange rate. We derive this noise to signal ratio as follows:

$$var\,(s) = var\,(f) + var\,(n) \tag{36}$$

where $var\,(s)$ is the variance of the simulated exchange rate, $var\,(f)$ is the variance of the fundamental and $var\,(n)$ is the residual variance (noise) produced by the non-linear speculative dynamics which is uncorrelated with $var\,(f)$. This the noise is to be interpreted as the volatility of the exchange rate which is unrelated to the volatility of the underlying fundamental variable. Rewriting (36), we obtain

$$\frac{var\,(n)}{var\,(f)} = \frac{var\,(s)}{var\,(f)} - 1 \tag{37}$$

The ratio $var\,(n)/var\,(f)$ can be interpreted as the noise to signal ratio. It gives a measure of how large the noise produced by the non-linear dynamics is with respect to the exogenous volatility of the fundamental exchange rate. A noise to signal ratio exceeding 1 means that the total volatility of the exchange rate is dominated by volatility which is unrelated to fundamental volatility. We simulate this noise to signal ratio for different values of the extrapolation parameter β (see Figure 7(a)). Each of these noise to signal ratios is computed using simulations of 1000 periods. We find that with increasing β the noise to signal ratio increases. This implies that when the chartists increase the degree with which they extrapolate the past exchange rate movements, the noise in the exchange rate, which is unrelated to fundamentals, increases. Thus, the signal about the fundamentals that we can extract from the exchange rate becomes more clouded when the chartists extrapolate more. It is important to note that since the fundamental variable follows a random walk, its variance increases with the length of the time interval over which it is computed.[16] We, therefore, also checked how the

[16]In the limit when $t \to \infty var\,(f) \to \infty$.

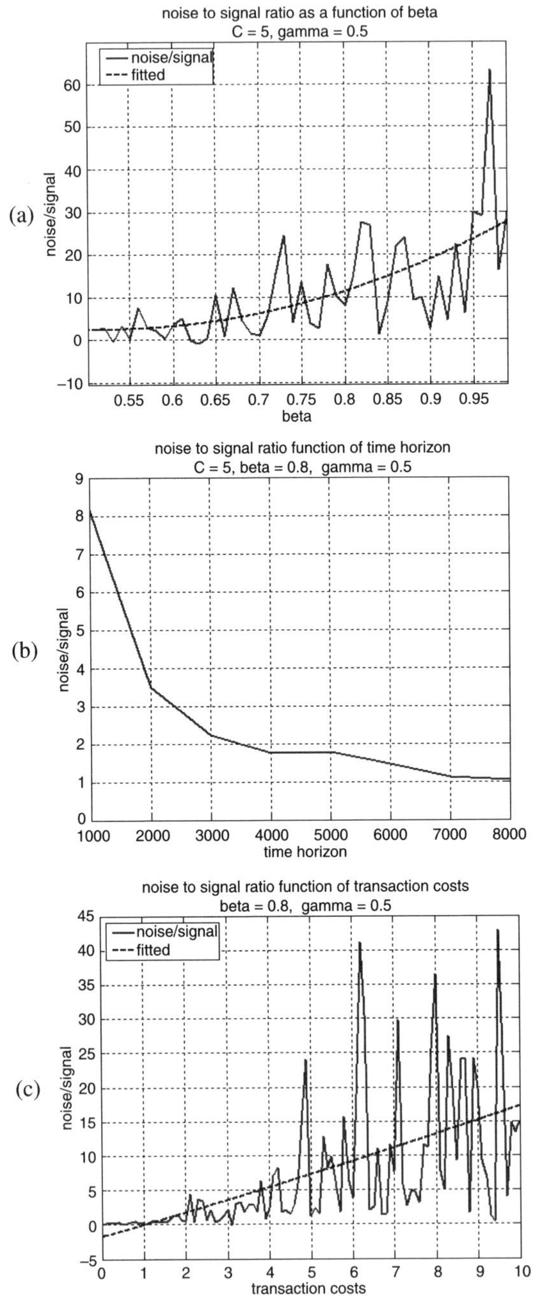
(a)
noise to signal ratio as a function of beta
C = 5, gamma = 0.5
noise/signal
fitted
60
50
40
30
20
10
0
−10
noise/signal
0.55 0.6 0.65 0.7 0.75 0.8 0.85 0.9 0.95
beta
(b)
noise to signal ratio function of time horizon
C = 5, beta = 0.8, gamma = 0.5
9
8
7
6
5
4
3
2
1
0
noise/signal
1000 2000 3000 4000 5000 6000 7000 8000
time horizon
(c)
noise to signal ratio function of transaction costs
beta = 0.8, gamma = 0.5
noise/signal
fitted
45
40
35
30
25
20
15
10
5
0
−5
noise/signal
0 1 2 3 4 5 6 7 8 9 10
transaction costs

Figure 7.

noise to signal ratio depends on the length of the time interval. We show the results in Figure 7(b) where we present the noise-to-signal ratios as a function of the length of time over which they are computed. We find that when the time horizon increases the noise-to-signal ratio declines. This is so because over long time horizons most of the volatility of the exchange rate is due to the fundamentals' volatility and very little to the endogenous noise. In contrast, over short time horizons the endogenous volatility is predominant and the signal that comes from the fundamentals is weak. This is consistent with the empirical finding concerning misalignments we discussed before.

It is also important to relate the noise-to-signal ratio to transaction costs in the goods market. Therefore, we show in Figure 7(c) how the noise-to-signal ratio changes with the size of transaction costs. We observe that the noise-to-signal ratio increases significantly with the size of transaction costs. An interpretation of this result is that as transaction costs increases the mean-reverting force from fundamentalists is weak while the chartists' force is strong. Thus, the noise created by chartists increases and clouds the signal coming from fundamentals.

6.3. *Non-normality of the Returns*

It is a well-established empirical fact that returns in financial markets are not normally distributed, exhibiting more density around the mean and fatter tails than the normal. This phenomenon was first discovered by Mandelbrot (1963) in commodity markets. Since then, fat tails and excess kurtosis have been discovered in many other asset markets including the exchange market. In particular, in the latter the returns have a kurtosis typically exceeding 3 and a measure of fat tails (Hill index) ranging between 2 and 5 (see Koedijk, Stork and de Vries, 1992; de Vries, 2001; Huisman *et al.*, 2002). It implies that most of the time the exchange rate movements are relatively small but that occasionally periods of turbulence occur with relatively large exchange rate changes. However, it has also been detected that the kurtosis is reduced under time aggregation. This phenomenon has been observed for most exchange rates (Lux, 1998; Calvet and Fisher, 2002). We checked whether this is also the case with the simulated exchange rate changes in our model.

We computed the kurtosis and the Hill index of the simulated exchange rate returns for different parameter values of the model using simulation runs of 2,000 periods. The Hill index was computed for 4 different samples of 2,000 iterations and we selected the median value. In addition, we considered three different cut-off points of the tails (2.5 percent, 5 percent, 10 percent). We show the results of the kurtosis and of the Hill index in Table 2. We find that for a broad range of parameter values the kurtosis exceeds 3 and the Hill index indicates the presence of fat tails. Finally we check if the kurtosis of our simulated exchange rate returns declines under time aggregation. In order to do so, we chose different time aggregation periods and we computed the kurtosis of the time-aggregated exchange rate returns. We found that the kurtosis declines under time aggregation. In Table 3, we show the results for some sets of parameter values.[17] This suggests that the non-linear dynamics of the model transforms normally distributed noise in the fundamental exchange rate into exchange rate movements with tails that are significantly fatter than the normal distribution and with more density around the mean. Thus our model mimics an important empirical regularity. It should

Table 2. Kurtosis and Hill index.

		Median Hill index		
Parameter values	Kurtosis	2.5 percent tail	5 percent tail	10 percent tail
$C = 5, \beta = 0.9, \gamma = 0.5$	5.65	4.92	4.98	3.98
$C = 5, \beta = 0.9, \gamma = 1$	4.39	4.06	4.46	3.90
$C = 5, \beta = 0.9, \gamma = 5$	6.30	4.42	3.00	2.40
$C = 5, \beta = 0.8, \gamma = 0.5$	8.33	4.39	4.19	3.80
$C = 5, \beta = 0.8, \gamma = 1$	7.92	4.15	4.37	3.73
$C = 5, \beta = 0.8, \gamma = 5$	11.08	3.63	3.90	3.54

[17]Another empirical regularity of the distribution of exchange returns is its symmetry. We computed tho skewness, and we could not reject that the distribution is symmetric.

Table 3. Kurtosis and time aggregation.

Parameter values	1 period returns	10 period returns	25 period returns	50 period returns
$C = 5, \beta = 0.9, \gamma = 0.5$	5.65	5.96	3.17	3.08
$C = 5, \beta = 0.9, \gamma = 1$	4.39	4.11	3.67	3.45
$C = 5, \beta = 0.9, \gamma = 5$	6.30	2.77	2.15	2.19
$C = 5, \beta = 0.8, \gamma = 0.5$	8.33	8.52	3.14	3.43
$C = 5, \beta = 0.8, \gamma = 1$	7.92	7.39	3.28	3.30
$C = 5, \beta = 0.8, \gamma = 5$	11.08	10.14	3.46	3.05

be noted that similar models with heterogenous agents applied to the stock markets have been equally successful in replicating fat tails and excess kurtosis (see Lux and Marchesi, 1999, 2000; Kirman and Teyssiere, 2002; LeBaron *et al.*, 1999; Gaunersdorfer and Hommes, 2000).[18]

7. Large and Small Shocks

In linear models, the size of the shocks does not affect the nature of the dynamics. In non-linear models the size of the shocks matters. In order to illustrate this in our model, we simulated it under two different assumptions about the variance of the shocks in the fundamental exchange rate. In the first case, we assume low variance of these shocks, in the second case we assume a high variance (ten times higher), i.e.:

low variance: $s_t^* = s_{t-1}^* + \epsilon_t$, where $\epsilon_t \sim iid$, $mean = 0$ and $standard\ deviation = 0.1$

high variance: $s_t^* = s_{t-1}^* + \epsilon_t$, where $\epsilon_t \sim iid$, $mean = 0$ and $standard\ deviation = 1$

The results of our simulations are presented in Figure 8. (The simulations shown here are representative for a wide range of parameter values).

[18]We have also found evidence of volatility clustering in the simulated exchange rates. Due to space limitations these are not reported here hut can be obtained from the authors.

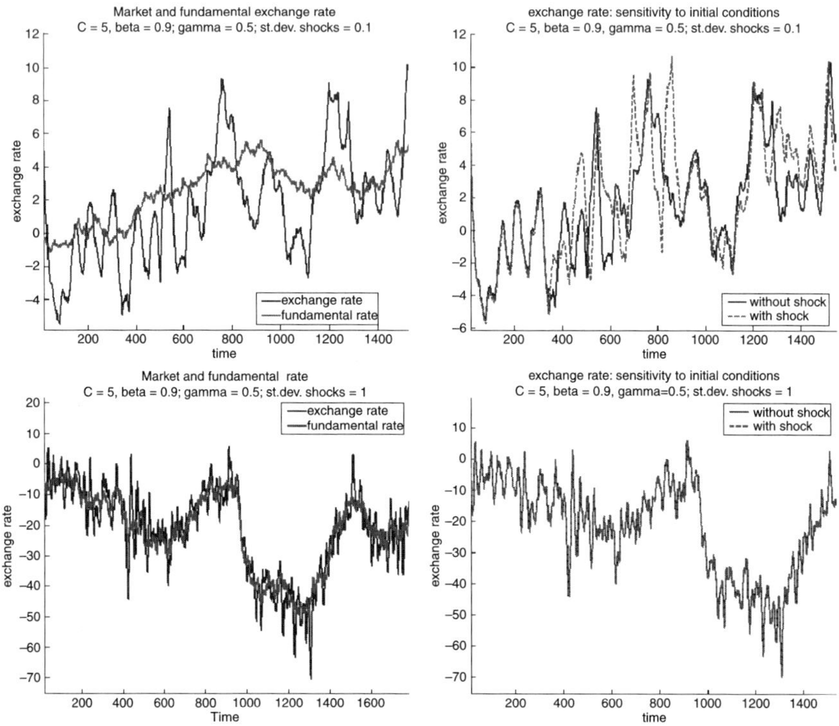

Figure 8.

Two conclusions follow from a comparison of the low and high variance cases. First, in the low variance case we observe sustained deviations from the fundamental exchange rate; this is not the case when the fundamental exchange rate is subject to large shocks (compare upper-left with lower-left panel in Figure 8). Second, the sensitivity to small changes in initial conditions is clearly visible when the variance of the exchange rate is low (see upper-right panel). When this variance is high, no such sensitivity can be observed (see lower-right panel). It is important to stress that the transactions cost band is the same in both cases. Thus, when the shocks are small relative to the given band of transactions costs, the movements of the exchange rate show more complexity than when the shocks are large.

The previous results are confirmed by a cointegration analysis like the one we performed in Section 6.1 (see Table 1) where this

Table 4. Error correction model high variance.

Error correction		Δs_{t-i}				Δs^*_{t-i}			
η	δ	ϑ_1	ϑ_2	ϑ_3	ϑ_4	φ_1	φ_2	φ_3	φ_4
−0.09	1.002	0.36	0.19	0.09	0.07	0.05	0.01	0.00	−0.01
−24.2	*156.2*	*27.5*	*13.2*	*6.7*	*5.1*	*3.3*	*0.9*	*0.06*	*−0.8*

analysis refers to a low variance environment. We show the results for the high variance regime in Table 4. These results contrast with those obtained in Table 1. The error correction coefficient is much larger in the high variance regime of Table 4 than in the low variance regime of Table 1. In the high variance case 9 percent of the deviation from equilibrium is adjusted for per period. This constrasts with a 0.3 percent found in the low variance case (see Table 1).

As in the low variance case we also performed a cointegration analysis over shorter sample periods. The results contrast with the tow variance case. For sample periods of 1,000 we find that the exchange rate and its fundamentals are always cointegrated. In the low variance case we do not find cointegration for all these sub-samples.

These results confirm what we observed from Figure 8, i.e., that in a regime of high variance of shocks the exchange rate is more tightly linked to the fundamentals, and that the speed of adjustment towards the equilibrium is higher than in low variance regimes.

The intuition of this result is that when the fundamental shocks are small the exchange rate regularly switches from the dynamics inherent within the transactions cost band to the one prevaling outside the band. This non-linearity produces a lot of noise and complexity in the dynamics of the exchange rate. When the shocks are large relative to transactions cost band the dynamics outside the band mostly prevails, leading to a tighter link between the exchange rate and the fundamental. This feature has also been found to hold empirically. In particular, it has been found that the PPP-relationship holds much tighter in high inflation countries than in low inflation countries (De Grauwe and Grimaldi, 2001). Put differently, in high inflation countries the link between the exchange rate and one of its most important fundamentals is tighter than in low inflation countries.

8. On the Success of Technical Analysis

There is a large literature showing that technical analysis is used widely in the foreign exchange market, also by large players (Taylor and Allen, 1992; Wei and Kim, 1997; James, 2003). This suggests that technical analysis (chartism) is profitable. Does our model replicate the empirical evidence of the success of chartism?

We investigate this issue by analyzing how chartism evolves under different conditions. In Figure 9, upper panel, we show the average chartists' weight for increasing values of the intensity of choice parameter γ in two different environments concerning the variance of the shocks in fundamentals. We obtained the chartists weights by simulating the model over 10,000 periods and computing the average weight over the last 5,000 periods. Our first finding is that chartism does not disappear, i.e, in all simulations for many different parameters configurations we find that the weight attached to chartists never goes to zero. On the contrary, we find that the chartists weight fluctuates around a market share, which exceeds 50 percent. (Note that in the steady state of the model the chartists' and fundamentalists' weights are 50 percent). These results are consistent with the empirical evidence of the importance of chartism in foreign exchange market. Second, the market share of chartists increases with the parameter γ which measures the intensity with which agents react to the relative profitability of the two rules. This result is related to the fact that increases in γ increase the volatility of the exchange rate. The increase in volatility is what chartists thrive on. Third, we find that, in general, chartism is more profitable in the low variance environment than in the high variance environment.[19] This is due to the fact that in a low variance environment the exchange rate movements are disconnected from the

[19]We defined low and high variance environments in the previous section.

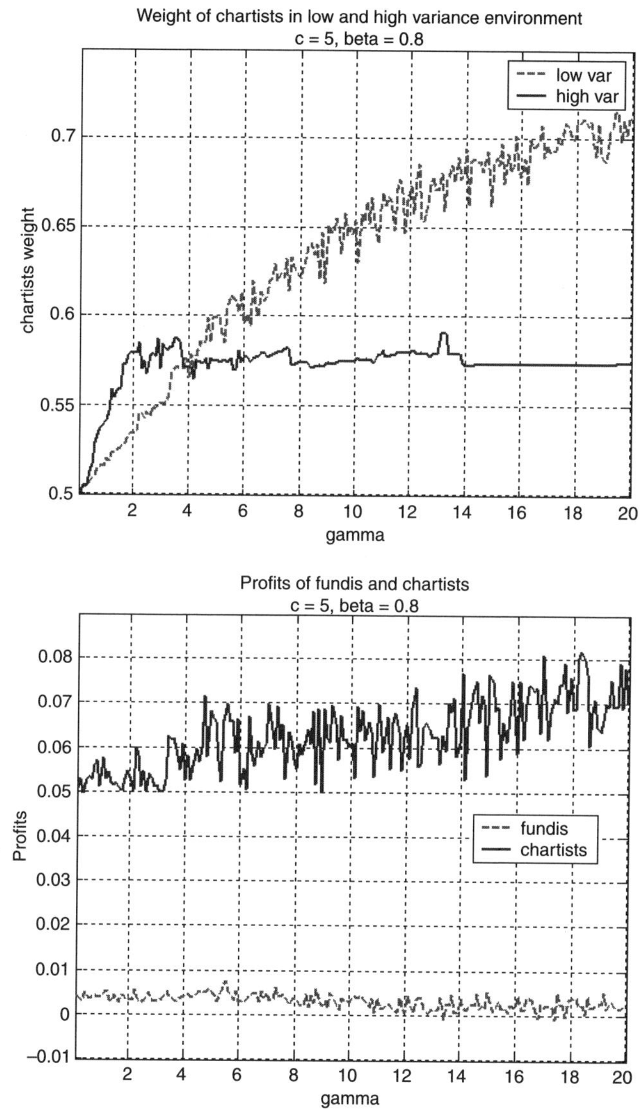

Figure 9.

fundamental most of the time making fundamentalist forecasting relatively unattractive. We show this feature in the lower panel of Figure 9 which presents the average realized returns of chartists and fundamentalists in the low variance environment. It is striking to see that in such an environment chartism appears to be much more profitable than fundamentalism.[20]

From the preceding analysis we conclude that chartism is generally more profitable than fundamentalism. In addition, there is a positive correlation between turbulence (noise) and the share of chartism in the market. With more noise there is more chartist profit and thus there are more chartists. The reverse is also true: with more chartists there is more noise and thus more profits for chartists. These results suggests that there is a selffulfilling evolutionary dynamics present in the system which can be described as follows. As the chartists increase in numbers, the noise they create makes the use of chartists rules more profitable. At the same time, the chartists have the effect of "creating smoke around the fundamentals," making fundamentalists' forecasting less profitable. Another way to interpret this result is that chartism creates noisy information that becomes the source of profitable speculation. The more chartists there are the more such information is created and the more profitable chartists' forecasting becomes. Thus, chartists create an informational environment which makes it rational to use chartists' rules.

Why doesn't all this not lead to a corner solution, i.e., a situation in which chartists drive out all fundamentalists? As we have seen in the previous paragraphs, the share of the chartists in the market is not driven to 1, it always settles below 1. The reason has to do with risk. When the weight of chartists increases in the market, so does volatility. Thus, as the weight of chartists in the market increases, both profitability and risk of using chartist rules increase. The increasing risk is strong enough to prevent the chartists from completely driving out the fundamentalists and taking over the market.

[20]Note that in the simulations reported here both chartists and fundamentalists make profits. This implies that there is a third group of agents, not modelled here, who make losses. These are traders who use the foreign exchange market as a hedge. The price they pay for hedging forms the counterpart of the profits realized by chartists and fundamentalists.

9. Conclusion

Using a mean variance optimisation framework we developed a simple non linear exchange rate model with transactions costs and with heterogeneous agents. Transactions costs in the goods markets produce an important non-linearity in the model. Agents are heterogenous in that they have different beliefs, i.e., they use different forecasting rules. The relative importance of these different types of agents is driven by the relative profitability of their forecasting rules and by the risk associated with the use of such rules. Thus agents are rational in the sense that they evaluate *ex post* the relative (risk-adjusted) profitability of the forecasting rules and switch to the better one. We argued that this *trial and error* process is a better way to model agents' behaviour than to assume that their expectations are rational. In rational expectations models with heterogenous agents the burden of collecting and processing information for individual agents is extraordinarily high, requiring God-like capacities. Not only must individual agents know the structure of the model, but they must also be able to read the minds of all the other agents. In traditional religions agents with such intellectual capacities were called Gods.

The model generates a multitude of fixed-point attractors depending on the initial conditions, i.e., for each initial condition there is a unique solution. By adding exogenous noise the model produces a complex dynamics that resembles a chaotic dynamics, although the deterministic part of the model is not chaotic. This feature has interesting implications. First, there is sensitivity to initial conditions, which implies that a small disturbance can drive the exchange rate on a different path. Second, the effect of a permanent shock in the fundamental exchange rate has a complex structure that might even be chaotic. This implies that the effect of a permanent shock in the fundamentals is largely unpredictable, i.e., one cannot forecast how the shock will affect the exchange rate in any particular point of time, but one can predict the average effect. We also find that the effect of such a shock depends on the exact timing of its occurrence. Thus, history matters. The market has a memory. This contrasts with exchange rate models based on the efficient market and rational expectations assumptions that tend to be a-historical.

The quality of a model should be judged by its empirical performance. We argued that the traditional rational expectations efficient market model has failed empirically. We analyse to what extent our model is capable of reproducing the exchange rate puzzles observed in reality. The first puzzle we analyse is the "disconnect puzzle" which has to do with the fact that the exchange rate movements are disconnected, most of the time, from the movements of the underlying fundamental variables. In our model "disconnection" is a natural outcome of the complex dynamics produced by the interactions between agents using different pieces of information.

Closely related to the disconnect puzzle is the presence of excess volatility of the exchange rate compared to the volatility of its fundamentals. This feature has been widely documented in the empirical literature. Our model mimicks this feature. We find that it is connected to the number of chartists in the market, i.e., the greater the share of chartists the larger is the noise to signal ratio in exchange rate movements.

Third, our model generates fat tails and excess kurtosis, a phenomenon which has been observed in exchange rate returns, and more generally in returns in most financial markets.

Fourth, the empirical evidence suggests that in environments with high variance of the fundamentals (e.g., in high inflation countries) the link between exchange rate changes and its fundamentals (e.g., inflation rates) is tighter than in low variance environments. We also obtain such a result in our model. This implies that in high variance environments predicting exchange rate changes using fundamental information should be easier than in low variance environments.

Finally, we found that chartism (technical trading) is a profitable strategy and often tends to dominate the market. This result is consistent with the empirical evidence of the importance of chartism in foreign exchange markets. We also detected a self-fullfilling character of chartist, profitability, i.e., when more chartists enter the market they create more noise and thereby make chartists rules more profitable, inducing more entry. Another way to interpret this result is that chartism creates noisy information that becomes the source of profitable speculation. Thus, chartists create an informational environment which makes it rational to use chartists' rules. This process is stopped, however, because of increasing risk generated by the increased noise that the same chartists produce. The self-fulfilling nature of chartists' profitability allows us to understand why chartism is generally observed to be important in foreign exchange markets.

A Appendix 1. The Variance Ratio $\sigma^2_{f,t}/\sigma^2_{c,t}$ in Steady State

In this Appendix, we show the ratio of the variance of the fundamentalist and chartists $\sigma^2_{f,t}$ and $\sigma^2_{c,t}$ as it converges to its steady state value. We simulated the model for different parameter configurations and different initial values of the exchange rate. In each case we found that the variance ratio converged to 1 as the system approached the steady state. In Section 3.2, we describe in more detail how these simulations are set up.

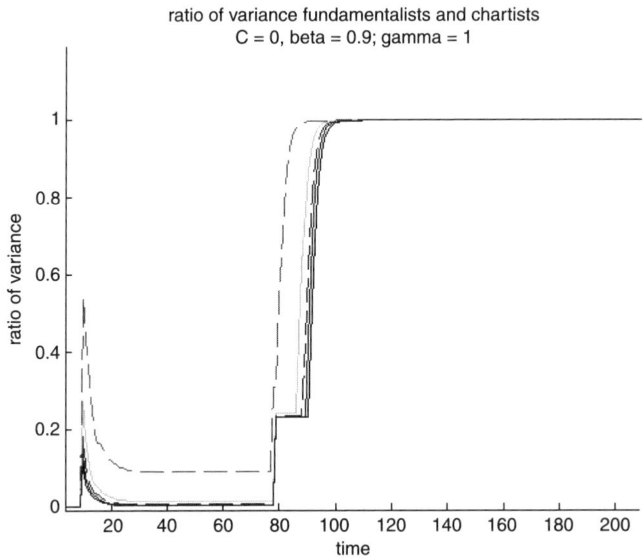

Figure 10.

B Appendix 2. Numerical Values of the Parameters Used in the Base Simulation

In the following table, we present the numerical values of the model. In the first column we listed the parameters of the model, in the second column we present the numerical values in the base simulations. The last column indicates whether or not we have performed a sensitivity analysis on these numerical values. If not, we use the same numerical value in all simulations.

Table 5. Numerical values of parameters.

Parameters	Values	Sensitivity analysis
ψ	0.2	No
$\alpha_1, \alpha_2, \alpha_3, \alpha_4, \alpha_5$	0.44, 0.26, 0.16, 0.09, 0.05	No
β	0.8	Yes
θ	0.6	No
γ	1	Yes
μ	1	No
C	5	Yes
r and r^*	0	No

References

Bacchetta, P and E van Wincoop (2003). Can information heterogeneity explain the exchange rate determination puzzle? NBER Working Paper No. 9498.

Baxter, M and A Stockman (1989). Business cycles and the exchange rate regime: Some international evidence. *Journal of Monetary Economics*, 23, 377–400.

Brock, W and C Hommes (1997). A rational route to randomness. *Econometrica*, 65, 1059–1095.

Brock, W and C Hommes (1998). Heterogeneous beliefs and routes to chaos in a simple asset pricing model. *Journal of Economic Dynamics and Control*, 22, 1235–1274.

Brunnermeier, M (2001). *Asset Pricing Under Asymmetric Information.* Oxford, UK: Oxford University Press.

Cheung, Y and K Lai (2000). On the purchasing power parity puzzle. *Journal of International Economics*, 52(2), 321–330.

Cheung, Y, K Lai and M Bergman (2002). Dissecting the PPP puzzle: The unconventional roles of nominal exchange rate and price adjustments. Paper presented at CES-Ifo Conference, Munich.

Chiarella, C, R Dieci and L Gardini (2002). Speculative behaviour and complex asset price dynamics. *Journal of Economic Behavior and Organization*, 49, 173–197.

Copeland, L (2000). *Exchange Rates and International Finance*, 3rd Edition. Upper Saddle River, NJ: Prentice Hall.

De Boeck, J (2000). The effect of macroeconomic "news" on exchange rates: A structural VAR approach. Mimeo: University of Leuven.

De Grauwe, P, H Dewachter and M Embrechts (1993). *Exchange Rate Theories. Chaotic Models of the Foreign Exchange Markets.* New Tork, NY: Blackwell.

De Grauwe, P and M Grimaldi (2001). Exchange rates, prices and money: A long run perspective. *International Journal of Finance and Economics*, 6(4), 289–314.

De Grauwe, P and I Vansteenkiste (2001). Exchange rates and fundamentals. A non-linear relationship? CESifo Working Paper No. 577.

de Vries, C (2000). Fat tails and the history of the guilder. *Tinbergen Magazine*, 4, 3–6.

De Long, JB, A Schleiffer, LH Summers and RJ Waldmann (1990). Noise trader risk in financial markets. *Journal of Political Economy*, 98(4), 703–738.

Dornbusch, R (1976). Expectations and exchange rate dynamics. *Journal of Political Economy*, 84(6), 1161–1176.

Dumas, B (1992). Dynamic equilibrium and the real exchange rate in a spatially separated world. *Review of Financial Studies*, 5(2), 153–180.

Engel, C (2000). Long run PPP may not hold after all. *Journal of International Economics*, 51(2), 243–273.

Engel, C and J Morley (2001). The adjustment of prices and the adjustment of the exchange rate. Discussion Paper, Department of Economics, University of Wisconsin.

Evans, M and R Lyons (1999). Order flow and exchange rate dynamics. NBER Working Paper No. 7317.

Faust, J, J Rogers, E Swanson and J Wright (2002). Identifying the effects of monetary policy shocks on exchange rates using high frequency data. International Finance Discussion Papers No. 739, Board of Governors of the Federal Reserve System, Washington, DC.

Flood, R and A Rose (1995). Fixing the exchange rate regime: A virtual quest for fundamentals. *Journal of Monetary Economics*, 36, 3–37.

Frankel, J and K Froot (1987). Understanding the US dollar in the eighties: The expectations of fundamentalists and chartists. NBER Working Paper No. R0957

Gaunersdorfer, A and C Hommes (2000). A nonlinear structural model for volatility clustering. CeNDEF Working Paper No. 00-02, University of Amsterdam.

Gaunersdorfer, A, C Hommes and F Wagener (2003). Bifurcation routes to volatility clustering. CeNDEF Working Paper No. 03-03, University of Amsterdam.

Goodhart, C (1989). News and the foreign exchange market. LSE Financial Markets Group Discussion Paper No. 71.

Goodhart, C and L Figliuoli (1991). Every minute counts in the foreign exchange markets. *Journal of International Money and Finance*, 10, 23–52.

Guillaume D (2000). *Intradaily Exchange Rate Movements.* Dordrecht, The Netherlands: Kluwer Academic Publishers.

Hallwood, P and R MacDonald (1994). *International Money and Finance*, 2nd Edition. Oxford, UK: Blackwell.

Huisman R, K Koedijk, C Kool and F Palm (2002). The tail-fatness of FX returns reconsidered. *De Economist*, 150, 299–312.

Hommes, C. Financial markets as nonlinear adaptive evolutionary systems. *Quantitative Finance*, 1, 149–167.

Isard, P (1995). *Exchange Rate Economics.* Cambridge, UK: Cambridge University Press.

James, J (2003). Simple trend-following strategies in currency trading. *Quantitative Finance*, 3(4), 75–77.

Johansen, S (1991). Estimation and hypothesis testing of cointegration vectors in Gaussian vector autoregressive models. *Econometrica*, 55, 1551–1580.

Kahnoman, D, J Knetsch and R Thaler (1991). The endowment effect, loss aversion and status quo bias. *Journal of Economic Perspectives*, 5, 193–206.

Kilian, L and M Taylor (2003). Why is it so difficult to beat the random walk forecast of exchange rates? *Journal of International Economics*, 60(1), 85–107.

Kirman, A and G Teyssiére (2002). Microeconomic models for long memory in the volatility of financial time series. *Studies in Nonlinear Dynamics and Econometrics*, 5, 281–302.

Kurz, M (1994). On the structure and diversity of rational beliefs. *Economic Theory*, 4, 877–900.

Kurz, M and M Motolese (2001). Endogenous uncertainty and market volatility. *Economic Theory*, 16, 497–544.

LeBaron, B, W Arthur and R Palmer (1999). Time series properties of an artificial stock market. *Journal of Economic Dynamics and Control*, 23, 1487–1516.

Li, K (1999). Testing symmetry and proportionality in PPP: A panel data approach. *Journal of Business and Economic Statistics*, 17(4), 409–418.

Lux, T (1998). The socio-economic dynamics of speculative markets: Interacting agents, chaos, and fat tails of return distributions. *Journal of Economic Behavior and Organization*, 33, 143–165.

Lux, T and M Marchesi (2000). Volatility clustering in financial markets: A microsimulation of interacting agents. *International Journal of Theoretical and Applied Finance*, 3(4), 675–702.

Lyons, R (2001). *The Microstructure Approach to Exchange Rates.* Cambridge, MA: MIT Press.

Mandelbrot, B (1963). The variation of certain speculative prices. *The Journal of Business*, 36, 394–419.

Meese, R and K Rogoff (1983). Empirical exchange rate models of the seventies: Do they fit out of sample? *Journal of International Economics*, 14, 3–24.

Michael, P, R Nobay and A Peel (1997). Transaction costs and non-linear adjustment in real exchange rates: An empirical investigation. *Journal of Political Economy*, 105(4), 862–879.

Obstfeld, M and K Rogoff (1996). *Foundations of International Macroeconomics.* Cambridge, MA: MIT Press.

Obstfeld, M and K Rogoff (2000). The six major puzzles in international macroeconomics: Is there a common cause? NBER Macroeconomics Annual, 15.

Rogoff, K (1996). The purchasing power parity puzzle. *Journal of Economic Literature*, 34, 647–668.

Schittenkopf, C, G Dorffner and E Dockner (2001). On nonlinear, stochastic dynamics in economics and financial time series. *Studies in Nonlinear Dynamics and Econometrics*, 4(3), 101–121.

Shleifer, A (2000). *Introduction to Behavioural Finance.* Gloucestershire: Clarendon Press.

Taylor, M and H Allen (1992). The use of technical analysis in the foreign exchange market. *Journal of International Money and Finance*, 11, 304–314.

Taylor, M, D Peel and L Sarno (2001). Non-linear mean reversion in real exchange rates: Towards a solution to the purchasing power parity puzzles. *International Economic Review*, 42, 1015–1042.

Wei, S-J and K Jungshik (1997). The big players in the foreign exchange market: Do they trade on information or noise? NBER Working Paper No. 6256.

Williamson, J (1985). The exchange rate system. *Journal of Banking and Finance*, 9(2), 333.

Empirical

Chapter 4

Exchange Rates in Search of Fundamentals: The Case of the Euro–Dollar Rate

Paul De Grauwe

1. Introduction

The decline of the euro during 1999–2000 has come as a surprise to most observers. Few people would have believed when the euro was launched on January 1, 1999, that in less than one and a half year it would lose 25 percent of its value against the dollar.

Many explanations have been given for this surprising phenomenon. Most of these explanations have invoked fundamental variables, in particular the stronger economic growth performance of the US economy in comparison with the European growth record. We cast doubt on this explanation. Our doubt is influenced by the empirical literature of exchange rate models, which we survey in Section 2. We then analyze how important observable fundamentals have been in explaining the movements of the euro–dollar exchange rate, we interpret the results, and we formulate an hypothesis explaining the weak link between the exchange rate and the fundamentals. We conclude with an analysis of the implications of this alternative view for the conduct of monetary policy and for the future of the euro.

Published in *International Finance*, 3(3), 329–356, 2000.
I am grateful to Magdalena Polan for research assistance and to Jan Abraham, Jan Bohets, Cláudia Costa, Hans Dewachter and Benn Steil for helpful comments. I am also indebted to an anonymous referee who suggested many improvements.

2. Exchange Rate Models: Theory and Empirical Evidence

Economists have developed several models that can guide us to identify the fundamentals that matter for the determination of the exchange rate. We briefly review these models.[1]

The flexible price monetary model

This model is built on the assumption that prices are flexible and that purchasing power holds continuously. It is usually written in the following form:

$$s_t = a_1(m_t - m_t^*) - a_2(y_t - y_t^*) + a_3(i_t - i_t^*) + u_t \tag{1}$$

where s_t is the exchange rate in period t, m_t and m_t^* are the domestic and foreign money stocks, y_t and y_t^* are the domestic and foreign output levels and i_t and i_t^* are the domestic and foreign interest rates. All variables (except the interest rates) are expressed in logarithms.

Invoking the Fisher relation

$$i_t = r_t + E_t\pi_{t+1} \tag{2}$$

$$i_t^* = r_t^* + E_t\pi_{t+1}^* \tag{3}$$

where r_t and r_t^* are the domestic and foreign real interest rates and $E_t\pi_{t+1}$ and $E_t\pi_{t+1}^*$ are the expected future rates of inflation in the home and foreign countries. Substituting Eqs. (2) and (3) into Eq. (1) yields

$$\begin{aligned} s_t = a_1(m_t - m_t^*) - a_2(y_t - y_t^*) + a_3(r_t - r_t^*) \\ + a_3(E_t\pi_{t+1} - E_t\pi_{t+1}^*) + u_t \end{aligned} \tag{4}$$

This simple model says that the fundamentals that matter for the exchange rate determination are the relative money supplies, the relative output levels, the real interest rate differentials and the differentials in the expected rate of inflation.

[1] For a more detailed discussion see e.g., Hallwood and MacDonald (1994), Isard (1995), Copeland (2000) or any good textbook of international economics.

As it stands, the model does not specify how expectations are formed. The academic consensus is that these expectations should be modelled in the context of rational expectations. Implementing this idea in the monetary model, leads to the conclusion that the exchange rate is determined by the current fundamentals and by the current expectations about the future fundamentals.[2] This analysis also leads to the important insight that changes in the exchange rate today can only come from "news" about the underlying fundamentals. Put differently, since the exchange rate today is determined by the current and expected future fundamentals, it will only change from today to tomorrow if new information about these fundamentals reaches the market.

The sticky-price monetary model (Dornbusch model)

This model has essentially the same underlying fundamentals as the previous one. The only difference is that the assumption of flexible prices is dropped, so that also the purchasing power parity does not hold at each instant in time. It only holds in the long run. The assumption of price stickiness in this model implies that not only the expected future inflation matters but that also past price changes can affect the current exchange rate. All the other conclusions derived from the previous models apply to the sticky price version of the monetary model, in particular the importance of news in the fundamentals for the explanation of changes in the exchange rate.

The portfolio balance model

This model has a different starting point than the monetary model. It recognizes that the decisions of portfolio holders should be introduced in the analysis. In these models the desire to diversify plays an important role in the determination of the exchange rate. As a result, in addition to the macroeconomic variables included in the monetary models, the portfolio balance models introduce measures

[2]For a proof, see e.g., Hallwood and MacDonald (1994), p. 161–164.

of risk premia and stocks of assets expressed in different currencies. In these models the current account has a prominent role because it measures the change in the net foreign asset position of nations and therefore influences the risk premia attached to investments in different currencies.[3]

The previous exchange rate models have been thoroughly tested since at least twenty years. Three major conclusions stand out from this vast empirical literature.

First, even if economic agents were able to perfectly forecast the future path of the fundamentals, this would not produce a better forecast of the future exchange rate compared to a forecast that does not rely at all on the fundamentals (e.g., random walk). This result was dramatised by the famous Meese and Rogoff's studies of the early 1980s who found that the random walk forecast typically works better than a forecast based on an economic model even when that model has access to perfectly anticipated future fundamentals. Although occasionally some researchers have claimed that their model could beat the random walk, the scientific consensus today is that the Meese and Rogoff results still stand.

There is some evidence that when forecasting over a longer horizon, say, more than one year, fundamentals based models sometimes outperform the random walk. It should be borne in mind though, that these fundamentalist forecasts (based on perfect foresight of future fundamentals) use an information set that is much larger than the information set needed to make random walk forecasts. This also implies that the long term forecasts based on the economic models use more information than the short-term forecasts. It is therefore not really surprising that they perform better. Independent evidence on PPP also suggests that if there is a long term mechanism driving the exchange rate, it is indeed a very long one.[4]

A second conclusion from the empirical literature is the following. Since the start of the floating exchange rate regime the variability

[3]For more details, see Hallwood and Macdonald (1994) and Copeland (2000).

[4]See Rogoff (1996). In this large literature on PPP, it is found that it takes 3 to 4 years for half of the adjustment towards PPP to be realised after a shock.

of the exchange rates (both nominal and real) has increased dramatically. At the same time there is no evidence to be found that the variability of the fundamentals identified by the theoretical models has increased compared to the fixed exchange rate period (see Baxter and Stockman, 1989; Flood and Rose, 1995). This is in contradiction with the models we have surveyed, which imply that the variability of the exchange rate can only increase when the variability of the underlying fundamental variables increases. This result has led to the view that the variability of the exchange rates is largely disconnected from the variability of the underlying fundamentals. In their recent paper Obstfeld and Rogoff (2000) have identified this phenomenon to be one of the six major puzzles in international macroeconomics.

A third conclusion relates to the "news" aspect of the models. As was stressed earlier, the theoretical models of the exchange rate use rational expectations. One important implication is that the exchange rates can only change at any given moment of time as a result of "news" in the fundamentals. It is fair to conclude now that this feature of the existing models has also been rejected by the data. There is evidence that a large part of the movements of the exchange rate cannot be associated with news (see Goodhart, 1989; Goodhart and Figliuoli, 1991). More recent analysis using structural VARs comes to a similar conclusion. Unanticipated shocks in the fundamental variables explain only a small fraction of the unanticipated changes in the exchange rates. Typically over forecast horizons of up to one year, news in output, inflation, and interest rates explains less than 5 percent of the total unanticipated variance of the exchange rate. About 95 percent of the latter is attributable to the news in the exchange rate itself (De Boeck, 2000).[5]

From this scientific evidence only one conclusion can be derived. The models linking the exchange rate to fundamental variables like inflation rates, output growth, interest rate differentials do not stand

[5]Again there is some evidence that over longer forecast horizons, the news in fundamentals becomes more important. It remains relatively low, however, remaining far below explaining 50 percent of the total variance.

when confronted with the empirical evidence. There is little scientific basis for a theory based on the idea that these fundamentals drive the exchange rate.[6] Instead the empirical evidence strongly suggests that the exchange rates of the major currencies are disconnected from fundamental economic variables most of the time. Only over the very long run is there some weak evidence that these fundamentals influence the exchange rate. But the long run is exceedingly long.

In the next section we study a recent period that demonstrates rather spectacularly how disconnected an exchange rate can be from its fundamentals. We will do this in the context of a case study of the euro–dollar exchange rate since 1999. Our analysis of the 1999–2000 period does not have the ambition to prove, but rather to illustrate what others have proved using more rigorous methods.

3. A Case Study: The Euro–dollar Rate During 1999–2000 and the Fundamentals

As argued in the previous section, standard exchange rate models have identified a number of fundamental variables that are potentially capable of influencing the exchange rate. Applying this theory to the euro–dollar rate the following set of fundamentals were selected: the growth rate of the US economy versus Euroland's economy, the inflation differential between the US and Euroland, the relative rates of return of US versus Euroland assets (both short and long term), the current account of the US and of Euroland. Typically these models also stress that it is the *unexpected* part of these variables that affect the change in the exchange rate. In other words, it is the news component in the fundamental variables that lead to changes in the exchange rate. Thus, if the US economy grows unexpectedly faster than Euroland's economy this leads to an appreciation

[6]Note that this conclusion can only be drawn for the exchange rates of the major currencies. There is evidence that the exchange rates of currencies experiencing very high inflation are responding to inflation differentials. This link, however, between inflation differentials and exchange rates tends to be extremely weak in low inflation environments that has been typical for the dollar, the German mark and the yen since the last twenty years.

of the dollar versus the euro.[7] Similarly, if the US inflation accelerates unexpectedly relative to Euroland's this leads to a depreciation of the dollar. A similar story can be told about the other fundamental variables. The role of the current account, however, is a little more problematic. An unexpected increase in the current account deficit can lead to an increase in the risk premium and thus to a depreciation of the domestic currency. Alternatively, it can be the result of a capital inflow induced by higher expected returns. In this case, the current account deficit will not be associated with a depreciation of the currency. We have to keep this in mind when interpreting the results.

We first present the data about these fundamental variables. Next, we estimate the news component in these data and compare these with the change in the dollar exchange rate.

3.1. *The Data*

Figure 1 presents the euro–dollar rate illustrating the steady decline of the euro since the start of 1999 until May 2000. The next figures present a number of fundamental variables. We first concentrate on variables relating to real economic activity. According to the monetary model, strong economic activity (relative to the rest of the world) leads to a strengthening of the domestic currency.[8] We observe that the growth rate of GDP has been consistently higher in the US than in Euroland, but that Euroland's growth rate accelerated faster than the US growth rate so that at the end of 1999 the growth gap had narrowed considerably (Figure 2). This trend seems to have continued in 2000. The data on industrial production confirm this picture. Although at the start of EMU the growth gap of industrial production was almost 3 percent in favor of the US, this growth differential had completely disappeared in early 2000 (Figure 3).

---

[7]Note that we follow the models discussed earlier when concluding that an increase in domestic output leads to an appreciation of the currency. If the output increase is the result of a supply shock we may get different results.

[8]We realize that this is a ceteris paribus statement. For a fully satisfactory analysis, the effects of other variables should be controlled for.

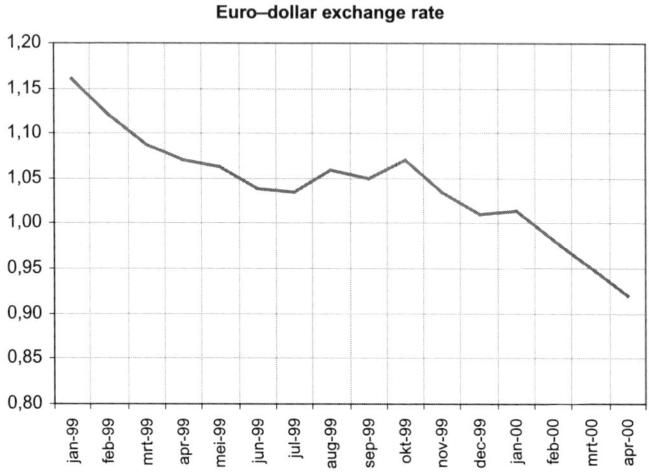

Figure 1.

Source: ECB, Monthly Bulletin, May 2000.

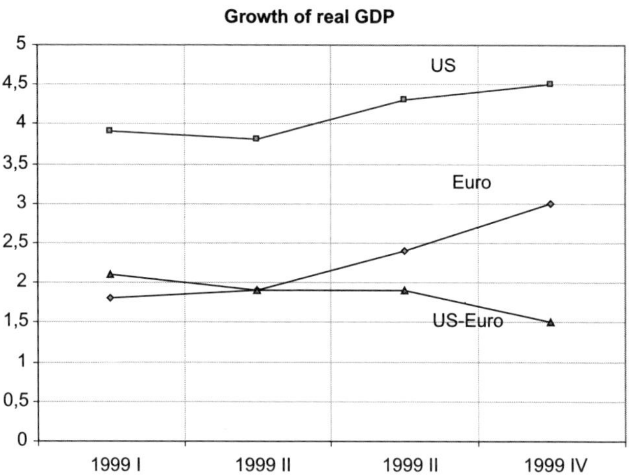

Figure 2.

Other measures of the real economy tell a similar story. The unemployment rate in the US has been far lower than the unemployment rate in Euroland (Figure 4). However, the differential narrowed somewhat throughout the period. Finally, the US current account

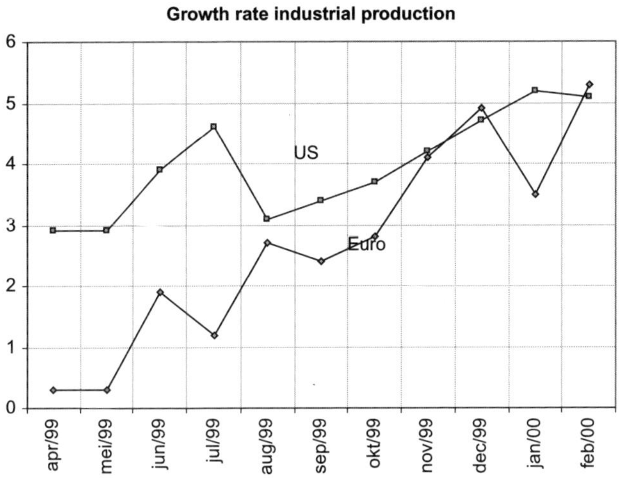

Figure 3.

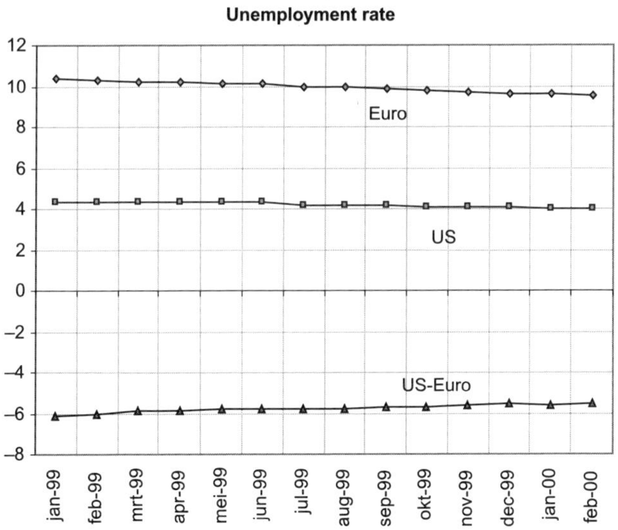

Figure 4.

Source: ECB, Monthly Bulletin, May 2000.

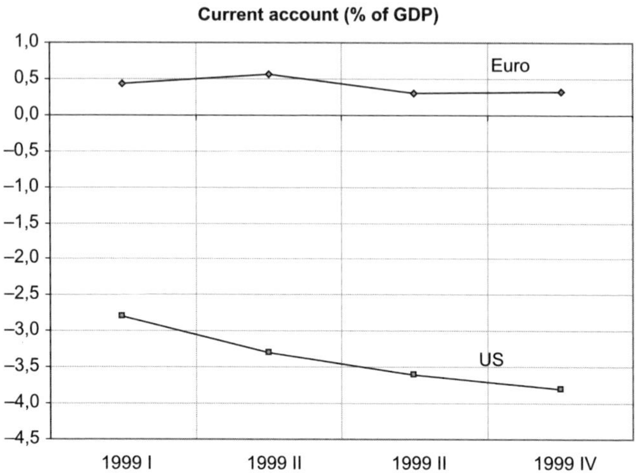

Figure 5.

Source: ECB, Monthly Bulletin, May 2000.

was significantly less favorable than Euroland's, and in addition it deteriorated substantially during the period (Figure 5). As mentioned earlier, however, the underlying forces driving the current account deterioration in the US may have been a higher expected return which led to a capital inflow. The high US current account deficit then reflects the favourable investment climate in that country.

The next set of fundamentals relates to financial and monetary data. Figs 6 to 8 provide information on the short and long nominal interest rates. We observe that the US rates were systematically higher than the Euro interest rates, but that the gap narrowed toward the end of the period. The difference between the US and the euro rates was more pronounced at the short than at the long end. As a result, the euro yield curve (as measured by the difference between long and short rates) was steeper than the dollar yield curve. This could be interpreted to mean that the markets expected a stronger economic recovery in Euroland than in the US.

Figure 9 shows the rates of inflation. The US experienced a faster inflation than Euroland throughout the period, and this differential increased during 2000. This inflation acceleration also shows up

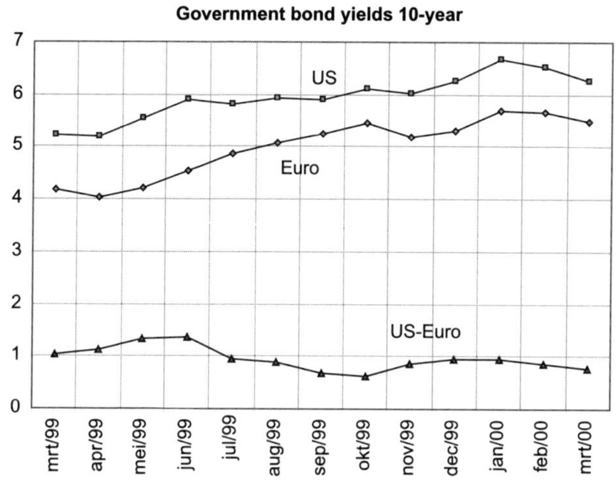

Figure 6.

Source: ECB, Monthly Bulletin, May 2000.

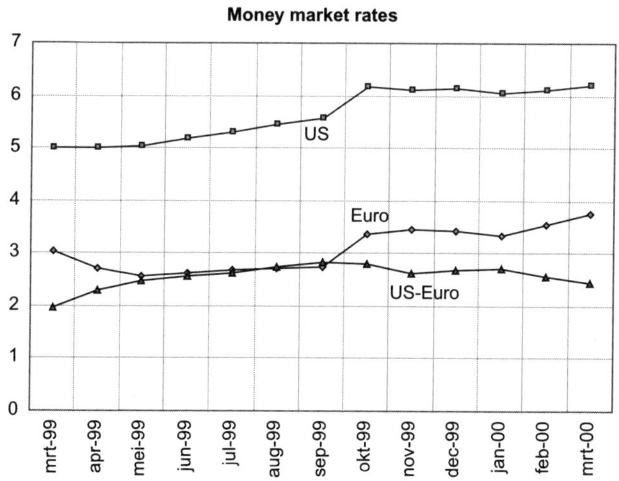

Figure 7.

Source: ECB, Monthly Bulletin, May 2000.

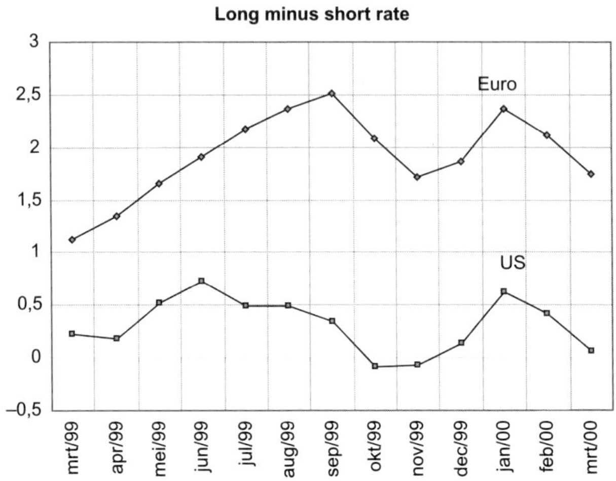

Figure 8.

Source: ECB, Monthly Bulletin, May 2000.

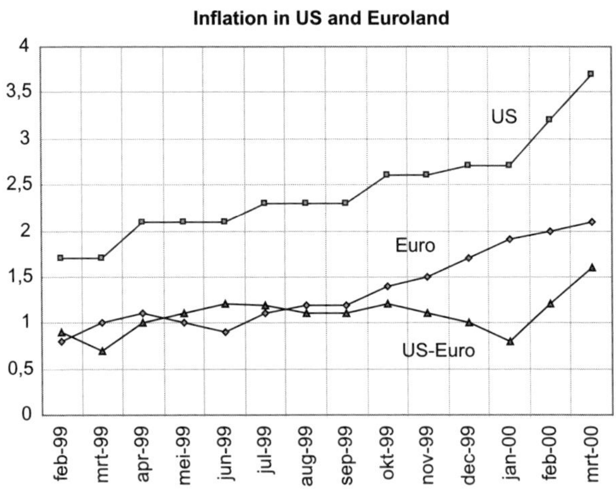

Figure 9.

Source: ECB, Monthly Bulletin, May 2000.

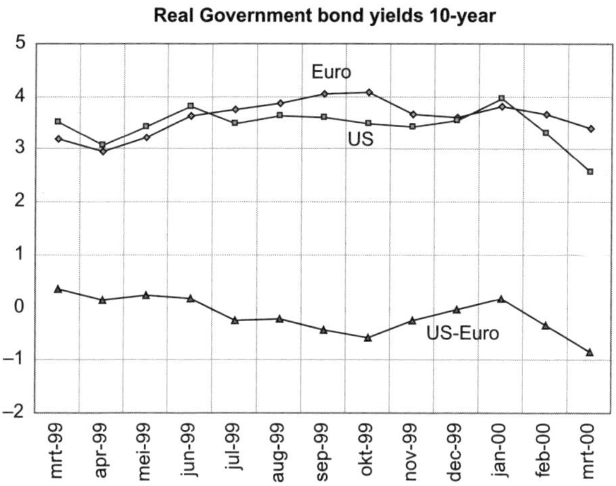

Figure 10.

Source: ECB, Monthly Bulletin, May 2000.

in the real interest rates. The real yield on long term government bonds was approximately equal in both countries (see Figure 10). In 2000, however, the US long-term real yield declined significantly below Euroland's. This phenomenon is mostly associated with the acceleration of the US inflation. Finally, the real short-term interest rate (Figure 11) was higher in the US than in Euroland throughout the period. However since the end of 1999 the gap narrowed. This could be interpreted to mean that on average the US monetary policy stance was more restrictive in the US than in Euroland. This difference in policy stance narrowed considerably since the start of 2000, however.

3.2. *The News Component in the Fundamentals*

As argued earlier, traditional exchange rate models tell us that changes in the exchange rates are driven by news in the fundamental variables. Given the limited number of observations about the euro–dollar rate and its determinants, it is not easy to estimate the news component. We took the view that these variables (i.e., the variables presented in the previous section) move pretty

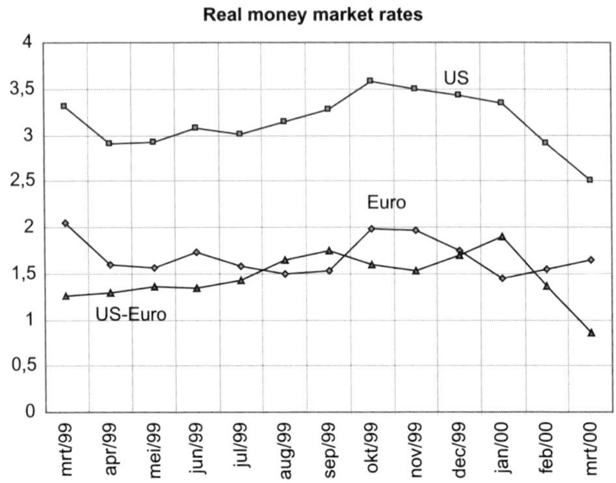

Figure 11.

Source: ECB, Monthly Bulletin, May 2000.

much like random walks. In that case, the changes in the variables can be considered as expressing news, i.e., we assume that the changes in the exchange rate and in its fundamentals (e.g., the change in the growth rates of GDP and industrial production, the change in the rate of inflation and in the real interest rates, the change in the current account) occurring at time t, are unanticipated. Admittedly, this is a crude assumption, which may affect our results. A more sophisticated analysis will have to wait until we have more data on the euro–dollar rate and its underlying fundamentals.[9]

We first show the news in the euro–dollar rate. An increase in the dollar relative to the euro is labeled *positive news* about the dollar, a decline is called *negative news*. Figure 12 confirms that there has been mostly positive news about the dollar since 1999, i.e., the dollar increased unexpectedly most of the time.

[9]Other measures of news require longer time series than those available. For example, we could have taken deviations from trend, or from a moving average. Given the short sample, such measures would not be meaningful. This holds even more strongly for news measures based on VAR. We find comfort from the fact that our results are perfectly consistent with the empirical evidence discussed in Section 2.

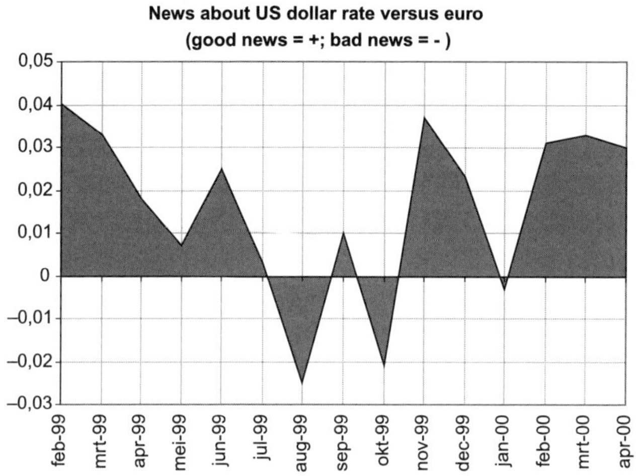

Figure 12.

Source: Computed from ECB, Monthly Bulletin, May 2000.

Can the good news about the dollar that prevailed during 1999–2000 be linked to comparable good news about the underlying fundamentals? We show the evidence in the Figs 13 to 14. We present the changes in the fundamental US variable relative to the Euro fundamental variable. We identify positive news about the US when the US variable improves relative to the euro variable and negative news when the opposite happens. Thus, the news about the US is always relative to the news about Euroland.

The evidence confirms the general conclusion derived from our survey of exchange rate models. Take the relative growth rates of GDP (Figure 13). We find that during the first, second and fourth quarters of 1999 the GDP growth rates in Euroland increased faster than the US growth rates, producing negative news about the US (positive news about Euroland). During the third quarter both growth rates changed by the same percentage, producing no news. Note that this evidence is not in contradiction with the observation that during most of 1999 the news about the US growth rate, considered in isolation, was mostly positive. However, the news about Euroland's growth rate was even more positive. It is the comparison

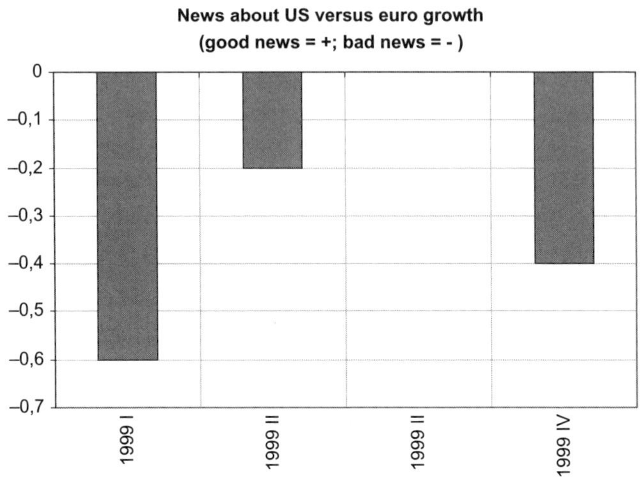

Figure 13.

Source: ECB, Monthly Bulletin, May 2000.

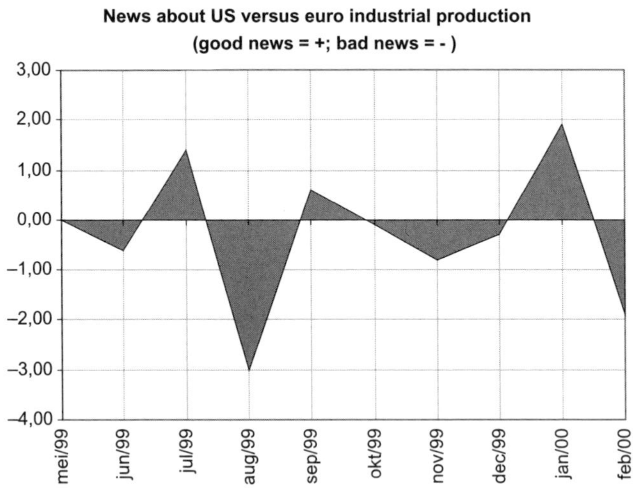

Figure 14.

Source: ECB, Monthly Bulletin, May 2000.

of the two that matters for the exchange rate. For some reason (to which we will return) market participants only seem to have looked at the positive US news.[10]

The news about the growth rates of industrial production is somewhat more mixed, although the negative US news is more prevalent than the positive news (Figure 14). This has to do with the observation made earlier that Euroland's industrial production recovered spectacularly during 1999 and 2000 so that in 2000 Euroland's growth rate of industrial production caught up with the buoyant US rate.

Something similar happened with unemployment (Figure 15). Despite the fact that the levels of unemployment were much lower in the US than in Europe, the unemployment in Euroland declined (marginally) faster than in the US, producing positive news about Euroland (negative news about the US).

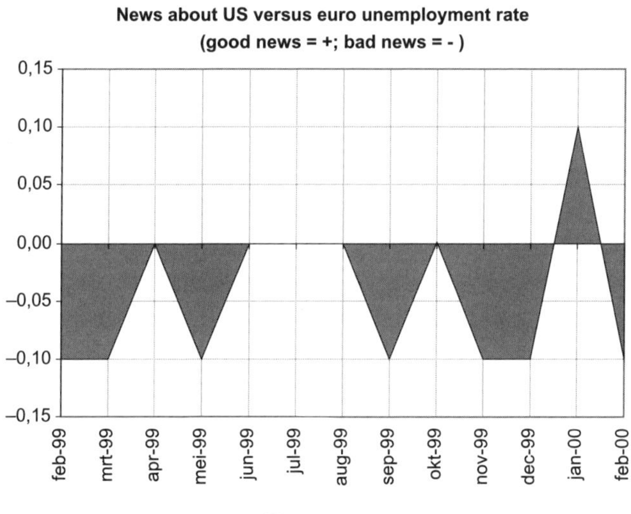

Figure 15.

[10]There is evidence that the random walk hypothesis we use to estimate the news component in the US data on economic growth has a negative bias. The general consensus of forecasters was that the US growth rate would go down in 1999 (see BIS, 2000). This did not materialise, however, so that there was a large positive surprise about the US growth performance during 1999. This bias seems to have been limited to the growth data and does not seem to have occurred in our estimates of the news in the other fundamental variables.

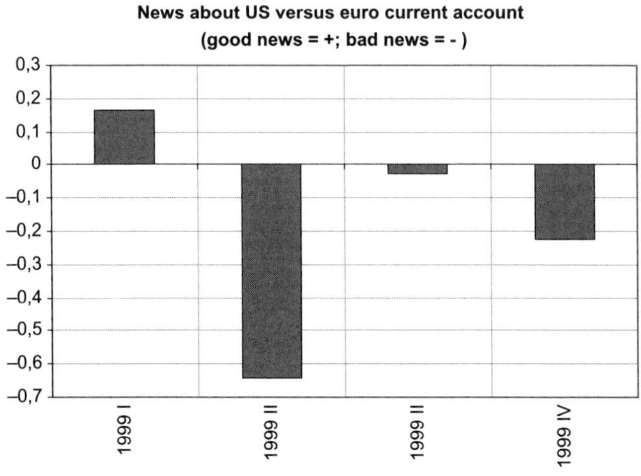

Figure 16.

As mentioned earlier, the news about the current account is more difficult to interpret (Figure 16). We have identified an increase of the US current account deficit as bad news for the dollar. But this may not be the correct interpretation. Part of the current account deficit may reflect capital inflows induced by better prospects for rates of return on investment. In that case, the deteriorating current account deficit may not be all bad news. There is evidence, however, that the deteriorating current account deficit is also related to a demand led economic recovery. On the whole the current account news remains difficult to interpret.

The empirical evidence about the news in the financial and monetary fundamentals is shown in Figs 17 to 21. Good news in the interest rates means that the interest rate differential favouring US assets increased unexpectedly, while bad news means that this differential declined unexpectedly. As far as the short rates are concerned, we observe that the good news for the US of the early part of the period turned into bad news in 2000. The results for the long-term bond yields are not as clear-cut.

The news about the inflation differential is shown in Figure 19 (note that an unexpected increase in the inflation differential between the US and Euroland should be interpreted as bad news for the US).

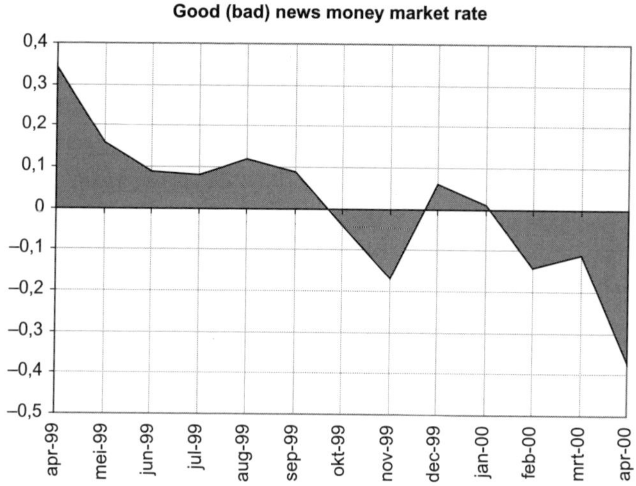

Figure 17.

Source: ECB, Monthly Bulletin, May 2000.

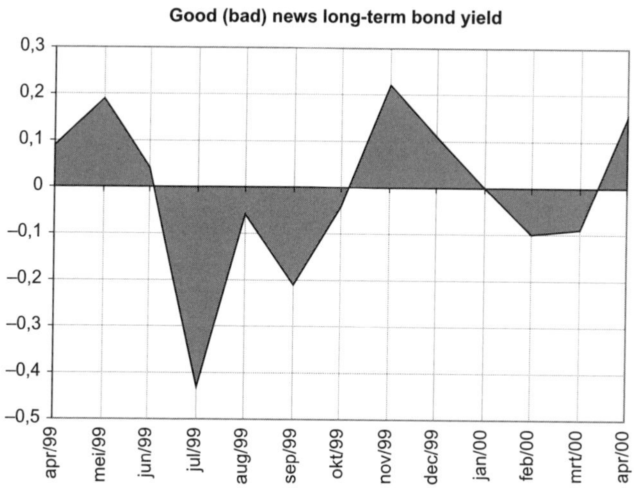

Figure 18.

Source: ECB, Monthly Bulletin, May 2000.

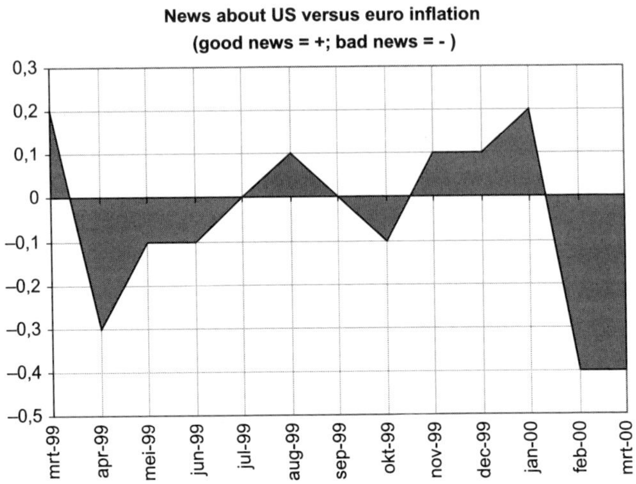

Figure 19.

Source: ECB, Monthly Bulletin, May 2000.

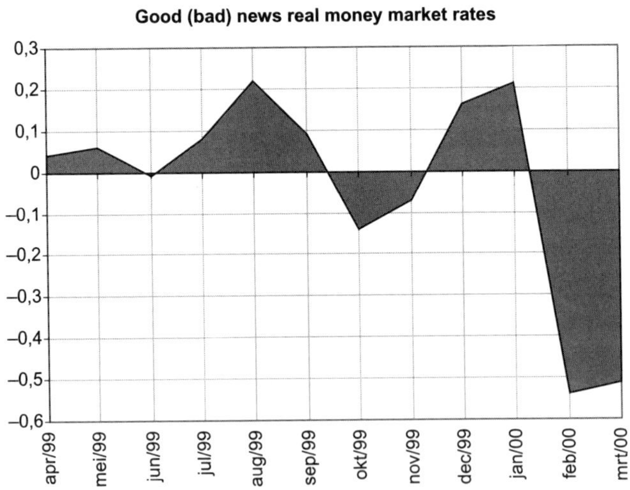

Figure 20.

Source: ECB, Monthly Bulletin, May 2000.

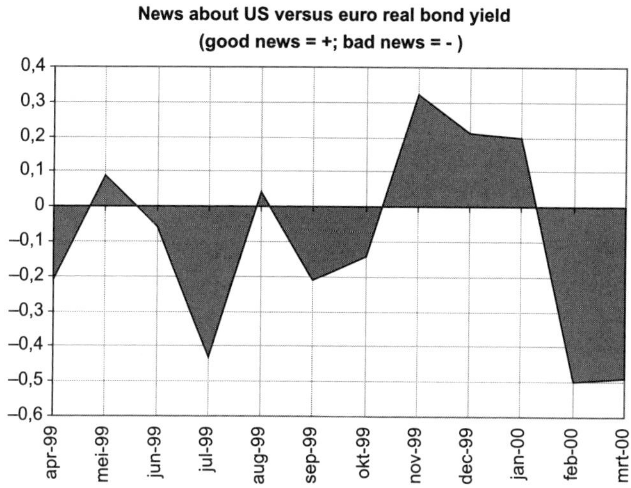

Figure 21.

Source: ECB, Monthly Bulletin, May 2000.

On the whole, bad news about the US dominates the good news. The striking fact here is the strong negative news for the US since the start of 2000, reflecting the acceleration of the US inflation rates. The evidence about the real rates (Figs 20–21) reveals a similar picture. Alternation of good and bad news (with somewhat more bad news as far as the long-term real rate is concerned), and a movement towards strong negative news since the start of 2000.

The previous evidence confirms the scientific evidence about the weak link between the exchange rate and the fundamentals as discussed in the previous section. Since the start of EMU the news about the dollar has been mostly positive, i.e., the dollar has appreciated quite unexpectedly. This positive news about the dollar cannot be associated with corresponding good news about the underlying fundamentals that the theory tells us drives the dollar. We found that on the whole the observable news about the US fundamentals has not been more favourable than the news about Eurolands's fundamentals.

The broader scientific evidence discussed in the previous section, together with the case study evidence about the recent movements in the euro–dollar rate raise a number of issues. On the one hand, the scientific evidence overwhelmingly rejects models that explain the movements of the exchange rates by the movements of underlying fundamentals. It is now a well-established scientific truth that the exchange rate is disconnected from fundamentals. If there is a relation between the exchange rate and the fundamentals it is a fuzzy and unstable one, that cannot be used to explain exchange rate movements, let alone to predict these.

On the other hand we observe that analysts and practical men continue to rely on these models (or fractions of these models) to explain the movements of the exchange rates. This raises the following question. Why is it that these practical men almost invariably explain exchange rate movements based on fundamental economic variables, while science tells us that there is no observably stable link between exchange rates and fundamentals? In the next section, we deal with this issue, focusing on the euro–dollar exchange rate.

4. The Exchange Rates in Search of Fundamentals

We propose the following explanation. There is great uncertainty about the true equilibrium value of the exchange rate. This uncertainty has two sources. The first one arises from the fact that it is very difficult to forecast the future value of the fundamentals. The other source of uncertainty comes from our lack of knowledge of the transmission process from the fundamentals to the exchange rate. The latter source of uncertainty has been underestimated in the academic literature which has focused mainly on our poor capacity to forecast future fundamentals.

The uncertainty about the nature of the transmission process from the fundamentals to the exchange rate can be called an endogenous uncertainty. It arises as a result of the speculative dynamics in the foreign exchange markets. In De Grauwe *et al.* (1993) it was shown that relatively simple models incorporating the interaction between chartists and fundamentalists create a complex (chaotic) dynamics of the exchange rate.[11] This dynamics has two features. The first one is that the exchange rate is dissociated from the underlying fundamentals. The second one is that for all practical purposes it is impossible to recover the economic structure underlying this dynamics with econometric techniques.

This endogenous uncertainty about the link between the fundamentals and the exchange rate has an important implication. The human mind does not easily accept agnosticism. It will try to fill the void. The movements in the exchange rate, when sustained in one or the other direction, set in motion a search of fundamental variables, including unobservable ones, that can explain this movement in the exchange rate. Thus, when the dollar starts moving up, this will be considered as evidence of strength of the US economy. Analysts will start a search of good news about the American economy, thereby carefully disregarding the bad news. Sure enough, good news will be found (high growth rates, new economy, US flexibility), and bad news will be erased (unsustainable consumer debt accumulation, large current account deficits, increasing inflation). This selection process makes sense. In a very uncertain world in which we do not know much about the link between (present and future) fundamental variables and the exchange rate, the movement in the latter becomes *prima facie* evidence that the fundamentals must be moving in the right direction. If some do not, they cannot be important, and they are eliminated. Thus, the upward movements of the dollar create beliefs about the strength of the US economy that can always be illustrated by a careful selection of fundamentals, observable and unobservable ones.[12]

The information processing described in the previous paragraph is akin to what economic psychologists have called "framing"

---

[11]Chartists make forecasts based on past movements of the exchange rate, while fundamentalists compute the equilibrium rate (based on fundamentals) and assume that the market exchange rate will return to the equilibrium value when it deviates. For empirical evidence on the importance of chartists, see Taylor and Allen (1992). For a well-known formalisation see Frankel and Froot (1986). For other formalisations of the same idea see De Long *et al.* (1990).

[12]Note that Kurz (1994) has formalized this idea and has called these beliefs "rational." See also Kurz and Motolese (2000).

(see e.g., Kahneman and Tsversky, 1981, 1984, Steil, 1992, Thaler, 1994).[13] In an uncertain world, agents are very much influenced by the way a problem or a piece of information are presented. In this context, readily available information or recent memories work as a frame within which information is interpreted. The movements of the exchange rate perform this framing function: recent increases in the dollar create a frame within which the strength of the US economy is evaluated. Thus, when the dollar strengthens, this creates a positive frame of mind, which leads agents to look at the US fundamentals in a benevolent way. Put differently, agents will tend to select mainly the positive news and to disregard the negative news because the increases in the dollar rate have created a positive frame within which they judge the American economy. This frame of mind and the ensuing selection of news then create positive beliefs about the American economy.

The mirror image for the euro can easily be told. When the euro starts declining this creates a frame within which the European economy is evaluated in a negative way. The decline of the euro, therefore, triggers a search for bad news about the European economy. Sure enough, bad news about European rigidities has been around for thirty years, waiting to be rediscovered in bad times by young analysts. At the same time the good news (unexpected high growth rates, better inflation record than the US) cannot be important because the euro is weak, and is disregarded. The declining euro creates beliefs of a weak European economy.

These beliefs then reinforce the movements of the exchange rate. The dollar increases further and the euro continues its decline, which in turn adds to the conviction that the beliefs are the true representations of reality. The increase in the dollar is treated as accumulating evidence in favour of the prevailing optimistic beliefs about the US economy. Exactly the reverse happens in Europe.

In a sense one can say that the market operates pretty much in the way scientific discoveries are made. Based on the movements

[13]This effect is sometimes called "anchoring." Steil (1992) has applied the idea of framing to interpret anomalies in corporate foreign exchange risk management.

of the exchange rate, theories (beliefs) are developed about the underlying economic structure. These theories are then confronted with the data. As long as no glaring inconsistencies between the data and the theories are detected the beliefs are maintained. The big difference between the market process of finding truth and science's way is that the former affects the observed data. Thus, as mentioned earlier, the optimistic beliefs about the US economy actually affect the dollar and reinforce the belief about the good health of the US economy.

This process can last for a while, like during 1980–1985 when optimistic beliefs about the US economy (Reagonomics and all that) and pessimistic beliefs about Europe (Eurosclerosis) were driving the market for five years. At some point, too many discrepancies between facts and beliefs accumulate, reducing the credibility of the latter. A small trigger that leads to a turn in the market can then reverse the process, leading after a while to a new process of rational construction of opposite beliefs.

During the 1980s, the small trigger may have been the agreement in early 1985 to intervene in the foreign exchange market, which initiated the decline of the dollar. After a while stories about weaknesses of the American economy started to appear on the Reuters screens and in the financial press. The main story of that day was the "short-termism" of the American financial markets that led American managers to care only about this quarters' profit. This then prevented them from making long-term strategic decisions. The reverse was told about Japan and Germany. Japanese and German managers were shielded from the pressure of short-term profitability because of their close relationship with banks and financial institutions. As a result, they made decisions that duly took into account the long-term interests of the companies. This "superior" model of finance and management became the rational belief of the day which "explained" the increasing strength of the mark and the yen.

The core of the explanation we propose here is that it is not the news in the fundamentals that drives the exchange rate changes, but rather the other way around. Changes in the exchange rate "frame" the beliefs of market participants and lead them to a selection of news about the fundamentals (present and future) that is consistent with the observed exchange rate changes. All this does not mean that the fundamentals do not matter. They do. Europe has a lot of rigidities; the European Central Bank still has to establish its credibility; conflicts within EMU could become a problem. But there is also a lot of good fundamental news about Europe that remained dormant during the first one and a half year of the existence of the euro, but that will be re-activated when a turnaround in the exchange rate occurs. The market will then start giving a much higher weight to this news than it was willing to do before when the prevailing beliefs prevented it from doing so.

The analysis presented here also allows us to better rationalize the importance of chartism and technical analysis in the foreign exchange markets. Economists have never been able to explain very well why sophisticated people rely so much on chartism. Our suggested explanation is that analyzing past patterns in the foreign exchange rate is a way to detect the frames that will influence agents beliefs about underlying strengths and weaknesses of the economies involved. It is therefore useful information in forecasting the future exchange rate.

5. Exchange Rates and Stock Prices

Theory tells us that like exchange rates, stock prices are driven by expectations about present and future fundamentals. When news about these fundamentals hit the market, the stock prices, will change. In the case of stock prices, these fundamentals are measures of profitability. The latter in turn are influenced by macroeconomic fundamentals such as the state of economic activity, inflation, interest rates. To a certain degree, therefore, stock prices, especially stock price indices, are influenced by the same fundamentals as the exchange rates.

In Figure 22, we show indices of share prices in Euroland and in the US. The most striking feature is the fact that while in the first part of the sample period both indices evolved in a similar way,

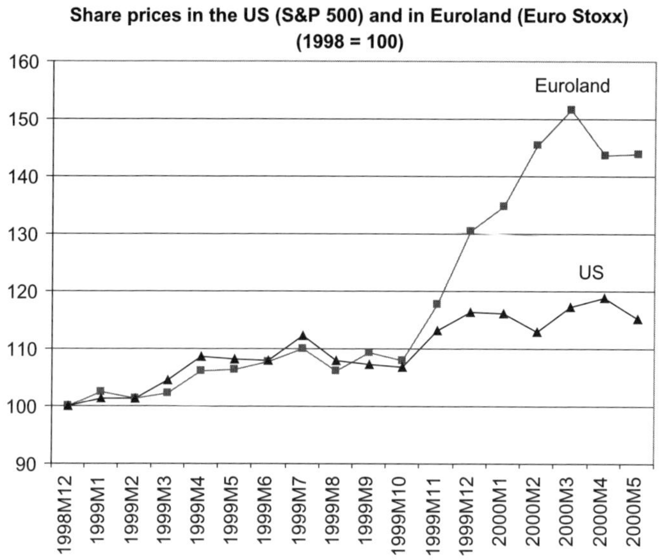

Figure 22.

Source: ECB, Monthly Bulletin, May 2000.

things were very different in the second half, when the Euroland stock prices experienced much higher increases than the US stock prices.

It is useful to compare the trend in the stock prices with the euro–dollar exchange rate. This is done in Figure 23, where we show the euro–dollar exchange rate together with the ratio of the share price indices of Euroland versus the US. We observe that from October 1999 to March 2000, when the euro experienced a steep decent, the correlation with the relative stock price index was negative, i.e., while the euro was declining sharply the stock markets in Euroland were booming much more strongly than in Wall Street. This is a puzzling phenomenon. The relative stock market index suggests that the stock markets were more optimistic about the European economy than about the US economy, while at the same time the euro–dollar exchange rate suggests that the exchange market was more optimistic about the US economy than about the European one. We leave it to future research to unravel this puzzle.

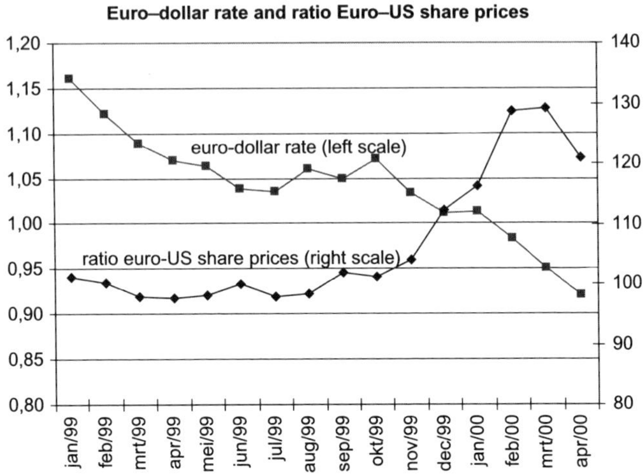

Figure 23.

Source: ECB, Monthly Bulletin, May 2000.

6. Some Additional Evidence

In recent papers Corsetti and Pesenti (1999) and Corsetti (2000) presented intriguing evidence indicating that the euro–dollar exchange rate during 1999–2000 was very well explained by (survey based) revisions of the forecasts of the growth rates of output in the US and in Euroland. When the growth rate in the US was expected to increase relative to Euroland this had the effect of increasing the value of the dollar relative to the euro. Corsetti and Pesenti noted that the expected growth rate differentials were the most important variable explaining the euro–dollar rate during 1999–2000. They also found, however, that this tight link between growth forecasts and exchange rates does not hold for other currencies during the same period (e.g., the yen–dollar exchange rate[14]). This tight link between

[14]One of the greatest puzzles of the 1999–2000 period is the fact that the growth rate of Japanese output was dismally low both compared to the US and to Europe, and yet the yen appreciated against the dollar.

growth forecasts and the dollar exchange rates in other periods does not seem to have been observed either.

This phenomenon can easily be explained by the hypothesis proposed in the previous section. Since the end of 1998 the markets have been increasingly influenced by positive beliefs about the growth potential of the US economy, which in turn have been very much influenced by stories concerning the marvels of the new economy. As a result of such beliefs, agents have focused on the one variable that provides evidence about these beliefs, i.e., the growth rate of output. At the same time, these agents have almost totally disregarded other fundamental variables that according to the theory are equally important to determine the exchange rate, e.g., inflation differentials, current accounts, and other variables. These have received close to zero weight. Thus, the tight fit between growth forecasts and the exchange rate is not the result of an immutable law that links the exchange rate to economic growth differentials, but rather to a passing belief that this is the only variable that matters. In other exchange markets (e.g., the yen–dollar market) or in other periods when beliefs were different, this strong link breaks down. During the 1970s, for example, the markets focused almost exclusively on inflation differentials and the growth rates of the money stock. They could not care less about growth differentials. Something similar happened during the 1990s with interesting results. During 1992–1996, the US economy grew at twice the rate observed in Germany (3.0 percent versus 1.5 percent per year). This did not prevent the dollar from depreciating *vis-à-vis* the German mark (from 2 to 1.9 DM). During that period nobody talked about new economy wonders and thus few observes cared to attach importance to a major differential in economic growth between the US and Germany.

This shifting selection of the variables that market participants care to look at, goes a long way in explaining the observed instability of the link between the exchange rate and the fundamental variables. This unstable relationship was dramatized by the empirical studies of Meese and Rogoff. Our explanation allows us to better understand this result.

7. Implications for Monetary Policies and for the Future of the Euro

The hypothesis formulated in this paper about how the exchange rates are determined has a number of implications. It should be stressed that much of the discussion that follows is speculative, as the main hypothesis requires further testing. Nevertheless, it is interesting to speculate about the possible implications of a theory that puts great emphasis on agents' beliefs. We will look first into the implications for monetary policies in general and then for foreign exchange market interventions. This analysis will also lead to some thoughts about the future evolution of the euro–dollar exchange rate.

7.1. *Monetary Policies and Beliefs*

The selection of particular variables by market participants to judge the economic success of a country has important implications for the transmission of monetary policies. To illustrate this, let us take the current focus of the markets on economic growth. The implication for the transmission of monetary policies can then be described as follows. Suppose the ECB raises the interest rate in order to bring back the rate of inflation to its targeted level of (at most) 2 percent. This restrictive policy has a negative effect on output growth. Since market participants focus on the latter variable to make forecasts about the euro–dollar rate their beliefs about a weak Euroland are reinforced. This leads to a further depreciation of the euro. Thus a monetary restriction leads to both a reduction of economic activity and a depreciation of the currency.[15] The effect on inflation is ambiguous. The reduction in aggregate demand produced by monetary restriction reduces inflation. However, the depreciation of the currency adds to inflation. In any case, one can conclude that the existence of beliefs that focus on economic growth performance reduces the effectiveness of monetary policies aimed at controlling inflation. Thus, as long as the beliefs in the foreign exchange markets are dominated by perceptions of strength in America and weakness in Europe, the ECB's

[15] Marani (1999) has formulated a similar hypothesis.

policies aimed at keeping inflation in check will be handicapped. The latter conclusion can also be made clear by analysing monetary policies in an environment where the market focuses on inflation.

The transmission of the same monetary policy when the markets focus on inflation (like they did in the 1970s) is very different. An increase in the interest rate induced by monetary restriction now leads to an appreciation of the currency. The reason is that the market anticipates that the monetary restriction will reduce inflationary pressures. Since inflation is the measure of strength of the currency, the markets applaud and expect an appreciation of the currency. The appreciation of the currency now reinforces the anti-inflationary stance of the central bank.

All this leads to the conclusion that the effectiveness of the central bank's monetary policies depends on the existing beliefs about strength and weakness of the economy. It also leads to the conclusion that the transmission of monetary policies is very unpredictable. Its sign depends on beliefs. Since these beliefs change, the same policies in different periods and countries can have drastically different effects on the exchange rate and on the price level.

There is some empirical evidence that substantiates this conclusion. VAR analysis of the transmission of monetary policies has detected a so-called price puzzle and an exchange rate puzzle, i.e., it has been found that during some periods and in some countries a monetary contraction leads to an increase in the price level and a depreciation of the currency.[16] Whether this finding is strong enough to be used as evidence for the hypothesis formulated in this paper remains to be seen. Nevertheless the idea that beliefs matter does not seem to be inconsistent with a number of puzzles that have been detected empirically.

The previous analysis also leads to a more general conclusion. When markets and policy-makers focus on different variables, the

---

[16]Sims (1992), Grilli and Roubini (1996), Koray and McMillin (1999) and Marani (1999) found an exchange rate puzzle for some currencies. Christiano, Eichenbaum and Evans (1994) and Fuhrer (1997) found price puzzles.

quality of policy-making is reduced. Thus, when markets focus on economic activity as a measure of economic success, while the monetary authorities focus on inflation, it will be more difficult to keep inflation in check, than when both the market and the authorities focus on the same variables. In the latter case the quality of policy-making is high. This may be the situation in which the US monetary authorities have found themselves over the last few years. Both the market and the authorities have focused on economic growth.[17]

It has not always been this way. During the 1970s when the markets were focusing on inflation as their measure of success, the US monetary authorities were following Keynesian policies of demand management. The inconsistency of these policies with the markets' yardstick of success (inflation) led to a poor quality of monetary policy-making, i.e., accelerating inflation and a depreciating currency.

7.2. *Foreign Exchange Market Interventions and Beliefs*

The preceding analysis has implications for the effectiveness of foreign exchange market interventions. The most obvious implication is that interventions in the foreign exchange markets only work if they affect prevailing beliefs. Since these interventions rarely do so, they are unlikely to have much effect. This conclusion holds whether or not interventions are sterilised or unsterilized. As will be remembered, sterilized interventions do not affect domestic monetary conditions (e.g., the interest rate) while unsterilized interventions do. This distinction has been very much stressed in the literature, leading to the consensus that unsterilized interventions are effective, while sterilized interventions are not. Our analysis makes clear that this distinction between sterilized and unsterilized intervention is irrelevant when the markets are guided by beliefs rather than facts. Paradoxically,

[17]This does not mean that the Fed did not care about inflation. It did, but it surely has attached less importance to fighting inflation than the ECB, and has concomitantly been willing to stimulate the economy more than the ECB probably would have done.

unsterilized intervention in the present context in which the markets focus on economic growth to measure the strength of a currency, may be worse than sterilized intervention. If the ECB were to engage in unsterilized intervention to push up the value of the euro, this would mean that the euro-interest rates increase. The negative effect this would have on economic activity would then, given the prevailing beliefs, weaken the euro further.

All this does not mean that foreign exchange market interventions never work. There are exceptional circumstances when they do. This will occur when the divergence between prevailing beliefs and economic reality becomes too great. This happened for example in 1985 when the dollar was pushed to record high levels. The concerted intervention by the US, the German and Japanese authorities led to a decline of the dollar and convinced the market that the high dollar rate was based on fiction. This then led to a precipitous decline of the dollar.

Something similar could happen in the future. It is likely, however, that the euro will have to decline significantly for interventions to produce the trigger effect that finally brings the market to realize that there is more than the growth rates of output to watch as a yardstick for the strength of a currency. At that moment, concerted intervention can trigger a turnaround in the market.

7.3. *Implications for the Future of the Euro*

It is very hazardous to make predictions about the future of the euro. Nevertheless some general insights can be gained from the previous analysis. A first insight is that beliefs change. The present beliefs about the strength of the US economy relative to the European economies are temporary. They will change when it becomes obvious that the US economy presents weaknesses that make the present rate of growth of the economy unsustainable. The market will then rediscover these weaknesses of the US economy and by the same token the relative strength of the European economies. This will then lead to a turnaround in the euro–dollar rate. When this will happen, however, is impossible to say.

A second insight has to do with the gap between the measures of success the market is focusing on and those the monetary authorities watch. The main reason for the weakness of the euro has to do with the fact that the market focuses almost exclusively on the growth rate of the economy, while the ECB focuses almost exclusively on price stability. When the ECB acts to achieve its measure of success (price stability), it worsens the measure of success the market is concentrating on (output growth). As long as this inconsistency exists the euro is likely to remain weak. How can the ECB deal with this? One possibility would be for the ECB to be a little more relaxed about inflation, and to measure success of its policy by taking into account the growth rate of economic activity. Given its strong mandate for price stability enshrined in its statutes, however, this possibility is very much limited. The important point, however, is that the ECB should take into consideration the "perverse" effects of interest rate increases on the value of the euro and on inflation when the market's measure of success is focused on economic growth.

As argued earlier, the present beliefs are unsustainable. When new beliefs gain prominence, the market will also switch from its single-minded focus on growth rates to other measures of success. This will strengthen the euro and make life easier for the ECB.

8. Conclusion

There is overwhelming empirical evidence that the exchange rates of the major currencies are mostly unrelated to the fundamentals that economic theory has identified. We illustrated this scientific discovery by a case study of the euro–dollar exchange rate during 1999–2000. Since the start of EMU until May 2000 the euro lost 25 percent of its value against the dollar. This decline was mostly unrelated to observable news about the underlying fundamentals. We found that, at least if we are willing to look at *all* the news that our economic models have identified as being of relevance, this news has been more favourable for Euroland than for the US.

We formulated the following interpretation of the lack of relation between the movements of the euro–dollar rate and its underlying fundamentals. There is great uncertainty among economists about how fundamentals affect the exchange rate. This uncertainty is due to the speculative dynamics of the exchange markets in which chartists interact with fundamentalists, producing complex movements of the exchange rate that are mostly unrelated to fundamentals. Because agents are so uncertain about the underlying fundamentals and their impact, the exchange rate movements themselves "frame" ("anchor") the market's perception of fundamental strength or weakness of the economy. Using these frames, agents go on a search for those fundamental variables that can corroborate their perception. This leads to beliefs about strength and weakness of the economies involved. Thus, when at the start of 1999 the dollar started to move upwards, this became a signal of fundamental strength of the US economy and fundamental weakness of Euroland's economy. This set in motion a search for good news about America and bad news about Europe. This search is usually successful because there is often conflicting evidence of underlying strength and weakness. The result of this process was to create (positive) beliefs about the US economy and negative beliefs about the European economy. These in turn reinforced the exchange rate movements.

There has been a lot of research in economic psychology on how agents process information in an uncertain environment. One conclusion of this research is that "framing" is important, i.e., agents are very much influenced by the way a problem or a piece of information is presented. We have relied on this research suggesting that the exchange rate movements themselves act as frames that affect the way agents will perceive the world and process information. This process leads to beliefs which in turn work as filters that allow the market to select the news that fit the prevailing beliefs. This filtering process often takes the form of focusing on one (or only a few) fundamental variables. In the euro–dollar market during 1999–2000 the focus of analysts was almost exclusively on the growth performance. However, in other markets (e.g., yen–dollar) during the same period and in the same market during other periods (e.g., DM–dollar during 1992–1996) economic growth does not seem to have attracted the analysts' attention at all. Thus, the filtering process leads to large shifts in the weight attached to fundamental variables. This also explains why econometric models of the exchange rate are marred by frequent structural shifts.

Obviously, this process of creating beliefs can only go on as long as the facts are not too inconsistent with these beliefs. If the gap between beliefs and facts become too large a turnaround in the exchange rate is imminent, and a new process of creation of beliefs is set in motion.

The view of the exchange market developed in this paper has interesting implications for the way monetary policies are transmitted in the economy. We argued that in a world where agents' forecasts are driven by beliefs, monetary policies can have very different effects on the exchange rate and the price level depending on the nature of these beliefs. We used this insight to claim that under the present set of beliefs that dominate the foreign exchange market, the ECB will find it difficult to control its main policy objective, i.e., the rate of inflation.

Our analysis also has implications for the effectiveness of foreign exchange market interventions. As long as the American economy is perceived to be fundamentally stronger than the European one, the ECB will find it difficult to trigger a turnaround in the euro–dollar exchange rate. Foreign exchange market intervention, however, can become very potent when the distance between beliefs and facts becomes large enough. At that moment, intervention can work as a trigger helping to unravel the prevailing beliefs as happened in 1985 when concerted intervention succeeded in bringing down the dollar. The downfall of the dollar quickly created new beliefs about fundamental weaknesses of the American economy.

References

Bank for International Settlements, 30 (2000). Annual Report, Basle, June.

Baxter, M and A Stockman (1989). Business cycles and the exchange rate regime: Some international evidence. *Journal of Monetary Economics*, 23, 377–400.

Copeland, L (2000). *Exchange Rates and International Finance*, 3rd Edition. Upper Saddle River, NJ: Prentice Hall.

Corsetti, G and P Pesenti (1999). Stability, asymmetry and discontinuity: The launch of European monetary union. *Brookings Papers on Economic Activity*, 2, 295–372.

Corsetti, G (2000). A perspective on the euro. Paper presented at the CFS Research Conference: The ECB and Its Watchers II, Frankfurt, June 26.

Christiano, L, M Eichenbaum and CL Evans (1998). Monetary policy shocks: What have we learned and to what end? NBER Working Paper No. 6400.

De Boeck, J (2000). The effect of macroeconomic "news" on exchange rates: A structural VAR approach. Mimeo: University of Leuven.

De Grauwe, P, H Dewachter and M Embrechts (1993). *Exchange Rate Theories: Chaotic Models of the Foreign Exchange Markets.* New York, NY: Blackwell.

De Long, JB, A Schleiffer, LH Summers and RJ Waldmann (1990). Noise trader risk in financial markets. *Journal of Political Economy*, 98(4), 703–738.

Frankel, J and K Froot (1986). The dollar as a speculative bubble: A tale of fundamentalists and chartists. NBER Working Paper No. 1963.

Flood, R and A Rose (1995). Fixing the exchange rate regime: A virtual quest for fundamentals. *Journal of Monetary Economics*, 36, 3–37.

Fuhrer, J (1997). The (un)importance of forward looking behavior of price specifications. *Journal of Money Credit and Banking*, 29(3), 338–350.

Goodhart, C (1989). News and the foreign exchange market. LSE Financial Markets Group Discussion Paper No. 71.

Goodhart, C and L Figliuoli (1991). Every minute counts in the foreign exchange markets. *Journal of International Money and Finance*, 10, 23–52.

Grilli, V and N Roubini (1996). Liquidity models in open economies: Theory and empiricial evidence. *European Economic Review*, 40, 847–859.

Gros, D and G Tabellini (2000). Second Report of the CEPS Macroeconomic Policy Group, Centre for European Policy Research, Brussels.

Hallwood, P and R MacDonald (1994). International money and finance. 2nd Edition. Oxford, UK: Blackwell.

Isard, P (1995). *Exchange Rate Economics.* Cambridge, UK: Cambridge University Press.

Kahneman, D and A Tversky (1984). Choices, values and frames. *American Psychologist*, 39(4), 341–350.

Kurz, M (1994). On the structure and diversity of rational beliefs. *Economic Theory*, 4, 877–900.

Kurz, M and M Motolese (2000). Endogenous uncertainty and market volatility. Mimeo: Stanford University.

Marani, U (1999). The monetary policy of the European central bank and the Euro–US dollar exchange rate. International Economics Research Paper No. 148, University of Leuven.

Meese, R and Rogoff (1983). Empirical exchange rate models of the seventies: Do they fit out of sample? *Journal of International Economics*, 14, 3–24.

Obstfeld, M and K Rogoff (2000). The six major puzzles in international macroeconomics: Is there a common cause? NBER Working Paper No. 7777.

Rogoff (1996). The purchasing power parity puzzle. *Journal of Economic Literature*, 34, 647–668.

Sims, C (1992). Interpreting the macroeconomic time series facts: The effects of monetary policy. *European Economic Review*, 36, 975–1011.

Steil, B (1993). Corporate foreign exchange risk management: A study in decision making under uncertainty. *Journal of Behavioral Decision Making*, 6, 1–31.

Svensson, L (1998). Inflation targeting as a monetary policy rule. IIES Seminar Paper No. 646.

Taylor, M and H Allen (1992). The use of technical analysis in the foreign exchange market. *Journal of International Money and Finance*, 11, 304–314.

Thaler, R (1994). *Quasi Rational Economics*. New York, NY: Russell Sage.

Tversky, A and D Kahneman (1981). The framing of decisions and the psychology of choice. *Science*, 211, 453–458.

Chapter 5

Exchange Rates and Fundamentals: A Non-Linear Relationship?

Paul De Grauwe and Isabel Vansteenkiste

We test whether the relationship between changes in the nominal exchange rate and changes in its underlying fundamentals has non-linear features. In order to do so, we extend the Markov-switching model as proposed by McConnell and Perez Quiros (2000) and Dewachter (2001) and test it using a sample of low- and high-inflation countries. The empirical analysis shows that for the high-inflation countries the relationship between news in the fundamentals and the exchange rate changes is stable and significant. This is not the case, however, for the low-inflation countries, where frequent regime switches occur. We develop a non-linear model based on the existence of transactions costs that could explain our empirical findings. We find that this simple non-linear model is capable of replicating the empirical evidence uncovered in this paper.

1. Introduction

Exchange rate economics has gone through different stages. The early theoretical models were developed mainly in the 1970s (monetary

Published in *International Journal of Finance and Economics*, 12, 37–54, 2007.
Keywords: nominal exchange rate; non-linearities; Markov-switching model.
JEL classification: F31, F37

model, Dornbusch model, portfolio balance model, and others). These "first-generation" models led to testable propositions in which the changes in the exchange rate are linearly related to news in the fundamentals (money stocks, prices, output, current accounts, etc.). After intensive empirical testing it is fair to conclude that the first-generation models were soundly rejected by the data, at least for the exchange rates of countries experiencing relatively low levels of inflation. Three serious anomalies of the first-generation models were detected.

First, in their celebrated empirical studies Meese and Rogoff (1983, 1988) found that the random walk forecast typically outperforms a forecast based on the first-generation models.[1] Although occasionally some researchers have claimed that their model could beat the random walk, the scientific consensus today is that the Meese and Rogoff results still stand at least as far as short-term (one-period ahead) forecasting is concerned. There is some recent evidence, however, indicating that non-linear models are capable of beating the random walk at medium-term horizons (see Kilian and Taylor, 2003).

A second anomaly detected in the empirical literature is the following. Since the start of the floating exchange rate regime the variability of the exchange rates (both nominal and real) has increased dramatically. At the same time there is no evidence to be found that the variability of the fundamentals identified by the theoretical models has increased compared to the fixed exchange rate period (see Baxter and Stockman, 1989; Flood and Rose, 1995). This is in contradiction with the first-generation models, which imply that the variability of the exchange rate can only increase when the variability of the underlying fundamental variables increases. This result has led to the view that the variability of the exchange rates is largely disconnected from the variability of the underlying fundamentals. In their recent paper Obstfeld and Rogoff (2000) have identified this

[1]There is some evidence that when forecasting over a longer horizon, say, more than one year, fundamentals-based models sometimes outperform the random walk (see, e.g. Mark, 1995). But also see Faust *et al.* (2003).

phenomenon to be one of the six major puzzles in international macroeconomics.

A third empirical anomaly relates to the "news" aspect of the first-generation models. The rational expectations assumption underlying the first-generation models implies that the exchange rates can only change at any given moment of time as a result of "news" in the fundamentals. Empirical analysis using structural VARs however comes to conflicting answers on this. On the one hand, Clarida and Gali (1994) and Farrant and Peersman (2005) find that a substantial part of real exchange rate fluctuations can in fact be explained by its underlying fundamentals. At the same time, De Boeck (2000) and Altavilla (2000) find that unanticipated shocks in the fundamental variables explain only a small fraction of the unanticipated changes in the exchange rates. Typically, over forecast horizons of up to one year, they find that news in output, inflation, and interest rates explains less than 5 percent of the total unanticipated variance of the exchange rate. About 95 percent of the latter is attributable to the news in the exchange rate itself.[2] From this evidence it appears that the first-generation models in which the exchange rate is driven by news in the fundamentals in a linear way must be called into question as a representation of the foreign exchange market.

The rejection of the first-generation models of the exchange rate has led researchers into different directions. The first one has led to what one could call the "second-generation" models, as exemplified by Obstfeld and Rogoff (1996). In these models, the starting point is utility maximization of a representative agent. These models typically lead to the conclusion that the coefficients of the reduced form equations of the first-generation models do not have to be constant. These coefficients vary as a result of the underlying stochastic disturbances and of changing policy regimes.

This is an important insight. The trouble, however, is that the "second-generation" models have led to few testable propositions

[2]Again there is some evidence that over longer forecast horizons, the news in fundamentals becomes more important. It remains relatively low, however, remaining far below explaining 50 percent of the total variance.

that would allow for their refutation. As long as these testable propositions are not formulated it is difficult to evaluate the scientific strength of these "second-generation" models.

A second direction taken by researchers in their search for an alternative to the "first-generation" models has been to introduce non-linearities into the model (see De Grauwe and Dewachter, 1993; Frankel and Froot, 1990; Kilian and Taylor, 2003; Kurz and Motolese, 1999). These models are characterized by the existence of several agents using different information sets (e.g., chartists and fundamentalists) and/or by the existence of transactions costs. The insight provided by these models is that they predict frequent structural breaks in linear exchange rate equations, and that they allow for changes in the exchange rates that are unrelated to news about the underlying fundamentals.

In this paper, we analyse the (possibly non-linear) nature of the relationship between exchange rate changes and the changes in the underlying fundamentals. More specifically, we test whether this relationship is subject to regime switches over time. In order to do so, we use a version of the Markov-switching autoregressive (MS-AR) model popularized by Hamilton (1989). We perform this analysis both on data of low- and high-inflation countries. This comparison between low- and high-inflation countries will allow us to gain additional insight about the nature of the relation between exchange rates and the fundamentals. Several recent studies have used similar Markov-switching models or ESTAR models to detect non-linearities in the exchange rate dynamics (see, e.g., Peel and Taylor, 2000; Taylor *et al.*, 2001). The additional value of our study is that it makes a distinction between low- and high-inflation countries. As will be shown, the level of inflation affects the non-linear nature of the exchange rate dynamics.

The rest of the paper is structured as follows. In Section 2, we present the Markov-switching model and discuss some of its features. In Section 3, we describe the estimation process and the data used, and in Section 4 we present the results. Next, in Section 5 we analyse the implications of our results for exchange rate modelling and then present in Section 6 a non-linear model that is capable of explaining our empirical findings.

2. The Model

The non-linear model we consider is derived from the Markov-switching autoregressive (MS-AR) models popularized by Hamilton (1989) as a way of characterizing expansions and contractions in empirical business cycle research. The MS-AR framework can be readily extended to various settings. In our analysis, we use the Markov-switching model to detect switches in the regressors and/or intercept of the benchmark model presented in Mark (1995) which includes a direct relationship between the (log of the) exchange rate and its (log) fundamental value. More specifically, our model is written as

$$\Delta e_t = e_t - e_{t-1} = \alpha_{s_t} - \beta z_{t-1} + \varepsilon_t, \quad \varepsilon_t \sim N(0, \sigma^2_{r_t})$$

where Δe_t represents the difference of the log exchange rate in month t relative to the previous month and z_{t-1} stands for the deviation of the (log of the) exchange rate from its fundamental value at time $t-1$, so

$$z_{t-1} = e_{t-1} - f_{t-1}$$

with f_{t-1} representing the date $(t-1)$ fundamental. Hence, we can write f_{t-1} as

$$f_{t-1} = \gamma_{1,q_{t-1}}(p_{t-1} - p^*_{t-1}) + \gamma_{2,u_{t-1}}(i_{t-1} - i^*_{t-1}) + \gamma_{3,v_{t-1}}(m_{t-1} - m^*_{t-1})$$

whereby $m_{t-1} - m^*_{t-1}$ represents the money stock differential, $p_{t-1} - p^*_{t-1}$ the price level differential, and finally $i_{t-1} - i^*_{t-1}$ the interest rate differential. Further, we postulate the existence of a number of unobserved variables that take on the value one or two. More specifically, we extend the set-up of McConnell and Perez Quiros (2000) and Dewachter (2001) and allow for up to five separate and independent latent variables (namely s_t, q_t, u_t, v_t and r_t) for the dynamics of the intercept, the regressor coefficients and the variance.[3] These variables characterize the state or regime that the process is in. We assume that the stochastic process generating these unobservable regimes is

[3]We postulate a separate and independent latent variable for the variance since we want to avoid that switches in the variances regime would influence our results for switches in the intercept or slope coefficients.

an ergodic, irreducible first-order Markov chain. Hence, the process for these unobserved variables is presumed to depend on past realizations of e and itself only through its first lag. To overcome the potential problem of multicollinearity between money growth and inflation differential, we estimate two variants of the above equation. More specifically, we estimate the equation once with money growth and interest rate differentials and once with inflation and interest rate differentials as explanatory variables.[4]

Note that an attractive feature of the model is that a variety of behaviors is allowed. No prior information regarding the dates or the sizes of the states is required. In particular, there could be asymmetries in the persistence of the states and we do not impose that the coefficients should be either significant or insignificant.[5,6]

---

[4]Note that since the results were qualitatively the same, we only report in the paper the results for the regression with inflation and interest rate differentials as explanatory variables.

[5]As an alternative to our specification, we could have made use of a TAR/STAR/ESTAR model (see, for instance, Kilian and Taylor, 2003). Such model specifications are based on the view that the nominal exchange rate reverts back to its *ppp-value* at least in the long run (or, in other words, that the real exchange rate is mean reverting). In our paper, however, we prefer to take a more agnostic approach. We start out by analysing the possible non-linear nature between the change in the nominal exchange rate and its underlying fundamentals, whereby the fundamentals include beyond inflation differentials also interest rate differentials and money growth differentials. Hence, we make use of a rather general model that does not impose any *a priori* relationship between the exchange rate and its underlying fundamental. In addition, the model allows for non-linear dynamics between the exchange rate and each of its underlying fundamentals separately (as each of the coefficients is governed by a separate and independent latent variable). As such, the approach is less restrictive than the TAR/STAR/ESTAR approach.

[6]Another alternative approach would be to estimate a model where the transition probabilities of the Markov chain depend on the dynamics in the underlying fundamentals. Such a set-up was, for instance, pursued by Vansteenkiste (2006) within a similar context. Results from that analysis would show that in general, a larger deviation from fundamentals would tend to increase the probability of switching to the regime where changes in the fundamentals determine significantly the exchange rate changes. However, the problem with this approach is that first it requires (as is the case for the TAR/STAR/ESTAR models) an assumption regarding the fundamental model driving the exchange rate (be it PPP or a monetary model). Moreover, it also involves a sacrifice with regards the number of fundamentals that could be included in the regression. In practice, this would imply that for technical reasons all fundamentals would be imposed to switch at the same time, which is a restriction we do not impose in this paper.

3. Estimation Process and the Variables Used

3.1. *The Variables*

To estimate the aforementioned models, we choose to work with monthly data on the exchange rates and various fundamentals. For the low-inflation countries, data on the home currency price for the exchange rate, the money supply, the price level and the domestic interest rate were obtained for Germany, France, Italy, Japan, the UK and the US. The data series for the low-inflation countries have been derived from the BIS except for the 10-year government bond yields which are obtained from the Global Financial Market database.

For the high-inflation countries, data on the same variables were obtained for Argentina, Bolivia, Brazil, Chile, Columbia and Ecuador.[7] Here IMF data were used only if the national statistical offices did not provide the data. It should be noted that for all country data consistency with the US data was ensured.

As regards the exchange rate data, while we use for low-inflation countries the standard official exchange rate series, for high-inflation countries, we complement our analysis by using market-determined (also known as "black" market or parallel) exchange rates as provided by Reinhart and Rogoff (2004). Using the parallel exchange rate could be beneficial since it has the advantage of being determined in a free market, and hence is not obviously contaminated by the distortionary effects of government policy.

Finally, we also need to determine the sample period over which the exchange rate in the high-inflation countries studied is floating. For this, we use as a starting point the exchange rate classification as presented by Reinhart and Rogoff (2004) but extend the analysis with information from the Latin American Development Bank.

3.2. *The Estimation Process*

In this paper, we follow the maximum likelihood approach to estimate the Markov-switching model. As the results from estimating

[7]For some high-inflation countries, data availability was restricted. More information about the samples and data availability can be found in Appendix A.

the model were consistent for official and black market exchange rate series, only the official exchange rate series results are reported below.[8] In order to increase the probability that we reach the global maximum of the likelihood function, we randomized a number of different starting values and we used the estimates associated with the highest likelihood value.[9]

To test the significance of the Markov-switching model across regimes, it was pointed out by Hansen (1992) that classical test statistics are not asymptotically χ^2 distributed in this case. These test statistics are all based on regularity conditions ensuring that the likelihood surface is locally quadratic and that the score-vector has a non-zero variance. These conditions are violated in the case of a Markov-switching model. Hence, the use of the standard distribution would cause a bias of the test against the null. To circumvent this problem, Hansen (1992) has proposed an alternative likelihood ratio test, in which empirical process theory is used to bound the asymptotic distribution of a suitable standardized likelihood ratio statistic, which is applicable when the assumptions of standard theory are violated. For the various regressions performed, the grid range and the size of the step have been made dependent on the regression outcome. For the probabilities, the grid always ranged between $[0.001, 0.991]$ in steps of 0.11.

4. The Results

4.1. *The Low-inflation Countries*

Table 1 shows the Hansen LR tests for the low-inflation countries.[10] As will be recalled the Hansen LR test allows us to test for the equality of the intercepts and the slopes in the different regimes identified

[8]The results for the black market exchange rate series are available upon request from the authors.

[9]Due to the computational complexity of the model, this number has been set to 30.

[10]For Italy, France and the UK the regression was also run including a German fundamental given that they were part of ERM for some part of the sample period. The German fundamental (i.e. German call money market rate or German M3) was, however, for all countries but Italy, not significant. For this reason, we prefer to present the regression results without the German fundamental.

Table 1. Hansen LR test results for low-inflation countries.

	Germany	France	Italy	UK	Japan
Switching in intercept and slope					
$\alpha_0 = \alpha_1$	0.2	0.1	0.9	0.1	0.7
$\gamma_{10} = \gamma_{11}$	2.1	6.1*	7.2*	9.3*	4.5*
$\gamma_{20} = \gamma_{21}$	5.4*	7.6*	2.1	6.6*	5.2*
Switching in intercept					
$\alpha_0 = \alpha_1$	0.6	0.5	0.5	0.9	0.2
Switching in slope					
$\gamma_{10} = \gamma_{11}$	11.2*	5.4*	6.7*	7.8*	9.4*
$\gamma_{20} = \gamma_{21}$	10.3*	5.5*	6.2*	9.7*	6.6*

Note: *Indicates a rejection of the null at a 5 percent significance level. Equation: $e_t - e_{t-1} = \alpha_i + \beta[e_{t-1} + \gamma_{1j}(p_{t-1} - p^*_{t-1}) + \gamma_{2k}(GBY_{t-1} - GBY^*_{t-1})]$ where $\varepsilon_t \sim N(0, \sigma^2_m), i, j, k, m = 0$ or 1. Further, e represents the (log of the) exchange rate, p the price level and GBY stands for the government bond yield. Note that the switches in the slope and volatility are not constrained to occur at the same moment in time.

by the Markov-switching model. We have considered three scenarios for the regime switches. In the first one we test whether there are switches in the intercept and the slope, in the second case we allow for switches in the intercept, and in the third case we only allow for switches in the slope.

A first conclusion from Table 1 is that the model identifies many significant switches in the slope coefficients. In particular, switches in the slope coefficients are almost always significant, except for the money stock differential.

Table 2 presents the estimates of the intercepts and slope coefficients obtained in the different regimes. The most remarkable result is that the slope coefficients often switch between significant and non-significant values (with the exception of the coefficients of the relative money supply which are in most cases never signi-ficant), suggesting that in one regime the variables in question have a significant effect on the exchange rate, while in the other regime their effect is not significantly different from zero. Moreover, it is often the case that if the slope coefficient of one fundamental is significant in the first regime, this implies significance of the other fundamental(s) in the second regime and *vice versa* (see Figure 1).

Table 2. Estimates fit to individual low inflation countries (74:8–98:11).

Parameter	Germany	France	Italy	UK	Japan
α	−0.938**	−2.547**	−13.651*	3.146**	−4.872**
	0.066	0.316	4.212	1.128	0.326
β	−0.038**	−0.121**	−0.002*	−0.002**	−0.008**
	0.014	0.024	0.001	0.000	0.002
γ_{10}	−2.687	−2.827**	3.829	−1.948	5.368
	1.666	0.770	8.853	2.149	4.882
γ_{11}	−0.491**	3.177	−2.020**	−8.867**	9.669**
	0.080	2.873	1.027	1.983	1.742
γ_{20}	0.233**	0.079	1.416**	0.000	0.588**
	0.104	0.070	0.313	0.233	0.215
γ_{21}	0.107	0.079**	−6.384	1.841**	3.071
	0.058	0.013	4.639	0.345	2.643
σ_0	0.005**	0.004**	0.001**	0.000**	0.002**
	0.001	0.001	0.001	0.000	0.000
σ_1	0.000	0.000	0.000	0.003**	0.004**
	0.002	0.002	0.004	0.001	0.001
q_{00}	0.730	0.991	0.783	0.457	0.996
q_{11}	0.666	0.977	0.777	0.911	0.344
u_{00}	0.881	0.488	0.958	0.759	0.949
u_{11}	0.704	0.985	0.633	0.291	0.525
r_{00}	0.380	0.868	0.954	0.862	0.573
r_{11}	0.594	0.877	0.947	0.987	0.696

Note: *Denotes significance at a 10 percent level, **at a 5 percent level. Equation: $e_t - e_{t-1} = \alpha + \beta[e_{t-1} + \gamma_{1j}(p_{t-1} - p^*_{t-1}) + \gamma_{2k}(GBY_{t-1} - GBY^*_{t-1})]$ where $\varepsilon_t \sim N(0, \sigma_i^2), j, k, l = 0$ or 1. Further, e represents the (log of the) exchange rate, p the price level, and GBY stands for the government bond yield. Note that the switches in the slope and volatility are not constrained to occur at the same moment in time. $q_{00}/q_{11}, u_{00}/u_{11}, r_{00}/r_{11}$ are the transition probabilities for the price level, interest rate, and volatility regimes, respectively.

4.2. *The High-inflation Countries*

How do these results compare with the results obtained for the high-inflation countries? Tables 3 and 4 give an answer to this question. In Table 3, we present the Hansen LR tests for the significance of the switches in regimes (intercepts and slopes) in the high-inflation countries. The contrast with the low-inflation countries is striking. We find significant regime switches in all countries, but these switches are never due to switches in the slope. They are caused (if they

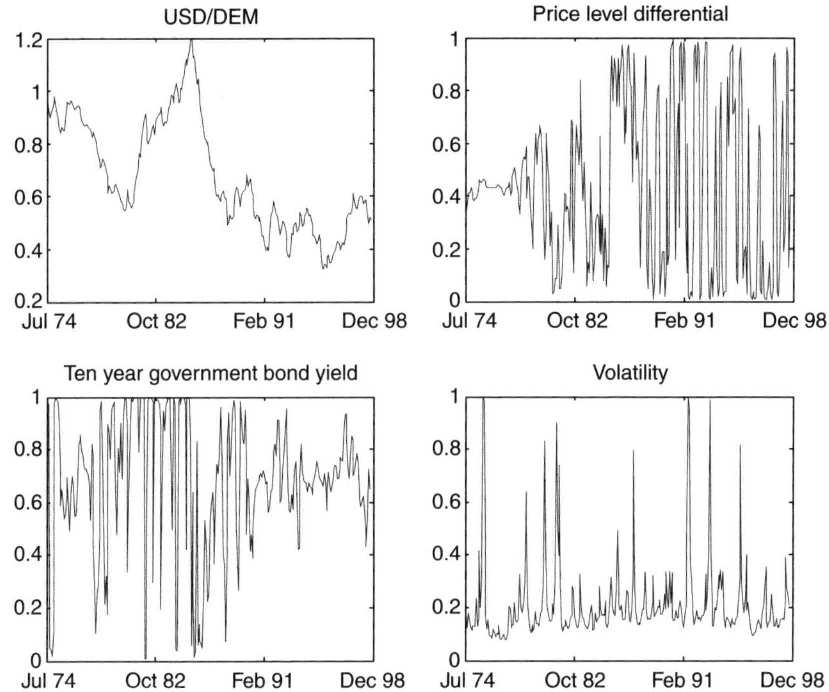

Figure 1. Smoothed probabilities for coefficient and volatility switches for German data.

happen at all) exclusively by switches in the intercept. Thus, in the high-inflation countries, there have been switches in the average level of appreciation, but the explanatory power of the independent variables (inflation, money supply, interest rate) has remained unchanged. This result contrasts with the results of the low-inflation countries in which the explanatory power of these independent variables appears to switch frequently.

In Table 4, we show the intercept and slopes in the different regimes for the high-inflation countries. We observe that, in contrast to the low-inflation countries, the slope coefficients are always significant and that often the switches only occur between two significant intercepts.[11] Hence, despite the more drastic economic and political

[11]In Table 4 we only report the Markov-switching model that allows for switches in the intercept but not in the slope. This is our preferred specification based on the Hansen

Table 3. Hansen LR test results for high-inflation countries.

	Argentina	Bolivia	Brazil	Chile	Ecuador
Switching in intercept and slope					
$\alpha_0 = \alpha_1$	6.5*	4.7*	7.8*	10.2*	9.3*
$\gamma_{10} = \gamma_{11}$	0.3	0.4	0.9	0.6	1.6
$\gamma_{20} = \gamma_{21}$	1.1	1.3	0.1	—	0.2
Switching in intercept					
$\alpha_0 = \alpha_1$	18.4*	14.5*	9.5*	15.4*	5.6*
Switching in slope					
$\gamma_{10} = \gamma_{11}$	0.2	0.4	0.8	0.5	0.7
$\gamma_{20} = \gamma_{21}$	0.4	0.9	0.2	—	0.4

Note: *Indicates whether the LR value found indicates a rejection of the null at a 5 percent significance level. Equation: $e_t - e_{t-1} = \alpha_i + \beta[e_{t-1} + \gamma_{1j}(p_{t-1} - p^*_{t-1}) + \gamma_{2k}(LR_{t-1} - LR^*_{t-1})]$ where $\varepsilon_t, \sim N(0, \sigma^2_m), i, j, k, m = 0$ or 1, where e represents the log of the official exchange rate, p the price level and LR stands for the lending rate. Note that no constraints were imposed on the timing, values or significance of the regime switches.

changes experienced in the high-inflation countries, the Hansen tests in Table 3 do not support the existence of statistically significant structural changes on the relationship between exchange rates and fundamentals of these economies. In other words, none of the changes on the macroeconomic and political environment seem to have forced a truly statistical change in the relationship between exchange rates and fundamentals (see Figure 2).

5. Theoretical Issues

The results discussed in the previous section can be summarized as follows. The relation between the exchange rate and the fundamentals of low-inflation countries is characterized by frequent regime shifts. We found that the coefficients of these fundamentals change over time quite often from significant values to insignificant ones, and *vice versa*. This feature is absent in the exchange rate equations of

LR test statistics in Table 3. However, it may be important to remark that under a Markov-switching model with both switches in the intercept and the slope, all coefficients estimated were always significant, hence confirming our stated conclusion.

Table 4. Estimates fit to high-inflation countries (with the official exchange rate-long sample).

Parameter	Argentina	Bolivia	Brazil	Chile	Ecuador
α_0	1.057**	2.224**	−2.343**	7.583**	6.969**
	0.406	0.162	0.957	1.013	0.254
α_1	0.834**	5.355**	−4.273**	3.210**	3.368**
	0.350	0.313	0.053	0.848	1.501
β	−0.002**	−0.325**	−0.391**	−0.025**	−0.021**
	0.001	0.108	0.071	0.007	0.006
γ_1	−0.068**	−1.435**	−1.004**	−0.889**	−1.048**
	0.016	0.210	0.035	0.068	0.051
γ_2	0.786**	−1.816**	−0.666**	0.341**	−5.009**
	0.223	0.625	0.138	0.040	0.664
σ_0	0.250**	0.647**	0.014	0.001	0.074**
	0.002	0.079	0.020	0.572	0.012
σ_1	0.001**	0.479**	0.021**	8.575**	0.016**
	0.000	0.078	0.002	4.243	0.001
s_{00}	0.858	0.984	0.939	0.715	0.982
s_{11}	0.928	0.996	0.853	0.933	0.000
r_{00}	0.703	0.793	0.493	0.476	0.555
r_{11}	0.869	0.724	0.937	0.377	0.903

Note: Standard errors are in parentheses, *denotes significance at a 10 percent level, **at a 5 percent level. Equation: $e_t - e_{t-1} = \alpha j + \beta[e_{t-1} + \gamma_1(p_{t-1} - p^*_{t-1}) + \gamma_2(LR_{t-1} - LR^*_{t-1})]$ where $\varepsilon_t \sim N(0, \sigma_i^2)$, i and $j = 0$ or 1, where e represents the log of the official exchange rate, p the price level, and LR stands for the lending rate. Note that no constraints were imposed on the timing, values or significance of the regime switches. $s_{00}/s_{11}, r_{00}/r_{11}$ are the transition probabilities for the intercept and volatility regimes, respectively.

high-inflation countries. In those countries we find that the coefficients of the fundamentals are quite stable (only the intercept switches).

These results suggest that for the high-inflation countries the linear first-generation model may be the right framework for explaining the movements of these countries' exchange rates. This is not the case for the low-inflation countries, whose exchange rates cannot be explained by a stable linear relation with underlying fundamentals.

Any explanation of these empirical results must be capable of accounting for the differences observed in the stability of the exchange rate equations between low- and high-inflation countries.

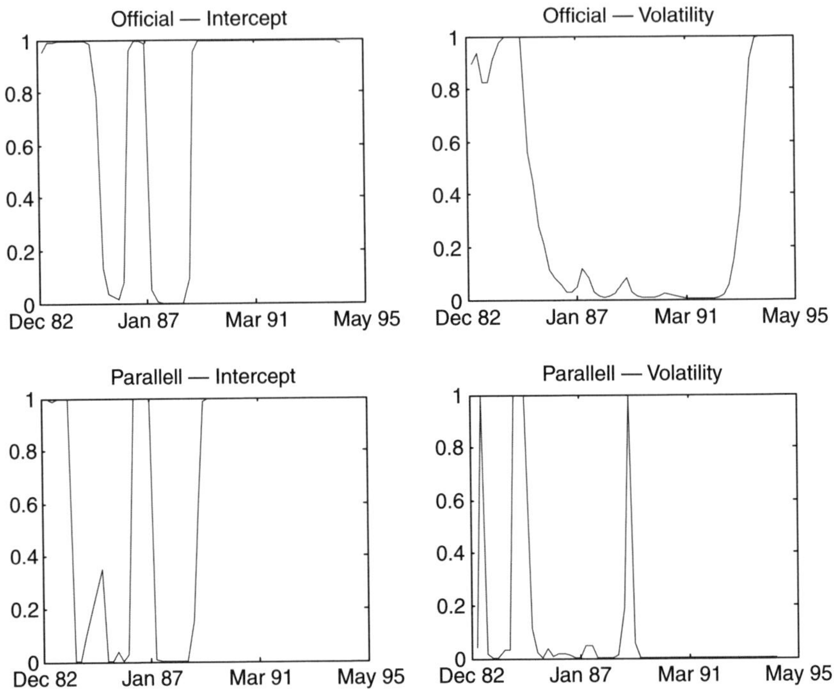

Figure 2. Smoothed probabilites for intercept and volatility switches for Brazilian data.

There are two alternative explanations. The first alternative is based on the second-generation model. We claim that this explanation is unsatisfactory. The second-generation model is based on explicit utility maximization of a representative agent. In this model, the structural instability of the coefficients in the exchange rate equations can be explained by shifts in the underlying stochastic structure, which may or may not be induced by changes in policy regimes. The contrasting evidence between high- and low-inflation countries, however, makes this explanation implausible. If anything, high-inflation countries experience stronger changes in the underlying stochastic structure (mainly induced by shifts in policy regimes) than low-inflation countries. And yet it is in the high-inflation countries that the linear first-generation model seems to be doing well while it fails for the low-inflation countries.

For this reason, our preferred explanation is based on non-linearities. In what follows, we outline the nature of non-linear features that in our view are capable of explaining the unstable relation between the exchange rate and its underlying fundamentals in low-inflation countries. In this section, we only briefly sketch the nature of these non-linearities and how these affect exchange rate models. In the next section, we present a simple model formalizing some of these ideas.

An important non-linearity has been stressed by Obstfeld and Rogoff (2000) who show that many of the current puzzles in international macroeconomics can be explained by transactions costs in the goods markets (see also Dumas 1992; Uppal *et al.* 1995; and De Grauwe and Grimaldi 2005). Transactions costs in the goods markets create a band of inaction within which international price differentials are not arbitraged away; only price differentials exceeding transactions costs (outside the band) are profitable to arbitrage. Transactions costs must be overcome for trade in goods to take place. To illustrate the magnitude of these transactions costs, De Grauwe and Grimaldi (2005) show the price dispersion of a sample of exactly the same products within the European Union. We observe price differentials of up to 40 percent. This suggests that producers price to market. Such pricing strategies can however only be applied successfully if transactions costs prevent arbitrage. Thus, these large price differentials suggest that transactions costs for traded goods are large, with the order of magnitude being between 20 percent and 40 percent.[12] In our case, introducing these transactions costs can contribute to understanding the difference in the relationship between the exchange rate and its fundamentals for low- and high-inflation countries.[13] To see this, consider the following set-up.

---

[12]It can be argued that for non-traded goods transaction costs are even higher (see Obstfeld and Rogoff, 2000).

[13]Transaction costs also exist in financial markets. However, here there is less consensus of the role of these transaction costs. In addition, the magnitudes are significantly smaller. Nevertheless, several studies indicate the importance of such transaction costs to account for the failure of, for instance, in the uncovered interest parity (see, for instance, Chang *et al.*, 2003).

The existence of transactions costs (say as a fixed proportion of the prices of products) defines a band in which arbitrage relations, such as the PPP relation, do not hold. This is the case in both the low- and high-inflation countries. Now introduce exogenous shocks in the underlying fundamental values of the exchange rate. In the low-inflation countries, many shocks tend to be small relative to the transactions cost band (e.g., differential inflation shocks are typically 1 or 2 percent per year). Hence, arbitrage will not be profitable in these cases and will remain absent. Some shocks, however, are large relative to the transactions cost band implying that arbitrage will take place. As a consequence, the relation between exchange rates and their underlying fundamentals will be unstable. In contrast, in the high-inflation countries, shocks in the fundamentals (especially nominal shocks) tend to be large relative to the transactions costs band, imposing strong arbitrage relations. This implies that the relation between the exchange rate and its fundamentals remains stable. The empirical importance of these transactions costs have also been confirmed empirically, for instance, in Taylor *et al.* (2001) and Kilian and Taylor (2003).

As stressed earlier, this is only a broad sketch of non-linearities in exchange rate models capable of explaining the results obtained in this paper. In the next section we present a simple non-linear model that allows us to capture some of the general ideas developed in this section.

6. A Simple Non-Linear Model with Transactions Costs

In this section, we develop a non-linear model that is as parsimonious as possible.

The exchange rate is e_t and its fundamental value is represented by f_t. The latter could be the price level, or more generally a vector of variables that determine the equilibrium value of the exchange rate. We assume that it is driven by a random walk process, i.e.:

$$f_t = f_{t-1} + \varepsilon_t \tag{1}$$

We assume fixed transactions costs, τ. The effect of these transactions costs is to prevent goods arbitrage. As a result, as long as the exchange rate is within its transactions cost band, there is no mechanism that drives the exchange rate towards its fundamental value. More formally, we postulate the following process. If

$$|e_t - f_t| < \tau, \quad e_t - e_{t-1} = \eta_t \tag{2}$$

where η_t is a white noise variable. If,

$$|e_t - f_t| > \tau, \quad e_t - e_{t-1} = \vartheta(f_{t-1} - e_{t-1}) + \eta_t \tag{3}$$

In words, when the difference between the exchange rate and its fundamental value is within the transactions cost band given by τ, the changes in the exchange rate are white noise. When the difference between the exchange rate and its fundamental value is larger than the fixed transactions costs, the exchange rate tends to return to its fundamental value. The speed with which this happens is determined by the parameter ϑ. In rational expectations models this parameter will typically be influenced by the structural parameters of the model, including the speed of adjustment in the goods market.[14]

Equations (1)–(3) present a very simple non-linear model of the exchange rate. In order to judge its empirical relevance, we simulate the above-presented model and use it to analyse whether the model is capable of replicating some of the empirical features analysed in the previous sections.[15] We will assume different values of the speed of adjustment parameter ∂ and of the transactions cost parameter τ. We then apply the Markov-switching and time-varying parameter methodology to analyse under what conditions this simple model produces regime switches that are similar to those detected in the data.

---

[14]The fact that the parameter ϑ is not infinite implies thus that there are some price rigidities that do not come from transactions costs.

[15]To simulate the model we assume that the fundamental consists of its past observations plus a random shock which is assumed to be Gaussian. We generate 300 such random shocks for each iteration. In total, we run the simulation 100 times.

We considered cases that come close to representing the situations of low- and high-inflation countries. More specifically, low-inflation countries are those for which the transactions cost band is high compared to the size of the shocks in the fundamentals. In addition, we assume that in these countries the speed of adjustment of prices is low. This is the case represented by $\vartheta = -0.02/\tau = 2$. In high-inflation countries the size of the transactions cost band is low compared to the size of the shocks in the fundamentals, and the speed of adjustment of prices is high. This is the case represented by $\vartheta = -0.04/\tau = 1$.[16] The parameters have been mainly based on findings from the empirical literature.

As regards the speed of adjustment parameter, there exists a vast literature on the determination and estimation of the half-life of deviations from PPP. In summarizing the results from studies using long-horizon data, Froot and Rogoff (1995) and Rogoff (1996) report the current consensus in the literature that the half-life of a shock (the time it takes for the shock to dissipate by 50 percent) to the real exchange rate is about 3–5 years, implying a slow parity reversion rate of between 13 percent and 20 percent per year.[17] However, in this paper we are more interested in the speed of convergence of the exchange rate towards a more broadly denned fundamental value. Here little estimates are available. Looking at the estimation results from Mark (1995) we find that half-life convergence would take around 4 years for low-inflation countries. Based on this information,

[16]We follow this procedure of setting the parameter τ (transaction cost band) different for low- and high-inflation countries because in the simulations we assume the same variance of the shocks in the fundamentals. Alternatively we could have assumed different variances (high for high-inflation countries and low for low-inflation countries) and the same values τ. The two procedures yield qualitatively the same results. What matters is that in the high-inflation countries the width of the transaction cost band is low relative to the size of the shocks. The opposite holds for the low-inflation countries.

[17]Abuaf and Jorion (1990) use data on bilateral real exchange rates between the US and several industrial countries during the twentieth century, and find average half-lives of deviations from parity of a little over 3 years. Frankel (1986) and Lothian and Taylor (1996) use two centuries of annual data on the sterling–dollar real exchange rate in calculating half-lives of about 5 years. Wu (1996) and Papell (1997) use panel data methods on quarterly post-Bretton Woods data to derive half-lives of between 2 and 3 years.

we select a speed of adjustment with a half-life of 2 years, which is on the lower bound of existing studies and a conservative input for our purpose (implying that ϑ equals -0.02 when assuming we use monthly observations). For high-inflation countries, few studies are available (even to determine the half-life of deviations from PPP), however the consensus is that the PPP relation holds much tighter in high-inflation countries than in low-inflation countries (see Frenkel, 1978; Chinn, 2001). González Anaya (2000), for instance, finds half-lives during the high-inflation episodes in Latin American countries of 6 months to 2 years. This result is further confirmed by Yazgan (2003) who finds a half-life of 1 year for Turkey. Hence, we set ∂ equal to -0.04 implying a half life of 1 year.

As regards the transactions cost parameter, it was already stressed in the previous section that these tend to be particularly large in the goods market of low-inflation, where observed price differentials suggest transactions costs for traded goods as large as 20 to even 40 percent whereas the size of the shocks to the underlying fundamentals are typically only a few percentage points per annum. Hence, for low-inflation countries, this would suggest that the exchange rate would hardly ever leave the transactions cost band. For our simulation exercise we opt for a parameter of $\tau = 2$ which would imply that for 96 percent of shocks to fundamentals the exchange rate would not leave the transactions cost band. By contrast, for high-inflation countries, we set $\tau = 1$ which means that for 32 percent of the shocks to fundamentals exceed the transactions cost band.

The results are shown in Tables 5 and 6. Our results are quite interesting. We find that the simple nonlinear model predicts that in low-inflation countries there are frequent switches in regimes, i.e., the slope coefficients of the fundamental variables switches regularly. No such regime switches in the slope coefficients are observed for the high-inflation countries. Similar results were obtained when estimating the time-varying parameter model. Here on average we found that for 42 observations out of 100 the slope coefficient was significantly different from zero for low-inflation countries whereas for high-inflation countries it was on average significantly different from zero in 98 observations out of 100.

Table 5. Hansen LR test results, number of simulations with null rejected at 5 percent level.

Switches in	intercept, slope and volatility			intercept	slope
H_o:	$\alpha_0 = \alpha_1$	$\gamma_0 = \gamma_1$	$\sigma_0 = \sigma_1$	$\alpha_0 = \alpha_1$	$\gamma_0 = \gamma_1$
$\vartheta = -0.02/\tau = 2$	Low-Inflation Country				
	2	92	76	5	96
$\vartheta = -0.04/\tau = 1$	High-Inflation Country				
	87	22	65	92	3

Note: 100 simulations with 300 observations each were run. For each simulation the Markov-switching model was next estimated and then the Hansen test was estimated. The estimated Markov-switching model is $e_t - e_{t-1} = \alpha_1 + \beta[\gamma_{1j}(fund_{t-1} - e_{t-1})] + \varepsilon_t$ where $\varepsilon_t \sim N(0, \sigma_k^2), i, j, k = 0$ or 1.

Table 6. Estimates fit to non-linear model, number of simulations with significant coefficient at 10 percent level.

	α_0	α_1	γ_0	γ_1
$\partial = -0.02/\tau = 2$ Low-Inflation Country	23	—	76	21
$\partial = -0.04/\tau = 1$ High-Inflation Country	98	76	100	—

Note: The results in the table show the number of simulations with significant coefficients (at 10 percent level) out of 100 simulations with 300 observations each were run. The estimated Markov-switching model for each simulation for the low-inflation countries is $e_t - e_{t-1} = \alpha + \beta[\gamma_{1j}(fund_{t-1} - e_{t-1})] + \varepsilon_t$ where $\varepsilon_t \sim N(0, \sigma_k^2), j, k = 0$ or 1 and for high-inflation countries it is $e_t - e_{t-1} = \alpha_j + \beta[\gamma_1(fund_{t-1} - e_{t-1})] + \varepsilon_t$ where $\varepsilon_t \sim N(0, \sigma_k^2), j, k = 0$ or 1. If in one of the two regimes the coefficient was significant, it was systematically classified as regime 0.

7. Concluding Remarks

Characterizing the nature of the relationship between exchange rate changes and the changes in its underlying fundamentals has long been an objective of empirical international macroeconomics. Although this research has contributed to our understanding of the behaviour of the exchange rates, it is also true that this empirical research has been unable to validate the existing theoretical models. In particular, the "first-generation models" of the exchange rates that were developed during the 1970s have been rejected at least when using data of the major industrial countries. The "second-generation models" based on explicit utility maximization of agents have not produced sharp enough testable propositions allowing for their refutation by the data. As a result, they have neither been confirmed nor refuted.

In this paper, we tested whether the relationship between the changes in the nominal exchange rate and the news in its underlying fundamentals has non-linear features. In order to do so, we developed a Markov-switching and applied it to a sample of low- and high-inflation countries.

The empirical analysis shows that for the high-inflation countries the first-generation models appear to work well: the relationship between news in the fundamentals and exchange rate changes is stable and always significant. This is not the case, however, for the low-inflation countries, where frequent regime switches occur.

We developed a non-linear model that is capable of explaining our empirical findings. The model is based on the existence of transactions costs in the goods markets. We found that this simple non-linear model is capable of replicating the empirical evidence uncovered in this paper. More specifically, the model predicts that in countries where shocks in fundamentals are low in comparison with the transactions cost band (low-inflation countries), frequent regime switches in the link between the exchange rate and its fundamentals must occur. This is not the case in high-inflation countries where the size of the shocks in fundamentals is large relative to the transactions cost band.

Appendix A: Data availability and sample selected

The countries included in the analysis are: Argentina, Bolivia, Brazil, Chile Colombia, Ecuador, France, Germany, Italy, Japan and the UK. Information on the home currency-dollar exchange rate and five fundamentals was retrieved on a monthly and quarterly basis. More specifically, this set of fundamentals covers:

1. The price level for the country concerned, defined as the consumer price level.

2. The money supply for the country under scrutiny, for all low-inflation countries this is M3 while for high-inflation countries this is M0.
3. The money market rate, which is used as a measure of the short-term interest rate for high-inflation countries.
4. The interbank rate, which is used as a measure of the short-term interest rate for low-inflation countries.
5. The lending rate and the long-term government bond yield which are both proxies of the long-term interest rate. The latter was however only available for the low-inflation countries.

In Table Al, the sample periods for the regressions are reported for the monthly data. For the quarterly observations, the same time periods were available then the figures were transformed to quarters rather than months.

Table A1. Sample periods used for estimations.

	Short sample		Long sample
Low-inflation countries			
Germany		1973M1-1998M12	
France		1973M1-1998M12	
Italy		1973M1-1998M12	
Japan		1988M1-2005M7	
UK		1973M1-2005M7	
High-inflation countries			
Argentina	1981M3-1985M6		1979M3-1991M3
Bolivia	1980M12-1985M12		1980M12-1986M12
Brazil	1989M4-1994M5		1982M12-1994M7
Chile	1971M7-1976M6		1962M4-1978M12
Ecuador		1983M1-1998M11	

Note: The short samples for the high-inflation countries are those where the exchange rate can be denned as floating. The long sample is the full sample for which we have data for the exchange rate of the country and all its fundamentals (except Chile where only information is available for inflation). During the full sample period various exchange rate regimes could happen though. In Ecuador the exchange rate was for the full sample for which we have data never floating.

Appendix B: The smoothed probabilities for low-inflation countries

France

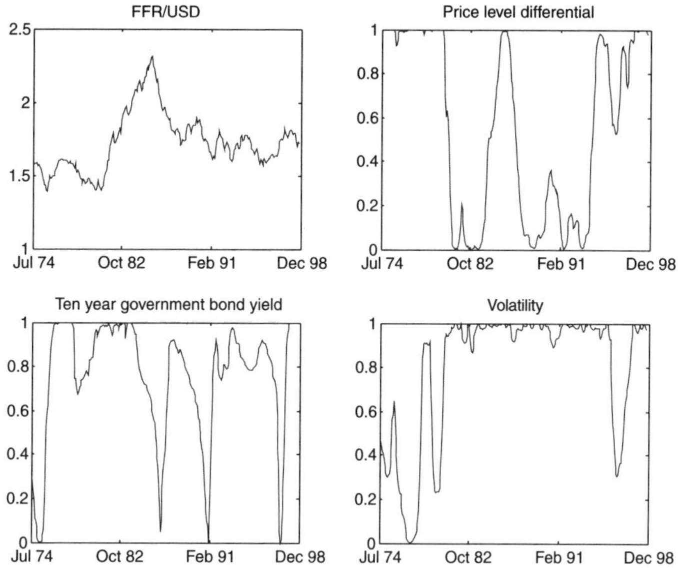

Italy

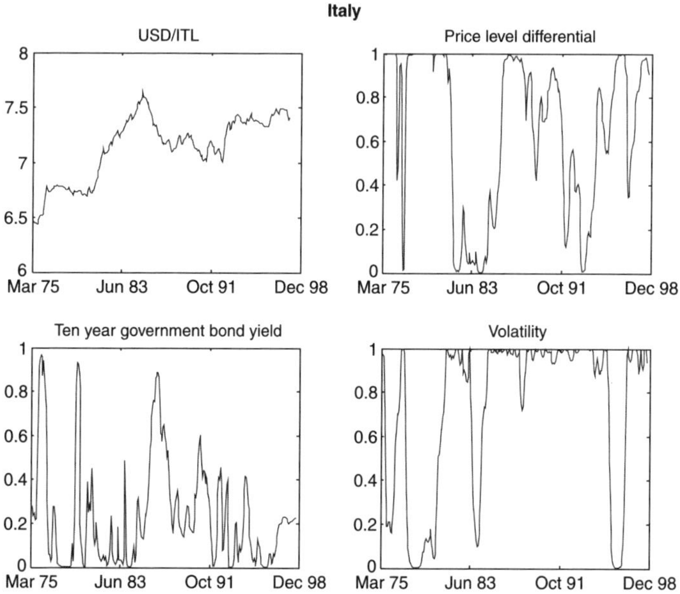

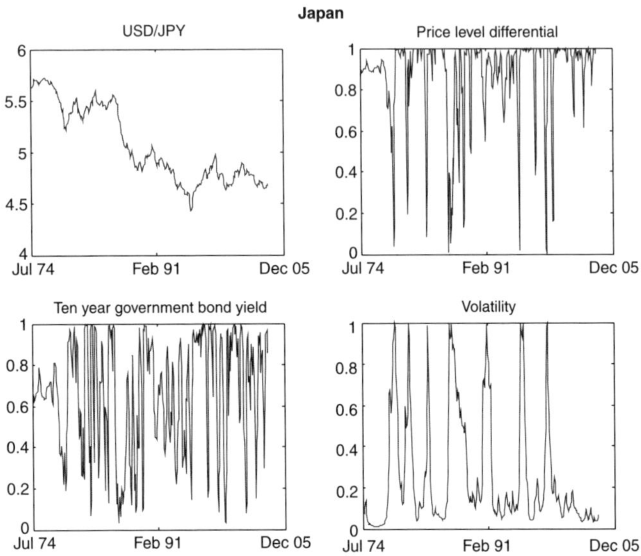
Japan
USD/JPY
6
5.5
5
4.5
4
Jul 74
Feb 91
Dec 05
Price level differential
1
0.8
0.6
0.4
0.2
0
Jul 74
Feb 91
Dec 05
Ten year government bond yield
1
0.8
0.6
0.4
0.2
0
Jul 74
Feb 91
Dec 05
Volatility
1
0.8
0.6
0.4
0.2
0
Jul 74
Feb 91
Dec 05

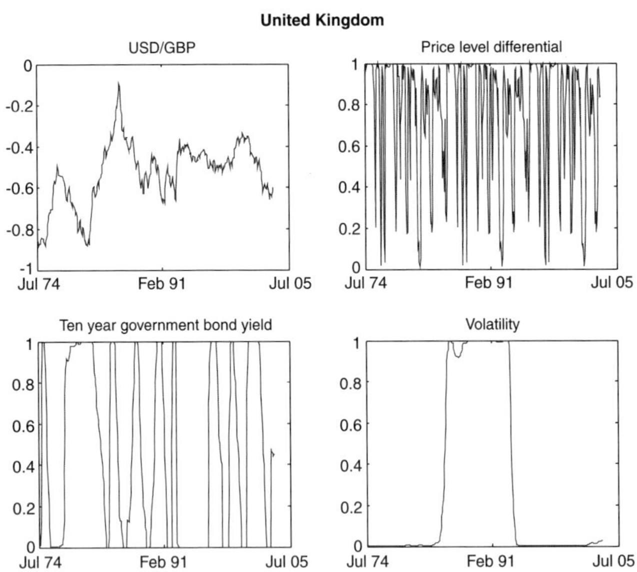
United Kingdom
USD/GBP
0
-0.2
-0.4
-0.6
-0.8
-1
Jul 74
Feb 91
Jul 05
Price level differential
1
0.8
0.6
0.4
0.2
0
Jul 74
Feb 91
Jul 05
Ten year government bond yield
1
0.8
0.6
0.4
0.2
0
Jul 74
Feb 91
Jul 05
Volatility
1
0.8
0.6
0.4
0.2
0
Jul 74
Feb 91
Jul 05

Appendix C: The smoothed probabilities for high-inflation countries

Argentina

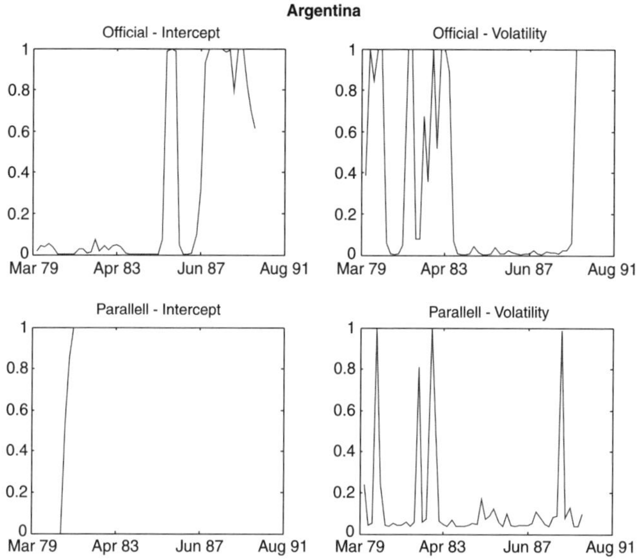

Bolivia

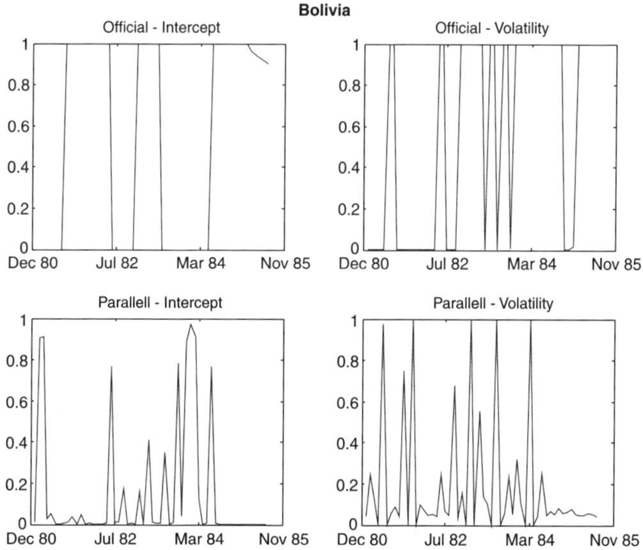

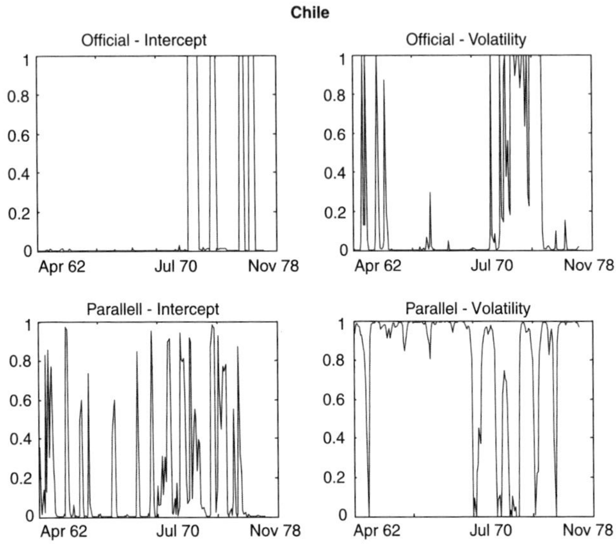

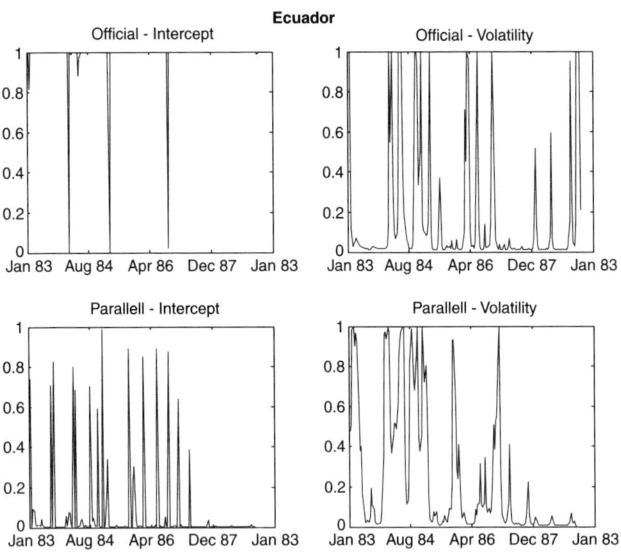

Acknowledgements

We are grateful to seminar participants at the European Central Bank, to participants at the 4th annual conference of the Dutch Central Bank (Amsterdam) for useful comments and interesting and constructive critiques on previous version of this paper. In particular, we wish to thank Ivan Alves, Lorenzo Cappiello, Maria Demertzis, Carsten Detken, Hans Dewachter and Peter McAdam for their valuable comments and remarks. The opinions expressed are not necessarily those of the European Central Bank. Responsibility of remaining errors is ours.

References

Abuaf, N and P Jorion (1990). Purchasing power parity in the long run. *Journal of Finance*, 45, 157–174.

Altavilla, C (2000). Measuring monetary policy asymmetries across the EMU countries. CES Discussion Paper No. 22.

Baxter, M and A Stockman (1989). Business cycles and the exchange rate regime: Some international evidence. *Journal of Monetary Economics*, 23(3), 377–400.

Chang, RP, S-H Lee, SF Reed and SG Rhei (2003). One-way arbitrage-based interest parity: An application of the Fletcher–Taylor approach in short-date markets. Working Paper, University of Hawai.

Chinn, M (2001). Menu costs and non-linear reversion to purchasing power parity among developed countries. Working Paper, University of Santa Cruz, San Diego.

Clarida, R and J Gali (1994). Sources of real exchange rate fluctuations: How important are nominal shocks? In *The Carnegie-Rochester Conference Series on Public Policy*, pp. 1–55, December.

De Boeck, J (2000). The effect of macroeconomic news on exchange rates: A structural VAR approach. Mimeo: Leuven.

De Grauwe, P and H Dewachter (1993). A chaotic model of the exchange rate: The role of fundamentalists and chartists. *Open Economies Review*, 4(4), 351–379.

De Grauwe, P and M Grimaldi (2005). Heterogeneity of agents, transactions costs and the exchange rate. *Journal of Economic Dynamics and Control*, 29, 691–719.

Dewachter, H (2001). Can markov switching models replicate chartist profits in the foreign exchange market? *Journal of International Money and Finance*, 20(1), 25–41.

Dumas, B (1992). Dynamic equilibrium and the real exchange rate in a spatially separated world. *Review of Financial Studies*, 5(2), 153–180.

Farrant, K and G Peersman (2005). Is the exchange rate a shock absorber of a source of shocks? New empirical evidence. *Journal of Money, Credit and Banking*, 38(4), 939–961.

Faust, J, J Rogers and JH Wright (2003). Exchange rate forecasting: The errors we've really made. *Journal of International Economics*, 60, 35–59.

Flood, R and A Rose (1995). Fixing exchange rates: A virtual quest for fundamentals. *Journal of Monetary Economics*, 36(1), 3–37.

Frankel, J (1986). International capital mobility and crowding out in the U.S. economy: Imperfect integration of financial markets or of goods markets? In *How Open Is the U.S. Economy?* R Hafter (ed.), pp. 33–67. Lexington, MA: Lexington Books.

Frankel, J and K Froot (1990). Chartists, fundamentalists, and trading in the foreign exchange market. *American Economic Review*, 80(2), 181–185.

Frenkel, JA (1978). Purchasing power parity: Doctrinal perspective and evidence from the 1920s. *Journal of International Economics*, 8, 169–191.

Froot, KA and K Rogoff (1995). Perspectives on PPP and long-run real exchange rates. In *Handbook of International Economics*, Vol. 3, G Grossman and K Rogoff (eds). Amsterdam: North Holland.

González Anaya, JA (2000). Exchange rate pass-through and partial dollarization: Is there a link? Center for Research on Economic Development and Policy Reform, Stanford University Working Paper No. 25.

Hamilton, J (1989). A new approach to the economic analysis of nonstationary time series and the business cycle. *Econometrica*, 57(2), 357–384.

Hansen, BE (1992). The likelihood ratio test under nonstandard conditions: Testing the Markov switching model of GNP. *Journal of Applied Econometrics*, 7, S61–S82.

Kiguel, MA and SA O'Connell (1995). Parallel exchange rates in developing countries. *World Bank Research Observer*, 10(1), 21–52.

Kilian, L and M Taylor (2003). Why is it so difficult to beat the random walk forecast of exchange rates? *Journal of International Economics*, 60(1), 1–29.

Kurz, M and M Motolese (1999). Endogenous uncertainty and market volatility. Fondazione Eni Enrico Mattei Note di Lavoro, 27/99.

Lothian, JR and MP Taylor (1996). Real exchange rate behavior: The recent float from the perspective of two centuries. *Journal of Political Economy*, 104(3), 488–509.

Mark, NC (1995). Exchange rates and fundamentals: Evidence on long-horizon prediction. *American Economic Review*, 85, 201–218.

McConnell, M and G Perez-Quiros (2000). Output fluctuations in the United States: What has changed since the early 1980s? *American Economic Review*, 90(3), 1464–1476.

Meese, R and K Rogoff (1983). Empirical exchange rate models of the seventies: Do they fit out of sample? *Journal of International Economics*, 14(1–2), 3–24.

Meese, R and K Rogoff (1988). Was it real? The exchange rate-interest rate differential relation over the modern floating-rate period. *Journal of Finance*, 43(4), 933–948.

Obstfeld, M and K Rogoff (1996). *Foundations of International Macroeconomics*. Cambridge, MA: MIT Press.

Obstfeld, M and K Rogoff (2000). The six major puzzles in international macroeconomics: Is there a common cause? NBER Working Paper No. 7777.

Papell, DH (1997). Searching for stationarity: Purchasing power parity under the current float. *Journal of International Economics*, 43, 313–332.

Peel, D and M Taylor (2000). Non-linear adjustment, long run equilibrium and exchange rate fundamentals. *Journal of International Money and Finance*, 19(1), 33–53.

Reinhart, C and K Rogoff (2004). The modern history of exchange rate arrangements: A reinterpretation. *The Quarterly Journal of Economics*, 119(1), 1–48.

Rogoff, K (1996). The purchasing power parity puzzle. *Journal of Economic Literature*, 34(2), 647–668.

Taylor, M, D Peel and L Sarno (2001). Nonlinear mean reversion in real exchange rates: Towards a solution to the purchasing power parity puzzles. *International Economic Review*, 42, 1015–1042.

Uppal, R, P Sercu and C van Hulle (1995). The exchange rate in the presence of transactions costs: Implications for tests of purchasing power parity. *Journal of Finance*, 50(4), 1309–1319.

Vansteenkiste, I (2006). Noise trading, fundamentals and exchange rate volatility. Mimeo: Katholieke Universiteit Leuven and European Central Bank.

Wu, Y (1996). Are real exchange rates nonstationary? Evidence from a panel-data test. *Journal of Money, Credit and Banking*, 28(1), 54–63.

Yazgan, MF (2003). The purchasing power parity hypothesis for a high inflation country: A re-examination of the case of Turkey. *Applied Economic Letters*, 10(3), 143–147.

Chapter 6

The Impact of FX Central Bank Intervention in a Noise Trading Framework

Michel Beine, Paul De Grauwe and Marianna Grimaldi

In this paper, we analyze the effectiveness of the direct central bank interventions using a new effectiveness criterion. To this aim, we investigate the effects of central bank interventions (CBI) in a noise trading model with chartists and fundamentalists. We first estimate a model in which chartists extrapolate past returns and fundamentalists forecast a mean reverting dynamics of the exchange rate toward a fundamental value. Then, we investigate the role of central bank interventions for explaining the switching properties between the two types of agents. We find evidence showing that in the medium run, interventions increase the proportion of fundamentalists and therefore exert some stabilizing influence on the exchange rate.

Published in *Journal of Banking and Finance*, 33(7), 1187–1195, 2009.
We would like to thank A. Bénassy for transmitting the exchange rate misalignment data used in this paper. This paper benefited from comments and suggestions by participants at presentations in Munich, Namur, Maastricht and Brussels. The usual disclaimer applies.
Keywords: FX markets; Central bank intervention effectiveness; Chartist-fundamentalist regimes; signalling channel.
JEL classification: C10, F31, F41

1. Introduction

Direct interventions in the foreign exchange (FX) market have often been used as a policy instrument by the major central banks. By sterilizing their operations, monetary authorities have used these interventions as a stabilization tool independent of monetary policy. While some authorities like the US Federal Reserve have been increasingly reluctant to use central bank interventions (CBIs hereafter), other major central banks like the European Central Bank (ECB) or the Bank of Japan (BoJ) have conducted several rounds of interventions over the last 5 years.

Despite the wide use of direct interventions by the central banks, researchers (as well as policy makers) have questioned the effectiveness of such an instrument. Within the literature devoted to the conduct of foreign exchange rate policies, the issue of effectiveness is the one which has received the greatest attention. Recent surveys (see Humpage, 2003) offer a useful review of this strand of the literature. One problem in assessing whether interventions have delivered the intended goal is that the objectives followed by the central banks are rarely known by external researchers. Several possible objectives have been mentioned including influencing trend movements, reversing past trends, smoothing exchange rate volatility or creating monetary base through unsterilized operations. While a couple of international agreements like the Plaza agreement in 1985 and the Louvre agreement in 1987 provide some insight about the ultimate goal of these interventions, the objectives are likely to change over time and to differ across central banks.[1]

In this paper, we develop an analysis directly consistent with a new criterion of effectiveness. A direct criterion of effectiveness used in the empirical literature is whether the exchange rate level reacts to the central bank purchases or sales of foreign currency in the intended direction the day of the intervention (Beine *et al.*, 2002). The adoption of this criterion stems from the fact that the most

[1]Lack of transparency in the FX policy is clearly one major source for identifying the explicit goals. The use of imprecise terms in central bank's statements also leads to some difficulty of interpretation.

frequent objective followed by central banks concerns the dynamics of the first moment of exchange rate returns. In general, the bulk of the empirical studies found that central bank interventions did not induce the intended changes in the exchange rate level. Some studies found even some moderate evidence of perverse results, which is difficult to rationalize (see nevertheless Bhattacharya and Weller, 1997). Quite recently however, new empirical approaches have provided more support for efficiency in the sense that the exchange rate was found to react significantly (and in the intended direction) to the central bank operation. Using intradaily data, Dominguez (2003) as well as Payne and Vitale (2003) indeed show that such an effect might show up in the very short run, i.e., within a few minutes after the occurrence of the operations.

While simple and straightforward, the use of this criterion of effectiveness raises two questions. First, the objective followed by the central bank might be less simple than influencing the level within the day or the hour of the intervention. For instance, the central bank might be willing to break a past depreciating or appreciating trend of its currency. In this case, insignificant results in terms of returns might lead to overemphasizing the poor performance of the operations. To tackle this point, some authors Fatum and Hutchison (2003) have conducted event studies that allow to introduce more flexibility in terms of the possible objectives followed by the central bank(s).[2] The second issue is the optimal horizon followed by central banks. While this horizon might differ across central banks and over time, central bank surveys (Neely, 2001) tend to show that central banks also care about the developments of the exchange rate beyond the day of the intervention. Promising outcomes generated by the

[2]While interesting, we do not follow here this kind of approaches that in turn raise some questions about their implementation. There are in particular two critical issues associated to the use of event studies for assessing the impact of FX interventions. The first one is the definition of an event and in particular the definition of clustered operations that should be considered as one single event. The second point concerns the endogenous definition of the event. For instance, if a particular central bank keeps intervening until the objective is reached, the use of event studies might lead to a bias in favor of efficiency. Interestingly, this general conclusion turns out to be more supported by this strand of the literature.

intervention in the very short run might thus be meaningless for central bankers if they are reversed later on. Conversely, the use of successive interventions that might signal commitment of the central bank to defend the currency might lead to more favorable results that can be difficult to identify in the (very) short run.

In this paper, we adopt another criterion for efficiency of the FX central bank interventions. We consider a given central bank intervention as efficient if it moves the exchange rate in a direction consistent with the fundamental equilibrium exchange rate. Central banks often claim that their interventions aim at restoring the value of exchange rates to a level consistent with the fundamentals. While central banks pursue other goals, the specific objective of minimizing the degree of misalignment has been extensively included in loss functions used in theoretical analyses (see Vitale, 1999 as well as De Grauwe and Grimaldi, 2006 among others). The adoption of such a policy has been advocated by several authors including for instance Neely (2004) claiming that the central bank should act as a long-term speculator in the FX market. Theoretical analyses such as De Grauwe and Grimaldi (2006) also suggest that central bank interventions might drive the exchange rate in a direction consistent with fundamentals. In contrast to the analysis of simple regression coefficients capturing some contemporaneous impact, the adoption of this criterion allows for some role for central bank interventions in the medium run. To this aim, we assess the impact of interventions conducted by the Bundesbank (ECB after the inception of the euro) and the Federal Reserve within a noise trading framework, i.e., a model allowing for the presence of two types of agents, namely chartists and fundamentalists. The noise trading framework has successfully been applied by authors to explain the discrepancy between the short and long-run exchange rate dynamics (De Grauwe and Dewachter, 1995). It reflects the complex dynamics produced by the interaction of two types of agents whose existence has been empirically supported by the results of surveys of practitionners (Cheung and Chinn, 2001 for instance). As originally done by Vigfusson (1996), the use of a two-regime Markov-switching regime allows to conduct an econometric analysis consistent with the theoretical assumption of two types of agents. Our analysis of central bank intervention in the context of a chartist-fundamentalist framework is related to the recent analysis of Reitz and Taylor (2008) but exhibits noticeable and important differences.[3]

The paper is organized as follows. In Section 2, we present a model of the foreign exchange market in which two types of agents, chartists and fundamentalists, interact. In Section 3, we test the prediction of this model and identify the effects of interventions. Section 4 briefly concludes.

2. The Underlying Theory

2.1. *The Theoretical Framework*

In this section, we present a simple exchange rate model. The model is based on De Grauwe and Grimaldi (2006a) and is explained there in greater detail. It starts from utility maximising agents selecting their optimal portfolio using a mean-variance utility framework. This allows to derive the standard optimal holding of foreign assets by agent i, $d_{i,t}$[4]

$$d_{i,t} = \frac{(1 + r^*)E_t^i(s_{t+1}) - (1 + r)s_t}{\mu\sigma_{i,t}^2}, \tag{1}$$

[3]Using a smooth transition model, Reitz and Taylor (2008) find evidence in favour of a coordination channel, i.e., the fact that interventions can move the exchange rate towards its equilibrium value. While we also conclude in favour of such a channel, our two-regime Markov Switching econometric analysis is, unlike their model, based on a structural model of chartist and fundamentalist agents. The proportion of those agents depend on the profitability of their respective forecasting rules. In our model, intervention will alter the dynamics of the exchange rate by changing the relative profitability of the rules, while in the Reitz and Taylor approach, intervention affects the confidence attached by the informed traders to the misalignment value of the exchange rate for processing their orders.

[4]If the model is interpreted as an asset pricing model of one risky asset (shares) and a risk free asset, the corresponding optimal holding of the risky asset becomes

$$d_{i,t} = \frac{E_t^i(s_{t+1} + y_{t+1}) - (1 + r)s_t}{\mu\sigma_{i,t}^2},$$

where s_{t+1} and y_{t+1} are the price and the dividend at $t + 1$, respectively, and of $\sigma_{i,t}^2 = V_t^i(s_{t+1} + y_{t+1})$ where s_{t+1} and y_{t+1} are the price and the dividend at $t+1$, respectively, and $\sigma_{i,t}^2 \equiv V_t^i(s_{t+1} + y_{t+1})$.

where s_t is the exchange rate (the price of the foreign currency in units of domestic currency) in period t, E_t^i is the forecast made about next period's exchange rate by agent i in period t, μ is the coefficient of risk aversion, r and r^* are the domestic and foreign interest rates respectively (assumed to be constant) and of $\sigma_{i,t}^2 = (1+r^*)^2 V_t^i(s_{t+1})$. Aggregating the individual demands and setting market demand equal to the market supply of net foreign assets, Z_t, allows us to derive the market clearing exchange rate:

$$s_t = \left(\frac{1+r^*}{1+r}\right)\frac{1}{\sum_{i=1}^N \frac{w_{i,t}}{\sigma_{i,t}^2}}\left[\sum_{i=1}^N w_{i,t}\frac{E_t^i(s_{t+1})}{\sigma_{i,t}^2} - \Omega_t Z_t\right], \tag{2}$$

where $w_{i,t} = \frac{n_{i,t}}{\sum_{i=1}^N n_{i,t}}$ is the weight (share) of agent i, and $\Omega_t = \frac{\mu}{(1+r^* \sum_{i=1}^N n_{i,t})}$.

Thus, the market clearing exchange rate is determined by the forecasts of the agents, E_t^i, about the future exchange rate, their respective weights $w_{i,t}$ and by the net supply of foreign assets Z_t. The latter is determined by the current account and the official interventions in the foreign exchange market. Note also that the forecasts are weighted by their respective variances of $\sigma_{i,t}^2$. When agent's i forecasts have a high variance the weight of this agent in the determination of the market exchange rate is reduced.

Two types of forecasting rules are assumed. One is called a "fundamentalist" rule, the other a "technical trading" (chartist) rule.[5] The agents using a fundamentalist rule, the "fundamentalists," base their forecast on a comparison between the market and the fundamental exchange rate, i.e., they forecast the market rate to return to the fundamental rate in the future. In this sense they use a negative feedback rule that introduces a mean reverting dynamics in the exchange rate.

The chartists are assumed to follow a positive feedback rule, i.e., they extrapolate past movements of the exchange rate into the future.

[5]The idea of distinguishing between fundamentalist and technical traders rules was first introduced by Frankel and Froot (1987).

Finally agents evaluate the fitness of these two forecasting rules, by comparing their (risk adjusted) profitability *ex post* and then deciding whether to keep the rule or switch to the other one. Thus, the model is in the logic of evolutionary dynamics, in which simple decision rules are selected. These rules will continue to be followed if they pass some "fitness" test (profitability test). This switching mechanism then determines the weights of chartists and fundamentalists w_{ct} and w_{ft}. For more detail see De Grauwe and Grimaldi (2006a). These authors show that the model is capable of generating all the empirical "puzzles" observed in the foreign exchange market. These empirical puzzles are first and foremost the disconnect phenomenon (see Obstfeld and Rogoff (2000) who coined the term "disconnect puzzle"). De Grauwe and Grimaldi (2006a,b) show that the model is capable of mimicking this disconnect puzzle. The mechanism producing this disconnect originates from the dynamic interaction of chartists and fundamentalists. A series of stochastic shocks can make chartist extrapolation profitable thereby attracting an increasing number of agents using extrapolative forecasting rules. This goes on producing misalignments of the exchange rate until it is reversed by shocks in the fundamentals that tend to make fundamentalist forecasting rules more profitable thereby increasing the importance of these rules in forecasting.

2.2. *Modelling Official Interventions in the Foreign Exchange Market*

The model presented in the previous section allows for an easy way to introduce the interventions of the central bank. The supply of foreign assets Z_t in Eq. (2) is determined by the current account position, i.e., a surplus (deficit) in the current account increases (decreases) the supply of foreign assets. The supply of foreign assets, however, can also be influenced by the intervention activities of the central bank. More specifically, when the central bank sells foreign exchange it increases the supply of foreign assets Z_t. This will generally put downward pressure on the exchange rate. This can also be seen from Eq. (2): the sign of Z_t is negative. Conversely when the central bank buys foreign exchange it reduces the supply of foreign assets putting upward pressure on the exchange rate.

It can be useful to analyze the impact effect of a surprise change in foreign assets on the exchange rate. We obtain this by isolating the effect of a change in Z_t in Eq. (3). Setting the expectational terms equal to zero, and using the definition of Ω_t we obtain

$$\Delta s_t = -\left(\frac{\mu}{1+r}\right)\frac{1}{\frac{w_{c,t}}{\sigma^2_{c,t}}+\frac{w_{f,t}}{\sigma^2_{f,t}}}X_t, \tag{3}$$

where $X_t = \Delta Z_t/N$, i.e., the supply of foreign assets per capita. We have also assumed that there are only two types of agents, i.e., chartists and fundamentalists (subscripted by c and f, respectively).

Eq. (3) makes clear that the effect of a foreign exchange market intervention on the exchange rate will be difficult to predict ex ante because it depends on the weights the chartists and fundamentalists have in the market, together with the forecast errors they have been making in the past. In other words the effect of interventions will depend on the market structure and the risk perceptions at the time of the intervention. Since these factors change continuously, the effect of interventions will also change.

It should also be stressed that we analyse the effects of sterilized interventions here, i.e., interventions that are not allowed to affect domestic money market conditions, including the domestic interest rate. Thus, we analyze interventions that do not affect the fundamentals.[6]

We investigate the question of the effectiveness of interventions assuming a simple intervention rule. The intervention rule we consider is one in which the central bank is continuously in the market smoothing the movements of the exchange rate by using a "leaning against the wind" intervention rule.[7] We specify this

[6]The interventions carried out by the ECB (Bundesbank) and the Fed over the investigated period in the empirical analysis are reported by the central banks to have been sterilized.

[7]This leaning-against-the wind type of behaviour has been supported by the estimation of empirical reaction functions for various central banks. See Almekinders and Eijffinger (1996) for the Bundesbank.

rule as follows:

$$\Delta Z_t = \zeta(\Delta s_{t-1}), \tag{4}$$

where $\zeta \geq 0$. Thus when the exchange rate increases (decreases), the central bank sells (buys) foreign exchange in the market so that the supply of foreign assets increases (decreases). The parameter ζ measures the intensity with which the central bank performs these operations. Note that as in the case of the private agents the current exchange rate is not in the information set of the central bank. The current exchange rate is the market clearing exchange rate that will be the outcome of the decisions of both the private agents and the central bank, but is not yet known when agents make their decision. This is in the logic of the behavioural finance model used here. Individual agents (both private and public) lack the cognitive skills to understand "the whole picture," i.e., they do not know the underlying model which they need to know to compute the market clearing exchange rate in period t (see De Grauwe and Grimaldi, 2006a).

This simple intervention rule can be implemented by substituting Eq. (4) into Eq. (2) and solving the model numerically taking into account the forecasting rules and the switching mechanism as presented in De Grauwe and Grimaldi (2006b). We show some results of simulating the model in the time domain in Fig. 1 using a particular configuration of parameters [in De Grauwe and Grimaldi (2006b) extensive sensitivity analyses are performed]. Panel (a) shows the exchange rate in the absence of any intervention ($\zeta = 0$). This is the free float solution. It exhibits large movements of the exchange rate around its fundamental. The next two panels (b) and (c) show the exchange rate for increasing intensity of intervention. In panel (b) we assume that $\zeta = 0.01$ and in panel (c) we assume that $\zeta = 0.1$. We find that as ε is increased the exchange rate is forced to move more tightly around its fundamental. Thus it appears that this simple rule is capable of reducing the large disconnection of the exchange rate from its fundamental in a free float environment. As a result, the application of this rule ensures that the exchange rate better reflects the underlying fundamental.

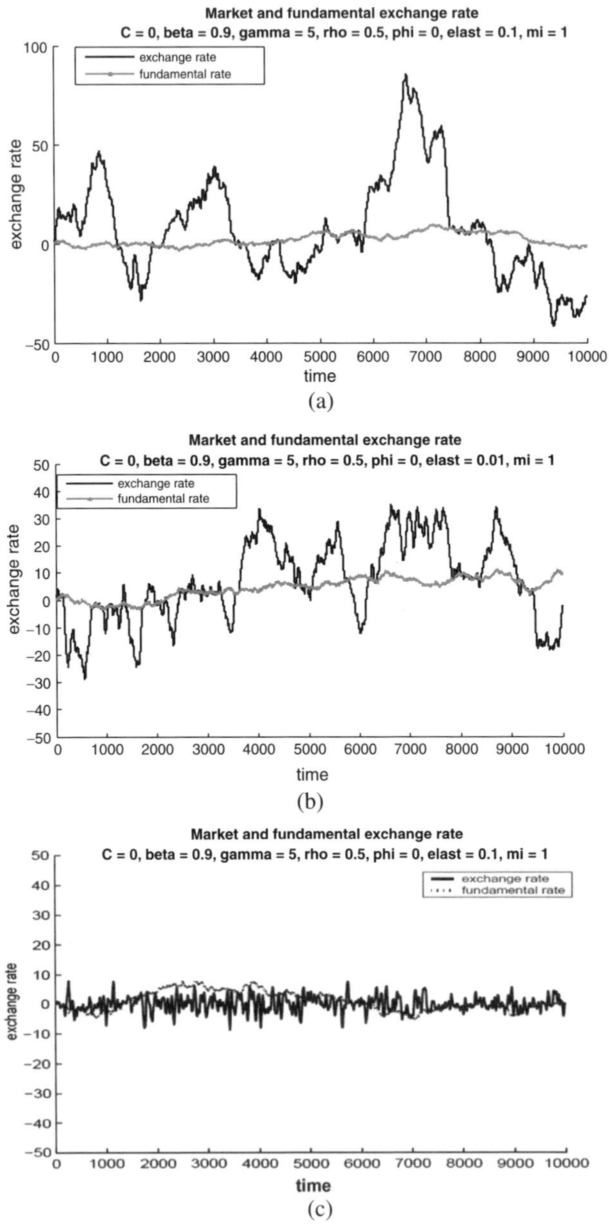

Figure 1. Simulated exchange rate under intervention rule.

The intuition behind this result is that the "leaning against the wind" strategy of the central bank reinforces the mean reverting dynamics in the market thereby strengthening the hand of the fundamentalists at the expense of the "trend chasers" (chartists). This stabilizes the market and reduces the probability of the emergence of bubbles. Thus the effect of this intervention is that the exchange rate follows the movements of the underlying fundamentals more closely.[8]

In order to shed additional light on the question of why a simple intervention rule can be effective, we show the average weight of the chartists and fundamentalists corresponding to the three scenarios in Table 1. We see that in the free float simulation the chartists have on average a weight of 90 percent in the market (the fundamentalists' weight is then 10 percent), while in the scenario of intense intervention ($\zeta = 0.1$) the average weight of the chartists declines to 76 percent (the average weight of fundamentalists increases to 24 percent). Thus when the central bank successfully stabilizes the exchange rate so that it closely reflects the fundamentals, the fundamentalists on average have a higher share in the market than when the central bank does not intervene. Put differently, systematic interventions by the central bank change the structure of the foreign exchange market, i.e., they reduce the importance of chartists

Table 1. Mean profits and weights of fundamentalists and chartists along with intervention intensity (ζ).

	Mean profits and weights of fundamentalists and chartists		
	$\zeta = 0$	$\zeta = 0.01$	$\zeta = 0.1$
Mean profit fundamentalists	0.0010	0.0045	0.0081
Mean weight fundamentalists	0.1	0.13	0.24
Mean profit chartists	0.1099	0.0971	0.0888
Mean weight chartists	0.9	0.87	0.76

[8]In De Grauwe and Grimaldi (2006a) we analyzed the target intervention rule as proposed by Miller and Williamson (1987). The results are very similar to the simple leaning against the wind rule analyzed here.

and increase the importance of fundamentalists. Thus, the "leaning against the wind" intervention rule of the central bank creates an environment in which the fundamentalists are more active thereby keeping the exchange rate close to its fundamental. The reason why this is made possible is that the intervention rule increases the mean reversion forces in the market thereby making fundamentalists forecasting rules more profitable. We show this in Table 1 where we present the average profits of chartists and fundamentalists in three scenarios. We find that in the intervention scenarios ($\zeta = 0.01$ and $\zeta = 0.1$) the fundamentalists make significantly more profits than in the free float scenario ($\zeta = 0$). The reverse is true for the chartists' profits. This confirms that the intervention rule of the central bank increases the relative profitability of fundamentalist forecasting rules, thereby enhancing the position of fundamentalists in the market and increasing their weight.[9] By the same token it reduces the weight of chartists in the market. Thus the stabilizing effect of the intervention rule comes about indirectly, i.e., it makes fundamentalist forecasting more attractive thereby allowing the market to discover the fundamental value of the exchange rate more effectively.

These results are consistent with the signalling channel of foreign exchange market interventions. In our model the interventions signal the central bank's commitment to avoid too large departures from the fundamental exchange rate. This signal has the effect of enhancing the influence of fundamental variables on the exchange rate.

The previous results assume a rule based intervention policy. The question that arises is how a stochastic intervention by the central bank affects these results. Using the same model as the one presented here, De Grauwe and Grimaldi (2006b) show that when the central bank intervenes in a random way, the effects of these interventions on the exchange rate are highly unpredictable. The reason why they obtain this result can readily be seen from Eq. (3). A random change in X has an unpredictable effect on the exchange rate because, as we argued earlier, it depends on market conditions prevailing at the

[9]Note that even in the intervention scenarios, chartism remains more profitable than fundamentalism.

time of the change in X. As a result, a given sale or purchase of foreign exchange can have very different effects on the exchange rate depending on the volatility in the market and the share of chartists at the time of the intervention.

3. The Empirical Investigation

3.1. *The Basic Chartists-fundamentalists Model*

In this section, we propose an empirical estimation of the impact of interventions, building on the theoretical framework developed in the previous section. The empirical counterpart of the theoretical model involves the modelling of chartist and fundamentalist traders whose proportions are ultimately affected by the occurrence of the central bank interventions. A natural way to do this is to specify a model with switching properties between a chartist and a fundamentalist regimes.

We focus on the dynamics of the USD against the Euro (DEM before 1999) over a period ranging from 1985 to 2003. We work at the bi-weekly frequency. On the one hand, the respective behaviours of the chartists and fundamentalists are clearly identifiable in the medium run. More precisely, typical chartists rule involve computations of moving average ranging from 14 to 200 days (see Neely, 2002 for instance). Fundamentalists basically react to deviations to equilibrium exchange rates which are computed at a macroeconomic frequency. On the other hand, central bank interventions are carried out at an intradaily frequency (the central bank typically reacts to short run exchange rate evolutions — see Neely, 2001) and the official data are available on a daily basis. The choice of the bi-weekly frequency for the data should therefore be seen as a compromise. It more or less matches the frequency that are typically used in previous estimations of this type of models (Vigfusson, 1996; Manzan and Westerhoff, 2007).[10]

[10]The choice of a trading rule based on a moving average pattern involving two months is consistent with the literature devoted to technical trading in the FX market. For instance, Schulmeister (2007) studies the profitability of such trading rules based on moving averages of various lengths. He finds that most of the selected models display a

The estimated model is a two-regime Markov switching model. Each regime captures the behavior of a particular type of agents trading in the FX market. At this stage, the switching properties of the model are not investigated further in the sense that the regime transition probabilities are supposed to be constant over time.[11] We denote e_t as the log of the euro–dollar exchange rate and we define the (bi-weekly) return as $r_t = 100[e_t - e_{t-1}]$.

In the first regime, the chartist regime, in line with the theoretical model, agents are supposed to use only past exchange rate developments to forecast future fluctuations of the currencies. The general specification of the chartist regime is given by:

$$r_{c,t} = C(r_{t-i}) + \varepsilon_{c,t}, \tag{5}$$

where $r_{c,t}$ is the forecasted value of r_t by chartists, $\varepsilon_{c,t}$ is the error term peculiar to chartists and C is the general function used by chartists for the purpose of forecasting.

In contrast to chartists, fundamentalists consider the exchange rate as reacting to misalignments of the current exchange rate level with the fundamental equilibrium value:

$$r_{f,t} = -\psi(e_{t-1} - f_{t-1}) + \varepsilon_{f,t}, \tag{6}$$

where $r_{f,t}$ is the forecasted value of r_t by fundamentalists, $\varepsilon_{f,t}$ is the error term peculiar to fundamentalists, ψ is the parameter used by fundamentalists to forecast the exchange rate using the known value of the exchange rate misalignment and f_{t-1} is the empirical counterpart of the log of the fundamental equilibrium exchange rate. Typically, parameter ψ should be negative in this regime to capture a mean reverting behaviour of the exchange rate towards the fundamental value (depreciation required to correct overvaluation).[12] In the Markov-switching model, the dynamics of the exchange rate

duration of profitable positions between 30 and 60 days. In contrast, trading rules based on short-term trends (say for duration less than 15 days) turn out to be less profitable.

[11]We will relax this assumption mater on in Section 3.4 when we will consider time-varying transition probabilities (TVTP).

[12]Of course, given the fact that the empirical specification slightly deviates from the theoretical model, we relax the assumption that Ψ is comprised between 0 and 1.

is driven by the value of a latent variable l_t that captures whether the prevailing regime is the chartist one ($l_t = c$) or the fundamentalist one ($l_t = f$). The special insight of the first-order Markov-switching model is that the dynamics of l_t is driven by first-order transition probabilities. In the basic Markov Switching model, these transition probabilities are assumed to be constant over time. In the case of two regimes, these transition probabilities are defined as:

$$p = Prob(l_t = c | l_{t-1} = c), \tag{7}$$

$$q = Prob(l_t = f | l_{t-1} = f). \tag{8}$$

In this model, p captures the probability of remaining in the chartist regime from one period to the other. It is therefore a measure of the persistence of the regime from which it is possible to compute theoretically the expected number of periods during which the economy will be in this regime.[13] For the sake of the future extension to the case of time-varying transition probabilities (TVTP), it may be useful to express p and q through a logistic specification of the type:

$$p = 1 - (1 + \exp(\pi_0))^{-1}, \tag{9}$$

$$q = 1 - (1 + \exp(k_0))^{-1}. \tag{10}$$

Notice that if the parameters π_0 and k_0 expressed on the logistic scale take both zero values, then p and q equal 0.5. In this case, the probability of remaining in the regime is equal to the probability of leaving the regime, suggesting that a Markov-switching approach is rather inappropriate to capture the dynamics of the exchange rate return. Although these specification tests may appear rather simple, Hamilton (1996) shows that t-tests applied to the transition probabilities of the type $[\hat{p} - p_0]/\hat{\sigma}_{\hat{p}}$ (where p_0 denotes the value of p under the null and $\hat{\sigma}_{\hat{p}}$ the estimate of the standard error of $\hat{p}$) can be trusted, both asymptotically and in finite samples.[14]

---

[13] Indeed, the respective expected numbers of periods are equal to $1/(1-p)$ and $1/(1-q)$.

[14] Hamilton provides some Monte Carlo analysis for $T = 50$ and $T = 100$, i.e., for much smaller samples sizes than the ones considered here ($T = 498$). The distributions of these t-statistics in small samples are found however to be skewed rightward.

3.2. *Preliminary Investigation*

In order to estimate model (5)–(7), we first need to tackle two points. The first one is the choice of an empirical measure of the fundamental equilibrium exchange rate f_t that plays an important role in the definition of the fundamentalist regime. Previous work (Vigfusson, 1996; Manzan and Westerhoff, 2007) has typically used the PPP value as a measure of the equilibrium exchange rate. However, while interesting, PPP levels capture only one type of equilibrium and rely on the relevance of the law of one price. As an alternative, we use here recent estimates of Bénassy-Quéré *et al.* (2004) of these equilibrium exchange rates. The specific insight of these estimates is that they provide levels consistent with a joint equilibrium of all countries included in their sample (broadly speaking, the OECD countries). Furthermore, the equilibrium value is defined as the one consistent with external and internal balance of these economies.

We first compute for a given year the value of the nominal equilibrium exchange rate for the Eurozone in terms of USD from the misalignment values estimated by Bénassy-Quéré *et al.* (2004) using the average value of the nominal exchange rate over the year. Since we compute misalignment values at much higher frequencies, we smooth this equilibrium value by interpolation in order to get rid of the artificial jumps due to changes of the calendar year. We then compute misalignment levels at the bi-weekly frequency by computing the distance of the (log of) the exchange rate from (the log of) this smoothed value of the equilibrium.[15] Figure 2 plots the evolution of the smoothed misalignment degree of the Euro against the dollar over the sample period (positive values refer to Euro undervaluation). From the figure, one can identify two distinct periods of dollar overvaluation: the first one ranges from the beginning of the sample

[15]As for the exchange rate quotation, we use values observed on Fridays at 21.00 GMT + 1 physical time. This choice ensures that interventions conducted by both central banks during the two last weeks occur before the quotation of the rate, assuming implicitly that these interventions take place on their own local markets. This assumption is supported by the evidence provided by Dominguez (2003) concerning the timings of the reported FX operation.

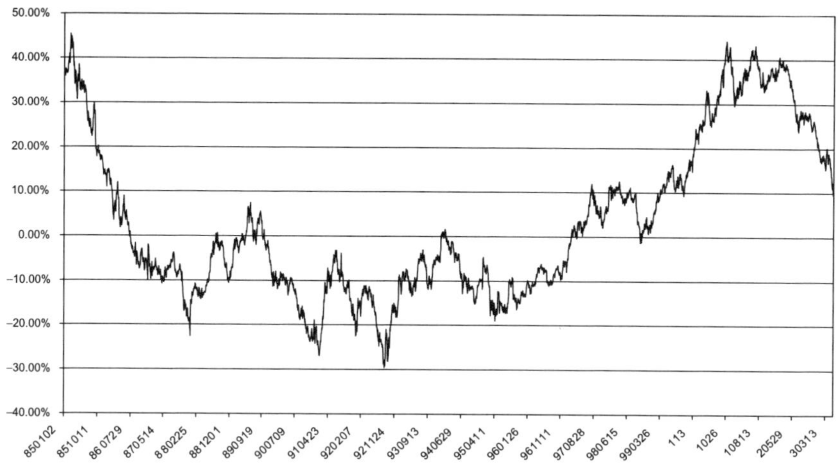

Figure 2. Misalignment of the euro against the US dollar (in percent).

(January 1985) to the end of 1986; the second one begins in mid 1998 and persists until the end of the sample (May 2003).

The second issue is the exact nature of the C function in the chartist regime (Eq. (5)). Chartists are usually reported to use a complex set of moving average rules leading to heterogeneous strategies across agents. This heterogeneity makes the identification of the aggregate chartist forecasting rule quite cumbersome. Since chartist behaviour is not directly observable, there is a large number of admissible specifications for Eq. (5), which need to be evaluated. The retained specification should be therefore selected on the basis of data adjustment. As a preliminary check, we have estimated simple AR-GARCH models of the following type:

$$r_t = r_0 + \sum_{i=1}^{g} \rho_i r_{t-i} - \lambda(e_{t-1} - f_{t-1}) + \varepsilon_t, \tag{11}$$
$$\sigma_t^2 = \omega + \varphi\varepsilon_{t-1}^2 + \eta\sigma_{t-1}^2,$$

where r_t is the return of the DEM/USD exchange rate, σ_t^2 is the conditional variance and r_0, ρ_i, λ, ω, φ and η are parameters to be estimated.[16] We find reasonable evidence of a mean reverting behaviour of r_t towards the equilibrium level with λ equal to a value close to 1.35 and a significance level slightly above 5 percent. We do not find any evidence of significant autoregressive coefficients for g up to 10. This is hardly surprising given that the model is a single regime model capturing some mixture of the dynamics between the chartist and the fundamentalist regimes. Nevertheless, almost all coefficients turn out to be positive, suggesting that agents make use of extrapolative moving average rules capturing the medium-run evolution of exchange rates. Replacing the autoregressive part $\sum_{i=1}^{g} \rho_i r_{t-i}$ by the past cumulated returns $[e_{t-1} - e_{t-(p+1)}]$, we find limited evidence of a positive relationship. In particular, we find that for $g = 4$, this term exhibits a positive relationship with a *p-value* slightly above 10 percent. This might suggest that on average chartists extrapolate returns using a 2-months window. We build on this preliminary evidence to find a suitable specification to Eq. (5) in the chartist regime.

3.3. *The Constant Transition Probabilities Case*

Based on the preliminary evidence and after testing competing models, the retained specification for the chartist equation is:

$$r_{c,t} = \alpha_1(e_{t-1}-e_{t-5})1_{\{|r_{t-1}|<\bar{b}\}}+\alpha_2(e_{t-1}-e_{t-5})1_{\{|r_{t-1}|<\bar{b}\}}+\varepsilon_{c,t}, \quad (12)$$

where 1 is the indicator function taking 1 if the condition within brackets is satisfied, 0 otherwise and $\bar{b}$ is some constant threshold. In this specification, chartists use past exchange rate trends defined over the last four periods (last 2 months) in a non linear way. The extrapolation rate is different whether short run volatility (captured by $|r_{t-1}|$) is below or above some threshold. To measure this threshold $b-$, we choose the average value of $|r_{t-1}|$ over the entire sample.[17] This specification therefore captures the fact that chartists

[16] In order to save place, we do not report the estimated values for r_0, ρ_i, ω, φ, and η but these can be obtained upon request.

[17] Note that given the fact that exchange rate volatility is often clustered over time, $|r_{t-1}|$ will also proxy the contemporaneous level of volatility.

will behave differently whether the level of exchange rate volatility has been relatively high or not.

The Markov-switching regimes are estimated by the Expected Maximum Likelihood (EML) procedure and rests on the Gaussian assumption for the underlying density.

Table 2 reports the estimates of the basic chartist-fundamentalist model for two alternative specifications. Several comments are in order. First, the model estimations clearly identify the fundamentalist regime. The ψ parameter is significantly positive, suggesting a mean-reverting behavior of e_t toward its fundamental value f_t. This finding is highly robust to alternative specifications and to

Table 2. The chartist-fundamentalist model: Euro–USD January 1985–May 2003.

	(1)	(2)
α_1	0.018	—
	[0.039]	
α_2	0.987*	1.007*
	[0.510]	[0.529]
ψ	1.574**	1.592**
	[0.785]	[0.778]
σ_c^2	2.583***	2.605***
	[0.235]	[0.246]
σ_f^2	1.658***	1.665***
	[0.161]	[0.160]
π_0	2.620***	2.516***
	[1.238]	[1.214]
K_0	2.687***	2.658***
	[0.916]	[0.869]
P	0.932***	0.925***
	[0.078]	[0.084]
q	0.935***	0.935
	[0.055]	[0.053]
N obs	981	981
Log Lik	−1042.9	−1043.03

Standard errors of EML estimates in brackets. S.E. of p and q computed with the delta method.
*Refers to significance at 10 percent.
**Refers to significance at 5 percent.
***Refers to significance at 1 percent.

the extension of the model to time-varying transition probabilities (see Section 3.4). Second, the model estimates suggest that in the chartist regime, agents tend to extrapolate past trends only when the short-run volatility is relatively high ($\alpha_2 > 0$). The p-value of this parameter is slightly above the 5 percent significance level (p-values of 5.3 percent and 5.7 percent for respectively specification (1) and specification (2)). In contrast, when the level of short-run volatility is historically low, chartists see the exchange rate as following a random walk: α_1 is insignificantly different from zero and is therefore excluded in the second specification (last column in Table 1). These results suggest that the chartist regime is at best non stabilizing for the exchange rate and can be even destabilizing in relatively turbulent markets. Importantly, the results are consistent with the theoretical framework in which chartists are supposed to follow a positive feedback rule.

3.4. *The Role of Interventions*

3.4.1. *The TVTP model*

In specification (9) and (10), the transition probabilities of remaining in a particular regime depend only on the previous state of the economy (l_{t-1}), i.e., the nature of the regime prevailing during the previous period. One possibility to capture the impact of exogenous variables is to make these transition probabilities dependent on these variables. In our analysis, we introduce central bank interventions that take place during the two preceding weeks. While specific, this extension is consistent with the theoretical model exposed in Section 2. Indeed, in the chartists-fundamentalists framework, the dynamics of the exchange rate is intrinsically related to the proportion of each type of agents. These proportions depend primarily on the profitability of the respective forecasting rules. In turn, the relative profitabilities are affected by the occurrence of the central bank interventions in the FX markets. As a result, as suggested by the simulation outcomes, the proportions of chartists and fundamentalists are affected by the central bank purchases and sales of foreign currency.

To implement the TVTP estimation, we follow Filardo (1994) and use a logistic specification. In this case, denoting by $I_{i,t-1}$ intervention of type i which has taken place between $t-1$ and t and building on Eqs. (9) and (10), we extend the chartist-fundamentalist model as:

$$p = Prob(l_t = c|l_{t-1} = c, I_{i,t-1}) = 1 - (1 + exp(\pi_0 +_{i=1}^{m} \pi_i I_{i,t-1})^{-1}, \tag{13}$$

$$q = Prob(l_t = f|l_{t-1} = f, I_{i,t-1}) = 1 - (1 + exp(k_0 +_{i=1}^{m} k_i I_{i,t-1})^{-1}. \tag{14}$$

The full model is made of Eqs. (6)–(14).

3.4.2. *CBI data*

The central bank intervention data used in this paper are direct purchases and sales of foreign currencies carried out by the Fed and the Bundesbank (ECB after the inception of the Euro) over the period ranging from January 1, 1985 to May 31, 2003.[18] We use daily official interventions, i.e. interventions released by the central banks themselves. These exclude false rumours of interventions. Given the available statistical information, there are several ways through which one can capture the activity of central banks in the FX markets.

First, one can measure central bank's activity through the total amounts sold or purchased on the markets. As an alternative, one can capture the presence of these central banks by either dummy variables or by the total number of intervention days over the period under investigation. Here, we disregard the amounts and use the

[18]We do not consider the BoJ interventions on the YEN/USD market for two important reasons. First, unlike the ECB or the Fed, it is very unlikely that the BoJ interventions aim at reducing the degree of exchange rate misalignment. For instance, over the second part of the investigation period, a lot of BoJ interventions have been conducted in a unsterilized way to raise inflation expectations, in line with the suggestions of Svensson (2001) among others. Second, unlike for the Fed and the BB, most recent interventions of the BoJ were secret, i.e., unreported to the FX traders. See Beine and Lecourt (2004) on this. This means that the signalling and the coordination channels that are central to our analysis cannot be operative for those interventions.

latter approach. Second, we use official data. However, using the mere number of official daily intervention days might be misleading in the sense that the exact number of interventions over the two previous weeks might also be unknown. As a result, we use two alternative measures. The first one computes the number of official intervention days over the two previous weeks by a given central bank. The second one uses a dummy variable capturing whether a particular central banks was active or not in the market during the previous period.

A final point concerns the distinction between concerted and unilateral operations. This distinction stems from two reasons. First, there is some evidence that coordinated operations might exert different impacts from unilateral interventions. The signalling theory that emphasizes the information content embedded by these operations also implies such an asymmetric effect. Nevertheless, this distinction has been especially relevant for studies using high frequency data and it is less clear that such a decomposition is needed when using bi-weekly data. From a statistical point of view, the distinction between concerted and unilateral operations also allows to reduce the observed degree of correlation between the intervention variables and to reduce the problems of multicollinearity (see Beine *et al.*, 2003 for some extensive evidence on weekly data). This high degree of correlation is due to the important proportion of concerted operations observed especially during the first part of the sample. This is particularly important when measuring central bank activity by the total number of intervention days over the previous period. As a result, we use two alternative measures of central bank activity. As a first measure, we use the number of intervention days of both central banks (ECB and the Fed), whether they are coordinated or not. As a second measure, we disentangle these operations into unilateral operations of each central bank and concerted operations.

3.5. *The Results*

Table 3 reports the estimation results of the full chartists-fundamentalists model with transition probabilities depending on the central bank interventions $I_{i,t-1}$. Each column reports the results

Table 3. FX interventions in the chartist-fundamentalist model: Euro–USD, January 1985–May 2003.

	(1)	(2)	(3)	(4)
α_1	−0.009	0.003	0.009	−0.006
	[0.039]	[0.030]	[0.032]	[0.040]
α_2	0.800	0.890**	0.834*	0.925*
	[0.535]	[0.438]	[0.430]	[0.504]
ψ	1.759***	1.996***	1.972***	1.592***
	[0.645]	[0.653]	[0.652]	[0.635]
σ_c^2	2.699***	2.555***	2.538***	2.723***
	[0.221]	[0.166]	[0.154]	[0.192]
σ_f^2	1.812***	1.709***	1.700***	1.775***
	[0.103]	[0.121]	[0.122]	[0.089]
π_0	4.331***	3.921***	3.966***	4.928***
	[0.767]	[0.780]	[0.819]	[1.087]
π_1 [Fed, c]	0.363	−0.071	—	5.093
	[0.599]	[0.414]		[4.934]
π_2 [ECB, c]	−0.924**	−0.830**	−0.891**	−3.989***
	[0.439]	[0.383]	[0.372]	[1.453]
π_3 [Coord, c]	—	−0.644	−1.157	−3.809**
		[0.551]	[1.064]	[1.760]
κ	6.066*	4.723***	4.784***	16.576
	[3.212]	[1.815]	[1.673]	[40.207]
κ_1 [Fed, f]	−2.423	−0.395	—	−16.375
	[2.005]	[0.433]		[40.163]
κ_2 [ECB, f]	−0.086	−1.051	−0.200	−15.247
	[0.923]	[0.990]	[0.682]	[40.207]
κ_3 [Coord, f]	—	−1.060	−1.807	−15.078
		[0.681]	[1.220]	[40.211]
Nobs	981	981	981	981
Log Lik	−1041.35	−1040.13	−1040.68	−1040.13
p-Value LRT	0.27	0.47	0.34	0.09

obtained with a different measure for $I_{i,t-1}$. Column (1) reports the results obtained with central bank activity measured by the total number of intervention days of the Fed (268 intervention days) and the Bundesbank (318 intervention days). As expected, given the share of coordinated interventions (161 intervention days) this results in a high degree of correlation (0.724), which may lead to imprecise estimates of the impact. This degree of correlation is very much reduced when measuring central bank activity by the number of unilateral and concerted operations.[19] The results specific to this specification are reported in column (2) of Table 3. Results of column (3) are obtained with the same specification, with the unilateral Fed interventions excluded to increase efficiency. Finally, results of column (4) are obtained with central bank activity captured by dummies rather than by the number of intervention days over the previous two-week period.[20]

On the whole, we find that the occurrence of interventions has induced some increase in the proportion of fundamentalists, especially when these operations took place when the chartist regime prevailed. Indeed we find that the transition probability of remaining in the chartist regime significantly decreases as a result of the occurrence of the FX interventions. This is the case for the Bundesbank interventions ($\pi_2 < 0$). We observe the same effect for coordinated interventions when central bank activity is captured through a single dummy variable (see $\pi_3 < 0$ in column 4). This may suggest that traders pay attention to the fact that the central banks were active during the past two weeks rather than to the pure number of occurrences of this type of operation.[21] Importantly, we do not find any evidence of some effect of interventions driving the exchange rate towards a value consistent with the chartist dynamics.[22]

We find evidence in favor of efficiency for the unilateral operations of the Bundesbank and to a lesser extent the concerted interventions. In contrast, the unilateral operations of the Fed display weak effects

[19]The correlation between concerted operations and unilateral Fed interventions (resp. BB interventions) amounts to 0.286 (resp. 0.391). The correlation between unilateral operations of the Fed and those of the Bundesbank is equal to 0.131.

[20]Using this measure, we observe 54, 45 and 62 occurrences for respectively the concerted, the Fed and the Bundesbank interventions.

[21]Once more, it should be stressed that traders are not necessarily able to observe the total number of operations in the short run. This is especially the case during the first part of the sample in which the quality of news wire services was relatively lower.

[22]For the central bank interventions taking place when the fundamentalist regime prevails, while negative, the impact is never significant due to the very high value of uncertainty obtained in the parameter estimation. This is for instance striking in column 4 of Table 2 (see k_1 k_2 and k_3 parameters). Such a blowing up of the standard deviation might reflect that very few interventions occur when such a regime prevails, leading to very poor estimations of these parameters.

in terms of the dynamics of chartists and fundamentalists. In the theoretical model, the adoption of an intervention rule that aims at reducing the degree of misalignment results in higher efficiency compared to interventions conducted in a random way. Almekinders and Eijffinger (1996) find that the Bundesbank intervened in reaction to deviations of the exchange rate from the CB target. To the extent that this target is similar to the equilibrium exchange rate, this suggests that the Bundesbank did not behave very differently compared with the representative central bank in the theoretical model. As for the recent period, the three unilateral interventions of the ECB in November 2000 took place when the Euro was obviously undervalued with respect to the dollar. While Almekinders and Eijffinger (1996) also found that the Fed adopted a leaning-against-the-wind policy before 1990, they also document a stronger reaction of the US authorities to exchange rate volatility. This suggests that the Fed is less keen to adopt a specific intervention rule aiming at reducing the degree of misalignment. This behaviour was confirmed in the nineties during which the official motivation to intervene was more to react to market disorders.[23]

To sum up, we find that if there is some effect of these operations at a 2-weeks horizon, the purchases or sales carried out by the central bank tend to push the exchange rate in a direction consistent with the fundamentals. This can be interpreted to mean that interventions were on average effective in the medium run. This contrasts with the usual claim that interventions are not effective (and even counterproductive) since they hardly manage to move the exchange rate in the intended direction.

4. Conclusion

This paper aims at revisiting the issue of effectiveness of central bank interventions in the FX market. As an alternative to what has been used in the literature, we define an effective operation as the one

[23]Interestingly, the quarterly report on the Treasury and Federal Reserve foreign exchange operations issued after the last intervention in 2000 states that the reason to intervene in support of the Euro was the prevailing excess exchange rate volatility.

driving the exchange rate closer to its fundamental value. To this aim, we analyse the effects of a central bank intervention rule within a theoretical framework capturing the interaction of the behaviour of chartist and fundamentalist traders in the FX market. The intervention is found to affect the relative profitability of the strategies developed by both type of agents, leading to an increase in the proportion of fundamentalist traders and hence a market exchange rate closer to the fundamental level.

We empirically assess the effectiveness of the interventions and focus on the effects of the operations carried out by the ECB (Bundesbank before the inception of the Euro) and the Federal Reserve in the Euro/USD market. We test to what extent the occurrence of the central bank interventions tended to affect the transition probabilities relative to the chartist and the fundamentalist regime. We find some evidence that in the medium run, the occurrence of some unilateral and to a lesser extent coordinated interventions led to a decrease in the proportion of chartists. To the extent that the chartist traders are found to extrapolate past exchange rate movements to forecast future values, we find that the interventions have the effect of bringing the exchange rate more in line with a value consistent with the fundamentals in the economy.

We take the view that our criterion of effectiveness of interventions is consistent with the general objectives pursued by central banks. It abstracts from simple criteria used before like the contemporaneous impact that can be inconsistent with the medium run goals followed by monetary authorities. Interestingly, while the bulk of previous studies often concluded against the effectiveness of the central bank interventions in the short run, our findings tend to give more support in favour of a reasonable degree of effectiveness in the medium run.

References

Almekinders, GJ and SCW Eijffinger (1996). A friction model of daily Bundes bank and federal reserve interventions. *Journal of Banking and Finance*, 20, 1365–1380.

Bhattacharya, U and P Weller (1997). The advantage of hiding one's hand: Speculation and central bank intervention in the FX market. *Journal of Monetary Economics*, 39, 251–277.

Beine, M, A Bénassy-Quéré and C Lecourt (2002). Central bank intervention and foreign exchange rates: New evidence from FIGARCH estimations. *Journal of International Money and Finance*, 21, 115–144.

Beine, M, S Laurent and C Lecourt (2003). Central bank intervention and exchange rate volatility: Evidence from a regime switching analysis. *European Economic Review*, 47(5), 891–911.

Beine, M and C Lecourt (2004). Reported and secret interventions in the foreign exchange markets. *Finance Research Letters*, 1(4), 215–225.

Bénassy-Quéré, A, P Duran-Vigneron, A Lahréche-Revil and V Mignon (2004). Burden sharing and exchange rate misalignments within the group of twenty. CEPII Working Paper No. 2004-13.

Cheung, Y-W and MD Chinn (2001). Currency traders and exchange rate dynamics: A survey of the US market. *Journal of International Money and Finance*, 20(4), 439–471.

De Grauwe, P and H Dewachter (1995). A chaotic model of the exchange rate: The role of fundamentalists and chartists. *Open Economies Review*, 4, 351–379.

De Grauwe, P and M Grimaldi (2006a). Exchange rate puzzles: A tale of switching attractors. *European Economic Review*, 50, 1–33.

De Grauwe, P and M Grimaldi (2006b). *The Exchange Rate in a Behavioural Finance Framework*. Princeton, NJ: Princeton University Press.

Dominguez, KM (2003). The market microstructure of central bank intervention. *Journal of International Economics*, 59, 25–45.

Fatum, R and MM Hutchison (2003). Is sterilized foreign exchange intervention effective after all? An event study approach. *The Economic Journal*, 113, 390–411.

Filardo, AJ (1994). Business cycles phases and their transitions. *Journal of Business and Economics Statistics*, 12, 299–308.

Frankel, JA and K Froot (1987). Using survey data to test standard propositions regarding the exchange rate expectations. *American Economic Review*, 77(1), 133–153.

Hamilton, JD (1996). Specification testing in Markov-switching time-series models. *Journal of Econometrics*, 70, 127–157.

Humpage, O (2003). Government intervention in the foreign exchange market. Working Paper No. 03-15, Federal Reserve Bank of Cleveland.

Manzan, S and F Westerhoff (2007). Heterogeneous expectations, exchange rate dynamics and predictability. *Journal of Economic Behavior and Organization*, 64(1), 111–128.

Miller, M and J Williamson (1987). *Targets and Indicators: A Blueprint for the International Coordination of Economic Policy* (*Policy Analyses in International Economics*). Washington, DC: Institute for International Economics.

Neely, CJ (2001). The practice of central bank intervention: Looking under the hood. *Federal Reserve Bank of Saint-Louis Review*, 83(3), 1–10.

Neely, CJ (2002). The temporal pattern of trading 1 rule returns and exchange rate interventions: Intervention does not generate technical trading profits. *Journal of International Economics*, 58(1), 211–232.

Neely, CJ (2004). The case for foreign exchange intervention: The government as a long-term speculator. Federal Reserve Bank of Saint-Louis Working Paper, November.

Obstfeld, M and K Rogoff (2000). The six major puzzles in international macroeconomics: Is there a common cause? NBER Working Paper No. 7777, July.

Payne, R and P Vitale (2003). A transaction level study of the effects of central bank interventions on exchange rates. *Journal of International Economics*, 61, 331–352.

Reitz, S and MP Taylor (2008). The coordination channel for foreign exchange intervention: A nonlinear microstructural analysis. *European Economic Review*, 55, 55–76.

Schulmeister, S (2007). Performance of technical trading systems in the YEN/Dollar Market. WIFO Working Paper No. 291/2007.

Svensson, LEO (2001). The zero bound in an open economy: A foolproof way of escaping from a liquidity trap. *Monetary and Economic Studies*, 19(S-l), 277–312.

Vigfusson, R (1996). Switching between chartists and fundamentalists: A Markov regime-switching approach. Bank of Canada Working Paper No. 96-1.

Vitale, P (1999). Sterilized central bank intervention in the foreign exchange market. *Journal of International Economics*, 49(3), 245–269.

PART II

MONETARY INTEGRATION

Chapter 7

Conditions for Monetary Integration: A Geometric Interpretation

Paul De Grauwe

1. Introduction

In recent years an important literature has developed on the conditions for a successful monetary integration of individual countries.[1] This literature has emerged partly as a result of the realization that the mere fixing of exchange rates is insufficient to guarantee a successful process of monetary integration.

The purpose of this paper is to set up a framework that allows for a systematic analysis of the conditions for a successful monetary integration. This analysis will be developed under two alternative assumptions concerning the inflation-unemployment trade-off. In a first version of the model the neo-Keynesian (Phillips curve) assumption will be used. In a second version the "monetarist" assumption is postulated. The purpose of this dual approach is to find out how these two views of the world affect the feasibility of a monetary union. In addition, it allows us to go one step further than the traditional

Published in *Weltwirtschaftliches Archiv*, 111, 634–646, 1975.
This paper was written as part of a project on European Monetary Unification financed by the Belgian Government. I am grateful to Frank Boll, Michele Fratianni, Theo Peeters, Jozef Vuchelen and the members of the EMU workshop at the Centrum voor Economische Studiën of the University of Louvain for valuable criticism and comment. This paper also benefited from comments received from a referee of this journal.
[1]A well-known survey is W. M. Corden (1972).

literature on the subject which is heavily influenced by the Phillips-curve assumption.[2]

The analysis will be made using a two-country framework. The advantage of a two country model is its simplicity. In addition, for the purposes of this paper two countries is really all what is needed. The generalization to n countries would not add anything substantial.

The model will be developed using graphical tools. It is evident that algebraic techniques could be used as well.

2. Monetary Integration in a Phillips-Curve World

In Figure 1, the basic model is represented. The north-east quadrant shows the Phillips curve of country 1; the south-east quadrant represents the Phillips curve of country 2. The positions and the

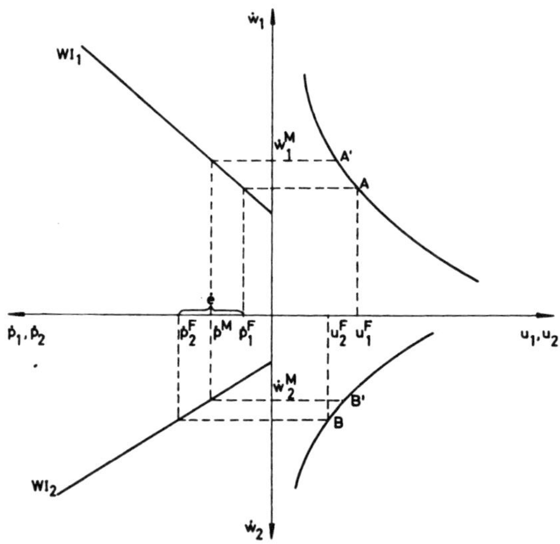

Figure 1. Monetary Union in a Phillips-curve world.

Notes:
u_1, u_2 = unemployment rate in country 1 resp. country 2
$\dot{w}_1, \dot{w}_2$ = rate of change of wages in country 1 resp. country 2 $\left(\dot{w} = \frac{1}{w}\frac{dw}{dt}\right)$
$\dot{p}_1, \dot{p}_2$ = rate of change of prices in country 1 resp. country 2
$\dot{e} = \dot{p}_2^F - \dot{p}_1^F$ = the rate of depreciation of currency 2

[2]See Fleming (1972).

slopes of these two curves, in general, will be different. The national authorities are assumed to have a particular preference ordering between unemployment and wage rate changes.[3] For instance, the authorities of country 1 determine that point A on the Phillips curve would maximize welfare in country 1. Similarly, the authorities of country 2 select point B as such a preferred point on their trade-off curve. Assuming that this selection of optimal points is more than pure wishful thinking, that is, that these points can be attained and maintained during a long enough period of time, they will determine the pairs of unemployment and wage rate changes in the two countries.

The north-west and south-west quadrants determine the inflation rates which correspond with the wage rate changes respectively in country 1 and country 2. This relationship between rates of changes of prices and wages is captured by the lines WI_1 and WI_2. The parameters which determine the specific form of these curves are the share of labor in the total product, the rate of productivity increase, and the degree of competition in the labor and product markets. Assuming perfect competition, WI_1 and WI_2 are straight lines with slopes equal to 1 in absolute value.[4] The intersection of WI_1 with the y-axis is determined by the rates of change of the labor share ($\dot{\alpha}_1$) and of the productivity of labor ($\dot{q}_1$). Assuming that the labor share is constant, the intercept of WI_1 is equal to the rate of change of productivity in country 1.[5] In Figure 1 this intercept is positive because it is assumed that the productivity change in country 1 is positive. In a similar way the intercept of WI_2 reflects the rate of change of productivity in country 2 ($\dot{q}_2$). In the following, it will be assumed that the rate of growth of productivity in country 1 is higher than in country 2. Therefore in Figure 1 the intercept of WI_1 is larger in

[3]This preference ordering is sometimes represented by a set of "social indifference curves" concave to the origin. This has not been done here. The process through which a national preference ordering comes about has been left unspecified.

[4]Using a Cobb–Douglas production function the competitive equilibrium relation between rates of change in prices and in wages can be shown to be $\dot{p} = \dot{w} - \dot{\alpha} - \dot{q}$, where α is the share of labor in total product and q is the average labor productivity.

[5]From footnote 2 it follows that with a constant labor share in country 1 $\dot{p}_1 = \dot{w}_1 - \dot{q}_1$. The intercept is found by setting $\dot{p} = 0$. One then has $\dot{w}_1 = \dot{q}_1 > 0$.

absolute value than the intercept of WI_2. This also implies that for a same wage rate increase in both countries the equilibrium price increase will be lower in country 1 than in country 2.

The model represented in Figure 1 illustrates how the two countries differ with respect to (a) the positions of their Phillips curves, (b) their rates of productivity growth, and (c) the preference of the two governments between unemployment and inflation. These differences explain why, in the absence of a monetary union, inflation rates in the two countries will be equal *only by accident.* In Figure 1, country 1 has an inflation rate which is lower than the inflation rate in country 2. It is therefore inevitable that the currency of country 2 depreciates vis-à-vis the currency of country 1. If this is allowed to happen, the system is in equilibrium and both countries are able to attain their targets represented by points A and B. In Figure 1 the equilibrium rate of depreciation of currency 2 is represented by $\dot{e} = \dot{p}_2^F - \dot{p}_1^F$.

Suppose now a monetary union is instituted between country 1 and 2. This implies that the exchange rate is irrevocably fixed, or, equivalently, that inflation rates in both countries cannot diverge. Thus one must have that $\dot{p}_1 = \dot{p}_2 (\dot{e} = 0)$.[6]

[6]This assumes absence of non-traded goods. If these are introduced, an irrevocably fixed exchange rate then only implies identical price changes of traded goods. Changes in the general price index in the two countries will diverge, if productivity growth rates diverge. Using the so-called Scandinavian model one can derive the equilibrium relation between the measured inflation rates in the two countries under monetary union ($\dot{e} = 0$). This turns out to be

$$\dot{p}_1 - \dot{p}_2 = \eta_1 [\dot{q}_{T_1} - \dot{q}_{N_1}] - \eta_2 [\dot{q}_{T_2} - \dot{q}_{N_2}] \tag{1}$$

where η_1 and η_2 are the shares of non-traded goods in gross domestic product in country 1 and 2, respectively; $\dot{q}_T$ and $\dot{q}_N$ are the productivity growth rates in the traded and non-traded goods sectors, respectively. Assuming equal shares η_1 and η_2 and equal growth rates of productivity in the non-traded goods sectors, this simplifies to

$$\dot{p}_1 - \dot{p}_2 = \eta [\dot{q}_{T_1} - \dot{q}_{T_2}] \tag{2}$$

Thus, the measured inflation rate in country 1 will exceed the measured inflation rate in country 2 if the growth rate of productivity in the traded goods sector in country 1 exceeds this growth rate in country 2. From (1) and (2) it is clear that the difference in inflation rates between the two countries is parametrically given. The introduction of (1) or (2) into our model would change its detail, but not its essence. For more detail on the Scandinavian model see e.g. Aukrust (1970).

From Figure 1 it is immediately evident which *minimum* condition must be satisfied for this arrangement to be feasible. Assuming a union inflation rate, $\dot{p}^M$, lying between the national inflation rates in the absence of monetary union, both countries will have to accept a combination of unemployment and inflation which is suboptimal from their national point of view.[7] It is conceivable, however, that one country imposes an inflation rate on the other. This would allow the former to maintain an optimal mix of inflation and unemployment, however, at the expense of the other country. The latter would have to accept that unemployment and inflation diverge even further from the nationally preferred one.

From the previous analysis a first conclusion emerges. A monetary union can only be maintained, if the national authorities abstain from setting national targets for the inflation-unemployment mix.[8] This condition is also sufficient, as long as the divergent movement in real wages (reflecting the difference in productivity growth) is left unhampered. In that case, no balance of payments problem can occur. The slow-productivity-growth country will be as "competitive" as the high-productivity-growth country because it accepts a lower increase in real wages.

The monetary union represented in Figure 1, therefore, implies unbalanced growth between country 1 and country 2. It has by now become widely accepted that in the long run this is an unacceptable arrangement, i.e., that monetary union should be accompanied by "balanced growth" between the countries joining in the union. The reason for this requirement of balanced growth is obvious. If the divergence in the growth rates of real income is left unchecked, pressures will build up which ultimately must lead to large scale movements of labor towards the high-productivity-growth countries. The costs, for individual countries, associated with such movements

---

[7]This point is elaborated in Fleming, *op. cit.*

[8]It is sometimes said that national authorities should bring their individual preferences for the trade-off between inflation and unemployment closer together. This is clearly not necessary. Cases could be imagined in which it would be necessary to let those preferences diverge in order to make a monetary union possible. Such cases will occur when the differences in productivity and/or in labor market conditions are large.

are, rightly or wrongly, deemed to be unacceptably high. It follows that if monetary union is to be accompanied by balanced growth, the condition that national authorities abstain from pursuing national targets for the inflation-unemployment mix is no longer sufficient (although still necessary). Much more is required. What is it?

Essentially, the requirement is that the curves WI_1 and WI_2 shift, so that at a given union inflation rate, changes in nominal wages and therefore real wages are equalized in the two countries. This is shown in Figure 2 where the WI_1 and WI_2 curves have shifted so as to satisfy the condition of equal wage rate change.

These shifts can be attained in two different ways. A first possibility is to introduce transfer payments from country 1 to country 2, without affecting the productivity growth rates. Redefining $\dot{w}_1$ and $\dot{w}_2$ as growth rates of nominal wages after tax (or subsidy), the downward shift of WI_1 is obtained by a wage tax in country 1, and the "upward" shift of WI_2 by a wage subsidy in country 2. Equilibrium is obtained when the fiscal transfer is such that net wage rate changes are equalized in the two countries.

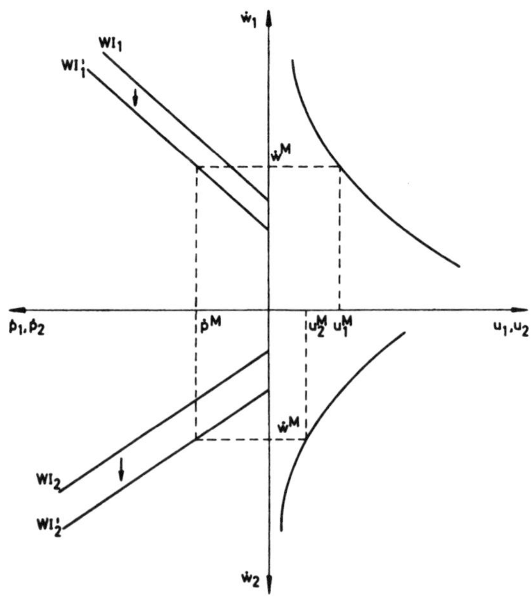

Figure 2. Monetary union cum balanced growth in a Phillips-curve world.

A second possibility is to introduce policies aimed at equalizing the growth rates of productivity of the two countries. A discussion of the kinds of policies required for such an equalization of productivity growth rates is outside the scope of this paper.[9] Two observations, however, should be made here. First, from the experience with regional policies in national context it is not clear that *effective* instruments of regional equalization of productivity growth exist, at this moment. If it cannot be established, with a reasonable degree of certainty, that regional policies on an international scale can be made to work effectively, a monetary union among countries with significantly different productivity growth rates is too much to hope for (except if one is willing to use transfer-payments from the high- to the low-productivity-growth country). Second, if equalization of the growth rates of productivity implies a reduction of the growth rate in the high-productivity-growth country, a monetary union will not look very attractive to the latter. Its decision to join the union then will depend on whether other benefits associated with a monetary union compensate for this loss in real income growth.

An important side issue arises as to how wage bargaining by labor unions affect the problems discussed until now. Suppose the introduction of a monetary union between the two countries leads to a unification of the trade unions. The question then is how wage bargaining should be conducted. Two cases can be considered.

The first case is the one in which productivity growth rates have been effectively equalized. In that case it is seen from Figure 3 that bargaining for equal wage rate changes on a union wide basis is a necessary condition for the monetary union to survive. If in country 1 the labor unions bargain for a higher nominal wage rate change, say $\dot{w}_1'$, than in country 2, a fixed exchange rate cannot be maintained, except if country 2 agrees to make transfer payments to country 1, so as to allow the residents of country 1 to enjoy a higher growth rate of real income. In terms of the model presented in Figure 3, these

[9]For such discussion see e.g., Study Group on Economic and Monetary Union, *European Economic Integration and Monetary Unification*, Commission of the European Communities, Brussels, October 1973.

transfer payments would have the effect of shifting WI_1 upwards and WI_2 downwards (northwards).

In the second case one starts with a monetary union without having equalized the productivity growth rates. As is shown in Figure 1 the necessary condition for the monetary union to survive, then, is that the trade unions bargain for different nominal wage rate changes in the two countries, i.e., for $\dot{w}_1^M$ and $\dot{w}_2^M$ respectively, reflecting the differences in productivity growth rates. If unions in both countries bargain for the same nominal wages, fixed exchange rates cannot be maintained, except if transfer payments are made from country 1 to country 2. These transfer payments would allow the residents of country 2 to enjoy the same living standard as country 1, however, without changing the underlying differences in real productivity growth rates.

Until now two kinds of monetary union have been described: a monetary union without a balanced growth requirement and a monetary union *cum* balanced growth. Conceivably a third kind of monetary union could be aimed at. This would be a monetary union *cum* balanced growth *cum* equal unemployment rates. It is evident from the model (see e.g., Figure 3) that a monetary union with balanced growth does not imply that unemployment rates are equalized in the two countries. True, shifts in the WI_1 and WI_2 curves affect the position of the respective Phillips curves. There is, however, no guarantee that policies aimed at equalizing productivity changes will tend to convergent shifts of the Phillips curves. Therefore, if the equalization of unemployment rates is deemed to be an essential part of any program for monetary union, additional policies aimed at equalizing conditions in the national labor markets will be necessary, so as to move the Phillips curves into the same position.

3. Monetary Integration in a Friedman-Phelps World

In recent years the concept of a trade-off between inflation and unemployment has come under increasing attack. It has been realized that if such a trade-off exists it must be of a very short-term nature. Too short to be of any use for policy makers.

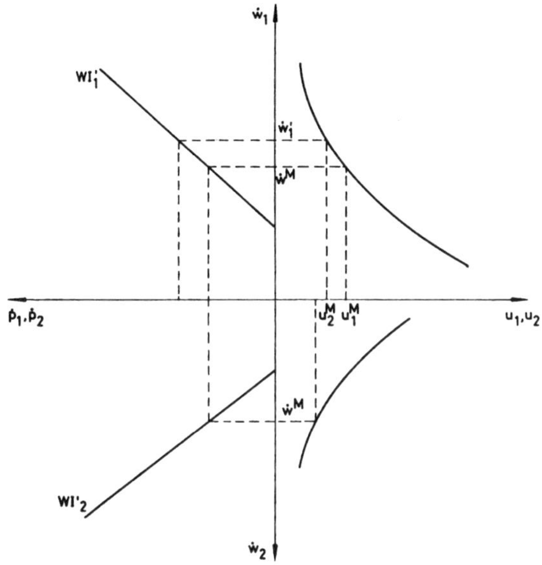

Figure 3. Monetary union and wage bargaining.

In the Friedman-Phelps view of the world the unemployment rate is independent of the rate of inflation, taking a time horizon exceeding the very short run. The unemployment rate is determined by "real" factors. Any attempt at fixing the unemployment rate below its "natural" rate will be self defeating and engender a process of *accelerating* inflation. The "Phillips curve" can conveniently be represented by a vertical line.

How does this view of the world affect the main issues discussed in the previous section? In Figure 4, the two country model is represented, assuming that the "Phillips curve" is vertical. This implies, of course, that national governments have been convinced that the rate of unemployment cannot be fixed at a level different from the natural rate, by manipulating the rate of monetary expansion.[10] If national authorities have attained such wisdom, it can easily be shown that

[10]A different model would result in the situation where national authorities do try to fix such an unemployment level using monetary policy, despite the fact that the underlying "Phillips curve" is vertical.

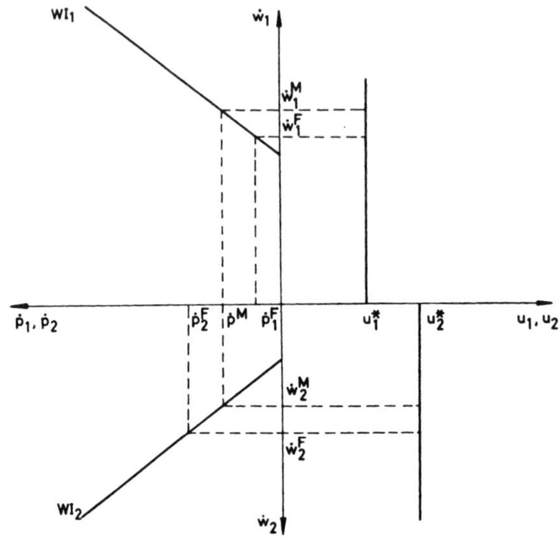

Figure 4. Monetary union in a Friedman–Phelps world.

Notes:
u_1^x, u_2^x = the natural rate of unemployment in country 1 resp. country 2. This is represented to be lower in the high-productivity-growth country, without thereby implying that this is a necessary outcome.

monetary union of the unbalanced growth variety can be realized without cost.

From Figure 4, it is clear that flexible rates allow the national authorities to determine their national rates of inflation independently. The exchange rate change (the depreciation of currency 2 in Figure 4) makes the two national inflation rates compatible. If the two countries join in a monetary union, they lose this power to determine the domestic rates of inflation independently. It will be clear, however, that there is no real cost in terms of employment associated with this loss of independence. The higher rate of inflation in country 2 ($\dot{p}_2^F$) does not "buy" less unemployment, as the latter is fixed at its natural rate. Nor does it allow country 2 to enjoy a higher growth rate in real income. The authorities of country 2 could fix the domestic inflation rate at the level of country 1's inflation rate ($\dot{p}_1^F$) without a loss in employment or in real income. It obviously follows that an agreement to join in a monetary union (i.e., to fix a common rate of inflation) does not introduce a loss of welfare for any of the two countries.

This conclusion can also be rephrased as follows. If national governments abstain from using monetary policies to influence the rate of unemployment and instead use monetary policy to control the domestic rate of inflation, they can as well decide on fixing a common rate of inflation. Monetary union in such a world is a costless operation.

Does this conclusion also hold for a monetary union *cum* balanced growth? From Figure 4, it is seen that it does not. The fixing of a common rate of inflation does not preclude a divergent movement in the rates of growth of nominal wages (and therefore of real wages). If this is to be avoided, transfer payments or policies aimed at bringing productivity growth rates in line would be necessary. These policies would have to be identical to the policies required to make a monetary union *cum* balanced growth feasible in a Phillips-curve world. A similar conclusion holds if monetary union implies, besides balanced growth, the equalization of the "natural" rates of unemployment. Again, additional policy instruments would have to be introduced so as to integrate the conditions in the different national labor markets.

As far as trade union integration is concerned, the same conclusion as in the previous section applies. As long as differences in productivity growth exist trade union bargaining for identical growth rates of nominal wages would be inappropriate. If these differences disappear, trade union bargaining for identical growth rates of nominal wages becomes a necessary condition for a successful monetary integration.

4. Conclusion

In this paper, a framework was set up to systematically analyze the minimum conditions for a monetary union to be feasible. Two kinds of monetary union were distinguished. Monetary union *tout court* and monetary union *cum* balanced growth.

In order to make the former possible, the necessary condition in a Phillips-curve world is that national authorities abstain from independently selecting points on the inflation-unemployment trade-off. The costs of this requirement are likely to be perceived as high by national authorities. If the world is a monetarist one (in the sense of a vertical Phillips curve) the necessary condition for the attainment of monetary union of the unbalanced variety is the equalization of national inflation rates. If in such a world the monetary authorities have been convinced that it is pointless to try to peg the unemployment rate at anything different than the natural rate and that monetary policy should be used exclusively to control the inflation rate, monetary union can be obtained without cost. By a suitable choice of monetary growth rules national inflation rates can be made to coincide.

The requirements for monetary union with balanced growth are obviously more stringent. In addition to the previous conditions such a monetary union requires a policy of transfers between countries and/or a policy aimed at equalizing national productivity growth rates. These requirements are identical whether in a Phillips-curve world or in a monetarist world.

Finally, differences in nominal wage rate changes in the monetary union should reflect differences in productivity growth rates. In other words, if labor unions bargain for equal nominal wages across countries, despite differences in productivity, the monetary union cannot survive without institutionalizing a policy of financial transfers from the high- to the low-productivity-growth country.

References

Aukrust, O (1970). PRIM I: A model of the price and income distribution mechanism of an open economy, *Review of Income and Wealth*, 16(1), 51–78.

Corden, WM (1972). *Monetary Integration.* Essays in International Finance, No. 93, Princeton, NJ.

Marcus Fleming, J (1971). On exchange rate unification. *The Economic Journal*, 8, 467.

Chapter 8

Is Europe an Optimum Currency Area? Evidence from Regional Data

Paul De Grauwe and Wim Vanhaverbeke

1. Introduction

The traditional theory of optimum currency areas, as developed by Mundell (1961), has identified the conditions under which a monetary union between regions or countries will work smoothly.[1] In a nutshell this theory says that when regions or countries are subjected to different disturbances (asymmetric shocks) the adjustment process will require either real exchange rates to adjust, or factors of production to move, or a combination of these two. In the absence of real exchange-rate flexibility and factor mobility, regional or national concentrations of unemployment will be inevitable.

The theory of optimum currency areas has also established a presumption that in a monetary union the adjustment mechanism will rely more on factor mobility than on real exchange-rate flexibility. Of course, in a monetary union the real exchange rates of regions can

Published in PE Masson and MP Taylor (eds.), *Policy Issues in the Operation of Currency Unions*, pp. 111–129. Cambridge, UK: Cambridge University Press (1993).
This paper is produced as part of a CEPR research programme on "Financial and Monetary Integration in Europe" supported by a grant from the Commission of the European Communities under its SPES Programme (No. E8900105/RES). We are grateful to Veerle Vermeulen for research assistance, and to Jürgen von Hagen and Ivo Maes for useful comments and suggestions.

[1]See also McKinnon (1963), Kenen (1969).

change, because of divergent regional movements of prices.[2] However, it is likely that the regional adjustment process following asymmetric shocks will rely less on these relative price changes than on mobility of labor. Exactly the opposite holds for countries with separate currencies. The presumption here is that more of the adjustment to asymmetric shocks will take the form of real exchange-rate changes than of labor mobility. The reason is that countries can change their nominal exchange rates (for a fundamental contribution see Vaubel, 1976 and Meltzer, 1986).

The purpose of this chapter is twofold. First it aims at contrasting the nature of the adjustment mechanism between regions of the same country, and between countries in Europe. Is this presumption as described by their theory of optimum currency areas correct?

Second, we want to find out whether the occurrence of asymmetric shocks is different as between regions of the same country and nations in Europe. Recently the European Commission (1990) has forcefully argued that further economic integration of Europe will reduce the likelihood of asymmetric shocks in European countries. If this is so, it may not matter much whether there is sufficient real exchange-rate flexibility and labor mobility. European countries may form a monetary union without fear that they will face large adjustment costs, because they will typically face the same shocks with similar effects in all countries. In this chapter we provide some evidence that can shed light on this issue. More particularly, we systematically compare the divergent movements of regional and national output and employment trends. We will ask the question of whether output and employment changes tend to be more asymmetric between countries than between regions of the same country. This issue of the asymmetry of shocks has recently been analyzed by several researchers (see Cohen and Wyplosz, 1989; Weber, 1990; EC-Commission, 1990; Eichengreen, 1990). The value added of the present chapter is that it contrasts the experience of regions with those of countries in Europe (for a similar recent study see von Hagen and Neumann, 1991).

[2]A recent paper by Poloz (1990) provides evidence that changes in these regional exchange rates in Canada are substantial.

In Sections 2 and 3 we focus the attention on the nature of the regional and national adjustment processes by presenting data on real exchange-rate variability (Section 2) and labor mobility (Section 3). In Section 4 we study the occurrence of asymmetric shocks by analyzing the degree of regional and national dispersion of output and employment trends. Finally in Section 5 the implications for economic and monetary union in Europe are drawn.

2. Real Exchange-Rate Variability — Regional and National

In this section, we compare systematically the degree of real exchange-rate variability of regions (within countries) and of countries.

Definitions and data

We concentrate our attention on the real exchange rates using *unit labor costs* as the price variable. We chose this definition because of data availability: using unit labor costs allowed us to cover a wider group of countries and regions than if we had used other price variables. In addition the unit labor cost is the most comprehensive measure of competitiveness.

For each country we define the real (effective) exchange rate as follows:

$$R_{it} = \sum_{j} \alpha_{ij}(S_{ijt}.P_{jt}/P_{it}) \tag{1}$$

where R_{it} is the real effective exchange rate of country i in period t; S_{ijt} is the nominal exchange rate of currency i with respect to currency j in period t expressed as an index; P_{jt} and P_{it} are the unit labor costs of country j and i respectively; α_{ij} is the weight of currency j in the effective exchange rate of country i, as measured by the share of trade of country j in country i's total trade.

In a similar way we define a real effective exchange rate of a region k in a particular country as follows:

$$R_{kt} = \sum_{m} \alpha_{km}(P_{mt}/P_{kt}) \tag{2}$$

Note that, since the currency is the same in that country, the nominal exchange rate is irrevocably fixed and drops out of the formula. Note also that α_{km} is defined here as the weight of region m in the effective exchange rate of region k. In this case of regional exchange rates we used the shares of region m in the total GDP of the country.[3]

The regional data come from Eurostat, *Banque de données régionales*. We used regional data of Germany, France, Spain, the UK, and the Netherlands. For the regions of the other countries we lacked the necessary data on unit labor costs. This yielded data of fifty regions during the sample period 1977–1985. (As a result of the limitations of regional data, this is the longest sample period that could be constructed.) The complete list of these regions is given in the appendix.

The data source of the national data is OECD, Economic Outlook. We used data of the following countries: Belgium, Denmark, France, Germany, Greece, Italy, Japan, the Netherlands, Portugal, Spain, the United Kingdom, and the United States.

Measures of real exchange-rate variability

We computed different measures of real exchange-rate variability. At first one aims at capturing the long-run variations of the real exchange rates. This measure should give us an idea of whether these real effective exchange rates of countries and regions have a tendency to move in a trend-like fashion or whether they return to some constant value.[4] We define this variability concept (LVR) as follows:

$$LVR = \sum_{i=1} \frac{1}{n}\frac{1}{m}\frac{|R_{i,tn} - R_{i,t0}|}{R_{i,t0}}$$

where n is the length of the period expressed in years, $R_{i,to}$ and $R_{i,tn}$ are the real exchange rates in the beginning and at the end of the period (respectively), and m is the number of countries (regions).

Two other measures of variability concentrate on the short-term movements of the real exchange rates. The first one is the mean of

[3]This implies that in Equation (2) $a_{km} = a_m$ for all k.

[4]It would have been more appropriate to use unit root tests. However, the limited number of (yearly) observations precluded such an approach.

the absolute yearly changes of the real exchange rate (MAYC). The second one is defined as the standard deviation of the yearly changes of the real exchange rate (SDYC).

Empirical results

In Table 1, we present the results of computing the average variability of the real exchange rates during 1977–1985.

We observe that the variability of the real exchange rates of nations is about twice as large as the one observed at the regional level.[5] In order to test for the significance of these differences, we computed t-ratios testing differences in the mean. The results are presented in Table 2.

Table 1. Real exchange-rate variability (in yearly percentage change).

Countries	Whole sample (1977–1985)	EMS (1977–1985)
Long-run variability:		
LVR	2.01	1.99
Short-run variability:		
MAYC	4.4	3.3
SDYC	4.5	3.6

Regions in	W. Germany (1977–1988)	Spain (1980–1985)	Netherlands (1977–1988)	UK (1980–1985)
Long-run variability:				
LVR	0.4	1.0	0.7	0.7
Short-run variability:				
MAYC	0.8	1.8	2.2	1.6
SDYC	0.9	1.9	1.5	1.6

Notes: MAYC is the mean absolute yearly change.
SDYC is the standard deviation of yearly changes.
Sources: The national data are from OECD, Economic Outlook.
The regional data are from Eurostat, Banque de données régionales.

[5]We also observe that the degree of variability of the regional exchange rates in West Germany is substantially lower than the one observed in other countries. We return to the differences between German regions and the other regions in Europe in a later section.

Table 2. Real exchange-rate variability (1980–1985): Tests of significance of differences in the mean.

Variability measures	Mean value		t-ratio
	Regions	Countries	
Long-run variability:			
LVR	0.75	2.01	−3.0
Short-run variability:			
MAYC	1.76	4.70	−4.4
SDYC	1.70	4.84	

Notes: See Table 1.
Sources: See Table 1.

The results of Table 2 confirm that the differences in the mean between regions and countries are significant. All the t-ratios indicate that these differences are significant at the 1 percent level. Thus, during the sample period 1977–1985 the long-run variability of the real exchange rates between regions of the same monetary union tended to be less than half as large as the one observed between sovereign nations. The same holds for the short-run variability measures.

Since the group of countries in the sample involve both EMS and non-EMS countries we also wanted to find out whether this significant difference between regional and national exchange-rate variability may not be affected by the fact that the real exchange-rate variability in the non-EMS countries was very high. We therefore computed the same average variability measures restricting ourselves to the EMS countries and the regions in EMS countries. The results are given in Table 3.

As expected, we observe from Table 3 that the variability of the real exchange rates is lower in the EMS than in the non-EMS countries. However, the difference between regional and national variability measures remains and is of a similar order of magnitude as in the previous table.

3. Regional and National Labor Mobility

The degree of labor mobility is an important factor in determining the nature of the adjustment when asymmetric shocks occur in

Table 3. Real exchange-rate variability: Tests of significance of differences in the mean.

Variability measures	Mean value		t-ratio
	EMS-Regions	EMS-Countries	
Long-run variability			
LVR	0.55	1.99	−3.4
Short-run variability			
MAYC	1.58	2.82	−1.9
SDYC	1.24	3.09	

Notes: See Table 1.
Sources: See Table 1.

regions or in countries. In this section we contrast the evidence about labor mobility between regions of the same country and between countries.

Our measure of labor mobility between regions will be the flow of migrants in one region from and to the other regions expressed as a percent of the population of the former region. Thus this measure is the sum of the immigrant and emigrant *flows* of a particular region (as a percent of the population of that region). Table 4 presents these measures of regional mobility for a number of European countries.

Table 4 allows to note some striking differences in inter-regional mobility of European countries. The two southern countries, Spain and Italy, have a much lower degree of inter-regional mobility than northern countries such as Germany, the UK, and France.

These differences are not due to aggregation bias, i.e., the size of the regions in these countries is approximately the same. This cannot be said of the smaller countries in the sample, whose regions are typically much smaller than regions in the larger countries. The smaller size of regions in small countries helps to explain the greater degree of inter-regional labor mobility observed in these countries. For West Germany we have also computed the same measures of inter-regional mobility after excluding the three "city-states" of the Federal Republic (Bremen, Hamburg, and West Berlin). These cities experience a much higher degree of mobility. The results are presented between brackets.

Table 4. Average flows of immigrants plus emigrants of regions to and from the rest of the country.

(as a percent of population of the region)

	1975	1980	1987	1975–1987 (yearly average)
Belgium	0.92	0.89	0.84	0.87
Denmark	1.29	1.12	1.17	1.17
W. Germany	1.32	1.33	1.07	1.21
	(1.06)*	(1.06)*	(0.85)*	(0.98)*
Spain	N.A.	0.40	0.46	0.36
France	1.24	1.15	N.A.	1.20
Italy	0.78	0.68	0.53	0.66
Netherlands	2.02	1.63	1.66	1.68
UK	N.A.	1.51	1.81	1.54

Notes: N.A. = not available.
* = these numbers exclude the German "city-states" Bremen, Hamburg, and West Berlin.
Source: Eurostat, Banque de données régionales.

The differences in the intensity of inter-regional mobility of labor between the south and the north of Europe is surprising. It is surprising because the regional differences in per capita income tend to be higher in the south than in the north.[6] These differences would tend to produce larger migratory flows in the south than in the north of Europe. The perception of a high inter-regional mobility in the south and a low one in the north does not correspond to the facts.

We next compare the inter-regional mobility measures of Table 4 to similar *inter-country* mobility measures in Europe. We could not find yearly *flow* data of inter-country mobility, however. Instead we had to rely on *stock* figures in a given year. These stock figures express the total number of migrants of a given country to and from the rest of the Community (as a percent of the population of the former country). Thus, these numbers have to be interpreted as the *cumulative flows* of all the preceding years. The results are given in Table 5. Due to data limitations we could only construct data for the original EC countries.

[6]See, e.g., EC Commission (1990) for evidence of regional disparities of income per capita.

Table 5. Stock of a country's immigrants plus emigrants from and to the rest of the EC, in 1984. (as a percent of population of the country)

Belgium	1.59
W. Germany	0.57
France	0.41
Italy	0.72
Netherlands	0.70
EC-6 average	0.64

Source: Calculations based on Straubhaar (1988).

Comparing Table 5 with Table 4 leads to the following conclusion. The migratory flows between regions of the same country are low and of a different order of magnitude than those between countries of the Community. This can be seen from the fact that the stock data of Table 5 are smaller (on average) than the yearly flow data of Table 4. If the average length of stay of migrants in EC countries is, say, ten years, this would imply that the yearly flows of migrants between the EC countries is less than one tenth of the yearly flow of migrants between regions.

The results presented so far can be summarized as follows. Adjustment mechanisms that can be relied upon to absorb shocks in regions and countries in Europe differ significantly. European countries experience a significantly higher degree of real exchange-rate variability than European regions. Conversely, regions experience a degree of labor mobility that is much higher than the one observed between countries in Europe. It is fair to say that the latter is almost absent as an adjustment mechanism.[7] These results confirm the presumption of the traditional optimum currency theory.

We have also observed that the degree of inter-regional mobility of labor is higher in the north than in the south of Europe (Spain and

[7]These results confirm the recent empirical studies of Eichengreen. See Eichengreen (1990b). In a recent study von Hagen and Neumann (1991) came to similar conclusions. However, from their study it appears that the degree of real exchange-rate variability among a core group of countries (Germany, Benelux, Austria) has declined significantly during the eighties.

Italy). We will take up this point when we consider the implications for European monetary unification.

4. Asymmetric Shocks in Regions and in Countries

The theory of optimum currency areas stresses that when asymmetric shocks occur, regions of an "optimal" monetary union are likely to adjust mainly by migration of the labor force, whereas countries that are not part of an "optimal" monetary union will rely more on real exchange-rate changes to adjust to those shocks. The empirical evidence discussed in the previous sections seems to confirm this traditional view.

Much of the recent discussion of the issue whether the EMS countries should form a monetary union has focused on the question whether large asymmetric shocks are likely to occur in a future European monetary union. If these are unlikely to happen, the lack of labor mobility between EMS countries may not matter much.

The recent European Commission's report "One Market, One Money" has taken a strong stand on this issue. It argues that the continuing economic integration in the Community will make the EC countries more alike, so that asymmetric shocks will become less important. The existing instruments of policy will be able to deal with these disturbances (see EC Commission, 1990, p. 136).

A major difficulty in identifying asymmetric shocks is that we only observe their effects on some endogenous variable (e.g., output and employment). These variables, however, are also influenced by economic policies. As a result, divergent movements in these variables can be evidence both of exogenous asymmetric shocks and of different national economic policies.

In this section we present some data on regional output and employment growth and compare these with the corresponding national data.

Regional and national output growth

Table 6 presents some evidence about divergencies in the growth rates of output between regions and between countries. We compute

Table 6. Short-term and long-term divergencies in regional and national growth rates of output.

(in yearly percentage change)

	Long-run divergence	Short-run divergence
Countries (76–90)		
Whole sample	0.48	1.66
EMS	0.48	
Regions in		
France (76–86)	0.78	2.04
W. Germany (76–86)	0.51	1.09
Netherlands (76–86)	0.71	3.85
Spain (81–86)	1.45	3.59
UK (76–88)	0.72	1.40

Note: The long-run divergence of regions is defined as the standard deviation of the average regional growth rates over the relevant periods. For nations we have the same definition. The short-run divergence is defined as the average of the yearly standard deviations of the regional (resp. the national) growth rates.
Sources: The national data are from OECD, Economic Outlook. The regional data are from Eurostat, Banque de données régionales.

measures of short-term and of long-term variability. As our measure of short-term regional divergencies of output growth, we take the average of the yearly standard deviations of the regional growth rates of output. We do the same for the short-term divergencies of national output growth.

As our measure of the long-term divergencies we compute the standard deviation of the average growth rate of regional output. We use a similar measure of long-term divergencies in growth rates of countries. Thus, this measure gives us insight into the question of whether long-term growth rates tend to diverge more between countries than between regions.

The results of Table 6 lead to some surprising conclusions. It appears that the long-run divergencies in *national* growth rates are substantially lower than the long-run divergencies in *regional* growth rates. Thus, regions belonging to the same countries in Europe tend to have a more unequal development of their output than nations.

As far as the short-term divergencies in growth rates are concerned, we find that there are fewer differences between regions and countries. The short-term deviations of the regional and the national growth rates are of comparable orders of magnitude.

We also note the special position of West Germany, where the regional dispersion of growth rates (both long-run and short-run) is small in comparison of what one observes in other countries.

Regional and national employment growth

In this section, we present data on the regional and national dispersion of the growth rates of employment. We use the same measures of dispersion as in the previous section. The results are presented in Table 7. Note that the sample of countries is not the same as in Table 6. This has to do with the different availability of regional employment data.

The conclusions that can be drawn from Table 7 are almost identical to the ones derived from Table 6. The long-fun dispersion of employment growth between regions of the same country is substantially larger than the dispersion of these growth rates between countries. For the short-term measures of dispersion we do not find the same pronounced difference between regions and countries.

Note again the special position of West Germany, which experiences a much more balanced regional development of employment than most other countries. Noteworthy is also the fact that the regional dispersion of employment growth is particularly pronounced in the southern European countries (Spain and Italy). Earlier we noted that the regional labor mobility is relatively low in these southern countries. These two features (unbalanced regional growth in employment and low mobility of labor) helps to explain the relatively large regional concentration of unemployment in these southern European countries. We show some evidence in Table 8. The differences between the north and the south of Europe are striking. The regional dispersion of unemployment appears to be much more

Table 7. Short-term and long-term divergencies in regional and national growth rates of employment.

(in yearly percentage change)

	Long-run divergence	Short-run divergence
Countries (1976–1990)		
Whole sample	0.30	1.13
EMS	0.26	
Regions in		
W. Germany (76–87)	0.38	0.63
France (76–87)	0.38	0.70
Italy (84–87)	0.89	2.18
Spain (81–88)	2.00	2.88
UK (82–86)	0.96	1.11

Note: The long-run divergence of regions is defined as the standard deviation of the average regional growth rates over the relevant periods. For nations we have the same definition. The short-run divergence is defined as the average of the yearly standard deviations of the regional (resp. the national) growth rates.

Table 8. Regional unemployment rates in 1989.

(in percent)

	Standard deviation	Maximum	Minimum	Difference
France	2.4	14.7	6.7	8.0
W. Germany	2.3	10.9	3.2	7.7
Great Britain*	2.3	10.5	4.0	6.5
Italy	6.4	21.8	4.1	17.7
Spain	4.5	26.5	13.7	12.8

Note: *Contrary to the data on the United Kingdom in the previous tables, the data in this table exclude Northern Ireland.
Source: Eurostat, Banque de données régionales.

substantial in Spain and especially in Italy as compared to Germany and Great Britain.

5. Real Exchange-Rate Flexibility and Asymmetric Shocks

In a previous section, we observed that the degree of real exchange-rate flexibility between regions of the same country is (on average) smaller than between countries. This, however, does not imply that real exchange-rate movements have no role to play in the regional adjustment process. In this section we provide some additional empirical evidence highlighting the role of real exchange-rate changes. We computed the correlations between variability measures of real output and of real exchange rates, for both regions and countries. We did the same exercise with employment. The results are shown in Tables 9 and 10.

We observe that the regional variability of output is relatively well correlated with the regional variability of the real exchange rates. The surprising thing is that this correlation is stronger and

Table 9. Correlations between measures of dispersion in real exchange rates and growth rates of output.

	Short-run	Long-run
All countries and regions	0.27**	0.23*
All countries	−0.03	−0.16
All regions	0.73***	0.28*
Regions in		
Germany	0.60**	0.07
Spain	0.79***	0.47**
Netherlands	0.95***	−0.2
UK	−0.41	0.18

Notes:
*** = significant at 1 percent level.
** = significant at 5 percent level.
* = significant at 10 percent level.
Source: Eurostat, Banque de données régionales.

Table 10. Correlations between measures of dispersion in real exchange rates and growth rates of employment.

	Short-run	Long-run
All countries and regions	0.22*	0.06
All countries	0.53*	0.10
All regions	0.50***	0.17
Regions in		
Germany	0.03	0.04
Spain	0.53**	−0.07
Netherlands	0.20	0.44
UK	−0.38	0.27

Notes:
*** = significant at 1 percent level.
** = significant at 5 percent level.
* = significant at 10 percent level.
Source: Eurostat, Banque de données régionales.

more significant at the regional than at the national level.[8] This suggests that, although the regional variability of real exchange rates is relatively small, it nevertheless plays a significant role in regional adjustment.

The correlations between the variability of real exchange rates and employment is much weaker. In addition, no strong differences are observed between the regional and the national correlations.

On the whole the evidence of Tables 9 and 10 suggests that real exchange rates do play some role in the adjustment process at the regional level. Regions experiencing large disturbances in real output tend to have relatively large movements in their real exchange rates. This is consistent with the hypothesis that asymmetric regional disturbances are absorbed by regional changes in the real exchange rates. And, since nominal exchange rates are fixed between regions, this can also be seen as evidence that relative prices play a role in the adjustment process. It is clear, however, that this evidence can only

[8]The EC Commission (1990) also found no evidence of a significant relationship between real exchange-rate changes and national growth rates of output. See EC Commission, 1990, p. 147.

be called suggestive. Correlation coefficients do not tell us anything about the direction of the causality. These correlations can also be interpreted to mean that relative price shocks cause variability in output and employment.

The evidence of this section adds some nuance to the presumption of the traditional optimum currency theory. It suggests that real exchange-rate changes continue to play a role in the adjustment process of regions. This has also been found by researchers in the context of other regions (see Poloz, 1990, for the Canadian provinces).

In this connection it is important to stress that there is evidence (which is not revealed by our correlation analysis) that real exchange-rate changes have also been quite important in the adjustment process of individual EMS countries, that have chosen to limit the changes in their nominal exchange rates. Countries like Belgium and the Netherlands, for example, allowed significant real depreciations of their currencies of 20–30 percent to occur during the early part of the eighties. These real depreciations were instrumental in the adjustment process of these countries following asymmetric shocks to which these countries were subjected at the start of the eighties.[9]

It is fair to conclude from this empirical evidence that real exchange-rate changes (relative price changes) will continue to play a role in regional adjustment in the future.

6. Conclusion: Implications for EMU

In this chapter we have presented descriptive statistics about regions and countries in Europe. This statistical analysis helps us to shed some light on the question of whether Europe is an optimal currency area. Our main findings are the following.

First, we have found that the presumption of the optimum currency theory holds for Europe provided some nuances are made. At the level of regions of the same country (monetary union) labor mobility plays a role in the adjustment process. Although the degree

[9]See De Grauwe and Vanhaverbeke (1990) for case studies of Belgium and the Netherlands.

of real exchange-rate flexibility between regions is limited, it does appear to play some role in the adjustment process of regions. At the national level, there is almost no labor mobility but significantly more exchange-rate variability. As the EMS moves toward monetary union the question arises whether and to what extent the smaller reliance on real exchange-rate flexibility can be compensated for by more labor mobility.

Second, there is no evidence that asymmetric shocks occur less at the regional than at the national level. The opposite seems to be the case. We found larger and more sustained divergencies of the growth rates of output and employment at the regional level than at the national level. Thus, national growth rates of output and employment tend to diverge less than the same growth rates at the level of regions of the same countries.

This evidence can lead to two interpretations about the prospects of a future EMU in Europe. One is optimistic, the other is pessimistic. The optimistic view, which can also be found in the recent "One Market, One Money" report of the EC Commission, is that the low occurrence of asymmetric shocks at the national level (which we find in our paper) makes it possible to move ahead with monetary union without one having to fear that major adjustment problems will arise in the future. In this view, as economic integration moves forward, the occurrence of asymmetric shocks will even decline in the future, reducing the adjustment costs.

There is, however, also a pessimistic interpretation of our results. Regions of the same country today are certainly more economically integrated with each other than countries in the Community. The large occurrence of asymmetric shocks at the regional level observed today suggests that economic integration does not make the occurrence of asymmetric shocks less likely. The opposite seems to be the case. Thus, a future EMU in Europe may be confronted with the same kind of divergencies in national output and employment trends as the one observed today at the regional level. This may lead to major changes in the adjustment process between countries, and may force labor mobility to play a greater role than it does today.

This more pessimistic view of the integration process stresses that the latter typically leads to regional concentration and agglomeration effects.[10] As a result, shocks that affect one particular industry also tend to have concentrated effects on particular regions. The experience of the US tends to confirm this view. The economic integration in the US is certainly more advanced than the integration achieved in the Community. At the same time one observes that the regional concentration of industrial production is much more pronounced in the US than in Europe (see Krugman, 1990, for evidence). As a result, sectoral shocks (say in the automobile industry, or in the textile industry) have pronounced regional effects, and require major regional adjustment efforts.

The interesting aspect of this phenomenon is that one finds evidence of relatively strong divergence of economic developments of highly integrated regions both at a relatively disaggregated level (i.e., regions within existing European countries) and at a more aggregated level (regions in the US of the size of existing European countries). This suggests that, if European countries integrate further, they are likely to move toward a model in which asymmetric shocks become more rather than less important.

Third, there are clearly two models of regional development in Europe. One is northern as typified by West Germany, the other is southern. The northern model of regional development is balanced. It involves a relatively large regional mobility of labor and low divergencies in output and employment. As a result, regional unemployment rates are relatively uniform. The southern model is one where labor is relatively immobile, divergencies in output and employment are relatively pronounced, and large regional concentrations of unemployment exist.

The major issue is to what model the monetary union in Europe will tend to converge. Neither of the two models will be without costs for individual countries. The northern model appears most attractive.

[10]For a recent formalization of this view see Krugman (1990). There are of course older writers who have stressed these effects of integration. See Giersch (1949), Myrdal (1957), and Scitovsky (1958).

One should bear in mind, however, that this model involves a sizeable amount of regional labor mobility. Thus, if this is the model to which Europe converges, relatively large movements of labor between countries will be necessary. The southern model does not require so much mobility of labor. It does lead to large regional divergencies in unemployment rates.

Which of the two models of monetary union will prevail in Europe is difficult to predict. If the mobility of labor between countries cannot be increased sufficiently, the southern model of monetary union may prevail. In that case not all regions and countries in Europe will profit from monetary union.

Appendix: List of Regions

BR Deutschland

Rl1	Schleswig-Holstein
R12	Hamburg
R13	Niedersachsen
R14	Bremen
R15	Nordrhein-Westfalen
R16	Hessen
R17	Rheinland-Pfalz
R18	Baden-Württemberg
R19	Bayern
R1A	Saarland
RIB	Berlin (West)

France

R21	Ile de France
R22	Bassin Parisien
R23	Nord-Pas-de-Calais
R24	Est
R25	Ouest
R26	Sud-Ouest
R27	Centre-Est
R28	Méditerranée
R29	Départements d'Outre-Mer

Italia

R31	Nord Ovest
R32	Lombardia
R33	Nord Est
R34	Emilia-Romagna
R35	Centro
R36	Lazio
R37	Campania
R38	Abruzzi-Molise
R39	Sud
R3A	Sicilia
R3B	Sardegna

Nederland

R41	Noord-Nederland
R42	Oost-Nederland
R47	West-Nederland
R45	Zuid-Nederland

United Kingdom

R71	North
R72	Yorkshire and Humberside
R73	East Midlands
R74	East Anglia
R75	South East
R76	South West
R77	West Midlands
R78	North West
R79	Wales
R7A	Scotland
R7B	Northern Ireland

Espana

RB11	Galicia
RB12	Asturias

RB13	Cantabria
RB21	Pais Vasco
RB22	Navarra
RB23	Rioja
RB24	Aragon
RB41	Castilla-Leon
RB42	Castilla-La Mancha
RB43	Extremadura
RB51	Cataluña
RB52	Comunidad Valenciana
RB53	Baleares
RB61	Andalucia
RB62	Murcia
RB63	Ceuta Y Melilla

References

Balassa, B (1961). *The Theory of Economic Integration.* New York, NY: Irwin.

Cohen, D and C Wyplosz (1989). The European monetary system: An agnostic evaluation. In *Macroeconomic Policies in an Interdependent World*, R Bryant, D Currie, J Frenkel, P Masson and R Portes (eds.), pp. 311–337. Washington, DC: International Monetary Fund.

De Grauwe, P and W Vanhaverbeke (1990). Exchange rate experiences in small EMS countries: Belgium, Denmark and the Netherlands. In *Choosing an Exchange Rate Regime: The Challenge of Smaller Industrial Countries*, V Argy and P De Grauwe (eds.). International Monetary Fund, Washington.

Eichengreen, B (1990a). One money for Europe? Lessons from the US currency Union. *Economic Policy*, 10, 117–187.

Eichengreen, B (1990b). Is Europe an optimum currency area? CEPR Discussion Paper No. 478, November.

European Commission (1990). One market, one money. European Economy, No. 44, October.

Giersch, H (1949). Economic union between nations and the location of industries. *Review of Economic Studies*, 17, 87–97.

Kenen, P (1969). The theory of optimum currency areas: An eclectic view. In *Monetary Problems of the International Economy*, R Mundell and A Swoboda (eds.). Chicago: University of Chicago Press.

Krugman, P (1990). Geography and trade. Gaston Eyskens Lectures, University of Leuven.

McKinnon, R (1963). Optimum currency areas. *American Economic Review*, 53, 717–725.

Meltzer, A (1986). Size, persistence, and interrelation of nominal and real shocks. *Journal of Monetary Economics*, 17, 161–194.

Mundell, RA (1961). A theory of optimum currency areas. *American Economic Review*, 51(4), 657–665.

Myrdal, G (1957). *Economic Theory and Underdeveloped Regions*. London, UK: Duckworth.

Poloz, S (1990). Real exchange rate adjustment between regions in a common currency area. In *Choosing an Exchange Rate Regime: The Challenge of Smaller Industrial Countries*, V Argy and P De Grauwe (eds.). International Monetary Fund, Washington.

Scitovsky, T (1958). *Economic Theory and Western European Integration*. Stanford, CA: Stanford University Press.

Straubhaar, T (1988). International labour migration within a common market: Some aspects of the EC experience. *Journal of Common Market Studies*, 27(1), 45–62.

Vaubel, R (1976). Real exchange rate changes in the European community: The empirical evidence and its implications for European currency unification. *Review of World Economics (Weltwirtschaftliches Archiv)*, 112, 429–470.

von Hagen, J and M Neumann (1991). Real exchange rates within and between currency areas: How far away is EMU? Discussion Paper No. 62, Indiana Center for Global Business, April.

Weber, A (1990). Emu and asymmetries and adjustment problems in the EMS: Some empirical evidence. CEPR Discussion Paper No. 448, August.

Chapter 9

Setting Conversion Rates for the Third Stage of EMU

Paul De Grauwe and Luigi Spaventa

1. Introduction

According to plans, the third stage of Monetary Union in Europe should start on January 1, 1999. After that date the exchange rates of the currencies of the participating countries will be irrevocably fixed, bilaterally and against the Euro, the single European currency. The decision on these conversion rates will be taken some time between the day when the decision about membership is announced and the starting day of the third stage of EMU.

In this chapter, we shall examine how the irrevocably fixed conversion rates can be set. In the next section, we shall first recall the few provisions of the Maastricht Treaty on the conversion procedure. They say little and set only one precise constraint: that the conversion procedure should not alter the external value of the

Published in *BNL Quarterly Review*, 201, 131–146, 1997.

This paper was presented on Match 10, 1997 to a meeting of the Consultative Group on the impact of the introduction of the euro on capital markets, instituted by the European Commission, Directorate General II.

The authors are grateful to Francesco Giavazzi, Maurice Obstfeld and Charles Wyplosz for their comments on an earlier draft. This version also benefits from the comments received at a seminar at the Europcn Monetary Institute.

ecu,[1] which, as decided by the Madrid Council, will be converted one to one into the euro. We shall then examine the (very) wide set of options which are apparently available. In Section 3, we shall show that, if there are currencies in the ecu basket that do not participate to the single currency, a whole subset of that set is incompatible with the Treaty provision on the external value of the ecu: conversion rates of the participating currencies cannot be set in advance in terms of the ecu, nor can they be set at the last moment in terms of central ERM ecu rates, without affecting (except in two wholly implausible cases) the external value of the ecu. The only possibility of setting euro rates for the inside currencies is to adopt as conversion rates the market ecu rates of those currencies on the last day before the start of the third stage: we argue that this is economically undesirable. Fixing instead bilateral conversion rates (no matter when and how) and then accepting the market value of the ecu as the euro conversion rate restores a degree of freedom and is compatible with the constraint on the external value of the ecu, as we argue in Section 4. There we also show that one of the rules, proposed for defining such rates — the so-called Lamfalussy rule — has undesirable consequences. Pre-announcing bilateral rates meets with two problems. First, market bilateral rates on the last day before the start of the third stage must have converged to the pre-announced rates in order to avoid a jump in the external value of the ecu. Second, a recent Council regulation on the legal framework for the use of the euro seems, if interpreted strictly, to rule out the possibility of fixing bilateral rates *and then* deriving the euro conversion rates: if this interpretation prevailed, the only undesirable choice left would be that of setting the euro conversion rates at the ecu market values on December 31, 1998. In Section 5, we propose a multi-stage solution to these two problems that is compatible with the Council regulation: announcement that the euro conversion rate will be set equal to the ecu market rate on the last day and a parallel agreement on the

[1]For a discussion of the different possible interpretations of this constraint see Kenen (1995). We will interpret this to mean that the conversion on January 1, 1999 should not lead to a change in the *external* value of the ecu from its level reached at the close of December 31, 1998.

desired structure of bilateral rates (arguably the central EMS rates) of the inside currencies. In the interim period the market bilateral rates should be steered towards previously agreed upon values.

2. The Treaty and the Options

2.1. *The Treaty*

The Maastricht Treaty states that: "At the starting date of the third stage [of Monetary Union], the Council shall, acting with the unanimity of the Member States without a derogation, on a proposal from the Commission and after consulting the ECB, adopt the conversion rates at which their currencies shall be irrevocably fixed and at which irrevocably fixed rate the ecu shall be substituted for these currencies, and the ecu will become a currency in its own right. This measure shall by itself not modify the external value of the ECU" (Article 1091 (4)).

The Madrid European Council of December 1995 confirmed "unequivocally that [the third] stage will commence on 1 January 1999 [...;] decided to name the single currency the 'Euro' [...] instead of the generic term 'ECU' used by the Treaty to refer to the European currency unit" and decided that "in the case of contracts denominated by reference to the official ECU basket of the European Community [...] substitution by the Euro will be at the rate one to one, unless otherwise provided by the contract." The Annex to the conclusions of the Madrid Council, on "the scenario for the changeover to the single currency," added that from January 1, 1999 "the Euro will be 'a currency in its own right' and the official ECU basket will cease to exist."

2.2. *The Options*

No decision has been taken so far on how the irrevocable conversion rates of the currencies of the member states fulfilling the conditions for admission will be set. The choice spans over several dimensions, so that a wide number of options is apparently available.[2]

[2]For a useful description of some options, see Arrowsmith (1996) and Gros and Lannoo (1996).

There is, first, a time dimension. By June 1998, at the latest, it will be known which member states are admitted to the third stage and hence for which currencies the irrevocable conversion rates are to be fixed. Conversion rates can be pre-announced before the latter date, or be announced on the eve of the third stage. In the latter case a method for setting the rates at the last moment may or may not be pre-announced.

Second, the conversion rates of the currencies of member states without a derogation, which from now on we shall call in-currencies, can be fixed bilaterally or in terms of the ecu. While fixed ecu rates imply a set of bilateral parities, the reverse is not true as long as there are currencies which are in the ecu basket but do not participate to the single currency.

A third dimension regards the choice of the conversion rates, be they bilateral or ecu rates. An obvious alternative is between central rates as defined in the exchange rate mechanism of the EMS, on the one hand, and, on the other, market rates, at the time of announcement, or on the last day before the irrevocable locking. Other possibilities are however conceivable and have been aired. The best known is the so-called Lamfalussy rule:[3] the conversion rate should be computed in terms of an average of past or of past and future market rates. Other candidates are forward rates, in the case of pre-announcement;[4] or pre-announced bilateral rates modified to take into account the interest rate differentials.

Even neglecting further distinctions arising from the possible behaviour of market participants — the pre-announced conversion rates may or may not be credible, the timing and the rule for setting the parities may or may not be expected — the combination of these three dimensions opens a very large number of options.

We shall see however that this *embarras de richesse* is to a large extent only apparent if, as is almost certain, some of the currencies entering into the ecu basket will not belong to the single currency

[3]Thus known as it was first put forward by the President of the European Monetary Institute.

[4]The forward rate rule is discussed by Brookes (1996).

from the start, because there are countries either not fulfilling the required conditions or having the right to opt out and deciding to do so.[5] In the following section, we shall begin our pruning by showing that it is impossible to either pre-announce conversion rates in terms of the ecu/euro or set euro conversion rates in terms of central ERM rates on January 1, 1999.

We shall neglect the problem arising from the fact that the value of the ecu computed from the basket does not coincide with the value of the private ecu quoted in the foreign exchange markets and shall refer only to the value of the official ecu, which coincides with its basket value.[6]

3. Setting Conversion Rates in Terms of the Ecu

We show in this section that setting the euro conversion rates of the in-currencies in terms of the ecu is either technically impossible or economically undesirable.

3.1. *A Set of Technically Impossible Solutions*

a) Pre-announcing ecu conversion rates

Let T be the last day before the commencement of the third stage, when the parities of the currencies of the in-countries are irrevocably fixed against the euro, and hence bilaterally. Suppose that of the N currencies belonging to the ecu basket I are of in-countries while $N - I$ are of out-countries, not joining the single currency at the outset. We ask the following question: is it possible to announce the parities of the I currencies against the ecu (equal to one euro) at

[5]The Fact that some currencies, like the Austrian shilling and the Finnish marka, which do not belong to the ecu basket because the latter was frozen by Article 109g of the Treaty, may instead participate to the single currency from the start is instead of no relevance.

[6]For some time the value of the private ecu in any given currency has been less than the value of the basket in that currency: the difference, which reached 250 basis points in the past, is now down to 40 basis points. A convincing explanation for the difference is provided in Folkerts-Landau and Garber (1995). See also Gonzalez-Pacheco and Steinherr (1996).

some time $t < T$, considering the constraint that the external value of the ecu at T should not be affected?

We denote by:

ecu_i the value of the ecu in terms of currency $i(i = 1, \ldots, I)$;

a_j, a_k the amounts of currency $j(j = 1, \ldots, I)$ and of currency $k(k = I + 1, \ldots, N)$ in the ecu basket;

$S_{ji,}, S_{ki}$ the exchange rate of currency $j(j = 1, \ldots, I)$ and of currency k $(k = I + 1, \ldots, N)$ in terms, respectively, of currency i (units of currency i per unit of currency j and of currency k).

From the basket definition of the ecu we know that:

$$\mathrm{ecu_i} = \sum_{j=1}^{I} \alpha_j S_{ji} + \sum_{k=I+1}^{N} \alpha_k S_{ki} \tag{1}$$

Is it possible that at time $t < T$ a fixed conversion rate into $ecu_i^* = euro_i^*$, is announced for each of the $i = 1, \ldots, I$ in-currencies?

Triangular arbitrage ensures that, by fixing the euro/ecu rates, the bilateral exchange rates for the in-currencies are also fixed, i.e.:

$$S_{ji}^* = \frac{\mathrm{ecu_i^*}}{\mathrm{ecu_j^*}} \tag{2}$$

Using (2) to rewrite (1) yields

$$\mathrm{ecu_i^*} = \sum_{j=1}^{I} \alpha_j \frac{\mathrm{ecu_i^*}}{\mathrm{ecu_j^*}} + \sum_{k=I+1}^{N} \alpha_k S_{ki} \quad \text{or} \tag{3}$$

$$\mathrm{ecu_i^*} \left(1 - \sum_{j=1}^{I} \alpha_j \frac{1}{\mathrm{ecu_j^*}}\right) = \sum_{k=I+1}^{N} \alpha_k S_{ki}, \tag{4}$$

for each in-currency $1, \ldots, I$.

As can be seen from (4), the left-hand side of the equation is a constant, determined by the chosen euro rates. Hence, also the right-hand side, which is the weighted exchange rate of the subset of out-currencies in the ecu against each in-currency, must be a constant. In other words, pre-fixing the euro rates of the in-currencies in advance of January 1, 1999 and guaranteeing the one-to-one conversion of ecus into euros requires that the weighted exchange rate of the subset of out-currencies with the in-currencies remains constant in the period between the announcement and the conversion. This can happen only in two cases: if all the outsiders decide to fix (unilaterally) their exchange rates with the insiders at the time of announcement and are able to defend those rates; or if, by some fluke, the movements of the exchange rate of the out-currencies against the in-currencies are such as to exactly offset each other. We may be allowed to say that the probability of the first case is very small and that of the second is nil for all practical purposes. Barring these two cases, pre-fixing the in-currencies' conversion rates in terms of euro violates the requirement that the external value of the ecu should not be affected by the conversion procedure. In particular, it would make the dollar value of ecu_i^* different from that of the ecu basket.

b) Adopting central ecu rates at the start of the third stage and the Lamfalussy rule in terms of ecu rates

A similar line of reasoning leads us to reject two more options: setting the in-currencies' conversion rates against the euro as the *central* ecu rates of the exchange rate mechanism; the Lamfalussy rule expressed in terms of average ecu market rates.

Let ecu_i^c be the ecu central rate of currency i and S_{ji}^c, S_{ki}^c the corresponding bilateral central rates of currencies $j (j=1,\ldots,I)$ and $k(k = I+1,\ldots,N)$ in terms of currency i, so that:

$$\mathrm{ecu_i^c} = \sum_{\mathrm{j=1}}^{\mathrm{I}} \alpha_\mathrm{j} \mathrm{S_{ji}^c} + \sum_{\mathrm{k=I+1}}^{\mathrm{N}} \alpha_\mathrm{k} \mathrm{S_{ki}^c} = \mathrm{euro_i} \tag{5}$$

which is currency i's euro-rate at T. The market ecu-rate on the previous day, $T-1$, will be:

$$\mathrm{ecu_i^{T-1}} = \sum_{\mathrm{j=1}}^{\mathrm{I}} \alpha_\mathrm{j} \mathrm{S_{ji}^{T-1}} + \sum_{\mathrm{k=I+1}}^{\mathrm{N}} \alpha_\mathrm{k} \mathrm{S_{ki}^{T-1}}, \tag{6}$$

so that

$$\mathrm{euro_i} - \mathrm{ecu}_\mathrm{i}^{\mathrm{T}-1} = \sum_{\mathrm{j}=1}^{\mathrm{I}} \alpha_\mathrm{j}(\mathrm{S}_\mathrm{ji}^\mathrm{c} - \mathrm{S}_\mathrm{ji}^{\mathrm{T}-1}) + \sum_{\mathrm{k}=\mathrm{I}+1}^{\mathrm{N}} \alpha_\mathrm{k}(\mathrm{S}_\mathrm{ki}^\mathrm{c} - \mathrm{S}_\mathrm{i}^{\mathrm{T}-1}). \quad (7)$$

Suppose that the in-countries manage to steer their bilateral exchange rates towards the central parities, so that the term in the first parenthesis on the right-hand side is zero. It is however most unlikely either that also the exchange rates of the out-currencies converge to their central parities or that their deviations from central parities are such as to exactly offset each other: the term in the second parenthesis will then in all probability be different from zero and, as a result, the procedure of conversion into euro will cause a jump in the external value of the ecu.

For precisely the same reason it is not possible to adopt a conversion rate into euro in terms of an average of ecu market rates. If the rule is announced before T, with reference to an average of future and possibly past rates, we come across the same problem as when the ecu rates are pre-announced. If the rule is adopted at T, with reference only to past rates, the possibility that market rates at $T-1$ coincide with an average of past market rates is even more remote than for central rates.

3.2. *Adopting the ecu Market Rate on the Last Day as the Conversion Rate: An Economically Undesirable Solution*

It follows from our argument above that, if there are out-currencies in the ecu basket, the only way of setting the euro rates in terms of the ecu while at the same time leaving the external value of the ecu unaffected is to fix the conversion rates as the market ecu rates on the last day before the third stage. This would however be a most unattractive procedure. First, there is a problem of indeterminacy of such rates, so that there would be no anchor for market expectations:[7] a problem made more relevant by the

[7]See Begg *et at.* (1997), where a forceful argument against letting the job of setting the (irrevocable) euro conversion rates for the in currencies to the market can be found.

uncontrollable movements of the exchange rates of the out-currencies present in the ecu basket (one of which will probably be an important international currency, like sterling). Second, that procedure may cause moral hazard problems with the in-countries. Once admission has been obtained, so that "severe tensions" in exchange rate movements[8] can no longer be invoked against it, and as long as the ERM remains in place with the wider 15 percent band, there would be a temptation to let one's currency depreciate within the band, thus engineering a *de facto* last devaluation in order to enter the third stage with a competitive advantage. Third, the markets would perceive all this, so that there may be speculative movements and in any case considerable and undesirable volatility in the interim period.

4. Bilateral Parities: Advantages and Problems

4.1. *Bilateral Conversion Rates*

If conversion rates are set as bilateral parities between the in-currencies, we restore a degree of freedom that allows this procedure to be compatible in principle with the external value constraint.

Consider first the case in which conversion rates are pre-announced. Equation (3) above now becomes:

$$\mathrm{ecu_i} = \sum_{\mathrm{j=1}}^{\mathrm{I}} \alpha_{\mathrm{j}} \mathrm{S^*_{ji}} + \sum_{\mathrm{k=I+1}}^{\mathrm{N}} \alpha_{\mathrm{ki}} \mathrm{S_{ki}}, \qquad (3')$$

where S^*_{ji} are the pre-set bilateral conversion rates of the in-currencies. At T the conversion rate of the latter with the euro will be the market rate of the ecu, which will depend in turn on the bilateral exchange rates of the out-currencies. The only consequence of fixing the in-currencies' bilateral rates is that, at T, the out-currencies will have appreciated or depreciated against each in-currency in exactly the same proportion.

[8] Article 3 of the Protocol on the convergence criteria referred to in Article 109j of the Treaty.

In principle the bilateral conversion rates could be the market rates at some time $t < T$, or the central EMS rates, or those derived from a Lamfalussy rule. Pre-setting bilateral rates, no matter how, meets however with an economic problem and with a potential legal difficulty. Before facing these issues, we can do some more pruning and exclude the Lamfalussy rule as a desirable option even if applied to bilateral parities.

4.2. *Ruling Out the Lamfalussy Rule*

Recall that the Lamfalussy rule prescribes that the conversion rate at T should be an average of market rates: between t, when the rule is announced, and T, or between some date before t and T, so as to give some weight also to the past. The alleged purpose of the proposal was to increase the credibility of the announcement of conversion rates, as central banks would not be obliged to intervene to defend a given parity. The rule suffers however from a number of defects, which make it unsuitable for practical application (see De Grauwe 1996).

First, at the moment of announcement of the rule, significant jumps in exchange rates are to be expected. This is possible also with alternative ways of setting conversion rates, but under the Lamfalussy rule there is an element of arbitrariness: if, as is quite possible, the market rate (which is the marginal rate) and the average rate move in an opposite direction at the moment of the announcement, the jump may occur in a direction opposite to that of market trends, producing artificial volatility unrelated to fundamentals. Second, use of the Lamfalussy rule does not prevent unpredictable drifts of the exchange rate after the announcement, causing significant uncertainty in the conversion rates to be applied after January 1, 1999.

We conclude that the Lamfalussy rule, though expressed in terms of bilateral rates, does not represent a satisfactory solution to the problem of setting conversion rates, even if applied to bilateral parities.

4.3. Problems with Setting Bilateral Parities

a) An economic problem

Our conclusion that bilateral conversion rates are, unlike ecu conversion rates, compatible with the external value constraint assumes that the announcement of the conversion rates is fully credible so that bilateral market rates are driven to their announced conversion rates on day $T-1$. It is however useful to analyse what could happen if the market distrusts this announcement so that on day $T-1$ the market rates diverge from the announced conversion rates. In that case the authorities face a difficult choice which can be made explicit as follows. Start from equation (7), which we can now rewrite as

$$\mathrm{euro_i} - \mathrm{ecu_i^{T-1}} = \sum_{\mathrm{j=1}}^{\mathrm{I}} \alpha_\mathrm{j}(\mathrm{S_{ji}^*} - \mathrm{S_{ji}^{T-1}}) + \sum_{\mathrm{k=I+1}}^{\mathrm{N}} \alpha_\mathrm{k}(\mathrm{S_{ki}} - \mathrm{S_{ki}^{T-1}}), \quad (7')$$

In order to make the one to one conversion of the ecu into the euro on day T possible, the left hand side of (7') must be zero. Since we only fix the bilateral rates of the in-currencies, there is no constraint on the bilateral rates of the out-currencies (as was the case in equation (7)). Thus, at the start of day T the bilateral market rates of the out-currencies are equal to those observed at the end of day $T-1$. This sets the second term on the right hand side of (7') equal to 0. It follows that if on day $T-1$ the bilateral market rates of the in-currencies, S_{ji}^{T-1}, diverge from the announced conversion rates, S_{ji}^*, the authorities are in trouble. Either they renege their announcement and select the market rates of day $T-1$ as bilateral conversion rates, which allows them to convert one ecu into one euro on day $T(euro_i - ecu_i^{T-1} = 0$ in (7')); or, if they want to stick to their announced conversion rates, they must drop the latter constraint and violate the Treaty provision.[9] This difficult trade-off can only be

[9]Obstfeld (1997) suggests that the only way to solve the problem created by the external value constraint is to abolish that constraint altogether by repealing Article 1091 of the Treaty. This would no doubt allow a more straightforward and satisfactory procedure for setting the conversion rates. To obtain this result, however, an agreement on,

avoided if the announced fixed bilateral conversion rates are made fully credible. In that case the latter will coincide with the market rates and the one to one conversion of the ecu into euros on day T does not pose problems.

b) A potential legal hurdle?

We have shown so far that, while setting ecu-conversion rates is technically impossible, unless the conversion rates are set as, or happen to coincide with, the market rates at T, there are no technical obstacles to fixing bilateral rates and taking the ecu market rate at T as the final ecu/euro conversion rate. We ruled out the Lamfalussy rule not because it was inconsistent with the requirements of the Treaty, but because it had other undesirable consequences.

A discretionary decision adopted by the Dublin Council on a proposal from the Commission seems however to rule out the whole set of options based on the adoption of bilateral conversion rates without previously passing through the ecu rate.

Pursuing the request of the Madrid Council that "a Council regulation entering into force on January 1, 1999 will provide the legal framework for the use of the euro" and "will have the effect that the national currencies and the euro will become different expressions of what is economically the same currency" (para. 9 of the Annex), in December 1996 the Ecofin and the Dublin European Council approved two regulations issued by the Commission of the European Communities (COM 96 499 final, 16.10.1996), of which the one "on some provisions regarding the introduction of the Euro" deals with the problem of setting the conversion rates.

The relevant provisions are the following (Article 4):

"(1) the conversion rates shall be adopted as one euro expressed in terms of each of the national currencies of the member states without a derogation. They shall be adopted with six significant figures.

---

and fifteen parliamentary approvals of, the formal repeal of a Treaty provision would be required: an unlikely event.

[...]

(3) The conversion rates shall be used for conversions either way between the euro unit and the national currency units. Inverse rates derived from the conversion rates shall not be used.

(4) Monetary sums to be converted from one national currency unit into another shall first be converted into a monetary sum expressed in the euro unit, rounded to at least three decimals, and then be converted into the other national currency."

The comment to the draft regulation states that "in order to avoid inaccuracies in conversions, the irrevocable fixing only includes the conversion rate between the euro and the national currency units", while "the bilateral rates between the,national currency units will be derived from these conversion rates." It adds that "Article 4 (4) [...] provides a binding algorithm for conversions between national currency units, given that those bilateral rates will not, according to the definition of conversion rates in Article 1, be defined directly."

The rationale of this decision is difficult to understand. At any rate the detailed provisions cited above go far beyond the need to stress that in the third stage what matters is the euro and not national currencies. A strict and narrow interpretation of those provisions would make it impossible to formally set the final conversion rates bilaterally — whether before T or at T — and then derive the ecu/euro conversion rate from the unconstrained ecu market rate. Having proved before that pre-announcing rates in terms of ecu, or setting them in terms of central ecu values, is inconsistent with the ecu external value constraint set by the Treaty, the only option left by this interpretation would be that of setting the in-currencies conversion rates in terms of the market value of the ecu at T: a most unattractive procedure, as we argued above.

We maintain however that a broader interpretation of the regulation is possible, under which euro conversion rates can be derived implicitly from previously agreed bilateral rates. We describe the procedure in the next Section, where we also consider briefly the problem of credibility.

5. Proposal

We propose an indirect decision-making process that involves several steps. First, the Council, soon after the selection of the in-currencies, announces *the method* that will be followed at the start of the third stage *to fix the ecu/euro conversion rates*, in compliance with the regulation: the euro conversion rates on Januaty 1, 1999 will be set equal to the market ecu rates of December 31, 1998. Second, the authorities of the in-countries will reach, and preferably announce, an agreement on the structure of the bilateral rates of their currencies that will be implicit in, and will constrain, the final euro conversion rate. This procedure is in our view compatible with the regulation, insofar as the formal decision will be taken in terms of euro/ecu rates; there is on the other hand no provision, either in the Treaty or in the regulation, that prevents the in-countries from agreeing on a set of bilateral rates.

It may be objected that there is going to be a last minute uncertainty regarding the precise values of the euro conversion rates. This uncertainty, however, only concerns the *levels* of these rates, but not their *ratios*. Thus, suppose that the decision has been taken that the FF/DM rate will be $S^*_{DM,FF}$ and that the bilateral market rate has converged to that level. As a result the ratio between the euro conversion rates of the two currencies will be $euro_{FF}/euro_{DM} = S^*_{DM,FF}$.

The uncertainty as to the last minute values of $euro_{FF}$, and $euro_{DM}$ will not concern that ratio, as the two ecu/euro rates will change in the same proportion. The uncertainty as to the levels has little economic relevance, as the choice of euro rates has an element of arbitrariness anyway: dividing or multiplying those rates by any arbitrary number would leave the structure of bilateral rates unaffected.

Next there is the problem of the credibility of the agreed upon bilateral rates. The authorities of the in-countries must take a firm commitment to steer their bilateral market exchange rates towards the agreed levels, by means of coordinated inframarginal interventions, to whatever extent is required, and of interest rate policies. Whether announced or not, the markets must be convinced that the commitment is unconditional and hence that the agreement is credible: if so, as the final date approaches, market rates will gradually converge to their target levels.[10]

How should the target bilateral rates be chosen? This is to no little extent a political problem. Central rates provide an unambiguous solution, which as such is preferable, but which may be objected to by those countries with a market exchange rate of their currencies depreciated with respect to the central rate. The choice of market rates at the time of decision may meet with opposite objections. One thing however is clear. Our proposal requires agreement on a specific and precise level of bilateral rates. This rules out more complicated solutions that leave the precise level of bilateral rates uncertain until the last moment, of which the Lamfalussy rule is one instance.

6. Conclusion

The two conditions, that the adoption of the irrevocably fixed conversion rates should not modify the external value of the ecu and that one euro should be equal to one ecu, severely constrain the choices about how to set the conversion rates for the third stage. In a nutshell, the constraint is that the conversion rates used on January 1, 1999 will have to be the market rates observed at the end of the previous day, whether they are expressed bilaterally or directly in terms of the euro. The constraints are however more binding if it is decided that the conversion rates must be set in euro: in this case it is not possible to announce fixed conversion rates in advance, so that the irrevocable conversion rates must necessarily be the ecu market rates of each participating currency on the last market day of 1998. This has several drawbacks: the temptation for some of the countries admitted to the single currency to engineer, *de facto*, a "last devaluation"; the markets' perception of this tempation; the fluctuations of the market ecu rates caused by the movements of the exchange

[10]Begg *et al.* (1997) argue in favour of letting market rates move freely in the interim period and bringing them in line with the announced rates by means of massive interventions on the last market day: a last-day intervention would leave the money supply of the euro-area unaffected. It may be noted that the procedure for setting the conversion rates that we have suggested has the merit of leaving a margin of tolerance for small last-minute deviations of market rates from the Jarget levels.

rates of the outside currencies. In the end, if it is decided to set euro conversion rates, the choice of those rates will be left to the market.

These constraints are less tight if it is decided to set the euro conversion rates indirectly, by first determining the bilateral rates. To make this legally possible, we suggest a procedure consisting of two parallel moves: announcing that the euro/ecu conversion rates to be adopted will be the ecu market rates on the last day before the third stage: reaching an agreement on the structure of bilateral rates prior to January 1, 1999, which may or may not be announced. The authorities of the countries concerned should then take a firm and explicit commitment to steer the market rates toward the agreed levels. If the commitment is credible, market rates will converge to the conversion rates before the latter are irrevocably set: the market ecu rates, which must equal the euro conversion rate, will then be compatible with the bilateral parities and not be the last minute outcome of the whims of the market.

References

Arrowsmith, J (1996). The role of exchange-rate arrangements in preparing for EMU. In *Making EMU Happen. Problems and Proposals*, Essays in International Finance, No. 199, P Kenen (ed.). Princeton: International Finance Section.

Begg, D, F Giavazzi, J von Hagen and C Wyplosz (1997). EMU: Gating the end-game right. Centre for Economic Policy Research, London.

Brookes, M (1996). Fixing the entry rates for EMU. EMU Briefing No. 7, Goldman Sachs, November.

De Grauwe, P. (1996). How to fix conversion rates at the start of EMU. CEPR Discussion Paper Series No. 1530, November.

Folkerts-Landau, D and P Garber (1995). Determining the value of a financial unit of account based on composite currencies: The case of the private ECU. *IMF Staff Papers*, 42(1).

Gonzalez-Pacheco, L and A Steinherr (1996). A proposal to stabilise the value of the ECU. EIB Papers, Special Issue on EMU, 1(1), European Investment Bank.

Gros, D and K Lannoo (1996). The passage to the Euro. Working Party Report No. 16, Centre for European Policy Studies, Brussels, December.

Kenen, P (1995). *Economic and Monetary Union in Europe.* Cambridge, UK: Cambridge University Press.

Obstfeld, M (1997). A strategy for launching the Euro. Unpublished manuscript.

Chapter 10

The Euro and Financial Crises

Paul De Grauwe

Can a financial crisis similar to the Asian one erupt in Europe? Our immediate answer is negative. These disturbing financial upheavals occur in "emerging" markets not in the bastions of stability that are found in Europe. The conditions that led to the financial crises in Asia are just not present in Europe.

The question of whether financial crises of the Asian kind can happen in Europe should not be brushed aside too lightly, however. From the Asian financial debacle we have learned the following about the conditions that can lead to financial instability. First, capital markets are liberalised creating the potential for vast international movements of financial assets. Second, countries keep their exchange rates pegged creating the perception that there is little risk involved moving funds from one market to the other. Third, the monetary regime (including the system of regulatory control) is not adapted to the new regime of liberal capital markets. These three factors have been present in one way or the other in the financial crises in Asia, but also in Latin America during the 1970s and 1980s. Of course, they do not always lead to disaster. There are also examples of countries that have avoided financial disturbances despite the fact that they went through the same process of liberalisation. Nevertheless it is

Published in the *Financial Times*, February 20 (1998).

fair to conclude that these three factors substantially increase the probability of major crises.

So, are these factors to be found in today's Europe? Obviously not. But Europe is soon going to move into EMU creating a totally different financial environment. It can be argued that the factors that create the conditions for financial disturbances may very well emerge in the future EMU.

EMU is certainly going to dramatically increase the degree of capital mobility within the euro area. Today, it is still the case that European capital markets are relatively closed. Financial institutions and insurance companies in Germany, France, Italy, etc. hold an overwhelming share of their total portfolio (often more than 90 percent) in domestic assets. The complete elimination of foreign exchange risk following the introduction of the euro and the disappearance of regulatory constraints on the holdings of "foreign" euro-assets will change all that, leading financial institutions to dramatically increase their holdings of "foreign" euro-assets. The result will be to open up financial markets in Europe in a more profound way than in the 1980s when most European countries eliminated their systems of capital controls. The size of the funds that will be freely moving within the euro area will make a quantum jump.

Against the background of this dramatic liberalization of Europe's financial markets there is the fact that the regulatory and institutional environment will not be adapted. Prudential control will still be done at the national level. This will handicap the regulators in assessing the risk of the institutions under their jurisdiction. In addition, financial institutions in each country of the euro area will, at least initially, overwhelmingly be national. The German financial markets will be dominated by German financial institutions, the French markets by French institutions, etc. Thus, institutionally the financial markets will still have a substantial domestic segmentation. This will make it difficult to efficiently spread the risk of asymmetric economic shocks, i.e., economic shocks occurring in one country and not in others.

The conditions that could lead to financial disturbances will, therefore, be present in the future euro area, at least during its initial phase when institutions have not yet adapted to the new environment. This, of course, does not mean that crises must inevitably occur. In order to gauge the risk of such occurrence let us analyse a particular scenario.

Suppose a country, which we arbitrarily call Spain, experiences a boom which is stronger than in the rest of the euro-area. As a result of the boom, output and prices grow faster in Spain than in the other euro-countries. This also leads to a real estate boom and a general asset inflation in Spain. Since the ECB looks at euro-wide data, it cannot do anything to restrain the booming conditions in Spain. In fact the existence of a monetary union is likely to intensify the asset inflation in Spain. Unhindered by exchange risk vast amounts of capital are attracted from the rest of the euro-area. Spanish banks that still dominate the Spanish markets, are pulled into the game and increase their lending. They are driven by the high rates of return produced by ever increasing Spanish asset prices, and by the fact that in a monetary union, they can borrow funds at the same interest rate as banks in Germany, France etc. After the boom comes the bust. Asset prices collapse, creating a crisis in the Spanish banking system.

Too far fetched to be realistic? The US monetary union provides many examples of such local booms and busts followed by financial crises that lead to large scale bail-out operations. Scenarios of local booms and bust, as the one just described, will almost certainly happen in the future euro-area. The essential ingredient triggering such crises is the existence of regional differences in rates of return on assets coupled with the fact that in a monetary union banks can borrow at the same interest rates.

These future euro financial crises, however, will in one crucial aspect be different from the financial crises recently experienced in Asia. They will not lead to speculative crises in the foreign exchange markets. Thus, if Spain is confronted by a banking crises this will not spill over into the Spanish foreign exchange market because there will be no such market. One source of further destabilisation of the markets will, therefore, be absent.

The founders of EMU have taken extraordinary measures to reduce the risk of debt default by governments. Maastricht convergence criteria and a stability pact have been introduced to guard EMU from the risk of excessive government debt accumulation. The Asian financial debacle teaches us that excessive debt accumulation by the private sector can be equally, of not more, risky. This has escaped the attention of the founders of EMU, concerned as they were by the dangers of too much government debt. In the meantime the EMU-clock is ticking, while he institutions that should guard EMU from financial and banking crises have still to be put into place.

Chapter 11

What Have We Learnt about Monetary Integration since the Maastricht Treaty?

Paul De Grauwe

The present governance of the euro area has been devised assuming that the world fits the monetarist-real-business-cycle theory. But that theory is not a correct representation of the world. The European monetary union is a remarkable achievement, but remains fragile because of the absence of a sufficient degree of political union.

1. Introduction

The late 1980s and the early 1990s are turning points in the history of monetary unification in Europe. It was the time of the Delors report which provided the intellectual basis of the Maastricht Treaty. The latter was signed in 1991 and developed the blueprint for monetary union in Europe. At the end of the 1990s monetary union became a fact of life in a large part of the European Union.

What have we learnt since the Treaty was signed? This is the question I attempt to answer in this article. Let us first look at the views prevailing at the time of the signing of the Treaty. We will then return to the question of what we have learned since then.

Published in *Journal of Common Market Studies*, 44(4), 711–730, 2006.
I am grateful for the comments of Waltraud Schelkle and two anonymous referees.

2. Mundell I and Mundell II

At the time of the signing of the Treaty, the economic profession was still struggling with the pros and cons of monetary union. This is also evident from my textbook *The Economics of Monetary Integration* first published in 1992, which could not make up its mind whether a monetary union in Europe was a good idea. The reason is that at the time there were really two theories competing for academic attention, with very different policy implications. Following McKinnon (2004), I will call the first of these theories, Mundell I, and the second theory, Mundell II. Mundell I provided the basis for widespread scepticism about the desirability of a monetary union in Europe, while Mundell II was used by the proponents of monetary union.

Mundell I is the traditional theory of optimal currency areas (OCA) pioneered by Mundell (1961) in the early 1960s and further elaborated by McKinnon (1963), Kenen (1969) and others. The OCA theory determines the conditions that countries should satisfy to make a monetary union attractive, i.e. to ensure that the benefits of the monetary union exceed its costs. This theory has been used most often to analyse whether countries should join a monetary union. It can also be used to study the conditions in which existing members of a monetary union will want to leave the union. (I will come back to this aspect of the theory later.)

The conditions that are needed to make a monetary union among candidate Member States attractive can be summarized by three concepts:

- Symmetry (of shocks)
- Flexibility
- Integration

Countries in a monetary union should experience macroeconomic shocks that are sufficiently correlated with those experienced in the rest of the union (*symmetry*). These countries should have sufficient *flexibility* in the labour markets to be able to adjust to asymmetric shocks once they are in the union. Finally they should have a sufficient degree of trade *integration* with the members of the union so as to generate benefits of using the same currency.

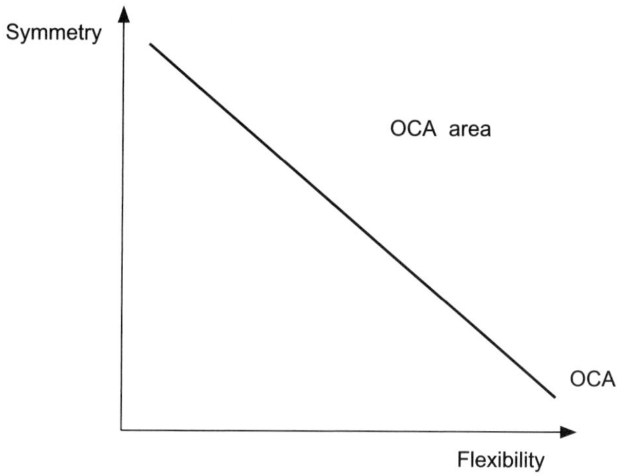

Figure 1. Symmetry and flexibility as OCA criteria.

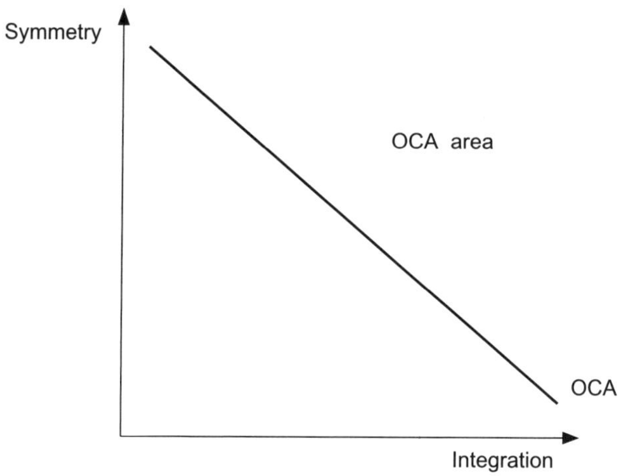

Figure 2. Symmetry and integration as OCA criteria.

One can summarize this theory in the form of graphical representations (see De Grauwe, 2005). This is done in Figures 1 and 2.

Figure 1 presents the minimal combinations of *symmetry* and *flexibility* that are needed to form an optimal currency area by the downward-sloping OCA line. Points on the OCA line define combinations of symmetry and flexibility for which the costs and the benefits of a monetary union just balance. It is negatively sloped because a declining degree of symmetry (which raises the costs) necessitates an increasing flexibility. To the right of the OCA line, the degree of flexibility is sufficiently large given the degree of symmetry to ensure that the benefits of the union exceed the costs. To the left of the OCA line, there is insufficient flexibility for any given level of symmetry.

Figure 2 presents the minimal combinations of *symmetry* and *integration* that are needed to form an optimal currency area. The OCA line represents the combinations of symmetry and integration among groups of countries for which the cost and benefits of a monetary union just balance. It is downward sloping for the following reason. A decline in symmetry raises the costs of a monetary union. These costs are mainly macroeconomic in nature. Integration is a source of benefits of a monetary union, i.e., the greater the degree of integration the more the member countries benefit from the efficiency gains of a monetary union. Thus, the additional (macroeconomic) costs produced by less symmetry can be compensated by the additional (microeconomic) benefits produced by more integration. Points to the right of the OCA line represent groupings of countries for which the benefits of a monetary union exceed its costs.

The presumption of many economists at the end of the 1980s was that the EU countries should be located to the left of the OCA lines in Figures 1 and 2, i.e., given the degree of integration achieved in the EU there was still too much asymmetry and too little flexibility for the EU to form a monetary union whose benefits would exceed the costs.

There was another intellectual tradition, however, going back to a relatively obscure paper of Mundell published in 1973 (Mundell, 1973). Its main insights can be summarized as follows. The new Mundell (Mundell II) starts from the situation of a world of free mobility of capital; a situation that was emerging in the 1970s but that seemed remote at the start of the 1960s. In a world of free mobility of capital, the exchange rate ceases to be a stabilizing force. Instead, according to Mundell II, the exchange rate becomes a target of destabilizing speculative movements and thus a source of large asymmetric shocks. Thus, the view of Mundell I implying that the exchange rate could be used to stabilize the economy after an asymmetric shock should be abandoned. In the world of Mundell II joining a monetary union should not be seen as a cost arising from the loss of the exchange rate as an adjustment mechanism, but as a benefit of eliminating a source of asymmetric shocks. For most countries, the exchange rate does not provide a degree of freedom but uses up a degree of freedom in their economic policy since they have to stabilize this asset price. Needless to say, this view is not very popular among the crowd of believers in the efficiency of the foreign exchange markets. In fact, the view expressed by Mundell II is based on the idea that foreign exchange markets are not efficient and should not be trusted to guide countries towards macroeconomic equilibrium.[1]

There is a second insight in Mundell II. This is that only in a monetary union can capital markets be fully integrated so that they can be used as an insurance mechanism against asymmetric shocks (see Asdrubali *et al.*, 1996). When countries remain outside a monetary union they cannot hope to profit from insurance against asymmetric shocks provided by capital markets in the rest of the world. The reason is that the large and variable exchange risk premia prevent these capital markets from providing insurance against asymmetric shocks.

Thus the world of Mundell II is one in which countries that stay outside a monetary union will have to deal with large asymmetric shocks that arise from the instability of international capital flows. In addition, these countries' ability to insure against traditional asymmetric shocks is severely restricted when they stay outside a monetary union. With such an analysis it should not be surprising that Mundell II became a major promoter of monetary union in large parts of the world, and in particular in Europe.

At the time the Maastricht Treaty was signed, most academic economists' minds were framed by Mundell I and scepticism about

[1]This view has received increased empirical backing. There is now substantial empirical evidence that the exchange rate is disconnected most of the time from its fundamental value and that its volatility cannot be explained by underlying fundamental volatility (see De Grauwe and Grimaldi, 2006, for evidence and implications of these findings).

the prospects of a monetary union was widespread. In the end Mundell II prevailed. Why did this happen?

There was first the collapse of the EMS in 1992–93. This historical episode made clear that in a world of free mobility of capital, fixed exchange rates were unsustainable as long as central banks maintained their own independent monetary policies. The EMS-crisis convinced many continental European economists that a choice had to be made for one of the two 'corner solutions' in exchange rate regimes, i.e., full flexibility of exchange rates or monetary union. Many decided that the latter would be the least bad choice. Mundell II triumphed on the European continent.

There was also the effect of an intellectual revolution that was started in the 1970s in the academic world and that reached the policy world during the 1980s. This was monetarism. Mundell I is very much a Keynesian theory, stressing that in a world of price and wage rigidities monetary policies, including exchange rate policies, can be used effectively to stabilize the economy. Monetarism, instead, stressed that activist monetary policies become sources of instability and that central banks should focus on their core business which is to maintain price stability. The logical consequence of monetarism was the view that central banks do not lose their capacity to stabilize their national economies when entering a monetary union, since they did not have such a capacity in the first place. In this monetarist vision (and Mundell II was also an outgrowth of monetarism) the costs of a monetary union are small. In terms of our Figures 1 and 2, the OCA line is located very close to the origin. The OCA-region is a vastly expanded one.

These developments explain why EMU became possible on the European continent. One of the paradoxes, however, is that as the Mundell II framework that explains the successful start of the euro area will be pushed into the background and will increasingly be forgotten, the Mundell I analysis will gain in importance again. This is already evident in a number of countries that have recently experienced large losses of competitiveness (an asymmetric shock). We show the real effective exchange rates in the euro area since 1998 (see Figure 3). The striking fact is the extent to which yearly

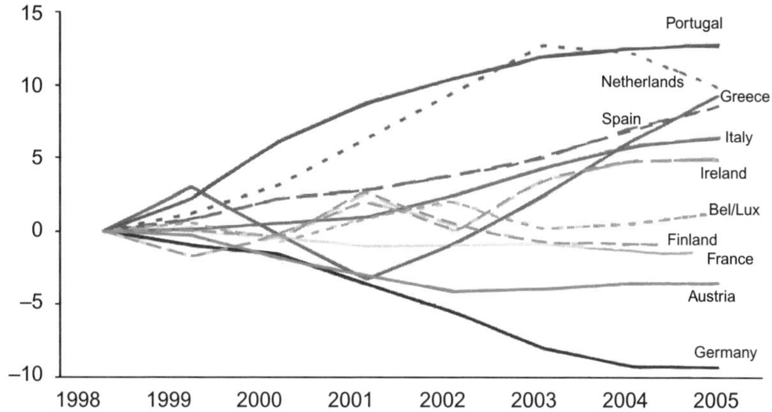

Figure 3. Intra-euro area real effective exchange rates (based on unit labour costs).

Source: Commission (2005).

inflation differentials have led to sustained changes in these real exchange rates. As a result of these trends, some countries (Portugal, Netherlands, Spain and Italy) have lost a significant amount of price competitiveness. Others, like Germany and Austria have gained a significant amount of price competitiveness.

This phenomenon will lead to the need to adjust in many countries.[2] In particular, the countries that have lost competitiveness will have to restore it. In a monetary union this can only come about by having lower rates of price and wage inflation than the average of the euro area. However, since the ECB is targeting a rate of inflation below 2 percent, the countries that have lost competitiveness will find it very difficult to lower their inflation rates below the euro area average without introducing outright deflation, and large increases in unemployment. As a result of the low inflation target, the whole process is costly in terms of output and employment.[3] This is Mundell I with a vengeance.

[2]Since the real exchange rates used here are based on unit labour costs, they take into account differential productivity growth. As a result divergent movements in these rates cannot be the result of the Balassa-Samuelson effect (see also Gros *et al.*, 2005).

[3]It can be argued that, by making it more difficult for countries to restore their lost competitiveness, the low inflation target of the ECB introduces a powerful rigidity in the

What have we learnt since the Treaty of Maastricht? I would like to focus on two ideas. The first one is the idea, first elaborated by Frankel and Rose (1998) of the endogeneity of the OCA criteria; the other idea relates to the governance of the monetary union.

3. Endogeneity of the OCA Criteria

Frankel and Rose (1998) came up with the idea that the OCA criteria are endogenous. By that they meant that these criteria are affected by the very decision to start a monetary union. Thus countries that before the start of the union fail to satisfy the OCA criteria may, by the very fact that they form a monetary union, change economic conditions in such a way that these conditions get satisfied. As a result the decision to start a monetary union has a self-fulfilling property. By starting the monetary union the conditions that are favourable for a monetary union get satisfied, making the decision to form a monetary union the right one. Conversely, a decision not to start a union when the conditions are not satisfied helps to maintain unfavourable conditions so that the negative decision also appears to have been the right one.

There are different mechanisms that can make the OCA criteria endogenous. First, monetary union can affect trade flows and intensify trade integration, thus increasing the benefits of the monetary union. Second, monetary integration leads to more intense financial integration thereby facilitating the emergence of insurance mechanisms. The latter reduce the costs of asymmetric shocks. Third, a monetary union affects the functioning of the labour markets and can potentially increase their flexibility, thereby reducing the costs of adjusting to asymmetric shocks in the monetary union.[4]

We show the effects of these mechanisms in Figures 4 and 5 which are the same as Figures 1 and 2. We have now put the euro area to the left of the OCA line, taking the view that when the euro area was

euro area. Thus paradoxically a higher inflation target would introduce more flexibility. It would also lead to less tension within the euro area.

[4]For a detailed discussion of these different mechanisms, see De Grauwe and Mongelli (2005).

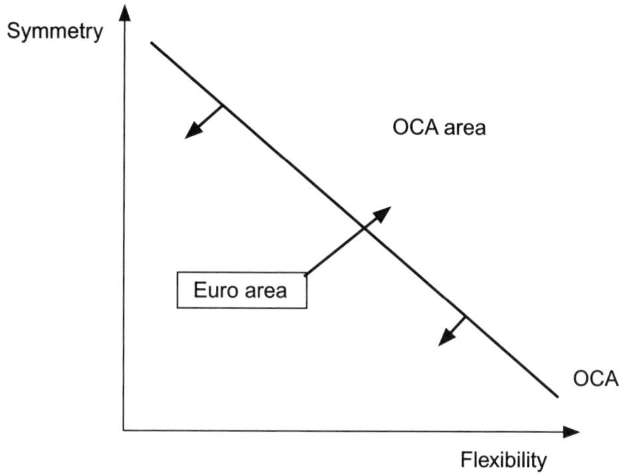

Figure 4. Symmetry and flexibility as OCA criteria.

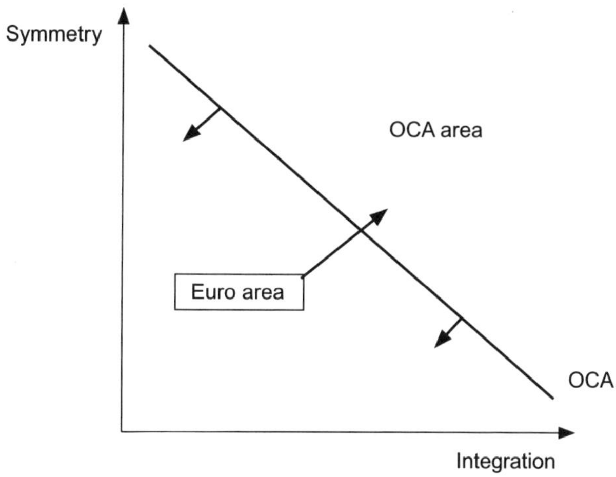

Figure 5. Symmetry and integration as OCA criteria.

started its members were not yet ready to form a monetary union. We do this not because we are convinced that this was necessarily the case, but rather because it allows us to show that even if this is the case, the future looks good for the union.

The endogenous mechanisms have the effect of moving the euro area towards the OCA area in Figures 4 and 5. This happens because monetary union increases the degree of economic (trade) integration (Figure 5). The spectacular studies of Rose (2000), Rose and van Wincoop (2001) suggest that this effect may be quantitatively very strong. Although later econometric studies have scaled down this "Rose effect" substantially (see, e.g., Mélitz, 2001; Bun and Klaassen, 2002; Micco *et al.*, 2003; and Baldwin, 2005), so that it is safe to conclude that a monetary union has a significant positive effect on economic integration, thereby moving the euro area towards the OCA area.

What about flexibility? If monetary union increases the pressure for labour markets to become more flexible, the decision to enter a monetary union also improves the OCA criteria tending to shift the euro area upwards towards the OCA area. It must be admitted that there is no consensus about this flexibility effect. Some authors (Bertola and Boeri, 2002; Blanchard and Giavazzi, 2003) argue that monetary union tends to increase the degree of flexibility of labour markets, while other authors (Sibert and Sutherland, 2000; Soskice and Iversen, 2001) conclude that a monetary union may not lead to more labour market flexibility.

The effect of monetary union on symmetry has been heavily debated among economists (see De Grauwe, 2005). No consensus seems to have emerged here, although the empirical work of Frankel and Rose (1998) indicating that trade integration and output correlation go hand-in-hand has become quite influential.

On the whole the theory and the evidence seem to suggest that there is a dynamics of endogeneity that has the potential of moving the euro area countries towards the OCA area. How important this endogeneity effect is, however, cannot be determined at this stage of our knowledge.

4. The Governance of Monetary Union

There is a fundamental difference between the monetary union among the US states and the European monetary union. The US federal government has a monopoly of the use of coercive power within the union and will surely prevent any state from seceding from the monetary union. The contrast with the Member States of the euro area is a very strong one.[5] There is no supranational institution in the EU that can prevent a Member State of the euro area from seceding. Thus, for the euro area to survive the Member States must continue to perceive their membership of the area to be in their national interest. If that is no longer the case, the temptation to secede will exist and at some point this temptation may lead to secession.[6]

This leads to the following question. In the absence of a coercive power that can keep the Member States within the union, what kind of governance can ensure that countries willingly stay in the union? This leads to the matter of the political ties that are essential to achieve this goal. Put differently, what is the nature of the political union that can maintain the cohesiveness of the monetary union? We return to the OCA theory to answer these questions.

Political Union in the OCA theory

The theory of optimal currency areas determines the conditions that countries should satisfy to make monetary union attractive, i.e., to ensure that the benefits of monetary union exceed its costs. This theory has been used almost exclusively to analyze whether countries should join a monetary union. It can also be used to study the conditions in which existing members of a monetary union will want to leave the union.

In this perspective, the OCA theory says that, if the benefits of the monetary union exceed the costs, member countries have no incentive to leave the union. They form an optimal currency area. Or, put differently, they are in a Nash equilibrium, and monetary union is sustainable. The same conditions of symmetry, flexibility and integration apply here, i.e., countries in a monetary union should experience

[5]For an insightful political analysis of monetary and economic integration, see Jones (2002). For a more general treatment of institutional and political dimensions of integration in general, see Wallace *et al.* (2005).

[6]Whether and when this happens also depends on the exit costs of the monetary union. If these are perceived to be large, the secession may not occur, or may take a long time to materialize. For a full analysis one would need to integrate the exit costs with the costs and benefits underlying the OCA analysis.

macroeconomic shocks that are sufficiently symmetric with those experienced in the rest of the union (*symmetry*) and they should have sufficient *flexibility* in the labour markets to be able to adjust to asymmetric shocks once they are in the union. Finally, they should have a sufficient degree of trade *integration* with the members of the union so as to generate benefits of using the same currency. If these criteria are not satisfied, monetary union will not be sustainable.[7]

Two issues arise here concerning the usefulness of the OCA theory to analyse the conditions under which secessions can arise. The criticism of the traditional OCA theory, Mundell I, as I have outlined earlier, could be construed to imply nothing less than that it is defunct as an economic theory. Its reintroduction to study the secession from a monetary union, therefore, requires some justification.

We have hinted to such a justification in Section 1. After a lapse of time Member States are likely to forget the reasons why they joined the union, i.e., to get rid of an exchange rate they found difficult to stabilize. Instead, the problems of adjustments to shocks that they are facing will get centre stage. We gave an example of the strong divergence in competitive positions observed during 1999–2005 as such an asymmetric shock to which member countries will have to adjust. All the problems analysed in the framework of the traditional OCA theory will become topical again.

A second problem with the use of the OCA theory to analyse the issue of secession from the union comes from the fact that when multinational monetary unions have broken up in the past, this was often for reasons other than those underlying the cost–benefit calculus of the OCA theory. Most often these other reasons had to do with political conflicts within the union, or outright political disintegration. This is certainly true, but this does not mean that the OCA analysis loses its usefulness. Economic and political shocks can arise that change the willingness of political leaders to maintain the union, and that lead to a political crisis. It is our ambition here to study how a political union feeds back into the OCA analysis and vice versa.

[7] For illuminating insights on the link between monetary and political union, see Alesina *et al.* (2001).

Let us return to the graphical analysis of Figures 1 and 2 to study how the nature of the political union can affect the cost–benefit analysis underlying the OCA theory. Let us now suppose that the euro area is safely located in the OCA area (to the right of the OCA line). How can political union be brought into the analysis? We take the view that the degree of political integration affects the optimality of a monetary union in several ways. First, political union makes it possible to organize systems of fiscal transfers that provide some insurance against asymmetric shocks. Thus, when one member country is hit by a negative economic shock, the centralized union budget will automatically transfer income from the Member States that experience good economic conditions to the Member State experiencing a negative shock. As a result, this Member State will perceive the adherence to the union to be less costly than in the absence of the fiscal transfer.

Second, political union reduces the risk of asymmetric shocks that have a political origin. To give some examples that are relevant for the euro area: today spending and taxation in the euro area remain in the hands of national governments and parliaments. As a result, unilateral decisions to lower (or to increase) taxes create an asymmetric shock. Similarly, social security and wage policies are decided at the national level. Again this creates the scope for asymmetric shocks in the euro area, like in the case of France when that country decided alone to lower the working week to 35 hours. From the preceding, it follows that political unification reduces the scope for such asymmetric shocks.

The way one can represent the effect of political unification is twofold. First, the existence of a centralized budget makes it possible to alleviate the plight of countries hit by a negative shock. Thus, the cost of the union declines for any given level of asymmetry. This has the effect of shifting the OCA lines downward in Figures 1 and 2.[8] Second, political union reduces the degree of asymmetry,

[8]It is important that these transfers be reversible to maintain their insurance character. If these transfers attain a permanent one-way character, they are likely to become unpopular in the 'donator' country, leading to a perception of a high cost of the monetary union. This calls for the use of transfers only to alleviate the effects of temporary asymmetric

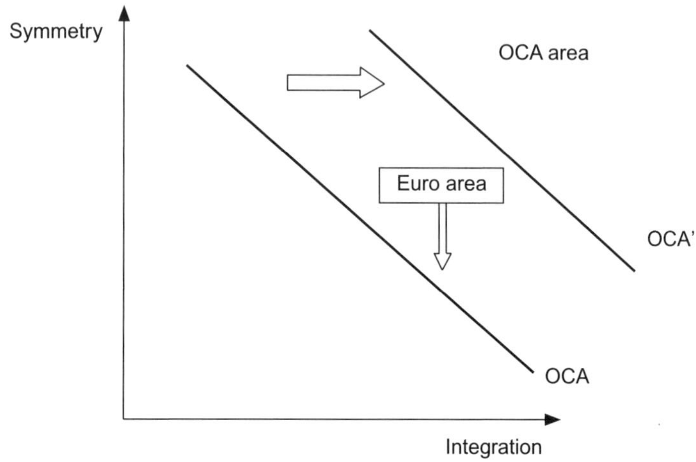

Figure 6. Political disintegration and the optimality of the euro area.

thereby shifting the euro area upwards. As a result of these two shifts political unification increases the long-term sustainability of monetary unions. Conversely political disintegration shifts the OCA lines upwards, thereby shrinking the OCA area and shifts the euro area downwards, creating the risk that the EU-12 ceases to be an optimal arrangement.[9] We represent the latter scenario in Figure 6. A political disintegration shifts the euro area downwards and shifts the OCA line to the right to the new position OCA'. As a result, it becomes more likely that the euro area ceases to be an optimal currency area, thereby undermining its long-term sustainability.[10]

A warning note should be sounded here. When we argue that some form of budgetary centralization is necessary to allow for an

shocks (business cycle movements) or, in the case of permanent asymmetric shocks, to make these transfers temporary allowing receiving countries to spread the adjustment cost over a longer time.

[9]For important additional insights into the link between monetary and political union, see von Hagen (1996), where it is argued that political unification can also lead to increased tensions between Member States. As a result, the link between monetary and political union is not a linear one.

[10]A similar analysis can be done using the symmetry-integration space of Figure 2. For a similar analysis, see von Hagen (1996).

insurance mechanism against asymmetric shocks, we should avoid the pitfalls of such mechanisms that have been observed within countries. These pitfalls have to do with moral hazard. We observe that this is often a serious problem when the transfers reduce the incentives of the receiving regions to adjust to shocks. As a result, temporary transfers can become chronic, thereby losing their insurance character. This feature will often lead to conflicts within the country (e.g., in Belgium) that are difficult to manage.

These moral hazard problems arise from the fact that the transfers within centralized countries are sizeable and unconditional. The insurance schemes envisaged for the euro area would remain relatively small compared to the national schemes given that the European budget today amounts to only 1 per cent of GDP while national budgets are often close to 50 per cent. It is quite inconceivable today that the European budget could approach national levels. We will therefore have to develop schemes that are much smaller and that, in addition, attach some conditionality on its use so as to reduce the moral hazard problems (for a discussion of such schemes, see Mélitz and Vori, 1993; and Hammond and von Hagen, 1993). Such relatively small and conditional insurance mechanisms, however, are an important ingredient in an integration effort whose aim is to create a sense of community of purpose. A union in which Member States show zero solidarity for the plight of other states cannot hope to have a reasonable chance of survival.

We conclude that, in order to enhance the sustainability of a monetary union it is important to have a central budget that can be used as a redistributive device between the Member States and it also matters to have some form of coordination of those areas of national economic policies that can generate macroeconomic shocks. The reason why this co-ordination is important is that these macroeconomic shocks spill over into the monetary union. For example, the decline in the working time in France was equivalent to a negative supply shock in France. This affected aggregate output in the euro area and thus the conduct of monetary policies by the ECB. This in turn influences all the other Member States of the euro area.

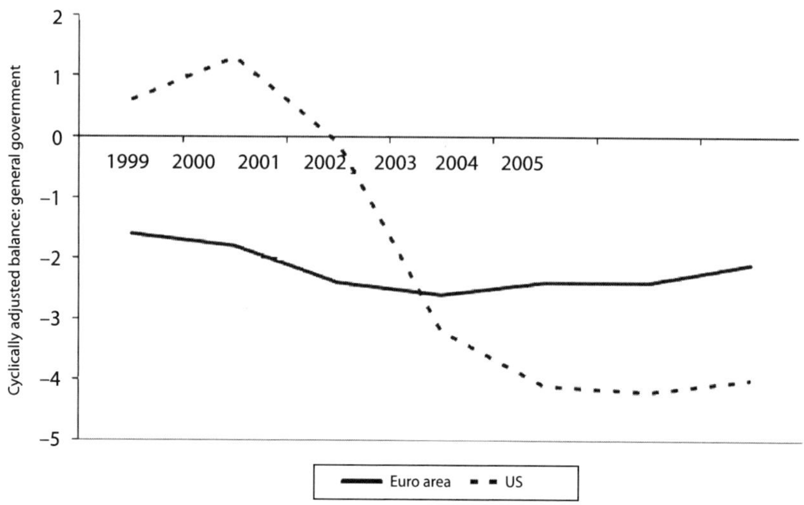

Figure 7. Cyclically adjusted budget balance in the euro area and the US.
Source: Commission (2005).

A central budget is important as a redistributive device. It also matters as a stabilizing instrument.[11] The absence of a central budget in the euro area implies that no budgetary policy aimed at stabilizing the business cycle in the union is available. The question that arises here is how important this is. In Figure 7 we show the contrast between the US and the euro area since 1999.

We observe that the US allowed its budget deficit to increase significantly as a response to the recession of 2001. There is no central budget in the euro area, but the aggregate of the national budget balances could work in a similar stabilizing way. The evidence of Figure 7, however, shows that this aggregate did not respond to the worsening economic conditions in the euro area from 2002 on. Thus, there is an absence of a system-wide budgetary policy in the euro area capable of performing a stabilizing role at the level of the euro area.

[11]Musgrave (1959) introduced the different functions of a government budget, as a distributive, a stabilizing and an allocative role.

The Brussels–Frankfurt consensus

The previous analysis and its conclusion that further political union is necessary for the long-run sustainability of the euro area is very much disputed by the Brussels–Frankfurt consensus, which has also become the official view. This view can be summarized as follows.

First, the way to deal with asymmetric shocks is to increase flexibility. As we showed in Figure 1, an increase in flexibility raises the sustainability of a monetary union. Thus a monetary union can be made sustainable by introducing structural reforms.

Second, the Stability and Growth Pact (SGP) provides all that countries need to use national fiscal policies as an instrument to deal with asymmetric shocks that have a cyclical (temporary) component. By following the SGP prescription of a balanced budget over the medium run, countries have enough flexibility to allow their budget deficit to increase up to 3 percent during an economic downturn. As a result, the euro area countries have the instrument to deal with business cycle movements.[12]

Third, there is no need to have a system-wide budgetary policy to stabilize the business cycle. ECB monetary policy is perfectly equipped to provide for macroeconomic stability in the euro area. By focusing on price stability the central bank does all that can be done to stabilize output movements at the euro area level. The reason is the following. If the output shocks are due to demand movements, inflation targeting will not only stabilize the rate of inflation but also the output movements. If these output movements are due to supply shocks they cannot be dealt with by monetary policies and/or budgetary policies.

The Brussels–Frankfurt consensus can be represented graphically in Figure 8. Structural reform has the effect of making the euro area countries more flexible, thereby shifting it to the right deep into the safe OCA-territory. At the same time the SGP rules allow for the

[12]One of the referees of this article pointed out that there is a certain coherence between the SGP and the need for flexibility. The SGP implements a fiscal framework for the monetary union that does not provide stabilizing transfers. As a result, not only does it put additional pressure on national budget consolidation, but it also increases the pressure to introduce more flexibility in the labour markets.

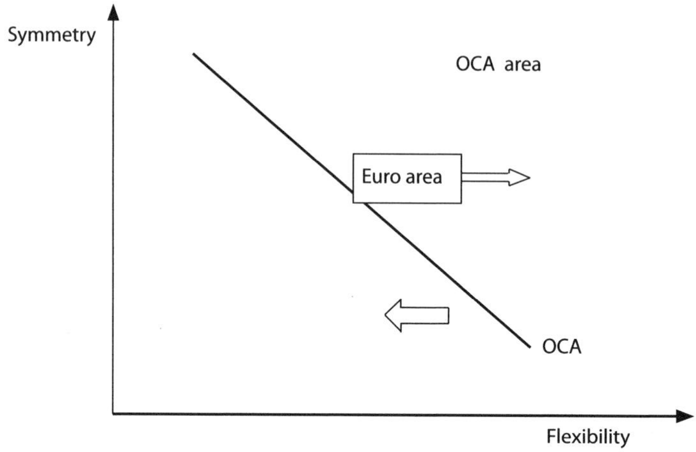

Figure 8. The Brussels–Frankfurt consensus.

use of national budgetary policies to alleviate the pain of asymmetric disturbances. This has the effect of shifting the OCA line to the left. The euro area can settle safely in the OCA area.

The conclusion from this analysis is that the present European institutions and their governance are appropriate to sustain the monetary union in the long run.[13] There is no need to increase the degree of political unification to make the monetary union sustainable. The euro area can survive in the long run without the need to create a European superstate.

An evaluation

What should we think of these two strongly opposing views? At the outset it can be interesting to focus on the underlying economic paradigms of these two views.

The Brussels–Frankfurt consensus is based on two academic theories. One is the monetarist theory which we discussed earlier, in which the central bank cannot do much to stabilize the economy. If it tries too hard to 'fine-tune' the economy it will end up with more

[13]See Padoa-Schioppa (2004) who as an insider develops a powerful criticism of this view which is implicit in the Brussels–Frankfurt consensus.

inflation. Thus the best thing a central bank can do is to stabilize the price level. This will have the incidental effect of producing the best possible outcome in terms of stability of the economic cycle. The second theory that influences the Brussels–Frankfurt consensus is the real business cycle theory. This says that the sources of economic cycles are shocks in technology (supply-side shocks) and changes in preferences (unemployment being mainly the result of workers taking more leisure). There is very little the central bank can do about these movements. The best is to keep the price level on a steady course. This will minimize the effects of these shocks. In addition, a macroeconomic policy based on the objective of price stability is the best thing the central bank can do to promote growth. As Lucas has stressed, the central bank's contribution to economic growth by maintaining price stability is immensely more important than an ephemeral success in reducing business cycle movements.

It will come as no surprise that if one adheres to these theories the present governance of the euro area is the right one: a central bank that cares about price stability and in so doing makes the best possible contribution to maintaining macroeconomic stability and to fostering economic growth; and national governments that keep budgetary discipline and do their utmost to introduce market flexibility. In such a world the productivity driven shocks can best be dealt with by governments keeping budgets in balance. Furthermore, in such a world the need to have an active budgetary policy at the euro area level does not exist.[14]

The theoretical underpinnings of the alternative OCA view are very different and are deeply rooted in Keynesian and neo-Keynesian ideas. In this view there are shocks in the economy that do not originate in the supply side but find their origin in the demand side. "Animal spirits," i.e., waves of optimism and pessimism capture consumers and investors. These waves have a strong element of self-fulfilling prophesy. When pessimism prevails, consumers and investors alike hold back their spending, thereby reducing output and

[14]It will also come as no surprise to those who have studied economic history that these were also the views that prevailed prior to the Great Depression.

income, and validating their pessimism. Similarly, when optimism prevails, consumers and investors will spend a lot, thereby increasing output and income, and validating their optimism.

The corollary of this effect is the well-known savings paradox. When pessimism prevails and consumers attempt to save more, the ensuing decline in income will prevent them from increasing their savings *ex post*. These phenomena were analysed by Keynes long ago, but have been thrown in the dustbins of economic history. Yet these ideas remain powerful, and have important influences on the governance of the monetary union.

In the logic of these Keynesian ideas, a monetary union needs a central budgetary authority capable of offsetting the desire of consumers gripped by pessimism to increase their savings, by dissaving of the central government. In addition, to the extent that there are asymmetric developments in demand at the national level, the existence of an automatic redistributive mechanism through a centralized budget can be a powerful stabilizing force. Finally, in this view the responsibility of a central bank extends beyond price stability (even if this remains its primary objective). There are movements in demand that cannot be stabilized by only caring about price stability.

From the preceding analysis it appears that the present governance of the euro area has been devised based on the assumption that the world is one which fits the monetarist-real-business-cycle (MRBC) theory. If the latter theory is indeed the correct view of the world, there is little need to move on with political integration in the euro area, and the present political governance of the euro area is perfectly adapted to the world in which we live.

But what if the MRBC theory is not a correct representation of the world? What if there are large movements in optimism and pessimism that affect consumers' and investors' behaviour? If we live in a world where such large movements are possible, then the euro area may have the wrong institutional design.

5. Conclusion

What have we learnt about monetary unions since the Treaty of Maastricht? A first idea which may have helped to convince the critics of monetary union is that, even if the euro area countries do not yet satisfy the OCA criteria, they will in the future as the monetary union sets in motion a process of more intense integration. This good-news-theory suggests that the euro area may be moving safely into the OCA area by the very fact that the euro area was started.

The existence of the euro area has also led economists to think about the governance of monetary union. The central idea here is that the absence of a political union is an important flaw in the governance of the euro area. For example, the lack of political union has had the unfortunate effect during the economic slowdown since 2001, of putting all the burden of macroeconomic management in the euro area on the shoulders of the ECB. The ECB, however, is neither ready nor willing to carry this burden. Yet the European population and its politicians will continue to expect the ECB to take on this role. It is clear, however, that the ECB alone cannot fulfil this role. This contrasts very much with the US where we have seen that both the central bank and the federal government have used their respective instruments to stabilize the business cycle.

The European monetary union is a remarkable achievement. Yet it also remains fragile because of a flaw in its governance. This is the absence of a sufficient degree of political union which includes a central European government with the power to spend and to tax, and which is independent of national governments. Such a government is necessary to complement the macroeconomic management of the euro area which is now entrusted exclusively to the ECB. In addition, a central European government is the only institution that can fully back the ECB.

Finally, the absence of a minimal degree of budgetary integration that can form the basis of an insurance mechanism is another flaw in the design of European monetary union. Such an insurance mechanism does not have to be as large and unconditional as those that exist within centralized countries. It is important, however, as a mechanism of solidarity even if its size is limited. It is difficult to conceive how a union can be politically sustainable if each time a country of the union gets into trouble because of asymmetric developments, it is told by the other members that it is entirely its own fault and that it should not count on any help. Such a union will not last.

The flaw in the design of the governance of the system that we have identified will have to be fixed. It should be clear, however, that it will be very difficult to do so. There is a general "integration fatigue" in Europe so that it is doubtful whether the European population wants to fix this flaw in the design of the euro system. At least it should be told that failure to do so implies that the European monetary union has no future.

References

Alesina, A, I Angeloni and F Etro (2001). The political economy of unions. NBER Working Papers.

Asdrubali, P, B Sorensen and O Yosha (1996). Channels of interstate risk sharing: United States 1963–1990. *Quarterly Journal of Economics*, 111, 1081–1110.

Baldwin, R (2005). The Euro's trade effects. Paper prepared for thre ECB Workshop What Effects is EMU Having on the Euro Area? Frankfurt, June.

Bertola, G (2000). Labor markets in the European Union. *Ifo-Studien*, 46(1), 99–122.

Bertola, G and T Boeri (2002). EMU labour market two years on: Microeconomic tensions and institutional evaluation. In *EMU and Economic Policy in Europe*, M Buti and A Sapir (eds.). Cheltenham: Edward Elgar.

Blanchard, O and F Giavazzi (2003). Macroeconomic effects of regulation and deregulation in goods and labor markets. *Quarterly Journal of Economics*, 118(3), 879–907.

Boeri T, A Brugiavini and L Calmfors (2001). *The Role of Unions in the Twenty-First Century-A Report for the Fondazione Rodolfo Debenedetti.* Oxford, UK: Oxford University Press.

Bun, M and F Klaassen (2002). Has the Euro increased trade? Tinbergen Institute Discussion Paper No. TI2002-108/2, Tinbergen Institute, Amsterdam/ Rotterdam.

Commission of the European Communities (2005). EMU after five years. European Economy, Special Report, Brussels, CEC.

Cukierman, A and F Lippi (2001). Labour markets and monetary union: A strategic analysis. *Economic Journal*, 111(473), 541–565.

De Grauwe, P (2005). *The Economics of Monetary Union*, 6th Edition. Oxford, UK: Oxford University Press.

De Grauwe, P and M Grimaldi (2006). *The Exchange Rate in a Behavioral Finance Framework.* Princeton, NJ: Princeton University Press.

Frankel, J and A Rose (1998). The endogeneity of the optimum currency area criteria. *Economic Journal*, 108, 1009–1025.

Gros, D, T Mayer and A Ubide (2005). The EMU at risk. 7th Annual Report of the CEPS Macroeconomic Policy Group, Brussels, Centre for European Policy Studies.

Hammond, G and J von Hagen (1993). *Regional Insurance Against Asymmetric Shocks: An Empirical Study for the European Community.* Mannheim: University of Mannheim.

Jones, E (2002). *The Politics of Economic and Monetary Union: Integration and Idiosyncrasy.* Lanham, MD/Oxford: Rowman and Littlefield.

Kenen, PB (1969). The optimum currency area: An eclectic view. In *Monetary Problems of the International Economy*, RA Mundell and A Swoboda (eds.). Chicago, IL: University of Chicago Press.

McKinnon, R (1963). Optimum currency areas. *American Economic Review*, 52, 712–725.

McKinnon, R (2004). Optimum currency areas and key currencies: Mundell I vs. Mundell II. *Journal of Common Market Studies*, 42(4), 689–715.

Mélitz, J (2001). Geography, Trade and Currency Union, CEPR Discussion Paper No. 2987, Centre for Economic Policy Research, London.

Mélitz, J and S Vori (1993). National insurance against unevenly distributed shocks in a European monetary union. *Recherches Economiques de Louvain*, 59, 1–2.

Micco, A, E Stein and G Ordonez (2003). The currency union effect on trade: Early evidence from EMU. *Economic Policy*, 37, 315–356.

Mundell, R (1961). A theory of optimal currency areas. *American Economic Review*, 51, 657–665.

Mundell, R (1973). Uncommon arguments for common currencies. In *The Economics of Common Currencies*, H Johnson and A Swoboda (eds.). London, UK: Allen & Unwin.

Musgrave, R (1959). *The Theory of Public Finance.* New York, NY: McGraw-Hill.

Padoa-Schioppa, T (2004). *The Euro and Its Central Bank: Getting United after the Union.* Cambridge, MA: MIT Press.

Rose, A (2000). One money, one market: The effect of common currencies on trade. *Economic Policy*, 30, 7–45.

Rose, A (2004). A meta-analysis of the effects of common currencies on international trade. NBER Working Paper No. 10373.

Rose, A and E van Wincoop (2001). National money as a barrier to trade: The real case for currency union. *American Economic Review, Papers and Proceedings*, 91(2), 386–390.

Sibert, A and A Sutherland (2000). Monetary union and labor market reform. *Journal of International Economics*, 51, 421–436.

Soskice, D and T Iversen (2001). Multiple wage bargaining systems in the single European currency area. *Empirica*, 28(4), 435–456.

von Hagen, J and G Hammond (1995). Regional insurance against asymmetric shocks. CEPR Discussion Paper No. 1170, Centre for Economic Policy Research, London.

von Hagen, J (1996). *Währungsunion, Fiskalunion, Politische Union.* Mannheim: University of Mannheim.

Wallace, H, W Wallace and M Pollack (2000). *Policy-Making in the European Union.* Oxford, UK: Oxford University Press.

Chapter 12

The Governance of a Fragile Eurozone

Paul De Grauwe

When entering a monetary union, member countries change the nature of their sovereign debt in a fundamental way; that is, they cease to have control over the currency in which their debt is issued. As a result, financial markets can force these countries' sovereigns into defaulting. This makes the monetary union fragile and vulnerable to changing market sentiments. It also makes it possible that self-fulfilling multiple equilibria arise. I analyze the implications of this fragility for the governance of the Eurozone. I argue that the role of the European Central Bank as a lender of last resort is crucial in reducing the fragility of the Eurozone. In addition, steps toward a budgetary union are key in structurally strengthening the union.

1. Introduction

In order to design the appropriate governance institutions for the Eurozone, it is important to make the right diagnosis of the nature of the debt crisis in the Eurozone. Failure to do so can lead to designing a governance structure that is inappropriate for dealing with the problems of the Eurozone. In this article, I argue that the governance structure that has emerged after a series of decisions of successive

Published in *Australian Economic Review*, 45(3), 255–268, 2012.
This article was prepared for the David Finch Lecture at the University of Melbourne, September 8, 2011. I am grateful to Daniel Gros, Martin Wolf and Charles Wyplosz for comments and suggestions.

European Council meetings, although an important step forwards, fails to address some fundamental problems in a monetary union.

2. A Paradox

I start with the paradox that is immediately visible from a comparison of Figs. 1 and 2. Figure 1 shows the debt to gross domestic

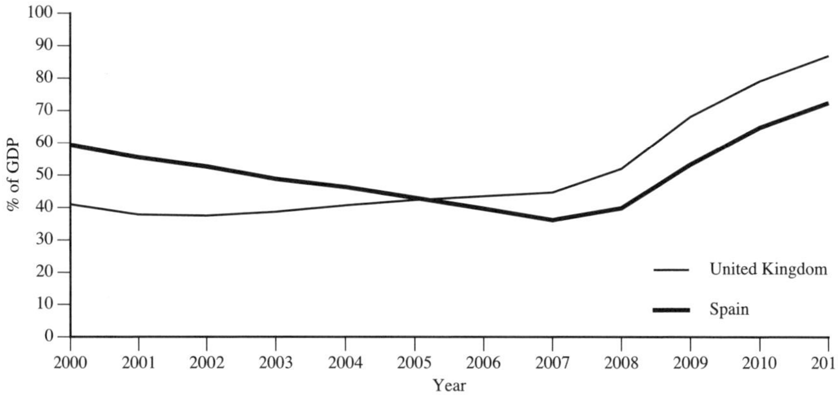

Figure 1. Gross government debt.

Source: AMECO, European Commission.

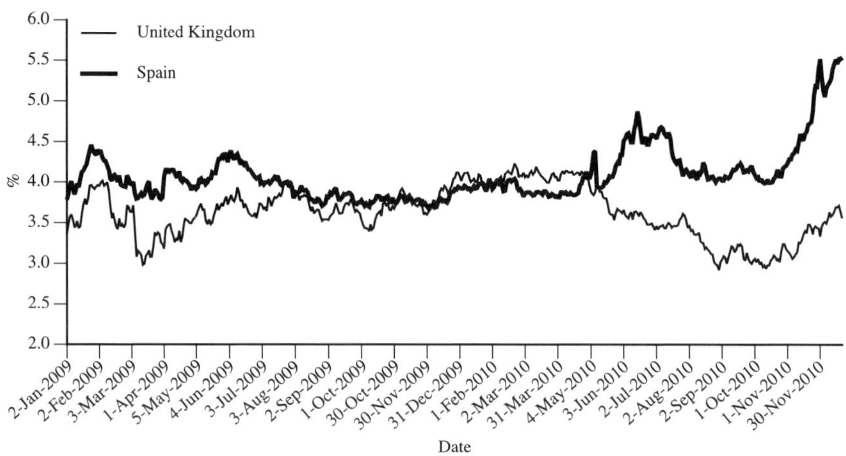

Figure 2. 10 year government bond rates, Spain and United Kingdom.

Source: Datastream.

product (GDP) ratios of the UK and Spain. It can be seen that, since the start of the financial crisis, the government debt ratio of the UK has increased more than that of Spain. As a result, in 2011 as a percentage of GDP, the UK Government's debt stood 17 percent higher than the Spanish Government's debt (89 percent versus 72 percent). Yet, from Figure 2, it appears that the financial markets have singled out Spain and not the UK as the country that could get entangled in a government debt crisis. This can be seen from the fact that, since the start of 2010, the yield on Spanish Government bonds has increased strongly relative to the UK, suggesting that the markets price in a significantly higher default risk on Spanish Government than on UK Government bonds. In early 2011, this difference amounted to 200 basis points. Why is it that financial markets attach a much higher default risk on Spanish Government than on UK Government bonds, while it appears that the UK faces less favourable sovereign debt and deficit dynamics?

One possible answer is that it may have something to do with the banking sector. This is unconvincing, though. The state of the UK banking sector is certainly not much better than the one of Spain. I will argue that this difference in the evaluation of the sovereign default risks is related to the fact that Spain belongs to a monetary union, while the UK is not part of a monetary union and therefore has control over the currency in which it issues its debt.

3. On the Nature of Sovereign Debt in a Monetary Union

In a nutshell, the difference in the nature of sovereign debt between members and non-members of a monetary union boils down to the following. Members of a monetary union issue debt in a currency over which they have no control. This has an important implication. It means that these countries' governments cannot guarantee the bond-holders that the cash will always be available to pay them out when the bonds mature. This is not the case in countries that are not part of a monetary union and have kept control over the currency in which they issue debt. Governments of these "standalone" countries give an implicit guarantee to the bond-holders that the cash will always be there to pay them out. The reason is that these governments can and will force the central bank to provide the cash in times of crisis (see Kopf, 2011).

The previous analysis suggests that there is an important, potentially destructive dynamic in a monetary union. Members of a monetary union are very susceptible to liquidity movements. When investors fear some payment difficulty (for example, triggered by a recession that leads to an increase in the government's budget deficit), liquidity is withdrawn from the national market (a "sudden stop"). This can set in motion a devilish interaction between liquidity and solvency crises. Once a member country gets entangled in a liquidity crisis, interest rates are pushed up. Thus, the liquidity crisis turns into a solvency crisis. Investors can then claim that it was right to pull out the money from a particular national market. It is a self-fulfilling prophecy: the country has become insolvent because investors fear insolvency.

Note that I am not arguing that all solvency problems in the Eurozone are of this nature. In the case of Greece, for example, one can argue that the Greek Government was insolvent before investors made their moves and triggered a liquidity crisis in May 2010. What I am arguing is that, in a monetary union, countries become vulnerable to self-fulfilling movements of distrust that set in motion a devilish interaction between liquidity and solvency crises.

From the preceding analysis, it follows that financial markets acquire great power in a monetary union.

4. Multiple Equilibria

The inherent volatility of financial markets leads to another fundamental problem. It can give rise to multiple equilibria, some of them good ones, others bad ones. This arises from the self-fulfilling nature of market expectations. In Appendix 1, I present a simple theoretical model showing more formally how multiple equilibria can arise.

Suppose markets trust government A. Investors then will show a willingness to buy government bonds at a low interest rate. A low interest rate embodies a belief that the default risk is low. But, the same low interest rate also has the effect of producing a low risk of defaulting. Markets trust that the UK Government will not default (despite having a high debt ratio). As a result, the UK Government enjoys a low interest rate. The solvency calculation then shows that indeed the UK Government is very solvent. Financial markets gently guide the UK toward a good equilibrium.

Suppose markets distrust government B. As a result, investors sell the government bonds. The ensuing increase in the interest rate embeds the belief that there is a default risk. At the same time, this high interest rate actually makes defaulting more likely. Thus, it appears that the market's distrust of the Spanish Government in a self-fulfilling way has made defaulting more likely. Financial markets push Spain towards a bad equilibrium.

The occurrence of bad equilibria is more likely with members of a monetary union, which have no control of the currency in which they issue their debt, than with standalone countries that have issued debt in a currency over which they have full control. Members of a monetary union face the same problem as emerging countries that, because of under-developed domestic financial markets, are forced to issue their debt in a foreign currency (see Calvo, 1988; Eichengreen, Hausmann and Panizza, 2005). In the words of Eichengreen, Hausmann and Panizza (2005), this works as the "original sin" that leads these countries into a bad equilibrium full of pain and misery.

To wrap up the previous discussion: members of a monetary union are sensitive to movements of distrust that have self-fulfilling properties and that can lead them to be pushed into a bad equilibrium. The latter arises because distrust can set in motion a devilish interaction between liquidity and solvency crises. Being pushed into a bad equilibrium has two further consequences. I analyze these in the following section.

5. The Bad News about a Bad Equilibrium

There are two features of a bad equilibrium that are worth analysing further. First, domestic banks are affected by the bad equilibrium in different ways. When investors pull out from the domestic bond market, the interest rate on government bonds increases. Since the domestic banks are usually the main investors in the domestic sovereign bond market, this shows up as significant losses on their balance sheets. In addition, domestic banks are caught up in a funding problem. As argued earlier, domestic liquidity dries up (the money stock declines), making it difficult for the domestic banks to roll-over their deposits, except by paying prohibitive interest rates. Thus, the sovereign debt crisis spills over into a domestic banking crisis, even if the domestic banks were sound to start with. This feature has played an important role in the case of Greece and Portugal, where the sovereign debt crisis has led to a full-blown banking crisis. In the case of Ireland, there was a banking problem prior to the sovereign debt crisis (which, in fact, triggered the sovereign debt crisis). The latter, however, intensified the banking crisis.

Second, once in a bad equilibrium, members of a monetary union find it very difficult to use automatic budget stabilizers: a recession leads to higher government budget deficits, which in turn lead to markets' distrust of the capacity of governments to service their future debt, triggering a liquidity and solvency crisis, of which the latter then forces them to institute austerity programs in the midst of a recession. In the stand-alone country (UK), this does not happen because the distrust generated by higher budget deficit triggers a stabilising mechanism.

Thus, member countries of a monetary union are downgraded to the status of emerging economies, which find it difficult if not impossible to use budgetary policies to stabilise the business cycle. This feature has been shown to produce pronounced booms and busts in emerging economies (see Eichengreen, Hausmann and Panizza, 2005).

This feature of a monetary union makes it potentially very costly. The automatic stabilisers in the government's budget constitute an important social achievement in the developed world as they soften the pain created by the booms and busts in capitalist societies for many people. If a monetary union has the implication of destroying these automatic stabilisers, it is unclear whether the social and political basis for such a union can be maintained. It is therefore important to design a governance structure that maintains these automatic stabilisers.

6. Imbalances and Sovereign Debt

The previous analysis allows us to connect sovereign debt dynamics and imbalance problems. It is now widely recognized that one of the fundamental imbalances in the Eurozone is the increased divergence in competitive positions of the members of the Eurozone since 2000. The phenomenon is shown in Figure 3. One may criticize this figure because of the choice of 2000 as the base year. Indeed, this choice assumes that, in 2000, there were no imbalances in competitive positions, so that any movement away from the 2000 level is a departure from equilibrium and thus problematic. This is surely not the case (see Alcidi and Gros, 2010). A number of countries may have been far from equilibrium in 2000, so that movements observed since that date could conceivably be movements towards equilibrium. In order to take this criticism into account, I present relative unit labor costs of the member countries using the long-term average over the

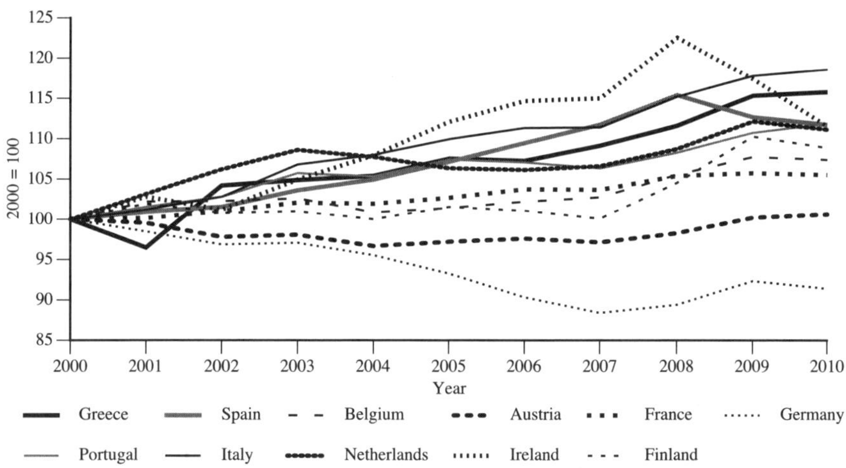

Figure 3. Relative unit labor costs in the Eurozone (2000 = 100).

Source: AMECO, European Commission.

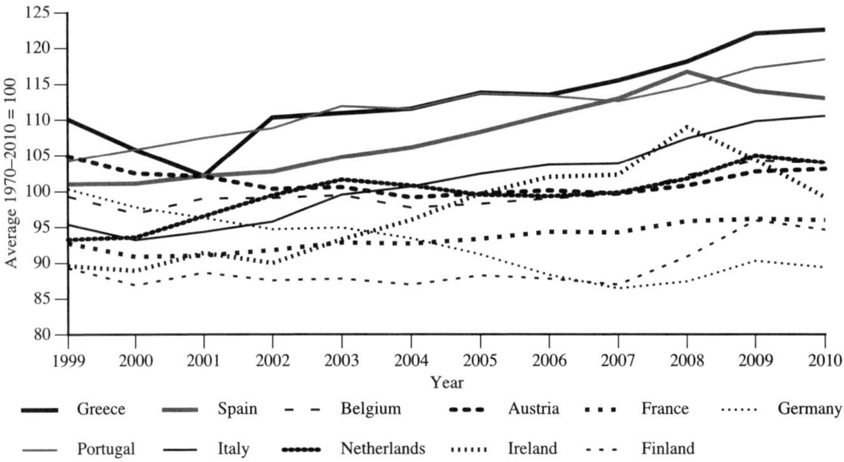

Figure 4. Relative unit labor costs in the Eurozone (average 1970–2010 = 100).

Source: AMECO, European Commission.

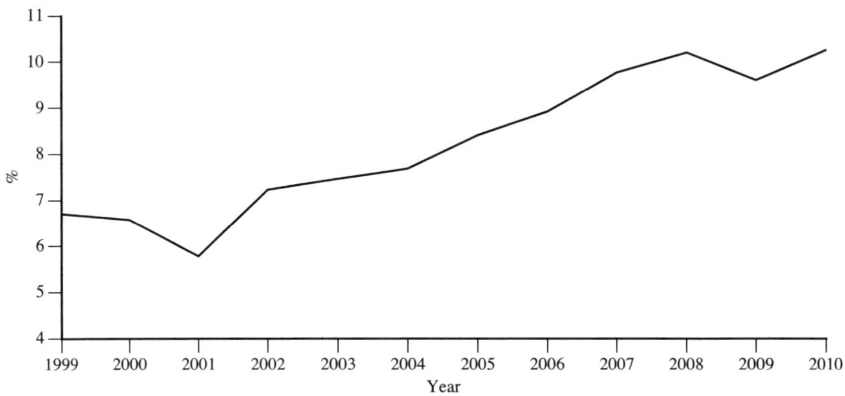

Figure 5. Standard deviation relative unit labor costs in the Eurozone.

Note: Computed using data of Figure 4.

period 1970–2010 as the base. The results are shown in Figure 4. The divergence is less spectacular, but still very significant. Figure 5 confirms this: the standard deviation of the yearly indices increased significantly since 1999.

The countries that lost competitiveness from 1999 to 2008 (Greece, Portugal, Spain and Ireland) have to start improving it. Given the impossibility of using a devaluation of the currency, an internal devaluation must be engineered; that is, wages and prices must be brought down relative to those of the competitors. This can only be achieved by deflationary macroeconomic policies (mainly budgetary policies). Inevitably, this will first lead to a recession and thus (through the operation of the automatic stabilisers) to increases in budget deficits.

Most of the analyses in textbooks now stop by noting that this is a slow and painful process. The analysis of the previous sections, however, allows us to go a little further and to link it with the debt dynamics described earlier. As countries experience increasing budget deficits while they attempt to improve their competitiveness, financial markets are likely to get nervous. Distrust may install itself. If strong enough, the latter may lead to a liquidity crisis, as described before. This then inevitably triggers a solvency crisis.

Thus, the period during which countries try to improve their competitiveness is likely to be painful *and* turbulent: painful because of the recession and the ensuing increase in unemployment and turbulent because, during the adjustment period, the country can be hit by sovereign debt and banking crises. If the latter occur, the deflationary spiral is bound to be intensified. For, in that case, the domestic long-term interest rate increases dramatically, forcing the authorities to apply even more budgetary austerity, which in turn leads to an even more intense recession. The banks that are trapped in a funding crisis reduce their credit to the economy. The country finds itself stuck in a bad equilibrium, characterized by austerity programs that fail to reduce budget deficits because they lead to a downward economic spiral and punishing interest rate levels. The path towards recovery for members of a monetary union is likely to be crisis-prone.

The contrast with stand-alone countries that have the capacity to issue debt in their own currency is stark. When these countries have lost competitiveness, they will typically try to restore it by allowing the currency to drop in the foreign exchange market. This makes it possible not only to avoid deflation, but also to avoid a sovereign debt crisis. As we have seen earlier, these countries' governments cannot be forced into defaulting by triggering a liquidity crisis. What is more, the whole adjustment process involving currency depreciation is likely to boost output and inflation, thereby improving the solvency of the sovereign.

7. What Kind of Governance?

In order to solve the problems that were analysed in the previous sections, collective action is necessary. Collective action can be taken at two levels. One is at the level of the central banks, the other is at the level of the government budgets.

Liquidity crises are avoided in stand-alone countries that issue debt in their own currencies, mainly because the central bank can be forced to provide all the necessary liquidity to the sovereign. This outcome can also be achieved in a monetary union if the common central bank is willing to buy the different sovereigns' debt. I discuss the role of the European Central Bank (ECB) as a lender of last resort in the government bond markets in Section 8.

Collective action can also be taken at the budgetary level. Ideally, a budgetary union is the instrument of collective action. By consolidating (centralizing) national government budgets into one central budget, a mechanism of automatic transfers can be organised. Such a mechanism works as an insurance mechanism that transfers resources to the country hit by a negative economic shock. In addition, such a consolidation creates a common fiscal authority that can issue debt in a currency under the control of that authority. In so doing, it protects the member states from being forced into defaulting by financial markets. It also protects the monetary union from the centrifugal forces that financial markets can exert on the union.

This solution of the systemic problem of the Eurozone requires a far-reaching degree of political union. Economists have stressed that such a political union will be necessary to sustain the monetary union in the long run (see Commission of the European Communities, 1977; De Grauwe, 1992). It is clear, however, that there is no willingness in

Europe today to significantly increase the degree of political union. This unwillingness to go in the direction of more political union will continue to make the Eurozone a fragile construction. I discuss a strategy of small steps in the process of budgetary unification in Section 9.

8. The European Central Bank as a Lender of Last Resort in the Government Bond Markets

The single most important argument for mandating the ECB to be a lender of last resort in the government bond markets is to prevent countries from being pushed into a bad equilibrium. The self-fulfilling nature of expectations creates a coordination failure; that is, the fear of insufficient liquidity pushes countries into a situation in which there will be insufficient liquidity for both the government and the banking sector. The central bank can solve this coordination failure by providing lending of last resort.

Failure to provide lending of last resort in the government bond markets of the monetary union carries the risk of forcing the central bank into providing lending of last resort to the banks of the countries that are hit by a sovereign debt crisis and this lending of last resort is almost certainly more expensive. The reason is that most often the liabilities of the banking sector of a country are many times larger than the liabilities of the national government. In 2008, bank liabilities in the Eurozone represented about 250 percent of GDP. This compares to a government debt to GDP ratio in the Eurozone of approximately 80 percent in the same year.

While the argument for mandating the ECB to be a lender of last resort in the government bond markets is a strong one, the opposition to giving the ECB this mandate is equally intense. Let me review the main arguments that have been formulated against giving a lender-of-last-resort role to the ECB.

8.1. *Risk of Inflation*

A popular argument against an active role of the ECB as a lender of last resort in the sovereign bond market is that this would lead to inflation. By buying government bonds, it is said, the ECB increases the money stock, thereby leading to a risk of inflation. Does an increase in the money stock not always lead to more inflation, as Milton Friedman taught us? Two points should be made here.

First, a distinction should be introduced between the money base and the money stock. When the central bank buys government bonds (or other assets), it increases the money base (currency in circulation and banks' deposits at the central bank). This does not mean that the money stock increases. In fact, during periods of financial crises, both monetary aggregates tend to become disconnected. An example of this is shown in Figure 6. One observes that, prior to the banking crisis of October 2008, both aggregates were very much connected. From October 2008, however, the disconnection became quite spectacular. In order to save the banking system, the ECB massively piled up assets on its balance sheets, the counterpart of which was a very large increase in the money base.[1] This had no effect on the money stock (M3) (see Figure 6). In fact, the latter declined until the

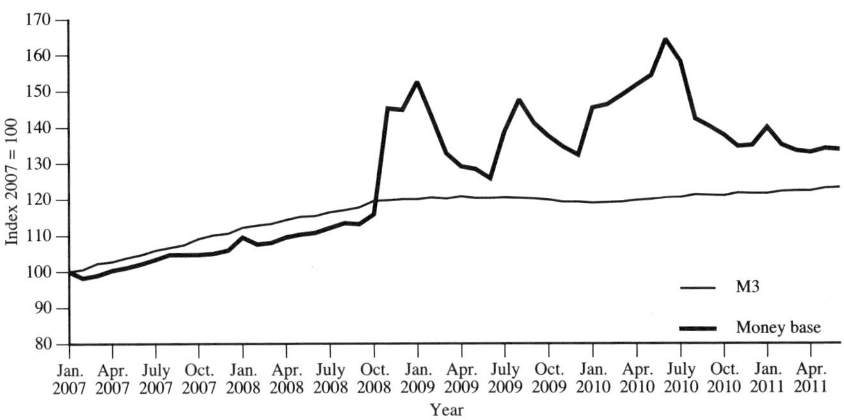

Figure 6. Money base and M3 in the Eurozone.

Source: Statistical Data Warehouse, European Central Bank.

[1]Note that, compared to the US Fed and the Bank of England, the expansion of the balance sheet of the ECB was much less pronounced. See the data in Appendix 1. It appears that the ECB has been a timid lender of last resort, compared to the Fed and the Bank of England.

end of 2009. The reason why this happened is that banks piled up the liquidity provided by the ECB without using it to extend credit to the non-banking sector. A similar phenomenon has been observed in the US and the UK.

Another way to understand this phenomenon is to note that, when a financial crisis erupts, agents want to hold cash for safety reasons. If the central bank decides not to supply the cash, it turns the financial crisis into an economic recession and possibly a depression, as agents scramble for cash. When instead the central bank exerts its function of lender of last resort and supplies more money base, it stops this deflationary process. That does not allow us to conclude that the central bank is likely to create inflation.

All this was very well understood by Milton Friedman, the father of monetarism, who cannot be suspected of favouring inflationary policies. In his classic book, co-authored with Anna Schwartz, *A Monetary History of the United States*, he argued that the Great Depression was so intense because the Federal Reserve failed to perform its role of lender of last resort and did not increase the US money base sufficiently (see Friedman and Schwartz 1961). In fact, Friedman and Schwartz produce a figure that is very similar to Figure 2, showing how, during the period 1929–33, the US money stock declined, while the money base ("high-powered money") increased (Friedman and Schwartz, 1961, p. 333). Friedman and Schwartz argued forcefully that the money base should have increased much more and that the way to achieve this was by buying government securities. Much to the chagrin of Friedman and Schwartz, the Federal Reserve failed to do so. Those who today fear the inflationary risks of lender-of-last-resort operations would do well to read Friedman and Schwartz.

8.2. *Fiscal Consequences*

A second criticism is that lender-of-last-resort operations in the government bond markets can have fiscal consequences. The reason is that, if governments fail to service their debts, the ECB will make losses. These will have to be borne by taxpayers. Thus, by intervening in the government bond markets, the ECB is committing future taxpayers. The ECB should avoid operations that mix monetary and fiscal policies (see Goodfriend, 2011).

All this sounds reasonable. Yet, it fails to recognise that all open market operations (including foreign exchange market operations) carry the risk of losses and thus have fiscal implications. When a central bank buys private paper in the context of its open market operation, there is a risk involved because the issuer of the paper can default. This will then lead to losses for the central bank.[2] These losses are in no way different from the losses that the central bank can incur when buying government bonds. Thus, the argument really implies that a central bank should abstain from any open market operation. It should stop being a central bank. The truth is that a central bank should perform (risky) open market operations. The fact that these are potentially loss-making should not deter the central bank. Losses can be necessary, even desirable, to guarantee financial stability.

There is another dimension to the problem that follows from the fragility of the government bond markets in a monetary union. I argued earlier that financial markets can, in a self-fulfilling way, drive countries into a bad equilibrium, where defaulting becomes inevitable. The use of the lender of last resort can prevent countries from being pushed into such a bad equilibrium. If the intervention by the central bank is successful, there will be no losses and no fiscal consequences.

8.3. *What About Moral Hazard?*

Like with all insurance mechanisms, there is a risk of moral hazard. By providing lender-of-last-resort insurance, the ECB gives an incentive to governments to issue too much debt. This is indeed a serious risk. But, this risk of moral hazard is no different from the risk of moral hazard in the banking system. It would be a terrible mistake if the central bank were to abandon its role of lender of last resort

[2]The same is true with foreign exchange market operations that can lead to large losses, as has been shown by the recent Swiss experience.

in the banking sector because there is a risk of moral hazard. In the same way, it is wrong for the ECB to abandon its role of lender of last resort in the government bond market because there is a risk of moral hazard.

The way to deal with moral hazard is to impose rules that will constrain governments in issuing debt, very much like how moral hazard in the banking sector is tackled by imposing limits on risk-taking by banks. In general, it is better to separate liquidity provision from moral hazard concerns. Liquidity provision should be performed by a central bank and the governance of moral hazard by another institution, the supervisor. This has been the approach taken in the strategy towards the banking sector: the central bank assumes the responsibility of lender of last resort, thereby guaranteeing unlimited liquidity provision in times of crisis, irrespective of what this does to moral hazard, while the supervisory authority takes over the responsibility of regulating and supervising the banks.

This should also be the design of the governance structure within the Eurozone. The ECB assumes the responsibility of lender of last resort in the sovereign bond markets. A different and independent authority takes over the responsibility of regulating and supervising the creation of debt by national governments. To use a metaphor: when a house is burning, the fire department is responsible for extinguishing the fire and another department (police and justice) is responsible for investigating wrongdoing and applying punishment if necessary. Both functions should be kept separate. A fire department that is responsible both for fire-extinguishing and punishment is unlikely to be a good fire department. The same is true for the ECB. If the latter tries to solve a moral hazard problem, it will fail in its duty to be a lender of last resort.

9. Budgetary Union: A Strategy of Small Steps

While a full budgetary union appears to be a perspective for the very long run, there is a strategy of small steps that could be implemented relatively quickly and that could show the way to a fuller budgetary union. This consists of the joint issue of Eurobonds.

By jointly issuing Eurobonds, the participating countries become jointly liable for the debt they have issued together. This is a very visible and constraining commitment that will convince the markets that member countries are serious about the future of the Euro (see Verhofstadt, 2009; Juncker and Tremonti, 2010). In addition, by pooling the issue of government bonds, the member countries protect themselves against the destabilising liquidity crises that arise from their inability to control the currency in which their debt is issued. A common bond issue does not suffer from this problem.

The proposal of issuing common Eurobonds has met stiff resistance in a number of countries (see Issing, 2009). This resistance is understandable. A common Eurobond creates a number of serious problems that have to be addressed.

The first problem is moral hazard. The common Eurobond issue contains an implicit insurance for the participating countries. Since countries are collectively responsible for the joint debt issue, an incentive is created for countries to rely on this implicit insurance and to issue too much debt. This creates a lot of resistance in the other countries that behave responsibly. It is unlikely that these countries will be willing to step into a common Eurobond issue unless this moral hazard risk is resolved.

The second problem (not unrelated to the previous one) arises because some countries, like Germany, Finland and the Netherlands, today profit from triple A ratings that allow them to obtain the best possible borrowing conditions. The question arises of what the benefits can be for these countries. Indeed, it is not inconceivable that, by joining a common bond mechanism that will include other countries enjoying less favourable credit ratings, countries like Germany, Finland and the Netherlands may actually have to pay a higher interest rate on their debt.

These objections are serious. They can be addressed by a careful design of the common Eurobond mechanism. The design of the common Eurobonds must be such as to eliminate the moral hazard risk and must produce sufficient attractiveness for the countries with favourable credit ratings. This can be achieved by working both on the quantity and the pricing of the Eurobonds.

Thus, my proposal would be to seek a combination of the Eurobond proposal made by De Grauwe and Moesen (2009) and the one made by Bruegel (Delpla and von Weizsäcker 2010). It would work as follows. Countries would be able to participate in the joint Eurobond issue up to 60 percent of their GDP, thus creating "blue bonds." Anything above 60 percent would have to be issued in the national bond markets ("red bonds"). This would create a senior (blue) tranche that would enjoy the best possible rating. The junior (red) tranche would face a higher risk premium. This existence of this risk premium would create a powerful incentive for the governments to reduce their debt levels. In fact, it is likely that the interest rate that countries would have to pay on their red bonds would be higher than the interest rate that they pay today on their total outstanding debt (see Gros, 2010, on this). The reason is that, by creating a senior tranche, the probability of defaulting on the junior tranche may actually increase. This should increase the incentive for countries to limit the red component of their bond issues.

The Bruegel proposal can be criticised on the following grounds. To the extent that the underlying risk of the government bonds is unchanged, restructuring these bonds into different tranches does not affect the risk. Thus, if the blue bond carries a lower interest rate, the red bond will have a higher interest rate, such that the average borrowing cost will be exactly the same as when there is only one type of bond (see Gros, 2010). This is an application of the Modigliani-Miller theorem which says that the value of a firm is unaffected by the way the liabilities of that firm are structured.

All this is true to the extent that the underlying risk is unchanged. The point, however, is that the common bond issue is an instrument to shield countries from being pushed into a bad equilibrium. If the common bond issue succeeds in doing so, the underlying risk of the bonds of these countries does indeed decline. In that case, these countries are able to enjoy a lower average borrowing cost. At the same time, the marginal borrowing cost is likely to be higher than the average. This is exactly what one wants to have: a decline of the average debt cost and an increase in the marginal cost of the debt. The former makes it easier to service the debt, the latter provides strong incentives towards reducing the level of the debt. This feature is important to reduce the moral hazard risk.

The second feature of my proposal works on the pricing of the Eurobonds and it follows the proposal made by De Grauwe and Moesen (2009). This consists of using different fees for the countries participating in the blue bond issue. These fees would be related to the fiscal position of the participating countries. Thus, countries with high government debt levels would face a higher fee and countries with lower debt levels would pay a lower fee. In practical terms, this means that the interest rate paid by each country in the blue bond tranche would be different. Fiscally prudent countries would have to pay a somewhat lower interest rate than fiscally less prudent countries. This would ensure that the blue bond issue would remain attractive for the countries with the best credit rating, thereby giving them an incentive to joint the Eurobond mechanism.

It should be noted that, if successful, such a common Eurobond issue would create a large new government bond market with a lot of liquidity. This in turn would attract outside investors, making the Euro a reserve currency. As a result, the Euro would profit from an additional premium. It has been estimated that the combined liquidity and reserve currency premium enjoyed by the US dollar amounts to approximately 50 basis points (Gourinchas and Rey, 2007). A similar premium could be enjoyed by the Euro. This would make it possible for the Eurozone countries to lower the average cost of borrowing, very much like the US has been able to do.

10. Conclusion

A monetary union is more than one currency and one central bank. Countries that join a monetary union lose more than an instrument of economic policy (interest rate or exchange rate). When entering the monetary union, they lose their capacity to issue debt in a currency over which they have full control. As a result, a loss of confidence of investors can, in a self-fulfilling way, drive the country into defaulting. This is not so for countries that are capable of issuing debt in their own currency. In these countries, the central bank can always provide the liquidity to the sovereign to avoid defaulting. This may lead to future inflation, but it shields the sovereign from a default that is forced by the market.

Thus, member countries of a monetary union become more vulnerable. Changing market sentiments can lead to "sudden stops" in the funding of the government debt, setting in motion a devilish interaction between liquidity and solvency crises. There is an important further implication of this increased vulnerability. This is that member countries of a monetary union lose much of their capacity to apply countercyclical budgetary policies. When during a recession the budget deficit increases, this risks creating a loss of confidence of investors in the capacity of the sovereign to service the debt. This has the effect of raising the interest rate, making the recession worse and leading to an even higher budget deficit. As a result, countries in a monetary union can be forced into a bad equilibrium, characterized by deflation, high interest rates, high budget deficits and a banking crisis.

These systemic features of a monetary union have not sufficiently been taken into account in the new design of the economic governance of the Eurozone. Too much of this new design has been influenced by the notion (based on moral hazard thinking) that, when a country experiences budget deficits and increasing debts, it should be punished by high interest rates and tough austerity programs. I have argued that this approach is usually not helpful in restoring budgetary balance.

A monetary union can only function if there is a collective mechanism of mutual support and control. Such a collective mechanism exists in a political union. In the absence of a political union, the member countries of the Eurozone are condemned to fill in the necessary pieces of such a collective mechanism. The debt crisis has made it possible to fill in a few of these pieces. What has been achieved, however, is still far from sufficient to guarantee the survival of the Eurozone.

Appendix 1: A Model of Good and Bad Equilibria

In this section, I present a very simple model illustrating how multiple equilibria can arise. The starting point is that there is a cost

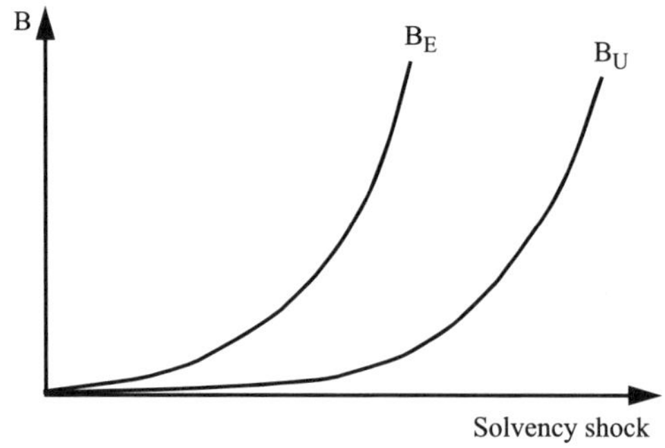

Figure A1. The benefits of defaulting after a solvency shock.

and a benefit of defaulting on the debt and that investors take this calculus of the sovereign into account. I will assume that the country involved is subject to a shock, which takes the form of a decline in government revenues. The latter may be caused by a recession or a loss of competitiveness. I will call this a "solvency shock". The higher this shock, the greater is the loss of solvency. I concentrate first on the benefit side. This is represented in Figure A1. On the horizontal axis, I show the solvency shock. On the vertical axis, I represent the benefit of defaulting. There are many ways and degrees of defaulting. To simplify, I assume this takes the form of a "haircut" of a fixed percentage. The benefit of defaulting in this way is that the government can reduce the interest burden on the outstanding debt. As a result, after the default it will have to apply less austerity; that is, it will have to reduce spending and/or increase taxes by less than without the default. Since austerity is politically costly, the government profits from the default.

A major insight of the model is that the benefit of a default depends on whether this default is expected or not. I show two curves representing the benefit of a default. B_U is the benefit of a default that investors do not expect to happen, while B_E is the benefit of a default that investors expect to happen. Let me first concentrate on the B_U curve. It is upward-sloping because when the solvency shock increases, the benefit of a default for the sovereign goes up. The reason is that when the solvency shock is large (that is, the decline in tax income is large), the cost of austerity is substantial.

Defaulting then becomes more attractive for the sovereign. I have drawn this curve to be non-linear, but this is not essential for the argument. I distinguish three factors that affect the position and the steepness of the B_U curve:

- The initial debt level: the higher is this level, the higher is the benefit of a default. Thus, with a higher initial debt level, the B_U curve will rotate upwards.
- The efficiency of the tax system: in a country with an inefficient tax system, the government cannot easily increase taxation. Thus, in such a country, the option of defaulting be comes more attractive. The B_U curve rotates upwards.
- The size of the external debt: when external debt takes a large proportion of total debt, there will be less domestic political resistance against defaulting, making the latter more attractive (the B_U curve rotates upwards).

I now concentrate on the B_E curve. This shows the benefit of a default when investors anticipate such a default. It is located above the B_U curve for the following reason. When investors expect a default, they will sell government bonds. As a result, the interest rate on government bonds increases. This raises the government's budget deficit, requiring a more intense austerity program of spending cuts and tax hikes. Thus, defaulting becomes more attractive. For every solvency shock, the benefits of defaulting will now be higher than they were when the default was not anticipated.

I now introduce the cost side of the default. The cost of a default arises from the fact that, when defaulting, the government suffers a loss of reputation. This loss of reputation will make it difficult for the government to borrow in the future. I will make the simplifying assumption that this is a fixed cost. I now obtain Figure A2, where I present the fixed cost (C) with the benefit curves.

I now have the tools to analyse the equilibrium of the model. I will distinguish between three types of solvency shocks: a small one, an intermediate one and a large one. Take a small solvency shock: this is a shock $S < S_1$. (This could be the shocks that Germany and the Netherlands experienced during the debt crisis.) For this small

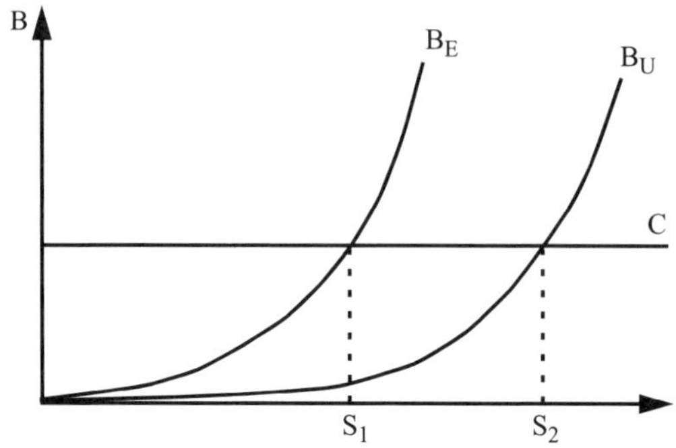

Figure A2. Costs and benefits of defaulting after a solvency shock.

shock, the cost of a default is always larger than the benefits (both of an expected and an unexpected default). Thus, the government will not want to default. When expectations are rational, investors will not expect a default. As a result, a no-default equilibrium can be sustained.

Let us now analyse a large solvency shock. This is one for which $S > S_2$. (This could be the shock experienced by Greece.) For all these large shocks, we observe that the cost of a default is always smaller than the benefits (both of an expected and an unexpected default). Thus, the government will want to default. In a rational expectations framework, investors will anticipate this. As a result, a default is inevitable.

I now turn to the intermediate case: $S_1 < S < S_2$. (This could be the shocks that Ireland, Portugal and Spain experienced.) For these intermediate shocks, I obtain an indeterminacy; that is, two equilibria are possible. Which one will prevail only depends on what is expected. To see this, suppose the solvency shock is S' (see Figure A3). In this case, there are two potential equilibria, D and N. Take point D. In this case, investors expect a default (D is located on the B_E line). This has the effect of making the benefit of a default larger than the cost C. Thus, the government will default. D is an equilibrium that is consistent with expectations.

But, point N is an equally good candidate to be an equilibrium point. In N, investors do not expect a default (N is on the B_U line).

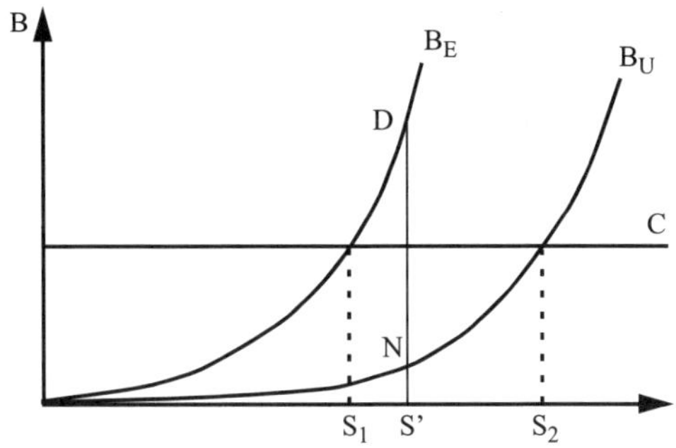

Figure A3. Good and bad equilibria.

As a result, the benefit of a default is lower than the cost. Thus, the government will not default. It follows that N is also an equilibrium point that is consistent with expectations.

Thus, we obtain two possible equilibria: a bad one (D) that leads to a default and a good one (N) that does not lead to a default. Both are equally possible. The selection of one of these two points only depends on what investors expect. If the latter expect a default, there will be one; if they do not expect a default, there will be none. This remarkable result is due to the self-fulfilling nature of expectations.

Since there is a lot of uncertainty about the likelihood of a default and since investors have very little scientific foundation to calculate probabilities of a default (there has been none in Western Europe in the last 60 years), expectations are likely to be driven mainly by market sentiments of optimism and pessimism. Small changes in these market sentiments can lead to large movements from one type of equilibrium to another.

The possibility of multiple equilibria is unlikely to occur when the country is a stand-alone country; that is, when it can issue sovereign debt in its own currency. This makes it possible for the country to always avoid an outright default because the central bank can be forced to provide all the liquidity that is necessary to avoid such an outcome. This has the effect that there is only one benefit curve. In this case, the government can still decide to default (if the solvency shock is large enough), but the country cannot be forced to do so by the whim of market expectations.

References

Alcidi, C and D Gros (2010). The European experience with large fiscal adjustments. Centre For European Policy Studies Policy Brief. Available at http://www.ceps.eu/book/european-experience-large-fiscal-adjustments.

Calvo, G (1988). Servicing the public debt: The role of expectations. *American Economic Review*, 78, 647–661.

Commission of the European Communities (1977). *Report of the Study Group on the Role of Public Finance in European Integration*. Brussels: European Commission.

De Grauwe, P (1992). *The Economics of Monetary Integration*, 1st Edition. Oxford, UK: Oxford University Press.

De Grauwe, P and W Moesen (2009). Gains for all: A proposal for a common eurobond. *Intereconomics*, May/June, 2–5.

Delpla, J and J von Weizsäcker (2010). The blue bond proposal. Bruegel Policy Brief No. 2010/03, Brussels.

Eichengreen, B, R Hausmann and U Panizza (2005). The pain of original sin. In *Other People's Money: Debt Denomination and Financial Instability in Emerging Market Economies*, B Eichengreen and R Hausmann (eds.). Chicago, IL: Chicago University Press.

Friedman, M and A Schwartz (1961). *A Monetary History of the United States*. Princeton, NJ: Princeton University Press.

Goodfriend, M (2011). Central banking in the credit turmoil: An assessment of federal reserve practice. *Journal of Monetary Economics*, 58, 1–12.

Gourinchas, P-O and H Rey (2007). From world banker to world venture capitalist: The US external adjustment and the exorbitant privilege. In *G7 Current Account Imbalances: Sustainability and Adjustment*, R Clarida (ed.). Chicago, IL: University of Chicago Press.

Gros, D (2010). The seniority conundrum: Bail out countries but bail in private short-term creditors. Centre for European Policy Studies Commentary,10 November.

Juncker, J-C and G Tremonti (2010). E-bonds would end the crisis. *Financial Times*, December, 5.

Issing, O (2009). Why a common eurozone bond isn't such a good idea. *Europe's World*, Summer, 77–79.

Kopf, C (2011). Restoring financial stability in the euro area. Centre for European Policy Studies Policy Brief.

Verhofstadt, G (2009). *De Weg uit de Crisis. Hoe Europa de Wereld Kan Redden*. Amsterdam: De Bezige Bij.

Chapter 13

Do Asymmetries Matter for European Monetary Policy?

Yunus Aksoy, Paul De Grauwe and Hans Dewachter

In this paper, we analyze the impact of economic and institutional (ECB decision rules) asymmetries on the effectiveness of monetary policy in Euroland. We consider a model where asymmetric shocks and divergent propagation of shocks in output and inflation are potential causes of tensions within the ECB concerning the conduct of common monetary (interest rate) policy. Welfare implications of the alternative decision procedures are discussed.

1. Introduction

The European Central Bank (ECB) has the sole responsibility for the conduct of monetary policies in Euroland. The Maastricht Treaty provides some general principles about the objectives to be pursued

Published in *European Economic Review*, 46, 443–469, 2002.
Filipa Correia provided excellent research assistance. We are grateful to two referees for their valuable comments and critiques on an earlier version of this paper. Also, we would like to thank Paul Bergin, Mathias Brueckner, Matt Canzoneri, Hanno Lustig, Jaques Melitz, Patrick Minford, Manfred Neumann, Andy Rose, Mark Salmon, Lars Svensson, Jurgen von Hagen, Casper de Vries and participants at conferences and seminars in Trouville (Denmark), Rotterdam, Berkeley, Harvard, Bonn (ZEI), Paris, the ASSA meeting (New York) and a CEPR meeting in Barcelona for useful comments on an earlier draft of this paper. Responsibility for remaining errors is ours.
Keywords: EMU; linear feedback rules; monetary stability.
JEL Classification: E52

by the ECB and has set the institutional framework within which the ECB will take its decisions. More precisely, the statutes of the ECB were enshrined in the Maastricht Treaty. The principles underlying these statutes are, first, that the primary objective of the ECB is the maintenance of price stability (Art. 105), and, second, that in order to achieve this objective, the ECB should be politically independent (Art. 107). The Treaty also formulates other objectives to be pursued by the ECB (e.g., high employment) but always adds the proviso that this should not interfere with the primary objective which is price stability.

The decision making body is the Governing Council (GC), which consists of the Governors (Presidents) of the National Banks of the euro-countries, and of the President, the Vice-President and the four Directors of the ECB. Each of the members have one vote. Although the statutes of the ECB mandate the members of the ECB-Council to represent the interests of Euroland as a whole, it is quite likely that there will be occasions when the national representatives will pursue national interests.[1]

One major question that arises in this context is the following. Will the national representatives in the ECB-Council take a union-wide perspective when deciding about monetary policies, or will they give a high weight to national economic conditions when taking these decisions? The question is important. For, if asymmetric shocks and/or adjustment speeds occur frequently in the future EMU, a nationalistic attitude of the ECB Council members, triggered by divergent economic conditions, may lead to frequent conflicts about the appropriate policies to be pursued. One can expect that, although each of the Governors will share similar preferences about inflation and output stabilization, these divergent economic conditions may lead them to take different positions on the desirable stance of monetary policies. When that happens, national

[1]For a more detailed description of the statutes of the ECB see Gros *et al.* (1999). See also Begg *et al.* (1998) and Gros *et al.* (1999) for a discussion of the decentralized nature of the European System of Central Banks.

viewpoints will loom large in the decision making process. As a result, the decision making process within the ECB will be made difficult.

At the end of the day, however, a common monetary policy must be implemented. The issue of divergent optimal (national) monetary policies thus leads to a need for decision procedures. These procedures will determine the way country-specific desires about monetary policies are aggregated into one common monetary policy. Obviously, the modalities of the decision procedure will matter in this aggregation problem and will also affect macro-economic performance and welfare of the individual countries.

This paper provides a first step in analyzing the effects of decision procedures in the GC on effectiveness of monetary policy and macroeconomic stabilization.[2] The paper proceeds in two steps. First, in Section 2 we assess empirically the magnitude of the divergence in "national interests" that may arise and their effects on the desired monetary policy reactions. This we achieve by using the benchmark Rudebusch and Svensson (1999) model for optimal monetary policy in an intertemporal setting. Second, having established the asymmetries in desired optimal monetary policy reactions, we formulate some rules for the decision process within the GC (Section 3). Four types of decision procedures will be analyzed: a consensus model, a purely nationalistic rule where all representatives only take into account their national interests, an intermediate case where the national representatives take a nationalistic perspective and the EMU-wide perspective prevails for the ECB representatives and an EMS-rule where German monetary preferences are applied. Effects of the decision procedures on macroeconomic stabilization will be discussed in Section 4. Finally, Section 5 contains a summary of the main findings of the paper.

[2]Recent papers have analyzed similar issues issues relating to workings of the European Central Bank. See Bindseil (1996), Bottazzi and Manasse (1998), Brueckner (1997) and Von Hagen and Sueppel (1994). See also Dornbusch, Favero and Giavazzi (1998) who study problems of voting in the ECB.

2. Optimal Policy Rules for Country Representatives

In this section we model central bank behavior, using the model presented in Rudebusch and Svensson (1999).[3] The central bank is assumed to have an explicit target for the goal variables such as an inflation target and output gap target. In order to reach these targets, the central banks use the short-run interest rate as an instrument. The implicit rule for the instrument (from now on policy rule) can then be derived from the first order condition of the explicit loss minimization. In general, this policy rule will depend on the current economic state of the country and the way the interest rate (over time) affecting the different explicit goal variables, i.e., inflation and output. The interest rate, as determined by the policy rule, will therefore be a function of (1) the preferences of the central bank over the different macro-economic variables, (2) the transmission of interest rates into these goal variables, (3) the actual state and structure of the economy, and finally (4) the stochastic shocks that alter the state of the economy. Each of these four components is likely to differ across countries such that optimal interest rate rules are likely to be country-specific and therefore a potential cause of tension within the ECB Governing Council.[4]

---

[3]We base our analysis on recent research concerning the use of monetary policy rules in a number of industrial countries (see Taylor, 1993; Clarida, Gali and Gertler, 1998). This research indicates that central banks in industrial countries generally target the rate of inflation and are also concerned about stabilizing the business cycle. The instrument used to perform these tasks is usually the short-term interest rate. This evidence has led Taylor (1993) to conclude that central banks (in particular the US Federal Reserve) raise the short term interest rate when inflation increases and when output grows relative to output capacity, and vice versa. Clarida, Gali and Gertler (1998) conclude that central banks of the major industrial countries (US, Japan, Germany, England) behave in a similar way, although the weight they attach to inflation and output varies. It is interesting to note that the Bundesbank which is the most outspoken about price stability as the primary objective of monetary policy, in practice attaches considerable importance to output stabilization (see also Bernanke and Mihov, 1997; Laubach and Posen, 1997; Issing, 1996; Neumann, 1997; von Hagen, 1995; and Peersman and Smets, 1999; on this issue).

[4]There is a large literature analysing these asymmetries in Europe. Some, like Bayoumi and Eichengreen (1993) or Bayoumi and Prasad (1997) analyze the asymmetries of shocks. More recently, there has been an upsurge of econometric analysis studying the assymetries in the tranmission mechnanism, of symmetric shocks. See, for example, Dornbusch, Favero and Giavazzi (1998), Ramaswamy and Sloek (1998), Peersman and

2.1. *State Space Representation*

To make the model similar in structure to the one used by central banks we follow Rudebusch and Svensson (1999) in focusing on the following three features: (1) the policy instrument used by the central bank is the short-run interest rate (i), (2) the model is defined in terms of the output gap, and (3) a standard autoregressive Phillips-curve is used. Note that the autoregressive Phillips curve is backward looking instead of the (theoretically) more appealing, forward looking, version. Empirical evidence, however, suggests that the former may, from an empirical point of view, be superior to the latter. For instance, Fuhrer (1997) finds that the backward looking version is much closer to the empirically observed inflation dynamics than the (purely) forward looking version. Recent research by Gali and Gertler (1999) shows that the use of the output gap can be a problem in forward looking specifications of the Phillips curve. Gali and Gertler find that the output gap leads the rate of inflation, a finding which is inconsistent with a forward looking Phillips curve. An additional reason why we did not use a forward looking Phillips curve is tractability. Although theoretical models for forward looking Phillips-curve models (see Svensson, 1999, 2000) and practically feasible estimation techniques exist (see for instance Clarida *et al.* 1998) for one country models, we face the situation where monetary policy is the outcome of possibly intricate decision procedures in the GC, involving seventeen agents. Implementation of the forward-looking Phillips-curve would imply explicitly (analytically) solving the decision procedure(s) and their effects on future inflation in each of the countries. Solving such a model for eleven countries is currently infeasible, forcing us to use the backward looking version for which expectations are easily identified.

Smets (1999), Giovannetti and Marimon (1998). Note that other recent studies focus on the likely impact of the differences in asset markets on the monetary transmission mechanism (see Maclennan, Muellbauer and Stephens, 1998) or stress the role of the financial and legal structures as a potential explanation of such asymmetries (see Cecchetti, 1999).

More formally, we assume that inflation (π) is determined by the output gap ($-y$) with a one period lag and past inflation rates:

$$\pi_{t+1} = \sum_{j=1}^{n} \alpha_{\pi,j}\pi_{t+1-j} + \alpha_y y_t + \varepsilon_{t+1}. \tag{1}$$

We decompose output into a permanent and a transitory component and interpret the permanent component of output as the output capacity of an economy. The transitory component y therefore measures the temporary over- or underutilisation of the output capacity. We adapt the standard Rudebusch and Svensson (1999) model to the European situation by explicitly modelling the trade-interactions among countries. More specifically, the output gap is assumed to depend on previous output gaps, a year lagged trade weighted output gaps of the other countries in the EMU (y^*_{t-12}) and the average real interest rate over the past 12 periods. More formally:

$$y_{t+1} = \sum_{j=1}^{m} \beta_{y,j} y_{t+1-j} + \beta^*_y y^*_{t-12} - \beta_r(\bar{i}_t - \bar{\pi}_t) + \eta_{t+1}, \tag{2}$$

where $\bar{i}_t$ and $\bar{\pi}_t$ denote a twelve month (moving) arithmetic average of current and past interest and inflation rates

$$\bar{i}_t = 1/(12)\sum_{i=0}^{11} i_{t-i} \quad \text{and} \quad \bar{\pi}_t = 1/12\sum_{i-0}^{11} \pi_{t-i} \tag{3}$$

and y^*_t denotes the bilateral trade weighted output gaps of the other EMU-members; This trade weighted output gap for country i is calculated as follows:

$$y^*_t = \sum_{j=1,j\neq i}^{11} w_{i,j}\, y_{j,t} \quad \text{with } w_{i,j} = \frac{X^i_j}{\sum_{k=1,k\neq i} X^i_k} \quad \text{and}$$

$$X^i_j \text{ export volume from country } i \text{ to } j. \tag{4}$$

Note that Eqs. (1) and (2) imply a particular transmission mechanism in response to changes in the policy instrument. More specifically, a change in the interest rate first affects the output gap and subsequently, with a one period lag, affects the inflation rate indirectly (through the effects of interest rate changes on the output gap). Evidently, the transmission of interest rate changes to output and inflation will be determined by the parameter values $\alpha_{\pi,l}$ and $\beta_{y,j}$ with $l = 1, \ldots, n$ and $j = 1, \ldots, m$.[5]

The state of the economy and its dynamics can be summarized by the state space representation of Eqs. (1) and (2). Denoting the state of the economy by X_t, an $(n + m + 2 + 11) \times 1$ vector, stacking consecutively π_t till π_{t-n}, y_t till y_{t-m}, y^*_{t-11} till y^*_{t-12} and i_{t-1} till i_{t-11}, its dynamics can be reformulated as (for a more detailed definition of A and B see Appendix A):

$$X_{t+1} = AX_t + Bi_t + v_{t+1} \tag{5}$$

Note that the above state space representation is not "closed". That is the dynamics of this state space representation depend on the dynamics of the interest rate level, which has not (yet) been modeled explicitly. To close the model we introduce in the next section the interest rate dynamics by deriving the optimal Taylor-rule for interest rates.

2.2. *Optimal Linear Feedback Rule*

The central bank has as objective to minimize its intertemporal loss function which is denned in terms of the time t expected difference between (yearly) inflation, the output gap $(-y)$ and their targeted values, c_1 and c_2, respectively.[6] Moreover, some degree of interest smoothing is assumed for the central bank. Formally, we assume the

---

[5]In order to satisfy the natural rate hypothesis a restriction of the α coefficients of the form

$$\sum_{j=1}^{n} \alpha_{\pi,j} = 1$$

should be imposed. In the empirical section, we use the unrestricted coefficient estimates for which the summed coefficients are in most cases reasonably close to and insignificantly different from 1. A formal test for long run neutrality is presented in Table 1 in the appendix.

[6]As y_t is being defined as the output gap one can conveniently set c_2 to zero.

following minimization problem:

$$\min_{i_t} \sum_{j=0}^{+\infty} \delta^j E_t[(\bar{\pi}_{t+j} - c_1)^2 + \lambda y_{t+j}^2 + v(i_{t+j} - i_{t+j-1})^2]. \tag{6}$$

If the frequency of meetings in the ECB is sufficiently high (say, monthly) such that the discount rate $\delta \to 1$, it can be shown that the above minimization problem can be restated in terms of an unconditional loss function (see Rudebusch and Svensson, 1998):

$$\min_{i_t} E[L_t] = Var[(\bar{\pi}_t - c_1)] + \lambda\, Var[y_t] + v\, Var[\Delta i_t]. \tag{7}$$

Again, following Rudebusch and Svensson (1999) we write the target variables, $\bar{\pi}_t, y_t$ and $i_t - i_{t-1}$ in function of the state variable X_t (a detailed definition of the matrices C_X and C_i can be found in appendix A):

$$Y_t = \begin{bmatrix} \bar{\pi}_t \\ y_t \\ i_t - i_{t-1} \end{bmatrix} = C_X X_t + C_i i. \tag{8}$$

The loss function can now be rewritten as[7]:

$$L_t = E[Y_t' K Y_t], \quad \text{where } K = \begin{bmatrix} 1 & 0 & 0 \\ 0 & \lambda & 0 \\ 0 & 0 & \nu \end{bmatrix}. \tag{9}$$

Given the empirical evidence that central banks base their interest rate policy on current (and previous) values of output and inflation we consider the class of linear feedback rules, that is linear rules based on the current economic states:

$$i_t = f X_t \tag{10}$$

where f denotes a $1 \times (n + m + 2 + 11)$ vector. Using the above relations and substituting the linear feedback rule we obtain the dynamics of the state variable, taking into account the actions of the central

[7]Note that in what follows we have implicitly deducted the mean from each of the target variables. In the empirical section we deal with this issue by doing the econometric analysis on the demeaned series.

bank (on interest rates), as:

$$X_{t+1} = MX_t + v_{t+1}, \quad M = A + Bf \tag{11}$$

and for the goal variables:

$$Y_t = CX_t, \quad C = C_X + C_i f. \tag{12}$$

Note that according to Eq. (10) the central bank can alter the dynamics of the economic state by conditioning its interest rate policy on the current state of the economy. The optimal linear feedback rule is then defined as that interest rate rule that generates a state-space dynamics that minimizes the loss function (8). Under the assumptions made so far, Rudebusch and Svensson (1999) show that the optimal (linear) policy rule is given by:

$$i_t \equiv fX_t = -(R + B'VB)^{-1}(U' + B'VA)X_t \tag{13}$$

where the matrix V is defined by:

$$V = Q + Uf + f'U' + f'Rf + M'VM \tag{14}$$
$$Q = C'_X KC_X, \quad U = C'_X KC_i \quad \text{and} \quad R = C'_i KC_i.$$

Inspection of the optimal linear feedback rule f shows that the desired interest rate levels can diverge across countries for two reasons: either in the feedback coefficients f or economic conditions X_t. First, the economic conditions, as summarized by the state variable, X, can differ and hence require different policy actions. Second, reaction coefficients (the vector f) can differ across countries basically for three reasons. First, the preferences of the central banks can differ (the K matrix). Second, the sensitivity of output to interest rate changes (the B vector) can differ across countries. And finally, countries can differ in the dynamic adjustment paths of the economy to shocks (the A matrix). So, if individual member-states try to pursue their own optimal economic policies within EMU, (country-specific) differences in economic state, transmission mechanisms and preferences over the three goal variables are a potential source of conflict in the conduct of the European monetary policy.

2.3. *Empirical Results*

In this section we empirically investigate the optimal feedback rules for each of the eleven EMU countries. First, we estimate the macro-model consisting of Eqs. (1) and (2). We use the Akaike Information Criterion in order to determine the lag structures for the aggregate demand supply equations.[8] Subsequently, we use the obtained estimates together with some assumptions about the preferences of the central bank (i.e., the matrix K) to compute the optimal feedback coefficients (contained in the vector f).

The sample consists of monthly observations for inflation and industrial production for the period 1979:1 till 1994:09.[9] Interest rates are monthly money market and call money rates (with the exceptions of STF rate for Ireland, average lending rate for Finland and lending rate for Portugal) as reported by the IFS statistics.[10] Monthly inflation series are constructed by taking first differences of (log) CPI data and the output gap was constructed by properly detrending the industrial production series.[11] For reasons of brevity we do not present the estimation results for all countries considered.[12] Table 1 summarizes some of the important features of the estimation results.

For our purpose, the presence of asymmetric propagation of shocks is of great importance. Therefore, we estimated the effects of interest rate changes on output and inflation for each of the countries. More specifically, we estimated the reaction of output and inflation

[8] Selected lag structures are presented in Table 1.
[9] Lack of data on industrial production for several countries, in particular for Portugal, prevented us from extending the sample to the current time.
[10] We asssume also that Belgian interest rate applies in Luxembourg.
[11] More specifically we used a multiplicative HP filter with a value for λ of 500, 000. This amounted to a linear detrending exercise for most countries involved. Only for Ireland we found evidence of a nonlinear trend. The output gap was then constructed by taking the logaritmic transform of the transitory part of the multiplicative HP filter. The resulting series captures very well the business cycle frequency.
[12] Regression diagnostics were reasonable for all estimated equations. No significant signs of remaining autocorrelations were reported. The R^2 for the output equation were relatively high explaining on average about 60 percent of variation. The R^2 for the inflation regressions were somewhat lower with an average around 40 percent. See Table 1. Estimation results and eigenvalues for the A matrix are available upon request.

Table 1. Statistical summary.

	AUS	BEL	FIN	FRA	GER	IRE	ITA	LUX	NET	POR	SPA
Eigenvalues											
M matrix	0.99	0.99	0.99	0.99	0.99	0.99	0.99	0.99	0.99	0.99	0.99
$\Sigma\alpha_{\pi,j}$	0.68	0.89	0.76	0.84	0.72	0.71	0.88	0.70	0.78	0.82	0.86
$\Sigma\beta_{\gamma,j}$	0.84	0.79	0.76	0.87	0.82	0.87	0.54	0.91	0.64	0.87	0.84
F Test	2,57*	1,98*	4,03*	9,85*	1.59	8,42*	5,25*	4,77*	2,86*	0.34	1,80*
Σf_n	0.46	0.67	1.52	1.65	0.76	0.61	1.44	0.75	0.20	0.77	0.18
Σf_y	0.38	0.47	−0.17	0.20	0.24	0.59	−0.02	0.89	−0.15	0.43	−0.23
$Sf_{\Delta i}$	0.50	0.24	0.39	0.81	0.55	0.70	−0.08	0.41	0.91	0.24	0.98
R^2 eq:π	0.20	0.46	0.40	0.75	0.24	0.30	0.78	0.46	0.45	0.39	0.36
R^2eq:y	0.72	0.65	0.90	0.80	0.77	0.59	0.72	0.71	0.42	0.81	0.78
Lag Lenghts											
π (Akaike)	12	13	20°	31°	14°	29	13	24	16°	11	15
y (Akaike)	11	11	31°	11°	11°	13	34	24	16°	13	18

*indicates that the hypothesis of long term neutrality is rejected in the 95% interval.
°indicates that the lag length as suggested by the AIC is applied and A and M matrices are stable. Otherwise we chose the lags in the close neighbourhood.

to a temporary (twenty-four months) increase of the interest rate by one percent. The results of these estimates can be obtained from the authors. In line with the existing empirical literature we find that both output and inflation decrease as a consequence of the increase in interest rate. Moreover, we find for all countries that the initial output response is larger than that of inflation. Also, the size of responses as well as the propagation of the increase in the interest rate differ considerably across countries.[13] Our results are broadly consistent with those of Ramaswamy and Sloek (1998). In line with their findings, we observe stronger impacts of changes in monetary policies for some countries such as Belgium, Finland and Germany, than in countries such as France and Spain. However, our results do not suggest a clear division of Euroland in two distinct groups of countries. Despite these differences, Ramaswamy and Sloek's main conclusion of significant differences of the direct impact and the transmission of shocks across countries is corroborated.

In order to construct the optimal feedback rules we need to specify the preferences of the central bank explicitly. We consider five preference configurations $diagK$: $(1, 1, .5), (1, .2, .5), (1, 5, .5), (1, 1, 1)$ and $(1, 1, 5)$. The first preference configuration will serve as our benchmark. Configurations two and three vary the output stabilization concern of the central bank to relatively low and high values respectively. The final two configurations increase the concern of the central bank for interest rate smoothing and financial stability.

Some observations are worth stating regarding the optimal feeback rule coefficients. First, in Figure 1 we plot the estimated optimal feedback rules (f-vector defined in (12)) for inflation and output for each individual country separately assuming the benchmark preference configuration $(1, 1, .5)$. We find that the initial feedback coefficient of output is considerably higher than the one of inflation, i.e. three to eight times higher depending on the country considered. This is clearly at odds with the standard Taylor rule, prescribing equal

[13]For some countries, notably Belgium and Ireland, we observe the so-called price puzzle (see Fuhrer, 1997; Christiano, Eichenbaum and Evans, 1996). That is, the price response to an increase in the interest rate is perverse, i.e., the price level increases (slightly) in response to an interest rate shock.

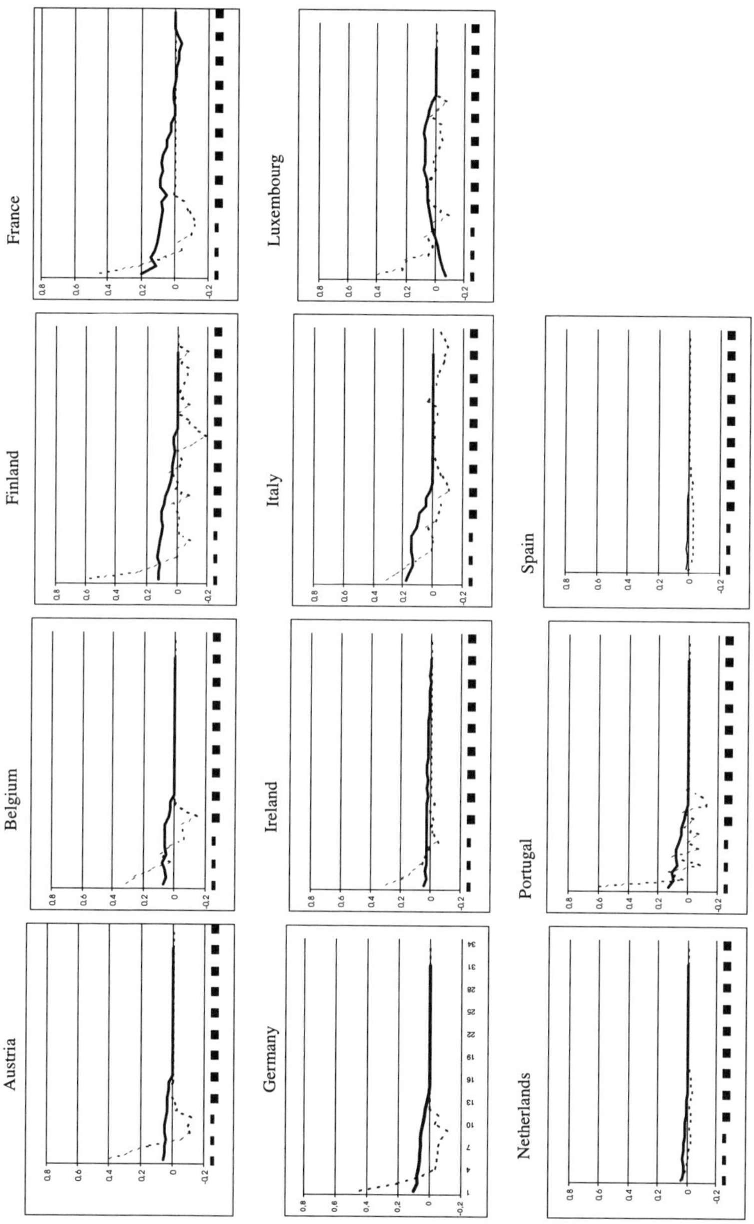

Figure 1. Optimal output gap (dashed line) and inflation (solid line) feedback coefficients ($\lambda = 1, v = 0.5$).

feedback coefficients of output and inflation. This finding is, however, qualitatively in line with the findings of Peersman and Smets (1999), who find a factor of three for quarterly data.[14] The sums of the optimal feedback coefficients are presented in Table 1. These suggest that the total feedback coefficient of inflation is systematically higher than the total feedback coefficient of output. Second, and in line with the intuition, the output coefficients in the feedback rules tend to increase with the weight on output stabilization (λ). Finally, as can be inferred from Table 1, the implementation of the optimal feedback rule by central banks does not lead to hysteresis effects. That is, the state-space representation remains stable after implementation of the optimal feedback rule. This can be inferred from the largest eigenvalue of the matrix M, which determines the dynamics of the state space under the linear feedback rule. As can be seen all maximal eigenvalues are below one.[15]

3. Institutional Framework: ECB Decision Rules

The monetary policy decisions are taken by the GC of the ECB which consists of seventeen representatives. Six members represent the ECB board and are likely to take a euro-wide view. The other eleven members are the governors of the national banks and are appointed by each of the individual member states. There is up till now no clear prescription about the procedures to be followed in the decision process. These procedures are at the discretion of the Council itself. As a result, one can argue that the ECB has instrument independence and although the Maastricht Treaty sets the price stability as the primary objective there is room for target independence. In other words, the ECB sets itself goals for inflation and possibly output stabilization,

[14] Estimating the optimal feedback rule for Germany on quarterly data we obtained coefficients close to the ones of Peersman and Smets, corroborating the relatively large weight on output.

[15] Note that the entries in Table 1 are only representative for the preference parameters 1, $\lambda = 1$ and $v = .5$. We also tested the stability for the other preference parameters. None of the cases considered yielded eigenvalues larger than 1. In other words, for all preference parameters considered, inflation, output and interest rates react only temporarily to demand and supply shocks.

designs its own strategy to meet these goals and moreover is the only one responsible for the design of the voting procedures in the GC as well.

To evaluate the effects of the decision procedures on the conduct of monetary policy we distinguish four procedures. The first one is denoted a nationalistic rule. In this case all the seventeen members of the Council determine the optimal interest rate rule based on the loss function of the country he represents. Thus, the optimal interest rate rule d for the representative of country j at time t can be written as:

$$d_{j,t} = i_{j,t} = -(R_j + B_j' V_j B_j)^{-1}(U_j' + B_j' V_j A_j) X_{j,t}, \quad j = 1, \ldots, 11. \tag{15}$$

The second rule is labelled the consensus rule. In this rule each representative takes a Euro-wide perspective, i.e. s/he takes into account the macro-economic situation of the whole union. We model this by assuming that such a representative would form the desired interest rate (rule) as a weighted average of the desired interest rates of the individual countries:

$$d_{EMU,t} = \sum_{j=1}^{11} w_j d_{j,t}. \tag{16}$$

The weights, $w_j\, j = 1, \ldots, 11$, represent the weight assigned to the country in the general loss function.[16] Equation (16) can be interpreted as a short cut to an Euro-wide optimal policy rule. As Gerlach and Schnabel (1998) show, the weighted average of Euro interest rates can be replicated well by a simple Taylor-rule on Euro aggregates of inflation and output. Therefore, we can interpret Eq. (16) as

[16]See Brueckner (1997) for a theoretical analysis on this issue. In the simulations we take the capital share (renormalized as to add up to 1) of every central bank in the ECB as the weight for the country. These weights are assumed to be a function of the countries population and GDP as a fraction of the aggregate EMU population and GDP. The weights are for Austria 0.0299, Belgium 0.0366, Finland 0.0177, France 0.2138, Germany 0.3093, Ireland 0.0106, Italy 0.1896, Luxemburg 0.0019, The Netherlands 0.0542, Portugal 0.0244 and Spain 0.1119.

an approximation of an optimal linear interest rate rule for euroland as a whole.

The third rule is called the ECB-rule. This is a combination of the previous two rules. More precisely, when this rule applies, we assume that the members of the ECB Board take a Euro-wide perspective, i.e., they apply Eq. (16), while the eleven national governors take a nationalistic perspective, i.e. they apply Eq. (15).

In all the three preceding rules we assume that the decision is taken by majority voting. Since the conditions of the median voter theorem apply, we select the desired interest rate of the representative located in the middle of the distribution of the desired interest rates. It is clear that other voting rules could be analyzed. In particular, the Governing Council may want to avoid applying majority voting so as to base its decisions on a broader consensual basis. We leave the study of this alternative to further research.[17]

Finally, in order to compare our results with a benchmark for the pre-EMU period, we have a fourth rule that we call the EMS-rule. Here, we assume that the desired interest rate of Germany holds as a Euro-wide interest rate.

Before discussing the results, it is useful to point out that the short-cut to a Euro-wide optimal policy rule represented by Eq. (16) can be given another interesting interpretation. One can write the following:

$$d_{EMU,t} = \sum_{j=1}^{11} w_j d_{j,t} = f_t^E X_t^E,$$

where X^E denotes the appropriately weighted average of the economic states of the different member countries and thus represents the EMU-wide economic state:

$$X_t^E = \sum_{j=1}^{11} w_j X_t^j,$$

[17]Issues related to the effects of the constitution of the ECB on macro-economic performance can also be found in Von Hagen (1995, 1998) and Von Hagen and Sueppel (1994).

and f_t^E denotes the EMU-wide (time varying) linear feedback rule. The k-th element in the feedback rule, $f_{t,k}^E$, is defined as:

$$f_{t,k}^E = \frac{\sum_{j=1}^{11} w_j X_{t,k}^j f_k^j}{\sum_{j=1}^{11} w_j X_{t,k}^j} \quad \text{for all } k.$$

In this interpretation the EMU-wide representatives take European aggregated economic conditions, i.e., X_t^E, as the basis for the linear feedback rule. However, in their response to this economic state they aggregate the optimal responses of the individual countries, f^j, using a weighted average which not only takes into account the size of the country, w_j, but also the particular economic conditions of that country, X_t^j. Economic responses are thus weighted using the severity of the economic situation in the country multiplied by the size of the country. Obviously, these weights will vary through time with the variation in the economic conditions.

4. Simulation Results

So far, we have modelled the country-specific desired interest rates and the decision procedures. In this section, we look into the macroeconomic effects of the different voting procedures on the different countries. We analyze the four decision rules listed above: the consensus rule, the ECB rule, the nationalistic rule and the EMS rule.

Some remarks with respect to the simulations are in order. The adjustment paths of inflation and output and the (correlation) structure of the shocks across the union are assumed not to be affected by the creation of EMU. In order to account for the comovements across the member states we use the residuals v_t of the state-space representation (5) for each country. Let S denote the variance-covariance matrix. A particularly useful decomposition of the matrix S is the Cholesky decomposition $S = LL'$, where L is a lower triangular matrix. In the simulations we construct shocks with the same covariance structure as observed in the past. Formally, this covariance structure can be recovered by constructing a vector of shocks $u_t = [u_{1,t}, \ldots, u_{11,t}]' = L\xi_t$, where ξ is standard normal, $N(0, I)$.

This procedure, of course, leaves us open to the Lucas critique: the new monetary regime is likely to affect the nature of the shocks and the transmission process. There is, however, very little one can do about this, except to wait for years before applying scientific analysis. In addition, we know very little about the question of how EMU will affect asymmetries. It is not even clear whether these will increase or decline. Finally, one can argue, following Peersman and Smets (1999), that the establishment of the ECB is not a totally new environment since a relatively long period of monetary convergence has preceded it.

4.1. *Interest Rate Behavior*

In this section we ask the question of how the interest rates desired by each country (i.e., those arising from the optimal interest rate rule) compare with the interest rate decided jointly in the GC for each of the rules considered. Large differences between these desired and decided interest rates are then a clear indication of potential conflicts.

We start by analyzing the correlation pattern between desired and decided interest rates. Table 2 presents the correlation of desired interest rates across countries, Table 3 summarizes the root mean squared error between desired and decided interest rates under alternative rules, and Table 4 contains the statistics about the median voter position.

Some results stand out. First, in the ECB-rule case, i.e., the situation where only the ECB-board members take an EMU-wide perspective, the proposal of the ECB-board will be accepted almost always. This can be deduced from the correlation coefficients between the interest rate desired by the ECB-Board and the decided interest rate, which are higher than 99 percent. It can also be seen from Table 4 which shows the number of times the ECB-board's desired interest rate coincides with the median voter's desired interest rate. We find that this is higher than 94 percent of the time. This dominating position of the ECB-board in the decision making process follows from the fact that the averaging procedure used by the ECB-board

Table 2. Correlations between desired and decided interest rates (%).

	AUS	BEL	FIN	FRA	GER	IRE	ITA	LUX	NET	POR	SPA	ECB
($\lambda = 0.2, v = 0.5$)												
EMS	96	90	26	94	100	93	49	25	98	51	98	40
ECB	87	80	23	90	93	84	49	3	97	59	97	100
NAT	92	80	37	92	93	86	20	−8	99	54	99	—
($\lambda = 1, v = 0.5$)												
EMS	77	60	24	89	100	64	27	27	94	23	93	57
ECB	56	51	10	89	83	39	42	−11	91	57	86	100
NAT	68	48	27	90	69	51	19	13	94	41	92	—
($\lambda = 5.0, v = 0.5$)												
EMS	54	41	14	79	100	46	35	32	90	6	86	70
ECB	37	53	14	70	74	23	33	10	76	27	67	100
NAT	45	47	20	79	51	43	21	23	85	24	77	—
($\lambda = 1.0, v = 1.0$)												
EMS	89	73	40	94	100	79	42	46	96	18	96	64
ECB	73	65	25	92	89	59	52	17	95	40	95	100
NAT	87	58	42	95	87	69	41	34	98	51	98	—
($\lambda = 1.0, v = 5.0$)												
EMS	98	97	61	99	100	95	33	76	99	77	99	34
ECB	94	90	41	98	97	82	75	48	99	77	98	100
NAT	97	93	73	99	97	89	17	46	99	79	99	—

puts the latter almost always right in the middle of the distribution of desired interest rates. Put differently, the ECB-board members who in this decision rule have the same desires and vote the same way, are almost always the median voter. As a result, in a majority voting system, the ECB-board almost always carries the day. So, unless desired interest rates are extremely skewed, the ECB-board's desires as a rule prevail. A corollary to this result is that it makes little difference whether the national representatives take an EMU-wide perspective or a nationalistic perspective. In both cases, the decision is the same, dictated as it is by the ECB-board's desires. It also follows that the consensus-rule and the ECB-rule give (almost always) the same result.

Table 3. Root mean squared error between desired and decided interest rates (%).

	AUS	BEL	FIN	FRA	GER	IRE	ITA	LUX	NET	POR	SPA
($\lambda = 0.2, v = 0.5$)											
EMS	1.0	1.7	12.2	1.3	0.0	1.3	4.5	5.3	0.7	5.4	0.6
ECB	0.8	1.0	12.1	1.1	0.6	0.9	1.9	4.2	0.4	5.1	0.4
NAT	0.8	1.2	8.6	1.1	0.8	1.0	3.3	4.5	0.4	5.2	0.4
($\lambda = 1.0, v = 0.5$)											
EMS	2.3	3.0	16.2	1.7	0.0	3.2	6.6	6.0	1.3	11.0	1.4
ECB	1.9	2.0	13.4	1.3	1.3	2.9	2.2	5.7	0.8	10.1	1.0
NAT	1.9	2.3	8.8	1.3	1.8	2.9	4.1	5.4	0.8	10.1	1.1
($\lambda = 5.0, v = 0.5$)											
EMS	5.9	7.6	30.3	4.0	0.0	7.3	12.8	10.4	2.8	24.5	3.6
ECB	4.6	3.9	25.4	3.0	3.2	6.5	5.4	8.5	1.8	21.7	2.7
NAT	4.7	5.3	15.9	3.0	4.5	6.5	9.2	8.9	2.1	21.7	3.0
($\lambda = 1.0, v = 1.0$)											
EMS	1.5	2.2	10.4	1.1	0.0	2.0	4.2	4.0	0.9	7.0	0.9
ECB	1.2	1.3	9.6	0.8	0.9	1.7	1.7	3.5	0.5	6.3	0.6
NAT	1.2	1.9	7.2	0.8	1.2	1.8	3.3	3.8	0.5	6.2	0.6
($\lambda = 1.0, v = 5.0$)											
EMS	0.6	1.1	3.8	0.4	0.0	1.0	3.8	1.9	0.4	2.6	0.4
ECB	0.5	0.6	5.9	0.3	0.3	0.7	0.9	1.4	0.2	2.6	0.2
NAT	0.5	0.8	2.8	0.3	0.4	0.8	2.5	1.7	0.2	2.5	0.2

Second, there appears to be a difference in the correlation coefficients of large and small countries (see Table 2). In general the correlation coefficients of large countries are significantly higher than those of small countries. (The only exceptions to this rule are The Netherlands as a relatively small country and Italy as a relatively large country). The interpretation is as follows. Large countries have a high weight in the averaging procedure followed by the ECB-board. As a result, the euro-average of the desired interest rates will generally be closer to the desired interest rates of the large countries. Some small countries (e.g., The Netherlands) may profit from this effect if their output and inflation shocks correlate well with one (or more) large countries. This result leads to the conclusion that,

Table 4. Median voters (%).

	AUS	BEL	FIN	FRA	GER	IRE	ITA	LUX	NET	POR	SPA	ECB
($\lambda = 0.2, v = 0.5$)												
ECB	0.33	0.27	0.07	0.13	0.53	0.07	0.27	0.00	0.40	0.00	0.60	0.97
NAT	5.47	3.40	1.00	8.13	14.27	5.80	4.40	1.00	27.00	1.27	28.27	—
($\lambda = 1.0, v = 0.5$)												
ECB	0.47	0.13	0.00	0.33	0.00	0.00	0.07	0.07	0.20	0.07	0.20	98.47
NAT	5.73	4.87	3.53	17.67	11.47	3.13	8.47	1.73	27.20	0.67	15.53	—
$\lambda = 5.0, v = 0.5$)												
ECB	0.40	0.20	0.00	0.73	0.13	0.20	0.13	0.40	0.33	0.00	0.53	96.93
NAT	5.27	5.47	3.67	20.07	13.67	4.53	7.73	3.13	21.00	2.00	13.47	—
($\lambda = 1.0, v = 1.0$)												
ECB	0.27	0.20	0.07	0.60	0.33	0.07	0.13	0.00	0.20	0.00	0.73	97.40
NAT	6.07	4.20	2.40	16.20	12.33	4.67	6.13	2.20	24.60	0.73	20.47	—
($\lambda = 1.0, v = 5.0$)												
ECB	0.27	0.53	0.07	1.47	1.13	0.27	0.13	0.13	0.67	0.20	0.60	94.53
NAT	5.67	3.20	2.33	24.80	13.87	3.80	1.80	1.27	26.13	1.27	15.87	—

generally speaking, small countries will experience more frustrations about the interest rate decisions taken in Frankfurt than the large countries.

Third, the correlation coefficients decline when the output stabilization weight, λ, increases. Thus, the more countries wish to stabilize output, the smaller are the correlation coefficients. This result can be given the following interpretation. When national authorities increase their ambition to stabilize output, their desired interest rate will react more to asymmetric shocks. There will, therefore, be a greater spread in the nationally desired interest rates, so that these will correlate less well with the one decided in Frankfurt (the median voter's desired interest rate). Put differently, when national authorities increase their ambitions to stabilize output, they will be more frustrated about decisions taken in Frankfurt. We also find that this degree of frustration (measured by low correlation coefficients) increases most for the small countries. Also, and not surprisingly, as the weight on interest rate stabilization increases, correlations between desired and decided interest rates increase substantially for most countries.

Finally, a relatively clear core-periphery dichotomy appears when one considers the deviation of the decided from the desired interest rate as measured by the RMSE (see Table 3). With the exception of Spain, the core countries of EMU tend to have the smaller deviations from the decided interest rates, while the others tend to have substantially larger average deviations between their desired interest rate and the decided (EMU-wide) rate. Note also that Table 3 confirms that large core countries' desires tend to be better served than those of the smaller peripheral countries.

4.2. *Welfare Analysis*

The ultimate objective of the monetary authorities is to minimize the loss functions as specified in Eq. (6). In this section we analyze how well the monetary authorities do this in the different decision rules. We, therefore, substituted the simulated output, inflation and interest rates into the loss functions and computed the average losses for each country, together with the contribution of each of the three variables in these losses. As before, we consider five cases concerning stabilization preferences: the standard case ($\lambda = 1, v = .5$), the low output stabilization case ($\lambda = 0.2, v = .5$), the high output stabilization case ($\lambda = 5, v = .5$) and two cases of increasing interest rate stabilization ($\lambda = 1, v = 1$) and ($\lambda = 1, v = 5$).

We add a benchmark to measure the losses. In this benchmark, each country is able to implement its own desired interest rate. This implies, of course, that each country maintains its monetary independence, i.e. that it does not take part in EMU. This is, of course, a very unrealistic benchmark since few countries have the capacity to enjoy full monetary independence, as defined here. We use this as a yardstick to give some perspective to the welfare analysis. In addition, we compare the losses generated under EMU with those obtained in the EMS. This comparison provides for a better evaluation of the welfare losses under EMU than the comparison of EMU with complete monetary independence.

Table 5. Losses in % ($\lambda = 1.0, v = 0.5$).

	AUS	BEL	FIN	FRA	GER	IRE	ITA	LUX	NET	POR	SPA
Benchmark											
Inflation	0,001	0,001	0,002	0,002	0,002	0,001	0,001	0,006	0,001	0,040	0,003
Output	0,091	0,109	0,081	0,057	0,060	0,213	0,043	0,153	0,093	1,154	0,135
Desired r	0,015	0,014	0,021	0,009	0,012	0,023	0,007	0,029	0,003	0,243	0,007
Decided r	—	—	—	—	—	—	—	—	—	—	—
Loss	0,099	0,117	0,094	0,064	0,068	0,225	0,047	0,174	0,096	1,315	0,142
ECB Rule											
Inflation	0,001	0,001	0,058	0,003	0,003	0,001	0,003	0,039	0,001	0,161	0,003
Output	0,111	0,132	1,424	0,063	0,074	0,252	0,072	0,317	0,093	1,839	0,144
Desired r	0,009	0,007	0,022	0,005	0,008	0,013	0,005	0,024	0,003	0,142	0,003
Decided r	0,003	0,003	0,003	0,003	0,003	0,003	0,003	0,003	0,003	0,003	0,003
Loss	0,113	0,135	1,484	0,067	0,079	0,254	0,077	0,357	0,095	2,001	0,149
Nationalistic Rule											
Inflation	0,001	0,001	0,028	0,003	0,004	0,001	0,008	0,036	0,001	0,154	0,003
Output	0,117	0,140	0,648	0,062	0,080	0,254	0,174	0,305	0,093	1,824	0,144
Desired r	0,009	0,007	0,016	0,006	0,009	0,013	0,006	0,024	0,004	0,141	0,004
Decided r	0,047	0,047	0,047	0,047	0,047	0,047	0,047	0,047	0,047	0,047	0,047
Loss	0,142	0,164	0,699	0,088	0,107	0,278	0,205	0,365	0,117	2,002	0,171
EMS Rule											
Inflation	0,001	0,001	0,084	0,003	0,002	0,001	0,011	0,039	0,001	0,184	0,003
Output	0,109	0,148	2,048	0,063	0,061	0,247	0,398	0,333	0,092	1,973	0,150
Desired r	0,013	0,011	0,033	0,012	0,012	0,019	0,011	0,031	0,010	0,144	0,012
Decided r	0,012	0,012	0,012	0,012	0,012	0,012	0,012	0,012	0,012	0,012	0,012
Loss	0,117	0,155	2,137	0,072	0,069	0,254	0,416	0,379	0,099	2,163	0,160

In Table 5, we show the results of the standard case (the cases of low and high stabilization parameter configurations are available upon request)[18] and in Table 6 we present results for relative losses across alternative decision rules. A first result to note is that the losses are higher in a monetary union compared to the benchmark of absence of monetary union. The differences, however, tend to

[18]Note that we do no longer present the case of the consensus rule separately. Given the discusssion in the previous section, it is obvious that all relevant values will almost exactly coincide with those reported under the heading ECB-rule. Results for the consensus rule are available upon request.

Table 6. Relative losses (%).

	AUS	BEL	FIN	FRA	GER	IRE	ITA	LUX	NET	POR	SPA
$\lambda = 0.2, v = 0.5$											
BEN/EMS	96	57	4	99	89	92	7	45	93	59	97
BEN/ECB	92	82	4	108	97	101	28	61	98	61	102
BEN/NAT	47	49	7	50	47	61	10	48	51	59	66
EMS/ECB	96	144	100	109	110	110	428	137	106	104	105
EMS/NAT	49	86	187	51	53	67	152	107	55	100	67
ECB/NAT	51	60	187	47	48	61	35	78	52	96	64
$(\lambda = 1.0, v = 0.5)$											
BEN/EMS	85	76	4	89	98	89	11	46	97	61	89
BEN/ECB	87	87	6	95	86	89	61	49	100	66	95
BEN/NAT	70	71	13	72	64	81	23	48	82	66	83
EMS/ECB	103	115	144	107	88	100	541	106	104	108	107
EMS/NAT	82	94	306	82	65	91	202	104	84	108	94
ECB/NAT	80	82	212	76	74	91	37	98	82	100	87
$(\lambda = 5.0, v = 0.5)$											
BEN/EMS	64	54	5	80	96	80	11	49	90	51	85
BEN/ECB	77	91	7	87	84	83	45	60	95	57	93
BEN/NAT	72	68	16	76	59	79	19	54	84	56	85
EMS/ECB	121	167	142	108	87	104	410	121	106	110	109
EMS/NAT	112	126	341	95	61	99	175	109	94	108	99
ECB/NAT	93	75	241	87	70	96	43	90	89	98	91
$(\lambda = 1.0, v = 1.0)$											
BEN/EMS	86	70	3	96	94	80	7	54	94	62	99
BEN/ECB	96	85	7	112	77	86	55	58	145	77	118
BEN/NAT	83	82	6	102	79	84	24	62	98	71	98
EMS/ECB	111	122	235	117	82	108	765	107	154	123	119
EMS/NAT	96	119	186	106	84	106	335	115	104	113	100
ECB/NAT	86	97	79	91	103	98	44	107	68	92	84
$(\lambda = 1.0, v = 5.0)$											
BEN/EMS	94	65	11	97	90	90	5	53	91	92	88
BEN/ECB	99	89	5	104	105	101	50	68	99	91	98
BEN/NAT	96	78	18	103	96	97	11	57	99	90	98
EMS/ECB	106	136	43	108	116	112	1,011	129	108	99	112
EMS/NAT	102	120	165	106	107	107	225	108	108	98	112
ECB/NAT	97	88	387	99	92	96	22	84	100	99	100

be limited especially when the stabilization parameter λ is not too high (the low and standard cases). With a high output stabilization parameter, these differences in the losses also become higher. This has to do with the fact that with a high stabilization preference individual countries' optimal interest rates are very much influenced by asymmetric output shocks. In a monetary union they find it more difficult to pursue their stabilization desires. As a result, losses increase.

A second result relates to the comparison between the ECB-rule and the nationalistic rule. The ECB-rule is welfare improving compared to the nationalistic rule. In general we find cases in which an ECB-rule leads to lower losses than the nationalistic rule, i.e. is a better rule to minimize the variability of output, inflation and the interest rate. There are, however, also cases where the opposite holds as for example Finland. This in a sense is not really surprising. The difference between the ECB-rule and the nationalistic rule boils down to a difference in the way in which information is processed. In the nationalistic rule each decision maker uses his own national information about output and inflation, and then votes. Majority rule then determines the outcome. In the ECB-rule some participants (the ECB-board) aggregate the national data on output and inflation, while others (the governors) use the "raw" national data. They then vote using the same majority rule. It is not a-priori obvious which of the two methods of aggregating national information is the most efficient, i.e., minimizes the losses of the individual countries. Put differently, the difference between the ECB-rule and the nationalistic rule boils down to a difference in the way national preferences are aggregated. These different aggregation procedures affect the effective voting power of the participants. Both rules stabilize output and inflation in approximately the same way. The nationalistic rule, however, generates in general a higher interest rate volatility. As a result, the losses generated under the nationalistic rule are systematically higher than those obtained under the ECB-rule.

A third result relates to the welfare implications of a switch from the EMS regime to EMU as presented in Table 6. Not surprisingly, the results show that, except for Austria, Finland and Germany, irrespective of their preferences all countries are better off moving

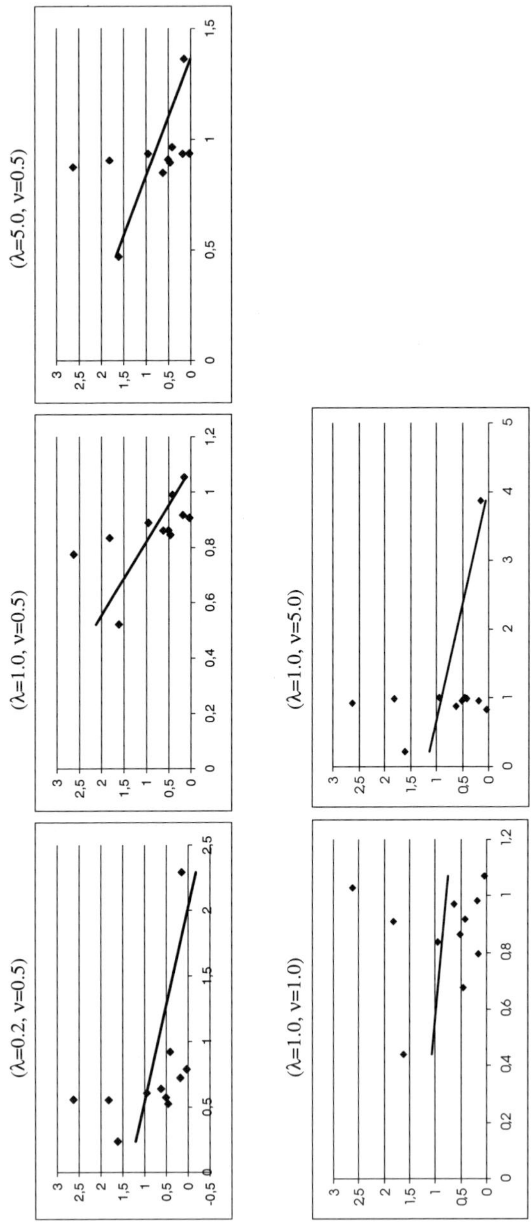

Figure 2. Voting power and relative losses.

from the EMS to EMU.[19] An interest rate dictated by the preferences of the German economic policymakers frustrates the other member states in their desire to stabilize output, inflation and interest rate. This result, however, only holds as long as the ECB-rule applies. Under the nationalistic rule, the superiority of EMU over EMS clearly depends on stabilization preferences.

Finally in Figure 2, we further analyze how the move from the nationalistic rule to the ECB-rule affects welfare of different countries. The two decision rules differ in the effective voting power they confer to individual countries.[20] Therefore, on the vertical axis we set out the ratio of the voting power of a country under the ECB rule and the voting power under the nationalistic rule. On the horizontal axis we set out the ratio of the losses under the ECB rule and under the nationalistic rule. We observe a negative relation, i.e., countries that gain (loose) voting power when moving from nationalism to ECB-rule in general improve (decrease) their welfare. We thus find that voting procedures clearly matter for welfare of the EMU-members.

5. Conclusions

In this paper we analyzed how different decision procedures in the Governing Council of the ECB affect economic conditions and welfare in the different member states, when shocks and transmission processes are asymmetric. In order to do so, we derived the optimal interest rates for each member state based on the optimal linear feedback rules as proposed by Rudebusch and Svensson (1999). We then applied majority rule assuming different procedures about the way

[19]Note that although the generated country specific "Cholesky filtered" shocks for output and inflation are identical across scenarios, the relative losses of Germany in the case of the benchmark and EMS rule do not exactly match. This is just because in the simulations we do take into account the "foreign" business cycle developments after interest rate changes in the two alternative scenarios. Whereas in the benchmark rule all countries can choose for their desired interest rate, in the EMS rule German desired interest rate applies which affects the business cycles in other countries that in turn affects the German business cycle through equation (2).

[20]We assume that the voting power under the ECB-scenario is given by the capital shares of the countries in the ECB, i.e., the weights used in the aggregation procedure in Eq. (15).

the members of the Council use national versus euro-wide aggregates. Our results can be summarized as follows.

First, when majority voting is used, the ECB can effectively control the GC and thus the monetary policy in EMU. That is, when all the ECB-board members take the same position on the desired interest rate based on a Euro-wide perspective, then the ECB-board's desires almost always prevail. The national governors then have a very small influence on the outcome when they take a nationalistic perspective, i.e., when their desired interest rate depends only on national economic conditions. This result has to do with the fact that the desires of the national governors tend to offset each other when asymmetries in the shocks or in the transmission process are high. This may lead to some frustration (measured by the difference between nationally desired interest rates and the decided interest rate) among these national central bankers. We also find that this frustration is typically larger for small countries.

Second, we find that when countries increase their desire to stabilize output they are increasingly frustrated about the decisions taken in Frankfurt. This result can be given the following interpretation. When national authorities increase their ambition to stabilize output, their desired interest rate will react more to asymmetric shocks. There will, therefore, be a greater spread in the nationally desired interest rates, so that these will correlate less well with the one decided in Frankfurt (the median voter's desired interest rate).

Third, welfare is in general improved by having an ECB-board take a euro-wide perspective (the "ECB-rule") compared with a regime in which all members of the Governing Council take a nationalistic view (the "nationalistic rule") or an EMS regime where Germany sets monetary policy. In general, we find that the ECB-rule leads to lower losses, i.e., is a better rule to minimize the variability of output, inflation and the interest rate, than the nationalistic rule and than the EMS-rule. The superiority of the ECB-rule is most pronounced with respect to the EMS-rule. This is not surprising. In the EMS-rule only information about German economic conditions is used to set the optimal interest rate of all the member states. This is generally a less efficient rule than a policy rule that uses information of all the countries in the system.

This paper has many limitations which invite further research. For instance, in the estimation of inflation and output equations we neglected the real exchange rate as a possible cause of output and inflation movements. Obviously, this external source of economic fluctuations may be of considerable importance for small open economies. Incorporating the real exchange rate along the lines of Peersman and Smets (1999) seems an interesting way to account for these external forces. However, it would also increase the dimension of the state space considerably, which is large already in the current setting. We plan to pursue this route of research in the near future.

Second, the optimal desired interest rate for Euroland as a whole has not been derived explicitly. Instead we assumed that a proxy for this variable was given by the weighted average of the desired interest rates of the member-states. The optimal desired interest rate could theoretically be obtained in much the same way as the national desired interest rates. Here the curse of dimensionality strikes again. At the end of the day, however, we would like to argue that the approach we took is a reasonable approximation for the ECB optimal linear feedback rule. Finally, we have only considered majority voting. Our results indicate that the use of majority voting can create significant conflicts between member-states in an environment characterized by asymmetric shocks. Therefore, the ECB may want to use other decision rules in which consensus plays a greater role. We hope to pursue this line of research in the future.

Appendix A

Here we present the matrix A, containing the autonomous dynamics of the state space in more detail. First, introduce the following notation: e_j denotes a $1 \times (n+m+2+11)$ vector with all elements equal to zero but the j-th which equals one; $e_{i:j}$ a $1 \times (n+m+2+11)$ vector with $1/12$ as element from row i up till row j and zeros elsewhere. The state space itself is constructed by stacking inflation output trade and interest rate variables into the state vector X. The matrix A summarizes the dynamics. The presentation of vectors and matrices below follows following notation: the first column specifies the variable in the matrix. The second column denotes the row in which the value enters.

$$X_t = \begin{bmatrix} \pi_t & 1 \\ \pi_{t-1} & 2 \\ \vdots & \downarrow \\ \pi_{t-n+1} & n \\ y_t & 1 \\ y_{t-1} & 2 \\ \vdots & \downarrow \\ y_{t-m+1} & m \\ y^*_{t-11} & 1 \\ y^*_{t-12} & 2 \\ i_{t-1} & 1 \\ \vdots & \downarrow \\ \vdots & \downarrow \\ i_{t-l} & l \end{bmatrix} \quad A = \begin{bmatrix} \sum_{j=1}^{n} \alpha_{\pi,j} e_j + \alpha_y e_{n+1} & 1 \\ e_1 & 2 \\ \vdots & \downarrow \\ e_n & n \\ \beta_r e_{1:11} + \sum_{j=1}^{m} \beta_{y,j} e_{n+j} + \beta^*_y e_{n+m+1} & 1 \\ -\beta_r e_{n+m+4m+m+2+l} & \\ e_{n+1} & 2 \\ \vdots & \downarrow \\ e_{n+m} & m \\ 0.999 c_{n+m+1} & 1 \\ c_{n+m+1} & 2 \\ e_0 & 1 \\ e_{n+m+4} & \downarrow \\ \vdots & \downarrow \\ e_{n+m+2+l} & l \end{bmatrix}$$

Note that we have imposed an autoregressive coefficient on the trade-weighted business cycle component of about .999. This value was obtained as the average of country by country AR model estimation.

The vector B is a vector containing zeros except for the element for y_{t-1} and the i_{t-1} where the coefficients are respectively $-\beta_r/12$ and 1. Finally we model the demand and supply shocks in the vector v.

$$B = \begin{bmatrix} 0 & 1 \\ 0 & 2 \\ \vdots & \downarrow \\ 0 & n \\ -\frac{\beta_r}{12} & 1 \\ 0 & 2 \\ \vdots & \downarrow \\ 0 & m \\ 0 & 1 \\ 0 & 2 \\ 1 & 1 \\ \vdots & \downarrow \\ \vdots & \downarrow \\ 0 & l \end{bmatrix} \quad \text{and} \quad v_t = \begin{bmatrix} \varepsilon_t & 1 \\ 0 & 2 \\ \vdots & \downarrow \\ 0 & n \\ \eta_t & 1 \\ 0 & 2 \\ \vdots & \downarrow \\ 0 & m \\ 0 & 1 \\ \vdots & 2 \\ \vdots & 1 \\ 0 & 2 \\ \vdots & \downarrow \\ \vdots & \downarrow \\ 0 & l \end{bmatrix} \tag{17}$$

Rewriting the target variables in terms of the state space:

$$Y_t = \begin{bmatrix} \bar{\pi}_t \\ y_t \\ i_t - i_{t-1} \end{bmatrix} = C_X X_t + C_i i_t,$$

$$\text{where } C_X = \begin{bmatrix} e_{1:12} \\ e_{n+1} \\ -e_{n+m+3} \end{bmatrix} \quad \text{and} \quad C_i = \begin{bmatrix} 0 \\ 0 \\ 1 \end{bmatrix} \tag{18}$$

References

Bayoumi, T and B Eichengreen (1993). Shocking aspects of european monetary unification. In *Adjustment and Growth in the European Monetary Union*, F Torres and F Giavazzi (eds.), pp. 193–229. Cambridge, UK: Cambridge University Press.

Bayoumi, T and E Prasad (1997). Currency unions, economic fluctuations and adjustment: Some empirical evidence. *IMF Staff Papers*, 44, 36–58.

Begg, D, P De Grauwe, F Giavazzi, H Uhlig and C Wyplosz (1998). *The ECB: Safe at Any Speed?* London: Monitoring the Central Bank, CEPR.

Bernanke, B and I Mihov (1997). What does the Bundesbank target? *European Economic Review*, 41, 183–228.

Bindseil, U (1996). A coalition form analysis of the allocation of voting rights in the council of the ECB. Unpublished manuscript.

Brueckner, M (1997). Voting and decisions in the ECB. EUI Working Papers No. 97/29, European University Institute, Florence.

Bottazzi, L and P Manasse (1998). Bankers versus workers Europe: Adverse selection in EMU. CEPR Discussion Paper No. 1846, March.

Cecchetti, SG (1999). Legal structure, financial structure and monetary policy transmission mechanism. *FRB of New York Economic Policy Review*, 5, 9–28.

Christiano, LJ, M Eichenbaum and C Evans (1996). The effects of monetary policy shocks: Some Evidence from the flow of funds. *Review of Economics and Statistics*, 78, 16–34.

Clarida, R, J Gali and M Gertler (1998). Monetary policy rules in practice: Some international evidence. *European Economic Review*, 42, 1033–1067.

Dornbusch, R, C Favero and F Giavazzi (1998). Immediate challenges for the European central bank. *Economic-Policy: A European Forum*, 26, 15–52.

Fuhrer, JC (1997). The (un)importance of forward-looking behavior of price specifications. *Journal of Money, Credit and Banking*, 29, 338–350.

Gali, J and M Gertler (1999). Inflation dynamics: A structural econometric analysis. *Journal of Monetary Economics*, 44, 195–222.

Gerlach, S and G Schnabel (1998). *The Taylor Rule and Average Interest Rates in the EMU-11 Area: A Note.* Mimeo: Bank for International Settlements.

Giovannetti, G and R Marimon (1998). An EMU with different transmission mechanisms. CEPR Discussion Paper No. 2016, November.

Ros, D, O Blanchard, M Emerson, HW Sinn, T Mayer and G St. Paul (1999). Macroeconomic policy in the first year of Euroland, CEPS Report, Brussels.

Issing, O (1996). Is monetary targeting in Germany still adequate? In *Monetary Policy in an Integrated World Economy: Symposium*, H Siebert (ed.), pp. 117–130. Tubingen: Mohr.

Laubach, T and A Posen (1997). *Disciplined Discretion: Monetary Targeting in Germany and Switzerland.* Princeton, NJ: Essays in International Finance.

Maclennan, D, J Muellbauer and M Stephens (1998). Asymmetries in housing and financial market institutions and EMU. *Oxford Review of Economic Policy*, 14, 54–80.

Neumann, M (1997). Monetary targeting in Germany. In *Towards More Effective Monetary Policy*, I Kuroda (ed.), pp. 176–198. Macmillan Press in Association with Bank of Japan.

Peersman, G and F Smets (1999). The Taylor rule: A useful monetary policy guide for the ECB. *International Finance*, 2, 85–116.

Ramaswamy, R and T Sloek (1998). The real effects of monetary policy in the European union: What are the differences? *IMF Staff Papers*, 45, 374–402.

Rudebusch, GD and LEO Svensson (1999). Policy rules for inflation targeting. In *Monetary Policy Rules*, JB Taylor (ed.), pp. 203–246. Chicago IL: University of Chicago Press.

Svensson, LEO (1999). Inflation targeting as a monetary policy rule. *Journal of Monetary Economics*, 43, 607–654.

Svensson, LEO (2000). Open-economy inflation targeting. *Journal of International Economics*, 50, 155–183.

Taylor, J (1993). Discretion versus policy rules in practice. *Carnegie Rochester Conference Series on Public Policy*, 39, 195–214.

Von Hagen, J (1995). Inflation and monetary targeting in Germany. In *Inflation Targets*, L Leiderman and L Svensson (eds.), pp. 107–121. London, UK: Centre for Economic Policy Research.

Von Hagen, J (1998). The composition of bank councils for monetary unions. Unpublished manuscript, ZEI, University of Bonn.

Von Hagen, J and R Sueppel (1994). Central bank constitutions for federal monetary unions. *European Economic Review*, 38, 774–782.

PART III

MACROECONOMICS AND MONETARY POLICY

Chapter 14

Is Inflation always and Everywhere a Monetary Phenomenon?

Paul De Grauwe and Magdalena Polan

Using a sample of about 160 countries over the last 30 years, we test for the quantity theory relationship between money and inflation. When analysing the full sample of countries, we find a strong positive relation between long-run inflation and the money growth rate. The relation is not proportional, however. The strong link between inflation and money growth is almost wholly due to the presence of high- (or hyper-) inflation countries in the sample. The relationship between inflation and money growth for low-inflation countries (on average less than 10 percent per annum over the last 30 years) is weak.

1. Introduction

Is inflation always and everywhere a monetary phenomenon?[1] Many economists today will argue that when analyzed over a sufficiently long period of time, inflation is indeed everywhere a monetary phenomenon. This "monetarist" view has not always been widespread,

Published in *Scandinavian Journal of Economics*, 107(2), 239–259, 2005.
We are grateful to Steinar Holden and to two anonymous referees for comments and suggestions.
Keywords: Inflation; money; quantity theory of money.
JEL classification: E40; E50

[1]Friedman (1963) wrote these now famous words, not as a question but in the affirmative; see also Friedman and Schwartz (1963).

however. Prior to the upsurge of inflation in the 1970s, many economists were not inclined to look at the money stock when analyzing the sources of the (low) inflation rates of that time. In this paper, we return to this issue using a sample of countries spanning the whole world over a period of 30 years. The key question we analyze concerns the link between inflation and the growth rate of money and how it depends on whether countries experience low or high rates of inflation.

The view that inflation is always and everywhere a monetary phenomenon has a long tradition based on the quantity theory of money (QTM). In its simplest form, the QTM says that changes in money supply growth are followed by equal changes in the inflation rate and, through the force of the Fisher effect, in the nominal interest rate. The QTM is a measure of the extent to which inflation movements can be explained by purely monetary forces.

The starting point of the QTM is the well-known identity:

$$MV = YP, \tag{1}$$

where M is money supply, V is the velocity of money, Y is real output, and P is the price level. If we move to growth rates, we can express this equation as:[2]

$$m + v = y + p, \tag{2}$$

where lowercase letters denote growth rates. Thus, inflation — or the growth rate of the price level — can be expressed as:

$$p = m - y + v. \tag{3}$$

These identities are transformed into a theory, the quantity theory, by the following two propositions. First, in the long run, there is a *proportionality* relation between inflation and the growth rate of

[2]These are, of course, instantaneous rates, not average rates. For low growth rates, this should not pose a problem; for high growth rates, however, the inflation rate will be underestimated by just adding growth rates of money, velocity and output.

money, i.e., in a regression of inflation on money growth, the coefficient of money is estimated to be 1. Second, over a sufficiently long period of time, output and velocity changes are *orthogonal* to the growth rate of the money stock.

Thus, there are two aspects of the quantity theory. The proportionality prediction says that a permanent increase in money growth leads to an equal increase in the rate of inflation in the long-run, while the orthogonality proposition — also referred to as the (super)neutrality of money — says that a permanent increase in the growth rate of money leaves output and velocity unaffected in the long run. If there is a positive effect of money growth on output, it only holds in the short run.

In this paper, we analyse these two propositions of the QTM. The way we proceed is to transform the identity into an econometric equation with testable propositions. Since we do not have independent estimates of velocity, we include velocity in the error term.[3] As a result, we estimate an equation of the form:

$$p_i = \beta_0 + \beta_1 m_i + \beta_2 y_i + \mu_i, \tag{4}$$

where p_i, m_i and y_i are the rate of inflation, the money growth and the output growth of country i, respectively, measured over a sufficiently long period of time (30 years). The QTM theory then predicts that $\beta_1 = 1, \beta_2 < 0$, and m_i and y_i are uncorrelated. We then test these propositions. Note that a potential bias may arise if the independent variables m_i and y_i are correlated with the error term (velocity). We provide indirect evidence that such a bias might exist.

The QTM does not specify which definition of money supply should be used in empirical tests of the theory. There is no theoretical reason why M1 or M2 should be used as the appropriate variable. Accordingly, many authors use both or other monetary aggregates to

[3]We could, of course, use the definitional equation to derive velocity. But this would not be very sensible as we would then estimate an identity.

compare the results obtained for various definitions of money. Since the empirical literature is not consistent in its opinion as to which monetary aggregate is more correlated with the price level, we use both M1 and M2 in our study.

2. Review of the Empirical Literature

There is a vast empirical literature concerning the long-run relation between money growth and inflation. We begin by briefly describing some of its aspects. This literature can be divided into three groups. The first uses cross-section data on a large number of countries over a long time span. Usually, a long-run average of money supply (or its growth rate) and price level (or the inflation rate) is calculated and used to compute the correlation between the two. All countries are treated equally, and there is no distinction according to monetary or economic regimes.

Authors in the second group use long series of higher frequency data (annual or quarterly) referring to only one country to describe a long-run relationship between money and the price level. Sometimes, the results are compared with other single-country findings.

The third group takes the shape of a historical investigation, sometimes reaching more than 200 years into the past. These studies often focus on one country only, but they suffer, as do studies of the second type, from the incomparability of the economic systems of a country across centuries.

Table 1 gives an overview of the representative articles of the first type of empirical studies, based on cross-sections of countries. The table also describes the data sets and the results. Authors of the articles listed in Table 1 try to either analyse data on the largest possible number of countries or focus on a smaller group of countries with similar economic systems. In the latter case, the results are only applicable to this particular group of countries, while the first method is supposed to yield universal results. In most cases, the relation between money supply and price level is strong and positive.

A common finding of these studies is that countries with low money growth (and low inflation) tend to create a horizontal cluster

Table 1. Main multi-country studies of long-run relationship between money supply and price level.

Author, year	Monetary aggregate	Prices	Data set	Time span	High-Low differentiation	Results
Vogel (1974)	Currency + demand deposits	CPI	16 Latin American countries	1950–1969, annual data	No	Proportionate changes in inflation rate within two years of changes in money growth
Dwyer and Hafer (1988)	M2	GDP deflator	62 countries	1979–1984, five-year averages	No	Strong positive correlation
Barro (1990)	Hand-to-hand currency	CPI	83 countries	1950–1987	No	Strong positive "association"
Pakko (1994)	Currency + bank deposits	CPI	13 former Soviet republics	1992 and 1993, four-quarter averages	No	Positive relationship
Poole (1994)	Broad money	n.a.	All countries in World Bank tables	1970–1980 and 1980–1991, annual averages	No	Strong positive relationship
McCandless and Weber (1995)	M0, M1, M2	CPI	110 countries reported in IMF IFS	1960–1990	No	Very strong positive correlation
Dwyer and Hafer (1999)	n.a.	GDP deflator	79 countries reported deflator in IMF IFS	1987–1997, two five-year averages	No	Strong and stable positive correlation

Note: "High–Low differentiation" indicates whether the author makes a distinction between low- and high-money growth countries.

in a plot where inflation (vertical axis) is set against money growth (horizontal axis). However, none of the papers surveyed here has attempted to analyse this phenomenon or study how the level of inflation affects the relation between money growth and inflation.

An interesting conclusion can be drawn from the article by Dwyer and Hafer (1999). These authors compare the relation between average money growth and average inflation rate in two periods, 1987–1992 and 1993–1997. In the second period, the average inflation rate (across all countries in the sample) is lower. The reduction in the average inflation rate leads to the creation of two horizontal clusters of observations close to the origin. Thus, the weakening relation between money growth and inflation, as we progress towards zero money growth, may be associated with the average money growth of a country.

The second type of empirical study uses single country time-series analysis. Within this class of studies, an initial approach has been to analyse the long-term quantity theory relationship after transforming time series into the frequency domain. Representative papers are Lucas (1980) and Fitzgerald (1999). These studies tend to confirm the proportionality prediction of the quantity theory, although their methodology has been criticised by McCallum (1984) and Rolnick and Weber (1995). McCallum (1984) warns us that associating high-frequency time series with long-run economic propositions is not always warranted.

More recently, researchers have adopted another — more satisfactory — approach in analysing the time-series properties of inflation, output and money. This consists of explicitly testing coefficient restrictions implied by the quantity theory in vector autoregression models. Important papers using this approach are Geweke (1986), Stock and Watson (1988), Boschen and Mills (1995), and King and Watson (1997). These authors confirm the long-run neutrality of money on output for the US economy. Similar results for G7 countries were obtained by Weber (1994).

In this context, the empirical studies using the P-star model should also be mentioned. This model, suggested by Hallman, Porter and Small (1991), was further explored by Vega and Trecroci (2002) and Gerlach and Svensson (2004); see also Jansen (2004) for a recent exposition. The P-star model may be regarded as a modern monetarist approach to modelling inflation. It starts by defining the price gap as the difference between the price level and the long-run equilibrium price level, which is implied by the long-run quantity relation. The model then specifies a direct effect from the lagged price gap and the current price level.

Studies designed to test the QTM using data on one or a few countries (the second group) often overlap with the third type of studies — very long-term historical analyses of the relation between money and prices, or investigations of this relation over a particular period in the past. One such long historical analysis was carried out by Smith (1988), who explores the relation between money and prices in the British colonies.

Studies analyzing a large set of countries typically do not take differences between countries into account. However, Rolnick and Weber (1995) show that such disregard can change the results of estimations. They prove that the strength of the long-run relationship between money and prices differs across countries operating under different monetary standards. When compared with fiat standards, commodity standards result in lower correlations of money growth and inflation, a higher correlation with output growth and a lower correlation of various monetary aggregates with each other. Inflation, money growth and output growth are generally lower under commodity standards than under fiat standards.

3. Cross-Section Evidence: The Long Run

We now turn to tests of the quantity theory using cross-section data on 30-year averages of money growth, inflation and output growth. (Later on, in Section 4, we use panel data to test the quantity theory.) We expect 30 years to be a sufficiently long period to be considered as "long-run." Therefore, we assume that our sample of data is sufficiently long to detect the type of relationship predicted by the quantity theory. We begin by presenting the data and then proceed to the regression analysis.

The Data

To explore the relationship between money growth and inflation, we chose the largest available sample of countries, covering the years 1969–1999. We used the International Financial Statistics of the IMF as the source of our data and tested the theory using two monetary aggregates, M1 and M2. Inflation is measured as a percentage increase in the consumer price index. Not all observations are shown in our graphs; five observations with an average inflation rate above 200 percent per annum were omitted. Including them would have compressed the remainder of the chart too much.

Figure 1 shows the full sample of observations on average annual inflation and money growth rates. As in the studies reviewed above, the observations are clustered around the 45° line. The correlation between average inflation and average M1 growth is 0.877, and 0.89 for the correlation with M2. Thus, the results are very similar to those obtained by Vogel (1974), Dwyer and Hafer (1988, 1999), Barro (1990), Poole (1994) and McCandless and Weber (1995). Note that our sample of countries is larger than the samples used in these studies.

Most of the observations are grouped in the lower-left part of the chart, close to the origin. To detect whether the relation between money supply growth and the inflation rate may vary between subsamples, we divided the set of all observations into groups in the following way. We started with a sample consisting of countries with

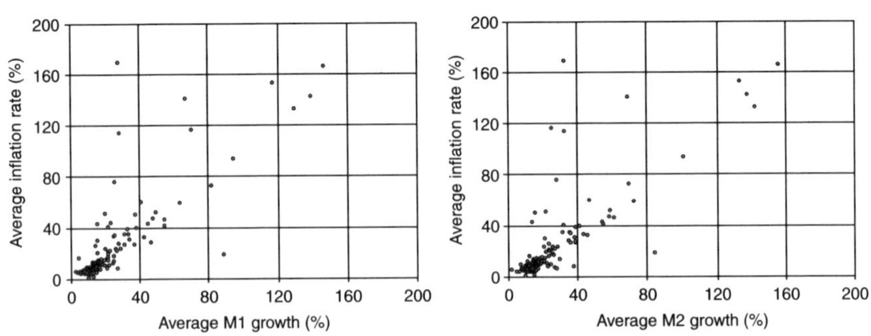

Figure 1. Inflation and the average growth of M1 and M2, 1969–1999 (up to 200 percent p.a.).

inflation and money growth below 10 percent. Then, we progressively expanded the sample by adding the observations of the next classes, i.e., 10 percent to 20 percent, 20 percent to 30 percent and so on. A selection of scatter diagrams is shown in Figures 2–4. It is immediately evident from the successive scatter diagrams that the positive relation between inflation and money growth seems to become more pronounced as observations of high-inflation countries are added to the sample. For low-inflation countries (less than 10 percent), the scatter diagram forms a shapeless, almost horizontal cloud. Thus, the relation between inflation and money growth obtained for the lowest inflation countries appears to be quite different from the results for the full sample. This feature of the cross-section analysis which, to

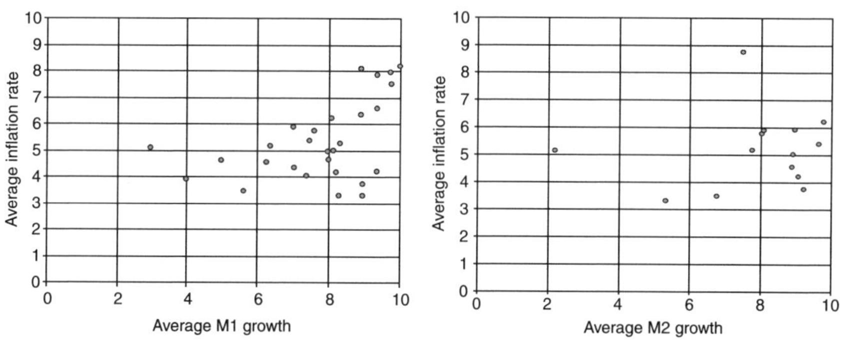

Figure 2. Inflation and money supply growth lower than 10 percent.

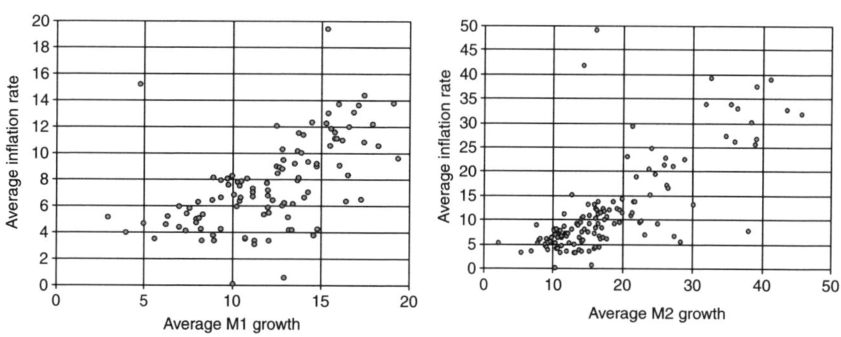

Figure 3. Inflation and money supply growth from 0 percent to 20 percent.

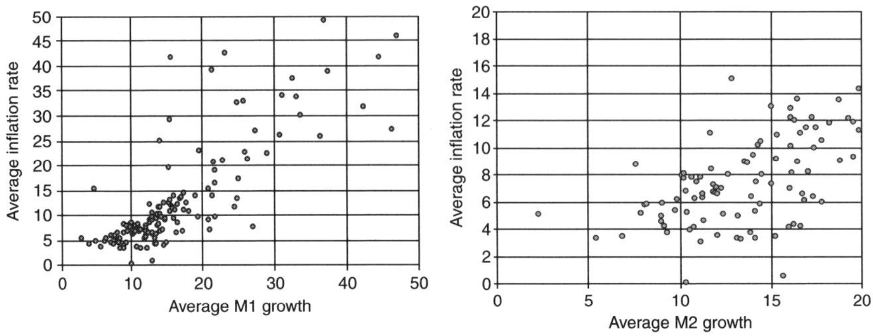

Figure 4. Inflation and money supply growth from 0 percent to 50 percent.

our knowledge, has not been analysed in the existing literature, is the focus of our analysis.

Cross-Section Empirical Analysis

Here, we test both the proportionality and the neutrality (orthogonality) propositions of the QTM. We begin by examining the whole sample, and then try to obtain additional insights into the QTM relationships by analyzing different subsamples.

Estimation over the Whole Sample

We start by estimating the regression Eq. (4) relating the long-term average inflation rate to the long-term average money supply growth, and the long-term growth rate of output (where the long term is 30 years).[4] The first sample (M1) contains 116 countries, the second (M2) 109. Since there is evidence of heteroscedasticity, we use White standard errors. The results of an OLS estimation are shown in Tables 2 and 3. We observe that the growth rates of M1 and M2 have the right sign and are highly significant. But the coefficients of M1 and M2 exceed one, and significantly so. The size of this coefficient, as predicted by the quantity theory of money,

[4]Some of the time series used in the calculations of averages differ in length. We have reestimated all equations using a sample consisting of time series with at least 20 observations. The results are very similar to those obtained for the full sample and are not reported here. They can be obtained from the authors on request.

Table 2. Results of the OLS estimation of $p_i = \beta_0 + \beta_1 m1_i + \beta_2 y_i + \mu_i$.

White HCSE & Covariance			Included observations: 116		
Variable	Coefficient	Std. error	t-Statistic	p-value	Test $\beta_1 = 1$
Constant	4.134	17.534	0.236	0.814	p-value
$m1$	1.639	0.161	10.195	0.000	0.0001
y	−2.826	3.476	−0.813	0.418	
Adjusted R-squared		0.858	Akaike information criterion 11.439		
Durbin-Watson statistic		1.793	p-value (F-test)		0.000

Note: The econometric package used for the regressions reported here and in the other tables is Eviews.

Table 3. Results of the OLS estimation of $p_i = \beta_0 + \beta_1 m2_i + \beta_2 y_i + \mu_i$.

White HCSE & Covariance			Included observations: 109		
Variable	Coefficient	Std. error	t-Statistic	p-Value	Test $\beta_1 = 1$
Constant	18.888	18.734	1.008	0.316	p-value
$m2$	1.451	0.164	8.836	0.000	0.007
y	−5.122	3.556	−1.440	0.153	
Adjusted R-squared		0.823	Akaike information criterion 11.716		
Durbin-Watson statistic		1.638	p-value (F-test)		0.000

should be one. However, for the full sample of countries analyzed over the 30-year period, this hypothesis is rejected. Later on, we return to this result, and argue that this coefficient is greatly influenced by hyperinflationary dynamics in the high-inflation countries, which leads to a positive correlation between money growth and velocity. This could then give rise to an upward bias in the coefficient of money growth.

The estimated coefficient of output growth has the expected sign and is surprisingly large in value, but it is not significant. Therefore, we cannot decisively confirm that output has no impact on inflation in any country.

As mentioned earlier, the quantity theory predicts that over a sufficiently long period, changes in the growth rate of money do not affect output growth. If a rise in money growth increases output growth, this effect is temporary. Over the time horizon of

30 years considered here, these temporary output effects of monetary expansions seem to have disappeared. To test the neutrality proposition, we estimated the following equation:

$$y_i = \gamma_0 + \gamma_1 m_i + \eta_i, \tag{5}$$

where the variables are defined as in (4). The results are reported in Tables 4 and 5. We find that although very small in absolute value, the effect of higher money growth on output growth is negative, and significantly so. This suggests two conclusions. First, the QTM prediction that an expansion of the money stock does not increase output in the long run is confirmed. Second, considering that the estimate is significant, countries having experienced higher money growth also experienced a lower output growth — a finding in line with the empirical evidence on the determinants of economic growth; see Barro and Sala-i-Martin (1995). However, this effect is quantitatively very small for low- and intermediate-inflation countries. For example, an increase in the yearly growth rate of money

Table 4. Results of the OLS estimation of $y_i = \gamma_0 + \gamma_1 m1_i + \eta_i$.

White HCSE & Covariance			Included observations: 116	
Variable	Coefficient	Std. error	t-Statistic	p-value
Constant	4.0508	0.2553	15.8615	0.0000
$m1$	−0.0054	0.0022	−2.5119	0.0134
Adjusted R-squared	0.0441		Akaike information criterion	4.6993
Durbin-Watson statistic	1.8769		p-value (F-test)	0.0134

Table 5. Results of the OLS estimation of $y_i = \gamma_0 + \gamma_1 m2_i + \eta_i$.

White HCSE & Covariance			Included observations: 109	
Variable	Coefficient	Std. error	t-Statistic	p-value
Constant	4.0736	0.2707	15.0459	0.0000
$m2$	−0.0046	0.0020	−2.2285	0.0279
Adjusted R-squared	0.0354		Akaike information criterion	4.7615
Durbin-Watson statistic	1.7961		p-value (F-test)	0.0279

M1 of 10 percentage points sustained over a 30-year period reduces yearly growth of output by 0.054 percent. For high-inflation countries which experience yearly growth rates of money of several hundred percentage points, this effect is quantitatively much more important. To gain insight into the quantitative importance of this effect, we multiplied the coefficients of money growth by one standard deviation of money growth observed in the sample. Due to the presence of very high-inflation countries in the sample, one standard deviation in the yearly rates of the money stocks is very high, i.e., 85 percent (for M1) and 122 percent (for M2). We find that a one-standard deviation increase in the average money growth reduces average output growth by approximately 0.5 percent.

Estimation over Subsamples

One of the main hypotheses we want to test is whether the quantity theory holds better (or less so) for different levels of inflation. To analyse this issue, we estimated the model for different subsamples. The intuitive choice would have been to use the level of inflation to define the subsamples; however, using the level of inflation (the LHS variable) to group observations creates a potential bias. Therefore, we grouped observations using money growth (a RHS variable). We performed the estimation in a recursive manner, i.e., enlarging the samples by adding observations with increasing values of money growth. The results are shown in Table 6. However, we also carried out all estimations dividing the countries according to their inflation rate, and obtained very similar results.

Table 6. Results of estimation of the equations: $p_i = \beta_0 + \beta_1 m_i + \beta_2 y_i + \mu_i$.

Variable	Coefficient	Std. error	*t*-Statistic	*p*-value	Test $\beta_1 = 1$
			M1		
Interval ($ml < 15$ percent p.a.; #obs. = 46)					
Constant	6.181	2.704	2.285	0.027	*p*-value
m1	0.224	0.262	0.856	0.397	0.003
y	−0.459	0.237	−1.943	0.059	

(*Continued*)

Table 6. (*Continued*)

Variable	Coefficient	Std. error	t-Statistic	p-value	Test $\beta_1 = 1$
Interval ($m1 < 20$ percent p.a.; #obs. = 70)					
Constant	2.398	2.314	1.036	0.303	p-value
m1	**0.795**	0.276	2.882	0.005	0.456
y	−0.874	0.509	−1.718	0.090	
Interval ($m1 < 30$ percent p.a.; #obs. = 88)					
Constant	0.636	3.385	0.188	0.851	p-value
m1	**1.243**	0.322	3.859	0.000	0.451
y	**−1.784**	0.754	−2.364	0.020	
Interval ($m1 < 100$ percent p.a.; #obs. = 106)					
Constant	6.919	5.003	1.383	0.169	p-value
m1	**1.344**	0.289	4.657	0.000	0.233
y	**−3.118**	1.191	−2.618	0.010	
Full sample (#obs. = 116)					
Constant	4.134	17.534	0.236	0.814	p-value
m1	**1.639**	0.161	10.195	0.000	0.000
y	−2.826	3.476	−0.813	0.418	
			M2		
Interval ($m2 < 15$ percent p.a.; #obs. = 32)					
Constant	4.75	4.745	2.145	0.035	p-value
m2	0.25	0.245	0.187	0.200	0.001
y	−0.28	−0.282	0.219	0.209	
Interval ($m2 < 20$ percent p.a.; #obs. = 58)					
Constant	0.592	2.212	0.268	0.790	p-value
m2	**0.888**	0.299	2.969	0.004	0.709
y	−1.095	0.613	−1.787	0.079	
Interval ($m2 < 30\%$ p.a.; #obs. = 79)					
Constant	1.012	2.479	0.408	0.684	p-value
m2	**1.059**	0.233	4.548	0.000	0.798
y	**−1.738**	0.756	−2.298	0.024	
Interval ($m2 < 100$ percent p.a.; #obs. = 101)					
Constant	11.250	6.685	1.683	0.096	p-value
m2	**1.316**	0.248	5.311	0.000	0.202
y	**−3.958**	1.113	−3.555	0.000	
Full sample (#obs. = 109)					
Constant	18.888	18.734	1.008	0.316	p-value
m2	**1.451**	0.164	8.836	0.000	0.006
y	−5.122	3.556	−1.440	0.153	

We observe that in the sample of low money growth countries (on average, a growth of M1 and M2 lower than 15 percent p.a.), the coefficients of the money variable are close to zero and not statistically different from zero. As we add observations of countries with high money growth, these coefficients increase in value and become significantly different from zero (already in the second subsample). Note that when we add the countries with the highest money growth, the coefficients of money growth become significantly higher than 1.

We conclude this section by noting that in the long term (30 years), the neutrality proposition of the quantity theory is confirmed, i.e., higher money growth has no permanently positive effect on output growth. For high-inflation countries, an increase in money growth reduces output growth. The prediction of proportionality is not maintained, however. For the sample as a whole, we find the coefficient of money to be systematically higher than 1. When we split the sample into subsamples according to the level of money growth, we find a very low and insignificant coefficient of money in the class of low-inflation countries. Thus, for low-inflation or low money growth countries, the quantity theory prediction that inflation is a monetary phenomenon is not confirmed. The situation is very different in the class of high-inflation, high money growth countries. There, we find a coefficient of money growth significantly higher than 1. Thus, in this group of countries, money growth has a more than proportional effect on inflation.

The picture emerging from this analysis is as follows:

(i) In the class of low-inflation countries, a higher growth rate of money does not lead to a proportional increase in inflation in the long run, nor does it affect the rate of output growth. This suggests that there must be a negative correlation between money growth and velocity growth, a conclusion following from the fact that $m + v = p + y$ is an identity.

This negative correlation between money growth and velocity growth in the class of low-inflation countries has two possible interpretations. One relies on the liquidity effect of an increase in money growth, i.e., when the growth of money increases, this leads to a decline in the nominal interest rate which, in turn, increases the demand for money (reduces velocity). This liquidity effect only occurs in the short run, however. In our sample, we relate 30-year average growth rates of money and velocity. It is difficult to believe that the short-term liquidity effect can be sustained over 30 years, so we discard this interpretation.

A second interpretation is that, in the class of low-inflation countries, velocity changes are exogenously driven. They are determined by technological and institutional changes in the payments system, most of which are unrelated to the growth rate of the money stock. Since, according to our previous results, output growth and inflation rates are disconnected from money growth, it follows that money growth adjusts to exogenous shocks in velocity in the class of low-inflation countries. If this interpretation is correct, the negative correlation between velocity (the error term) and money growth creates a downward bias in the estimated coefficient of money in the class of low-inflation countries. Another way of phrasing this interpretation is as follows. Most of the inter-country differences in money growth reflect different experiences in velocity. As a result, the observed cross-country differences in money growth do not reflect systematic differences in monetary policies, but the "noise" coming from differences in velocity. It follows that the observed differences in money growth will not well explain differences in inflation across countries; for a similar interpretation, see Gerlach (2002).

(ii) In the class of high-inflation countries, money growth has a more than proportional effect on inflation, without affecting output growth to any large extent. Thus, the quantity theory identity ($m+v = p+y$) suggests money growth and velocity growth to be positively correlated. This phenomenon can easily be interpreted by hyperinflationary dynamics, i.e., an increase in the growth rate of the money stock leads to an acceleration of velocity which, in turn, reinforces the hyperinflationary dynamics. This phenomenon has been well documented in studies of hyperinflation; see e.g., Cagan (1956). This also suggests that the positive correlation between money growth and velocity (the error term) leads to an upward bias in the estimated coefficient of money growth in the class of high-inflation countries.

The results above suggest that theoretical models which specify velocity as a function of the interest rate (and thus inflation) are a better representation of long-run empirical relations than models considering velocity to be fixed, such as cash-in-advance models and the early generation of search models.

4. Panel Data Evidence: Less than the Long Run

Next, we consider panel data models to further explore the relation between money supply growth and the inflation rate. The use of panel data implies that we now focus on the relation between money growth and inflation over shorter horizons (typically a year). We should not expect high-frequency observations of the type used here to reveal the long-run relationship between money growth and inflation as predicted by the QTM. However, these panel data are interesting for two reasons. First, they allow us to test whether there are subsamples of countries (e.g., those of high-inflation countries) for which the QTM prediction could occur even with high-frequency data. Second, we use these yearly observations as a first step towards gradual aggregation of the observations over longer time spans.

Here, the use of panel data also introduces the necessity of checking for the existence of unit roots in the annual data. Applying unit root tests, we found that some of the time series are stationary, while others are not. This means that our panel is heterogeneous, which appears even within cross-sections. Unfortunately, in such a situation, we could not apply standard procedures of handling nonstationarity of panel models, since they are designed to be used with homogeneous panels.

We proceed as follows. First, we specify and estimate a fixed-effect model using yearly observations of all countries in the sample. Second, we examine the same models with different time aggregation and dummy variables.

The fixed-effect model is specified as follows:

$$p_{it} = \beta_{oi} + \beta_1 m_{it} + \xi_{it}, \tag{6}$$

where the subscript i refers to countries and the subscript t to time (years), β_1 is common for all countries and each country gets its own constant β_{0i}. The latter represent time-invariant, country-characteristic factors, which influence the inflation rate. These country-specific factors include the long-term growth rates of output and trend changes in velocity.

We applied this model to both the M1 and M2 definitions of money. Due to data availability, the second panel is slightly smaller than the first. The yearly data are the same as those used to compute the average rates, analysed in detail in preceding sections. The model was estimated using GLS, assuming the presence of cross-section heteroscedasticity. Table 7 reports the results of the estimations. We find significant but small effects of money growth on inflation. The coefficient of M1 growth is 0.096, while the coefficient of M2 growth is 0.2. As argued earlier, the small size of the coefficients should not come as a surprise, since the QTM is a theory about the long-run effects of money.

Figures 5 and 6 show the fixed effects (vertical axis) and relate these to the average money growth rates of each country (horizontal axis). The relation appears to be highly non-linear. That is why we also show the relation on a logarithmic scale in the right-hand panel.

Table 7. Estimation of fixed effects

Variable	Coefficient	Std. error	t-Statistic	p-value
		M1		
$m1$	0.0961	0.0073	13.2381	0.0000
Adjusted R-squared	0.3033		Durbin-Watson statistic	1.0627
		M2		
$m2$	0.2005	0.0039	51.1270	0.0000
Adjusted R-squared	0.6392		Durbin-Watson statistic	1.2290

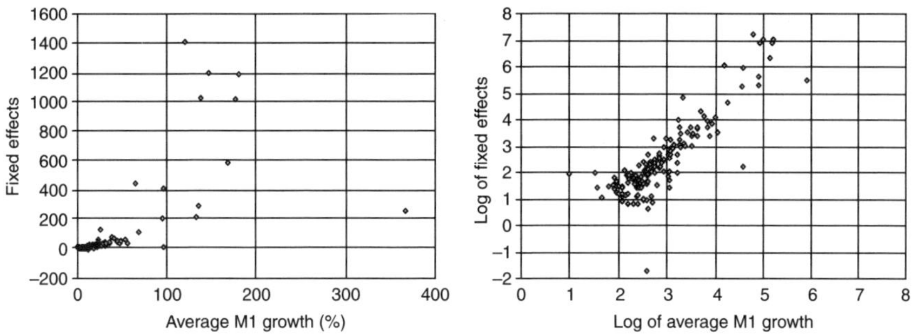

Figure 5. Fixed effects and money growth (M1). Left panel — prime data; right panel —logs.

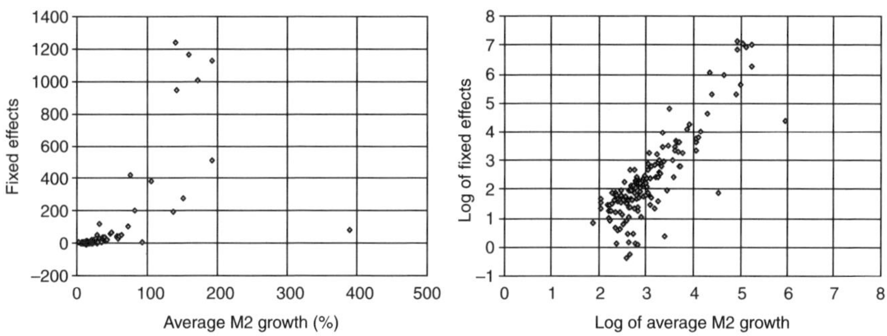

Figure 6. Fixed effects and money growth (M2). Left panel — prime data; right panel — logs.

We find a strong correlation between the average money growth rates and the fixed effects (the correlation coefficients are 0.69 and 0.67 for M1 and M2 samples, respectively). The non-linear nature of this relation implies that as the average growth rates of money increase, the fixed effects (country-specific effects) tend to increase more than proportionately. Our favoured interpretation, which is also in line with our earlier conclusion, runs as follows: when money growth becomes very high, the dynamics of hyperinflation is set in motion, thereby producing strong increases in the velocity of money. This tends to increase inflation more than proportionately; see the classical paper by Cagan (1956).

We choose to focus on the fixed-effects model for a number of reasons. In a situation where a panel is constructed of time series representing single countries or large companies or industries ("one of a kind") and we want to make predictions for one cross-section or a group of them, it is usually advisable to use a fixed-effects model. Since, in such a situation, the observations cannot be assumed to be randomly drawn from a certain underlying (common) distribution, determining the individual characteristics of cross-sections is important in interpreting the results of the estimation.

A clear sign of the situation where a fixed-effects model should be preferred is correlation between fixed effects and the regressor. If there is correlation, the random effects estimator is inconsistent, since it ignores this correlation. Therefore, after observing high correlation between fixed effects and money growth, we limit the analysis to the estimation of the fixed-effects model; see Verbeek (2000).

Note that the Hausman test which can be used to select a random-effects model over a fixed-effects model is not informative in our case. We only estimate one parameter (we have one regressor), which implies that we have to use critical values from a χ^2 distribution with only one degree of freedom. Therefore, our test statistic is very likely to fall in the confidence interval and make us accept the null hypothesis of no difference between random-and fixed-effects models. As a result, we rely solely on the strong correlation between money growth and fixed effects as the argument in favour of the fixed-effects model.

The next step in the analysis consists of testing for different effects of money growth on inflation, depending on the level of inflation. For this purpose, we created six dummies for increasing levels of inflation (D1: 0 to 10 percent, D2: 10 percent to 20 percent,. . . ,D6: more than 50 percent). Then, we multiplied these dummies by m to obtain a slope coefficient (coefficient of m) for each group of inflation. The panel-data model was re-estimated including these dummies. The results are shown in Table 8. All slope coefficients are significant for both *m1* and *m2*. As predicted, they are higher for countries with higher average inflation rates. The differences are quite substantial. Countries with low inflation (less than 10 percent per year) exhibit very low coefficients of money growth. Only high-inflation countries have coefficients which come close to that predicted by the

Table 8. Estimation of panels with a distinction between inflation groups (fixed–effect models).

Variable	Coefficient	p-value $\beta = 0$	Variable	Coefficient	p-value $\beta = 0$
$m1{*}D1$	0.0604	0.0000	$m2{*}D1$	0.1663	0.0000
$m1{*}D2$	0.0605	0.0010	$m2{*}D2$	0.1446	0.0000
$m1{*}D3$	0.5880	0.0000	$m2{*}D3$	0.6794	0.0000
$m1{*}D4$	1.2343	0.0000	$m2{*}D4$	0.8346	0.0000
$m1{*}D5$	1.0738	0.0000	$m2{*}D5$	0.6890	0.0000
$m1{*}D6$	1.1470	0.0000	$m2{*}D6$	1.2248	0.0000
Benchmark	0.0961		Benchmark	0.2005	

Note: The sizes of the different subsamples are: D1–83; D2–35; D3–12; D4–9; D5–7; D6–20.

QTM. Thus, in high-inflation countries, we cannot reject the QTM prediction on a *yearly* basis, i.e., when inflation is very high, the prediction that inflation and money growth are proportional holds even in high-frequency observations. This result suggests that the speed at which inflation adjusts to increases in the growth rate of money is not constant. It increases with the level of inflation. In high-inflation regimes, prices adjust quickly to monetary shocks. This is consistent with historical evidence about the speed of adjustment of prices in hyperinflationary regimes; see Bresciani-Turroni (1937).

The final step in our analysis of the panel data is to apply different levels of time aggregation. We start with a panel constructed with non-overlapping, two-year averages of money growth and inflation. We then turn to averages over three years or more, and finish with a panel of six-year averages. By analysing these panels, we want to see how the influence of money growth on inflation changes as we pass through increasing levels of time aggregation.

We estimate the following model:

$$P_{it\tau} = \delta_{0\tau} + \delta_{1\tau} m_{it\tau} D_j + \zeta_{it\tau}, \tag{7}$$

where i denotes the country, t the time period, τ is the length of the period over which averages are computed ($\tau = 1, \ldots, 6$),

Table 9. Estimated coefficients of m1 and m2 for different levels of inflation (D1, ..., D6) and different levels of time aggregation (1,...,6 years).

	1 year	2 years	3 years	4 years	5 years	6 years
M1						
D1	0.0465	0.2486	0.5322	0.2004	0.2555	−0.3061
D2	0.1574	0.3684	0.5747	0.0007	0.3685	0.0007*
D3	0.5159	0.7576	0.7377	0.8163	0.9060	0.5807
D4	0.9162	1.0300	1.0739	1.0583	1.0128	0.8550
D5	1.0592	1.0728	1.0603	1.0707	1.0228	0.9662
D6	1.1105	1.3864	1.3130	1.1136	1.0463	0.8265
M2						
D1	0.1641	0.3883	0.4276	0.2608	0.3174	0.0906*
D2	0.2032	0.3545	0.4067	0.3367	0.3760	0.2198
D3	0.4601	0.6920	0.7156	0.6161	0.6715	0.5730
D4	0.7051	0.8183	0.9595	0.8692	0.9416	0.7937
D5	0.9821	0.9126	1.1264	0.9446	0.9960	1.0382
D6	1.1001	1.1797	0.9623	0.9903	1.0348	0.8241

*Not significant at the 5% level.

D_j denotes the dummy variable, and j is the number of the inflation group ($j = 1, \ldots, 6$).

This model allows us to study how the level of time aggregation affects the coefficients of money growth. The QTM predicts that with increasing time aggregation, the effect of money growth on inflation increases. Similarly, the model allows us to study how the level of inflation affects the coefficients of money growth for different levels of time aggregation. Here, we concentrate on the coefficients of *m1* and *m2*, which are shown in Table 9. (Full and detailed results are available on request.) The results lend themselves to the following interpretation. First, the coefficients of money growth increase with the level of inflation, for all levels of time aggregation.

Second, time aggregation increases the value of the coefficients of *m1* and *m2* for low-inflation countries. When moving from one-yearly averages to three-yearly averages, we see that the coefficients of low-inflation countries *(D1)* increase to approximately 0.5. Further time aggregation reduces this coefficient, however.

5. Conclusions

The quantity theory of money is based on two propositions. First, in the long run, there is *proportionality* between money growth and inflation, i.e., when money growth increases by x percent inflation also rises by x percent. Second, in the long run, there is *neutrality* between money growth on the one hand and output growth and velocity changes on the other.

We subjected these statements to empirical tests using a sample which covers most countries in the world during the last 30 years. Our findings can be summarised as follows. First, when analyzing the full sample of countries, we find a strong positive relation between the long-run growth rate of money and inflation. However, this relation is not proportional.

Our second finding is that this strong link between inflation and money growth is almost wholly due to the presence of high-inflation or hyperinflation countries in the sample. The relation between inflation and money growth for low-inflation countries (on average less than 10 percent per year over 30 years) is weak, if not absent. However, we also find that this lack of proportionality between money growth and inflation is not due to a systematic relationship between money growth and output growth. We find that, in low-inflation countries, money growth and output growth are independent in the long run. This finding is consistent with the large number of econometric analyses using time series of single countries. Most of these studies have found money to be neutral in the long run.

A third finding (obtained from a panel-data analysis) indicates that country-specific effects become increasingly important when the rate of inflation increases. We interpret this to mean that velocity accelerates with increasing inflation, thereby leading to inflation rates exceeding the growth rates of the money stock. This also explains why in cross-section regressions, inflation rates increase more than proportionately to money growth in high-inflation countries.

Fourth, the panel-data analysis revealed "long-run" to be a relative concept, i.e., the time it takes for the long-run effects of monetary expansions to be realised depends on the level of inflation.

We found the transmission of money growth into inflation to be established within a year in high-inflation countries.

Finally, we found that in the class of low-inflation countries, money growth and velocity changes are inversely related, while in the class of high-inflation countries the reverse holds, i.e., money growth and velocity growth are positively related. The latter confirms our interpretation of the positive correlation between money growth and fixed effects in our panel-data model.

These results can be given the following interpretation. In the class of low-inflation countries, inflation and output growth seem to be exogenously driven phenomena, mostly unrelated to the growth rate of the money stock. As a result, changes in velocity necessarily lead to opposite changes in the stock of money (given the definition $p + y = m + v$). Put differently, most of the inter-country differences in money growth reflect different experiences in velocity. As a result, the observed cross-country differences in money growth do not reflect systematic differences in monetary policies, but the "noise" coming from velocity differences. It thus follows that the observed differences in money growth have a poor explanatory power with respect to differences in inflation across countries in the class of low-inflation countries.

For high-inflation countries, on the other hand, an increase in the growth of the money stock leads to an increase in both inflation and velocity. The latter reinforces the inflationary dynamics. This is also the reason why, in the class of high-inflation countries, we find a coefficient of money growth typically exceeding 1. This process has been well documented in empirical studies of hyperinflation and it is confirmed by our results; see Cagan (1956).

Our results have some implications for the question regarding the use of the money stock as an intermediate target in monetary policy. As is well known, the European Central Bank continues to assign a prominent role to the growth rate of the money stock in its monetary policy strategy.[5] The ECB bases this strategy on the view

[5]In May 2003, the ECB announced that it would downplay, but not eliminate, the prominent role it assigns to the evolution of the money stock in its monetary policy strategy.

that "inflation is always and everywhere a monetary phenomenon."[6] This may be true for high-inflation countries. Our results, however, indicate that there is no evidence for this statement in relatively low-inflation environments, which happen to be a characteristic of the EMU countries. In these environments, money growth is not a useful signal of inflationary conditions, because it is dominated by "noise" originating from velocity shocks. It also follows that the use of the money stock as a guide for steering policies towards price stability is not likely to be useful for countries with a history of low inflation.

References

Barro, R (1990). *Macroeconomics*, 3rd Edition. New York, NJ: John Wiley.

Barro, R and X Sala-i-Martin (1995). *Economic Growth.* Cambridge, MA: MIT Press.

Boschen, J and L Mills (1995). Tests of the relation between money and output in real business cycle models. *Journal of Monetary Economics*, 22, 355–374.

Bresciani-Turroni, C (1937). *The Economics of Inflation.* London, UK: Allen & Unwin.

Cagan, P (1956). The monetary dynamics of hyperinflation. In *Studies in the Quantity Theory of Money*, M Friedman (ed.). Chicago, IL: University of Chicago Press.

Dwyer, GP Jr. and RW Hafer (1988). Is money irrelevant? *Federal Reserve Bank of St. Louis Review*, 70, 3–17.

Dwyer, GP Jr. and RW Hafer (1999). Are money growth and inflation still related? *Federal Reserve Bank of Atlanta Economic Review*, 84, 32–43.

Fitzgerald, TJ (1999). Money growth and inflation: How long is the long-run? Federal Reserve Bank of Cleveland Economic Commentary.

Friedman, M (1963). *Inflation: Causes and Consequences.* New York, NY: Asia Publishing House.

Friedman, M and A Schwartz (1963). *A Monetary History of the United States, 1867–1960.* Princeton, NJ: Princeton University Press.

Gerlach, S and L Svensson (2004). Money and inflation in the euro area: A case for monetary indicators. *Journal of Monetary Economics*, 50, 1649–1672.

Gerlach, S (2002). *The ECB's Two Pillars.* Mimeo: Hong Kong Monetary Authority.

Geweke, J (1986). The superneutrality of money in the United States: Interpretation of the evidence. *Econometrica*, 54, 1–21.

[6]The monetary policy strategy of the ECB is described in the *Monthly Bulletin* of January 1999. On p. 47, the section describing the role of money in this strategy starts with the statement: "Inflation is ultimately a monetary phenomenon."

Hallman, J, R Porter and H Small (1991). Is the price level tied to the M2 monetary aggregate in the long-run? *American Economic Review*, 81, 841–858.

Jansen, E (2004). Modelling inflation in the euro area. ECB Working Paper No. 322, Frankfurt.

King, R and M Watson (1997). Testing long-run neutrality. *Federal Reserve Bank of Richmond Quarterly*, 83, 69–101.

Lucas, RE Jr. (1980). Two illustrations of the quantity theory of money. *American Economic Review*, 70, 1005–1014.

McCallum, BT (1984). On low frequency-estimates of long-run relationships in macroeconomics. *Journal of Monetary Economics*, 14, 3–14.

McCandless, GT Jr. and WE Weber (1995). Some monetary facts. *Federal Reserve Bank of Minneapolis Quarterly Review*, 19, 2–11.

Pakko, MR (1994). Inflation and money growth in the former Soviet Union. International Economic Contributions, Federal Reserve Bank of St. Louis.

Poole, W(1994). Keep them in monetary policy, jobs & capital. Milken Institute for Job & Capital Formation, Santa Monica, CA.

Rolnick, A and W Weber (1998). Money, inflation, and output under fiat and commodity standards. *Federal Reserve Bank of Minneapolis Quarterly Review*, 22, 11–17.

Smith, BD (1988). The relationship between money and prices: Some historical evidence reconsidered. *Federal Reserve Bank of Minneapolis Quarterly Review*, 12, 18–32.

Stock, J and M Watson (1988). Interpreting the evidence on money income causality. *Journal of Econometrics*, 40, 161–182.

Vega, J and C Trecroci (2002). The information content of m3 for future inflation. *Weltwirtschaftliches Archiv*, 138, 22–53.

Verbeek, M (2000). *A Guide to Modern Econometrics.* Chichester: John Wiley.

Vogel, RC (1974). The dynamics of inflation in Latin America, 1950–1969. *American Economic Review*, 64, 102–114.

Weber, A (1994). Testing long-run neutrality: Empirical evidence for G6-countries with special emphasis on Germany. *Carnegie-Rochester Conference Series on Public Policy*, 41, 67–117.

Chapter 15

Monetary Policy and the Real Economy

Paul De Grauwe and Cláudia Costa Storti

Introduction

How effective is monetary policy in influencing output and employment? How long do the effects of monetary policy last? These questions have been hotly debated. In the 1970s and 1980s, they led to a major schism in the economics profession between Monetarists and Keynesians. This schism seems to have been resolved now, and a mainstream view can be said to have emerged.

The mainstream view today has been influenced by several theoretical developments. First, there is the real business cycle theory, which has introduced the idea that macroeconomic models should be based on sound micro-foundations in which individual agents continuously maximize their utilities in a dynamic framework and in which these agents understand and use the full complexity of the underlying model in forecasting the future (rational expectations). Second, building on this methodological innovation, macroeconomists have introduced price and wage rigidities into their models. This has led to the so-called Neo-Keynesian models in which representative agents optimize their utilities and have rational expectations but face some constraints in that they cannot adjust prices and wages instantaneously (see e.g., Clarida *et al.*, 1999; Christiano *et al.*, 2001). This

Published in R Schettkat and J Langkau (eds.), *Economic Policy Proposals for Germany and Europe*. New York: Routledge (2008).

last feature provides the basis for monetary policy to affect output and employment.

These theoretical developments have led to the consensus view, first, that monetary policy has significant short-term effects on output and employment; second, that these effects are temporary. This consensus can be represented by a hump-shaped curve showing the time profile of the effect of an unexpected decline in the short-term interest rate on output. This curve is typically obtained from an impulse response analysis of the effect of an unanticipated decline in the short-term interest rate in an empirical version of Neo-Keynesian macroeconomic models (see e.g., Smets and Wouters, 2003; Walsh, 2003). Much of the discussion, today, among macroeconomists has shifted to the issue of whether this empirical regularity can be exploited by the monetary authorities and whether rules should govern the conduct of monetary policy.

In this chapter, we provide additional evidence of the effects of monetary policies on output and on the timing of these effects. In order to do so, we will use meta-analysis as our methodology. We will focus on both the output and price effects of monetary policies, mainly because the issue of how effective monetary policy is in influencing output cannot be dissociated from the price effects of these policies.

A Meta-Analysis of the Effects of Monetary Policy on Output and Prices

The econometric analysis of the effect of monetary policies has changed considerably during the 1990s mainly as a result of the advance of econometric techniques and, in particular, as a result of the increasing use of VAR and structural VAR (SVAR) techniques. This has led to a proliferation of econometric evaluations of the effectiveness of monetary policies in many countries.

In order to analyze the effectiveness of monetary policies in changing output, we will use a "meta-analysis." This technique is frequently used in medical sciences and has sporadically been used in economics (see e.g., Knell and Stix, 2003; Nijkamp and Poot,

2004; Rose, 2004).[1] The objective of this analysis is first to statistically analyze the estimated effects of monetary policy shocks on output and prices and second to identify the factors that can explain the differences in these estimated effects.

The way to proceed is to first collect data on the parameters that measure the effect of monetary policy on output and prices and that have been estimated in econometric studies. We will distinguish between the short-term and the long-term effects on output and price levels. The parameters collected from these studies will then be used as the dependent variable in an econometric analysis that aims at explaining the variation in these parameters.

The data

The source of the data we used is the empirical studies on the effects of monetary policies. We restricted the empirical studies to those published after 1990. The main reason is that during the 1990s, the new econometric technology using VARs came into use in studies evaluating monetary policies. Since this has become the new state-of-the-art econometric technology, we decided to restrict the analysis to a period in which this technology was introduced.

We used a search of Econlit and also searched in well-known discussion paper series (NBER, CEPR, and CESifo) and the discussion paper series of central banks. We obtained 83 studies that report numbers on the effect of monetary policy. There are of course many more papers that analyse the transmission of monetary policies, but many of these papers provide no or incomplete quantitative evidence of the effects of monetary policy, or report results that cannot be made comparable to other results.

We were interested in four different parameters measuring the effect of monetary policy. These are:

- the short-term effect on output;
- the long-term effect on output;

[1]See Stanley (2001) for a critical analysis of the use of meta-analysis in economics.

- the short-term effect on the price level;
- the long-term effect on the price level.

We decided that the effects after one year measure the short run, while the effects obtained after five years measure the long run. In fact, all the long-run coefficients reported in the studies relate to periods from five to seven years. We would have liked to use a longer time span, but no coefficients measuring the effects after seven years were found. It is clear that this procedure introduces some arbitrariness in what we call short-run and long-run effects. In particular, one could argue that five to seven years is not really the long run. Yet, finding output effects of monetary policies lasting five to seven years comes close to what one could label the long run.

The way the empirical results are reported is far from harmonized. The VAR and SVAR studies report impulse response functions that measure the impact of a monetary policy shock (typically a short-term unanticipated interest rate increase) on output and prices. We harmonized these numbers so that each number measures the effect of a 1 percent increase of the interest rate on output and the price level at the respective horizons.[2]

There are very few studies that use the money stock as the policy variable. Almost no VAR or SVAR studies use the money stock. As a result, we restricted the analysis to those studies that use the interest rate as the policy variable.

There are also a number of studies using structural econometric models.

These studies typically report the effect of a monetary policy shock on output (prices) as the difference between the simulated output (price) level obtained with and without the policy shock.[3] We used these numbers and applied the same harmonization so that

[2]Many VAR and SVAR studies only report the graphs of the impulse response functions. We therefore enlarged these graphs considerably allowing us to measure the coefficients of the impulse response functions with great precision.

[3]Thus, the parameter estimates obtained from econometric models do not distinguish between anticipated and unanticipated interest rate shocks. Typically, VAR-based estimates relate to unanticipated interest rate shocks.

these parameters measure the effect of a shock in the interest rate (money stock) of 1 percent.

Many of the 83 studies selected report results for more than one country. As a result, we obtained 278 parameters measuring the short-term and long-term output effects of monetary policy shocks. For the effects of monetary policy on the price level, we only obtained 185 parameters because a number of studies focus only on the output effects of monetary policy.

Some descriptive statistics

Before engaging in the econometric analysis, it is useful to present some descriptive statistics of the different parameters measuring the effects of monetary policies. We do this in the form of histograms. We First concentrate on the estimated output effects. In Figures 2 and 3, we show the histograms of the short-term and long-term effects of an interest rate increase of 1 percent obtained from our sample of econometric studies. We eliminated some outliers, i.e. in the case of the short-term effects, all the coefficients lower than -1 and higher than $+1$, and in the case of the long-term effects, all the coefficients

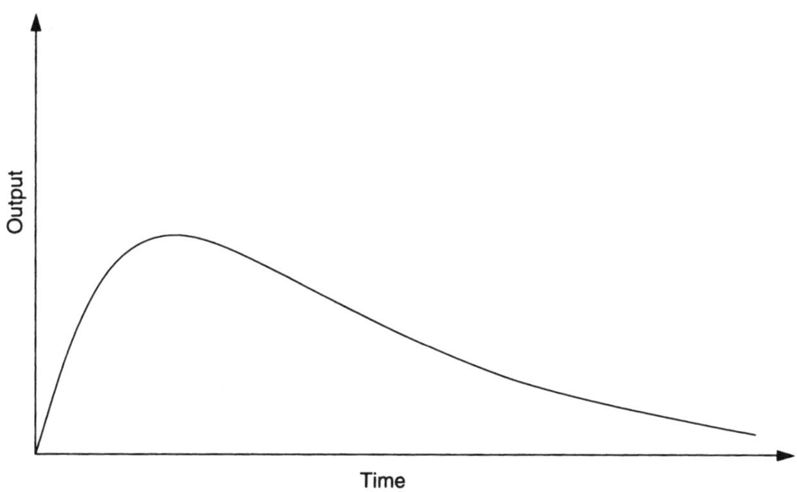

Figure 1. Stylized impulse response function of output following an expansionary monetary policy.

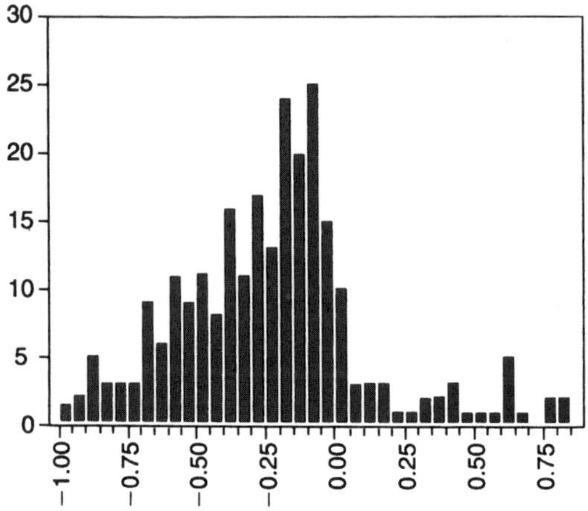

Series: OUTPUTSTOUT	
Sample 1,278	
Observations 253	
Mean	−0.232073
Median	−0.218000
Maximum	0.846154
Minimum	−0.992908
Standard deviation	0.342539
Skewness	0.586143
Kurtosis	3.914012
Jarque–Bera	23.29361
Probability	0.000009

Figure 2. Frequency distribution of the estimated short-term output effect of a 1 percent increase in the short-term interest rate.

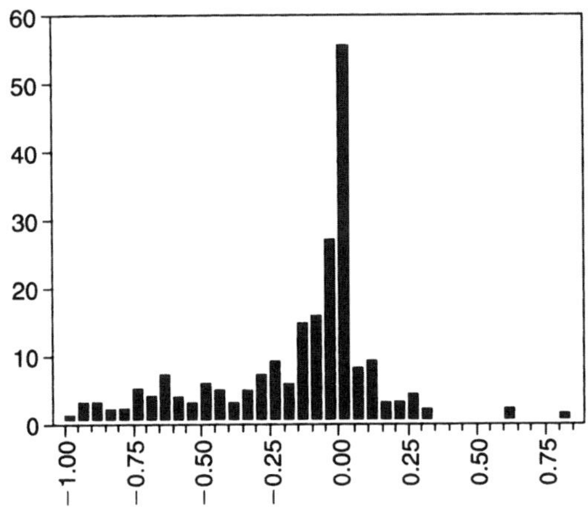

Series: OUTPUTLTOUT	
Sample 1,278	
Observations 221	
Mean	−0.157541
Median	−0.040000
Maximum	0.811000
Minimum	−0.981432
Standard deviation	0.300833
Skewness	−0.695962
Kurtosis	3.700205
Jarque–Bera	22.35543
Probability	0.000014

Figure 3. Frequency distribution of the estimated long-term output effect of a 1 percent increase in the short-term interest rate.

lower than −1. However, for the sake of completeness, we present the full sample in Appendix 1.

We focus first on the short-term output effects in Figure 2 (effect after one year). We find that the mean coefficient is −0.23, i.e., after one year, a 1 percent (unanticipated) increase in the short-term interest rate leads to a decline in output of 0.23 percent. We also observe, however, that there is a large variance of the estimated coefficients. One of the purposes of the meta-analysis will be to identify the factors that explain this large variance.

The long-term output effects shown in Figure 3 lead to similar observations. The mean long-term coefficient is −0.16 which is lower than the short-term coefficient. This finding is in accordance with the hump-shaped time profile of the effects of monetary policy shown in Figure 1, which suggests that the short-term effect of a monetary policy shock on output is larger than its long-term effect. We also find that the variance in these estimated coefficients is rather high.

We perform a similar descriptive analysis of the price effects of monetary policy shocks. We show these in Figures 4 and 5.

From Figure 4, we observe that the mean coefficient measuring the short-term effect of an increase in the short-term interest rate is close to zero. The coefficient measuring the long-run effect (Figure 5) is relatively large (in absolute value). Thus, the econometric studies confirm that there is price stickiness. In the short-run (one year), monetary policy shocks do not affect prices. These effects appear only in the long run. Note again that the variance around the mean coefficients is very high.

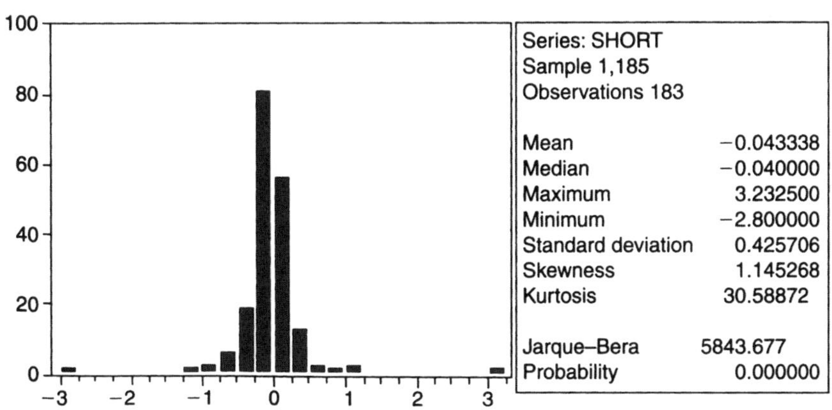

Figure 4. Frequency distribution of the estimated short-term price effect of a 1 percent increase in the short-term interest rate.

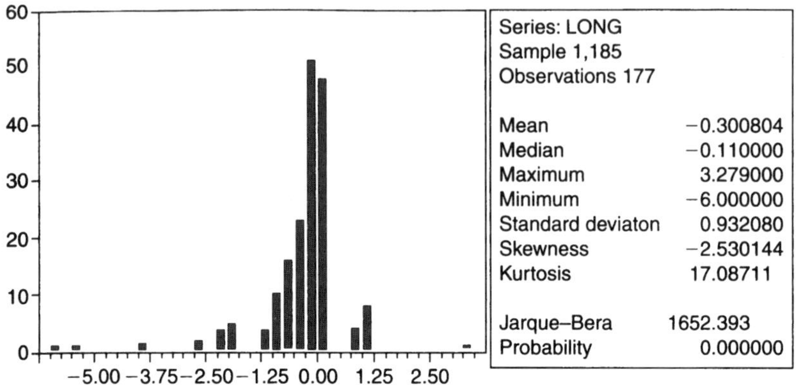

Figure 5. Frequency distribution of the estimated long-term price effect of a 1 percent increase in the short-term interest rate.

Econometric analysis: Output effects

In this section, we specify an econometric equation explaining the different parameters described in the previous section. The purpose is to control for a number of variables that can affect the size of the estimated coefficients. This will allow us to explain part of the large variance in the estimated coefficients.

The econometric equation is specified as follows:

$$PS_i = a + \sum_k \beta_k D_k + \varepsilon_i \tag{1}$$

$$PL_i = c + \sum_k \eta_k D_k + \omega_i \tag{2}$$

where PS_i and PL_i are the observed short-term and long-term parameters measuring the effect of monetary policy.

The variables D_k are variables expressing a particular characteristic of the study from which parameter i was obtained or from the country involved. We distinguish between the following characteristics:

- The countries analysed in the study: in this case, each country is represented by a separate dummy variable.
- The econometric technique used. We distinguish between five types of econometric methods. The first one uses “plain vanilla” VARs,

i.e., the method used to impose identifying restrictions is based on imposing a recursiveness ordering (Choleski decomposition). The second one uses SVARs. This is a VAR method that relies on an economic theory to impose prior restrictions on (some) parameters of the model. Quite often, this method imposes a restriction on the long-term effect of monetary policy (e.g., a zero restriction on the long-term output effect). The third one, FAVAR, uses dynamic factor analysis, and the fourth one, MARKOV, uses switching in regimes. Finally, the fifth technique relies on traditional econometric modelling.[4]

- The variable used to measure output. We distinguish between GDP, industrial production (PROD), and output gap (GAP). Each of these measures is represented by a separate dummy.
- The sample period during which the studies were performed. We distinguish between studies in which the sample period starts in the 1960s, the 1970s and the 1980s. This distinction is introduced to find out whether the coefficients measuring the effectiveness of monetary policy have changed over time. We introduce three dummy variables: SIXTIES, SEVENTIES, and EIGHTIES.
- The exchange rate regime. We distinguish between two exchange rate regimes, fixed and flexible. The countries on a flexible exchange rate regime are the UK, the US, Japan and Germany. The others (EMS countries and emerging countries) are on a fixed exchange rate regime.[5]

A final issue concerns the weights given to the different publications. The quality of the different studies is not the same. One would therefore like to adjust for the quality of the studies. It is, however, very difficult to do this without introducing subjective judgment. This could lead to the possibility of a selection bias, whereby the researcher gives a higher weight to those studies, which come close to his priors. We have not attempted to do this. The only quality

[4]There is, of course, scope for further distinctions in the econometric techniques.

[5]One could introduce finer distinctions between different exchange rate regimes. For example, one could use the IMF classification of exchange rate regimes. This classification has been criticized, however. See Calvo and Reinhart (2000).

criterion we have maintained is the length of the sample periods of the different studies.[6] Thus, studies that use a longer sample period, and thus more information, receive a higher weight than studies using a shorter sample period. The way we do this is by weighting each study by the length of the sample period (expressed as a percent of the longest sample period). We will present results using both weighted and unweighted data.

We show the results for the *short-term output effects* in Table 1.[7] We have structured the model in such a way that we have one dummy variable for each country. For the other variables (econometric method, output measure, and sample period), we eliminate one of them, i.e., we eliminate VAR, GDP, and SIXTIES. As a result, the country coefficients represent the effects of monetary policy in each country in studies using VAR as an econometric method, GDP as a measure of output, with a sample period starting in the 1960s. In this way, we eliminate differences between countries that have to do with the use of different econometric methods, output measures, and sample periods. The coefficients of the remaining variables then measure how the different econometric methods, the output measures, and the sample periods affect these country coefficients on average.

We observe that the country coefficients are very similar and in most cases statistically different from zero. This suggests that studies estimating the effects of monetary policy using VARs, GDP as the measure of output, and samples starting in the 1960s (the benchmark case) find significant short-term effects on output in most countries in the sample.

There are a few additional observations one can make from Table 1. First, the way output is measured does not seem to affect the size of the coefficients. Second, the use of different econometric methods matters. Studies using SVARs produce short-term output

[6]Another possible quality criterion could be the significance of the estimated coefficients. The trouble with this is that many studies do not report confidence levels of the estimated coefficients.

[7]The variable FLOAT was dropped. We did not find any significant difference between countries with floating and fixed exchange rates.

Table 1. Regression results of Equation (1): Short-term output coefficients.

	Unweighted regression		Weighted regression	
Variable	Coefficient	*t*-statistic	Coefficient	*t*-statistic
Austria	−0.38	−2.83	−0.24	−2.93
Belgium	−0.31	−2.09	−0.22	−2.46
Denmark	−0.16	−0.76	−0.15	−1.21
Eurozone	−0.22	−0.84	−0.22	−1.34
Finland	−0.38	−2.64	−0.25	−2.92
France	−0.32	−2.94	−0.22	−3.42
Germany	−0.34	−1.72	−0.30	−2.24
Ireland	−0.19	−1.02	−0.18	−1.61
Italy	−0.22	−2.07	−0.16	−2.48
Netherlands	−0.29	−2.13	−0.20	−2.39
Portugal	−0.28	−1.70	−0.18	−1.84
Spain	−0.25	−2.03	−0.18	−2.50
Sweden	−0.43	−1.95	−0.31	−2.29
Greece	−0.23	−0.93	−0.24	−1.61
Luxembourg	−0.26	−0.75	−0.19	−0.91
UK	−0.28	−1.38	−0.27	−1.97
USA	−0.31	−1.77	−0.25	−2.12
Japan	−0.06	−0.27	−0.16	−1.08
Australia	−0.31	−0.81	−0.32	−1.35
Canada	−0.28	−0.99	−0.31	−1.75
Emerging	0.03	0.25	−0.09	−1.16
IND	−0.04	−0.62	−0.03	−0.67
GAP	0.14	1.16	0.06	0.86
SVAR	0.17	1.88	0.11	2.02
ECON	0.16	2.85	0.07	2.16
FAVAR	−0.29	−1.96	−0.18	−2.01
MARKOV	0.02	0.09	−0.06	−0.55
SEVENTIES	−0.02	−0.19	0.03	0.52
EIGHTIES	−0.08	−1.10	0.07	1.38
MONEY	0.16	1.54	0.13	2.14
FLOAT	0.01	0.05	0.05	0.46
R-squared	0.18		0.15	
S.E. of regression	0.33		0.20	
Sum-squared resid.	23.30		8.30	
Log-likelihood	−61.80		57.10	

coefficients that on average are significantly smaller (in absolute value) than the coefficients obtained with VARs. The same is true for studies using econometric models. The opposite holds for studies using VARs that combine dynamic factor analysis. Third, there is some evidence (in the weighted regressions) that the coefficients are smaller (in absolute value) in the studies with sample periods starting in the 1980s.

The results of estimating Eq. (2) for the long-term output coefficients are shown in Table 2. A first striking observation is that the long-term output coefficients in the different countries are generally not zero. In many cases, they are statistically different from zero. This is surprising, as the consensus view described in the introduction tells us that in the long run the output effects of monetary policy shocks should be zero. This result, however, strongly depends on the econometric method that is used. As in Table 1, the country coefficients in Table 2 represent the benchmark case, i.e., the use of VARs, GDP, and the 1960s as starting sample period. An analysis of the coefficients of SVAR, ECON, FAVAR, and MARKOV in Table 2 reveals that in the studies that use SVARs and econometric models, the long-term output coefficients are much lower (in absolute value) and are close to zero. The use of dynamic factor analysis, however, again leads to an increase in the long-term output coefficients.

Thus, we find that econometric methods that use SVARs and econometric models produce results that are in accordance with the consensus view. This is not really surprising. These methods typically impose the long-term condition that the output effect is zero. In contrast, the econometric methods that do not impose such a long-run restriction, the "plain vanilla" VAR, find that in the long run (after five years), there are still significant output effects of monetary policies in most countries. Put differently, if one "allows the data to speak," the consensus view of monetary policy neutrality does not seem to hold.

An important issue that arises here is whether five years can be considered the long run. One could argue that a fair test of the neutrality proposition should extend the time horizon beyond five years. We look into this problem in Section "The role of macroeconomic

Table 2. Regression results of Equation (2): Long-term output coefficients.

Variable	Unweighted regression		Weighted regression	
	Coefficient	*t*-statistic	Coefficient	*t*-statistic
Austria	−0.36	−3.03	−0.24	−3.18
Belgium	−0.17	−1.42	−0.15	−1.90
Denmark	−0.13	−0.83	−0.14	−1.35
Finland	−0.14	−1.13	−0.15	−1.88
France	−0.23	−2.37	−0.16	−2.64
Germany	−0.18	−1.17	−0.22	−2.04
Ireland	−0.17	−1.16	−0.18	−1.95
Italy	−0.09	−0.96	−0.11	−1.75
Netherlands	−0.29	−2.38	−0.21	−2.65
Portugal	−0.30	−2.19	−0.22	−2.53
Spain	−0.20	−1.73	−0.18	−2.44
Greece	−0.47	−2.18	−0.40	−2.92
Luxembourg	−0.25	−0.84	−0.21	−1.13
Eurozone	−0.20	−0.93	−0.21	−1.53
Sweden	−0.14	−0.76	−0.17	−1.43
UK	−0.10	−0.63	−0.15	−1.40
USA	−0.14	−1.02	−0.22	−2.38
Japan	0.09	0.48	−0.08	−0.70
Australia	−0.24	−0.75	−0.28	−1.34
Canada	−0.21	−0.80	−0.20	−1.20
Emerging	−0.15	−1.35	−0.14	−1.88
IND	−0.10	−1.54	−0.06	−1.36
GAP	0.17	1.81	0.10	1.77
SVAR	0.24	3.23	0.14	2.92
ECON	0.16	2.76	0.08	2.26
FAVAR	−0.37	−3.35	−0.14	−2.06
MARKOV	0.12	0.85	0.08	0.85
SEVENTIES	−0.05	−0.74	0.01	0.30
EIGHTIES	0.10	1.41	0.13	2.85
FLOAT	−0.09	−0.77	0.01	0.13
MONEY	−0.16	−1.73	−0.07	−1.21
R-squared	0.26		0.25	
S.E. of regression	0.28		0.18	
Sum-squared resid.	16.08		6.27	
Log-likelihood	−23.27		78.19	

variables." We note, however, that the finding that monetary policy effects on output last five years or more in many countries is troublesome for the consensus view described in the introduction.

Finally, it is worth mentioning here that as in the case of the short-term coefficients, the size of the long-term output coefficient appears to have declined in the studies using more recent sample periods (after 1980).

Econometric analysis: Price effects

In this section, we analyze the short-term and long-term price effects of monetary policies. We will proceed in the same way as in the previous section. We estimate the econometric model consisting of Eqs. (1) and (2), where PS_i and PL_i now represent the estimated short-term and long-term price effects of monetary policy shocks. A note of warning is necessary here. Because not all the empirical studies of the effect of monetary policies report results of the effects on the price level, we have fewer data points in the sample (185). As a result, the statistical quality of the econometric results is weaker than in the previous section.

We first concentrate on the short-term price effects (Eq. (1)). We show the results of estimating Eq. (1) in Table 3, both for the weighted and for the unweighted data. We find that most of the country coefficients are close to zero. None is statistically different from zero. This contrasts with the short-term output coefficients which were found to be statistically different from zero for most countries. These results are in line with the well-known empirical regularity discussed earlier, i.e., that prices are stickier than output. In the short run (i.e., after one year), prices do not react to monetary policy shocks.

The next step in the analysis consists in performing the same analysis for the long-term price coefficients. The results are shown in Table 4. We now find country coefficients that are statistically different from zero in almost all cases. Thus, in the long-run (after five years or more), monetary policy shocks have significant effects on the aggregate price levels in almost all countries. We also note that

Table 3. Regression results of Equation (1): Short-term price coefficients.

	Unweighted regression		Weighted regression	
Variable	Coefficient	*t*-statistic	Coefficient	*t*-statistic
Austria	−0.15	−1.28	−0.05	−0.79
Belgium	−0.11	−0.94	−0.04	−0.62
Denmark	0.002	0.01	0.01	0.04
Eurozone	0.03	0.16	0.03	0.24
Finland	−0.06	−0.47	−0.06	−0.80
France	0.003	0.04	−0.003	−0.07
Germany	0.02	0.19	0.004	0.07
Greece	−0.06	−0.34	−0.04	−0.39
Ireland	−0.09	−0.66	−0.03	−0.41
Italy	−0.03	−0.33	−0.02	−0.35
Japan	0.30	2.67	0.15	2.29
Luxembourg	−0.02	−0.08	0.02	0.17
Netherlands	−0.20	−1.64	−0.07	−0.99
Portugal	−0.13	−0.90	−0.04	−0.56
Spain	−0.05	−0.41	−0.01	−0.17
Sweden	−0.03	−0.17	0.03	0.41
UK	−0.02	−0.20	0.002	0.05
USA	−0.06	−1.25	−0.03	−1.21
Australia	−0.08	−0.32	−0.04	−0.26
Canada	−0.27	−1.55	−0.19	−1.95
Emerging	0.08	1.00	0.020	0.40
SVAR	0.01	0.23	−0.003	−0.11
ECON	−0.02	−0.31	−0.04	−1.02
FAVAR	0.001	0.01	0.01	0.12
SEVENTIES	0.02	0.28	−0.003	−0.08
EIGHTIES	−0.07	−1.11	−0.02	−0.42
MONEY	0.50	2.53	0.42	3.68
R-squared	0.18		0.17	
S.E. of regression	0.24		0.14	
Sum-squared resid.	8.59		2.81	
Log-likelihood	10.18		99.64	

the statistical quality of the regression is higher when we use weighted data (higher R^2 and more significant coefficients). In addition, the country coefficients are more similar in the weighted regressions.

The use of different econometric techniques does not affect the previous results very much. In particular, SVARs produce pretty

Table 4. Regression results of Equation (2): Long-term price coefficients.

	Unweighted regression		Weighted regression	
Variable	Coefficient	t-statistic	Coefficient	t-statistic
Austria	−0.34	−2.13	−0.24	−2.87
Belgium	−0.36	−2.29	−0.25	−2.99
Denmark	−0.22	−0.98	−0.22	−1.80
Eurozone	−0.26	−0.86	−0.23	−1.46
Finland	−0.30	−1.83	−0.22	−2.47
France	−0.29	−2.33	−0.22	−3.28
Germany	−0.29	−2.47	−0.24	−3.81
Greece	−0.45	−2.05	−0.32	−2.76
Ireland	−0.27	−1.62	−0.22	−2.49
Italy	−0.18	−1.63	−0.19	−3.22
Japan	−0.06	−0.46	−0.16	−2.24
Luxembourg	−0.37	−1.22	−0.22	−1.39
Netherlands	−0.34	−2.34	−0.25	−3.15
Portugal	−0.33	−1.92	−0.25	−2.79
Spain	−0.47	−3.40	−0.33	−4.45
Sweden	−0.40	−2.08	−0.28	−2.73
UK	−0.35	−2.84	−0.26	−3.89
USA	−0.41	−6.53	−0.27	−8.24
Australia	−1.03	−3.40	−0.56	−3.42
Canada	−1.13	−4.39	−0.79	−5.70
Emerging	−0.14	−1.36	−0.16	−2.79
SVAR	0.11	1.41	0.06	1.47
ECON	0.16	1.96	0.03	0.72
FAVAR	−0.07	−0.67	−0.02	−0.36
SEVENTIES	0.08	0.80	0.09	1.71
EIGHTIES	0.12	1.44	0.16	3.55
MONEY	1.10	4.59	0.81	6.29
R-squared	0.35		0.43	
S.E. of regression	0.28		0.15	
Sum-squared resid.	9.41		2.68	
Log-likelihood	−8.40		79.21	

much the same results as "plain vanilla" VARs. This contrasts with the results obtained in the previous section dealing with the output effects. Similarly, there is little evidence that the price effects have changed over time. The coefficients of the SEVENTIES and EIGHTIES dummies are not statistically different from zero.

Finally, there is some evidence that the long-term price effects of monetary policies have tended to become smaller. This can be seen from the coefficient of the EIGHTIES variable that is positive and significant in the case of the weighted regression. This is probably related to the fact that since the 1980s, inflation has come down significantly thus reducing its sensitivity to monetary shocks.

Are the Effects of Monetary Policy Different in the US and the Eurozone?

In this section, we analyse the issue of whether the effectiveness of monetary policies in the United States and in the Eurozone countries is different. A consensus seems to have emerged that because of the existence of labour market rigidities, monetary policies in the Eurozone are less effective in influencing output than is the case in the United States. The argument is quite often phrased as follows: "rigidities in the labour markets tend to limit the pace at which an economy can grow without fueling inflationary pressures" (European Central Bank, 2004:21). Thus, when the ECB lowers the interest rate to stimulate the Eurozone economy, this will quickly be transmitted into higher prices with only limited effects on output. Since the US economy is less rigid, the Federal Reserve can more easily stimulate the economy without introducing inflationary pressures.

An influential paper substantiating this view is Angeloni *et al.* (2003). These authors came to the conclusion that a one percentage point increase in the short-term interest rate tends to have a substantially stronger output effect in the US than in the Eurozone. In addition, they identified this difference to be due to a significantly higher consumption effect of monetary policy changes in the US as compared to the Eurozone. As an example, we show the effects of monetary policy on output, consumption, and investment in the US and the Eurozone as obtained by Angeloni *et al.* (2003) in Table 5. It can be seen that the output effects of monetary policy changes are more than twice as strong in the US than in the Eurozone and that most of this difference comes from much larger consumption effects in the United States than in the Eurozone.

Table 5. Effect of one percentage point increase in the short-term interest rate on a number of macroeconomic variables in the US and in the Eurozone.

	USA			Eurozone		
	1 year	2-years	3-years	1 year	2-years	3-years
CPI	−0.07	−0.41	−1.01	−0.09	−0.21	−0.31
GDP	−0.35	−1.28	−1.37	−0.22	−0.38	−0.31
Consumption	−0.37	−1.35	−1.44	−0.12	−0.23	−0.19
Investment	−0.31	−1.79	−3.16	−0.34	−1.04	−1.22

Source: Angeloni *et al.* (2003).

This evidence has strengthened the perception that while an activist monetary policy such as the one followed by the Federal Reserve during the last decade may be sensible for the United States, it is not appropriate for the Eurozone where as a result of rigidities, such an activist monetary policy would barely affect output, while it would mainly lead to more inflation. This view of the relative ineffectiveness of monetary policy in the Eurozone has now become the conventional one and is often formulated in the popular financial press (see e.g. *The Economist*, 2005, p. 20).

There is a large literature on the relation between price and wage rigidities and the optimal design of monetary policies. This literature has led to a number of propositions that can be summarized as follows. First, in a world of perfectly flexible wages and prices, monetary policy has no effect on output (Woodford 2003). In such a world, there is also no need for using monetary policy to stabilize output. Second, in a world characterized by price and wage rigidities, monetary policy can be quite potent in influencing output at least in the short run (see e.g., Fischer, 1977; Taylor, 1980; Clarida *et al.*, 1999). In fact, it is only because prices and wages are rigid that monetary policy can affect output in the short run (see also our discussion in the introduction). In this sense, the view that monetary policies in the Eurozone are ineffective because of the existence of rigidities is surprising. Without rigidities, monetary policy cannot affect output. This leads to a third proposition. The effectiveness of monetary policy depends on the nature of these rigidities. The consensus today is that *nominal* wage rigidities *increase* the output effects of monetary policy shocks. In contrast, *real* wage rigidities *reduce* the effectiveness of monetary policies in affecting output (see Gylfason and Lyndbeck, 1994; Soskice and Iversen, 2000; Tabellini, 2001). It follows that it is important to specify the nature of the structural rigidities to understand how these affect the transmission of monetary policies. Some rigidities increase the effectiveness of monetary policies in affecting output, others reduce this effectiveness. Thus, the issue of how rigidities affect the effectiveness of monetary policies is an empirical one to which we now turn.

The way we proceed in our empirical analysis is to perform Wald tests for equality of the coefficient of the US and the Eurozone countries reported in the different tables of the previous section. We do this for the output and price coefficients. Note that the statistical testing procedure is such that when we test for equality, we control for differences in econometric methodology, differences in the measurement of output, and differences in the sample period.

We first show the results for the output coefficients in Table 6. The Wald test on the short-term coefficients reveals that we cannot reject the hypothesis that these coefficients are equal. The results concerning the long-term coefficients are more subtle. We find that when we apply the test on all these coefficients, we should reject the hypothesis that these are equal. It turns out, however, that if we remove the outlier (Greece in the weighted regression), we cannot reject the hypothesis that the US and Eurozone long-term output coefficients are equal.

Table 6. Wald test: Equality of the US and Eurozone output coefficients.

Short-term coefficients (Equation (1)) weighted regression			
F-statistic	0.255	Probability	0.99
Chi-square	3.320	Probability	0.99
Long-term coefficients (Equation (2)) weighted regression			
F-statistic	0.590	Probability	0.85
Chi-square	7.679	Probability	0.86
Long-term coefficient (Equation (2)) weighted regression, outlier Greece excluded			
F-statistic	0.395	Probability	0.96
Chi-square	4.743	Probability	0.96

From the preceding analysis, we can conclude that there is little evidence that the transmission of monetary shocks into output in the Eurozone is any different from the transmission in the United States. Both the short-term and the long-term output coefficients in the Eurozone countries and in the United States appear to be of the same order of magnitude if we control for differences in econometric methodology, differences in the measurement of output, and differences in the sample periods.

As argued earlier, the hypothesis that monetary policies in the Eurozone are ineffective in influencing output has a corollary as far as the transmission into prices is concerned. It implies that a monetary expansion in the Eurozone will be transmitted more quickly and more completely into price increases (see European Central Bank, 2004, p. 21). We now test this corollary by applying similar Wald tests on the price coefficients. We show the results in Table 7. We cannot reject the hypothesis that both the short-term and the long-term price coefficients are equal. We conclude from this that there is no evidence that monetary policy shocks lead to a quicker and stronger transmission into prices in the Eurozone than in the US. The hypothesis that Eurozone monetary policy is less effective than US monetary policy because of a quicker and stronger transmission of Eurozone monetary policies into prices has no empirical backing.

The role of macroeconomic variables

Macroeconomic variables also matter in explaining the differences in the output and price coefficients. In this section, we analyse the importance of macroeconomic variables. We do this by adding

Table 7. Wald test: Equality of the US and Eurozone price coefficients.

Short-term coefficients (Equation (1)) weighted regression			
F-statistic	0.218	Probability	0.99
Chi-square	2.837	Probability	0.99
Long-term coefficients (Equation (2)) weighted regression			
F-statistic	0.435	Probability	0.95
Chi-square	5.657	Probability	0.96

macroeconomic variables that describe the nature of the macroeconomic regime of the countries involved in the empirical studies to our econometric Eqs. (1) and (2). The econometric equation is now specified as follows:

$$PS_i = a + \Sigma_k \beta_k D_k + \sum_j \gamma_j M_j + \varepsilon_i \tag{3}$$

$$PL_i = c + \Sigma_k \eta_k D_k + \sum_j \gamma_j M_j + \omega_i \tag{4}$$

where PS_i and PL_i are the observed short-term and long-term parameters measuring the effect of monetary policy.

As before, the variables D_k are dummy variables expressing a particular characteristic of the study from which parameter i was obtained.

The variables M_j are macroeconomic variables associated with country i (that is represented by parameter i). We use the following variables:

- The openness of the country involved, as measured by the ratio of its exports to its GDP. We expect that the output effects of domestic monetary policy shocks are smaller in relatively open countries than in relatively closed ones.
- The size of countries as measured by their GDP in dollars.
- The exchange rate regime. We distinguished between two exchange rate regimes, fixed and flexible. The countries on a flexible exchange rate regime are the UK, the US, Japan, and Germany. The others (EMS countries and emerging countries) were on a fixed exchange rate regime.[8]
- The rate of inflation that prevailed on average during the sample period over which the output coefficient was estimated. There is a theoretical presumption that the effect of a monetary expansion on output declines with the level of inflation. Several theoretical models can be invoked to substantiate this. The most influential is

[8]One could clearly introduce finer distinctions between different exchange rate regimes. For example, one could use the IMF classification of exchange rate regimes. This classification has been criticized, however. See Calvo and Reinhart (2000).

Lucas (1973) "island model." In this model, the aggregate supply equation depends on the relative variance of real and nominal disturbances. The implication is that in a regime of high nominal variability, an increase in prices is more likely to be interpreted as resulting from an aggregate price increase than in a regime of low nominal variability. As a result, the real effects of such an increase in prices will be reduced. A similar analysis can be performed using the Philips curve as a tool. In such a framework, the Philips curve is also non-linear in the rate of inflation. Thus, when inflation is high, one will need a stronger monetary surprise to generate a given increase in output (decline in unemployment) than when inflation is low.[9] This proposition was also tested-by Lucas (1973).

- The importance of the banking sector as measured by the ratio of the consolidated balance sheet of the banking sector over GDP. The theory is not clear about how this variable affects the output effects of monetary policy shocks. We introduce this variable here to find out whether differences in the size of the banking sector can explain the differences in the estimated output coefficients. Because of the limited availability of data, we had to estimate Eqs. (3) and (4) on a smaller sample of coefficients than in the previous sections. In addition, the country dummies are now highly correlated with some of the macroeconomic variables (size, openness, and inflation). Using Wald tests, we found that the differences in the country dummy coefficients are not statistically significant. As a result, we estimated Eqs. (3) and (4) restricting the country coefficients to be equal.

The results are shown in Tables 8 and 9. The constant term in Tables 8 and 9 represents the effect of the omitted dummies. As before, the omitted dummies are VAR, GDP, and SIXTIES. Thus, the constant term measures the coefficient of studies using VAR methods, using GDP as the measure of output, and using a sample period starting in the 1960s. The most important results can be summarized as follows.

[9]See Ball *et al.* (1988) and Wyplosz (2001).

Table 8. Short-term output coefficients (Equation (3)). Included observations: 127.

	Unweighted data		Weighted data	
Variable	Coefficient	*t*-statistic	Coefficient	*t*-statistic
C	−1.333	−4.543	−1.067	−4.536
SVAR	−0.388	−2.555	−0.124	−0.872
ECON	−0.125	−0.841	−0.012	−0.104
IND	0.140	0.967	0.061	0.469
GAP	−0.174	−0.853	−0.163	−0.910
SEVENTIES	0.066	0.415	0.058	0.470
EIGHTIES	−0.275	−1.646	−0.213	−1.415
INFLATION	0.038	1.895	0.023	1.372
FIX	0.046	0.294	0.064	0.489
PUBDATE	0.075	2.821	0.048	2.197
SIZE	3.9E-05	0.979	5.02E-05	1.308
OPEN	0.141	0.781	0.126	0.816
BANKING	0.067	0.599	0.052	0.711
R-squared	0.194		0.130	
Adjusted R-squared	0.117		0.046	
Mean-dependent VAR	−0.394		−0.366	

As the results of the study characteristies are similar to those obtained in Section "A meta-analysis of the effects of monetary policy on output and prices", we concentrate our analysis on the coefficients of the macroeconomic variables. Our major result is that the level of inflation matters. We find that inflation tends to reduce the output effect of monetary policy, both in the short run and in the long run. From Table 8, we find that for every percentage point increase in inflation the short-term output parameter declines (in absolute value) by approximately 0.04. This effect is significant in the regression using unweighted data but is less so in the regression using weighted data. We find a similar result for the long-term output coefficients Table 9). This result is conforming to economic theory.

It is interesting to have an insight in the quantitative importance of the effect of inflation. The median inflation rate in the sample is 5.2 percent. (In Appendix 3.1, we show the distribution of the inflation rates in the sample of countries.) Thus, for the median inflation

Table 9. Long-term output coefficients (Equation (4)). Included observations: 122.

	Unweighted data		Weighted data	
Variable	Coefficient	t-statistic	Coefficient	t-statistic
C	−0.769	−2.689	−0.848	−2.528
SVAR	0.282	1.829	0.411	1.977
ECON	0.378	2.413	0.500	2.882
IND	0.208	1.390	0.210	1.087
GAP	0.467	2.341	0.560	2.182
SEVENTIES	−0.140	−0.879	−0.260	−1.432
EIGHTIES	0.152	0.901	0.118	0.538
INFLATION	0.039	1.909	0.038	1.597
FIX	0.228	1.447	0.273	1.446
PUBDATE	−0.007	−0.301	−0.009	−0.309
SIZE	4.73E-05	1.191	5.10E-05	0.927
OPEN	0.198	1.103	0.283	1.263
BANKING	−0.023	−0.213	−0.005	−0.051
R-squared	0.194		0.256	
Adjusted R-squared	0.111		0.181	
Mean-dependent VAR	−0.252		−0.304	

rate, the short-term output coefficient is reduced by 0.2. For the highest inflation country in the sample (16 percent), the short-term output coefficient is reduced by 0.622. Thus, the short-term output effect is reduced by half compared to the benchrmark in the highest inflation country.

We obtain similar results for-the long-term coefficients. We find that for the median inflation country, the long-term output coefficient is reduced by 0.21, while for the highest inflation country, it is reduced by 0.64. As a result, for the highest inflation countries in the sample, the long-term output effects of monetary policies are close to zero. The interesting aspect of this result is that for the low inflation countries, these long-term output effects are strong and significant.

The other variables in the regression equation do not have a significant effect on the output coefficients. The macroeconomic variables such as openness, size of the countries, and the importance of the banking sector do not create significant differences in the output effects of monetary policy shocks. This may seem surprising. For example, one may expect that openness and size matter. In Particular, the output effects of monetary policies should be smaller in relatively small and open economies because much of the domestically generated monetary shocks spill over to the rest of the world. However, in small open economies, most of the monetary policy shocks are not generated by domestic monetary authorities. They are typically the result of monetary policy shocks originating in large countries. To give an example: when the German Bundes bank increased its interest rate, central banks of countries like the Netherlands and Belgium routinely increased their short-term interest rates a few minutes later. As a result, the monetary policy shock occurred in many countries at the same time. It is therefore not so surprising that monetary policy shocks can have similar effects in large and small countries.

We conclude this section by discussing the results of estimating Eqs. (3) and (4) for the price effects, which are presented in Tables 10 and 11. We find as before that in the short run, monetary policy shocks (increase in the interest rate) have no significant effect on

Table 10. Short-term price coefficients (Equation (3)). Included observations: 86.

	Unweighted data		Weighted data	
Variable	Coefficient	*t*-statistic	Coefficient	*t*-statistic
C	0.216	0.942	0.219	1.047
SVAR	−0.257	−2.658	−0.364	−3.224
ECON	−0.089	−0.767	0.114	0.989
INFLATION	−0.022	−1.276	−0.025	−1.395
SIZE	4.03E-06	0.120	3.46E-05	0.893
OPEN	−0.018	−0.145	−0.051	−0.366
BANKING	0.050	0.642	0.064	0.997
PUBDATE	−0.021	−1.247	−0.028	−1.662
FIX	0.134	1.159	0.256	1.984
R-squared	0.116		0.201	
Adjusted R-squared	0.024		0.117	
Mean-dependent VAR	−0.098		−0.096	

Table 11. Long-term price coefficients (Equation (4)). Included observations: 84.

	Unweighted data		Weighted data	
Variable	Coefficient	*t*-statistic	Coefficient	*t*-statistic
C	−1.230	−1.989	−1.154	−1.887
SVAR	0.320	1.156	0.292	0.851
ECON	0.640	1.814	0.908	2.453
INFLATION	0.010	0.211	0.005	0.095
SIZE	0.0001	1.281	0.0001	1.172
OPEN	0.216	0.621	0.342	0.814
BANKING	0.034	0.164	0.014	0.075
PUBDATE	0.022	0.433	0.005	0.104
FIX	0.624	1.795	0.589	1.449
SEVENTIES	−0.829	−2.182	−0.996	−2.593
EIGHTIES	−0.013	−0.034	0.015	0.035
R-squared	0.195		0.261	
Adjusted R-squared	0.085		0.160	
Mean-dependent VAR	−0.403		−0.493	

prices. In the long run, these price effects are strong and significant. We also find that the sign of the inflation variable in the short-run equation is correct, although its significance is weak (see Table 10). Thus, in high inflation countries, the monetary policy shock appears to a stronger impact on prices than in the low inflation countries. This is the corollary of what we found for the short-term output effects, i.e. in high inflation countries, monetary policy shocks have a weaker effect on output than in low inflation countries.

From Table 10, we conclude that in the long run, there is no difference in the price effects of monetary policies between low and high inflation countries.

Conclusion

The issues of whether monetary policies affect output and, if so, how long this effect lasts have been hotly debated by economists. The consensus today is that monetary policies do affect output. What is less clear is how long these effects last. In this chapter, we have analysed these questions using a meta-analysis of the effects of monetary policies on output and prices.

We can summarize the main results concerning the *output* effects of monetary policy as follows. First, there is a large variation in the reported output effects of monetary policies. This is the case both with the short-term and with the long-term effects. Second, we are able to explain part of these large variations by a number of variables, although much remains unexplained. Third, a significant part of the wide variation in the long-term output effects is due to the use of different econometric techniques. In particular, the use of VARs produces long-term effects of monetary policies, while the use of SVARs leads to significantly lower long-term effects. This result is not without importance. It suggests that techniques that use economic theory to constrain parameters lead to significantly different effects from those techniques that "allow the data to speak." More specifically, SVARs typically impose the condition that the long-term output effects of monetary policies should be zero. This condition is based on the now prevailing theoretical insights influenced by monetarism and the real business cycle theory that money is neutral in the long run. The worrisome aspect of these theories is that one has to assume this condition to hold in order to validate it empirically. Put differently, in those econometric studies that do not impose long-run neutrality, the long-run neutrality of money is rejected. This certainly calls into question one of the fundamental tenets of the new consensus in macroeconomics.

It should be pointed out that there is still the issue of how long the long run is. In the meta-analysis, we have used as a cut-off point five years or more. It could be argued that the long run is longer than five years and that a fair test of the long-run neutrality proposition would be to analyse longer time horizons. This has not been done in this chapter, because the reported econometric studies typically do not report results that go beyond a time horizon of five to seven years.

A fourth result of our analysis is that the level of inflation affects the effectiveness of monetary policies. More particularly, we found that in the countries which experienced low inflation, the output effects of monetary policy shocks are substantial. This is the case both for the short-term and for the long-term effects. In the high inflation countries of our sample, these output effects are much smaller. Moreover, the long-term output effects of monetary policies all but vanish for the highest inflation countries. This confirms the theory, which suggests that in a low inflation environment, monetary policies are quite effective in influencing output, both in the short run and in the long run. In other words, like in the US and the Eurozone countries, one should expect that monetary policies have relatively strong output effects in comparison to countries like Argentina with a history of high inflation.

Fifth, we could not find any significant differences in the output and price effects of monetary policies in the US and in the Eurozone countries. There is a popular view according to which monetary policies in the Eurozone are ineffective in boosting output because supply rigidities quickly lead to higher inflation, while in the US, monetary policies are capable of boosting output without strong inflationary effects. The existing econometric estimates of the output and price effects of monetary policies in the US and the Eurozone countries do not allow us to draw such a conclusion. Since the effectiveness of monetary policies very much depends on the nature of price and wage rigidities, these results suggest that the US and the Eurozone are less different in terms of wage and price rigidities than is commonly thought.

Much of the discussion today among macroeconomists has shifted to the issue of whether the output effects of monetary policies can be exploited by the monetary authorities and whether rules should govern the conduct of monetary policy. The consensus view today, based on the use of monetarist and real business cycle models, is that monetary authorities should not actively try to fine-tune output movements.

Although the issues concerning monetary policy rules were not the focus of our research, our results allow us to shed some light on these questions. In particular, our finding that the long-run neutrality of money has a weak empirical basis calls into question the use of models whose central theoretical building block is the long-run neutrality of money. These models are now used for policy purposes, and they have led to the widespread view among policymakers that monetary policy should only be used to stabilize the price level and should not be employed for other purposes. It should be clear, however, that these conclusions have more to do with theoretical convictions about how the world should work, than with hard empirical evidence of how the world actually works.

Appendix: Descriptive Statistics, Full Sample

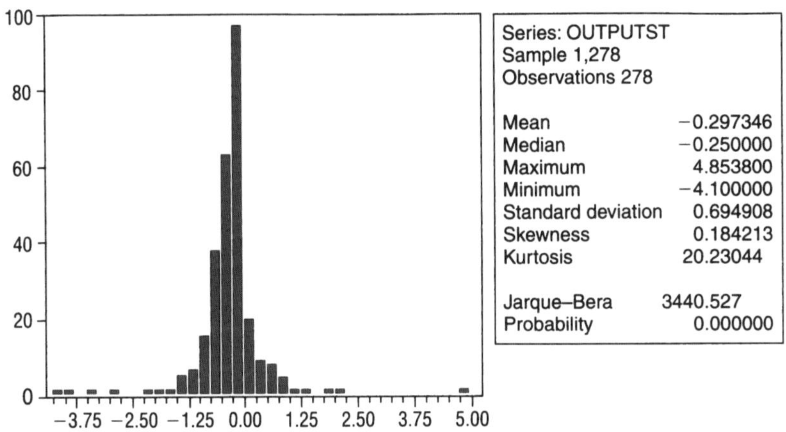

Short-term output coefficient (OUTPUTST), full sample.

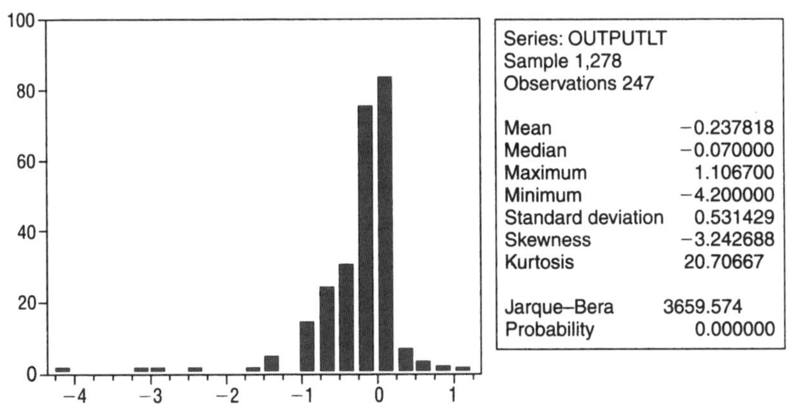

Long-term output coefficients (OUTPUTLT), full sample.

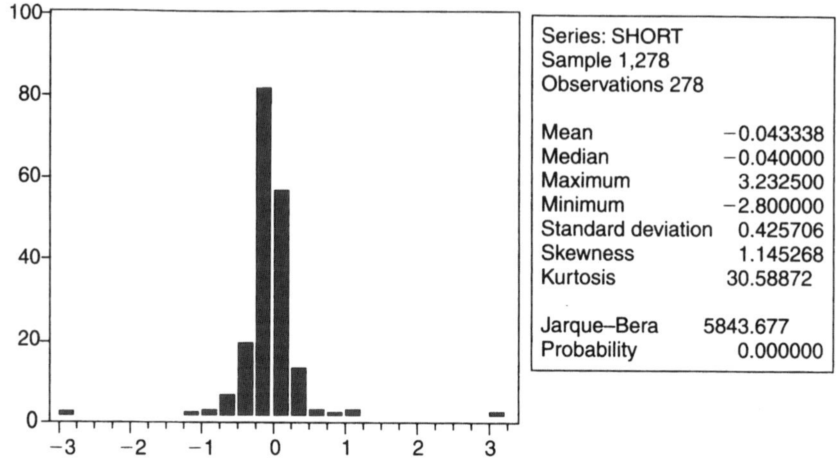

Short-term price coefficient (SHORT), full sample.

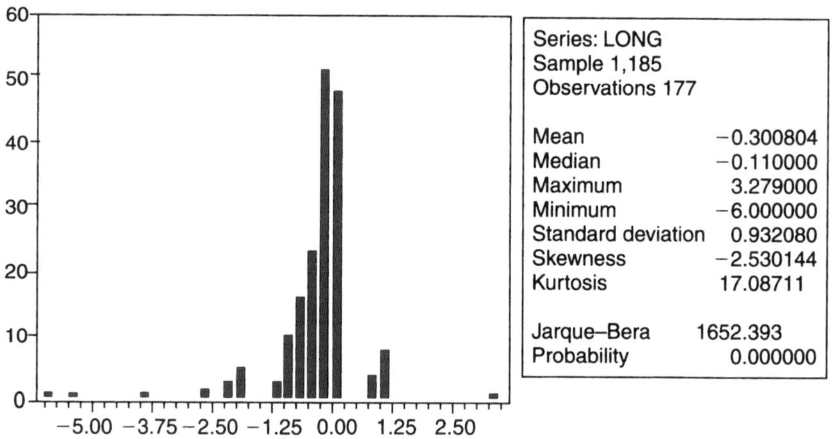

Long-term price coefficient (LONG), full sample.

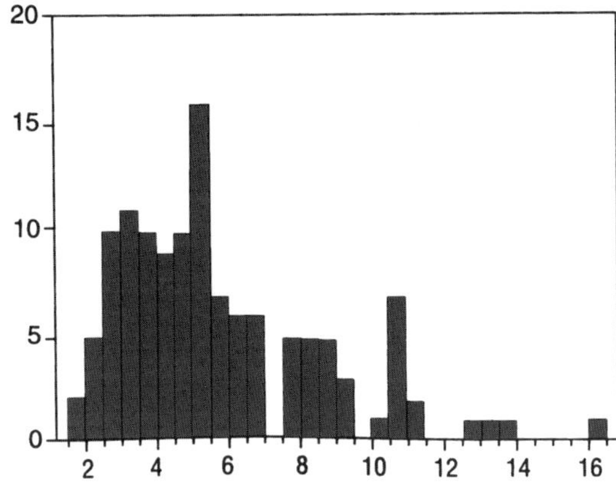

Series: INFLATION	
Sample 1,139	
Observations 124	
Mean	5.824748
Median	5.209471
Maximum	16.05292
Minimum	1.925000
Standard deviation	2.847042
Skewness	1.088077
Kurtosis	3.883654
Jarque–Bera	28.50187
Probability	0.000001

Frequency distribution of inflation rates.

References

Angeloni, I, A Kashyap, B Mojon and D Terlizzese (2003). The output composition puzzle: A difference in the monetary transmission mechanism in the euro area and the US. European Central Bank Working Paper No. 268, September.

Ball, L, G Mankiw and D Romer (1988). The new keynesian economics and the output-inflation trade-off. *Brookings Papers on Economic Activity*, 1, 1–82.

Calvo, GA and CM Reinhart (2000). Fear of floating. NBER Working Papers No. 7993.

Christiano, L, M Eichenbaum and C Evans (2001). Nominal rigidities and the dynamic effects of a shock to monetary policy. Federal Reserve Bank of Cleveland Working Paper.

Clarida, R, J Gali and M Gertler (1999). The science of monetary policy. *Journal of Economic Literature*, 37(4), 1661–1707.

European Central Bank (2004). The monetary policy of the ECB. Frankfurt: European Central Bank.

Fischer, S (1977). Long-term contracts, rational expectations and optimal money supply rules. *Journal of Political Economy*, 85, 191–206.

Greene, W (1997). *Econometric Analysis*, 3rd Edition. Upper Saddle River, NJ: Prentice Hall.

Gylfason, T and A Lyndbeck (1994). The interaction of monetary policy and wages. *Public Choice*, 79, 33–46.

Knell, M and H Stix (2003). How robust are money demand estimations? A meta-analytic approach. Discussion Paper No. 81, Austrian National Bank.

Lucas, R (1973). Some international evidence on output-inflation tradeoffs. *The American Economic Review*, 63(3), 326–334.

Nijkamp, P and J Poot (2004). Meta-analysis of the effect of fiscal policies on long-run growth. *European Journal of Political Economy*, 20, 91–124.

Rose, A (2004). The effect of common currencies on international trade: A meta-analysis. In *Monetary Unions and Hard Pegs: Effects on Trade, Financial Development and Stability*, GM von Furstenberg (ed.). Oxford, UK: Oxford University Press.

Smets, F and R Wouters (2003). An estimated dynamic stochastic general equilibrium model of the euro area. *Journal of the European Economic Association*, 1(5), 1123–1175.

Soskice, D and T Iversen (2000). The non-neutrality of monetary policy with large price or wage setters. *Quarterly Journal of Economics*, 14, 110–124.

Stanley, T (2001). Wheat from chaff: Meta-analysis as quantitative literature review. *Journal of Economic Perspectives*, 15(3), 131–150.

Tabellini, G (2001). Comment on The Case for Price Stability by Marvin Good Friend and Robert King. In *Why Price Stability? Proceedings of the First ECB Central Banking Conference*, G Herrero, M Hoogduin and Winkler (eds.). Frankfurt: ECB.

Taylor, J (1980). Aggregate dynamics and staggered contracts. *Journal of Political Economy*, 88, 1–22.

The Economist (2005). The great thrift shift: A survey of the world economy. *The Economist*, September 24.

Walsh, C (2003). Monetary *Theory and Policy*, 2nd Edition. Cambridge, MA: MIT Press.

Woodford, M (2003). *Interest and Prices: Foundations of a Theory of Monetary Policy*. Princeton, NJ: Princeton University Press.

Wyplosz, C (ed.) (2001). *The Impact of EMU on Europe and the Developing Countries*. Oxford, NY: Oxford University Press.

Chapter 16

Lessons from the Banking Crisis: A Return to Narrow Banking

Paul De Grauwe

1. The Basics of Banking

In order to draw the lessons from the banking crisis it is useful to start from the basics of banking.[1] Banks are in the business of borrowing short and lending long. In doing so they provide an essential service to the rest of us, i.e., they create credit that allows the real economy to grow and expand.

This credit creation service, however, is based on an inherent fragility of the banking system. If depositors are gripped by a collective movement of distrust and decide to withdraw their deposits at the same time, banks are unable to satisfy these withdrawals as their assets are illiquid. A liquidity crisis erupts.

In normal times, when people have confidence in the banks, these crises do not occur. But confidence can quickly disappear, for example, when one or more banks experience a solvency problem due to non performing loans. Then bank runs are possible. A liquidity crisis erupts that can bring down sound banks also. The latter become innocent bystanders that are hit in the same way as the insolvent banks by the collective movement of distrust.

Published in *Journal for International Comparisons*, 7(2), 2009.

[1] A very useful book is Goodhart and Illing (2002).

The problem does not end here. A devilish interaction between liquidity crisis and solvency crisis is set in motion. Sound banks that are hit by deposit withdrawals have to sell assets to confront these withdrawals. The ensuing fire sales lead to declines in asset prices, reducing the value of banks' assets. This in turn erodes the equity base of the banks and leads to a solvency problem. The cycle can start again: the solvency problem of these banks ignites a new liquidity crisis and so on.

The last great banking crisis occurred in the 1930s. Its effects were devastating for the real economy. After that crisis the banking system was reformed fundamentally. These reforms were intended to make such a banking crisis impossible. The reforms had three essential ingredients. First, the central bank took on the responsibility of lender of last resort. Second deposit insurance mechanisms were instituted. These two reforms aimed at eliminating collective movements of panic. A third reform aimed at preventing commercial banks from taking on too many risks. In the US, this took the form of the Glass–Steagall Act, which was introduced in 1933 and which separated commercial banking from investment banking.

Most economists thought that these reforms would be sufficient to produce a less fragile banking system and to prevent large scale banking crises. It was not to be. Why? In order to answer this question it is useful to first discuss "moral hazard."

The insurance provided by central banks and governments in the form of lender of last resort and deposit insurance gives bankers strong incentives to take more risks. To counter this, authorities have to supervise and regulate, very much like any private insurer who wants to avoid moral hazard will do.

And that's what the monetary authorities did during most of the post-war period. They subjected banks to tight regulation aimed at preventing them from taking on too much risk. But then something remarkable happened.

2. The Efficient Market Paradigm

From the 1970s on, economists were all gripped by the intellectual attraction of the efficient market paradigm. This paradigm which originated in academia became hugely popular also outside academia. Its main ingredients are the following.

First, financial markets efficiently allocate savings toward the most promising investment projects thereby maximizing welfare. Second, asset prices reflect underlying fundamentals. As a result, bubbles cannot occur, and neither can crashes. The third ingredient of the efficient market paradigm is the capacity of markets for self-regulation. The proponents of this paradigm told us that financial markets can perfectly regulate themselves and that regulation by governments or central banks is unnecessary, even harmful (Greenspan, 2007).

The efficient markets paradigm was extremely influential. It was also captured by bankers to lobby for deregulation. If markets work so beautifully there was no need for regulation anymore. And bankers achieved their objective. They were progressively deregulated in the US and in Europe. The culmination was the repeal of the Glass–Steagall act in 1999 by the Clinton administration. This allowed commercial banks to take on all the activities investment banks had been taking, e.g. the underwriting and the holding of securities; the development of new and risky assets like derivatives and complex structured credit products. Thus banks were allowed to take on all risky activities that the Great Depression had thought us could lead to problems. The lessons of history were forgotten.

The efficient market paradigm provided the intellectual backing for deregulation of financial markets in general and the banking sector in particular. At about the same time financial markets experienced a burst of innovations. Financial innovations allowed designing new financial products. These made it possible to repackage assets into different risk classes and to price these risks differently. It also allowed banks to secuterize their loans, i.e., to repackage them in the form of asset backed securities (ABSs) and to sell these in the market.

This led to the belief, very much inspired by the optimism of the efficient market paradigm, that securitization and the development of complex financial products would lead to a better spreading of the risk over many more people, thereby reducing systemic risk and reducing the need to supervise and regulate financial markets. A new era of free and unencumbered progress would be set in motion.

3. Are Financial Markets Efficient?

Deregulation and financial innovation promised to bring great welfare improvements: better risk spreading; lower costs of credit, benefitting firms who would invest more and benefitting millions of consumers who would have access to cheap mortgages.

The trouble is that financial markets are not efficient. We illustrate this lack of efficiency in the two dimensions that matter for the stability of the banking sector.[2] First, bubbles and crashes are an endemic feature of financial markets. Second, financial markets are incapable of regulating themselves. Both failures would in the end bring down the new banking model that had been allowed to emerge and that was predicated on financial markets being efficient.

3.1. *Bubbles and Crashes are Endemic in Financial Markets*

Nobody has written a better book on the capacity of financial markets to generate bubbles and crashes than Kindleberger in his masterful "Manias, panics and crashes."[3] Kindleberger showed how the history of capitalism is littered with episodes during which asset markets are caught by a speculative fever that pushes prices to levels unrelated to fundamental economic variables. But lessons of history were forgotten.

Let us look at some of the bubbles and crashes that littered financial markets during the last twenty five years. Take the US stock market during 2006–2008. We show the Dow Jones and the Standard and Poor's in Figure 1.

What happened in the US economy between July 2006 and July 2007 to warrant an increase of 30% in the value of stocks? Or put

---

[2]The empirical evidence against the efficiency of Financial markets has been building up over the last decade. For useful overviews see Shleiffer (2000) and Shiller (2000).

[3]See Kindleberger (2005). Chancellor (1999) also provides a vivid account of the many bubbles and crashes in the history of financial markets.

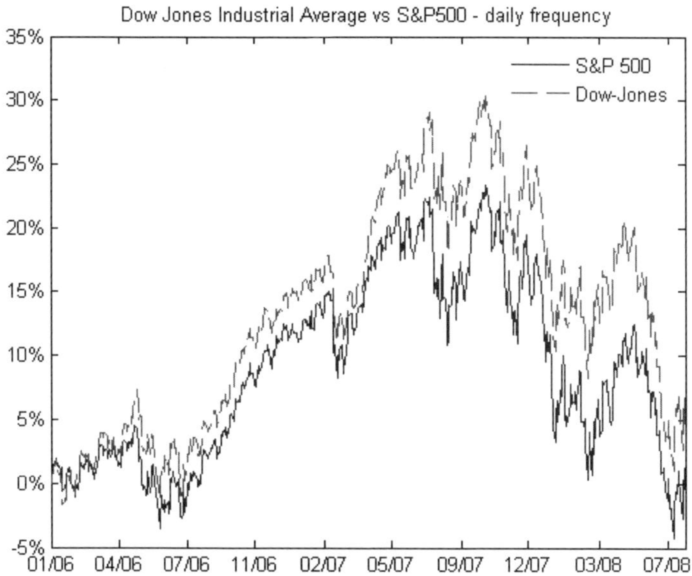

Figure 1. The Dow Jones and the S&P500 2006–2008.

Source: Yahoo Finance.

differently. In July 2006, US stock market capitalization was $11.5 trillion. One year later it was $15 trillion. What happened to the US economy to make it possible that $3.5 trillion was added to the value of US corporations in just one year? During the same year GDP increased by only 5 percent ($650 billion).

The answer is: almost nothing. Fundamentals like productivity growth increased at their normal rate. The only reasonable answer is that there was excessive optimism about the future of the US economy. Investors were caught by a wave of optimism that made them believe that the US was on a new and permanent growth path for the indefinite future. Such beliefs of future wonders can be found in almost all bubbles in history, as is made vividly clear in Kindleberger's book.

Then came the downturn with the credit crisis. In one year time (July 2007 to July 2008) stock prices dropped by 30%, destroying $3.5 trillion of value. The same amount as the one that had been created the year before. What happened? Investors finally realized

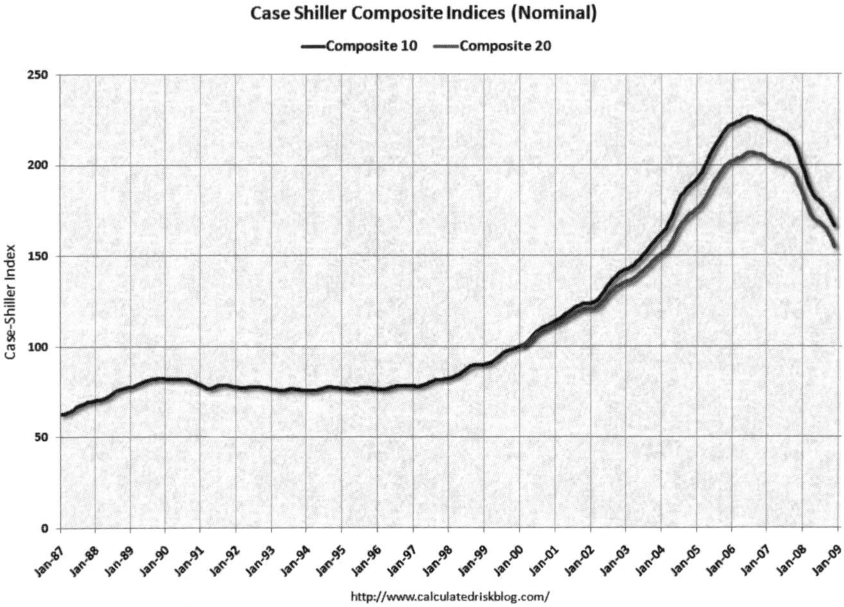

Figure 2.

Source: Standard&Poor's.

that there had been excessive optimism. The wave turned into one of excessive pessimism.

A similar story can be told about the US housing market. Figure 2 shows the Case-Shiller house price index from 2000 to 2008. During 2000–2007 US house prices more than doubled. What happened with economic fundamentals in the US warranting a doubling of house prices in seven years time? Very little. Again the driving force was excessive optimism. Prices increased because they were expected to increase indefinitely into the future. This was also the expectation that convinced US consumers that building up mortgage debt would not create future repayment problems.

These episodes illustrate the endemic nature of bubbles and crashes in capitalist systems. They happened in the past and will continue to occur in the future.

The deregulation of the banking sector that started in the 1980s fully exposed the banks to the endemic occurrence of bubbles and

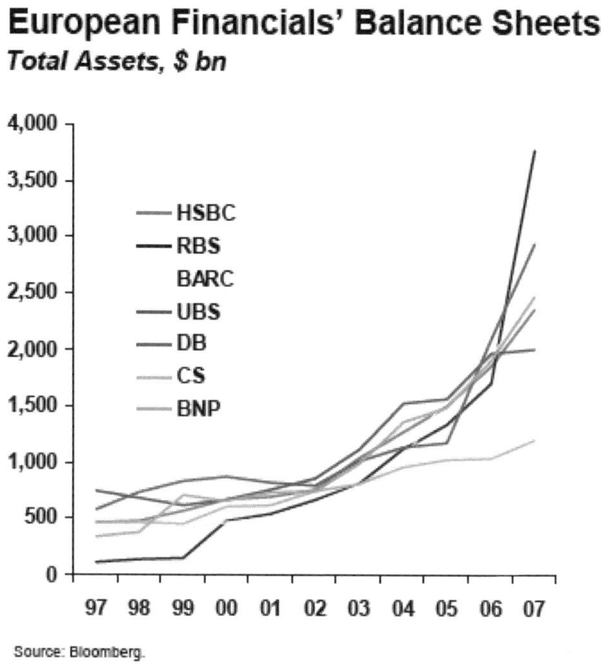

Figure 3.

Source: Bloomberg.

crashes in asset markets. Because banks were allowed to hold the full panoply of financial assets, their balance sheets became extremely sensitive to bubbles and crashes that gripped these assets. This is shown in a spectacular way in Figure 6. It illustrates how since the start of the decade the balance sheets of the major European banks exploded, reflecting the various bubbles that occurred at that time (housing bubble, stock market bubbles, commodities bubbles).

While commercial banks were increasingly involving themselves in financial markets and thus were taking over activities that were reserved to investment banks, the opposite occurred with investment banks. The latter increasingly behaved like banks, i.e., they borrowed short and lent long, thereby moving into the business of credit creation. To give an example. Investment banks (e.g., Lehman

Brothers) moved into the business of lending money to hedge funds and accepted stocks or other securities as collateral. They then went on and lent that collateral to others so as to make extra money. Thus, investment banks had become banks in that they were creating credit. In the process they created an unbalanced maturity structure of assets and liabilities. Their assets were long term and illiquid while their liabilities had a very short maturity.

Thus, as a result of deregulation a double movement occurred: Commercial banks moved into investment bank territory and investment banks moved into commercial bank territory. This led to a situation in which both the commercial banks and the investment banks built up a lethal combination of credit and liquidity risks.

3.2. *The Mirage of Self-regulation of Financial Markets*

A centerpiece of the efficient market theory was that financial markets were capable of self-regulation, making government regulation redundant. Two mechanisms were seen as central in making self-regulation work. One was the role of rating agencies; the other was the use of mark-to-market rules.

Rating agencies would guarantee a fair and objective rating of banks and their financial products. It did not happen. The reason was that there was massive conflict of interest in the rating agencies. These both advised financial institutions on how to create new financial products and later on gave a favourable rating to the same products. Their incentives, instead of leading to the creation of sound and safe financial products were skewed towards producing risky and unsafe products.

The other piece in the belief that markets would regulate themselves was the idea of mark-to-market. If financial institutions used mark to market rules the discipline of the market would force them to price their products right. Since prices always reflected fundamental values mark-to-market rules would force financial institutions to reveal the truth about the value of their business, allowing investors to be fully informed when making investment decisions.

The trouble here again was the efficiency of markets. As we have illustrated, financial markets are regularly gripped by bubbles and crashes. In such an environment mark-to-market rules, instead of being a disciplining force, worked pro-cyclically. Thus during the bubble this rule told accountants that the massive asset price increases corresponded to real profits that should be recorded in the books. Now the reverse is happening. Mark to market rules force massive write-downs, correcting for the massive overvaluations introduced the years before, intensifying the sense of gloom and the economic downturn.

4. Long-Term Solutions: A Return to Narrow Banking

It is time to start working on the rules for a new banking system. There are two ways to go forward. One can be called the Basle-approach, the other the Glass-Steagall approach.

The Basle approach accepts as a *fait accompli* that banks will go on performing both traditional and investment bank activities. This approach then consists in defining and implementing rules governing the risks that these banks can take. Its philosophy is that a suitable analysis of the risk profile of the banks' asset portfolios allows for calculating the required capital to be used as a buffer against future shocks in credit risk. Once these minimum capital ratios are in place, credit risk accidents can be absorbed by the existing equity, preventing banks from going broke and thereby avoiding the devilish spillovers from solvency problems into liquidity problems.

This approach has completely failed. It was first implemented in the Basle 1 accord, but was massively circumvented by banks that profited from the loopholes in the system. Basle 2 attempted to remedy this by allowing banks to use internal risk models to compute their minimum capital ratios. The underlying assumption was that scientific advances in risk analysis would make it possible to develop a reliable method of determining minimum capital ratios.

This approach at managing risks of banks does not work and will never do because it assumes efficiency of financial markets; an assumption that must be rejected.[4] Banks that fully participate in the financial markets subject themselves to the endemic occurrence of bubbles and crashes. These lead to large tail risks that with our present knowledge cannot be quantified. There is no prospect for gaining substantial knowledge about tail risks in the near future. The Basle approach must be abandoned.

This leaves only one workable approach. This is a return to the Glass–Steagall Act approach, or put differently, a return to narrow banking in which the activities banks can engage in are narrowly circumscribed. In this approach banks are excluded from investing in equities, derivatives and complex structured products. Investment in such products can only be performed by financial institutions, investment banks, which are forbidden from funding these investments by deposits (either obtained from the public of from other commercial banks).

In a nutshell, a return to narrow banking could be implemented as follows. Financial institutions would be forced to choose between the status of a commercial bank and that of investment bank. Only the former would be allowed to attract deposits from the public and from other commercial banks and to transform these into a loan portfolio with a longer maturity (duration). Commercial banks would benefit from the lender of last resort facility and deposit insurance, and would be subject to the normal bank supervision and regulation. The other financial institutions that do not opt for a commercial bank status would have to ensure that the duration of their liabilities is on average at least as long as the duration of their assets. This would imply, for example, that they would not be allowed to finance their illiquid assets by short-term credit lines from commercial banks. Thus, while commercial banks would be barred from engage themselves in activities of investment banks, the reverse would also hold, i.e. investment banks would not be allowed to borrow short and to lend long thereby taking on liquidity risks.

[4]There is a second reason why it will not work and that is conflict of interests. Supervisors should not trust complex risk models produced by bankers because the latter have a strong incentive not to reveal their true risk exposures.

Thus, we would return to a world where banking activities are tightly regulated and separated from investment banking activities. This also implies that commercial banks would not be allowed anymore to sell (securitize) their loan portfolio. Securitization leads to a build-up of the credit pyramid. When a bank secuterizes a loan, it obtains new liquidities that can be used to grant new loans, which in turn can be used to secuterize further. As a result, a credit expansion is made possible which occurs outside the supervision and control of the central bank (which, however, will be called upon to buy these assets when it becomes the lender of last resort). Put differently, securitization allows the credit multiplier to increase for any given level of the money base provided by the central bank. Credit gets out of control, endangering the whole banking system, including the central bank. It is worth stressing the latter point. The massive credit expansion made possible by securitization also endangers the balance sheet of the central bank. This is so because in times of crisis, the central bank is called upon to function as a lender of last resort. As a result, it will be faced with the need to accept as collateral secuterized assets that were created by banks. Allowing banks to secuterize thus means that the central bank takes on a substantial part of the risk.

The preceding argument also implies that the "originate and distribute model" that banks have increasingly used in the recent past must be abandoned. Recent proposals to save it by requiring banks to hold a fraction of the secuterized assets on their balance sheets are inappropriate as they do not eliminate the risk arising from the multiplication of credit described in the previous paragraph.

A return to narrow banking will necessitate a cooperative international approach. When only one or a few countries return to narrow banking, the banks of these countries will face a competitive disadvantage. They will lose market shares to banks less tightly regulated. As a result, they will have forceful arguments to lobby domestically against the tight restrictions they face. In the end, the governments of these countries will yield and the whole process of deregulation will start again.

References

Chancellor, E (1999). *Devil Take the Hindmost: A History of Financial Speculation.* New York, NY: Farrar, Straus and Giroux.

Goodhart, C and G Illing (ed.) 2002. *Financial Crises, Contagion, and the Lender of Last Resort: A Reader.* Oxford, UK: Oxford University Press.

Greenspan, A (2007). *The Age of Turbulence: Adventures in a New World.* London, UK: Penguin Books.

Kindleberger, C (2005). *Manias, Panics, and Crashes*, 5th Edition. New York, NY: Wiley.

Minsky, H (1986). *Stabilizing an Unstable Economy.* New York, NY: McGraw-Hill.

Shiller, R (2000). *Irrational Exuberance.* Princeton, NJ: Princeton University Press.

Shleifer, A (2000). *Clarendon Lectures: Inefficient Markets.* Oxford, UK: Oxford University Press.

Chapter 17

The Scientific Foundation of Dynamic Stochastic General Equilibrium (DSGE) Models

Paul De Grauwe

DSGE-models provide a coherent framework of analysis. This coherence is brought about by restricting acceptable behavior of agents to dynamic utility maximization and rational expectations. The problem of the DSGE-models (and more generally of macroeconomic models based on rational expectations) is that they assume extraordinary cognitive capabilities of individual agents. In addition, these models need a lot of *ad-hoc* assumptions to make them fit the data. I argue that we need models that take into account the limited cognitive abilities of agents. One can introduce rationality in such models by assuming "trial and error" learning. I propose such a model and I analyze its implications.

Published in *Public Choice*, 144, 413–443, 2010.

This paper was presented at the Symposium in Honour of Gebhard Kirchgässner's 60th Birthday, Wartensee, April 18–19, 2008. The paper is based on a previous version written while I was visiting the ECB as a Wim Duisenberg Fellow during October–December 2007.

I am grateful to Stephan Fahr, Richard Harrison, Romain Houssa, Pablo Rovira Kaltwasser, Christian Keuschnigg, Giovanni Lombardo, Lars Ljungqvist, Ilbas Pelin, Frank Smets, Leopold von Thadden, and Tony Yates for their comments and suggestions. The paper profited greatly from the comments of two anonymous referees. The hospitality and the financial support of the ECB are gratefully acknowledged.

Keywords: Behavioral macroeconomics; DGSE models; inflation; methodology of macroeconomics; output gap.

JEL classification: E13, E17, E30.

1. Introduction

One of the surprising developments in macroeconomics is the systematic incorporation of the paradigm of the utility maximizing forward looking and fully informed agent into macroeconomic models. This development started with the rational expectations revolution of the 1970s, which taught us that macroeconomic models can be accepted only if agents' expectations are consistent with the underlying model structure. The real business cycle theory (RBC) introduced the idea that macroeconomic models should be "micro-founded," i.e., should be based on dynamic utility maximization. While RBC models had no place for price rigidities and other inertia, the New Keynesian School systematically introduced rigidities of all kinds into similar micro-founded models. These developments occurred in the ivory towers of academia for several decades until in recent years these models were implemented empirically in such a way that they have now become tools of analysis in the boardrooms of central banks. The most successful implementation of these developments are to be found in the Dynamic Stochastic General Equilibrium models (DSGE-models) that are increasingly used in central banks for policy analysis (see Smets and Wouters, 2003; Christiano *et al.*, 2007; Smets and Wouters, 2007; Adjemian *et al.*, 2007).

These developments are surprising for several reasons. First, while macroeconomic theory enthusiastically embraced the view that agents fully understand the structure of the underlying models in which they operate, other sciences like psychology and neurology increasingly uncovered the cognitive limitations of individuals (see e.g., Damasio, 2003; Kahneman, 2002; Camerer *et al.*, 2005). We learn from these sciences that agents understand only small bits and pieces of the world in which they live, and instead of maximizing continuously taking all available information into account, agents use simple rules (heuristics) in guiding their behavior and their forecasts about the future. This raises the question of whether the micro-founded macro-economic theory that has become the standard is well-grounded scientifically.

A second source of surprise in the development of macroeconomic modeling in general and the DSGE-models in particular is that other branches of economics, like game theory and experimental economics have increasingly recognized the need to incorporate the limitations agents face in understanding the world. This has led to models that depart from the rational expectations paradigm (see e.g., Thaler, 1994).

Standard macroeconomics has been immune for these developments. True, under the impulse of Sargent (1993) and Evans and Honkapohja (2001) there has been an attempt to introduce the notion in macroeconomic models that agents should not be assumed to be cleverer than econometricians and that therefore they should be modeled as agents who learn about the underlying model as time passes. This has led to learning in macroeconomics. The incorporation of learning in macroeconomics, however, has up to now left few traces in standard macroeconomic models and in the DSGE-models.

In the first part of this paper, we subject the DSGE-models to a methodological analysis using the main insights we have obtained from other disciplines. We will ask the question of whether these models are scientifically well founded. In a second part, we develop an alternative stylized version of a macroeconomic model that incorporates the idea that agents use simple rules (heuristics) in forecasting and we contrast the results of this "behavioral model" with a stylized version of the DSGE-model, which will be labeled the "rational model."

2. The Scientific Foundation of the DSGE-Models

The DSGE-models embody the two central tenets of modern macroeconomics. The first one is that a macroeconomic model should be based ("micro founded") on dynamic utility maximization of a representative agent. The second one is that expectations should be model-consistent which implies that agents make forecasts based on the information embedded in the model. This idea in turn implies that agents have a full understanding of the structure of the underlying model.

There can be no doubt that this approach to macroeconomics has important advantages compared to previous macroeconomic models. The main advantage is that it provides for a coherent and self-contained framework of analysis. This has great intellectual appeal. There is no need to invoke *ad-hoc* assumptions about how agents behave and how they make forecasts. Rational expectations and utility maximization introduce discipline in modeling the behavior of agents.

The scientific validity of a model should not be based on its logical coherence or on its intellectual appeal, however. It can be judged only on its capacity of making empirical predictions that are not rejected by the data. If it fails to do so, coherent and intellectually appealing models should be discarded. Before turning our attention to the empirical validation of models based on dynamic utility maximization and rational expectations, of which the DSGE-models are now the most prominent examples, we analyze the plausibility of the underlying assumptions about human behavior in these models.

There is a very large literature documenting deviations from the paradigm of the utility maximizing agent who understands the nature of the underlying economic model. For recent surveys, see Kahneman and Thaler (2006) and Della Vigna (2007). This literature has followed two tracks. One was to question the idea of utility maximization as a description of agents' behavior (see Kirchgässner, 2008 for an illuminating analysis of how this idea has influenced social sciences). Many deviations have been found. A well-known one is the framing effect. Agents are often influenced by the way a choice is framed in making their decisions (see Tversky and Kahneman, 1981). Another well-known deviation from the standard model is the fact that agents do not appear to attach the same utility value to gains and losses. This led Kahneman and Tversky (1973) to formulate prospect theory as an alternative to the standard utility maximization under uncertainty.

We will not deal with deviations from the standard utility maximization model here, mainly because many (but not all) of these anomalies can be taken care of by suitably specifying alternative utility functions. Instead, we will focus on the plausibility of the rational expectations assumption and its logical implication, i.e., that agents understand the nature of the underlying model.

It is no exaggeration to say that there is now overwhelming evidence that individual agents suffer from deep cognitive problems limiting their capacity to understand and to process the complexity of the information they receive.

Many anomalies that challenge the rational expectations assumption were discovered (see Thaler, 1994 for spirited discussions of these anomalies; see also Read and van Leeuwen, 1998; Della Vigna, 2007). We just mention "anchoring" effects here, whereby agents who do not fully understand the world in which they live are highly selective in the way they use information and concentrate on the information they understand or the information that is fresh in their minds. This anchoring effect explains why agents often extrapolate recent movements in prices.

In general the cognitive problem which agents face leads them to use simple rules ("heuristics") to guide their behavior (see Gabaix *et al.*, 2006). They do this not because they are irrational, but rather because the complexity of the world is overwhelming. In a way it can be said that using heuristics is a rational response of agents who are aware of their limited capacity to understand the world. The challenge when we try to model heuristics will be to introduce discipline in the selection of rules so as to avoid that "everything becomes possible."

One important implication of the assumption that agents know the underlying model's structure is that all agents are the same. They all use the same information set including the information embedded in the underlying model. As a result, DSGE-models routinely restrict the analysis to a representative agent to fully describe how all agents in the model process information. There is no heterogeneity in the use and the processing of information in these models. This strips models based on rational expectations from much of their interest in analyzing short-term and medium-term macroeconomic problems which is about the dynamics of aggregating heterogeneous behavior and beliefs (see Colander *et al.*, 2009).[1]

[1]There have been attempts to model heterogeneity of information processing in rational expectations models. These have been developed mainly in asset market models. Typically, it is assumed in these models that some agents are fully informed (rational) while others, the noise traders, are not. See e.g., De Long *et al.* (1990).

It is fair to conclude that the accumulated scientific evidence casts doubts about the plausibility of the main assumption concerning the behavior of individual agents in DSGE-models, i.e., that they are capable of understanding the economic model in which they operate and of processing the complex information distilled from this model. Instead the scientific evidence suggests that individual agents are not capable of doing so, and that they rely on rules that use only small parts of the available information.

One could object here and argue that a model should not be judged by the plausibility of its assumptions but rather by its ability to make powerful empirical predictions. Thus, despite the apparent implausibility of its informational assumption, the macroeconomic model based on rational expectations could still be a powerful one if it makes the right predictions. This argument, which was often stressed by Milton Friedman, is entirely correct. It leads us to the question of the empirical validity of the rational macromodels in general and the DSGE-models in particular.

The main problem of the "pure" micro-founded macro-model with forward looking agents appears to be that it underestimates the degree of inertia in wages and prices. For example, it predicts that when new information reaches the market rational agents will immediately change their optimal plans, leading to instantaneous price changes. This prediction flies in the face of empirical evidence that shows quite universally that prices have a strong inertial component and react sluggishly to shocks (see Nelson, 1998; Estrella and Fuhrer, 2002 for empirical evidence; see also Walsh, 2003).

Thus, right from the start, the micro-founded macroeconomic models had to be sent back to the repair shop. Once in the repair shop, macro theorists diluted their ambition to "micro-found" the macro-theory by introducing *ad-hoc* assumptions about why agents do not adjust their plans instantaneously and why prices are rigid. The pure micro-founded model received a "New Keynesian" treatment (see e.g., Clarida *et al.*, 1999; Woodford, 2002). The main characteristics of this "repair shop treatment" were to add lags into the model so as to create the necessary inertia observed in the data. This was done in several ways.

First, consumers were modeled as agents subject to habit formation. This trick allowed one to introduce lagged consumption in the utility function and added welcome inertia. Few theorists, however, bothered about the inconsistency of assuming super-rational agents that can continuously optimize using the latest available information and yet are prone to strange habits that prevent them from acting according to the optimal plan and from using all available information.

A second popular way to introduce inertia in the model has been to invoke Calvo pricing in which firms are constrained in adjusting prices instantaneously (Christiano, Eichenbaum and Evans, 2001). Again the inconsistency was brushed under the carpet. Why is it that in a world where everybody understands the model and each other's rationality, agents would not want to go immediately to the optimal plan using the optimal price?

The use of Calvo-pricing rules is often justified by invoking institutional restrictions that limit the freedom of action of individual firms. But again the question arises here why rational and perfectly informed agents would accept institutions that limit their freedom to set optimal plans. After all, it is against their own interest to accept such limitations. It is not only against the interests of the firms, but also of consumers and workers, who in the rational macroeconomic models are agents who perfectly understand the world and their own interests and will always want to maximize their utilities. Any limitation on their optimizing behavior reduces their welfare. Thus, in the context of DSGE-models these limitations should not be invoked. If they exist in the real world, it is proof that this should be interpreted as evidence against DSGE-models. We are forced to conclude that Calvo pricing is an *ad hoc* assumption forced unto the model to create enough inertia so that it would fit the data better.

Other limitations on optimizing behavior (e.g., rule of thumb consumers) have been introduced that can be interpreted in a similar way.

Thus, when the models came out of the repair shops, they were changed fundamentally by the addition of features that have no micro-foundations. These changes were not just innocent ones. They were crucial in making the model fit the data. In a way it can be said that habit formation, Calvo-pricing, and rule of thumb consumers have been ways to introduce heuristics into the DSGE-models through the back door.

The issue then is how much is left over from the paradigm of the fully informed rational agent in the existing DSGE-models? How important have the heuristics become in generating the dynamics in these models? Since the heuristics has been added in an *ad-hoc* and haphazard way it is difficult to answer this question. The suspicion exists that the heuristics may drive most of the dynamics in the DSGE models (see Chari *et al.*, 2009). We return to this issue in Section 4.

This leads to the question of whether it is not preferable to admit that agents' behavior is guided by heuristics, and to incorporate these heuristics into the model from the start, rather than to pretend that agents are fully rational but to rely in a nontransparent way on heuristics to improve the fit of the model. That is what we plan to do in the next section.

3. A Behavioral Model

In this part of the paper, we describe how an alternative modeling strategy could be developed. We do this by presenting a standard aggregate-demand, aggregate supply model augmented with a Taylor rule. The novel feature of the model is that agents use simple rules, heuristics, to forecast the future. These rules are subjected to a selection mechanism. Put differently, agents endogenously will select the forecasting rules that have delivered the greatest fitness in the past. This selection mechanism acts as a disciplining device on the kind of rules that are acceptable. Since agents use different heuristics we also obtain heterogeneity. This, as will be shown, creates endogenous business cycles.

We will contrast the behavior of this model with a similar model that incorporates rational expectations and that we interpret as a stylized version of DSGE-models. This comparison will also allow us to focus on some crucial differences in the transmission of shocks, in particular of monetary policy shocks.

Obviously, the approach presented here is not the only possible one. In fact, a large literature has emerged attempting to introduce imperfect information into macroeconomic models. These attempts have been based mainly on the statistical learning approach pioneered by Sargent (1993) and Evans and Honkapohja (2001). This literature leads to important new insights (see, e.g., Gaspar and Smets, 2006; Orphanides and Williams, 2004; Milani, 2007). However, we feel that this approach still loads individual agents with too many cognitive skills that they probably do not possess in the real world. A similar criticism can be developed against another approach to modeling imperfect information based on "rational inattention" (see Mackowiak and Wiederholt, 2005; Sims, 2005).

Our approach is also not the first attempt to introduce heuristics into macroeconomic models. Recently, Brazier *et al.* (2006) have done so in the context of an overlapping generations model. In addition, there is a large literature of behavioral finance models that now incorporate the view that agents are limited in their cognitive skills and use heuristics to guide their behavior and forecasting (see Brock and Hommes, 1997; Lux and Marchesi, 2000; De Grauwe and Grimaldi, 2006).

3.1. *The Model*

The model consists of an aggregate demand equation, an aggregate supply equation and a Taylor rule.

The aggregate demand equation can be derived from dynamic utility maximization. This produces an Euler equation in the same vein as in DSGE-models. We obtain

$$y_t = a_1 \tilde{E}_t y_{t+1} + (1 - a_1) y_{t-1} + a_2 (r_t - \tilde{E}_t \pi_{t+1}) + \varepsilon_t \tag{1}$$

where y_t is the output gap in period t, r_t is the nominal interest rate, π_t is the rate of inflation, and ε_t is a white noise disturbance term. $\tilde{E}_t$ is the expectations operator where the tilde above E refers to expectations that are not formed rationally. We will specify this process subsequently. We follow the procedure introduced in DSGE-models of adding lagged output in the demand equation. This is usually justified by invoking habit formation. We criticized this approach for being an *ad-hoc* departure from the assumption of rational forward-looking agents. In a model where agents cannot fully understand the world it is a more reasonable assumption to make. In addition, given that we want to compare the behavioral model with the DSGE-rational expectations model we follow the same procedure as in the latter. Finally, we will show in Section 4 that we do not really need these inertia-building devices to generate inertia in the endogenous variables.

The aggregate supply equation can be derived from profit maximization of individual producers. We assume as in DSGE-models a Calvo pricing rule, which leads to a lagged inflation variable in the equation.[2] The supply curve can also be interpreted as a New Keynesian Philips curve. We obtain:

$$\pi_t = b_1 \tilde{E}_t \pi_{t+1} + (1 - b_1)\pi_{t-1} + b_2 y_t + \eta_t \tag{2}$$

Finally the Taylor rule describes the behavior of the central bank

$$r_t = c_1(\pi_t - \pi_t^*) + c_2 y_t + c_3 r_{t-1} + u_t \tag{3}$$

where π_t^* is the inflation target which for the sake of convenience will be set equal to 0. Note that we assume, as is commonly done, that the central bank smoothes the interest rate. This smoothing behavior is represented by the lagged interest rate in Eq. (3). Ideally, the Taylor rule should be formulated using a forward looking inflation variable, i.e., central banks set the interest rate on the basis of their forecasts about the rate of inflation. We have not done so here in order to maintain simplicity in the model.

[2]It is now standard in DSGE-models to use a pricing equation in which marginal costs enter on the right hand side. Such an equation is derived from profit maximisation in a world of imperfect competition. It allows introducing more detail into the model and makes it possible to specify productivity shocks better. It also allows for analyzing how shocks in markups affect the economy. We have not tried to introduce this feature here (see Gali, 2008; Smets and Wouters, 2003).

We assume that agents use simple rules (heuristics) to forecast output and inflation. The way we proceed is as follows. We start with a very simple heuristics for forecasting and apply it to the forecasting rules of future output. We assume that because agents do not fully understand how the output gap is determined, their forecasts are biased. We assume that some agents are optimistic and systematically bias the output gap upwards, others are pessimistic and systematically bias the output gap downwards.

$$\text{The optimists are defined by } \tilde{E}_t^{opt} y_{t+1} = g \tag{4}$$

$$\text{The pessimists are defined by } \tilde{E}_t^{pes} y_{t+1} = -g \tag{5}$$

where $g > 0$ expresses the degree of bias in estimating the output gap. We will interpret $2g$ to express the divergence in beliefs among agents about the output gap.

Note that we do not consider this assumption of a simple bias to be a realistic representation of how agents forecast. Rather is it a parsimonious representation of a world where agents do not know the "truth" (i.e., the underlying model). As a result of their cognitive limitations the rule they use is biased. This does not mean that the agents are "dumb" and that they do not want to learn from their errors. We will specify a learning mechanism later in this section in which these agents continuously try to correct for the bias by switching from one rule to the other.

The market forecast is obtained as a weighted average of these two forecasts, i.e.,

$$\tilde{E}_t y_{t+1} = \alpha_{opt,t} \tilde{E}_t^{opt} y_{t+1} + \alpha_{pes,t} \tilde{E}_t^{pes} y_{t+1} \tag{6}$$

$$\tilde{E}_t y_{t+1} = \alpha_{opt,t} g - \alpha_{pes,t} g \tag{7}$$

and

$$\alpha_{opt,t} + \alpha_{pes,t} = 1 \tag{8}$$

where $\alpha_{opt,t}$ and $\alpha_{pes,t}$ are the weights of optimists, receptively, pessimists in the market.

A methodological issue arises here. The forecasting rules (heuristics) introduced here are not derived at the micro level and then aggregated. Instead, they are imposed *ex post*, on the demand and supply equations. This has also been the approach in the learning literature pioneered by Evans and Honkapohja (2001). Ideally, one would like to derive the heuristics from the micro-level in an environment in which agents experience cognitive problems. Our knowledge about how to model this behavior at the micro level[3] and how to aggregate it is too sketchy, however, and we have not tried to do so.

As indicated earlier, agents are rational in the sense that they continuously evaluate performances of their forecasts. We apply notions of discrete choice theory (see Anderson, de Palma and Thisse, 1992; Brock and Hommes, 1997) in specifying the procedure agents follow in this evaluation process. Discrete choice theory analyzes how agents decide between different alternatives. The theory takes the view that agents are boundedly rational, i.e., utility has a deterministic component and a random component. Agents compute the forecast performance of the different heuristics as follows:

$$U_{opt,t} = -\sum_{k=1}^{\infty} \omega_k [y_{t-k} - \tilde{E}_{opt,t-k-1} y_{t-k}]^2 \tag{9}$$

$$U_{pes,t} = -\sum_{k=1}^{\infty} \omega_k [y_{t-k} - \tilde{E}_{pes,t-k-1} y_{t-k}]^2 \tag{10}$$

where $U_{opt,t}$ and $U_{pes,t}$ are the forecast performances of the optimists and pessimists, respectively. These are defined as the mean squared forecasting errors (MSFEs) of the optimistic and pessimistic forecasting rules; ω_k are geometrically declining weights.

Applying discrete choice theory the probability that an agent will use the optimistic forecasting rule is given by the expression (Anderson, de Palma and Thisse, 1992; and Brock-Hommes, 1997).

$$\alpha_{opt,t} = \frac{\exp(\gamma U_{opt,t})}{\exp(\gamma U_{opt,t}) + \exp(\gamma U_{pes,t})} \tag{11}$$

[3]Psychologists and brains scientists struggle to understand how our brain processes information. There is as yet no generally accepted model we could use to model the micro-foundations of information processing.

Similarly the probability that an agent will use the pessimistic forecasting rule is given by:

$$\alpha_{pes,t} = \frac{\exp(\gamma U_{pes,t})}{\exp(\gamma U_{opt,t}) + \exp(\gamma U_{pes,t})} = 1 - \alpha_{opt,t} \quad (12)$$

Equation (12) says that as the past forecast performance of the optimists improves relative to that of the pessimists agents are more likely to select the optimistic belief about the output gap for their future forecasts. As a result the fraction of agents using the optimistic rule increases. Equation (13) has a similar interpretation. The parameter γ measures the "intensity of choice." It parameterizes the extent to which the deterministic component of utility determines actual choice. When $\gamma = 0$ utility is purely stochastic. In that case the probability of being an optimist (or pessimist) is exactly 0.5. When $\gamma = \infty$ utility is fully deterministic and the probability of using an optimistic rule is either 1 or 0.

Note that this selection mechanism is the disciplining device introduced in this model on the kind of rules of behavior that are acceptable. Only those rules that pass the fitness test remain in place. The others are weeded out. In contrast to the disciplining device implicit in rational expectations models, which implies that agents have superior cognitive capacities, we do not have to make such an assumption here.

It should also be stressed that although individuals use biased rules in forecasting the future, this does not mean that they fail to learn. On the contrary, the fitness test is a learning mechanism based on "trial and error." When observing that the rule they use performs less well than the alternative rule, they are willing to switch to the better performing rule. Put differently, the rules are biased because agents have a poor understanding of the underlying model. But these agents are not "dumb." They avoid making systematic mistakes by constantly being willing to learn from past mistakes and to change their behavior. This "trial and error" learning mechanism ensures that the market forecasts are unbiased.

Agents also make forecasts of inflation in this model. At this stage of the analysis we will simply assume that all agents perceive the central bank's announced inflation target π_t^* to be fully credible. They use this value as their forecast of future inflation, i.e., $\tilde{E}_t\pi_{t+1} = \pi_t^*$ (where for the sake of simplicity we assume the inflation target to be equal to 0). We will extend this simple inflation forecasting process in a later section when we will also assume that there is heterogeneity of beliefs in the inflation forecasting process. We keep homogeneity of beliefs here to focus on the impact of heterogeneity in the forecasting of future output gaps.

The solution of the model is found by first substituting (3) into (1) and rewriting in matrix notation. This yields:

$$\begin{bmatrix} 1 & -b_2 \\ -a_2c_1 & 1-a_2c_2 \end{bmatrix} \begin{bmatrix} \pi_t \\ y_t \end{bmatrix} = \begin{bmatrix} b_1 & 0 \\ -a_2 & a_1 \end{bmatrix} \begin{bmatrix} \tilde{E}_t\pi_{t+1} \\ \tilde{E}_t y_{t+1} \end{bmatrix} + \begin{bmatrix} 1-b_1 & 0 \\ 0 & 1-a_1 \end{bmatrix} \begin{bmatrix} \pi_{t-1} \\ y_{t-1} \end{bmatrix} + \begin{bmatrix} 0 \\ a_2c_3 \end{bmatrix} r_{t-1} + \begin{bmatrix} \eta_t \\ a_2u_t + \varepsilon_t \end{bmatrix}$$

or

$$AZ_t = B\tilde{E}_t Z_t + CZ_{t-1} + br_{t-1} + v_t \tag{13}$$

where bold characters refer to matrices and vectors. The solution for Z_t is given by

$$Z_t = A^{-1}\lfloor B\tilde{E}_t Z_t + CZ_{t-1} + br_{t-1} + v_t \rfloor \tag{14}$$

The solution exists if the matrix A is non-singular, i.e., if $(1 - a_2c_2) - a_2b_2c_1 \neq 0$. The system (14) describes the solution for y_t and π_t given the forecasts of y_t and π_t. The latter have been specified in Eqs. (4) to (12) and can be substituted into (14). Finally, the solution for r_t is found by substituting y_t and π_t obtained from (14) into (3).

Our research strategy consists in comparing the dynamics of this behavioral model with the same structural model (aggregate demand Eq. (1), aggregate supply Eq. (2) and Taylor rule Eq. (3)) under rational expectations which we interpret as a stylized DSGE-model.

The model consisting of Eqs. (1) to (3) can be written in matrix notation as follows:

$$\begin{bmatrix} 1 & -b_2 & 0 \\ 0 & 1 & -a_2 \\ -c_1 & -c_2 & 1 \end{bmatrix} \begin{bmatrix} \pi_t \\ y_t \\ r_t \end{bmatrix} = \begin{bmatrix} b_1 & 0 & 0 \\ -a_2 & a_1 & 0 \\ 0 & 0 & 0 \end{bmatrix} \begin{bmatrix} E_t\pi_{t+1} \\ E_t y_{t+1} \\ E_t r_{t+1} \end{bmatrix} + \begin{bmatrix} 1-b_1 & 0 & 0 \\ 0 & 1-a_1 & 0 \\ 0 & 0 & a_3 \end{bmatrix} \times \begin{bmatrix} \pi_{t-1} \\ y_{t-1} \\ r_{t-1} \end{bmatrix} + \begin{bmatrix} \eta_t \\ \varepsilon_t \\ u_t \end{bmatrix}$$

$$\Omega \mathrm{Z_t} = \Phi \mathrm{E_t Z_t} + \Lambda \mathrm{Z_{t-1}} + \mathrm{v_t} \tag{15}$$

$$\mathrm{Z_t} = \Omega^{-1}[\Phi \mathrm{E_t Z_t} + \Lambda \mathrm{Z_{t-1}} + \mathrm{v_t}] \tag{16}$$

This model can be solved under rational expectations using the Binder-Pesaran (1996) procedure.

3.2. *Calibrating the Behavioral and the Rational Model*

We proceed by calibrating the model. In Appendix A, we present the parameters used in the calibration exercise. We have calibrated the model in such a way that the time units can be considered to be months. In Section 7, we present a sensitivity analysis of the main results to changes in the main parameters of the model.

We show the results of a simulation exercise in which the three shocks (demand shocks, supply shocks and interest rate shocks) are i.i.d. with standard deviations of 0.5 percent.

We first present a simulation in the time domain. Figure 1 shows the time pattern of output and inflation produced by the behavioral model. We observe a strong cyclical movement in the output gap. The source of these cyclical movements is seen to be the weight of optimists and pessimists in the market (see second panel of Figure 1). The model in fact generates endogenous waves of optimism and pessimism. During some periods pessimists dominate and this translates

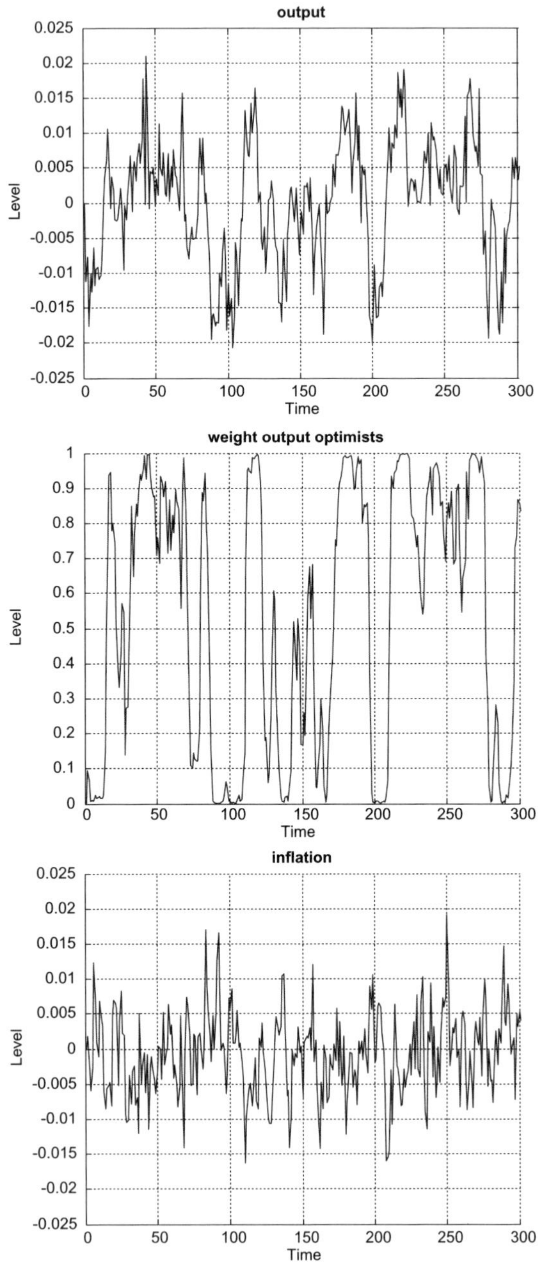

Figure 1. Output gap and inflation in behavioral model.

into below average output growth. These pessimistic periods are followed by optimistic periods when optimistic forecasts tend to dominate and the growth rate of output is above average. These waves of optimism and pessimism are essentially unpredictable. Other realizations of the shocks produce different cycles.

These endogenously generated cycles in output are reminiscent of what Keynes called "animal spirits." In our model these animal spirits are created by a self-fulfilling mechanism that can be described as follows. A series of random shocks creates the possibility that one of the two forecasting rules, say the optimistic one, delivers a higher payoff, i.e., a lower MSFE. This attracts agents that were using the pessimistic rule. The "contagion-effect" leads to an increasing use of the optimistic belief to forecast the output-gap, which in turn stimulates aggregate demand. Optimism is therefore self-fulfilling. A boom is created. At some point, either because of negative stochastic shocks or because during a boom the central bank raises the interest rate (using the Taylor rule, Eq. (3)) a dent in the MSFE of the optimistic forecasts is made. The pessimistic belief becomes attractive and therefore fashionable again. The economy turns around.

From Figure 1 (third panel) we observe that inflation is relatively stable and fluctuates around the target (set at 0) in a relatively narrow band. This result has everything to do with our assumption that agents are homogeneous in giving full credibility to the inflation target of the central bank. We will return to this when we introduce heterogeneity among agents in their perception of the credibility of the central bank's inflation target.

We contrast these results with those obtained using the model under rational expectations. We use the same structural model with the same parameter values for the aggregate demand, supply and Taylor equations. In addition the shocks are the same with the same i.i.d. structure.

We show the results in Figure 2. Two differences stand out. First the rational expectations model does not produce clear cyclical movements in the output gap. In a way this is not surprising: the shocks are white noise and the transmission mechanism exhibits a minimal degree of inertia. In full-fledged DSGE-models the inertia is more

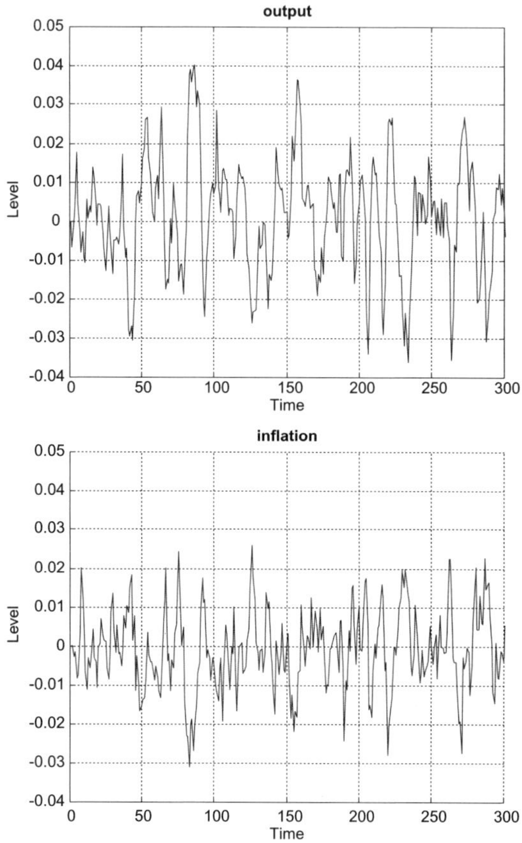

Figure 2. Output gap and inflation in the rational model.

complex and the shocks typically exhibit autoregressive patterns that are important in producing cyclical movements in output. Thus, our results illustrate that the cycles produced in the DSGE models come to a large extent from outside the model. We return to this issue in Section 4 where we analyze the degree of inertia produced by the two models.

Second, output and inflation are more volatile in the rational expectations model compared to the behavioral model. This can also be seen from Table 1 where we show the standard deviations of the output gap and inflation in the two models. Again this has to do with the minimal inertia assumed in the underlying structural model.

Table 1. Standard deviations of output gap and inflation.

	Behavioral model	Rational model
output gap	0.86	1.35
inflation	0.56	0.89

Note: These standard deviations are the averages obtained from simulating the model 1000 times, each time over 1000 periods.

Much of the attempt to fit the rational expectations model (DSGE-models) has consisted in adding additional lags so as to produce more persistence and less short-term volatility.

3.3. *Impulse Responses in the Behavioral and the Rational Model*

The next step in the analysis is to compute the impulse responses to shocks. Here we focus on the impulse responses to an interest rate shock, defined as plus one standard deviation of the shock in the Taylor equation.

The peculiarity of the behavioral model is that for the same parameters of the model the impulse responses are different for each realization of the stochastic shocks. This contrasts with the rational expectations model where the impulse response functions are not sensitive to the realization of the stochastic shocks (keeping the parameters unchanged).

Figure 3 shows the mean impulse responses to an interest rate shock. We constructed the mean response by simulating the model 100 times with 100 different realizations of the shocks. We then computed the mean response together with the standard deviations. Figure 3 shows the mean response (the dotted lines are the mean response + and -2 standard deviations; note also that we introduced the shock after 100 periods). We obtain the standard result of an interest rate shock on output and inflation. However, the uncertainty surrounding this result is considerable at least in the short run.

Where does this uncertainty come from? Not from parameter uncertainty. We use the same parameters in constructing all our

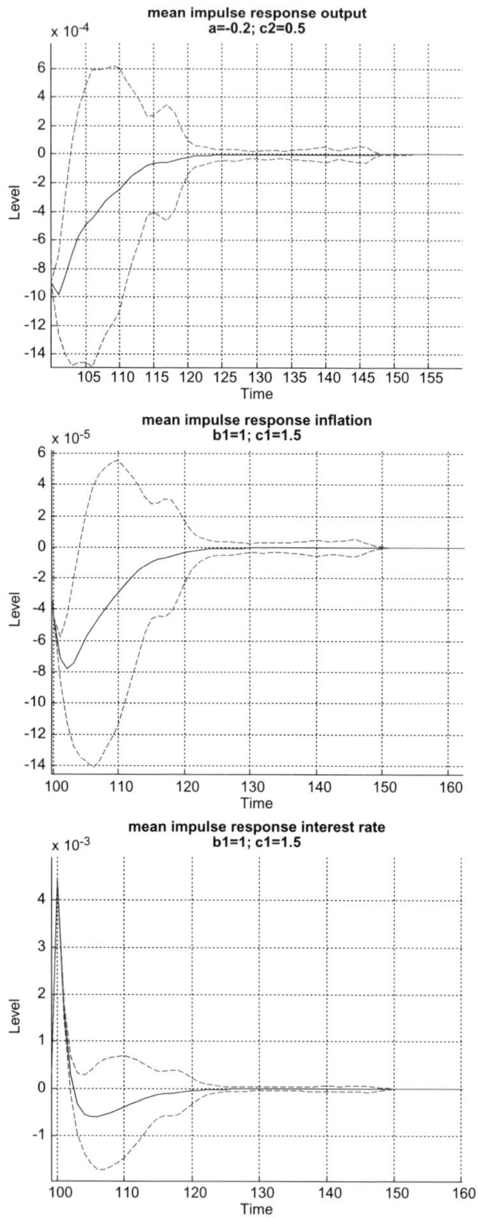

Figure 3. Mean impulse responses to interest rate shock in the behavioral model. *Note*: The dotted lines represent the impulse responses with $+/-2$ standard deviations.

impulse responses. The answer is that in this behavioral model each realization of the shocks creates different waves of optimism and pessimism. We could also call this "market sentiments." Thus, a shock that occurs in period 100 in one simulation happens in a different market sentiment than the same shock in another simulation. In addition, the shock itself affects market sentiments. As a result, the short-term effects of the same interest rate shock become very hard to predict.

Another way to interpret this result is to say that the timing of the shock is important. The same shocks applied at different times can have very different short-term effects on inflation and output. In other words, history matters. This contrasts with what rational expectations models tell us. In a rational expectations world the timing of the shock does not matter. In this sense the rational expectations model is a-historic.[4]

Note that the uncertainty about the impulse responses tends to disappear in the long run, as the effect of short-term differences in market sentiments disappears.

This difference in the nature of uncertainty in a heuristic and a rational expectations model has everything to do with the fact that the former has non-linear features while the latter is linear. Thus the additional uncertainty produced by the behavioral model, i.e., the dependence of the impulse response functions on the state of the economy is the outcome of its non-linearity. Rational expectations models including the DSGE-models traditionally impose some linearization procedure. This is done for the sake of mathematical simplicity. It leads to a problem though. If the micro foundation of the model leads to a non-linear model, it is important to know how this non-linearity (which is part of the micro-foundation) affects the dynamics generated by the model. Eliminating these non-linearities amounts to destroying information that is relevant to predict the transmission of shocks. This may not matter much for the long run,

[4]Michael Woodford has claimed that rational expectations models of the kind analyzed here have an element of historic dependence. This follows from the fact the existence of lags in the model. The historic dependence we are talking about here is of another nature.

but since the DSGE-models have the ambition of forecasting the transmission process, it is of significant importance.

3.4. *The Extended Behavioral Model*

In this section, we extend the behavioral model by allowing the inflation forecasters to be heterogeneous. We follow Brazier *et al.* (2006) in allowing for two inflation forecasting rules. One rule is based on the announced inflation target (as in the previous section); the other rule extrapolates inflation from the past into the future. One may argue that this is quite a different pair of heuristics than in the case of output forecasting. The difference between inflation forecasting and output forecasting is that in the former case there is a central bank that announces a particular inflation target. This target works as an anchor for the forecasts of agents. Such an anchor is absent in the case of output forecasting.

The "inflation targeters" use the central bank's inflation target to forecast future inflation, i.e., $\tilde{E}_t^{tar} = \pi_t^*$, where as before we set the inflation target $\pi_t^* = 0$

The "extrapolators" are defined by $\tilde{E}_t^{ext} = \pi_{t-1}$.

The market forecast is a weighted average of these two forecasts, i.e.,

$$\tilde{E}_t\pi_{t+1} = \beta_{tar,t}\tilde{E}_t^{tar}\pi_{t+1} + \beta_{ext,t}\tilde{E}_t^{ext}\pi_{t+1} \tag{17}$$

or

$$E_t\pi_{t+1} = \beta_{tar,t}\pi_t^* + \beta_{ext,t}\pi_{t-1} \tag{18}$$

and

$$\beta_{tar,t} + \beta_{ext,t} = 1 \tag{19}$$

We use the same selection mechanism as in the previous section based on the mean squared forecasting errors produced by the two rules to determine the proportions of agents trusting the inflation target and those who do not trust it and revert to extrapolation of past inflation, i.e.,

$$\beta_{tar,t} = \frac{\exp(\gamma U_{tar,t})}{\exp(\gamma U_{tar,t}) + \exp(\gamma U_{ext,t})} \tag{20}$$

$$\beta_{ext,t} = \frac{\exp(\gamma U_{ext,t})}{\exp(\gamma U_{tar,t}) + \exp(\gamma U_{ext,t})} \tag{21}$$

where $U_{tar,t}$ and $U_{ext,t}$ are the weighted averages of past squared forecast errors using targeter and extrapolator rules, respectively. These are defined in the same way as in (9) and (10).

This inflation forecasting heuristics can be interpreted as a procedure of agents to find out how credible the central bank's inflation targeting is. If this is very credible, using the announced inflation target will produce good forecasts and as a result, the proportion of agents relying on the inflation target will be large. If on the other hand the inflation target does not produce good forecasts (compared to a simple extrapolation rule) it will not be used much and therefore the proportion of agents using it will be small.

We calibrated the model using the same parameters as in the previous section. We first show the results in the time domain and then discuss the impulse response functions.

Figure 4 presents the results for the output gap in the time domain. We find the same cycles in the output gap as in the previous section. Again these cycles are related to the waves of optimism and pessimism in the forecasting (second panel in Figure 4).

The results concerning the time path of inflation are shown in Figure 5. We first concentrate on the second panel of Figure 5. This shows the proportion of "extrapolators," i.e., the agents who do not trust the inflation target of the central bank. We can identify two regimes. There is a regime in which the proportion of extrapolators fluctuates around 50 percent which also implies that the proportion of forecasters using the inflation target as their guide (the "inflation targeters") is around 50 percent. This is sufficient to maintain the rate of inflation within a narrow band of approximately + and −1 percent around the central bank's inflation target. There is a second regime though which occurs when the extrapolators are dominant. During this regime the rate of inflation fluctuates significantly more.

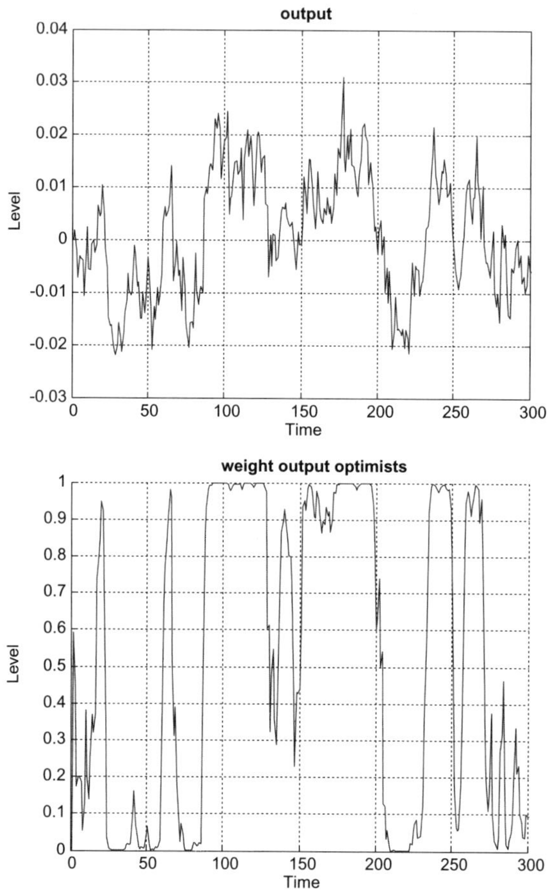

Figure 4. Output gap in the extended behavioral model.

Thus the inflation targeting of the central bank is fragile. It can be undermined when forecasters decide that relying on past inflation movements produces better forecast performances than relying on the central bank's inflation target. This can occur quite unpredictably as a result of stochastic shocks.

How can the central bank strengthen the inflation targeting regime? The previous simulations assumed an inflation coefficient of 1.5 in the Taylor equation. This is a value often found in empirical work. As an alternative the central bank could apply a larger

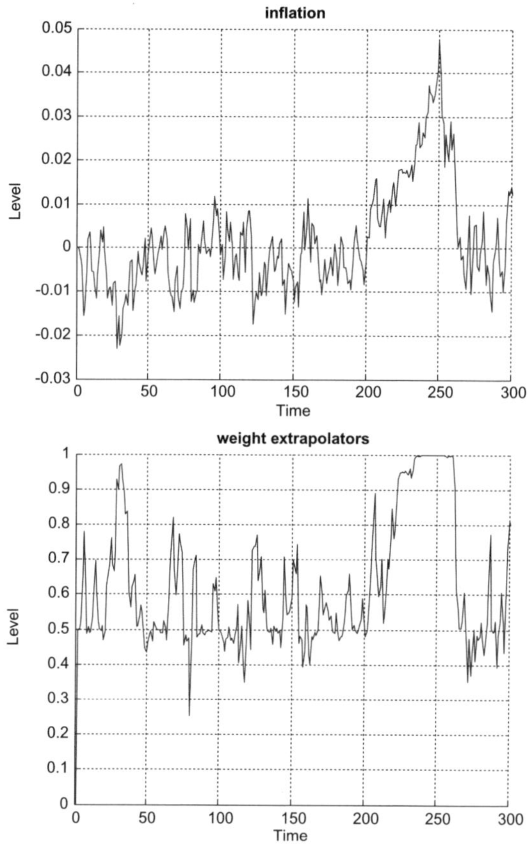

Figure 5. Inflation in the extended behavioral model.

inflation coefficient, implying that it reacts more strongly to changes in inflation from its target. We show the results of a simulation when the central bank sets this coefficient equal to 2.5 in Figure 6. We now observe that this stricter inflation targeting policy has the effect of keeping the rate of inflation within the narrow band of $+/-1$ percent most of the time. There are occasional "dérapages" into the second more turbulent regime but these are less frequent and less persistent. This has all to do with the fact that a sufficiently large proportion of agents continue to trust the central bank's inflation target as a guide in forecasting.

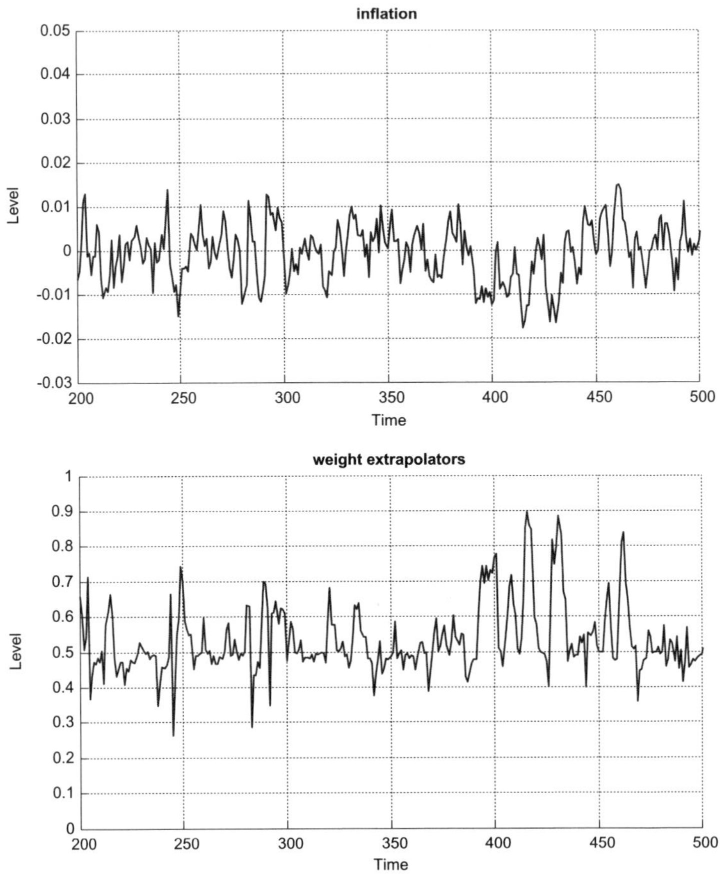

Figure 6. Inflation in the extended behavioral model with strict inflation targeting.

3.5. *Impulse Responses in the Extended Behavioral Model*

In this section, we present the impulse responses to a positive interest rate shock of one standard deviation. Two results stand out. First the uncertainty surrounding the effects of interest rate shocks is greater and lasts longer than in the simple behavioral model with homogenous inflation forecasting. Second, there is in this extended model considerably more inertia in inflation adjustment than in output adjustment following the interest rate shock. This feature whereby

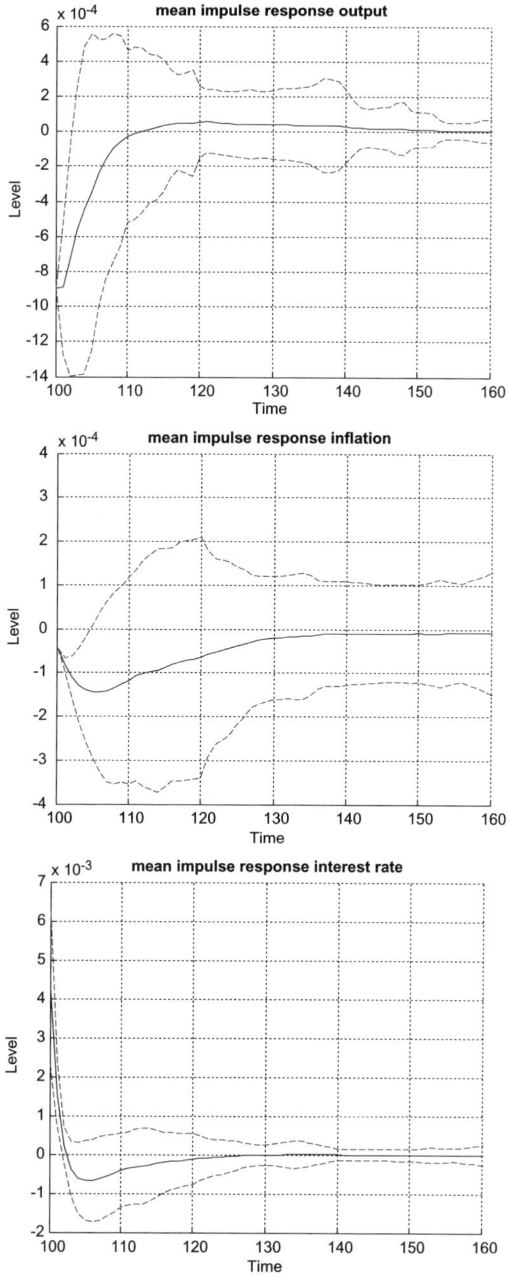

Figure 7. Mean impulse responses to an interest rate shock in the extended behavioral model.

there is more inertia in inflation adjustment than in output adjustment after a shock is routinely found in VAR estimates of interest rate surprises. The inertia generated by the model finds its origin in the evolutionary process inherent in the fitness criterion guiding the selection of forecasting rules.[5]

3.6. *A Further Extension: A Three Agent Model*

The heuristics used in the forecasting of the output gap assumes that agents are biased either in the positive or in the negative sense. It does not allow for the possibility that agents may (even by chance) use an unbiased rule. In this section we analyze the question of how the model is affected if we allow for a third, unbiased, forecasting rule. We implement this idea by defining a third forecasting rule to be

$$\tilde{E}_t^{un} y_{t+1} = 0 \tag{22}$$

where $\tilde{E}_t^{un} y_{t+1}$ is the unbiased forecasting rule.

We now assume as before a switching rule, whereby agents can switch between the three rules. This implies first that agents compute the performance (utility) of using these rules as in Eqs. (9) and (10) for the optimistic and pessimistic rules. For the unbiased rule this becomes

$$U_{un,t} = -\sum_{k=1}^{\infty} \omega_k [y_{t-k} - \tilde{E}_{un,t-k-1} y_{t-k}]^2 \tag{23}$$

The corresponding probabilities of using the three rules now become:

$$\alpha_{opt,t} = \frac{\exp(\gamma U_{opt,t})}{\exp(\gamma U_{opt,t}) + \exp(\gamma U_{pes,t}) + \exp(\gamma U_{un,t})} \tag{24}$$

$$\alpha_{pes,t} = \frac{\exp(\gamma U_{pes,t})}{\exp(\gamma U_{opt,t}) + \exp(\gamma U_{pes,t}) + \exp(\gamma U_{un,t})} \tag{25}$$

$$\alpha_{un,t} = \frac{\exp(\gamma U_{un,t})}{\exp(\gamma U_{opt,t}) + \exp(\gamma U_{pes,t}) + \exp(\gamma U_{un,t})} \tag{26}$$

[5] A similar result was obtained by Anagastopoulos *et al.* (2006).

We simulated the model in the time domain using the same calibration as in Sections 3.4 and 3.5 (the extended behavioral model). We show the results in Figure 8. The top panel shows the output gap in the time domain; the middle panel shows the fractions (probabilities) of the agents using the optimistic forecasting rule; and the bottom panel shows the fractions using the unbiased rule. (Note that the pessimistic fractions are equal to 1 minus the previous two fractions).

We obtain rather interesting results. We find that the existence of unbiased predictors does not eliminate the occurrence of waves of optimism and pessimism. As one can see from the bottom half of Figure 8, there are regularly periods during which the market is dominated by optimism, despite the fact that there are agents that use the unbiased forecasts. Similarly, there are periods where the market is dominated by pessimistic forecasts. These waves of optimism then affect output in a self-fulfilling way. Note also that the unbiased rules do not vary much and fluctuate around 1/3 of the market. As a result, they have only a limited impact on the movements of the output gap.

In order to find out how important animal spirits are in shaping fluctuations in the output gap we correlated the simulated output gap with the fraction of optimists in the market. We did this both for the three-agent model and for the two-agent model of the previous sections. We find an average correlation coefficient of 0.83 in the three-agent model and one of 0.86 in the two-agent model. This means that the addition of a third unbiased rule does not reduce the correlation of the output gap and the "animal spirits" in a significant way. Thus, our main results that waves of optimism and pessimism (animal spirits) can emerge, is maintained even in a world where agents have access to unbiased forecasts.

4. Trade-Offs Between Inflation and Output Variability

The business of central banks is to make choices which arise from the existence of trade-offs. We analyze these trade-offs both in the

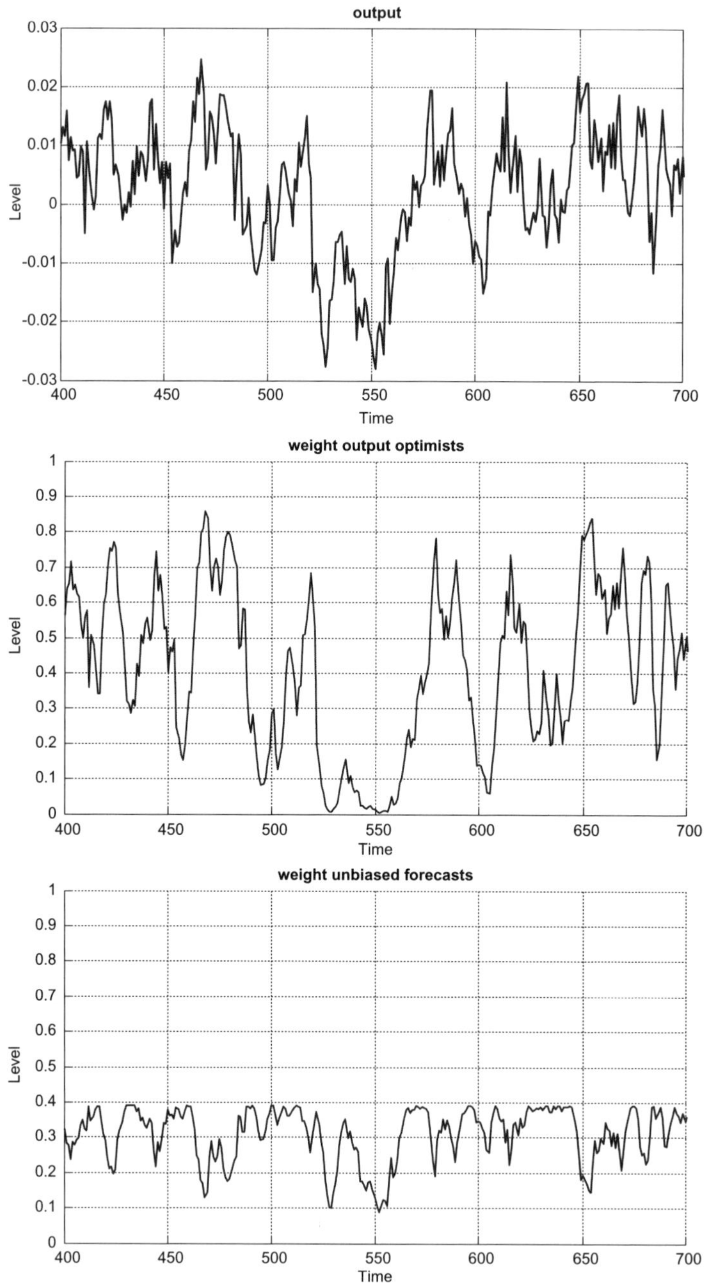

Figure 8. Output gap and animal spirits in a three-agent model.

Behavioral model

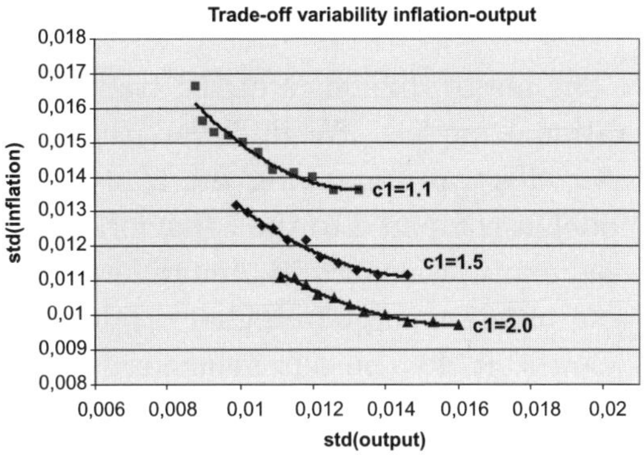

Rational model

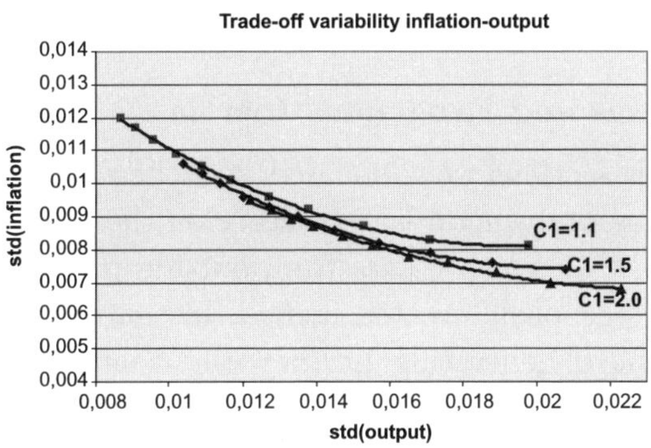

Figure 9. Trade-offs between inflation and output variability.

behavioral and the rational expectations models. We return to the two-agent model used earlier.

Figure 9 presents the trade-offs. These are obtained by varying the output coefficient in the Taylor rule (c_2) from 0 to 1 and computing the inflation and output variability for each of these values. These variabilities in inflation and output are set out on the vertical and horizontal axes of Figure 9. The trade-offs we obtain shows that a central bank applying more output stabilization (by increasing c_2) manages to reduce output variability at the expense of more inflation variability. We obtain this result in both the behavioral and the rational model. We also note that the trade-off improves when

c_1 increases, i.e., when the central bank reacts more forcefully to an inflation upsurge, it can achieve both lower inflation and output variability.

We observe one major difference in the trade-offs of the behavioral and the rational models. We find that the value of c_1 has a significantly lesser effect on improving the trade-off in the rational expectations model as compared to the behavioral model. Put differently, in a rational expectations world a more forceful reaction of the central bank to an inflation surge (a higher c_1) does not improve the trade-off significantly. It does in our behavioral model. The reason is that a more credible inflation targeting regime also reduces the intensity of the waves of optimism and pessimism, thereby reducing both inflation and output variability.

5. Endogenous and Exogenous Inertia

In the previous sections we contended that the rational model introduces inertia by imposing a lag structure on the transmission mechanism, the logic of which comes from outside the model. We could call this an exogenously created inertia. In contrast, the behavioral model is capable of generating inertia without introducing lags in the transmission process. This could be called endogenous inertia. We illustrate this difference by analyzing the behavioral and the rational model in the absence of lags in the transmission process in the demand and the supply equations. We achieve this by setting $a_1 = 0$ in Eq. (1) and $b_1 = 1$ in Eq. (2). We then applied the same i.i.d. shocks in both the heuristic and the rational model and computed the autocorrelation coefficients of the simulated series of output gaps and inflation. We show the results in Table 2. We observe that the behavioral model produces inertia (positive autocorrelation) in the output gap and in inflation even if there are no lags in the transmission of shocks. Our rational model produces no inertia in the output gap and in inflation.

Table 2 then shows the autocorrelation coefficients obtained in models that assume lags in the transmission. These coefficients are obtained when we set $a_1 = 0.5$ in Eq. (1) and $b_1 = 0.5$ in Eq. (2).

Table 2. Autocorrelation coefficients in output gap and inflation.

	Behavioral model	Rational model
No lags in transmission		
Output gap	0.77	0.07
Inflation	0.69	−0.02
Lags in transmission		
Output gap	0.89	0.79
Inflation	0.90	0.61
Lags in transmission and autoregressive shocks		
Output gap	0.99	0.98
Inflation	0.98	0.97

Note: The autocorrelation coefficients are the averages obtained from simulating the model 1,000 times, each time over 1,000 periods.

These are also the numerical values assumed in all the simulations reported in the previous sections. We now observe that inertia in the output gap and in inflation increases in both models.

Finally we simulate the models assuming both lags in the transmission process and an autoregressive pattern in the error terms. We assumed a first order autocorrelation of the error terms of 0.8 in both models. We now observe that the autocorrelation coefficients of output and inflation converge to the same high values in both models. From this exercise, it can be concluded that most of the inertia obtained in the rational model is the result of lags in the transmission process and autoregressive errors. This is not the case in the behavioral model that produces a significant level of endogenous inertia that is independent of the transmission process and the autoregressive nature of the shocks.

This difference between the two models is quite fundamental. In the rational model there is no uncertainty about how the shock is transmitted in the model. Thus in the absence of lags in transmission, agents immediately find the optimal levels of output and inflation. In order to produce the required inertia (and the business cycle movements), lags in transmission preventing instantaneous adjustment to the optimal plan, are necessary together with autoregressive shocks. In the behavioral model, agents do not fully understand how the shock will be transmitted. As a result they follow a procedure (heuristics together with a selection mechanism) that functions as a "trial and error" learning mechanism aimed at revealing information about shocks and the transmission process. This is a slow process that also uses backward evaluation processes. It generates an endogenous inertia (and business cycle) into the model.

The inertia obtained in our behavioral model could also be called informational inertia. In contrast to the rational expectations model, agents in the behavioral model experience an informational problem. They do not fully understand the nature of the shock, nor its transmission. They try to understand it by applying a trial and error learning rule, but they never succeed in fully understanding the complexity of the world. This cognitive problem then creates the inertia in output and prices. Thus we obtain very different theories of the business cycles in the two models.

Critics of the behavioral model presented here may argue that the comparison between the rational and the behavioral model is unfair for the rational model. For the behavioral model generates inertia because the evaluation process of the different heuristics is backward looking. This is the reason why the behavioral model does not need lags in the transmission process to generate inertia. This latter is correct. However, we claim that this evaluation process can only be backward, and as a result, the lags that are present in the behavioral model are completely within the logic of that model. This contrasts with the lags introduced in the rational model: they come from outside the logic of the model.

6. Sensitivity Analysis

In this section we analyze how sensitive the results are to different numerical values of the "learning parameters" in the model. These are the parameters describing how agents use and select forecasting rules. There are three such parameters in our model. First, there is the divergence between the optimists' and pessimists' beliefs. We will call this the divergence parameter, which we define as $2g$ (remember that g is the bias of the optimists and −g is the bias of the pessimists).

Second, there is the memory agents have when calculating the performance of their forecasting. This was represented by the parameter ω_k in Eqs. (9)–(10) and is a series of declining weights attached to past forecast errors. We define $\omega_k = (1-\rho)\rho^k$ (and $0 \leq \rho \leq 1$). The parameter ρ can be interpreted as a measure of the memory of agents. When $\rho = 0$ there is no memory, i.e., only last period's performance matters in evaluating a forecasting rule; when $\rho = 1$ there is infinite memory.

Finally, there is the parameter γ which measures the intensity with which agents are willing to switch to a better performing rule (see Eqs. (11)–(12)).

We discuss the sensitivity of the results with respect to these parameters by showing how they affect the volatility and the degree of inertia (autocorrelation) of inflation and output.

6.1. *Sensitivity to Divergence in Beliefs*

The upper panels of Figure 9 show how the volatility of output and inflation depends on the degree of divergence in beliefs in forecasting output. We observe that when divergence increases the volatility of output increases substantially. No such increase occurs with inflation which is not surprising as the divergence parameter relates to differences in beliefs about future output.

The lower panels of Figure 10 indicate that increasing divergence tends to increase inertia in output (autocorrelation), with little effect on inflation inertia.

6.2. *Sensitivity to Memory*

The memory agents use when they evaluate their past performance, plays an important role in the dynamics of the model. This is illustrated by Figure 11. The upper part shows the volatility of output and inflation for different values of the memory parameter (ρ). It is striking to find that with longer memory the volatility of these variables declines significantly. Note however that the relationship

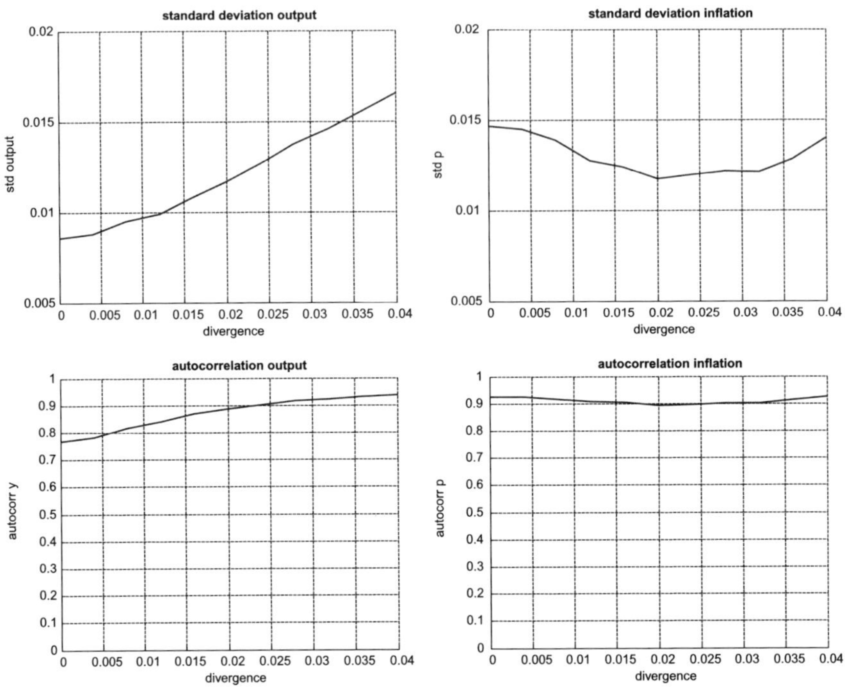

Figure 10. Standard deviation and autocorrelation of output gap and inflation.

Note: The standard deviations and autocorrelation coefficients are the averages obtained from simulating the model 1,000 times, each time over 1,000 periods.

is non-linear. One needs a large value of ρ for the volatility to start declining. In the simulations presented in the previous sections we set $\rho = 0.5$. The volatility obtained for this parameter value is very close to the volatility obtained when $\rho = 0$ (i.e., when agents have no memory and only the performance of the last period matters).

We obtain similar results with the autocorrelation coefficients of output and inflation. For low and medium values of ρ the autocorrelation coefficients are relatively constant. One needs a sufficiently large value of the memory parameter to reduce the autocorrelation coefficients significantly. We conclude that long memory tends to stabilize output and inflation and to reduce inertia in these variables.

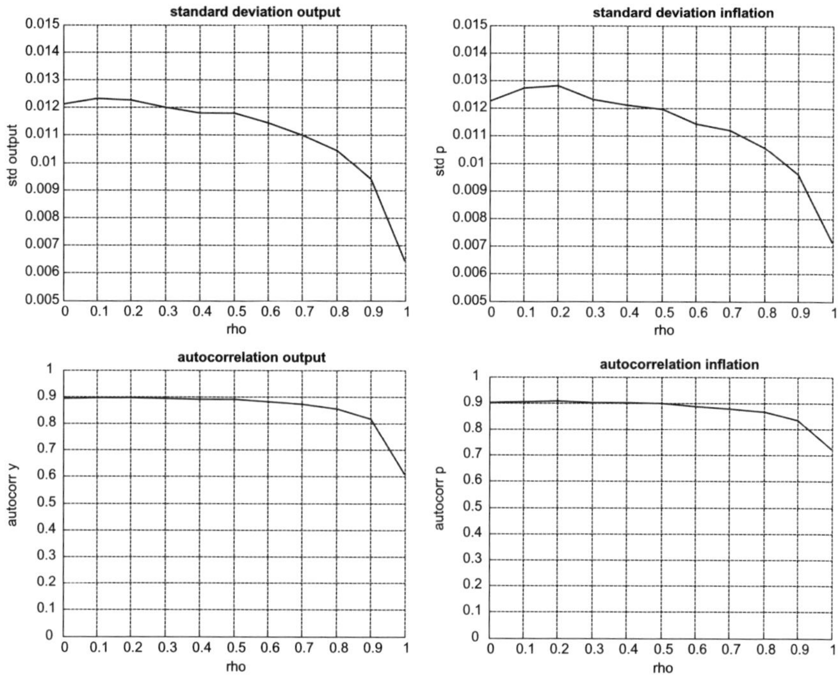

Figure 11. Standard deviation and autocorrelation of output gap and inflation.
Note: The standard deviations and autocorrelation coefficients are the averages obtained from simulating the model 1,000 times, each time over 1,000 periods.

6.3. *Sensitivity to Intensity of Choice*

The intensity of choice parameter controls the degree with which agents switch from one rule to the other when the performances of the forecasting rules change. In general, we find that, as this parameter increases, volatility and inertia tend to increase. This is illustrated in Figure 12. The upper panel shows the volatility of output and inflation as a function of the intensity of choice parameter. We observe a clear positive relation. The lower panel shows how the autocorrelation coefficients increase when intensity of choice is increased.

We conclude that as agents react more forcefully to changes in performance of their forecasting rules, the volatility of output and inflation and their inertia increases. The intuition for this result is the following. With a low intensity of choice parameter agents do

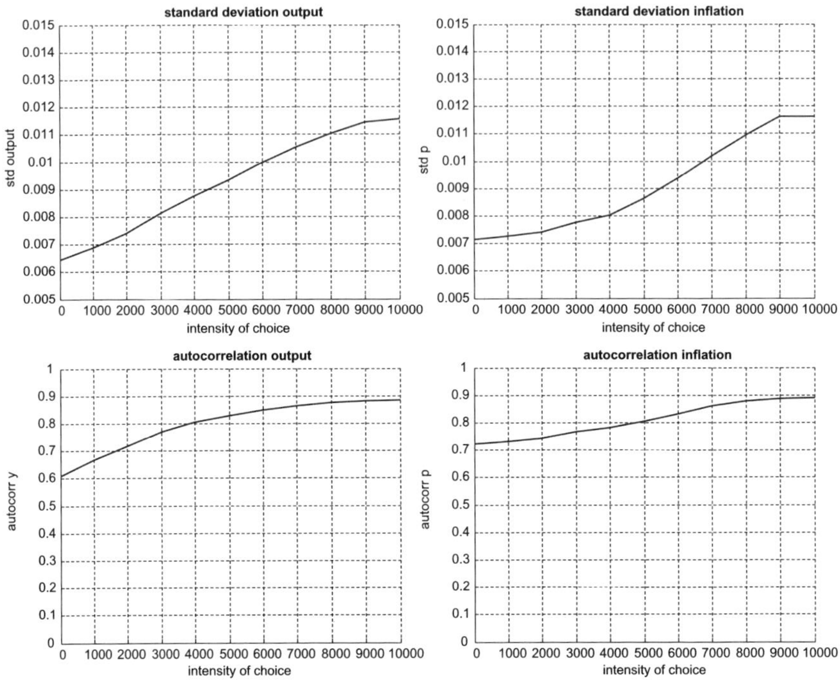

Figure 12. Standard deviation and autocorrelation of output gap and inflation.
Note: The standard deviations and autocorrelation coefficients are the averages obtained from simulating the model 1,000 times, each time over 1,000 periods.

not let their decision to switch depend much on past performance. The switching behaviour is then mostly driven by chance. Waves of optimism and pessimism cannot then come off the ground easily, leading to output changes that come close to i.i.d. changes. As the intensity of choice parameter increases in value, agents react more forcefully to performance. This sets in motion the endogenous waves of optimism and pessimism. As a result, both the volatility and the autoregressive pattern increase.

7. Conclusion

DSGE-models provide a coherent framework of analysis. This coherence is brought about by restricting the acceptable behavior of agents to dynamic utility maximization and rational expectations. These features explain the intellectual appeal of these models and their recent success in academic circles and among policymakers.

The problem of the DSGE-models (and more generally of rational expectations macroeconomic models) is that they assume extraordinary cognitive capabilities of individual agents. Recent developments in other disciplines including psychology and brain science overwhelmingly document that individual agents struggle with limited cognitive abilities, restricting their capacity to understand the world. As a result, individual agents use small bits of information and simple rules to guide their behavior.

The fact that the assumption of rational expectations is implausible does not necessarily mean that models using such an assumption cannot be powerful tools in making empirical predictions. The problem, however, is that rational expectations macroeconomic model make systematically wrong predictions, in particular about the speed with which prices adjust. This empirical failure could have led the profession of macroeconomists to drop the model and to look for another one. Instead, macroeconomists decided to stick to the rational expectations model but to load it with a series of *ad-hoc* repairs that were motivated by a desire to improve its fit. These repair operations most often involved adding lags to the models so as to create sufficient inertia in variables. These operations were successful in the sense that the fit was significantly improved. In another sense, however, they were failures because the inertia building tricks are really departures from rationality. As a result, the present DSGE-models create a dynamics the largest part of which is the result of the ad-hoc repair operations. These have nothing to do with optimizing behavior and rationality of expectations. In a way it can be said that these ad-hoc repairs introduced heuristics in the model through the back door.

We argued that if it is necessary to introduce heuristics into the model in order to make it empirically palatable, one might as well introduce these heuristics explicitly and right from the start. That is what we did in this paper. The advantage of this approach is that one can also specify explicitly what kind of heuristics is acceptable. We did this by introducing a selection mechanism guiding the use of heuristics.

The ensuing "behavioral model" produces a number of results that distinguishes it from the rational expectations models. First, the behavioral model is capable of generating endogenous cycles based on waves of optimism and pessimism. This dynamics is akin to what Keynes called animal spirits. Second, in contrast to the DSGE-models the inertia in output and prices is generated within the model, instead of being "imported." Third, the behavioral model produces a degree of uncertainty about the transmission of monetary policy shocks that is very different from the uncertainty obtained in DSGE-models. In the latter models, uncertainty about the effects of monetary policy shocks arises because of the lack of precision in the estimation of the structural parameters of the model. In the behavioral model there is an additional dimension to uncertainty. This is that the same policy shock can have very different effects depending on what we have called market conditions, i.e., the degree of optimism and pessimism agents have about the future.

The success of the DSGE-model has much to do with the story it tells about how the macroeconomy functions. This is a story in which rationality of superbly informed and identical agents reigns. Shocks from the outside occur continuously forcing these agents to re-optimize repeatedly, which they are eager to do. Unfortunately and inexplicably, the outside world imposes restrictions on this behavior creating distortions and departures from optimality. It also generates cycles in output and inflation. This in turn creates a stabilizing responsibility for the central bank.

We have questioned this story by presenting an alternative one. This is a story in which agents do not understand the model well, and use a trial and error learning strategy to discover its underlying logic. Such a model generates cycles endogenously. Thus in contrast with the DSGE-world where the shocks come from outside, in the behavioral world some shocks are generated within the model. As a result, the degree of uncertainty about how monetary policy is transmitted is of a higher order of magnitude.

There is another dimension in the difference between the two models. In his famous AER article Hayek (1945) stressed that individuals have only very small parts of the available information in their brains. No individual can ever hope to understand and to process the full complexity of the world in which he lives. That's why markets are so important. They are institutions that efficiently aggregate the diverse bits of information stored in individual brains. The socialist economists at the time in contrast assumed that there was one individual, "the planner," who understood the whole picture. By giving him all the power this all-knowing individual could compute all the relevant prices and so force the optimum on the system. Markets were not necessary in this view.

Paradoxically, the rational expectations revolution that was so much influenced by the Chicago School created a model that, like in the socialist models of the past, assumes an all-knowing individual, who can compute the optimal plans and set the optimal prices. In such a world, markets are indeed not necessary to coordinate the actions of heterogeneous individuals. The representative agent does it all in his mind. In the behavioral model presented here, we go back to the old Hayekian idea that we need markets to aggregate the information that is spread out in tiny little bits in individuals' brains. It is this aggregation process that creates macroeconomic fluctuations.

Appendix A: Parameter Values of the Calibrated Model

Behavioral model

pstar = 0;	% the central bank's inflation target
a1 = 0.5;	% coefficient of expected output in output equation
a2 = −0.2;	% a is the interest elasticity of output demand
b1 = 0.5;	% b1 is coefficient of expected inflation in inflation equation
b2 = 0.05;	% b2 is coefficient of output in inflation equation

```
c1 = 1.5;             % c1 is coefficient of inflation in Taylor
                        equation
c2 = 0.5;             % c2 is coefficient of output in Taylor equation
c3 = 0.5;             % interest smoothing parameter in Taylor
                        equation
g = 0.01;             % output forecasts optimists
gamma = 10000;        % switching parameter gamma in Brock
                        Hommes
sigma1 = 0.005;       % standard deviation shocks output
sigma2 = 0.005;       % standard deviation shocks inflation
sigma3 = 0.005;       % standard deviation shocks Taylor
rho = 0.5;            % rho measures the speed of declining weights
                        omega in mean squares errors
```

Rational model

```
pstar = 0;            % the central bank's inflation target
a1 = 0.9;             % coefficient of expected output in output
                        equation
a2 = -0.2;            % a is the interest elasticity of output demand
b1 = 0.5;             % b1 is coefficient of expected inflation in
                        inflation equation
b2 = 0.05;            % b2 is coefficient of output in inflation equation
c1 = 1.5;             % c1 is coefficient of inflation in Taylor equation
c2 = 0.5;             % c2 is coefficient of output in Taylor equation
c3 = 0.5;             % interest smoothing parameter in Taylor
                        equation
sigma1 = 0.005;       % standard deviation shocks output
sigma2 = 0.005;       % standard deviation shocks inflation
sigma3 = 0.005;       % standard deviation shocks Taylor
```

Appendix B

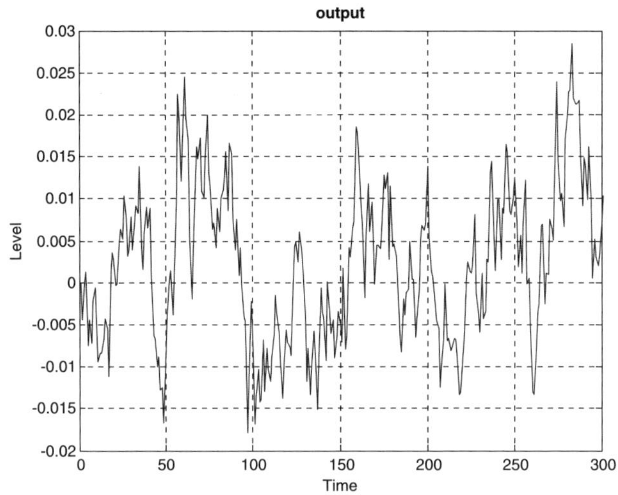
output
Level
Time
0.03
0.025
0.02
0.015
0.01
0.005
0
-0.005
-0.01
-0.015
-0.02
0
50
100
150
200
250
300

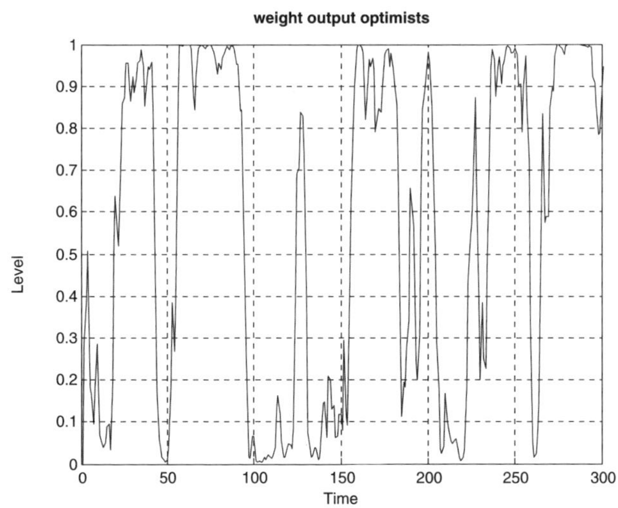
weight output optimists
Level
Time
1
0.9
0.8
0.7
0.6
0.5
0.4
0.3
0.2
0.1
0
0
50
100
150
200
250
300

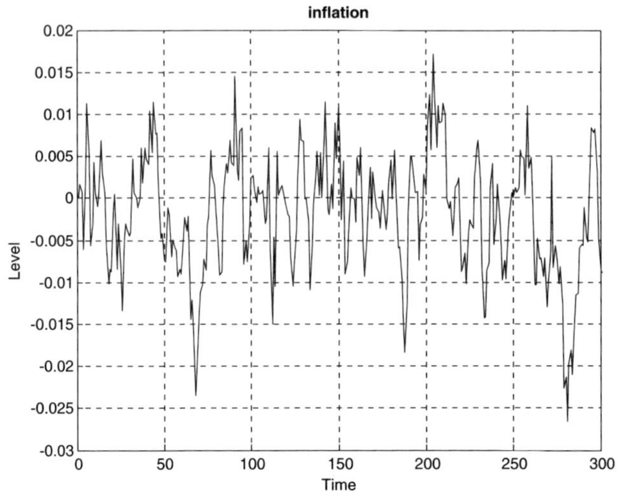

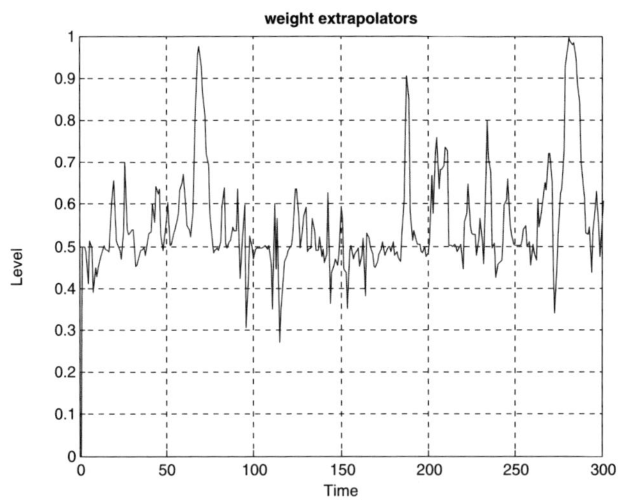

References

Anagnostopoulos, A, O Licandro, I Bove and K Schlag (2007). An evolutionary theory of inflation inertia. *Journal of the European Economic Association*, 5, 433–443.

Adjemian, S, M Darracq Pariès and S Moyen (2007). Optimal monetary policy in an estimated DSGE-model for the euro area. Working Paper No. 803, European Central Bank.

Anderson, S, A de Palma and J-F Thisse (1992). *Discrete Choice Theory of Product Differentiation.* Cambridge, MA: MIT Press.

Binder, M and MH Pesaran (1996). Multivariate rational expectations models and macroeconomic modeling: A review and some results. In *Handbook of Applied Econometrics: Macroeconomics*, MH Pesaran and M Wickens (eds.), London, UK: Blackwell.

Branch, W and G Evans (2006). Intrinsic heterogeneity in expectation formation. *Journal of Economic Theory*, 127, 264–295.

Brazier, A, R Harrison, M King and T Yates (2006). The danger of inflating expectations of macroeconomic stability: Heuristic switching in an overlapping generations monetary model. Working Paper No. 303, Bank of England.

Brock, W and C Hommes (1997). A rational route to randomness. *Econometrica*, 65, 1059–1095.

Camerer, C, G Loewenstein and D Prelec (2005). Neuroeconomics: How neuroscience can inform economics. *Journal of Economic Literature*, 63, 9–64.

Chari, V, P Kehoe and E McGrattan (2009). New Keynesian models: Not yet useful for policy analysis. *American Economic Journal: Macroeconomics*, 1, 242–266.

Christiano, L, M Eichenbaum and C Evans (2001). Nominal rigidities and the dynamic effects of a shock to monetary policy. NBER Working Paper No. 8403, July.

Christiano, L, R Motto and M Rostagno (2007). Shocks, structures or monetary policies. Working Paper No. 774, European Central Bank.

Clarida, R, J Gali and M Gertler (1999). The science of monetary policy: A new Keynesian perspective. *Journal of Economic Literature*, 37, 1661–1707.

Colander, D, P Howitt, A Kirman, A Leijonhufvud and P Mehrling (2008). Beyond DSGE-models: Toward an empirically based macroeconomics. *American Economic Review, Papers and Proceedings*, 98, 236–240.

Damasio, A (2003). *Looking for Spinoza, Joy, Sorrow and the Feeling Brain.* Orlando: Harcourt.

De Grauwe, P and M Grimaldi (2006). *The Exchange Rate in a Behavioral Finance Framework.* Princeton, NJ: Princeton University Press.

Della Vigna, S (2007). Psychology and economics: Evidence from the field. NBER Working Paper No. 13420.

De Long, J, B Bradford, A Shleifer and L Summers (1990). Noise trader risk in financial markets. *Journal of Political Economy*, 98, 703–738.

Estrella, A and J Furher (1992). Dynamic inconsistencies: Counterfactual implications of a class of rational expectations models. *American Economic Review*, 92, 1013–1028.

Evans, G and S Honkapohja (2001). *Learning and Expectations in Macroeconomic.* Princeton: Princeton University Press.

Gabaix, X, D Laibson, G Moloche and S Weinberg (2006). Costly information acquisition: Experimental analysis of a boundedly rational model. *American Economic Review*, 96(4), 1043–1068.

Gali, J (2008). *Monetary Policy, Inflation and the Business Cycle: An Introduction to the New Keynesian Framework.* Princeton, NJ: Princeton University Press.

Gaspar, V, F Smets and D Vestin (2006). Adaptive learning, persistence and optimal monetary policy. Working Paper Series No. 644, European Central Bank.

Goodhart, C (2007). The continuing muddles of monetary theory: A steadfast refusal to face facts. Mimeo: Financial Markets Group, London School of Economics.

Hayek, FA (1945). The use of knowledge in society. *American Economic Review*, 35, 519–530.

Kahneman, D and A Tversky (1973). Prospect theory: An analysis of decisions under risk. *Econometrica*, 47, 313–327.

Kahneman, D and A Tversky (2000). *Choices, Values and Frames.* Cambridge, UK: Cambridge University Press.

Kahneman, D (2002). Maps of bounded rationality: A perspective on intuitive judgment and choice. Nobel Prize Lecture, December 8, Stockholm.

Kahneman, D and R Thaler (2006). Utility maximization and experienced utility. *Journal of Economic Perspectives*, 20, 221–234.

Kirchgässner, G (2008). *Homo Oeconomicus: The Economic Model of Behaviour and Its Applications to Economics and Other Social Sciences.* New York, NJ: Springer.

Mackowiak, B and M Wiederholt (2005). Optimal sticky prices under rational inattention. Discussion Paper, Humboldt University, Berlin.

Milani, F (2007). Learning and time-varying macroeconomic volatility. Mimeo, Irvine: University of California.

Nelson, E (1998). Sluggish inflation and optimizing models of the business cycle. *Journal of Monetary Economics*, 42, 303–322.

Orphanides, A and J Williams (2004). Robust monetary policy with imperfect information. Board of Governors of the Federal Reserve System.

Sargent, T (1993). *Bounded Rationality in Macroeconomics.* Oxford, UK: Oxford University Press.

Sims, C (2005). Rational inattention: A research agenda. Discussion Paper No. 34/2005, Deutsche Bundesbank.

Smets, F and R Wouters (2003). An estimated dynamic stochastic general equilibrium model. *Journal of the European Economic Association*, 1, 1123–1175.

Smets, F and R Wouters (2007). Shocks and frictions in US business cycles. Working Paper No. 722, European Central Bank.

Stanovich, K and R West (2000). Individual differences in reasoning: Implications for the rationality debate. *Behavioral and Brain Sciences*, 23, 645–665.

Thaler, R (1994). *Quasi Rational Economics.* New York, NY: Russell Sage Foundation.

Tversky, A and D Kahneman (1981). The framing of decisions and the psychology of choice. *Science*, 211, 453–458.

Walsh, C (2003). *Monetary Theory and Policy.* Cambridge, MA: MIT Press.

Woodford, M (2003). *Interest and Prices: Foundations of a Theory of Monetary Policy.* Princeton, NY: Princeton University Press.

Chapter 18

Animal Spirits and Monetary Policy

Paul De Grauwe

I develop a behavioral macroeconomic model in which agents have cognitive limitations. As a result, they use simple but biased rules (heuristics) to forecast future output and inflation. Although the rules are biased, agents learn from their mistakes in an adaptive way. This model produces endogenous waves of optimism and pessimism ("animal spirits") that are generated by the correlation of biased beliefs. I identify the conditions under which animal spirits arise. I contrast the dynamics of this model with a stylized DSGE-version of the model and I study the implications for monetary policies. I find that strict inflation targeting is suboptimal because it gives more scope for waves of optimism and pessimism to emerge thereby destabilizing output and inflation.

1. Introduction

The idea that "animal spirits" drive the business cycle has been at the core of the macroeconomic dynamics described by Keynes. These

---

Published in *Economic Theory*, 47, 423–457, 2010.
This research was supported by a grant of the European Commission (POHLIA). I am grateful to Yunus Aksoy, Tony Atkinson, Stephan Fahr, Daniel Gros, Richard Harrison, Romain Houssa, Pablo Rovira Kaltwasser, Christian Keuschnigg, Alan Kirman, Giovanni Lombardo, Lars Ljungqvist, Patrick Minford, John Muellbauer, Ilbas Pelin, Frank Smets, Leopold von Thadden, David Vines, and Tony Yates for their comments and suggestions on previous versions of this paper. I am also indebted to an anonymous referee whose comments and suggestions have led to significant improvements.
Keywords: Animal spirits; heuristics; behavioral macroeconomics; rational expectations.
JEL classification: E10, E32, D83.

"animal spirits" are defined as waves of optimism and pessimism gripping investors and consumers, and by having self-fulfilling properties, influencing output and investment. Although elusive as a concept, it has maintained a great popularity in analyses of the business cycle outside academia.

As a result of the systematic incorporation of rational expectations in macroeconomic models, the concept of "animal spirits" plays almost no role in mainstream macroeconomic theory. In the currently fashionable DSGE models that incorporate the rational expectations hypothesis together with a new Keynesian framework of wage and price rigidities, there is no room for waves of optimism and pessimism to exert an independent influence on economic activity. In these models, all fluctuations in investment and output are the result of exogenous shocks in preferences, endowments and technologies that are slowly transmitted into the economy. This combination of exogenous shocks and slow transmission (inertia) creates cyclical movements in these models. In this sense, the cyclical movements in output and prices in DSGE-models are created exogenously.

There have been serious attempts to incorporate the notion of "animal spirits" in dynamic general equilibrium models. This literature started with Azariadis (1981) and was further extended by Farmer and Guo (1994), and Benhabib and Farmer (1994). These authors aim at developing rigorous models of the business cycle in which expectations are rational and aggregate fluctuations are driven by animal spirits. Typically these models produce multiple equilibria (sunspots). Together with random shocks they are capable of generating endogenous business cycles. It must be admitted though that these models have not become a part of mainstream macroeconomic thinking.

In this paper, an alternative approach to modeling animal spirits is presented. This is done because the notions of "animal spirits" and rational expectations do not mix well. The assumption of rational expectations implies that agents understand the underlying model structure and the distribution of the shocks. It also means that agents use the same information set, and can, therefore, be represented by one individual, the representative agent, who understands the "truth." In such a framework, it is difficult to see how agents could be gripped by collective waves of optimism and pessimism.

The notion of animal spirits as understood in this paper is based on the fact that individuals do not understand the "truth." Individuals only understand small parts of the total information set, and they are not capable of describing the statistical distribution of economic shocks. The cognitive limitations of individuals have now been abundantly documented by psychologists and brain scientists (For recent surveys, see Kahneman and Thaler, 2006; Della Vigna, 2007; Thaler, 1994; Clarida *et al.*, 1999). As a result of these cognitive limitations, there is also heterogeneity in the use of information (see also the classic analysis of Hayek, 1945).

It is now also generally recognized that the cognitive limitations of individuals in understanding and processing information leads them to use simple rules ("heuristics") to guide their behavior (see Gaspar *et al.*, 2006). They do this not because they are irrational, but rather because the complexity of the world is overwhelming. In a way it can be said that using heuristics is a rational response of agents who are aware of their limited capacity to understand the world. Because agents have limited cognitive abilities, these rules will also typically be biased. The challenge when we try to model such heuristics is twofold. First, we have to introduce discipline in the selection of rules so as to avoid that "everything becomes possible." We will achieve this discipline by subjecting the selection of rules to a "fitness" criterion. Second, we want to use a selection mechanism that allows agents to learn from their mistakes (their biases). We will use a "trial and error" (adaptive) learning mechanism to achieve this. Thus our concept of rationality is one in which agents are aware of the fact that their beliefs are biased but are willing to learn from the mistakes these biases produce.

The modeling approach presented in this paper is not the only possible one to model agents' behavior under bounded rationality. In fact, a large literature has emerged attempting to introduce bounded rationality into macroeconomic models. These attempts have been based mainly on the statistical learning approach pioneered by Sargent (1993) and Evans and Honkapohja (2001). This literature leads to important new insights (see e.g., Gaspar *et al.*, 2006; Orphanides and Williams, 2005; Milani, 2007a; Branch and Evans, 2009). However, we feel that this approach still loads individual agents with too many cognitive skills that they probably do not posses in the real world.[1]

A similar criticism can be leveled against another approach at modeling imperfect information which is based on the notion of "rational inattention" (see Mackowiak and Wiederholt, 2005; Sims, 2005; Ball *et al.*, 2005). In these models, the processing of information is costly. As a result, the use of new information is slowed down, leading to inertia in prices. After the passage of time, however, agents are able to use all available information, so that they then have conventional rational expectations. Imperfect information, in our model, is different in nature. Agents never acquire the cognitive skills to understand the full complexity of the underlying model. The heuristics agents use and the switching process between different heuristics is a learning process by which these agents try to understand the world, the complexity of which, however, they never fully grasp. This view contrasts with both the "rational inattention" and the "statistical learning" literatures which are fundamentally optimistic about the capacity of individuals to find out the ultimate "truth." Ours is a less optimistic view, although agents never stop trying to understand.

Our approach is also not the first attempt to introduce heuristics into macroeconomic models. Recently, Brazier *et al.* (2008) have done so in the context of an overlapping generations model. Branch and Evans (2006) have developed models in which agents must choose between misspecified models. Thus, although agents may have full information, for a variety of reasons, such as concerns about degrees of freedom, they may be fitting overly parsimonious models (see also Anufriev *et al.*, 2009). Kurz (1994) and Kurz and Motolose (2007) use models in which agents develop "rational beliefs." In addition, there is a large literature of behavioral finance models that now incorporate the view that agents are limited in their cognitive skills and

[1]See the fascinating book of Gigerenzer and Todd (1999) on the use of simple heuristics as compared to statistical (regression) learning.

use heuristics to guide their behavior and forecasting (see Kirman, 1993; Brock and Hommes, 1997; Lux and Marchesi, 2000; De Grauwe and Grimaldi, 2006).

In this paper, a parsimonious model capable of generating endogenous and self-fulfilling waves of optimism and pessimism (animal spirits) in an otherwise standard setup is developed. Parsimony makes it possible to find out what the simplest possible model is needed to generate such cycles. As will become clear extremely simple rules are capable of generating a very complex dynamics.

2. A Behavioral Macroeconomic Model

In this the modeling strategy is described. This is done by presenting a standard aggregate–demand–aggregate supply model augmented with a Taylor rule. The novel feature of the model is that agents use simple rules, heuristics, to forecast the future. These rules are subjected to an adaptive learning mechanism, i.e., agents endogenously select the forecasting rules that have delivered the highest performance ("fitness") in the past. This selection mechanism acts as a disciplining device on the kind of rules that are acceptable. Since agents use different heuristics one obtains heterogeneity. This, as will be shown, creates endogenous business cycles.

This behavioral model is contrasted with a similar model that incorporates rational expectations, and that is interpreted as a stylized version of DSGE-models. This comparison will make it possible to focus on some crucial differences in the transmission of shocks, in particular of monetary policy shocks.

2.1. *The Model*

The model consists of an aggregate demand equation, an aggregate supply equation and a Taylor rule.

The aggregate demand equation is specified in the standard way, i.e.,

$$y_t = a_1 \tilde{E}_t y_{t+1} + (1 - a_1) y_{t-1} + a_2 (r_t - \tilde{E}_t \pi_{t+1}) + \varepsilon_t \tag{1}$$

where $0 \leq a_1 \leq 1$, $a_2 < 0$, y_t is the output gap in period t, r_t is the nominal interest rate, π_t is the rate of inflation, and ε_t is a white noise disturbance term. $\tilde{E}_t$ is the expectations operator where the tilde above E refers to expectations that are not formed rationally. This process will be specified subsequently. I follow the procedure introduced in DSGE-models of adding a lagged output in the demand equation. This is usually justified by invoking habit formation. I keep this assumption here as I want to compare the behavioral model with the DSGE-rational expectations model. However, I will show in Section 3 that I do not really need this inertia-building device to generate inertia in the endogenous variables.

The aggregate supply equation can be derived from profit maximization of individual producers. As in DSGE-models a Calvo pricing rule and some indexation rule used in adjusting prices is assumed. This leads to a lagged inflation variable in the equation.[2] The supply curve can also be interpreted as a New Keynesian Philips curve:

$$\pi_t = b_1 \tilde{E}_t \pi_{t+1} + (1 - b_1)\pi_{t-1} + b_2 y_t + \eta_t \tag{2}$$

where $0 \leq b_1 \leq 1$ and $b_2 > 0$.

Finally, the Taylor rule describes the behavior of the central bank

$$r_t = c_1(\pi_t - \pi^*) + c_2 y_t + c_3 r_{t-1} + u_t \tag{3}$$

where $c_1, c_2 > 0$, $0 \leq C_3 \leq 1$ and π^* is the inflation target which for the sake of convenience will be set equal to 0. Note that, as is commonly done, the central bank is assumed to smooth the interest rate. This smoothing behavior is represented by the lagged interest rate in Eq. (3). Ideally, the Taylor rule should be formulated using a forward looking inflation variable, i.e., central banks set the interest rate on the basis of their forecasts about the rate of inflation. This was not done here in order to maintain simplicity in the model.

[2]It is now standard in DSGE-models to use a pricing equation in which marginal costs enter on the right hand side. Such an equation is derived from profit maximisation in a world of imperfect competition. It can be shown that under certain conditions the aggregate supply Eq. (2) is equivalent to such a pricing equation (see Galí, 2008; Smets and Wouters, 2003).

Agents are assumed to use simple rules (heuristics) to forecast the future output and inflation. The way I proceed is as follows. I start with a very simple heuristics for forecasting and apply it to the forecasting rules of future output. Because agents do not fully understand how the output gap is determined, their forecasts are assumed to be biased. Some agents are optimistic and systematically bias the output gap upwards, others are pessimistic and systematically bias the output gap downwards.

$$\text{The optimists are defined by } \tilde{E}_t^{\text{opt}} y_{t+1} = g_t \tag{4}$$

$$\text{The pessimists are defined by } \tilde{E}_t^{\text{pes}} y_{t+1} = -g_t \tag{5}$$

where $g_t > 0$ expresses the degree of bias in estimating the output gap. The expression $d_t = 2g_t$ can be interpreted as the divergence in beliefs among agents about the output gap. This divergence in beliefs is assumed to be a function of the volatility of the output gap. Thus

$$d_t = \beta + \delta\sigma(y_t) \tag{6}$$

where $\beta \geq 0$, $\delta \geq 0$ and $\sigma(y_t)$ is the unconditional standard deviation of the output gap (computed over a fixed window of past observations[3]). The logic is that when the volatility of the output gap increases, the uncertainty surrounding the movements of the output gap increases, leading the agents' beliefs about the true output gap to diverge more. However, the special case where $\delta = 0$, i.e., the divergence in beliefs is constant and equal to β, will also be analyzed. In that case g_t in Eqs. (4) and (5) is constant and equal to $\frac{\beta}{2}$.

The forecasting rule used here may appear ad hoc. Indeed it is when one assumes that agents know the underlying model and the statistical distribution of shocks. There would then be no reason for these agents not to use that information. This is not so, however, in a world where uncertainty, i.e., non-quantifiable risk reigns. In such an uncertain world there is no scientific basis for making predictions.

[3]In the numerical implementation this window is set at 50 periods.

All that is left over is beliefs about the future. In this paper we assume the simplest possible set of beliefs, i.e., optimistic and pessimistic beliefs. Clearly, this set of beliefs can be extended (we perform such an extensions in Section 5).

The rule agents use is biased. This does not mean that the agents are "dumb" and that they do not want to learn from their errors. I will specify a learning mechanism later in this section in which these agents continuously try to correct for the bias by switching from one rule to the other.

The market forecast is obtained as a weighted average of these two forecasts, i.e.,

$$\tilde{E}_t y_{t+1} = \alpha_{\mathrm{opt},t} \tilde{E}_t^{\mathrm{opt}} y_{t+1} + \alpha_{\mathrm{pes},t} \tilde{E}_t^{\mathrm{pes}} y_{t+1} \tag{7}$$

$$\tilde{E}_t y_{t+1} = \alpha_{\mathrm{opt},t} g_t - \alpha_{\mathrm{pes},t} g_t \tag{8}$$

and

$$\alpha_{\mathrm{opt},t} + \alpha_{\mathrm{pes},t} = 1 \tag{9}$$

where $\alpha_{\mathrm{opt},t}$ and $\alpha_{\mathrm{pes},t}$ are the probabilities that agents use an optimistic, respectively, a pessimistic rule. As will be made clear later, this market forecast will turn out to be unbiased on average.

A methodological issue arises here. The forecasting rules (heuristics) introduced here are not derived at the micro level and then aggregated. Instead, they are imposed ex post, on the demand and supply equations. This has also been the approach in the learning literature pioneered by Evans and Honkapohja (2001). Ideally one would like to derive the heuristics from the micro-level in an environment in which agents experience cognitive problems. Our knowledge about how to model this behavior at the micro level[4] and how to aggregate it is too sketchy, however, and I have not tried to do so.

[4]Psychologists and brains scientists struggle to understand how our brain processes information. There is as yet no generally accepted model we could use to model the micro-foundations of information processing.

As indicated earlier, agents are rational in the sense that they continuously evaluate their forecast performance. I apply notions of discrete choice theory (see Anderson *et al.*, 1992; Brock and Hommes, 1997) in specifying the procedure agents follow in this evaluation process. Discrete choice theory analyzes how agents decide between different alternatives. The theory takes the view that agents are boundedly rational, i.e., utility has a deterministic component and a random component. Agents compute the forecast performance of the different heuristics as follows:

$$U_{\text{opt},t} = -\sum_{k=1}^{\infty} \omega_k [y_{t-k} - \tilde{E}_{\text{opt},t-k-1} y_{t-k}]^2 \tag{10}$$

$$U_{\text{pes},t} = -\sum_{k=1}^{\infty} \omega_k [y_{t-k} - \tilde{E}_{\text{pes},t-k-1} y_{t-k}]^2 \tag{11}$$

where $U_{\text{opt},t}$ and $U_{\text{pes},t}$ are the forecast performances (utilities) of the optimists and pessimists, respectively. These are defined as the mean squared forecasting errors (MSFEs) of the optimistic and pessimistic forecasting rules; ω_k are geometrically declining weights.

Applying discrete choice theory the probability that an agent will use the optimistic forecasting rule is given by the expression (Anderson *et al.*, 1992; Brock and Hommes, 1997):

$$\alpha_{\text{opt},t} = \frac{\exp(\gamma U_{\text{opt},t})}{\exp(\gamma U_{\text{opt},t}) + \exp(\gamma U_{\text{pes},t})} \tag{12}$$

Similarly the probability that an agent will use the pessimistic forecasting rule is given by:

$$\alpha_{\text{pes},t} = \frac{\exp(\gamma U_{\text{pes},t})}{\exp(\gamma U_{\text{opt},t}) + \exp(\gamma U_{\text{pes},t})} = 1 - \alpha_{\text{opt},t} \tag{13}$$

Equation (12) says that as the past forecast performance of the optimists improves relative to that of the pessimists agents are more likely to select the optimistic belief about the output gap for their future forecasts. As a result the fraction of agents using the optimistic rule increases. Equation (13) has a similar interpretation. The parameter γ measures the "intensity of choice." It parameterizes the extent to which the deterministic component of utility determines actual choice. When $\gamma = 0$, utility is purely stochastic. In that case agents decide to be optimist or pessimist by tossing a coin and the probability to be optimist (or pessimist) is exactly 0.5. When $\gamma = \infty$, utility is fully deterministic and the probability of using an optimistic rule is either 1 or 0. The parameter γ can also be interpreted as expressing a willingness to learn from past performance. When $\gamma = 0$ this willingness is zero; it increases with the size of γ.

Note that this selection mechanism is the disciplining device introduced in this model on the kind of rules of behavior that are acceptable. Rules that perform better (are fitter) are used more; those that perform less well are used less.[5] In contrast with the disciplining device implicit in rational expectations models which implies that agents have superior cognitive capacities, we do not have to make such an assumption here.

It should also be stressed that although individuals use biased rules in forecasting the future, this does not mean that they fail to learn. In fact the fitness criterion used should be interpreted as a learning mechanism based on "trial and error." When observing that the rule they use performs less well than the alternative rule, agents are willing to switch to the more performing rule. Put differently, the rules may be biased, but agents reduce this bias by constantly being willing to learn from past mistakes and to change their behavior.

Agents also make forecasts of inflation in this model. At this stage of the analysis I will simply assume that all agents perceive the central bank's announced inflation target π^* to be fully credible. They use this value as their forecast of future inflation, i.e., $\tilde{E}_t\pi_{t+1} = \pi^*$ (where for the sake of simplicity we assume the inflation target to be equal to 0). I will extend this simple inflation forecasting process in a later section when I will also assume that there is heterogeneity

[5]The rule used here contrasts with replicator dynamics, in which poorly performing rules are gradually weeded out. For a paper that compares the two dynamics, see Branch and McGough (2008).

of beliefs in the inflation forecasting process. I keep homogeneity of beliefs here to focus on the impact of heterogeneity in the forecasting of future output gaps.

The solution of the model is found by first substituting Eq. (3) into Eq. (1) and rewriting in matrix notation. This yields:

$$\begin{bmatrix} 1 & -b_2 \\ -a_2c_1 & 1-a_2c_2 \end{bmatrix} \begin{bmatrix} \pi_t \\ y_t \end{bmatrix} = \begin{bmatrix} b_1 & 0 \\ -a_2 & a_1 \end{bmatrix} \begin{bmatrix} \tilde{E}_t\pi_{t+1} \\ \tilde{E}_t y_{t+1} \end{bmatrix} + \begin{bmatrix} 1-b_1 & 0 \\ 0 & 1-a_1 \end{bmatrix} \begin{bmatrix} \pi_{t-1} \\ y_{t-1} \end{bmatrix} + \begin{bmatrix} 0 \\ a_2c_3 \end{bmatrix} r_{t-1} + \begin{bmatrix} \eta_t \\ a_2u_t + \varepsilon_t \end{bmatrix}$$

or

$$\boldsymbol{AZ}_t = \boldsymbol{B\tilde{E}}_t\boldsymbol{Z}_{t+1} + \boldsymbol{CZ}_{t-1} + \boldsymbol{br}_{t-1} + \boldsymbol{V}_t \tag{14}$$

where bold characters refer to matrices and vectors. The solution for Z_t is given by

$$\boldsymbol{Z}_t = \boldsymbol{A}^{-1}[\boldsymbol{B\tilde{E}}_t\boldsymbol{Z}_{t+1} + \boldsymbol{CZ}_{t-1} + \boldsymbol{br}_{t-1} + \boldsymbol{V}_t] \tag{15}$$

The solution exists if the matrix A is non-singular, i.e., if $(1 - a_2c_2)a_2b_2c_1 \neq 0$ which is satisfied given the conditions imposed on the parameters in Eqs. (1)–(3). The system (15) describes the solution for y_t and π_t given the forecasts of y_{t+1} and π_{t+1}. The latter have been specified in Eqs. (4)–(13) and can be substituted into Eq. (15). Finally, the solution for r_t is found by substituting y_t and π_t obtained from Eq. (15) into Eq. (3).

My research strategy consists in comparing the dynamics of this heuristic model with the same structural model [aggregate demand Eq. (1), aggregate supply Eq. (2) and Taylor rule Eq. (3)] under rational expectations which we interpret as a stylized DSGE-model.

The model consisting of Eqs. (1)–(3) can be written in matrix notation as follows:

$$\begin{bmatrix} 1 & -b_2 & 0 \\ 0 & 1 & -a_2 \\ -c_1 & -c_2 & 1 \end{bmatrix} \begin{bmatrix} \pi_t \\ y_t \\ r_t \end{bmatrix} = \begin{bmatrix} b_1 & 0 & 0 \\ -a_2 & a_1 & 0 \\ 0 & 0 & 0 \end{bmatrix} \begin{bmatrix} E_t\pi_{t+1} \\ E_t y_{t+1} \\ E_t r_{t+1} \end{bmatrix}$$

$$+ \begin{bmatrix} 1-b_1 & 0 & 0 \\ 0 & 1-a_1 & 0 \\ 0 & 0 & a_3 \end{bmatrix}$$

$$\times \begin{bmatrix} \pi_{t-1} \\ y_{t-1} \\ r_{t-1} \end{bmatrix} + \begin{bmatrix} \eta_T \\ \varepsilon_t \\ u_t \end{bmatrix}$$

$$\boldsymbol{\Omega Z}_t = \boldsymbol{\Phi E}_t \boldsymbol{Z}_{t+1} + \boldsymbol{AZ}_{t-1} + \boldsymbol{V}_t \tag{16}$$

$$\boldsymbol{Z}_t = \boldsymbol{\Omega}^{-1}[\boldsymbol{\Phi E}_t \boldsymbol{Z}_{t+1} + \boldsymbol{AZ}_{t-1} + \boldsymbol{V}_t] \tag{17}$$

This model can be solved under rational expectations using the Binder and Pesaran (1996) procedure.

2.2. *Calibrating the Model*

I proceed by calibrating the model. In Appendix A, the parameters used in the calibration exercise are presented. The model was calibrated in such a way that the time units can be considered to be months. I find that the model is determinate under rational expectations. In Section 2.5, a sensitivity analysis of the main results to changes in the main parameters of the model is presented. The three shocks (demand shocks, supply shocks and interest rate shocks) are i.i.d. with standard deviations of 0.5 percent.

First simulations in the time domain are presented. Figure 1 shows the time pattern of output and inflation produced by the behavioral model. A strong cyclical movement in the output gap can be observed. The source of these cyclical movements is seen to be the fractions of optimists and pessimists in the market (see second panel of Figure 1). The model in fact generates endogenous waves of optimism and pessimism. During some periods pessimists dominate and

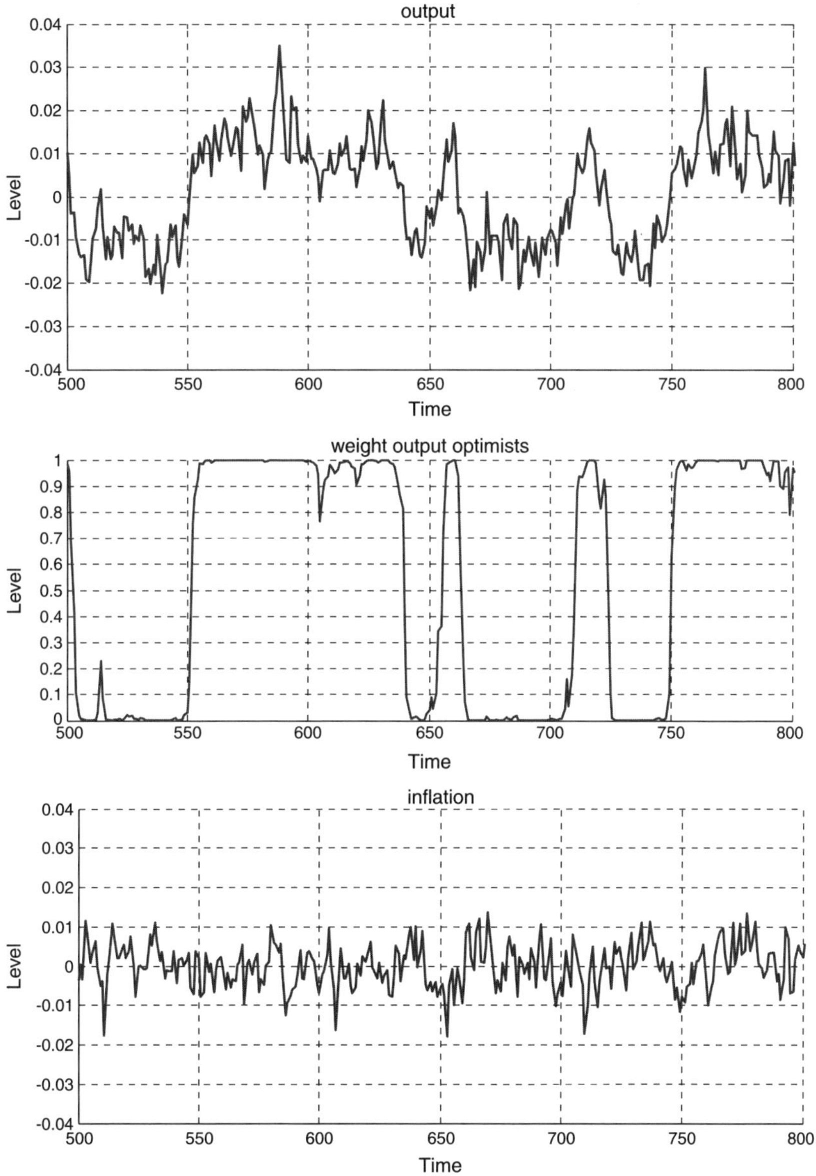

Figure 1. Output gap and inflation in behavioral model.

this translates into below average output growth. These pessimistic periods are followed by optimistic ones when optimistic forecasts tend to dominate and the growth rate of output is above average. These waves of optimism and pessimism are essentially unpredictable. Other realizations of the shocks produce different cycles with the same general characteristics.

These endogenously generated cycles in output are made possible by a partially self-fulfilling mechanism that can be described as follows. A series of random shocks creates the possibility that one of the two forecasting rules, say the optimistic one, delivers a higher payoff, i.e., a lower mean squared forecast error (MSFE). This attracts agents that were using the pessimistic rule. The "contagion-effect" leads to an increasing use of the optimistic belief to forecast the output-gap, which in turn stimulates aggregate demand. Optimism is therefore self-fulfilling. A boom is created. At some point, negative stochastic shocks and/or the reaction of the central bank through the Taylor rule make a dent in the MSFE of the optimistic forecasts. The pessimistic belief becomes attractive and therefore fashionable again. The economy turns around.

These waves of optimism and pessimism can be understood to be searching (learning) mechanisms of agents who do not fully understand the underlying model but are continuously searching for the truth. An essential characteristic of this searching mechanism is that it leads to systematic correlation in beliefs (either optimistic or pessimistic ones). This systematic correlation is at the core of the booms and busts created in the model. Note, however, that when computed over a significantly large period of time the average error in the forecasting goes to zero. In this sense, the forecast bias tends to disappear asymptotically.[6]

From Figure 1 (third panel), one observes that inflation is relatively stable and fluctuates around the target (set at 0) in a relatively narrow band. This result has everything to do with the assumption

[6]This is not an artefact arising from the symmetry assumption that the positive and negative bias are equal as implied in Eqs. (4) and (5). In a model with asymmetric beliefs the bias also disappears asymptotically because the fractions of optimists endogenously adjust to the potential bias introduced by asymmetric beliefs.

that agents are homogeneous in giving full credibility to the inflation target of the central bank. I will return to this when I introduce heterogeneity among agents in their perception of the credibility of the central bank's inflation target.

These results can be contrasted with those obtained using the model under rational expectations. I use the same structural model with the same parameter values for the aggregate demand, supply and Taylor equations. In addition, the shocks are the same with the same iid structure. The results are shown in Figure 2. (Note that with the chosen parameters the RE-model is determinate). Comparing this

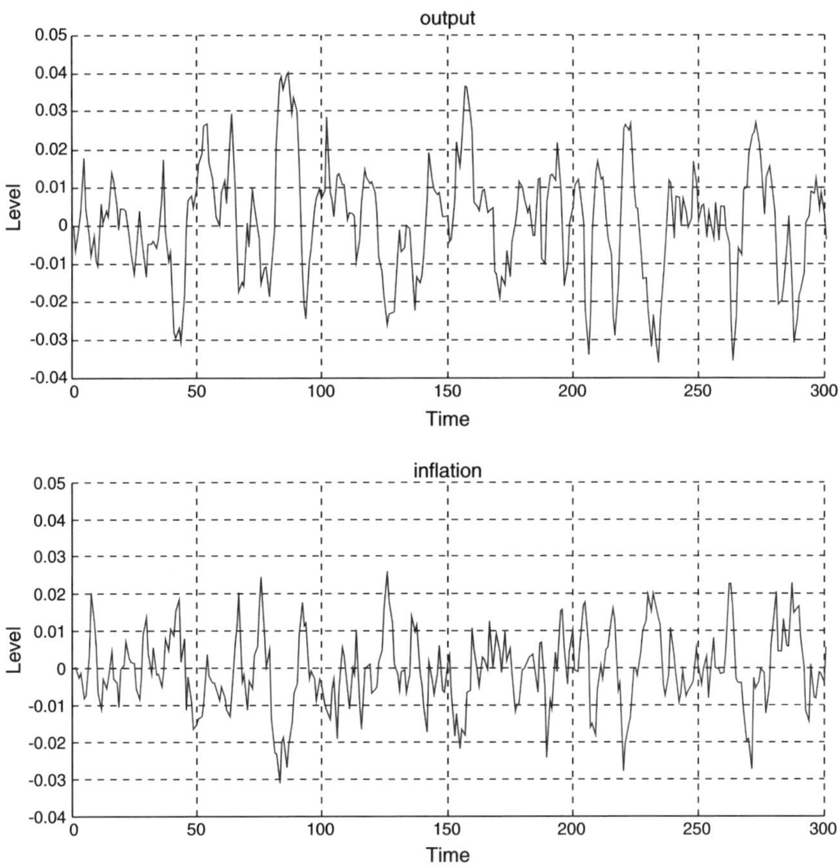

Figure 2. Output gap and inflation in the rational model.

figure with Figure 1 one observes that rational expectations model does not produce clear cyclical movements in the output gap. In a way this is not surprising: the shocks are white noise and the transmission mechanism exhibits a minimal degree of inertia. In full-fledged DSGE-models the inertia is more complex and the shocks typically exhibit autoregressive patterns that are important in producing cyclical movements in output (see Chari *et al.*, 2009 who argue that most of the movements of output and inflation in standard DSGE-models come from the shocks). Thus the results confirm that the cycles produced in the DSGE models come to a large extent from outside the model. This issue will be analyzed further in Section 3.

One could argue that the comparison of the behavioral model with the stylized version of the DSGE-model is not entirely fair. DSGE-models have been extended not only by introducing more transmission lags and autoregressive shocks but also by adding credit amplification effects that can generate booms and busts. But these can also be added to the behavioral model. The attractive feature of the behavioral model is that one does not need these additional complexities to generate business cycle movements.

2.3. *Impulse Responses in the Behavioral and the Rational Model*

The next step in the analysis is to compute the impulse responses to shocks. Here I focus on the impulse responses to an interest rate shock, defined as plus one standard deviation of the shock in the Taylor equation. Since this is a non-linear model, during the post-shock period I continue to allow for random disturbances. Thus, the impulse response measures the response to the interest rate shock in an environment in which the random disturbances are the same for the series with and without the interest rate shock.

The peculiarity of the behavioral model is that for the same parameters of the model the impulse responses are different for each realization of the stochastic shocks. This contrasts with the rational expectations model where the impulse response functions are not sensitive to the realization of the stochastic shocks (keeping the parameters unchanged). I will return to this difference and give it an interpretation.

Figure 3 shows the mean impulse responses to an interest rate shock. These were constructed by simulating the model 100 times with 100 different realizations of the shocks. The mean response together with the standard deviations were then computed. Figure 3 shows the mean response (the dotted lines are the mean response + and −2 standard deviations; note also that we introduced the shock after 150 periods[7]), exhibiting the standard result of an interest rate shock on output and inflation. However, the uncertainty surrounding this result is considerable at least in the short run.

Where does this uncertainty come from? Not from parameter uncertainty. The same parameters are used in constructing all our impulse responses. The answer is that in this behavioral model each realization of the shocks creates different waves of optimism and pessimism (animal spirits). One could also call these "market sentiments." Thus a shock that occurs in period 150 in one simulation happens in a different market sentiment than the same shock in another simulation. In addition, the shock itself affects market sentiments. As a result, the short-term effects of the same interest rate shock become very hard to predict.

Another way to interpret this result is to say that the timing of the shock is important. The same shocks applied at different times can have very different short-term effects on inflation and output. In other words, history matters. Note that the uncertainty about the impulse responses tends to disappear in the long run, as the effect of short-term differences in market sentiments disappears.

This difference in the nature of uncertainty in a behavioral and a rational expectations model has everything to do with the fact that the former has non-linear features while the latter is linear. Thus the additional uncertainty produced by the behavioral model, i.e., the dependence of the impulse response functions on the state of the economy is the outcome of its non-linearity. Rational expectations

[7]Actually the impulse response analysis is started after letting the program run 1,000 initial periods to make sure that the system has converged to its ergodic distribution.

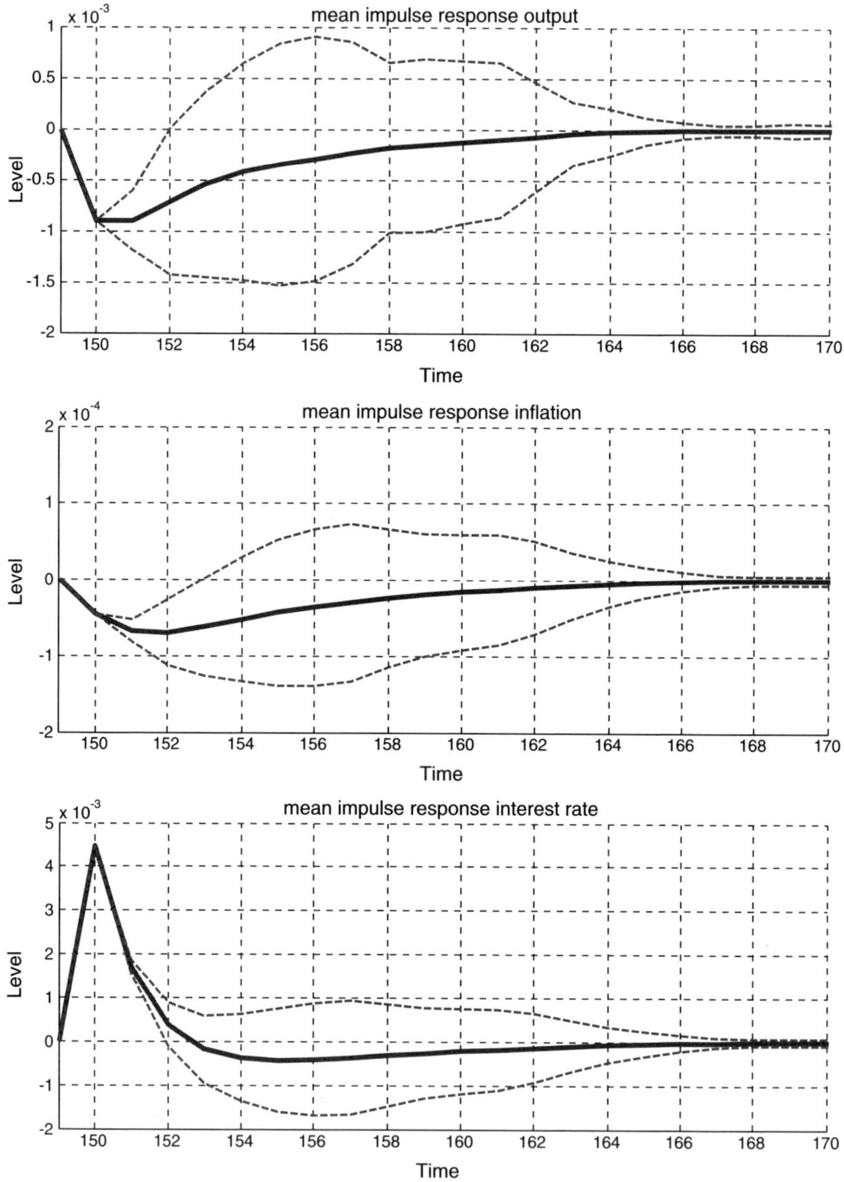

Figure 3. Mean impulse responses to interest rate shock in the behavioral model. *Dotted lines* represent the impulse responses with ±2 standard deviations.

models including the DSGE-models traditionally impose some linearization procedure. It would be valuable to extend the approach of this paper to DSGE-models that retain their nonlinear structure (See Benhabib *et al.*, 2001; Evans *et al.*, 2008).

2.4. *The Extended Behavioral Model*

In this section, the behavioral model is extended by allowing the inflation forecasters to be heterogeneous. I follow Brazier *et al.* (2008) in allowing for two inflation forecasting rules. One rule is based on the announced inflation target (as in the previous section); the other rule extrapolates inflation from the past into the future. One may argue that this is quite a different pair of heuristics than in the case of output forecasting. The difference between inflation forecasting and output forecasting is that in the former case there is a central bank that announces a particular inflation target. This target works as an anchor for the forecasts of agents. Such an anchor is absent in the case of output forecasting.

The "inflation targeters" use the central bank's inflation target to forecast future inflation, i.e.,

$$\tilde{E}_t^{\text{tar}} \pi_{t+1} = \pi^* \tag{18}$$

where as before the inflation target $\pi^* = 0$

The "extrapolators" are defined by $E_t^{\text{ext}} \pi_{t+1} = \pi_{t-1}$ (19)

The market forecast is a weighted average of these two forecasts, i.e.,

$$\tilde{E}_t \pi_{t+l} = \beta_{\text{tar},t} \tilde{E}_t^{\text{tar}} \pi_{t+l} + \beta_{\text{ext},t} \tilde{E}_t^{\text{ext}} \pi_{t+1} \tag{20}$$

or

$$\tilde{E}_t \pi_{t+1} = \beta_{\text{tar},t} \pi^* + \beta_{\text{ext},t} \pi_{t-l} \tag{21}$$

and

$$\beta_{\text{tar},t} + \beta_{\text{ext},t} = 1 \tag{22}$$

The same selection mechanism is used as in the previous section to determine the probabilities of agents trusting the inflation target and those who do not trust it and revert to extrapolation of past inflation, i.e.,

$$\beta_{\text{tar},t} = \frac{\exp(\gamma U_{\text{tar},t})}{\exp(\gamma U_{\text{tar},t}) + \exp(\gamma U_{\text{ext},t})} \tag{23}$$

$$\beta_{\text{ext},t} = \frac{\exp(\gamma U_{\text{ext},t})}{\exp(\gamma U_{\text{tar},t}) + \exp(\gamma U_{\text{ext},t})} \tag{24}$$

where $U_{\text{tar},t}$ and $U_{\text{ext},t}$ are the weighted averages of past squared forecast errors of using targeter and extrapolator rules, respectively. These are defined in the same way as in Eqs. (10) and (11).

This inflation forecasting heuristics can be interpreted as a procedure of agents to find out how credible the central bank's inflation targeting is. If this is very credible, using the announced inflation target will produce good forecasts and as a result, the probabilities that agents will rely on the inflation target will be high. If on the other hand the inflation target does not produce good forecasts (compared to a simple extrapolation rule) the probability that agents will use it will be small.

The model is calibrated using the same parameters as in the previous section. First the results in the time domain are shown and then the impulse response functions are discussed.

Figure 4a presents the results for the output gap in the time domain. The same cycles in the output gap are found as in the previous section. Again these cycles are related to the waves of optimism and pessimism in the forecasting (second panel in Figure 4a). In this particular simulation, the correlation coefficient between the fraction of optimists and the output gap is 0.86.

The results concerning the time path of inflation are shown in Figure 4b. First concentrate on the second panel of Figure 4b. This shows the fraction of agents using the extrapolator heuristics, i.e., the agents who do not trust the inflation target of the central bank. One can identify two regimes. There is a regime in which the fraction of extrapolators fluctuates around 50% which also implies that the fraction of forecasters using the inflation target as their guide (the "inflation targeters") is around 50 percent. This is sufficient to

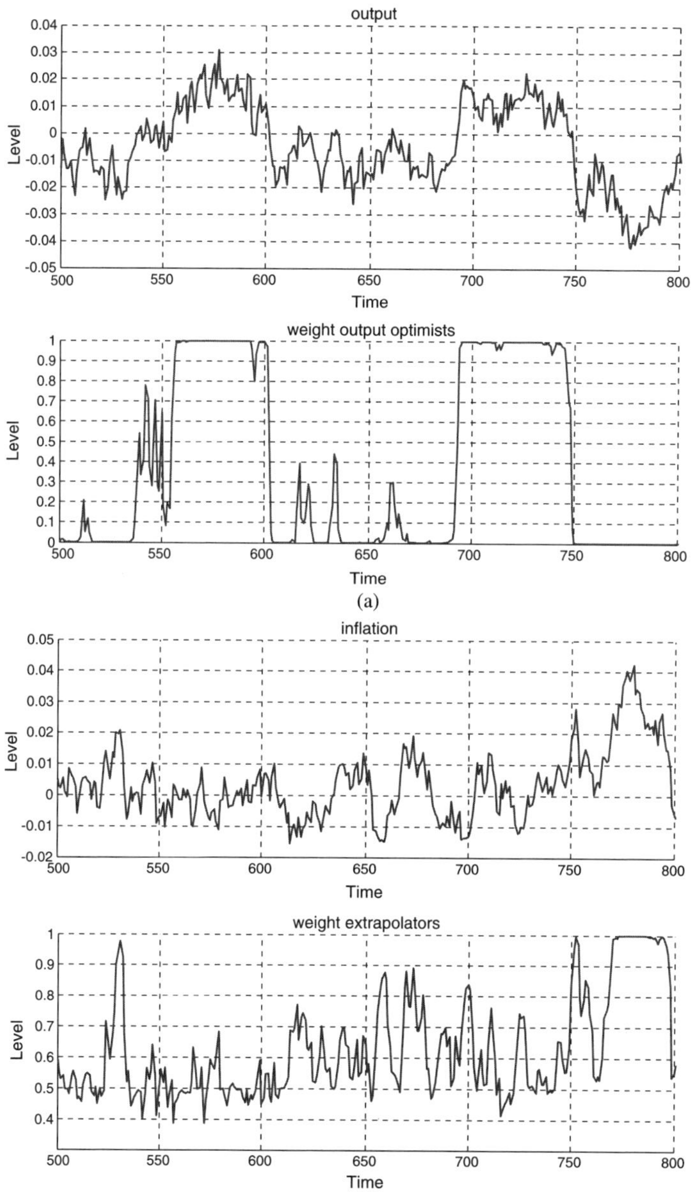

Figure 4. (a) Output gap in the extended behavioral model, (b) inflation in the extended behavioral model.

maintain the rate of inflation within a narrow band of approximately + and -1 percent around the central bank's inflation target. There is a second regime though which occurs when the extrapolators are dominant. During this regime the rate of inflation fluctuates significantly more. Thus the inflation targeting of the central bank is fragile. It can be undermined when forecasters decide that relying on past inflation movements produces better forecast performances than relying on the central bank's inflation target. This can occur quite unpredictably as a result of stochastic shocks in supply and/or demand.

How can the central bank strengthen the inflation targeting regime? This issue is taken up in Section 4 where the tradeoffs between output and inflation variability are analyzed.

2.5. *Animal Spirits, Learning and Forgetfulness*

The simulations reported in the previous section assumed a given set of numerical values of the parameters of the model. It was found that for this set of parameter values animal spirits (measured by the movements in the fraction of optimists) emerge and affect the fluctuations of the output gap. The correlation coefficient between the fraction of optimists and the output gap in the simulation reported in Figure 4 is 0.86. One would like to know how this correlation evolves when one changes the parameter values of the model. I concentrate on three parameter values here,[8] the intensity of choice parameter (γ), the sensitivity of divergence in beliefs to the volatility of the output gap (δ), and the memory agents have when calculating the performance of their forecasting. The latter is represented by the parameter ω_k in Eqs. (9)–(10) and is a series of declining weights attached to past forecast errors. I define $\omega_k = (1-\rho)\rho^k$ (and $0 \leq \rho \leq 1$). The parameter ρ can then be interpreted as a measure of the memory of agents. When $\rho = 0$ there is no memory; i.e., only last period's performance matters in evaluating a forecasting rule; when $\rho = 1$ there is infinite

[8] In appendix, I shows the results of more extensive sensitivity analyses.

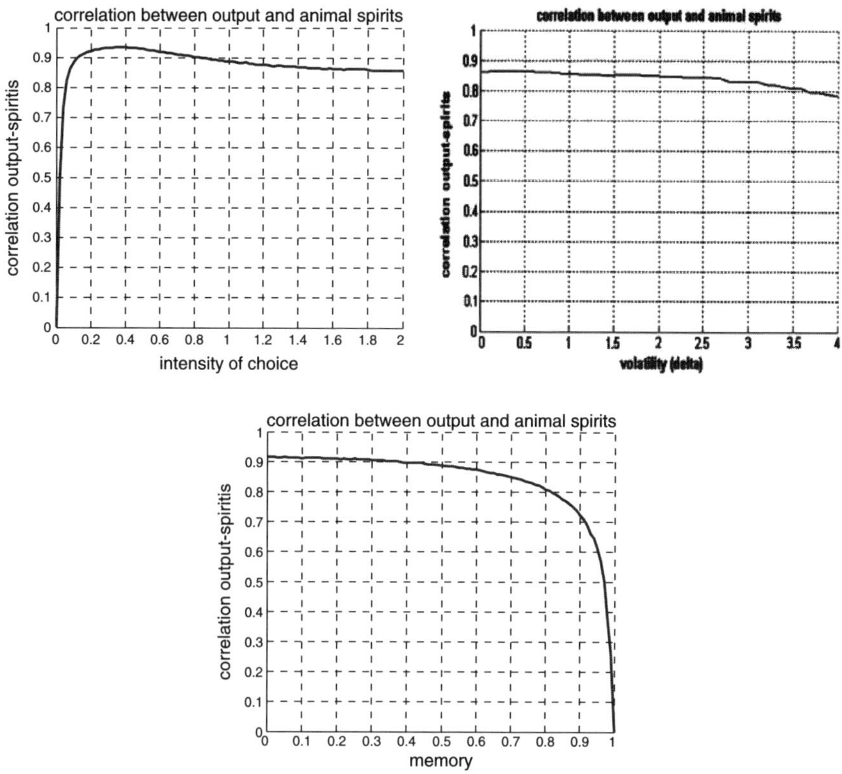

Figure 5. Correlations between output gap and fraction of optimists.

memory, i.e., all past errors, however far in the past, obtain the same weight.

The results of the sensitivity analysis are shown in Figure 5. The upper left hand panel shows the correlation between the output gap and the fraction of optimists for increasing values of the intensity of choice parameter, γ. It can be seen that when γ is zero (i.e., the switching mechanism is purely stochastic), this correlation is zero. The interpretation is that in an environment in which agents decide purely randomly, i.e., they do not react to the performance of their forecasting rule, there are no systematic waves of optimism and pessimism (animal spirits) that can influence the business cycle. When y increases, the correlation increases sharply. Thus in an environment in which agents learn from their mistakes, animal spirits arise. Thus one needs a minimum level of rationality (in the sense of a willingness to learn) for animal spirits to emerge and to influence the business cycle. It appears from Figure 5 that this is achieved with relatively low levels of γ.

The upper right panel shows the correlation between output gap and the fraction of optimists for increasing values of the parameter δ. We observe that this correlation is relatively little affected by δ. It is significant to note that when $\delta = 0$ (i.e., the divergence of beliefs is constant and unaffected by the uncertainty surrounding the movements of the output gap), the correlation is high. This means that the emergence of animal spirits does not depend on the value of δ.

The lower panel shows the correlation between the output gap and the fraction of optimists for increasing values of the memory parameter ρ. It can be seen that when $\rho = 1$ the correlation is zero. This is the case where agents attach the same weight to all past observations, however, far in the past they occur. Put differently, when agents have infinite memory; they forget nothing. In that case animal spirits do not occur. Thus, one needs some forgetfulness (which is a cognitive limitation) to produce animal spirits. Note that the degree of forgetfulness does not have to be large. For values of ρ below 0.9 the correlations between output and animal spirits are quite high.[9]

2.6. *Impulse Responses in the Extended Behavioral Model*

In this section, the impulse responses to a positive interest rate shock of one standard deviation are presented. Two results stand out (see Figure 6). First the uncertainty surrounding the effects of interest rate shocks is greater and lasts longer than in the simple behavioral model with homogenous inflation forecasting based on full

[9]The importance of the degree of forgetting is also emphasized by Branch and Evans (2006). They find that the most interesting time-series dynamics arise when the "gain" under dynamic predictor selection (their term for the degree of forgetting) is not too small.

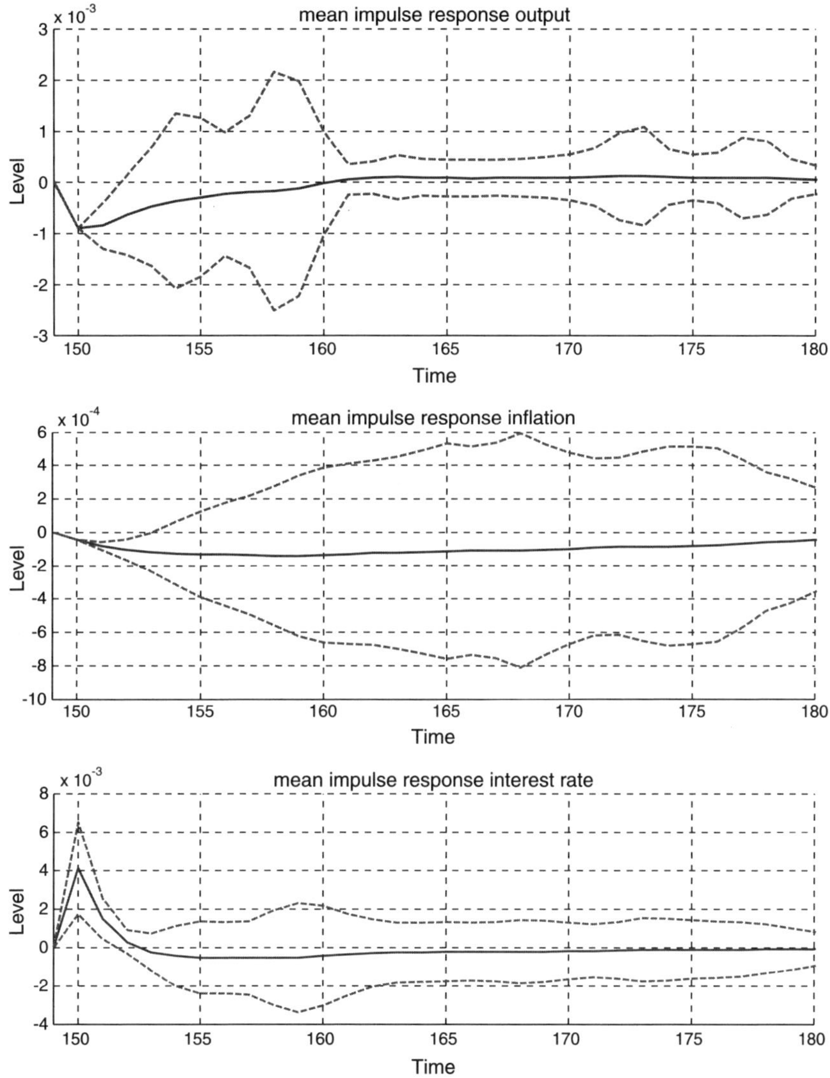

Figure 6. Mean impulse responses to an interest rate shock in the extended behavioral model.

credibility of the announced inflation target. Second, there is in this extended model considerably more inertia in inflation adjustment than in output adjustment following the interest rate shock. This feature whereby there is more inertia in inflation adjustment than in output adjustment after a shock is routinely found in VAR estimates of interest rate surprises. The inertia generated by the model finds its origin in the evolutionary process inherent in the fitness criterion guiding the selection of forecasting rules.[10]

3. Endogenous and Exogenous Inertia

Business cycle movements in the DSGE-models arise as a result of exogenous shocks (in productivity and preferences) and lags in the transmission of these shocks to output and inflation. Thus, inertia in output and inflation are the result of the lagged transmission of exogenous shocks.

One could call the inertia (and the business cycles) introduced in the DSGE-model exogenously created phenomena. In contrast, the behavioral model presented here is capable of generating inertia (and business cycles) without imposing lags in the transmission process. This could be called endogenous inertia. This difference is illustrated by analyzing the behavioral and the rational models in the absence of lags in the transmission process in the demand and the supply equations. This is achieved by setting the parameters of the forward looking variables $a_1 = 1$ in Eq. (1) and $b_1 = 1$ in Eq. (2). The same i.i.d. shocks are then applied in both the behavioral and the rational models and the autocorrelation coefficients of the simulated series of output gaps and inflation are computed. The results are shown in Table 1. It can be seen that the behavioral model produces inertia (positive autocorrelation) in the output gap and in inflation even if there are no lags in the transmission of shocks. The rational model produces no inertia in the output gap and in inflation.

Table 1 also shows the autocorrelation coefficients obtained in models that assume lags in the transmission. These coefficients are obtained when $a_1 = 0.5$ in Eq. (1) and $b_1 = 0.5$ in Eq. (2). These are also the numerical values assumed in all the simulations reported in the previous sections. One now observes that inertia in the output gap and in inflation increases in both models. However, it can be

[10] A similar result was obtained by Anagastopoulos *et al.* (2006).

Table 1. Autocorrelation coefficients in output gap and inflation.

	Behavioral model	Rational model
No lags in transmission		
Output gap	0.77	0.07
Inflation	0.69	−0.02
Lags in transmission		
Output gap	0.89	0.79
Inflation	0.90	0.61

The autocorrelation coefficients are the averages obtained from simulating the model 1,000 times, each time over 1,000 periods.

concluded that all of the inertia obtained in the rational model is the result of the lags in the transmission process. This is not the case in the behavioral model where most of the inertia is produced endogenously.

The inertia obtained in the behavioral model could also be called informational inertia. In contrast to the rational expectations model, agents in the behavioral model experience an informational problem. They do not fully understand the nature of the shock nor its transmission. They try to understand it by applying a trial and error learning rule, but they never succeed in fully understanding the complexity of the world. This cognitive problem then creates the inertia in output and prices. Thus one obtains very different theories of the business cycles in the two models.[11]

Mankiw and Reis (2002, 2006) have introduced a similar concept which they call "sticky information." In their model information inertia arises because agents find it costly to gather and make use of information. As a result, agents update their information sets

[11]Critics of the heuristic model presented here may argue that the comparison between the rational and the heuristic model is unfair for the rational model. Indeed the heuristic model generates inertia because the evaluation and selection process of the different heuristics is backward looking. This is the reason why the heuristic model does not need lags in the transmission process to generate inertia. However, it can be argued that this evaluation and selection process can only be backward looking, and as a result, the lags that are present in the heuristic model are within the logic of that model. This contrasts with the lags introduced in the rational model: they come from outside the model. See Milani (2007b) who makes a similar point contrasting rational expectations models with learning models.

infrequently. Thus, firms form expectations that are rational, given their information set, but in any given period most firms do not update their information set. This has the effect that the economy never reaches a full information rational expectations equilibrium.

4. Trade-offs between Inflation and Output Variability

In this section the tradeoff between output and inflation variability is analyzed in the context of the extended behavioral model.

The tradeoffs are constructed as follows. Figure 7 shows how output variability (Figure 7a) and inflation variability (Figure 7b) change as the output coefficient (c_2) in the Taylor rule increases from 0 to 1. Each line represents the outcome for different values of the inflation coefficient (c_1) in the Taylor rule.

Figure 7a showing the evolution of output variability exhibits the expected result, i.e., as the output coefficient increases (inflation targeting becomes less strict) output variability tends to decrease. One would now expect that this decline in output variability resulting from more active stabilization comes at the cost of more inflation variability. This, however, is not found in Figure 7b. One observes that the relationship is non-linear. As the output parameter is increased from zero, inflation variability first declines. Only when the output parameter increases beyond a certain value (in a range 0.6–0.8) inflation variability starts increasing. Thus, the central bank can reduce both output and inflation variability when it moves away from strict inflation targeting ($c_2 = 0$) and engages in some output stabilization, not too much though. Too much output stabilization turns around the relationship and increases inflation variability.

Figure 7 allows us to construct the tradeoffs between output and inflation variability. These are shown in Figure 8 for different values of the inflation parameter c_1. Take the tradeoff AB. This is the one obtained for $c_1 = 1$. Start from point A on the tradeoff.

In point A, the output parameter $c_2 = 0$ (strict inflation targeting). As output stabilization increases we first move downwards. Thus increased output stabilization by the central bank reduces

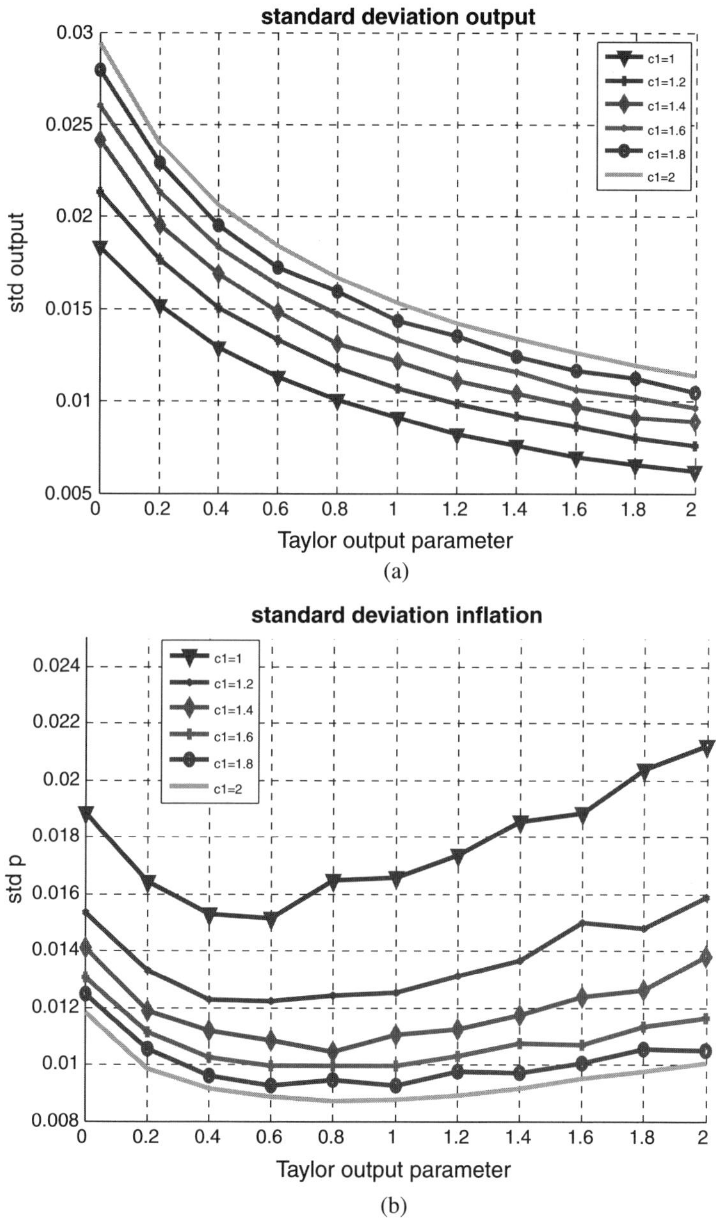

Figure 7. Output and inflation variability.

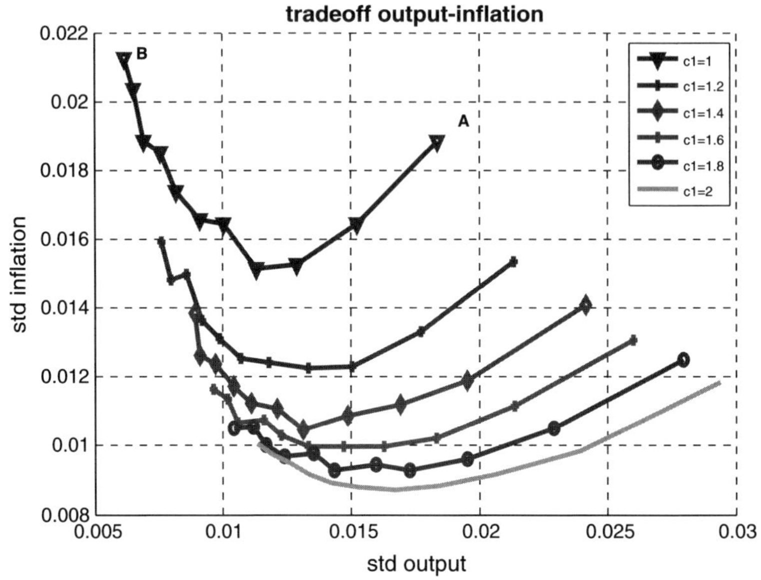

Figure 8. Trade-offs in the extended behavioral model.

output and inflation variability. The relation is non-linear, however. At some point, with too high an output stabilization parameter, the tradeoff curve starts increasing, becoming a "normal" tradeoff, i.e., a lower output variability is obtained at the cost of increased inflation variability.

How can we interpret these results? Let us start from the case of strict inflation targeting, i.e., the authorities set $c_2 = 0$. There is no attempt at stabilizing output at all. The ensuing output variability intensifies the waves of optimism and pessimism (Animal spirits). These larges waves lead to higher inflation variability. Thus, some output stabilization is good; it reduces both output and inflation variability by preventing too large swings in animal spirits. With no output stabilization at all ($c_2 = 0$) the forces of animal spirits are so high that the high output variability also increases inflation volatility through the effect of the output gap on inflation (supply equation). Too much output stabilization, however, reduces the stabilization bonus provided by a credible inflation target. When the central bank attaches too much importance to output stabilization it creates more scope for better forecasting performance of the inflation extrapolators, leading to more inflation variability.

Figure 8 also tells us something important about inflation targeting. We note that increasing the inflation parameter in the Taylor rule (c_1) has the effect of shifting the tradeoffs downwards, i.e., the central bank can improve the tradeoffs by reacting more strongly to changes in inflation.[12] The central bank achieves this improvement in the tradeoff because by reacting more intensely to changes in inflation it reduces the probability that inflation extrapolators will tend to dominate the market, and as a result it reduces the probability that inflation targeting looses credibility. Such a loss of credibility destabilizes both inflation and output. Thus maintaining credibility of inflation targeting is an important source of macroeconomic stability in our behavioral model.

The previous results suggest that there is a relationship between the parameters c_1 and c_2 in the Taylor equation and the credibility of the inflation target. This relationship can be analyzed in more detail. Inflation credibility can be given a precise definition in the model. It can be defined as the fraction of agents who use the inflation target to forecast inflation ("inflation targeters"). Thus when more agents use the announced inflation target to forecast inflation, credibility increases. Figure 9 presents the relationship between inflation credibility and the parameters c_1 and c_2. On the horizontal axis, the parameter c_2 (output parameter) is set out; on the vertical axis the inflation credibility. The latter is obtained by simulating the model 200 times and computing the mean fraction of inflation targeters for different values of the c_1 and c_2. Each curve represents the relation between credibility and the output parameter (c_2) for different values of the inflation parameter (c_1). It has a non-linear feature, i.e., when the output parameter c_2 increases this has the effect of first increasing inflation credibility until a maximum is reached. Then credibility

[12] A similar result on the importance of strict inflation is also found in Orphanides and Williams (2005), and Gaspar *et al.* (2006) who use a macroeconomic model with least squares learning. Our paper stresses that in addition to setting a sufficiently high value for the inflation parameter in the Taylor rule, it also matters to set a sufficiently high value for the output parameter.

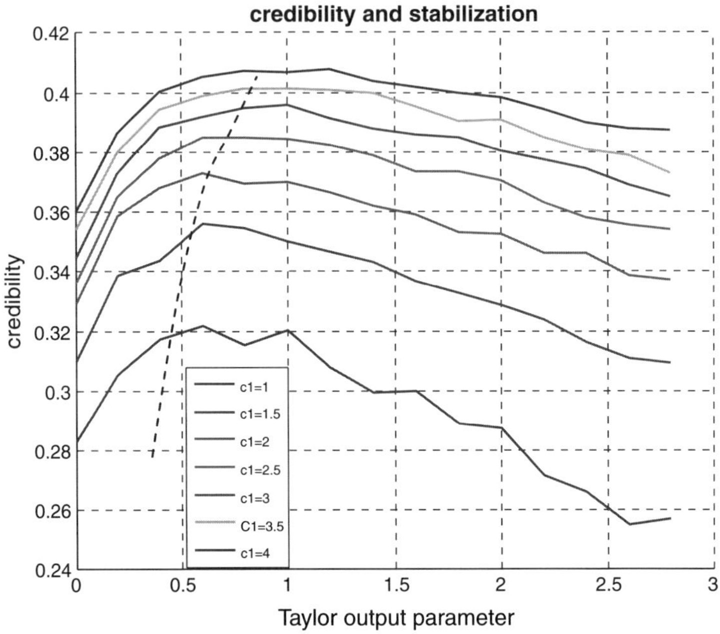

Figure 9. Credibility and stabilization.

starts declining when c_2 increases further. This non-linear feature is found for all values of c_1. Note that the maximum points obtained in Figure 10 correspond to the minimum point of the tradeoffs in Figure 8.

These results have the following interpretation. When the central bank increases its effort to stabilize output this has at first a positive effect on the credibility of its inflation target. The reason, as was discussed earlier, is that by stabilizing output, the central bank also reduces the amplitude of the animal spirits thereby stabilizing output and inflation.

Finally, Figure 9 shows that for increasing values of c_1 the credibility curves increase. Thus a central bank can improve its inflation credibility by reacting more strongly to changes in inflation. This feature then underlies the result found in Figure 8 that higher values of c_1 improve the tradeoff between inflation and output variability.

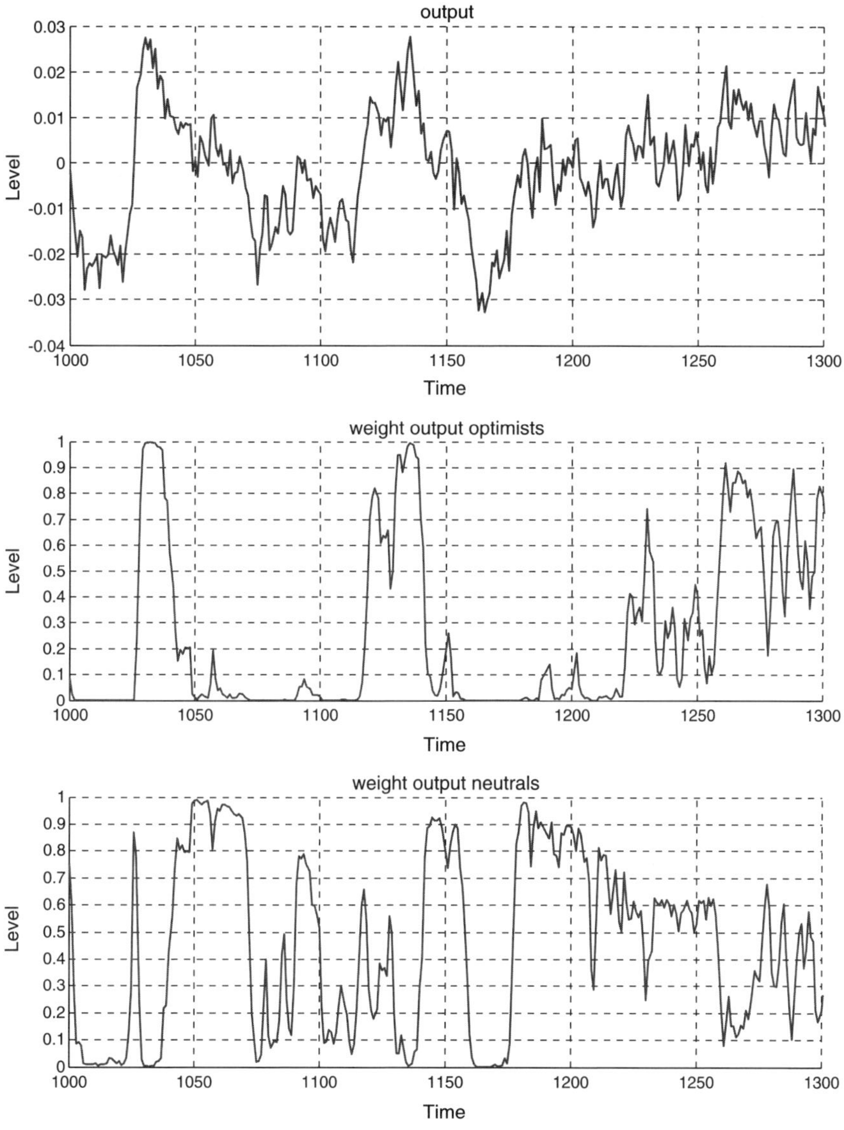

Figure 10. Output gap and animal spirits in a three-agent model.

5. A Further Extension: A Three-Agent Model

The heuristics used in the forecasting of the output gap assumes that agents are biased either in the positive or in the negative sense. It does not allow for the possibility that agents may (even by chance) use an unbiased rule. In this section, the question is analyzed of how the model is affected if we allow for a third, unbiased, forecasting rule. This idea is implemented by defining a third forecasting rule to be

$$\tilde{E}_t^{\mathrm{un}} y_{t+1} = 0 \tag{25}$$

where $\tilde{E}_t^{\mathrm{un}} y_{t+1}$ is the unbiased forecasting rule.

As before a selection mechanism is assumed, whereby agents can switch between the three rules. This implies first that agents compute the performance (utility) of using these rules as in Eqs. (10) and (11) for the optimistic and pessimistic rules. For the unbiased rule this becomes

$$U_{\mathrm{un},t} = -\sum_{k=1}^{\infty} \omega_k [y_{t-k} - \tilde{E}_{\mathrm{un},t-k-1} y_{t-k}]^2 \tag{26}$$

The corresponding probabilities of using the three rules now are:

$$\alpha_{\mathrm{opt},t} = \frac{\exp(\gamma U_{\mathrm{opt},t})}{\exp(\gamma U_{\mathrm{opt},t}) + \exp(\gamma U_{\mathrm{pes},t}) + \exp(\gamma U_{\mathrm{un},t})} \tag{27}$$

$$\alpha_{\mathrm{pes},t} = \frac{\exp(\gamma U_{\mathrm{pes},t})}{\exp(\gamma U_{\mathrm{opt},t}) + \exp(\gamma U_{\mathrm{pes},t}) + \exp(\gamma U_{\mathrm{un},t})} \tag{28}$$

$$\alpha_{\mathrm{un},t} = \frac{\exp(\gamma U_{\mathrm{un},t})}{\exp(\gamma U_{\mathrm{opt},t}) + \exp(\gamma U_{\mathrm{pes},t}) + \exp(\gamma U_{\mathrm{un},t})} \tag{29}$$

The model was simulated in the time domain using the same calibration as in Section 2.4 (the extended behavioral model). The results are shown in Figure 10. The top panel shows the output gap in the time domain; the middle panel shows the fractions (probabilities) of the agents using the optimistic forecasting rule; and the bottom panel shows the fractions using the unbiased rule. (Note that the pessimistic fractions are equal to 1 minus the previous two fractions).

The results are rather interesting. The existence of unbiased predictors does not eliminate the occurrence of waves of optimism and pessimism. As one can see from the center panel of Figure 10, there are regularly periods during which the market is dominated by optimism, despite the fact that there are agents that use the unbiased forecasts. Similarly, there are periods where the market is dominated by pessimistic forecasts. These waves of optimism then affect output in a self-fulfilling way.

In order to find out how important animal spirits are in shaping fluctuations in the output gap the simulated output gap was correlated with the fraction of optimists in the market. This was done both for the three-agent model and for the two-agent model of the previous sections. The average correlation coefficient is 0.84 in the three-agent model and 0.86 in the two-agent model. This means that the addition of a third unbiased rule does not reduce the correlation of the output gap and the "animal spirits" in a significant way. Thus, one of the main results of this paper, i.e., that waves of optimism and pessimism (animal spirits) can emerge, is maintained even in a world where agents have access to unbiased forecasts.

6. Animal Spirits in the Macroeconomic Literature

As mentioned in the introduction our model is not the first one to formalize the idea of animal spirits, i.e., expectations driven business cycle movements. In fact there is a very large literature that has done so in various ways. In this section we compare our approach to these different strands of the literature.

There is a first important strand of literature producing models with sunspot-equilibria. This literature started with Shell (1977) and Azariadis (1981), and includes Azariadis and Guesnerie (1986). Models with sunspot equilibria are found both in the RBC-framework (see Benhabib and Farmer, 1994 and Farmer and Guo, 1994 as in the New-Keynesian framework Clarida *et al.*, 2000). In these models there are multiple REE solutions, which include "self-fulfilling" solutions that depend on extraneous variables ("sunspots"). These models provide for a fully rational way to model animal spirits, implementing the basic insights of Keynes.

A very similar strand of literature is provided by models generating global indeterminacies. Howitt and McAfee (1992), Evans *et al.* (1998), and Evans and Honkapohja (2001) develop models with externalities that lead to multiple steady states. These papers exhibit equilibria with random switching between high and low activity steady states (or, in the Evans *et al.*, 1998, paper, between high and low growth rates). The rational expectations solutions in these models depend on an exogenous two-state Markov variable that acts to coordinate expectations and triggers the shifts between high (optimistic) and low (pessimistic) states.[13]

The common characteristics of these multiple equilibria models is an exogenous process that leads to switches between these different equilibria. The model presented in the present paper differs from these multiple equilibria models in that it does not rely on extraneous "sunspots." The economic fluctuations are driven instead by the intrinsic random shocks of the model.

The latter is also the case in Evans and Honkapohja (2001, Chapter 14), in which the fluctuations are driven by productivity shocks, with the learning rule leading to occasional shifts between equilibria. However, our model differs from this and the previous models in that it does not have multiple equilibria under Rational Expectations. Instead, the multiplicity is the result of the restricted list of forecast rules from which the agents can choose.

Our model comes closest to Branch and Evans (2007) who also use a discrete choice framework inside a simple monetary model and who find regime-switching behavior driven by the shocks in the model. The shifts in expectations, as agents occasionally move from pooling on one forecast rule to pooling on the other rule, is a kind of self-fulfilling phenomenon. The similarity with our model is that in the Branch and Evans (2007) model there is a unique equilibrium under Rational Expectations, but because agents must choose between two misspecified models, there are multiple equilibria (of a type that the authors carefully define). Under real-time updating of the discrete-choice type, this leads to regime-switching behavior over time. However, in Branch and Evans (2007), the switching is

[13]It should be noted that in each of these models fluctuations can also arise as the outcome of a boundedly rational learning process.

between high and low volatility regimes, whereas in our paper it is also between high and low activity states, generating business cycle effects that are of first order. Although the two set-ups differ in a number of other details, the critical one is that in our paper the choice of the two forecast rules is between two "biased" rules, i.e., between an optimistic forecast rule and a pessimistic one. The tendency for agents at any moment to pool on one of the forecast rules then leads to the results.

7. Conclusion

The idea that the business cycle is driven by waves of optimism and pessimism has a long tradition. It was made popular by Keynes who called these waves "animal spirits." Outside academia, this idea continues to enjoy a wide acceptability in explaining movements in economic activity. Only recently has it obtained some academic respectability again (see Akerlof and Shiller 2009).

As a result of the systematic incorporation of rational expectations in macroeconomic theory the idea that waves of optimism and pessimism can have an independent influence on economic activity has been discarded from mainstream academic thinking. The DSGE-models which have now achieved a near monopoly in macroeconomics, view business cycles as the result of a combination of exogenous shocks and slow transmission of these shocks into output and prices. In these models there is no place for endogenously generated business cycles.

The problem of the DSGE-models (and more generally of macroeconomic models based on rational expectations) is that they assume extraordinary cognitive capabilities of individual agents. Recent developments in other disciplines including psychology and brain science document that individual agents struggle with limited cognitive abilities, restricting their capacity to understand the world. As a result, individual agents use small bits of information and simple rules to guide their behavior.

I have used these new insights to develop a macroeconomic model in which the cognitive limitations of agents take center stage.

Once one moves into a world of cognitive limitations one faces the problem that agents use simple and biased rules to forecast output and inflation. In order to provide discipline in the use of these rules a learning mechanism was introduced that allows for the selection of those rules that are more profitable than others. This learning mechanism ensures that although agents use biased rules the market forecasts are unbiased.

The ensuing "behavioral model" produces a number of results that distinguishes it from the rational expectations models. First, the behavioral model creates correlations in beliefs which in turn generate waves of optimism and pessimism. The latter produce endogenous cycles which are akin to the Keynesian "animal spirits." These animal spirits are found to become more important when agents are willing to learn from the errors produced by biased beliefs. But, at the same time, there must be some forgetfulness about errors made long ago for animal spirits to emerge and to influence the business cycle.

Second, due to its non-linearity, the behavioral model produces a degree of uncertainty about the transmission of monetary policy shocks that is different from the uncertainty obtained in DSGE-models. In the latter linear models, uncertainty about the effects of monetary policy shocks arises only because of the lack of precision in the estimation of the structural parameters of the model. In the behavioral model there is an additional dimension to uncertainty. This is that the same policy shock can have different effects depending on the state of the economy, including the degree of optimism and pessimism agents have about the future. As a result, the transmission of policy shocks depends on the timing of these shocks.

A third result is that the inflation targeting regime turns out to be of great importance to stabilize the economy in a behavioral model. In a regime in which inflation targeting is credible, inflation and output variability are greatly reduced. The reason is that credibility also helps to reduce correlations in beliefs and the ensuing self-fulfilling waves of optimism and pessimism. In a regime of imperfect credibility, these waves are more pronounced.

However, and fourth, strict inflation targeting is not an optimal policy. Some output stabilization (given a credible inflation target) also helps in reducing the correlation of biased beliefs thereby reducing the scope for waves of optimism and pessimism to emerge and to destabilize output and inflation.

Finally, the behavioral model provides for a very different theory of the business cycle as compared to the business cycle theory implicit in the DSGE-models. In the DSGE-models, business cycle movements in output and prices only arise because rational agents cannot adjust their optimal plans instantaneously after an exogenous disturbance. Price and wage stickiness prevent such instantaneous adjustment. As a result, these exogenous shocks produce inertia and business cycle movements.

Agents in the behavioral model not only cannot instantaneously adjust their prices but they also experience an informational problem. They do not fully understand the nature of the shock nor its transmission. They use a trial and error learning process aimed at distilling information. This cognitive problem then creates inertia in output and prices in addition to the price inertia originating from the fact that contracts cannot be changed instantaneously. Thus, a richer theory of the business cycles is obtained.

These differences also have policy implications. In order to reduce output volatility in the DSGE-models more flexibility in prices and wages is required. That's why many central banks call for more flexibility of wages and prices. In a more flexible world, central banks will not be called upon so often to stabilize output, and thereby set price stability at risk.

In the behavioral model, business cycle movements in output arise from informational inertia. Thus, even if prices and wages become more flexible, this will not necessarily reduce the business cycle movements in output. As a result, society's desire to stabilize output will not be reduced. And central banks that inevitably respond to these desires will face the need to stabilize output.

The behavioral model proposed in this paper can be criticized for being "ad hoc." There is no doubt that the model has ad hoc features, i.e., assumptions that cannot be grounded on some deeper principle, and therefore have to be taken for granted. In defence of this "ad hoc querie", the following should be stressed. Once we leave the comfortable world of agents who experience no limits to their cognitive abilities, ad hoc assumptions are inevitable. This is due to the fact that we do not fully comprehend the way individuals with cognitive limitations process information.

The research presented in this paper should be considered to be preliminary. In order to be convincing as an alternative modeling strategy, the predictions of the model will have to be confronted more systematically with the data. In addition, the menu of heuristics which is extremely small in this paper, will have to be broadened so that the selection of the "fittest" rules can occur using a wider pool of possible rules.

Appendix A: Parameter values of the calibrated model

Behavioral model

$\pi^* = 0$ % the central bank's inflation target,
$a_1 = 0.5$ % coefficient of expected output in output equation,
$a_2 = -0.2$ % interest elasticity of output demand,
$b_1 = 0.5$ % coefficient of expected inflation in inflation equation,
$b_2 = 0.05$ % coefficient of output in inflation equation,
$c_1 = 1.5$ % coefficient of inflation in Taylor equation,
$c_2 = 0.5$ % coefficient of output in Taylor equation,
$c_3 = 0.5$ % interest smoothing parameter in Taylor equation,
$\beta = 1$ % fixed divergence in beliefs,
$\delta = 2$ % variable component in divergence of beliefs,
$\gamma = 1$ % intensity of choice parameter,
$\rho = 0.5$ % ρ measures the speed of declining weights in mean squares errors (memory parameter),
sigma1 = 0.5 % standard deviation shocks output gap.
sigma2 = 0.5 % standard deviation shocks inflation,
sigma3 = 0.5 % standard deviation shocks Taylor.

Rational model

This uses the same parameter values as in the heuristic model.

Appendix B: Sensitivity Analysis

In this Appendix, I analyze how sensitive the results are to different numerical values of the "learning parameters" in the model. These are the parameters describing how agents use and select forecasting rules. There are three such parameters in the model. First, there is the divergence between the optimists' and pessimists' beliefs. I analyze the sensitivity to the coefficient β in Eq. (6) which measures the sensitivity of the divergence of beliefs to output uncertainty.

Second, there is the memory agents have when calculating the performance of their forecasting, as represented by the parameter ρ.

Finally, there is the parameter γ which measures the intensity with which agents are willing to switch to a better performing rule [see Eqs. (12)–(13)].

The sensitivity of the results with respect to these parameters are discussed by showing how these parameters affect the volatility of inflation and output, and the degree of inertia (autocorrelation) in these variables.

B.1 *Sensitivity to uncertainty*

The upper panels of Figure 11 show how the volatility of output and inflation depends on the degree to which the divergence in beliefs depends on output volatility (uncertainty). One observes that when uncertainty increases, the volatility of output and inflation increases substantially. The lower panels of Figure 11 indicate that increasing uncertainty tends to increase inertia in output (autocorrelation), with little effect on inflation inertia.

B.2 *Sensitivity to memory*

The memory agents use when they evaluate their past performance, plays an important role in the dynamics of the model. This is illustrated by Figure 12. The upper part shows the volatility of output and inflation for different values of the memory parameter (ρ). It is striking to find that with increasing memory the volatility of these variables declines significantly. Note however that the

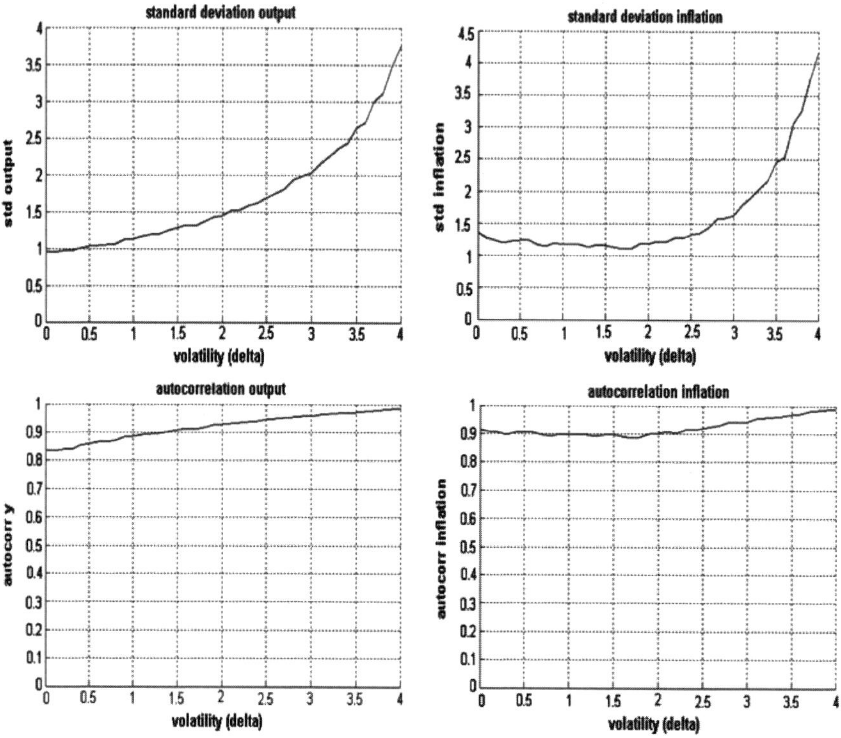

Figure 11. Standard deviation and autocorrelation of output gap and inflation. The standard deviations and autocorrelation coefficients are the averages obtained from simulating the model 1,000 times, each time over 1,000 periods.

relationship is non-linear. One needs a large value of ρ for the volatility to start declining. In the simulations presented in the previous sections $\rho = 0.5$. The volatility obtained for this parameter value is very close to the volatility obtained when $\rho = 0$ (i.e., when agents have no memory and only the performance of the last period matters).

Similar results are obtained with the autocorrelation coefficients of output and inflation. For low and medium values of ρ the autocorrelation coefficients are relatively constant. One needs a sufficiently large value of the memory parameter to reduce the autocorrelation coefficients significantly. Thus long memory tends to stabilize output and inflation and to reduce inertia in these variables.

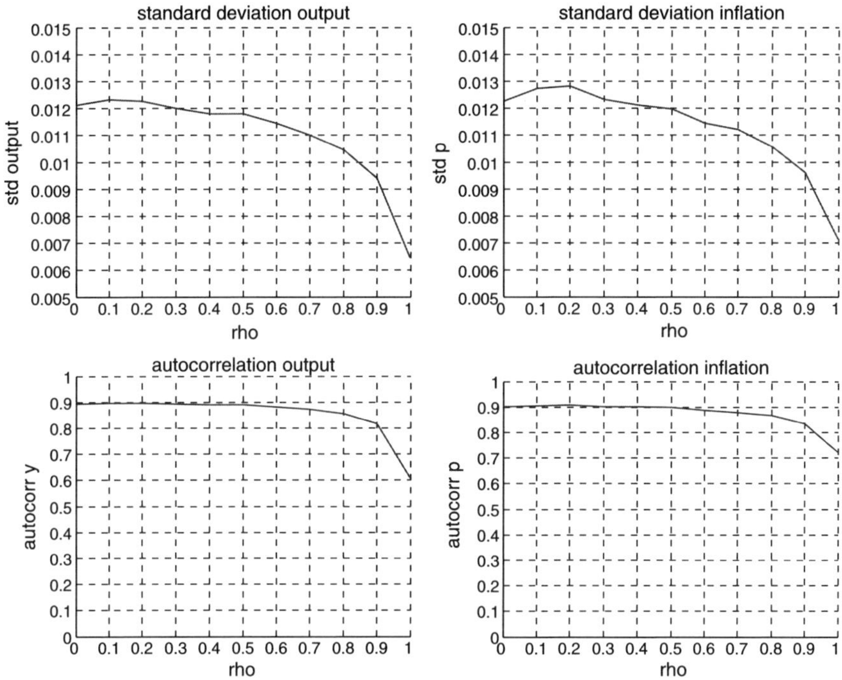

Figure 12. Standard deviation and autocorrelation of output gap and inflation. The standard deviations and autocorrelation coefficients are the averages obtained from simulating the model 1,000 times, each time over 1,000 periods.

B.3 *Sensitivity to intensity of choice*

The intensity of choice parameter γ parametrizes the extent to which the deterministic component of utility determines actual choice. When $\gamma = 0$ utility is purely stochastic. In that case the probability to be optimist (or pessimist) is constant and exactly 0.5. When $\gamma = \infty$ utility is fully deterministic and the probability of using an optimistic rule is either 1 or 0 depending on whether the optimistic rule outperforms the pessimistic one or not.

Figure 13 shows that an increase in γ raises volatility and inertia. The upper panel shows the volatility of output and inflation as a function of γ. A clear positive relation can be observed. The lower panel shows how the autocorrelation coefficients increase when intensity of choice is increased.

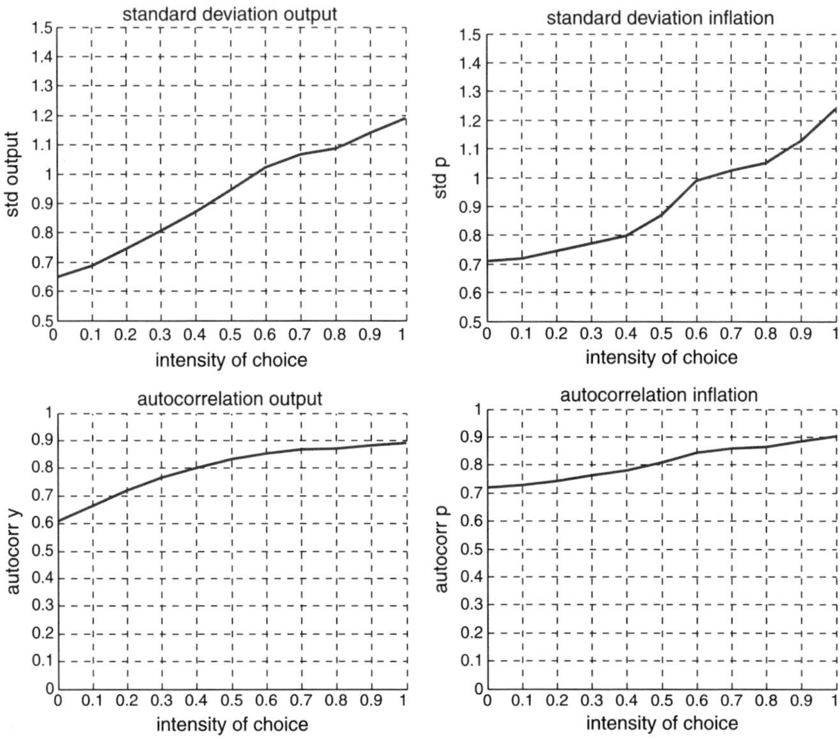

Figure 13. Standard deviation and autocorrelation of output gap and inflation. The standard deviations and autocorrelation coefficients are the averages obtained from simulating the model 1,000 times, each time over 1,000 periods.

It can be concluded that as utility becomes more deterministic, i.e., agents come closer to rational behavior (in the sense of increasing willingness to learn), the volatility of output and inflation and their inertia increase.

References

Adjemian, S, M Darracq Pariés and S Moyen (2007). Optimal monetary policy in an estimated DSGE-model for the euro area. Working Paper No. 803, European Central Bank.

Akerlof, G and R Shiller (2009). *Animal Spirits: How Human Psychology Drives the Economy and Why It Matters for Global Capitalism.* Princeton, NJ: Princeton University Press.

Anagnostopoulos, A, O Licandro, I Bove and K Schlag (2007). An evolutionary theory of inflation inertia. *Journal of the European Economic Association*, 5, 433–443.

Anderson, S, A de Palma and J-E Thisse (1992). *Discrete Choice Theory of Product Differentiation.* Cambridge, MA: MIT Press.

Anufriev, M, T Assenza, C Hommes and D Massaro (2009). *Interest Rate Rules and Macroeconomic Stability under Heterogeneous Expectations, CeNDEF.* Amsterdam: University of Amsterdam.

Azariadis, C (1981). Self-fulfilling prophecies. *Journal of Economic Theory*, 25, 380–396.

Azariadis, C and R Guesnerie (1986). Sunspots and cycles. *Review of Economic Studies*, 53(5), 725–738.

Ball, L, G Mankiw and R Reis (2005). Monetary policy for inattentive economies. *Journal of Monetary Economics*, 52(4), 703–725.

Benhabib, J and REA Farmer (1994). Indeterminacy and increasing returns. *Journal of Economic Theory*, 63, 19–46.

Benhabib, J and U Schmitt-Grohe (2001). The perils of Taylor rules. *Journal of Economic Theory*, 96, 40–69.

Binder, M and MH Pesaran (1996). Multivariate rational expectations models and macroeconomic modeling: A review and some results. In *Handbook of Applied Econometrics. Macroeconomics*, MH Pesaran and M Wickens (eds.), pp. 139–187.

Branch, W and G Evans (2006). Intrinsic heterogeneity in expectation formation. *Journal of Economic Theory*, 127, 264–295.

Branch, W and G Evans (2007). Model uncertainty and endogenous volatility. *Review of Economic Dynamics*, 10, 207–237.

Branch, W and G Evans (2010). Monetary policy with heterogeneous expectations. SIRE Discussion Papers No. 2010-32.

Branch, W and B McGough (2008). Replicator dynamics in a Cobweb model with rationally heterogeneous expectations. *Journal of Economic Behavior and Organization*, 65(2), 224–244.

Brazier, A, R Harrison, M King and T Yates (2008). The danger of inflating expectations of macroeconomic stability: Heuristic switching in an overlapping generations monetary model. *International Journal of Central Banking*, 4, 219–254.

Brock, W and C Hommes (1997). A rational route to randomness. *Econometrica*, 65, 1059–1095.

Camerer, C, G Loewenstein and D Prelec (2005). Neuroeconomics: How neuroscience can inform economics. *Journal of Economic Literature*, 63(1), 9–64.

Chari, V, P Kehoe and E McGrattan (2009). New Keynesian models: Not yet useful for policy analysis. *American Economic Journal: Macroeconomics*, 1(1), 242–266.

Christiano, L, M Eichenbaum and C Evans (2005). Nominal rigidities and the dynamic effects of a shock to monetary policy. *Journal of Political Economy*, 113, 1–45.

Christiano, L, R Motto and M Rostagno (2007). Shocks, structures or monetary policies. Working Paper No. 774, European Central Bank.

Clarida, R, J Gali and M Gertler (1999). The science of monetary policy, a new Keynesian perspective. *Journal of Economic Literature*, 37, 1661–1707.

Clarida, R, J Gali and M Gertler (2000). Monetary policy rules and macroeconomic stability. *Quarterly Journal of Economics*, 37, 1661–1707.

Curtin, R (2007). Consumer sentiment surveys: Worldwide review and assessment. *Journal of Business Cycle Measurement and Analysis*, 3, 1–37.

De Grauwe, P and M Grimaldi (2006). *The Exchange Rate in a Behavioral Finance Framework.* Princeton, NJ: Princeton University Press.

Della Vigna, S (2007). Psychology and economics: Evidence from the field. NBER Working Paper No. 13420.

De Long, JB, A Schleiffer, LH Summers and RJ Waldmann (1990). Noise trader risk in financial markets. *Journal of Political Economy*, 98, 703–738.

Estrella, A and J Furher. Dynamic inconsistencies: Couterfactual implications of a class of rational expectations models. *American Economic Review*, 92(4), 1013–1028.

Evans, G, S Honkapohja and P Romer (1998). Growth cycles. *American Economic Review*, 88, 495–515.

Evans, G and S Honkapohja (2001). *Learning and Expectations in Macroeconomics.* Princeton, NJ: Princeton University Press.

Evans, G, E Guse and S Honkapohja (2008). Liquidity traps, learning and stagnation. *European Economic Review*, 52, 1438–1463.

Farmer, REA and J-T Guo (1994). Real business cycles and the animal spirits hypothesis. *Journal of Economic Theory*, 63, 42–73.

Farmer, REA (2006). Animal spirits. Palgrave Diet Econ.

Gabaix, X, D Laibson, G Moloche and S Weinberg (2006). Costly information acquisition: Experimental analysis of a boundedly rational model. *American Economic Review*, 96(4), 1043–1068.

Gali, J, D López-Salido and J Vallés (2004). Rule of thumb consumers and the design of interest rate rules. *Journal of Money, Credit and Banking*, 36(4), 739–764.

Gali, J (2008). *Monetary Policy, Inflation and the Business Cycle.* Princeton, NJ: Princeton University Press.

Gaspar, V, E Smets and D Vestin (2006). Adaptive learning, persistence and optimal monetary policy. *Journal of the European Economic Association*, 4, 376–385.

Gigerenzer, G and PM Todd (1999). *Simple Heuristics That Make Us Smart.* New York, NY: Oxford University Press.

Goodhart, C (2007). The continuing muddles of monetary theory: A steadfast refusal to face facts, Mimeo, Financial Markets Group. London, UK: London School of Economics.

Hayek, F (1945). The use of knowledge in society. *American Economic Review*, 35(4), 519–530.

Howitt, P and RP McAfee (1992). Animal spirits. *American Economic Review*, 82, 493–507.

Kahneman, D and A Tversky (1973). Prospect theory: An analysis of decisions under risk. *Econometrica*, 47, 313–327.

Kahneman, D and A Tversky (2000). *Choices, Values and Frames.* Cambridge, UK: Cambridge University Press.

Kahneman, D (2002). Maps of bounded rationality: A perspective on intuitive judgment and choice. Nobel Prize Lecture, December 8, Stockholm.

Kahneman, D and R Thaler (2006). Utility maximization and experienced utility. *Journal of Economic Perspectives*, 20, 221–234.

Katona, G (1951). *Psychological Analysis of Economic Behavior*. New York, NY: McGraw-Hill.

Keynes, JM (1936). *The General Theory of Employment, Interest and Money*. New York, NY: MacMillan and Co.

Kirman, A (1993). Ants, rationality and recruitment. *Quarterly Journal of Economics*, 108, 137–156.

Kurz, M (1994). On rational belief equilibria. *Economic Theory*, 4, 859–876.

Kurz, M and M Motolese (2010). Diverse beliefs and time variability of risk premia. *Economic Theory*.

Ludvigson, S (2004). Consumer confidence and consumer spending. *Journal of Economic Perspectives*, 18, 29–50.

Lux, T and M Marchesi (2000). Volatility clustering in financial markets: A micro simulation of interacting agents. *International Journal of Theoretical and Applied Finance*, 3, 675–702.

Mackowiak, B and M Wiederholt (2005). Optimal sticky prices under rational inattention. Discussion Paper, Humboldt University, Berlin.

Mankiw, NG and R Ricardo (2002). Sticky information versus sticky prices: A proposal to replace the new Keynesian Phillips curve. *Quarterly Journal of Economics*, 117(4), 1295–1328.

Mankiw, NG and R Ricardo (2006). Pervasive stickiness. *American Economic Review*, 96(2), 164–169.

Milani, F (2007). *Learning and Time-Varying Macroeconomic Volatility*. Irvine: University of California.

Milani, F (2007). Expectations, learning and macroeconomic persistence. *Journal of Monetary Economics*, 54, 2065–2082.

Nelson, E (1998). Sluggish inflation and optimizing models of the business cycle. *Journal of Monetary Economics*, 42(2), 303–322.

Orphanides, A and J Williams (2005). Robust monetary policy with imperfect information. In *The Inflation Targeting Debate*, NBER Book Series Studies in Business Cycles, B Bernanke and M Woodford (eds.). NBER.

Sargent, T (1993). *Bounded Rationality in Macroeconomics*. New York, NY: Oxford University Press.

Shell, K (1977). Monnaie et allocation intertemporelle. CNRS Séminaire Roy-Malinvaud, Paris, November.

Sims, C (2005). Rational inattention: A research agenda. Discussion Paper No. 34/2005, Deutsche Bundesbank.

Smets, E and R Wouters (2003). An estimated dynamic stochastic general equilibrium model. *Journal of the European Economic Association*, 1, 1123–1175.

Smets, F and R Wouters (2007). Shocks and frictions in US business cycles. Working Paper No. 722, European Central Bank.

Stanovich, K and R West (2000). Individual differences in reasoning: Implications for the rationality debate. *Journal of Behavioral and Brain Science*, 23, 645–665.

Svensson, L (1997). Inflation forecast targeting: Implementing and monitoring inflation targets. *European Economic Review*, 41, 111–146.

Thaler, R (1994). *Quasi Rational Economics.* New York, NY: Russell Sage Foundation.

Tversky, A and D Kahneman (1981). The framing of decisions and the psychology of choice. *Science*, 211, 453–458.

Walsh, C (2003). *Monetary Theory and Policy*, 2nd Edition. Cambridge, MA: MIT Press, pp. 612.

Woodford, M (2003). *Interest and Prices: Foundations of a Theory of Monetary Policy.* Princeton, NJ: Princeton University Press.

Chapter 19

Booms and Busts in Economic Activity: A Behavioral Explanation

Paul De Grauwe

Booms and busts in economic activity are a regular occurrence. They lead to a strong empirical regularity, i.e. that output gaps and output growth are non-normally distributed. Mainstream macroeconomic models explain this phenomenon by invoking exogenous shocks that are non-normally distributed. This is not a very satisfactory explanation as it shifts our ignorance one step further. I propose an explanation based on a behavioral macroeconomic model, in which agents are assumed to have limited cognitive abilities and thus develop different beliefs. This model produces waves of optimism and pessimism in an endogenous way (animal spirits) and provides for a better

Published in *Journal of Economic Behavior and Organization*, 88(3), 484–501, 2012.
I am grateful to Yunus Aksoy, Tony Atkinson, Robert Boyer, Casper de Vries, Stephan Fahr, Daniel Gros, Richard Harrison, Romain Houssa, Gerhard Illing, Pablo Rovira Kaltwasser, Christian Keuschnigg, Alan Kirman, Giovanni Lombardo, Lars Ljungqvist, Patrick Minford, John Muellbauer, Ilbas Pelin, Andrea Roventini, Willi Semmler, Frank Smets, Robert Solow, Leopold von Thadden, David Vines, Volker Wieland and Tony Yates for their comments and suggestions. I am also grateful to an anonymous referee for insightful suggestions.
Keywords: Non-normality; imperfect information; heuristics; animal spirits.
JEL classification: E10, E32, D83.

(endogenous) explanation of the observed non-normality in output movements. I also analyze the implications for monetary policy.

1. Introduction

One of the most robust empirical regularities in the movements of the output gap and the growth rates of output in industrialized countries is the fact that these movements are non-normally distributed. We show, as an example, the US output gap data and their distribution during 1960–2010 in Figures 1 and 2. The latter clearly illustrates that the distribution is non-Gaussian, exhibiting excess kurtosis and fat tails. A simple Jarque–Bera test rejects normality. The same regularity has been analyzed in great detail by Fagiolo *et al.* (2008, 2009). These authors confirm that output growth rated in most OECD-countries are non-normally distributed, with tails that are much fatter than those in a Gaussian distribution and that fat tails in the distribution of these series is a robust feature. Fagiolo *et al.* (2009) find the same features in the US output gap data.

The fact that output gap and output growth are non-normally distributed exhibiting excess kurtosis and fat tails is an important property of the dynamics of the business cycle. It implies that

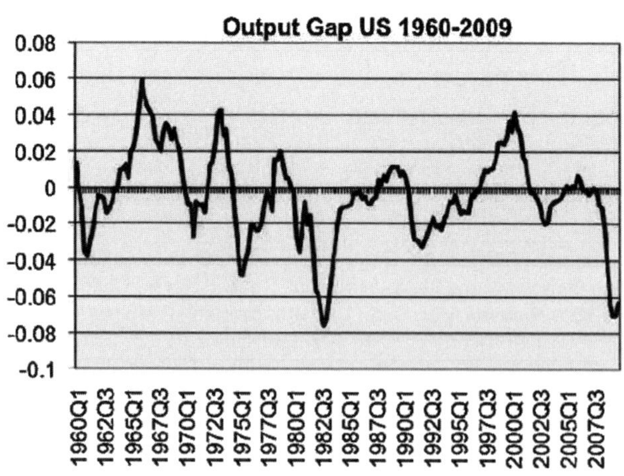

Figure 1.

Source: US Department of Commerce and Congressional Budget Office.

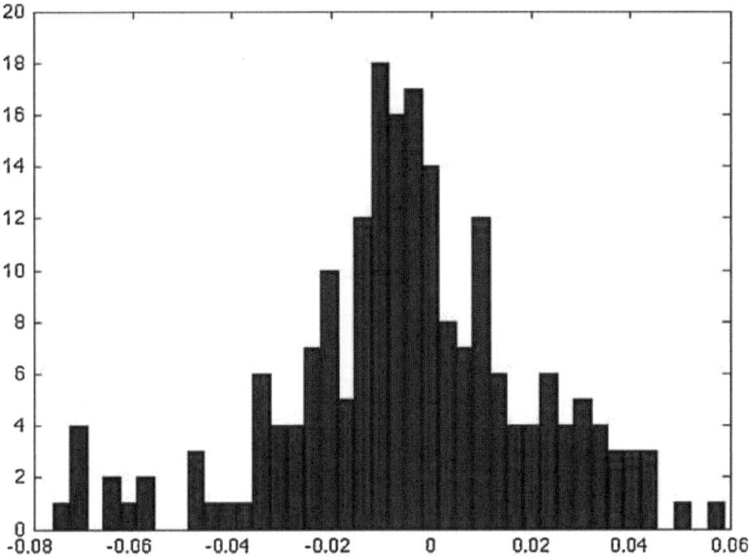

Figure 2. Frequency distribution of US output gap (1960–2009).

Source: US Department of Commerce and Congressional Budget Office.

business cycle movements are characterized by periods of relatively small changes in output interrupted by (infrequent) periods of large changes. Thus much of the time tranquillity reigns followed (unpredictably) by bursts of booms and busts. The financial and economic crisis of 2007–2009 was preceded by a period of tranquillity that was characterized as a period of "Great Moderation."

Mainstream DSGE-models have been struggling to provide a good explanation. In these models the existence of occasionally large booms and busts is explained by the occurrence of large exogenous shocks. This is not a very attractive theory. The explanation comes as a "Deus ex Machina" in which nothing in the macroeconomy tends to lead to non-normality. The latter comes from the outside world. This shifts the burden of explanation one step further leading to the question of why the outside shocks are not normally distributed.

A satisfactory macroeconomic theory should try to explain the occurrence of non-normality in the movements in output from within the theory. This is what I attempt to do in this paper using a behavioral macroeconomic model in which endogenously generated "animal spirits" take center stage. Section 2 presents the behavioral macroeconomic model. Its basic assumption is that agents have cognitive limitations, i.e., they only understand small bits and pieces of the whole model and use simple rules (heuristics) to guide their behavior. I will introduce rationality in the model through a selection mechanism in which agents evaluate the performance of the rule they are following and decide to switch or to stick to the rule depending on how well the rule performs relative to other rules.

The approach presented in this paper is not the only possible one to model agents' behavior under imperfect information. In fact, a large literature has emerged attempting to introduce imperfect information into macroeconomic models. These attempts have been based mainly on the statistical learning approach pioneered by Sargent (1993) and Evans and Honkapohj a (2001). This literature leads to important new insights (see e.g., Gaspar *et al.*, 2006; Orphanides and Williams, 2004; Milani, 2007; Branch and Evans, 2009). However, I feel that this approach still loads individual agents with too many cognitive skills that they probably do not posses in the real world.[1]

2. A Behavioral Macroeconomic Model

In this section the modeling strategy is described. This is done by presenting a standard aggregate-demand-aggregate supply model augmented with a Taylor rule. The novel feature of the model is that agents use simple rules, heuristics, to forecast the future. These rules are subjected to an adaptive learning mechanism, i.e., agents endogenously select the forecasting rules that have delivered the highest performance ("fitness") in the past. This selection mechanism acts as a disciplining device on the kind of rules that are acceptable. Since agents use different heuristics one obtains heterogeneity. This, as will be shown, creates endogenous business cycles.

[1]See the fascinating book of Gigerenzer and Todd (1999) on the use of simple heuristics as compared to statistical (regression) learning.

2.1. *The Model*

The model consists of an aggregate demand equation, an aggregate supply equation and a Taylor rule. The aggregate demand equation is specified in the standard way, i.e.

$$y_t = a_1 \tilde{E}_t y_t + (1 - a_1) y_{t-1} + a_2 (r_t - \tilde{E}_t \pi_{t+1}) + \varepsilon_t \tag{1}$$

where y_t is the output gap in period t, r_t is the nominal interest rate, π_t is the rate of inflation, and ε_t is a white noise disturbance term. $\tilde{E}_t$ is the expectations operator where the tilde above E refers to expectations that are not formed rationally. This process will be specified subsequently. I follow the procedure introduced in DSGE-models of adding a lagged output in the demand equation. This is usually justified by invoking habit formation. I keep this assumption here.

The aggregate supply equation can be derived from profit maximization of individual producers. As in DSGE-models a Calvo pricing rule and some indexation rule used in adjusting prices is assumed. This leads to a lagged inflation variable in the equation.[2] The supply curve can also be interpreted as a New Keynesian Philips curve:

$$\pi_t = b_1 \tilde{E}_t \pi_{t+1} + (1 - b) \pi_{t-1} + b_2 y_t + \eta_t \tag{2}$$

Finally the Taylor rule describes the behavior of the central bank

$$r_t = c_1 (\pi_t - \pi^*) + c_2 y_t + c_3 r_{t-1} + u_t \tag{3}$$

where π^* is the inflation target which for the sake of convenience will be set equal to 0. Note that, as is commonly done, the central bank is assumed to smooth the interest rate. This smoothing behavior is represented by the lagged interest rate in Eq. (3). Ideally, the Taylor rule should be formulated using a forward looking inflation variable, i.e. central banks set the interest rate on the basis of their

[2] It is now standard in DSGE-models to use a pricing equation in which marginal costs enter on the right hand side. Such an equation is derived from profit maximisation in a world of imperfect competition. It can be shown that under certain conditions the aggregate supply Eq. (3) is equivalent to such a pricing equation (see Galí, 2008; Smets and Wouters, 2003).

forecasts about the rate of inflation. This was not done here in order to maintain simplicity in the model.

2.1.1. *Introducing heuristics in forecasting output*

Agents are assumed to use simple rules (heuristics) to forecast the future output and inflation. The way I proceed is as follows. I start with a very simple forecasting heuristics and apply it to the forecasting rules of future output. I assume two types of forecasting rules. A first rule can be called a "fundamentalist" one. Agents estimate the steady state value of the output gap (which is normalized at 0) and use this to forecast the future output gap.[3] A second forecasting rule is an "extrapolative" one. This is a rule that does not presuppose that agents know the steady state output gap. They are agnostic about it. Instead, they extrapolate the previous observed output gap into the future.

The two rules are specified as follows

$$\text{The fundamentalist rule is defined by } \tilde{E}_t^f y_{t+1} = 0 \tag{4}$$

$$\text{The extrapolative rule is defined by } \tilde{E}_t^e y_{t+1} = y_{t-1} \tag{5}$$

This kind of simple heuristic has often been used in the behavioral finance literature where agents are assumed to use fundamentalist and chartist rules (see Brock and Hommes, 1997; Branch and Evans, 2006; De Grauwe and Grimaldi, 2006). It is probably the simplest possible assumption one can make about how agents, which experience cognitive limitations, use rules that embody limited knowledge to guide their behavior. In this sense they are bottom-up rules. They only require agents to use information they understand, and do not require them to understand the whole picture (see also Hayek, 1945 on this information assumption).

Some additional observations about these forecasting rules should be made here. First, the fundamentalists are assumed to know the model's structure since they can compute the steady state value of

[3]In De Grauwe (2010) this assumption is relaxed by assuming that agents do not know the steady state output gap with certainty and only have biased estimates of it. This extension does not alter the model qualitatively.

the output gap. Yet they do not have rational expectations. The latter would require them also to know the behavior of the extrapolators. We take the view here that the cognitive abilities of agents are too restricted for them to be able to know this. Second, there is a timing problem for the forecasters in our model. Agents do not know the value of the output gap in period $t(y_t)$, which is the period in which they make their forecasts of the output gap in $t + 1$. In fact they cannot know y_t. In order to know y_t they would have to compute the effect of their own forecasts and of those of the other agents on contemporaneous output. This they can only do under rational expectations.

Thus the specification of the heuristics in (4) and (5) should not be interpreted as a realistic representation of how agents forecast. Rather is it a parsimonious representation of a world where agents do not know the "truth" (i.e., the underlying model including the forecasting rules of all the other agents). The use of simple rules does not mean that the agents are dumb and that they do not want to learn from their errors. I will specify a learning mechanism later in this section in which these agents continuously try to correct for their errors by switching from one rule to the other.

The market forecast is obtained as a weighted average of these two forecasts, i.e.:

$$\tilde{E}_t y_{t+1} = \alpha_{f,t}\tilde{E}_t^f y_{t+1} + \alpha_{e,t}\tilde{E}_t^e y_{t+1} \tag{6}$$

$$\tilde{E}_t y_{t+1} = \alpha_{f,t}0 + \alpha_{e,t}y_{t-1} = \alpha_{e,t}y_{t-1} \tag{7}$$

and

$$\alpha_{f,t} + \alpha_{e,t} = 1 \tag{8}$$

where $\alpha_{f,t}$ and $\alpha_{e,t}$ are the probabilities that agents use a fundamentalist, respectively, an extrapolative rule.

A methodological issue arises here. The forecasting rules (heuristics) introduced here are not derived at the micro level and then aggregated. Instead, they are imposed ex post, on the demand and supply equations. This has also been the approach in the learning literature pioneered by Evans and Honkapohja (2001). One could argue, therefore, that my modeling technique is still not fully bottom-up. Ideally one would like to derive the heuristics from the micro-level in an environment in which agents experience cognitive problems. Our knowledge about how to model this behavior at the micro level and how to aggregate it is too sketchy, however, and I have not tried to do so.[4] Clearly, this is an area that will have to be researched in the future.

As indicated earlier, agents are rational in the sense that they continuously evaluate their forecast performance. I apply notions of discrete choice theory (see Anderson *et al.*, 1992; Brock and Hommes, 1997) in specifying the procedure agents follow in this evaluation process. Discrete choice theory analyzes how agents decide between different alternatives. The theory takes the view that agents are boundedly rational, i.e., utility has a deterministic component and a random component. Agents compute the forecast performance of the different heuristics as follows:

$$U_{f,t} = -\sum_{k=0}^{\infty} \omega_k [y_{t-k-1}]^2 \tag{9}$$

$$U_{e,t} = -\sum_{k=0}^{\infty} \omega_k [y_{t-k-1} - \tilde{E}_{e,t-k-2} y_{t-k-1}]^2 \tag{10}$$

where $U_{f,t}$ and $U_{e,t}$ are the forecast performances (utilities) of the fundamentalists and extrapolators, respectively. These are defined as the mean squared forecasting errors (MSFEs) of the optimistic and pessimistic forecasting rules; ω_k are geometrically declining weights.

Applying discrete choice theory the probability that an agent will use the fundamentalist forecasting rule is given by the expression

[4]Psychologists and brains scientists struggle to understand how our brain processes information. There is as yet no generally accepted model we could use to model the micro-foundations of information processing. There are some attempts to provide micro-foundations of models with agents experiencing cognitive limitations, though. See e.g., Kirman (1993) and Delli Gatti *et al.* (2005).

(Anderson *et al.*, 1992; Brock and Hommes, 1997):

$$\alpha_{f,t} = \frac{\exp(\gamma U_{f,t})}{\exp(\gamma U_{f,t}) + \exp(\gamma U_{e,t})} \tag{11}$$

Similarly the probability that an agent will use the extrapolative forecasting rule is given by:

$$\alpha_{e,t} = \frac{\exp(\gamma U_{e,t})}{\exp(\gamma U_{f,t}) + \exp(\gamma U_{e,t})} = 1 - \alpha_{f,t} \tag{12}$$

Equation (11) says that as the past forecast performance of the fundamentalists improves relative to that of the extrapolators agents are more likely to select the fundamentalist rule about the output gap for their future forecasts. As a result the probability that agents use the fundamentalist rule increases. Equation (12) has a similar interpretation. The parameter γ measures the "intensity of choice." It parametrizes the extent to which the deterministic component of utility determines actual choice. When $\gamma = 0$ utility is purely stochastic. In that case agents decide to be fundamentalist or extrapolator by tossing a coin and the probability to be fundamentalist (or extrapolator) is exactly 0.5. When $\gamma = \infty$ utility is fully deterministic and the probability of using a fundamentalist rule is either 1 or 0. The parameter γ can also be interpreted as expressing a willingness to learn from past performance. When $\gamma = 0$ this willingness is zero; it increases with the size of γ.

Note that this selection mechanism is the disciplining device introduced in this model on the kind of rules of behavior that are acceptable. Only those rules that pass the fitness test remain in place. The others are weeded out. In contrast with the disciplining device implicit in rational expectations models, which implies that agents have superior cognitive capacities, we do not have to make such an assumption here.

It should also be stressed that although individuals use simple rules in forecasting the future, this does not mean that they fail to learn. In fact the fitness criterion used should be interpreted as a learning mechanism based on "trial and error". When observing that the rule they use performs less well than the alternative rule, agents are willing to switch to the more performing rule. Put differently, agents avoid making systematic mistakes by constantly being willing to learn from past mistakes and to change their behavior. This also ensures that the market forecasts are unbiased.

The mechanism driving the selection of the rules introduces a self-organizing dynamics in the model. It is a dynamics that is beyond the capacity of any one individual in the model to understand. In this sense it is a bottom-up system. It contrasts with the mainstream macroeconomic models in which it is assumed that some or all agents can take a bird's eye view and understand the whole picture. These agents not only understand the whole picture but also use this whole picture to decide about their optimal behavior. Thus there is a one-to-one correspondence between the total information embedded in the world and the individual brains.

2.1.2. *Introducing heuristics in forecasting inflation*

Agents also have to forecast inflation. A similar simple heuristics is used as in the case of output gap forecasting, with one rule that could be called a fundamentalist rule and the other an extrapolative rule (see Brazier *et al.*, 2006, for a similar setup). The fundamentalist rule is based on the announced inflation target, i.e. agents using this rule have confidence in the credibility of this rule and use it to forecast inflation. They can also be called "true believers" as they have full confidence in the central bank's announcement even though there is no commitment device in place that is necessary to produce the required confidence. The extrapolative rule is used by agents who do not trust the announced inflation target. Instead they extrapolate inflation from the past into the future.

The fundamentalist rule will be called an "inflation targeting" rule. It consists in using the central bank's inflation target to forecast future inflation, i.e.:

$$\tilde{E}_t^{tar} \pi_{t+1} = \pi^* \tag{13}$$

where the inflation target π^* is normalized to be equal to 0

$$\text{The “extrapolators” are defined by} \quad \tilde{E}_t^{ext}\pi_{t+1} = \pi_{t-1} \tag{14}$$

The market forecast is a weighted average of these two forecasts, i.e.:

$$\tilde{E}_t\pi_{t+1} = \beta_{tar,t}\tilde{E}_t^{tar}\pi_{t+1} + \beta_{ext,t}\tilde{E}_t^{ext}\pi_{t+1} \tag{15}$$

or

$$\tilde{E}_t\pi_{t+1} = \beta_{tar,t}\pi^* + \beta_{ext,t}\pi_{t-1} = \beta_{ext,t}\pi_{t-1} \tag{16}$$

and

$$\beta_{tar,t} + \beta_{ext,t} = 1 \tag{17}$$

The same selection mechanism is used as in the case of output forecasting to determine the probabilities of agents trusting the inflation target and those who do not trust it and revert to extrapolation of past inflation, i.e.:

$$\beta_{tar,t} = \frac{\exp(\gamma U_{tar,t})}{\exp(\gamma U_{tar,t}) + \exp(\gamma U_{ext,t})} \tag{18}$$

$$\beta_{ext,t} = \frac{\exp(\gamma U_{ext,t})}{\exp(\gamma U_{tar,t}) + \exp(\gamma U_{ext,t})} \tag{19}$$

where $U_{tar,t}$ and $U_{ext,t}$ are the weighted averages of past squared forecast errors of using targeter and extrapolator rules, respectively. These are defined in the same way as in (9) and (10).

This inflation forecasting heuristics can be interpreted as a procedure of agents to find out how credible the central bank's inflation targeting is. If this is very credible, using the announced inflation target will produce good forecasts and as a result, the probability that agents will rely on the inflation target will be high. If on the other hand the inflation target does not produce good forecasts (compared to a simple extrapolation rule) the probability that agents will use it will be small.

The solution of the model is found by first substituting (3) into (1) and rewriting in matrix notation. This yields:

$$\begin{bmatrix} 1 & -b_2 \\ -a_2c_1 & 1-a_2c_2 \end{bmatrix}\begin{bmatrix} \pi_t \\ y_t \end{bmatrix} = \begin{bmatrix} b_1 & 0 \\ -a_2 & a_1 \end{bmatrix}\begin{bmatrix} \tilde{E}_t\pi_{t+1} \\ \tilde{E}_t y_{t+1} \end{bmatrix} + \begin{bmatrix} 1-b_1 & 0 \\ 0 & 1-a_1 \end{bmatrix}\begin{bmatrix} \pi_{t-1} \\ y_{t-1} \end{bmatrix} + \begin{bmatrix} 0 \\ a_2c_3 \end{bmatrix} r_{t-1} + \begin{bmatrix} \eta_t \\ a_2u_t + \varepsilon_t \end{bmatrix}$$

or

$$\boldsymbol{AZ}_t = \boldsymbol{B}\tilde{\boldsymbol{E}}_t\boldsymbol{Z}_{t+1} + \boldsymbol{CZ}_{t-1} + \boldsymbol{b}r_{t-1} + \boldsymbol{v}_t \qquad (20)$$

where bold characters refer to matrices and vectors. The solution for $\mathbf{Z}_t$ is given by

$$\boldsymbol{Z}_t = \boldsymbol{A}^{-1}[\boldsymbol{B}\tilde{\boldsymbol{E}}_t\boldsymbol{Z}_{t+1} + \boldsymbol{CZ}_{t-1} + \boldsymbol{b}r_{t-1} + \boldsymbol{v}_t] \qquad (21)$$

The solution exists if the matrix $\mathbf{A}$ is non-singular, i.e., if $(1-a_2c_2)a_2b_2c_1 \neq 0$. The system (21) describes the solution for y_t and π_t given the forecasts of y_t and π_t. The latter have been specified in Eqs. (4)–(12) and can be substituted into (21). Finally, the solution for r_t is found by substituting y_t and π_t obtained from (21) into (3).

2.2. *Calibrating the Model*

I proceed by calibrating the model. In Appendix A the parameters used in the calibration exercise are presented. The model was calibrated in such a way that the time units can be considered to be months. A sensitivity analysis of the main results to changes in some of the parameters of the model will be presented. The three shocks (demand shocks, supply shocks and interest rate shocks) are i.i.d. with standard deviations of 0.5 percent.

3. Animal Spirits, Booms and Busts

In this section simulations of the behavioral model in the time domain are presented and interpreted. The upper panel of Figure 3 shows the

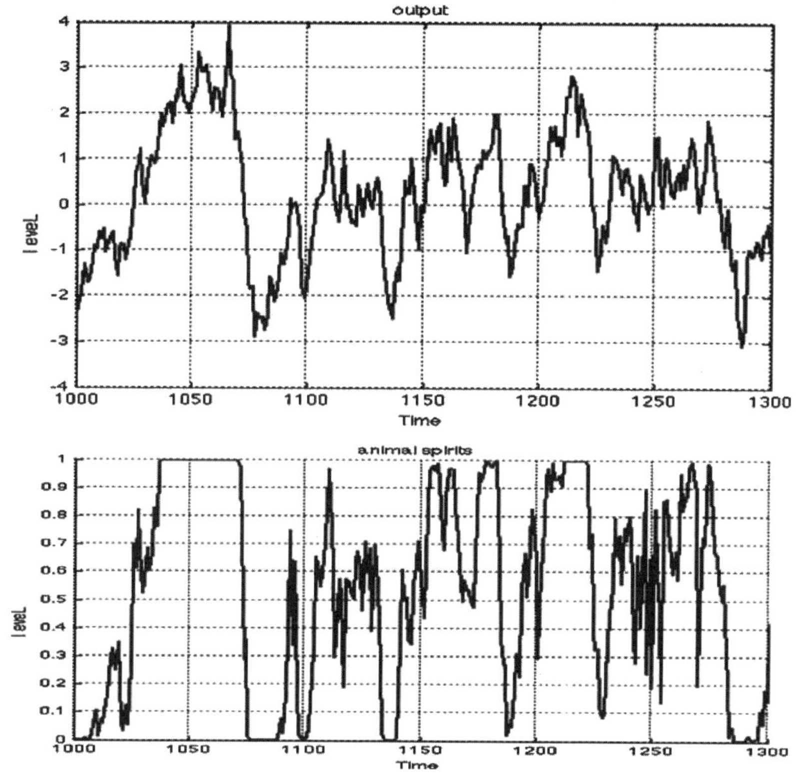

Figure 3. Output gap in behavioral model.

time pattern of the output gap produced by the behavioral model. A strong cyclical movement in the output gap can be observed. The lower panel of Figure 3 shows a variable called "animal spirits".[5] It represents the evolution of the fractions of the agents who extrapolate a positive output gap. Thus when the curve reaches +1 all agents are extrapolating a positive output gap; when the curve reaches 0 no agents are extrapolating a positive output gap. In fact in that case they all extrapolate a negative output gap. Thus the curve shows the

[5]See Mario Nuti (2009) on the different interpretations of "Animal Spirits." The locus classicus is Keynes (1936). See also Farmer and Roger (2006) and the recent book of Akerlof and Shiller (2009).

degree of optimism and pessimism of agents who make forecasts of the output gap.

Combining the information of the two panels in Figure 3 it can be seen that the model generates endogenous waves of optimism and pessimism. During some periods optimists (i.e., agents who extrapolate positive output gaps) dominate and this translates into above average output growth. These optimistic periods are followed by pessimistic ones when pessimists (i.e., agents who extrapolate negative output gaps) dominate and the growth rate of output is below average. These waves of optimism and pessimism are essentially unpredictable. Other realizations of the shocks produce different cycles with the same general characteristics.

It should be noted that these irregularly oscillating time patterns in the output gap are the result of the non-linearities in the fractions $\alpha_{i,t}$ and $\beta_{k,t}$. Put differently, the model produces a unique equilibrium with oscillations around it produced by time dependent and non-linear fractions of optimists and pessimists.

These endogenously generated cycles in output are made possible by a self-fulfilling mechanism that can be described as follows. A series of random shocks creates the possibility that one of the two forecasting rules, say the extrapolating one, delivers a higher payoff, i.e., a lower mean squared forecast error (MSFE). This attracts agents that were using the fundamentalist rule. If the successful extrapolation happens to be a positive extrapolation, more agents will start extrapolating the positive output gap. The "contagion-effect" leads to an increasing use of the optimistic extrapolation of the output-gap, which in turn stimulates aggregate demand. Optimism is therefore self-fulfilling. A boom is created. At some point, negative stochastic shocks and/or the reaction of the central bank through the Taylor rule make a dent in the MSFE of the optimistic forecasts. Fundamentalist forecasts may become attractive again, but it is equally possible that pessimistic extrapolation becomes attractive and therefore fashionable again. The economy turns around.

These waves of optimism and pessimism can be understood to be searching (learning) mechanisms of agents who do not fully understand the underlying model but are continuously searching for the truth. An essential characteristic of this searching mechanism is that it leads to systematic correlation in beliefs (e.g., optimistic extrapolations or pessimistic extrapolations). This systematic correlation is at the core of the booms and busts created in the model. Note, however, that when computed over a significantly large period of time the average error in the forecasting goes to zero. In this sense, the forecast bias tends to disappear asymptotically.

It can now be shown that this behavioral model is capable of mimicking the empirical regularities documented in the introduction, i.e., the non-normality of the output gap. I show this by presenting the histogram of the output gaps obtained from Figure 3. The result is presented in Figure 4. The frequency distribution of the output gap deviates significantly from a normal distribution. There is excess kurtosis (kurtosis = 4.4), i.e., there is too much concentration of observations around the mean for the distribution to be normal. In addition

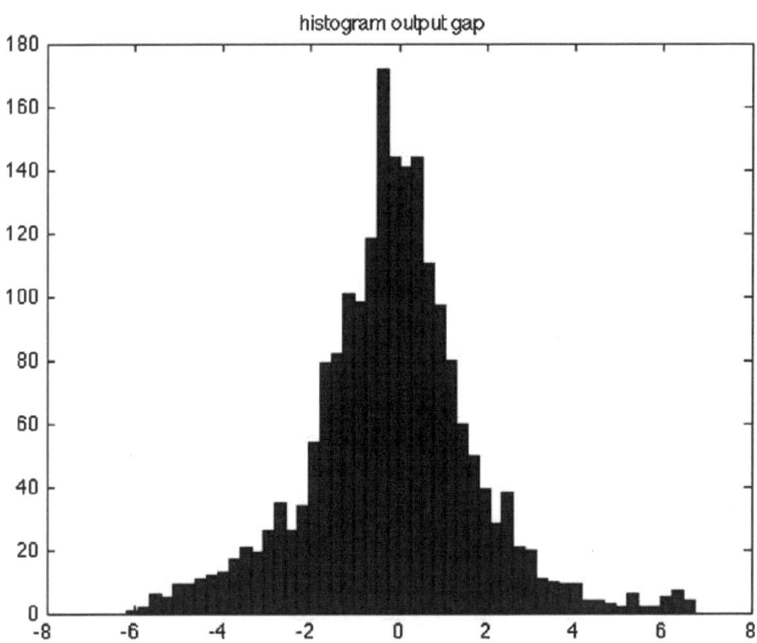

Kurtosis = 4.4, Jarque - Bera = 178.4 (*p*-value = 0.001)

Figure 4. Frequency distribution of simulated output gap.

there are fat tails. This means that there are too many observations that are extremely small or extremely large to be compatible with a normal distribution. I also applied a more formal test of normality, the Jarque–Bera test, which rejects normality. Note that the non-normality of the distribution of the output gap is produced endogenously by the model, as we feed the model with normally distributed shocks.

It is fine to observe this phenomenon. It is even better to have an explanation for it. The behavioral model provides such an explanation. It is based on the particular dynamics of "animal spirits." I illustrate this in Figure 5. This shows the frequency distribution of the animal spirits index (defined earlier), which is associated with the frequency distribution of the output gap obtained in Figure 4. From Figure 5 one observes that there is a concentration of the animal spirits at the extreme values of 0 and 1 and also in the middle of the distribution (but more spread out). This feature provides the key explanation of the non-normality of the movements of the output gap.

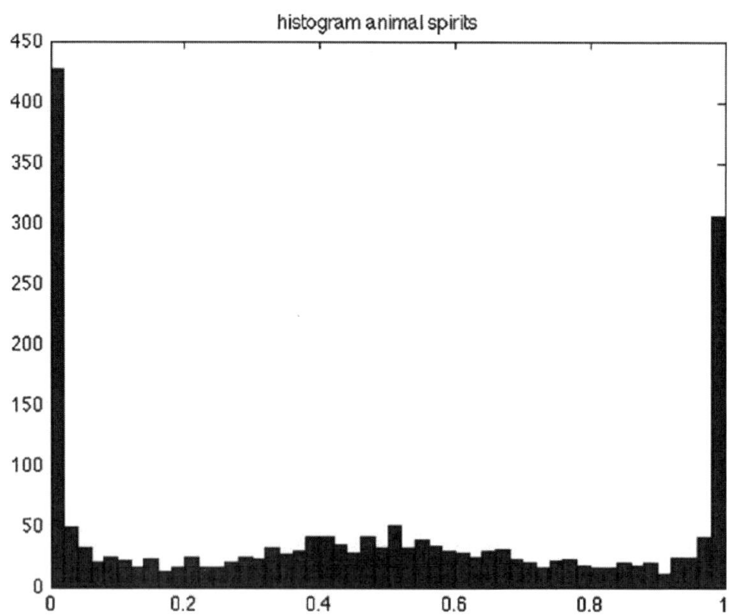

Figure 5. Frequency distribution simulated animal spirits.

When the animal spirits index clusters in the middle of the distribution we have tranquil periods. There is no particular optimism or pessimism, and agents use a fundamentalist rule to forecast the output gap. At irregular intervals, however, the economy is gripped by either a wave of optimism or of pessimism. The nature of these waves is that beliefs get correlated. Optimism breeds optimism; pessimism breeds pessimism. This can lead to situations where everybody has become either optimist of pessimist. These periods are characterized by extreme positive of negative movements in the output gap (booms and busts).

From the previous discussion it follows that the behavioral macroeconomic model has a strong prediction about how the movements of the output gap are distributed. These movements should be non-normal. This is also what one observes in reality.

4. Inflation Cycles

In this section the results concerning the movements of inflation are presented. The results concerning the time path of inflation are shown in Figure 6. First concentrate on the lower panel of Figure 6. This shows the fraction of agents using the extrapolator heuristics, i.e., the agents who do not trust the inflation target of the central bank. One can identify two regimes. There is a regime in which the fraction of extrapolators fluctuates around 50 percent, which also implies that the fraction of forecasters using the inflation target as their guide (the "inflation targeters") is around 50 percent. This is sufficient to maintain the rate of inflation within a narrow band of approximately + and −1% around the central bank's inflation target. There is a second regime though which occurs when the extrapolators are dominant. During this regime the rate of inflation fluctuates significantly more. Thus the inflation targeting of the central bank is fragile. It can be undermined when forecasters decide that relying on past inflation movements produces better forecast performances than relying on the central bank's inflation target. This can occur quite unpredictably as a result of stochastic shocks in supply and/or demand.

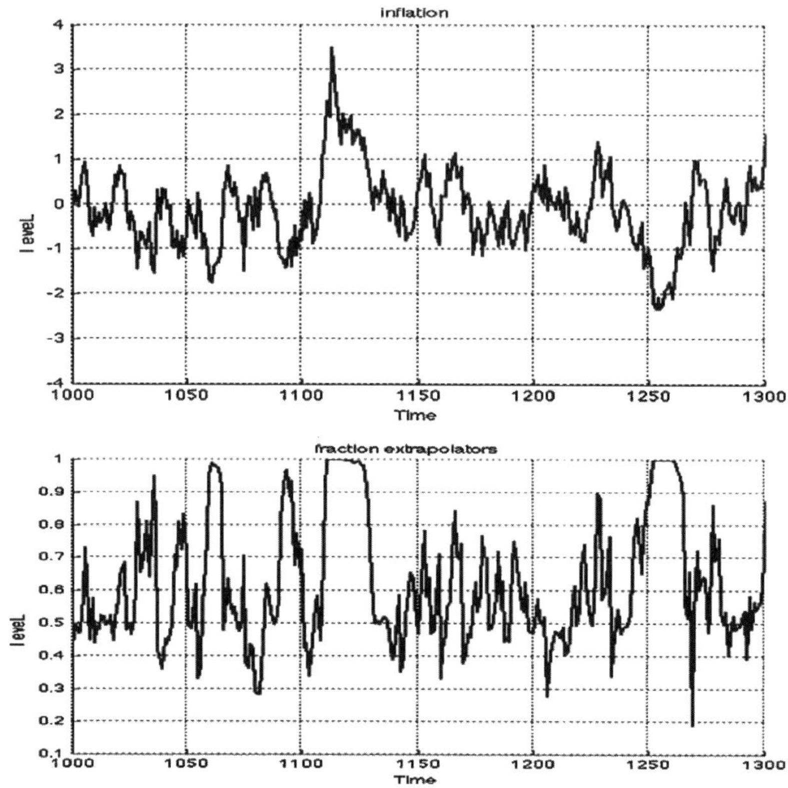

Figure 6. Inflation in behavioral model.

5. Animal Spirits and the Nature of Shocks

How important is the nature of the shocks hitting the economy? Macroeconomists have long recognized that demand and supply shocks have very different macroeconomic effects. In general, supply shocks are seen to be more uncomfortable. The main reason is that a supply shock moves inflation and output in opposite directions. A negative supply shock reduces output and increases inflation; a positive supply shock raises output and reduces inflation. This feature leads to an uncomfortable choice for the monetary authorities. They face a trade-off between stabilizing output and inflation. If, following a negative supply shock, they choose to fight inflation by raising the interest rate, they will have to sacrifice some output (at least in the short-run).

No such trade-off exists when a demand shock hits the economy. In that case inflation and output move in the same direction. This makes life easier for the monetary authorities. Thus, if as a result of a positive demand shock inflation and output increase, the authorities can reduce both by the same increase in the interest rate. This has led to the view that provided shocks are primarily demand shocks, a strict inflation targeting strategy will do a good job both at stabilizing inflation and output.

In this section I analyze the importance of the nature of the shocks in our behavioral macroeconomic model. The way I proceed is to analyze the model first when only supply shocks exist, and then to do the same when only demand shocks.

Thus in the scenario when only supply shocks occur, I set the error term in the aggregate demand Eq. (1) equal to zero. In the alternative scenario I set the error term in the supply Eq. (2) equal to zero. I present the results of simulating the model under these two scenarios in Figures 7 and 8. The contrast is striking. When only supply shocks occur (Figure 7) we obtain the results that was also found earlier: there are strong cyclical movements in output gap; these cyclical movements are highly correlated with the animal spirits (correlation coefficient $= 0.89$); the output gap is not normally distributed and this feature is related to the fact that the markets are regularly gripped by extreme optimism or extreme pessimism.

These results are very different from those found in the scenario where only demand shocks occur (Figure 8). In this case the cyclical movements of the output gap are much weaker and show much less amplitude. Animal spirits are a weak force. There are never moments where everybody is either optimist or pessimist. The result of all this is that the output gap is normally distributed, and the market is never gripped by extreme optimism and pessimism.

How can these striking differences be explained? The answer has to do with what was noted earlier. In the demand-shocks-only scenario, the central bank has an easy job in stabilizing both inflation and output. There is never a choice to be made. This has the effect

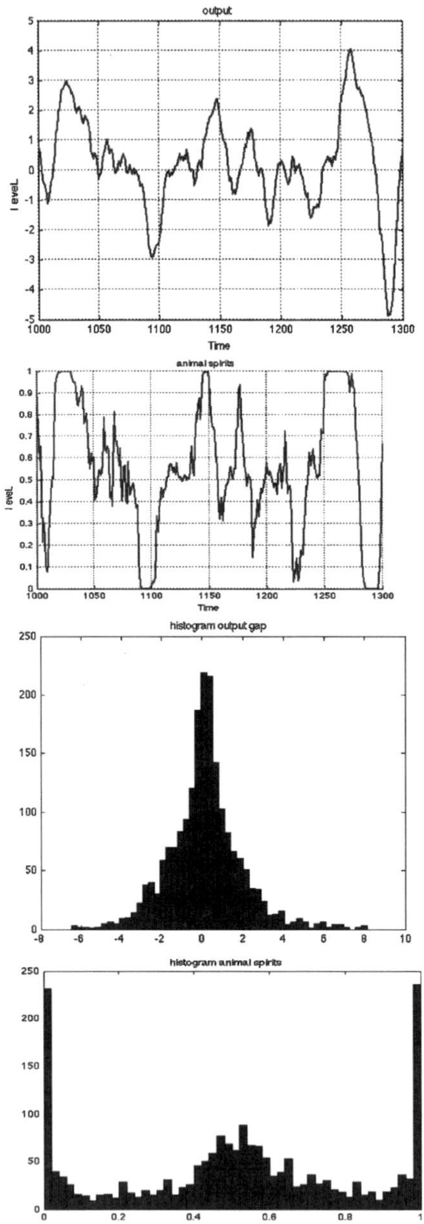

Figure 7. Only supply shocks.

Note: Jarque–Berra = 538; kurtosis = 5.2.

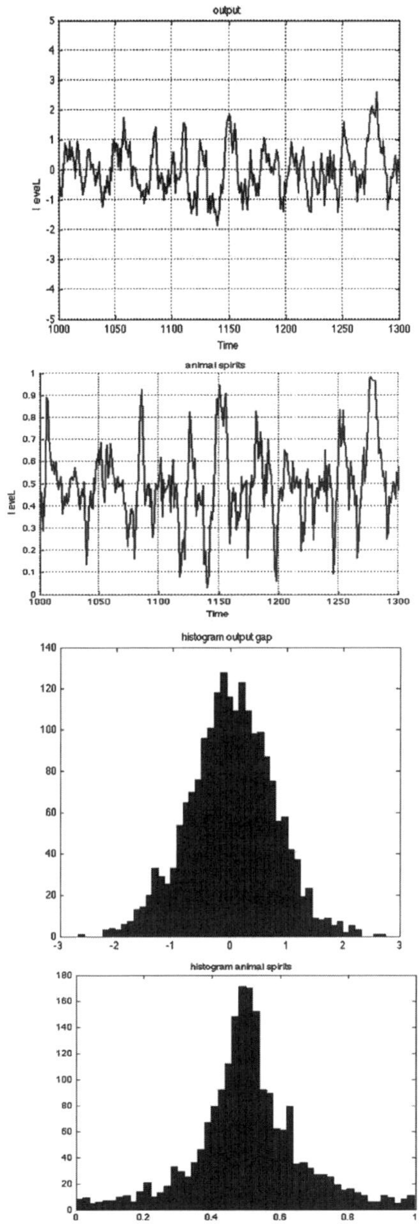

Figure 8. Only demand shocks.

Note: Jarque–Berra = 3.1; kurtosis = 3.2.

that by stabilizing output and inflation, the animal spirits are also "tamed", so that extreme optimism or pessimism have no chance to emerge. (Note that the Taylor rule equation applies and we impose the same coefficients as in Eq. (3)).

In the supply-only-shocks scenario, the central bank faces the difficult trade-off between stabilizing inflation and output. As a result, stabilization is very imperfect giving scope for animal spirits to do their work in destabilizing output. Thus, one obtains non-normality in the movements of the output gap when supply shocks dominate.

Does that mean that when only demand shocks occur, movements in the output gap are always normally distributed? The answer to this question is not obvious. Underlying the previous results is the assumption that the central bank stabilizes inflation *and* output (the coefficients c_1 and c_2 in the Taylor rule are positive). This may influence the result that in the demand-only-shocks scenario animal spirits are weak, and the output gap movements are non-normally distributed.

In order to illustrate this, I simulated the demand-shocks-only scenario assuming strict inflation targeting. The latter means that the central bank does not aim at stabilizing output (the output coefficient in the Taylor rule is zero). Figure 9 shows the result. One now observes that the output gap becomes much more volatile and that animal spirits become the main driving force behind this volatility. Animal spirits now switch between extreme optimism and pessimism. This can also be seen in the lower two panels of Figure 9. The output gap now ceases to be normally distributed and this is due to the extreme values animal spirits regularly take. Thus we are back in the world of non-normality, despite the fact that shocks only occur in the demand equation. The reason we obtain this result is that the central bank applies strict inflation targeting thereby allowing animal spirits to be set loose and to destabilize output and inflation. Thus, even when only demand shocks occur non-normality will emerge when central banks fail to stabilize output.

In order to shed more light on the importance of output stabilization as a tool to reduce the fat tails in the distribution of the output gap I computed the Jarque–Bera statistic (JBstat) for different values

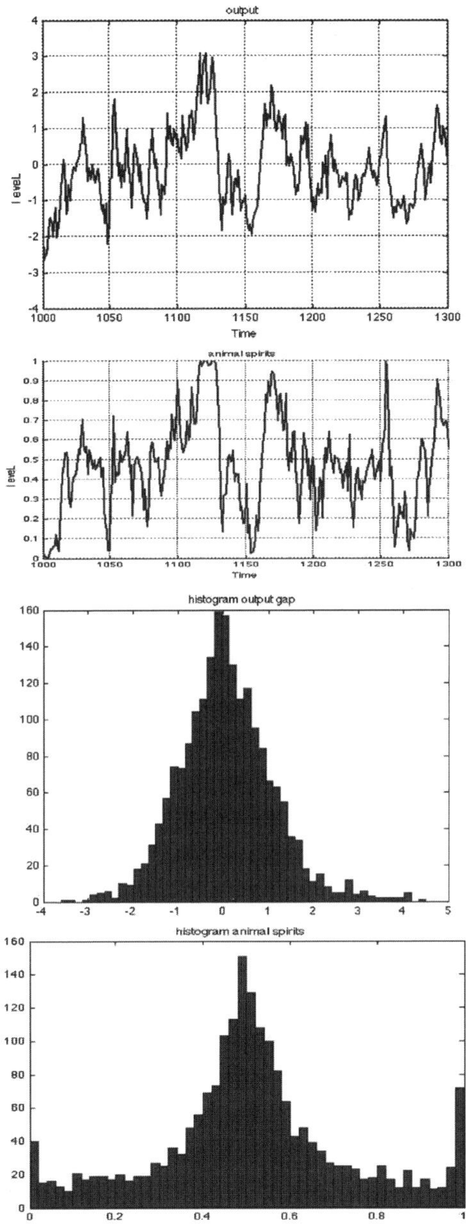

Figure 9. Demand-shocks-only scenario and strict inflation targeting.

Note: kurtosis: 4.2; JB = 175.

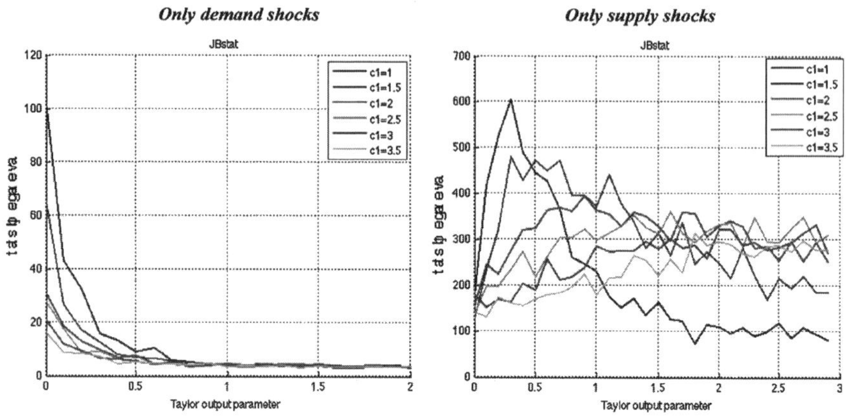

Figure 10. Normality test for different values of Taylor output parameter when only demand shocks occur.

of the output parameter in the Taylor equation. This statistic tests for normality of the distribution. The critical value is around 3. When JBstat exceeds 3 one can reject the hypothesis that the distribution of the output gap is normal. The results are plotted in Figure 10 for both the scenarios of demand and supply shocks.

When only demand shocks occur we find that for values of the Taylor output parameter less than 0.5, the distribution of the output gap is non-normal. Thus when the central bank does not apply enough stabilization ($c_2 < 0.5$) the distribution of the output gap exhibits fat tails, i.e., there will regularly be large booms and busts in output. This can be avoided by applying a sufficient amount of output stabilization ($c_2 > 0.5$). In that case the central bank does not give a chance to animal spirits to "show their ugly heads", and to trigger large booms and busts.

When only supply shocks occur the distribution of the output gap is non-normal for all values of the Taylor output parameter. We observe though that as the central bank applies more output stabilization the Jarque–Bera statistic (JBstat) declines, suggesting that the departures from normality are reduced. Thus when supply shocks dominate, the central bank cannot eliminate the booms and busts driven by animal spirits, but they can mitigate these.

6. The Tradeoff Between Inflation and Output Volatility in Behavioral Model

Modern macroeconomics in general, and DSGE-models in particular, have provided the intellectual foundation of inflation targeting. Until the eruption of the financial crisis in 2007, inflation targeting strategies had become the undisputed policy framework modern central banks should adopt. And most did. The official holders of macroeconomic wisdom declared that this step toward inflation targeting constituted a great victory of macroeconomics as a science (Woodford, 2009). From now on we would be living in a more stable macroeconomic environment, a "Great Moderation." How things can change so quickly.

Inflation targeting, of course, does not imply that there is no role for output stabilization. DSGE-modelers who have put a New Keynesian flavor in their models, have always stressed that wage and price rigidities provide a rationale for output stabilization by central banks (see Clarida *et al.*, 1999; Galí, 2008). This idea has found its reflection in "flexible" inflation targeting (Svensson, 1997; Woodford, 2003). Because of the existence of rigidities, a central bank should not attempt to keep inflation close to its target all the time. When sufficiently large shocks occur that lead to departures of inflation from its target, the central bank should follow a strategy of gradual return of inflation to its target. The rationale is that in a world of wage and price rigidities too abrupt attempts to bring back inflation to its target would require such high increases in the interest rate as to produce too strong declines in output.

Output stabilization in the DSGE-world, however, is very much circumscribed. The need to stabilize arises because of the existence of rigidities in prices that makes it necessary to spread out price movements over longer periods. The limited scope for output stabilization is based on a model characterized by a stable equilibrium. There is no consideration of the possibility that the equilibrium may be unstable or that fluctuations in output have a different origin than price rigidities. Should the scope for output stabilization be enlarged? In order to shed some light on this issue I derive the tradeoff between output and inflation variability in the context of the behavioral model, and I formulate some policy conclusions.

The tradeoffs are constructed as follows. The model was simulated 10,000 times and the average output and inflation variabilities were computed for different values of the Taylor rule parameters. Figure 11 shows how output variability (panel a) and inflation variability (panel b) change as the output coefficient (c_2) in the Taylor rule increases from 0 to 1. Each line represents the outcome for different values of the inflation coefficient (c_1) in the Taylor rule.

Panel a showing the evolution of output variability exhibits the expected result, i.e. as the output coefficient (c_2) increases (inflation targeting becomes less strict) output variability tends to decrease. One would now expect that this decline in output variability resulting from more active stabilization comes at the cost of more inflation variability. This, however, is not found in panel b. One observes that the relationship is non-linear. As the output coefficient is increased from zero, inflation variability first declines. Only when the output coefficient increases beyond a certain value (in a range 0.6–0.8) inflation variability starts increasing. Thus the central bank can reduce both output *and* inflation variability when it moves away from strict inflation targeting ($c_2 = 0$) and engages in some output stabilization. Not too much though. Too much output stabilization turns around the relationship and increases inflation variability.

Figure 11 allows us to construct the tradeoffs between output and inflation variability. These are shown in Figure 12 for different values of the inflation parameter c_1. Take the tradeoff AB. This is the one obtained for $c_1 = 1$. Start from point A on the tradeoff. In point A, the output parameter $c_2 = 0$ (strict inflation targeting). As output stabilization increases we first move downwards. Thus increased output stabilization by the central bank reduces output and inflation variability. The relation is non-linear, however. At some point, with too high an output stabilization parameter, the tradeoff curve starts increasing, becoming a "normal" tradeoff, i.e., a lower output variability is obtained at the cost of increased inflation variability.

How can we interpret these results? Let us start from the case of strict inflation targeting, i.e., the authorities set $c_2 = 0$. There

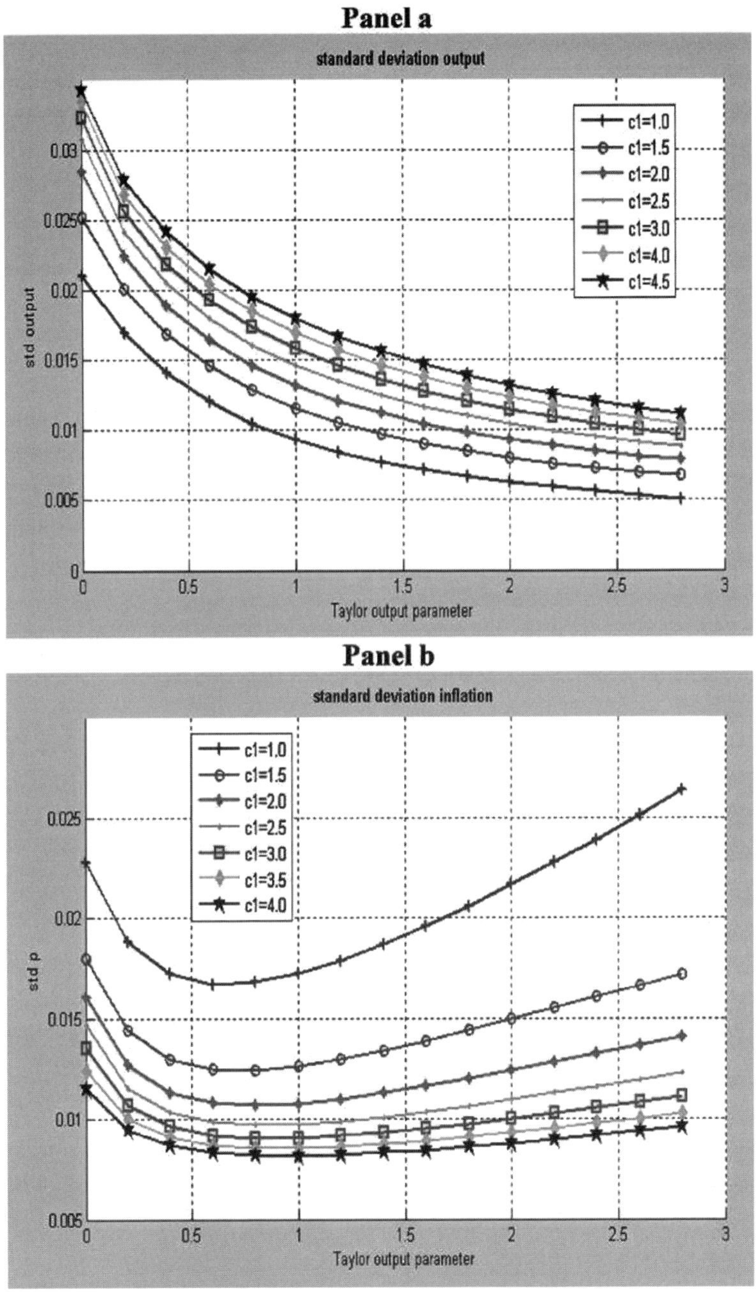

Figure 11. Output and inflation variability.

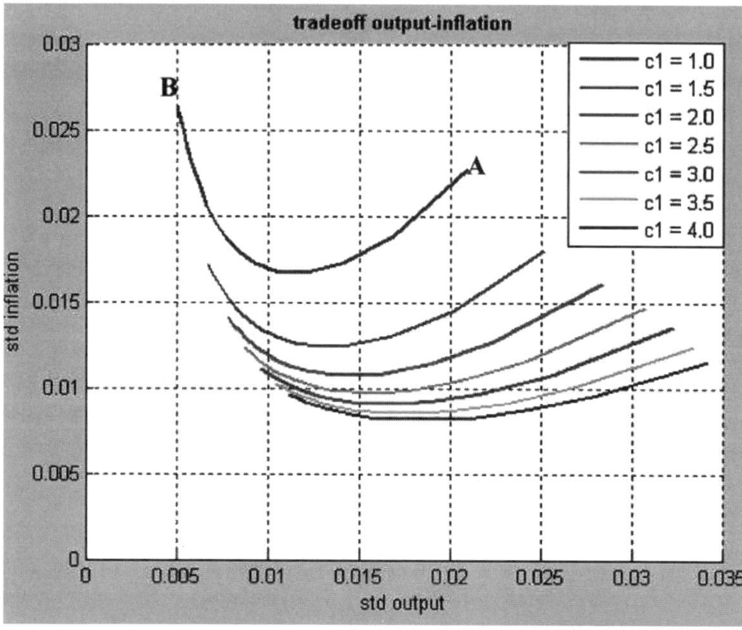

Figure 12. Trade-offs in the behavioral model.

is no attempt at stabilizing output at all. The ensuing output variability intensifies the waves of optimism and pessimism (animal spirits), which in turn feed back on output volatility. These larges waves lead to higher inflation variability. Thus, some output stabilization is good; it reduces both output and inflation variability by preventing too large swings in animal spirits. With no output stabilization at all ($c_2 = 0$) the forces of animal spirits are so high that the high output variability also increases inflation volatility through the effect of the output gap on inflation (supply equation). Too much output stabilization, however, reduces the stabilization bonus provided by a credible inflation target. When the central bank attaches too much importance to output stabilization it creates more scope for better forecasting performance of the inflation extrapolators, leading to more inflation variability.

Figure 12 also tells us something important about inflation targeting. We note that increasing the inflation parameter in the Taylor rule (c_1) has the effect of shifting the tradeoffs downwards, i.e., the central bank can improve the tradeoffs by reacting more strongly to changes in inflation.[6] The central bank achieves this improvement in the tradeoff because by reacting more intensely to changes in inflation it reduces the probability that inflation extrapolators will tend to dominate the market, and as a result it reduces the probability that inflation targeting looses credibility. Such a loss of credibility destabilizes both inflation and output. Thus maintaining credibility of inflation targeting is an important source of macroeconomic stability in our behavioral model.

Finally it should be stressed that the tradeoffs derived in this section only take into account the second moments, i.e., the standard deviations in output gap and inflation. They are silent about the higher moments, kurtosis and fat tails. As was stressed in the previous sections, these are also important. There we illustrated how the central banks can by changing the intensity of their stabilization efforts affect these higher moments. In fact we found that by increasing its stabilization effort the central bank can reduce the fatness of the tails in the distribution of the output gap, thereby contributing to less intense booms and busts in economic activity. Figure 13 confirms this. It shows how the Jarque-Bera normality test behaves as a function of the Taylor output parameter, when shocks occur both in the demand and supply equations.

7. Sensitivity Analysis

The simulations reported in the previous sections assumed a given set of numerical values of the parameters of the model. It was found that for this set of parameter values animal spirits (measured by the movements in the fraction of optimistic extrapolators) emerge and affect the fluctuations of the output gap.

One way to measure the importance of animal spirits in shaping the movements of the output gap is to compute the correlation coefficient between the fraction of optimists and the output gap.

[6]A similar result on the importance of strict inflation is also found in Gaspar *et al.* (2006) who use a macromodel with statistical learning.

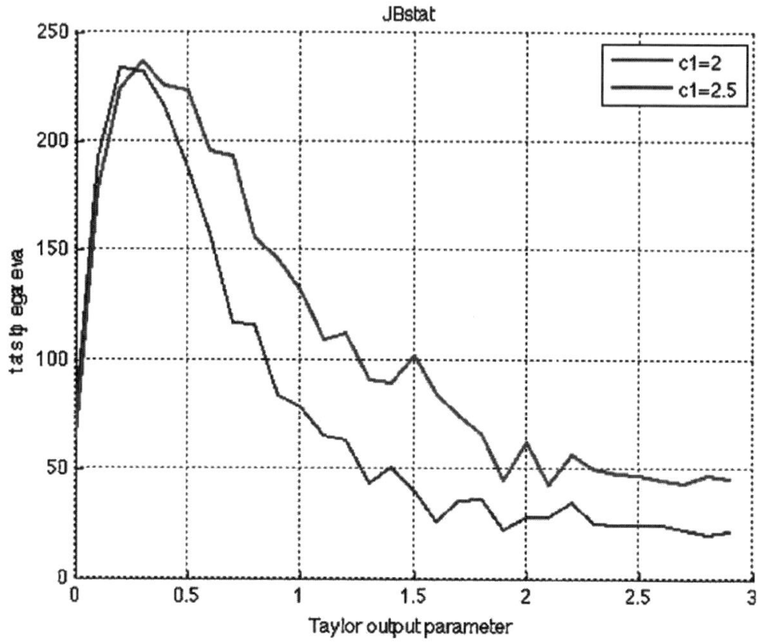

Figure 13. Normality test (JBStat) with demand and supply shocks.

In the simulation reported in Figure 3 this correlation coefficient is 0.86. One would like to know how this correlation evolves when one changes the parameter values of the model. I concentrate on two parameter values here, the intensity of choice parameter, γ, and the memory agents have when calculating the performance of their forecasting. The latter is represented by the parameter ω_k in Eqs. (9) and (10) and is a series of declining weights attached to past forecast error. I define $\omega_k = (1-\rho)\rho^k$ (and $0 \leq \rho \leq 1$). The parameter ρ can then be interpreted as a measure of the memory of agents. When $\rho = 0$ there is no memory, i.e., only last period's performance matters in evaluating a forecasting rule; when $\rho = 1$ there is infinite memory, i.e., all past errors, however far in the past, obtain the same weight.

The results of the sensitivity analysis are shown in Figure 14. The left hand panel shows the correlation between the output gap and the fraction of optimistic extrapolators (animal spirits) for increasing

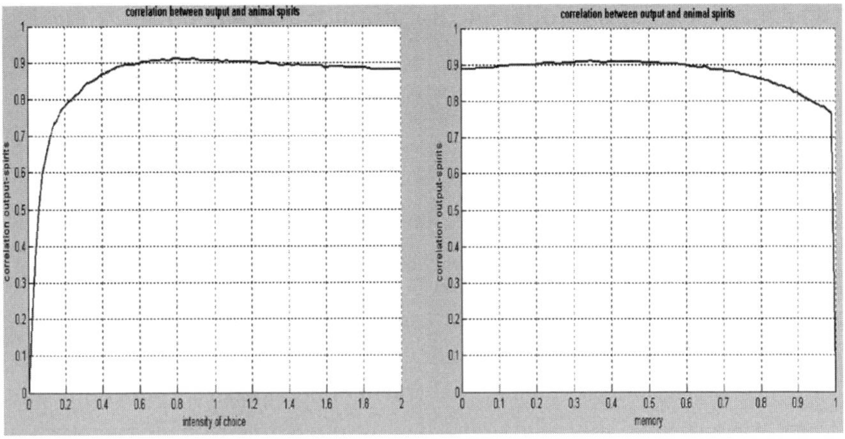

Figure 14. Correlations between output gap and fraction of optimists.

values of the intensity of choice parameter, γ. It can be seen that when γ is zero (i.e., the switching mechanism is purely stochastic), this correlation is zero. The interpretation is that in an environment in which agents decide purely randomly, i.e., they do not react to the performance of their forecasting rule, there are no systematic waves of optimism and pessimism (animal spirits) that can influence the business cycle. In this case the output gap is normally distributed. When γ increases, the correlation increases sharply. Thus in an environment in which agents learn from their mistakes, animal spirits arise, and the output gap becomes non-normally distributed. Thus one needs a minimum level of rationality (in the sense of a willingness to learn) for animal spirits to emerge and to influence the business cycle. It appears from Figure 14 that this is achieved with relatively low levels of γ.

The right hand panel shows the correlation between the output gap and the fraction of optimists for increasing values of the memory parameter ρ. It can be seen that when $\rho = 1$ the correlation is zero. This is the case where agents attach the same weight to all past observations, however, far in the past they occur. Put differently, when agents have infinite memory, they forget nothing. In that case animal spirits do not occur. Thus, one needs some forgetfulness (which is a cognitive limitation) to produce animal spirits. Note that the degree of forgetfulness does not have to be large. For values of ρ below 0.98 the correlations between output and animal spirits are quite high.

8. Conclusion

Booms and busts are an endemic feature of capitalism. Economic activity is often subjected to strong growth followed by sharp declines. As a result, the frequency distribution of output gap (and output growth) is non-normal, exhibiting excess kurtosis and fat tails. The latter means that if we are basing our forecasts on the normal distribution we tend to underestimate the probability that in any one period a large increase or decrease in the output gap can occur.

Mainstream macroeconomic models (DSGE-models) experience difficulties in explaining this phenomenon. In DSGE-model, large booms and busts can only be explained by large exogenous shocks. Price and wage rigidities then lead to wavelike movements of output and inflation. Thus booms and busts are explained exogenously. The fat tails observed in the frequency distribution of the output gap arise because there are large shocks hitting the economy. Thus the typical DSGE-trained macroeconomist will explain the eruption of the financial crisis by an exogenous shock, like a meteor, and not by some internal dynamics of the macroeconomy. This explanation of non-normality in macroeconomic movements comes as a "Deus ex Machina." This leads to the unanswered question of why the outside world is full of non-normally distributed shocks while the macroeconomy behaves according to a Gaussian distribution.

The behavioral model presented in this paper allows us to give a more satisfactory explanation of the observed non-normality in the distribution of the output gaps. The agents in our model have limited cognitive limitations, which forces them to use simple rules (heuristics). The interactions between these agents create correlations in beliefs, which in turn generate waves of optimism and pessimism. The latter produce endogenous cycles, which are akin to the Keynesian animal spirits. Occasionally this correlation of beliefs leads to extreme optimism (explaining booms) followed by extreme pessimism (explaining busts). Thus the behavioral model provides for an endogenous explanation of business cycle movements. Our model allows us to better understand the booms and busts that have been characteristic of market systems, up to the latest boom (2003–07) and bust (2008–09).

The behavioral model leads to a different view about the responsibility of the central bank. As in the mainstream DSGE model, we find that a credible policy of inflation targeting is important to stabilize inflation and output. However, we also find that strict inflation targeting is never optimal. Some output stabilization (given a credible inflation target) helps in reducing the correlation of biased beliefs thereby reducing the scope for waves of optimism and pessimism to emerge and to destabilize output and inflation. We also find that output stabilization by the central bank is important to reduce the higher moment volatilities (by fat tails) observed in the output gap.

The behavioral model proposed in this paper can be criticized for being "ad hoc." There is no doubt that the model has ad hoc features, i.e. assumptions that cannot be grounded on some deeper principle, and therefore have to be taken for granted. In defence of this "ad hocquerie," the following should be stressed. Once we leave the comfortable world of agents who experience no limits to their cognitive abilities, ad hoc assumptions are inevitable. This is due to the fact that we do not fully comprehend the way individuals with cognitive limitations process information. In contrast, there is no secret in how the superbly informed individuals in the rational expectations world process information. They understand the model, and therefore there is only one way to write down how they form their expectations. This feature may give the model builder intellectual satisfaction, but it is unclear whether such a model is useful to understand a world in which agents' cognitive capacities are severely restricted.

An important shortcoming of the behavioral model presented in this paper is that is does not introduce financial markets and the banking sector. Financial markets have been shown to be gripped by movements of optimism and pessimism leading to bubbles and crashes. It will be interesting to extend the model to incorporate these features and to see how they interact with the animal spirits analyzed in this paper.

Appendix A. Parameter Values of the Calibrated Model

Behavioral model

$p_{\text{star}} = 0$ % the central bank's inflation target
$a_1 = 0.5$ % coefficient of expected output in output equation
$a_2 = -0.2$ % a is the interest elasticity of output demand
$b_1 = 0.5$ % b_1 is coefficient of expected inflation in inflation equation
$b_2 = 0.05$ % b_2 is coefficient of output in inflation equation
$c_1 = 1.5$ % c_1 is coefficient of inflation in Taylor equation
$c_2 = 0.5$ % c_2 is coefficient of output in Taylor equation
$c_3 = 0.5$ % interest smoothing parameter in Taylor equation
$\beta = 1$ % fixed divergence in beliefs
$\delta = 2$ % variable component in divergence of beliefs
$\sigma = 1$ % intensity of choice parameter
$\sigma_1 = 0.5$ % standard deviation shocks output
$\sigma_2 = 0.5$ % standard deviation shocks inflation
$\sigma_3 = 0.5$ % standard deviation shocks Taylor
$\rho = 0.5$ % ρ measures the speed of declining weights in mean squares errors (memory parameter)

Rational model

$p_{\text{star}} = 0$ % the central bank's inflation target
$a_1 = 0.5$ % coefficient of expected output in output equation
$a_2 = -0.2$ % a is the interest elasticity of output demand
$b_1 = 0.5$ % b_1 is coefficient of expected inflation in inflation equation
$b_2 = 0.05$ % b_2 is coefficient of output in inflation equation
$c_1 = 1.5$ % c_1 is coefficient of inflation in Taylor equation
$c_2 = 0.5$ % c_2 is coefficient of output in Taylor equation
$c_3 = 0.5$ % interest smoothing parameter in Taylor equation

$\sigma_1 = 0.5$ % standard deviation shocks output
$\sigma_2 = 0.5$ % standard deviation shocks inflation
$\sigma_3 = 0.5$ % standard deviation shocks Taylor

References

Akerlof, G, R Shiller (2009). *Animal Spirits: How Human Psychology Drives the Economy and Why It Matters for Global Capitalism.* Princeton, NJ: Princeton University Press.

Anderson, S, A de Palma and JF Thisse (1992). *Discrete Choice Theory of Product Differentiation.* Cambridge, MA: MIT Press.

Branch, W and G Evans (2006). Intrinsic heterogeneity in expectation formation. *Journal of Economic Theory*, 127, 264–295.

Branch, W and G Evans (2009). *Monetary Policy with Heterogeneous Expectations.* Mimeo: Stanford University.

Brazier, A, R Harrison, M King and T Yates (2006). The danger of inflating expectations of macroeconomic stability: Heuristic switching in an overlapping generations monetary model. Working Paper No. 303, Bank of England.

Brock, W and C Hommes (1997). A rational route to randomness. *Econometrica*, 65, 1059–1095.

Clarida, R, J Gali and M Gertler (1999). The science of monetary policy, a new Keynesian perspective. *Journal of Economic Literature*, 37, 1661–1707.

De Grauwe, P and M Grimaldi (2006). *The Exchange Rate in a Behavioural Finance Framework.* Princeton, NJ: Princeton University Press.

Delli Gatti, D, C Di Guilmi, E Gaffeo, G Giuloni, M Gallegati and A Palestrini (2005). A new approach to business fluctuations: heterogenous interacting agents, scaling laws and financial fragility. *Journal of Economic Behavior and Organization*, 56, 489–512.

Evans, G and S Honkapohja (2001). *Learning and Expectations in Macroeconomics.* Princeton, NJ: Princeton University Press.

Fagiolo, G, M Napoletano and A Roventini (2008). Are output growth rate distributions fat-Tailed: Evidence for OECD-countries. *Journal of Applied Econometrics*, 23, 639–669.

Fagiolo, G, M Napoletano, M Piazza and A Roventini (2009). Detrending and the distributional properties of U.S. output time series. *Economics Bulletin*, 29, 4.

Farmer, REA (2006). Animal spirits. *Palgrave Dictionary of Economics.*

Galí, J (2008). *Monetary Policy Inflation and the Business Cycle.* Princeton, NJ: Princeton University Press.

Gaspar, V, F Smets and D Vestin (2006). Adaptive learning, persistence a and optimal monetary policy. Working Paper Series No. 644, European Central Bank.

Gigerenzer, G and PM Todd (1999). *Simple Heuristics that Make Us Smart.* New York, NY: Oxford University Press.

Hayek, F (1945). The use of knowledge in society. *American Economic Review*, 35(4), 519–530.

Keynes, JM (1936). *The General Theory of Employment Interest and Money.* MacMillan and Co.

Kirman, A (1993). Ants, rationality and recruitment. *Quarterly Journal of Economics*, 108, 137–156.

Milani, F (2007). Learning and time-varying macroeconomic volatility. Mimeo, Irvine: University of California.

Orphanides, A and J Williams (2004). Robust monetary policy with imperfect information. Board of Governors of the Federal Reserve System.

Sargent, T (1993). *Bounded Rationality in Macroeconomics.* New York, NY: Oxford University Press.

Smets, F and R Wouters (2003). An estimated dynamic stochastic general equilibrium model. *Journal of the European Economic Association*, 1, 1123–1175.

Svensson, L (1997). Inflation forecast targeting: implementing and monitoring inflation targets. *European Economic Review*, 41, 111–146.

Woodford, M (2003). *Interest and Prices: Foundations of a Theory of Monetary Policy.* Princeton, NJ: Princeton University Press.

Woodford, M (2009). Convergence in macroeconomics: Elements of the new synthesis. *American Economic Journal: Macroeconomics*, 1(1), 267–297.

Index